DICTIONARY OF LATINO CIVIL RIGHTS HISTORY

F. Arturo Rosales

Arte Público Press
Houston, Texas

This volume is made possible through grants from the Charles Stewart Mott Foundation; the Ewing Marion Kauffman Foundation; the Rockefeller Foundation; the Exemplar Program, a program of Americans for the Arts in Collaboration with the LarsonAllen Public Services Group, funded by the Ford Foundation; and the City of Houston through The Cultural Arts Council of Houston / Harris County.

Recovering the past, creating the future

Arte Público Press
University of Houston
452 Cullen Performance Hall
Houston, Texas 77204-2004

Cover design by Exact Type
Cover art by José Ramírez & Bread and Roses

Rosales, Francisco A. (Francisco Arturo)
    Dictionary of Latino Civil Rights History / F. Arturo Rosales.
        p.   cm.
    Includes index.
    ISBN-10: 1-55885-347-2 (alk. paper)
    ISBN-13: 978-1-55885-347-8
    1. Hispanic Americas—Civil rights—History—Dictionaries. 2. Civil rights movements—United States—History—Dictionaries. 3. United States—Ethnic relations—Dictionaries. I. Title.
E184.S75R69 2006
323.1168'07303—dc22   2005054512
                                                                CIP

♾ The paper used in this publication meets the requirements of the American National Standard for Information Sciences—Permanence of Paper for Printed Library Materials, ANSI Z39.48-1984.

6 7 8 9 0 1 2 3 4 5   10 9 8 7 6 5 4 3 2 1

Dedication

*To my sisters, Margie and Gina, who struggled valiantly
to make the last few years of our parents
Cuca (1915–2003) and George (1908–2005)
as comfortable and happy as possible.*

Table of Contents

Acknowledgments

After many years of researching and writing about Latino civil rights, it occurred to me that I had collected enough resources to provide another type of venue for the millions of readers interested in this topic: a dictionary. Indeed, the same rationale prompted me to produce my historical documents book, *Testimonio: A Documentary History of the Mexican-American Struggle for Civil Rights*. In both cases, I collaborated closely with my old friend and mentor, Nicolás Kanellos of Arte Público Press in Houston.

As it turned out, my own considerable trove of resources did not contain nearly enough materials to produce a comprehensive civil rights dictionary, especially after Kanellos suggested that the piece transcend the civil rights struggles of Chicanos to include the civil rights struggles of all of the Latino groups in the United States. Fortunately, I had conducted research on other Latinos for an extensive chapter written for the original *Hispanic Almanac* in the early 1990s; so the task did not seem impossible. But that piece focused on Mexican Americans, Puerto Ricans, and Cuban Americans. Since its publication, the actual size and the variety of other Latino groups has grown dramatically and enough time has elapsed since their initial settling in the United States for their sojourns and experiences truly to be considered historical. Today, for example, Dominicans outnumber Puerto Ricans, and Salvadorans also number in the millions. Needless to say, I spent a few years researching more data. Still the emphasis of this work is on Mexican Americans, Puerto Ricans, and Cubans, whose history in U.S. territory is the most extensive. Nonetheless, I have included as much as I could find on their fellow Latinos.

The criteria employed to determine what qualifies a person, event, organization, etc., to merit an entry is flexible: anyone or anything manifesting a form of defense, resistance, assistance for social mobility, cultural reinforcement, and survival is legitimately eligible.

As in my other publications with Arte Público Press, my experience with the staff and with Nicolás Kanellos has been most gratifying. This work has had a long gestation period, and I am appreciative for the patience, support, and the numerous editorial suggestions made by Kanellos. I owe much gratitude to my graduate students, Jeannie Carlisle, Marcos Popovich, and Eric

Meringer, who provided invaluable assistance in the early years of compilations. I am grateful to Joxán Barrón and my daughter, Sara Rosales, for their tremendous help with the index.

I also wish to thank the persons who responded to my e-mail queries about themselves, other people, organizations, or events for which I needed more information. I relied on both conventional articles and books as well as on Internet sources, all of which receive credit in the documentation. Some sources on the Internet have no author credit, except for the URL address of the web page—I am thankful to those writers who did not sign their Internet entries.

The final work does not pretend to be definitive, for Latino civil rights have never been documented in such detail before, and this civil rights history is still very much ongoing and evolving. Arte Público Press fully intends to update this dictionary periodically.

F. Arturo Rosales
Arizona State University

Introduction

During recent years, Arte Público Press has supported the development of a dedicated series of books on Latino civil rights history. The series principally features first time works on the public record by Latino authors. It is intended to overcome the still-surprising dearth of books that treat Latino contributions to U.S. democracy and civic culture from the perspective of Hispanic Americans themselves. To date, the series has produced more than twenty new volumes of autobiographical and biographical works, non-fiction collections of essays and academic articles, and commentaries by some of the leading Latino and Latina civil rights advocates and scholars of the 20th and 21st centuries.

A still somewhat underrepresented aspect of the series has been the publication of reference books offering information and contextual analyses of major figures, organizations, and developments germane to the modern Latino civil rights field. F. Arturo Rosales' *Dictionary of Latino Civil Rights History* offers a robust response to the pressing need for more published works of this sort. The dictionary promises to be an important new tool for researchers and scholars, journalists, civil rights advocates, and other interested observers of the national Latino community's rich social justice history in the United States.

Many readers of this volume—including even more informed readers —will be surprised by the breadth of Rosales' work, covering here more than 500 pages of text and nearly 1,000 entries. Though primarily focused on the Mexican American experience, which Rosales knows so well being one of the nation's most prestigious Mexican American historians, it also extends to the legacies of other key U.S. Latino groups and in doing so provides one of the most comprehensive overviews of the Latino civil rights experience in America ever produced in a reference format.

Even despite Rosales' achievement, I note in my own review of the *Dictionary*'s contents that a few important names and events I expected to find there are not included. The arguable absence of certain worthy individuals and historical developments, however, is in the eye of the beholder and makes for interesting intellectual discussion and debate. It also speaks to the prospective need and opportunity to produce additional work in this rich and still-not-fully-mined field of inquiry, building on Rosales' excellent first effort.

The work Rosales has assembled in the *Dictionary* is undeniably thoughtful and painstaking. It reveals a broad command of the major aspects of Hispanic evolution in America that have been informative simultaneously of the U.S. Latino community's public identity and of the broader American community's social evolution.

Arte Público Press is proud to include F. Arturo Rosales' landmark *Dictionary of Latino Civil Rights History* as the latest entry in its continuing civil rights book series. Through the production and broad dissemination of works like this one, we hope to expand public appreciation of Latino America's many contributions to our national narrative and U.S. democratic principals.

Henry A. J. Ramos
Executive Editor
Hispanic Civil Rights Series
Arte Público Press

How to Use the *Dictionary of Latino Civil Rights History*

The entries to this dictionary are arranged alphabetically. Within entries, there are cross references, indicated by an asterisk(*), to names of events, individuals, and concepts that have their own separate entries. For example, "César Chávez"* appears numerous times throughout the dictionary and has an asterisk at each mention to indicate that this person also has an entire entry devoted to him.

The titles of the vast majority of the entries are also included in the index at the end of this volume, even if a particular title appears only once in the dictionary. The index does not include the word civil rights because it is an integral notion within most entries; a listing of the pages corresponding to this process would prove unwieldy to the reader. Instead, I have put the word civil rights under other entries such as cities or ethnic groups. Thus the category "Cuban Americans," which will obviously have many sub-categories, will include one called "civil rights." The index can also be used to find individuals, events, and organizations that do not have separate entries in this volume but which appear one or more times throughout the dictionary.

I have used numerous identifiers throughout the volume, such as "Latino," "Hispanic," "Boricua," "Chicano," "Cuban American," "Dominican," "Central American," "Mexican American," "Puerto Rican," "Hispano," as pertains to people and organizations who self-identify themselves in this manner. "Latino" and "Hispanic" are used to denote the aggregate when a specific group name is not relevant or specified a source of information. "Chicanos" and "Mexican Americans" are the same group, as are "Boricua" and "Puerto Ricans," "Latinos" and "Hispanics." In all, I have strived to remain faithful to the sources and the subjects of information.

At the end of each entry, those particular sources are referenced, as they are also in the Bibliography. It is hoped that this will assist the reader in obtaining further information on the particular subject.

All photos are from the Arte Público Press archives, except for the following:

Arizona Historical Society	Alianza Hispano-Americana
California Historical Society	Pío de Jesús Pico
The Catholic Herald	Mariel boatlift receiving refugees
Herman Gallegos	Community Services Organization convention with Saul Alinsky, César Chávez, Edward Roybal, Fred Ross, and Herman Gallegos
Houston Public Library	First LULAC Convention in Corpus Christi, LULAC Convention in Houston, LULAC Women's Auxiliary, Felix Tijerina, Repatriation photo from Houston Chronicle (Houston Metropolitan Research Center)
Hunter College, CUNY	Pura Belpré, Luisa Capetillo, Jesús Colón, Puerto Rican Day Parade, La Liga Puertorriqueña e Hispana (El Centro de Estudios Puertorriqueños)
Laredo Public Library	Benavides Brothers in Confederate Army
Library of Congress	Herman Badillo, Fulgencio Batista, Dennis Chávez, Henry B. González, Octaviano Larrazolo, Edward Pastor, Ileana Ross-Lehtinen, Edward R. Roybal, Esteban E. Torres, Nydia M. Velásquez, Youth stripped of zoot suit by servicemen
National Steinbeck Center	Californa Rural Legal Assistance, César Chávez, Héctor de la Rosa and Enrique Cantú Flores
The San Jacinto Museum of History	Lorenzo de Zavala
The Southwest Museum Los Angeles	Antonio Coronel
Texas State Library	Texas Rangers showing of dead bodies of "bandits" killed
University of Texas	Border Patrol (Harry Ransom Center)
University of Texas	Vicente Ximenes (Lyndon Baines Johnson Library)
Wayne State University	Picketing for the United Farm Workers National boycott (Archives of Labor and Urban Affairs)

We gratefully acknowledge their permissions

DICTIONARY
OF LATINO
CIVIL RIGHTS
HISTORY

ACADEMIA DE LA NUEVA RAZA, *see* **ATENCIO, TOMÁS**

ACCIÓN PUERTORRIQUEÑA

Students at Princeton University organized Acción Puertorriqueña in the 1970s in order to build a united Puerto Rican community with a strong cultural identity. The organization has also provided a lively social environment while promoting an interest in scholarly interests that are not addressed by the existing Princeton curriculum. Acción Puertorriqueña encourages those who identify with the heritage of Puerto Ricans, regardless of ethnic origin, to participate in the activities of the group. In addition, the organization takes positions on issues that impinge on the civil rights of Latinos in this country and encourages its members to engage in activism that will impede the erosion of these rights. Moreover, the organization played a key role in the creation of Latino Studies at Princeton. [SOURCE: http://www.princeton.edu/~accion/about.htm]

ACOSTA BAÑUELOS, RAMONA (1925-)

Ramona Acosta Bañuelos became the first Hispanic treasurer of the United States. Born in Miami, Arizona, Bañuelos was forcefully deported with her parents during the Depression. In 1944, she resettled in Los Angeles and soon thereafter founded a tortilla factory. By 1969, she was named Outstanding Businesswoman of the Year in Los Angeles. She was sworn in as treasurer on December 17, 1971. [SOURCE: Meier and Feliciano, *Dictionary of Mexican American History*, 33.]

ACTION GENERAL RESOLUTION ON CENTRAL AMERICAN REFUGEES

In 1984 the Unitarian Universalist Association adopted an Action General Resolution on Central American Refugees which provided for the following aspects:

WHEREAS, civil war in El Salvador has resulted in more than 45,000 political deaths; and

WHEREAS, there is no significant change in officially sanctioned violence, and death squads continue to operate with impunity; and

WHEREAS, almost all asylum requests have been denied by the U.S. Immigration and Naturalization Service (INS);

BE IT RESOLVED: That the 1984 General Assembly of the Unitarian Universalist Association supports specific rectifying legislation, H.R. 4447, sponsored by Rep. Joe Moakley of Massachusetts and others, and S. 2131, sponsored by Sen. Dennis DeConcini of Arizona, which provides for the temporary suspension of deportation of certain aliens who are nationals of El Salvador and for Presidential and Congressional review of conditions in El Salvador; and

BE IT FURTHER RESOLVED: That this Assembly urges that refugees in the U.S. from Guatemala be also protected under the same legislation; and

BE IT FURTHER RESOLVED: That this Assembly urges Unitarian Universalists to support actively those Unitarian Universalist societies and other religious communities which offer sanctuary to El Salvadoran and other Central American refugees.

In 1961, the Unitarian Universalist Association formed as a result of the consolidation of two religious denominations: the Universalists, organized in 1793, and the Unitarians, organized in 1825. The organization now represents the interests of more than one thousand Unitarian Universalist congregations across the hemisphere. [SOURCE: http://www.uua.org/actions/international/84refugees.html; http://www.vua.org/aboutus.html]

ACUÑA, RODOLFO (1932-)

Rodolfo Acuña is considered to be one of the most influential scholars in the field of Chicano* Studies, an interdisciplinary field examining the life and culture of Mexicans on both sides of the border. Born in 1932 in the Boyle Heights, he grew up and attended public schools in Los Angeles, where that community is located. While studying for his doctoral degree in Latin American Studies at the University of Southern California, in1966 he taught the first Chicano History class ever offered in the United States, at the community college level. After completing his Ph.D. in 1968, Acuña established one of the first Chicano Studies departments in the country, in 1969. In 1972, as member of the faculty at San Fernando Valley State College (now California State University, Northridge), he published the most-read survey of Chicano history, *Occupied America: A History of Chicanos.** Acuña acknowledges that he used a unique paradigm to write this book because he felt that mainstream historians had neglected the history of Mexicans in the United States. The book traces the conquest of northern Mexico by the United States and the ensuing conflicts over land, language, and civil rights of Chicanos from the 1800s to the present.

In his career as an historian, Acuña also became an advocate for the rights of ethnic Mexicans living in the United States and served as a pioneer in helping shape the course of the Mexican-American civil rights movement during the 1960s. To a large degree, participants in this movement were influenced by Acuña's writing and teaching in rejecting the strategy of earlier organizations struggling to gain civil rights objectives through litigation, electoral power, and diplomatic appeals. Acuña and other Chicano intellectuals offered a new paradigm to combat racism and discrimination through militancy and confrontation in order to dramatize social injustices toward ethnic Mexicans and to intimidate establishment officials into effecting change.

Acuña published an additional fourteen books and continues to inspire academic researchers and students alike. *U.S. Latino Issues*, published in 2003, addresses such issues as migration, intermarriage, and the use of the term "Latino" itself, as well as examining civil rights issues that affect other Latinos. [SOURCE: Acuña, *Occupied America*; Rosales, *Chicano!*, 254.]

ADAMS-ONÍS TREATY

In the final years of the Spanish regime in North America, John Quincy Adams and Luis de Onís, the Spanish ambassador to the United States, negotiated an agreement that determined the boundaries of the Spanish Empire in North America. The final proviso became known as the Adams-Onís Treaty of 1819. Among the many provisions in the treaty, the one that specified the western boundary of the Louisiana Territory rankled Americans the most. Detractors, especially those living close to Texas, felt that Spain had kept too much territory on the Louisiana-Texas border. The Arkansas River served as an international boundary between Spain and the United States after the Adams-Onís Treaty was signed; many Americans had hoped lands south of the River would be available for settlement but were disappointed with the resultant boundary, which was considered an obstacle to what would become the doctrine of Manifest Destiny.* [SOURCE: Campa, *Hispanic Culture in the Southwest*, 131, 179.]

AFRICAN AMERICANS AND HISPANICS IN MIAMI

Between 1959 and 1989, an adversarial relationship developed between the African-American citizens and the Cuban refugees pouring into Miami in flight from Communist Cuba. During this period, the civil rights movement was struggling to provide political and economic opportunities for blacks at the same time that the government was providing public assistance to the Cuban refugees. In comparison to blacks in other southern cities, however, Miami blacks had to compete for jobs and housing with a more-educated Cuban community, which quickly experienced mobility in both the public and private economic sectors. Blacks often remained confined to menial jobs while still living in poverty-stricken ghettos. As a consequence, the perception that Cubans and other Hispanics were obstacles to improving the condition of the black community, caused deep resentment and triggered several riots [SOURCE: Mohl, "On the Edge: Blacks and Hispanics in Metropolitan Miami since 1959."]

LA AGRUPACIÓN PROTECTORA MEXICANA

San Antonio Mexicans started La Agrupación Protectora Mexicana in 1911 to provide "legal protection for its members whenever they faced Anglo-perpetuated violence or illegal dispossession of their property." Such concerns dated from the nineteenth century and primarily affected native Tejanos and northern Mexicans who arrived early enough to become land owners, tenants and sharecroppers. By 1911, members of La Agrupación were predominantly immigrants, probably Mexican northeasterners. That La Agrupación was centered in San Antonio was an indication of its appeal to urban Mexicans, as well. In Houston, a chapter was started by Mexican school teacher J.J. Mercado.* The chapter worked with the Mexican consul to remedy Mexican grievances about employers, such as compensation for accidents at work. Members of La Agrupación in 1911 attended Texas' first major Mexican civil rights meeting, El Primer Congreso Mexicanista.* [SOURCE: De León, *Mexican Americans in Texas*, 38.]

AGUIRRE, EDUARDO (1945-)

On June 17, 2005, Eduardo Aguirre, Jr. of Houston, Texas, was sworn in as ambassador to Spain. Aguirre had been the director of U.S. Citizenship and Immigration Services for the Homeland Security Department since 2003. Born in 1945 in Cuba, Aguirre's parents sent him in 1960 to Louisiana through a program called Operation Peter Pan,* a project which transported many children from Cuba so that the Communist indoctrination of Fidel Castro's* regime would not affect them. In Louisiana, he was sheltered by a Catholic charity and after graduating from high school in New Orleans, Aguirre attended Louisiana State University in Baton Rouge, where he received a degree in finance in 1967. In 1970, Aguirre obtained a master's degree from the National Commercial Lending Graduate School at the University of Oklahoma. Before heading the Citizenship and Immigration Services, Aguirre was vice chairman and chief operating officer of the Export-Import Bank, a presidential appointment he accepted in 2001 after working for 24 years at Bank of America as an executive officer. Governor George W. Bush appointed Aguirre to the Board of Regents of the University of Houston System for a six-year term, where he became chairman from 1996 to 1998. [SOURCE: http://uscis.gov/graphics/aguirre_bio.htm]

AIR TRAGEDY, 2001

American Airlines Flight 587 crashed November 12, 2001, after taking off from New York's JFK airport. About 70 percent of the 251 passengers were

Dominicans, and their deaths highlighted the transnational lives that many Dominicans have lead through much of the twentieth and twenty-first centuries. On November 27, 2001, New York Mayor-elect Michael Bloomberg traveled to the Dominican Republic and met some twenty grieving relatives of victims who died aboard the ill-fated flight. He pledged help and espoused solidarity with the homeland of immigrants, who were rapidly achieving political clout in the city. Bloomberg also convened a private meeting with President Hipólito Mejía, in which he agreed to co-operate in aiding the victims' families. The two also touched on another of Mejía's major concerns: the issues and problems facing Dominican immigrants in New York City. [SOURCE: http://www.skicanadam-ag.com/TravelNewsNYCrash/011127_tribute-ap.html]

ALBIZU CAMPOS, PEDRO (1891–1965)

To Puerto Ricans who support independence of the island from U.S. rule, Pedro Albizu Campos, who was born in Tenerías Village, Ponce, on September 12, is considered a hero and martyr. By his own admission, his relationship with the United States became estranged after he experienced first-hand racial discrimination in an African-American unit during World War I. Albizu Cam-pos joined the Nationalist Party of Puerto Rico in 1924 after receiving two degrees from Harvard (B.S. 1916, L.L.B. 1923) and was elected president of that organization in 1930. He was imprisoned on the mainland from 1937 to 1943 after being convicted of seeking to overthrow the U.S. government. He returned to Puerto Rico in 1947 and helped orchestrate an unsuccessful cam-paign in the 1948 elections. He was arrested again in 1950 and sentenced to a 53-year prison term for masterminding an attack on the governor's mansion in Puerto Rico. Alvizu Campos was also a suspect in an assassination attempt on President Harry S.

Pedro Albizu Campos

Truman on October 31, 1950. In 1953, Governor Luis Muñoz Marín* offered a conditional pardon to Alvizu Campos, only to withdraw it after Puerto Rican nationalists attacked the U.S. House of Representatives the next year. Albizu Campos spent most of his remaining years imprisoned and in poor health. A year before his death in Hato Rey, Puerto Rico, on April 21, 1965, he received another pardon. [SOURCE: http://welcome.topuertorico.org/culture/famous-prA-C.shtml#albizupedro]

ALBUQUERQUE WALKOUT

Some leaders from traditional Mexican-American organizations, such as the League of United Latin American Citizens (LULAC),* the Mexican American Political Association (MAPA),* La Alianza Hispano-Americana,* and the Political Association of Spanish-Speaking Organizations (PASSO),* showed militancy when they walked out of the 1966 Equal Employment Opportunity Commission (EEOC)* in Albuquerque. Triggering the action was the perception that President Lyndon B. Johnson,* who promised in his 1965 "Great Society" inaugural address a "War on Poverty," did not follow through when it came to Mexican Americans. The initial promise by Johnson buoyed the hopes of Mexican-American leaders that programs to combat poverty and patronage jobs would be forthcoming. This optimism was dashed, however, when Johnson's Great Society set its sights more directly on America's black population. Most Mexican-American conservatives saw their dignity disparaged and their leadership positions endangered by these organizations' militant tactics. But for younger, less-compromised Chicanos,* and for some from the Mexican-American generation, this paved the way to using confrontation in obtaining or safeguarding civil rights.

In response to the protests, President Johnson named Vicente Ximenes* to the EEOC, who in turn established the Inter-Agency Cabinet Committee on Mexican American Affairs.* In October of 1967, Ximenes scheduled hearings at El Paso that coincided with the much-heralded ceremony in which the United States returned to Mexico the disputed Chamizal territory. [SOURCE: Rosales, *Chicano!*, 108, 166.]

ALEGRÍA, RICARDO E. (1921-)

Through Professor Ricardo Alegría's efforts, the influential Institute of Puerto Rican Culture was established in 1955. He served as director of the institute from its founding to 1972. In 1993, he was awarded the Picasso Medal from the United Nations Educational, Scientific, and Cultural Organization, becoming the first Latin American to receive such an honor. That same year, he accepted the Charles Frankel Award of the Humanities from President Bill Clinton. [SOURCE: http://welcome.topuertorico.org/culture/famousprA-C.shtml#alegriaricardo]

ALEMANY, JOSÉ SADOC (1814-1888)

A bishop, and later archbishop, Alemany came to the United States from Spain in 1840. After the Mexican-American War, he was named as bishop of the diocese of Monterey and in 1853 became the archbishop of the San Francisco diocese, which had jurisdiction over all of California. Alemany was successful in regaining title to many of the missionary properties that had been secularized or lost for the Catholic Church during the changes in dominion from Mexico to the United Sates. He resigned in 1884 and returned to Spain. [SOURCE: Meier and Rivera, *A Dictionary of Mexican American History*, 10.]

ALIANZA

Latino students founded Wellesley College's Alianza in the early 1980s to increase cultural and social awareness of Latin Americans and Iberians on the Wellesley campus and to advance the common concerns of these people. It provided, then and now, a familiar atmosphere in which students of these backgrounds can share their similar/different experiences and establish friendships through various activities such as salsa/merengue classes, lectures, discussions, etc. [SOURCE: http://www.wellesley.edu/Activities/homepage/alianza/html/index.html]

ALIANZA FEDERAL DE LAS MERCEDES

In the 1950s, as New Mexico's population grew, land competition fostered tension between Hispano farmers and outsider landowners. To stem their economic erosion, Hispano villagers formed the Corporation of Abiquiu. In the 1960s, an evangelist Texan, Reies López Tijerina,* took over the new organization just as the U.S. Forest Service* had issued stricter codes regulating grazing, wood cutting, and water use on federal lands. The restrictions, combined with López Tijerina's announcement that the land claims of Hispanos could be legitimized by Treaty of Guadalupe Hidalgo* provisions, increased the popularity of the fledgling organization. In 1963, the Corporation of Abiquiu's headquarters moved from Tierra Amarilla to Albuquerque and changed its name to Alianza Federal de las Mercedes.

To persuade officials to investigate their land claims, Alianza members marched from Albuquerque to the steps of the state capital in Santa Fe in July 1966, only to have their claims rejected. Frustrated, in October of 1966 the *aliancistas* occupied Echo Amphitheater, a National Forest campground, and evicted the forest rangers. Officials arrested López Tijerina and some of his followers, but released them shortly thereafter.

Members of the group were again arrested in May 1966, when they tried to plan another occupation of San Joaquín del Río de Chama* land. López Tijerina and other *aliancistas* on June 5 attempted to free their comrades from the jail in Río Arriba and wounded two officers in the process. Within hours, the governor mobilized the National Guard and embarked on one of the most massive manhunts in New Mexico history.

Eventually, local officials arrested all of the Alianza raiders and charged them with second-degree kidnapping, assault to commit murder, and an unlawful assault on a jail. In his trial, López Tijerina defended himself and obtained a not guilty verdict. At a federal trial, however, López Tijerina and

four others present at the Echo Amphitheater confrontation were found
guilty on two counts of assault against forest rangers. A federal judge sentenced him to two years in prison. After the courthouse raid, however,
extreme violence characterized all activities surrounding the land-grant
movement, both by and against the *aliancistas,* a situation that began to
erode López Tijerina's hold on leadership.

On June 6, 1969, *aliancistas* converged on Coyote and set up a tent city
on private land to camp out while they held their annual conference. At the
conference, López Tijerina clashed physically with Forest Service employees and was charged with a number of felonies. He was sentenced to prison,
but was released on July 26, 1971. In 1975, he went to prison again. The
Alianza movement died on the vine as much of its activities turned to dealing with the personal legal problems besetting López Tijerina. [SOURCE:
Nabokov, *Tijerina and the Courthouse Raid.*]

LA ALIANZA HISPANA

La Alianza Hispana (The Hispanic Alliance) was founded in 1970 in
Roxbury, Massachusetts. It is a community-based, nonprofit organization
dedicated to promoting Latino self-determination, it advocates equal access
to basic services, and combats the effects of poverty, discrimination, and the
stress of migration. [SOURCE: http://www2.wgbh.org/MBCWEIS/LTC/
LAH/Welcome.html]

Alianza Hispano-Americana Parade

ALIANZA HISPANO-AMERICANA

The Alianza Hispano-Americana (Hispanic American Alliance) was founded in Tucson, Arizona, in 1894 as a mutual aid society. Its principal founders, Carlos Velasco and Manuel Samaniego, were middle-class immigrants from Sonora, Mexico. It spread throughout the Southwest and by the 1920s, the organization had ten thousand members. Although its main purpose continued to be to provide social and health benefits to its members, it also accumulated a respectable record in protecting civil rights for Mexicans. La Alianza, as it became known, joined other associations in efforts to save Mexicans condemned to the gallows. During the Great Depression, the internal problems beset the organization and its leadership, a factor that diminished its effectiveness.

Following World War II, the organization refocused on civil rights issues and education problems. In Arizona, Alianza member and lawyer, Ralph Estrada, with the help of local community leaders, argued the 1952 *Sheely v. González** case, which abolished segregation in Tolleson, a town near Phoenix. The Alianza continued to exert pressure on segregated schools in Arizona and, in 1954, the Peoria school district caved in and voluntarily ended the segregation of Mexicans—this was the last hold-out in the state. The initiative foiled the desires of school officials, who stubbornly clung to the idea that Mexican Americans required separation because of their different culture. During this same period, the educator Ralph Guzmán organized a civil rights department within the Alianza, and the organization also began scholarship programs for for Mexican Americans. By the end of the 1950s, internal leadership problems again plagued the organization and led to its demise. [SOURCE: Meier and Rivera, *A Dictionary of Mexican American History*, 12.]

ALLEE ET AL V. MEDRANO ET AL

A class action suit brought against the Texas Rangers* and Captain A.Y. Allee, following the 1966-1967 farmworkers strike in the lower Rio Grande Valley, *Medrano v. Allee* charged that the rangers had interfered in a variety of ways with the workers' right to organize and strike, depriving them of constitutional rights guaranteed by the First and Fourteenth Amendments. In 1972, in *Allee et al v. Medrano et al,* a federal district judge ruled in favor of the farmworkers, who were represented by the lead plaintiff, Francisco Medrano, a union organizer. The court ruled that the rangers could not block such efforts by workers, and any arrests must be made due to probable cause. Although appealed, the U.S. Supreme Court in 1974 upheld the decision and ruled that the Rangers had maliciously manipulated the law to the extreme. [SOURCE: http://caselaw.lp.findlaw.com/scripts/getcase.pl?court=us&vol=416&invol=802]

ALL NATIONS FOUNDATION

As immigration from Mexico increased into Los Angeles between 1910 and 1930, Protestant reformers made proselytizing among the immigrants and eradicating their poverty and squalor their primary goals. Half a million dollars were earmarked for this purpose by the early 1920s. In 1915, the Methodist-Episcopal Church led the way in this commitment with the founding of the All Nations Foundation in the downtown area of Los Angeles. The foundation had an employment agency, a craft shop, a music department, a clinic, health clubs, choral clubs, sewing clubs for girls, sports clubs for boys, and an orphanage. Underlying all of these services was Protestant Christian training. By 1935, the Hollenbeck Center was created by All Nations in Boyle Heights. In stark contrast, the Catholic Church provided few social services until after World War II. Even then, the level of Mexican charity work never approximated that done by the Protestants. [SOURCE: Monroy, *Rebirth: Mexican Los Angeles,* 59.]

THE ALMA CURRICULUM AND TEACHER TRAINING PROJECT

In July 1996, the Goals 2000 Partnerships for Educating Colorado Students awarded a grant to the Denver Public Schools to create the Alma Curriculum and Teacher Training Project. This program has facilitated the development of instructional units on the history, contributions, and issues pertinent to Latinos and Hispanics in the southwest United States in the Denver public schools. The project has also involved outside expert consultants, volunteers, and community organizations in the development of content in history, literature, science, art, and music, as well as in teacher training. In addition, the project has also formed partnerships with various colleges and universities, a decision that was mutually beneficial for all of the participating institutions. [SOURCE: http://almaproject.dpsk12.org/stories/storyReader$89]

ALURISTA (1947-)

The San Diego-poet Alberto Baltazar Urista, more popularly known as Alurista, became the quintessential promoter of Chicanismo and a return to indigenous roots during the 1960s. This most widely read of the Chicano* poets was born in Mexico City in 1947 and moved to the United States as a teenager. He earned a B.A. in Psychology from San Diego State University (SDSU) and then later an M.A. in Spanish literature from the University of California, San Diego. Besides becoming one of the Chicano Movement's* most renowned poets, he co-founded the Movimiento Estudiantil Chicano de Aztlán (MECHA)* and the Chicano Studies Department at SDSU, in 1969. His poetry from 1960 to 1970 idealized the pre-Columbian past and essentialized such mundane aspects of culture as the corn tortilla. His most well-known role was the drafting of El Plan Espiritual de Aztlán (The Spiritual

Alurista

Plan of Aztlán)* at the National Chicano Youth Liberation Conference* sponsored by the Denver-based Crusade for Justice* in the Spring of 1969. In addition, he is credited with applying the concept of Aztlán, the mythical original home of the Aztecs to the Southwest, where the majority of Mexican Americans lived and which had belonged to Mexico before the Mexican-American War. As happened to Luis Valdez,* Alurista was also faulted by Chicano Marxists and other critics for dwelling too much on cultural fantasies. [SOURCE: http://chicano.nlcc.com/bios.html; Rosales, *Chicano!*, 56, 182, 262.]

ALVAREZ, JULIA (1950–)

Julia Alvarez, one of the most popular Latina writers in the United States, received wide acclaim with *How the García Girls Lost Their Accents* and it is considered one of the most significant fictional treatments of the Latina experience. Born in 1950 in New York City, she returned with her family to the Dominican Republic, where she grew up in an extended family of aunts, uncles, and cousins—an experience that has served as an inspiration for her fiction. In 1960, the family was forced to flee the island at a time when the dictator Rafael Leonides Trujillo was losing his grip on power and had embarked on a campaign of repression and violence. The family came to Queens, New York, where Alvarez continued her education and eventually earned degrees in literature and writing. [SOURCE: http://www.geocities.com/Athens/Forum/6517/ everything/latinas.html]

ALVAREZ, ROBERTO R. (1919-2003) *see also* SEGREGATION, *ALVAREZ V. LEMON GROVE*

In 1931, at age twelve, Roberto R. Alvarez was selected as the plaintiff in what would become a landmark Superior Court case to desegregate the Lemon Grove School District, a community near San Diego, California. The Lemon Grove School Board had decided to build a separate school for Mexicans, explaining that Spanish-speaking children needed special instruction. The parents of the Mexican children, most from tight-knit families with origins in Baja California, upon discovering the plan, organized themselves into Los Vecinos de Lemon Grove (The Lemon Grove Neighbors) and won the court battle to keep their children in a school designated for whites only. The court ruled in favor of Alvarez, who represented the hopes of the Mexican community, on the grounds that separate facilities for Mexican-American students were not necessary to achieve Americanization and English-language development in the Spanish-speaking children. Alvarez was selected as plaintiff because of his exemplary academic record at the Lemon Grove School District. He was born in La Mesa, California, in 1919 after his parents Roberto and Ramona Castellanos had migrated from Baja California. Roberto Jr. went on to finish high school and served in the Navy during World War II. He became a successful businessmen specializing in importing and marketing agricultural produce. He died of heart disease in 2003. [SOURCE: Rosales, *Testimonio*, 128-129; http://www.laprensa-sandiego.org/archieve/february28-03/alvarez.htm]

ALVAREZ V. LEMON GROVE see also ALVAREZ, ROBERT R., SEGREGATION

Mexican immigrant leaders in the early twentieth century mounted numerous challenges to the segregation of their children. The most encompassing court victory in this era occurred in Lemon Grove, California, a community near San Diego, during 1930 after the Lemon Grove School Board had decided to build a separate school for Mexicans, explaining that Spanish-speaking children needed special instruction. The parents of the Mexican children, most from tight-knit families with origins in Baja California, upon discovering the plan organized into Los Vecinos de Lemon Grove (The Lemon Grove Neighbors), prevailed in the law suit to keep their children in a school designated for whites only. The court ruled in favor of the Mexican community on the grounds that separate facilities for Mexican-American students were not necessary to achieve Americanization and English-language development in the Spanish-speaking children. [SOURCE: Rosales, *Testimonio*, 128-129; Alvarez, *La Familia: Migration and Adaptation in Baja and Alta California*, 153-155.]

AMERICAN BAPTIST NATIONAL HISPANIC CAUCUS

In May 1970, under the leadership of Reverend Vahac Mardirosian,* a southern California activist minister in the Baptist church, 16 Hispanic ministers decided to confront the church leadership during the annual Baptist convention held in Cincinnati, Ohio. The group demanded equality for Hispanics within Baptist denominational entities. Although Baptist missionary work in the United States dated back to the first decade of the twentieth century, the Hispanic Caucus, as the dissident Hispanic ministry came to be known, felt that church resources were not distributed equally and that not enough attention was paid to the social needs of Hispanic members. This was the first time the denomination had been challenged by the Hispanic ministry, "not by a group that extended its hands as beggars, but as equals." This action resulted in a dramatic reallocation of Baptist denominational resources and in the caucus establishing vigilance to maintain these gains.

The American Baptist National Hispanic Caucus today comes together during the American Baptist Biennials to discuss pertinent issues and elect caucus officers. [SOURCE: http://www.abc-usa.org/hispanic/indexeng.htm]

AMERICAN COMMITTEE FOR THE PROTECTION OF THE FOREIGN BORN, UNITED NATIONS PETITION

In 1959, the American Committee for the Protection of the Foreign Born presented a petition to the United Nations on behalf of Mexican Americans as an "oppressed national minority." According to members of the committee, including activists Ralph Acevedo and Eliseo Carrillo, the petition was necessary because the United States government in ignoring the mistreatment of Mexicans was violating the United Nation's Universal Declaration of Human Rights. The group charged that Mexican-American communities suffered from a state of permanent insecurity because of discrimination, segregation, raids, and repeated deportation drives. [SOURCE: Gutiérrez, *Walls and Mirrors*, 173.]

AMERICAN COORDINATING COUNCIL OF POLITICAL EDUCATION

The 1960 Viva Kennedy clubs* conducted by Mexican Americans as part of the effort to elect John F. Kennedy as president energized many Hispanic leaders to achieve political power at the national level. The Political Association of Spanish-Speaking Organizations (PASSO),* which was primarily based in Texas, served as a vanguard in this effort. In the early 1960s, PASSO laid the groundwork to expand into Arizona and continue political organizing in that state by establishing the American Coordinating Council of Political Education (ACCPE) in Phoenix, Arizona. The Arizona organizers, however, sought a course independent of PASSO, citing the unique needs of Arizona's Mexican Americans, which required home-grown strategies. ACCPE soon established organizations throughout the state and served to bolster the political power of Mexican Americans in Arizona's smaller communities. At its height, the organization boasted 2,500 members and succeeded in supporting the election of Mexican Americans to city councils and school boards in rural communities. ACCPE, however, could not translate success at the local level into state and federal elections and eventually folded. [SOURCE: Meier and Rivera, *A Dictionary of Mexican American History*, 15.]

AMERICAN COUNCIL OF SPANISH-SPEAKING PEOPLE

Dr. George I. Sánchez,* the quintessential intellectual leader of the World War II generation of Mexican-American leaders and a stalwart in the League of United Latin American Citizens (LULAC),* founded the American Council of Spanish-Speaking People in 1950 to serve as a forum for protecting the civil rights of Mexican Americans. Convinced that discrimination in employment, education, and housing, as well as lack of political representation, served as major obstacles to the advancement of Mexican Americans, Sánchez encouraged the organization to struggle for the elimination of these evils. The organization also joined other civil rights groups, such as LULAC and the American G.I. Forum,* in their fight to desegregate schools during this era of intense segregation of Mexican-American children. [SOURCE: Meier and Rivera, *A Dictionary of Mexican American History*, 16.]

THE AMERICAN FEDERATION OF LABOR CONFERENCE

During the early twentieth century, as the union movement in the United States was attempting to gain a foothold throughout the Western Hemisphere, the American Federation of Labor (AF of L) made efforts to reach out to the Mexican labor movement in order to resolve issues common to workers on both sides of the border. In November 1918, Samuel Gompers, president of the AF of L called a meeting in Laredo, Texas, to bring together Mexican labor union leaders like Luis Morones, head of Confederación Regional de Obreros Mexicanos (Regional Confederation of Mexican Workers-CROM) and American government officials such as Secretary of Labor William B. Wilson. Mexican workers in the United States became a major point of discussion. CROM delegates charged that the immigrants encountered myriad problems stemming from discrimination, workplace exploitation, and recurring bouts of unemployment during economic downturns. They asked the AF of L to use its influence to reduce this mistreatment. [SOURCE: Rosales, *Testimonio*, 239-240.]

AMERICAN G.I. FORUM

A dynamic organization that zealously sought the protection of civil rights for veterans was the American G.I. Forum. Mexican-American World War II veterans organized the organization in response to the refusal of a funeral director in Three Rivers, Texas, to bury Felix Longoria,* a soldier killed in the Pacific theater. Key figures in the group were Dr. Héctor P. García,* a former Army medical officer who saw action in Europe, and civil rights lawyer Gus García. Longoria's remains were finally buried at Arlington Cemetery with full honors after Congressman Lyndon B. Johnson* intervened. The organization, nonetheless, became permanent, opened up its membership to veterans and went on to become a leading advocate for civil rights. Unlike LULAC,* whose avowed policy was not to involve itself directly in electoral politics, the forum openly advocated getting out the vote and endorsing candidates. In recent years, the number of once vibrant grassroots chapters of the forum have declined, reflecting the aging and demise of the World War II generation leaders. Dr. García himself died on July 26, 1996. Since the 1970s, the mantle of leadership from the World War II era Forumeers, most of whom did not attend college, passed to younger, college-educated members. The forum, as a result, has become more of a national

Dr. García with Corky Gonzales and American G.I. Forumeers

advocacy organization with full-time lobbyists in Washington, D.C. [SOURCE: Ramos, *The American G.I. Forum;* García, *Hector P. García.*]

AMERICAN IMMIGRATION LAWYERS ASSOCIATION

Founded in 1946 and based in Washington, D.C., the American Immigration Lawyers Association (AILA) is a nonpartisan, nonprofit organization that provides its continuing legal education, information, and professional services to its members. It is made up of more than 8,000 attorneys and law professors who practice and teach immigration law. AILA's members have helped thousands of U.S. clients obtain U.S. permanent residence for spouses, children, and other close relatives. AILA has worked with the private sector to obtain work status for highly skilled foreign workers when employers have proven the unavailability of U.S. workers. In addition, AILA represents foreign students, entertainers, athletes, and asylum seekers, often on a pro bono basis. AILA is an Affiliated Organization of the American Bar Association and is represented in the ABA House of Delegates. [SOURCE: http://www.aila.org/contentdefault.aspx?docid=1021]

AMERICAN LATIN LEAGUE

In 1919, relations between Mexico and the United States became extremely tense as a consequence of border violence stemming from the revolution in Mexico. That year Reginald del Valle, a descendent of an old Californio family, and J.J. Uriburu started the American Latin League in Los Angeles to help Mexican workers obtain better treatment, housing, and wages. During 1919, the United States was threatening to invade Mexico, thus the Mexican government opposed the organization's founding after the Los Angeles Mexican consul heard rumors that the league's purpose was Americanization, an allegation both Uriburu and del Valle vehemently denied. [SOURCE: Rosales, *Pobre Raza!*, 36.]

EL AMIGO DEL HOGAR

The weekly newspaper *El Amigo del Hogar* (Friend of the Home, 1925) was founded by the Círculo de Obreros Católicos San José in East Chicago, Indiana. The organization attracted a number of Mexican immigrant refugees who supported the Cristero Rebellion in Mexico (anti-government uprising by Catholics) and often railed against the repression of that movement. But its pages were not limited to issues of religious persecution and exile, extending to general news, literature, and culture. It also defended the local community by such actions as leading a battle to desegregate local movie houses. [SOURCE: Kanellos, *Hispanic Periodicals in the United States*, 26–27.]

AMIGOS EN AZUL

Founded in 1982 in Austin, Texas, as a Hispanic police officers' association, Amigos en Azul's main goals are to promote a positive image of law enforcement in the Hispanic community. Specifically, the members participate in such youth programs as mentoring at Mendez Jr. High and "Bowling for Badges." In addition, the group broadens the lines of communication by participating in programs and projects of other Hispanic community organizations. Since its inception, Amigos has sponsored an annual picnic and a Christmas dance for members and their families, activities that emphasize positive family values. By conducting extensive community outreach, Amigos encourages Hispanic youths to consider law enforcement careers and provides them with role models. Perhaps the most important aspect of Amigos is the advocating of policies and programs that result in equitable representation and treatment of Hispanics in the Austin Police Department. [SOURCE: http://www.ci.austin.tx.us/empassoc/eaamigos.htm#]

ANAYA, RUDOLFO ALFONSO (1937-)

Born on October 30, 1937, Rudolfo Alfonso Anaya grew up as the fifth of seven children in the rural village of Pastura, New Mexico. The experiences of growing up in a small village became the inspiration for his future writing. At 15, Anaya moved to Albuquerque and graduated from high school in 1956. A few years later, he began studying accounting at a private business school, but found this career unfulfilling. He later obtained a B.A. in English from the University of New Mexico at Albuquerque. While teaching in a small New Mexico town, he discovered that his passion was writing; he continued to practice his writing every day. His wife Patricia Lawless, whom he married in 1966, supported his ambition to write and served as his editor.

Although Anaya continued to teach during the 1960s, he found time to write until he developed his own unique literary voice. His first novel, the monumental *Bless Me, Última* (1972), dealt with the role of a faith healer in rural culture. Other novels such as *Heart of Aztlán* in 1976 and *Tortuga* in 1979 have all been well-received throughout the world. Anaya has continued to write; he taught at the University of New Mexico until he retired in 1993. [SOURCE: http://www.galegroup.com/free_resources/chh/bio/anaya_ r.htm#b_ Essay]

ANDRADE DECISION

On December 12, 1936, Timoteo Andrade stood before Judge John Knight of the First Federal Circuit Court in Buffalo awaiting a citizenship swearing-in ceremony. Andrade was shocked when Knight rejected his application because of his American-Indian heritage. Until the 1950s, naturalization laws denied citizenship to many non-Whites, but the exclusion did not apply to Mexicans, primarily because of the 1897 *Rodríguez v Texas* decision, allowing Mexicans to naturalize as estipulated by the 1848 Treaty of Guadalupe Hidalgo.* Judge Knight, using a legal interpretation provided by the California-based Joint Immigration Committee, ruled the Rodríguez decision to be unconstitutional. He based much of his judgment on a more recent case denying citizenship to a Canadian Native American. Alonso Mclatchey, chairman of the Committee and a member of the family publishing the nativist *Sacramento Bee*, persuaded John Murf, the naturalization officer in charge of Andrade's proceedings, to collude with Judge Knight and reject Andrade's application.

The Mexican government, alarmed over the possibility that such a decision would prevent future immigration, considered appealing the case. After a legal analysis, Mexican officials concluded that the Knight decision was constitutionally defensible. They opted for behind-the-scenes diplomacy. Meanwhile, Sumner Welles, the State Department Latin American affairs specialist, concerned with the potential damage to President Franklin D. Roosevelt's Good Neighbor Policy, assured the Mexican ambassador in Washington that immigration officials would permit Mexicans to enter the United States in spite of the decision. The consul general in New York City then paid $4,000 to a prominent attorney and close friend of the judge to influence Knight to expunge the decision. In this manner, a history-changing event did not take place. Andrade, a native of Jalisco, was sworn in as a citizen, according to his widow, "with a lot of pride and with no ill-feelings against the United States." [SOURCE: Lukens Espinosa, "Mexico, Mexican Americans and the FDR Administration's Racial Classification Policy."]

ANGLO CLAIMS TO CALIFORNIA

California's occupation by Anglo Americans proceeded gradually, impelled by the prospect of financial profit and a desire for expansion. Trappers, the first to move overland, were soon followed by farmers in search of more fertile land. Traders and merchants followed them, arriving in California coastal cities and bringing manufactured goods, which they traded with Californios for hides and tallow. The Californios welcomed the Yankees, who made their lives more comfortable and enjoyable. Unfortunately for the Californios, squatters and gold seekers, who had no desire to interact with Hispanic Californians, soon superceded earlier Anglo settlers. This entry of a large number of Anglo Americans into California served as an historical precursor to the inevitability of the United States occupation of the West Coast.

Throughout this period, England was an obstacle to United States plans for the occupation of California. England had long wanted to occupy California and it had already claimed the Oregon Territory. A controversy over this latter area almost brought the two nations to war in 1843, a conflict which was not settled until 1846 through a compromise which ceded the part of the territory south of the 49th parallel to the United States. Now the path was cleared for United States desires for California. [SOURCE: Campa, *Hispanic Culture in the Southwest*, 98.]

ANNUAL ERNESTO GALARZA COMMEMORATIVE LECTURE

The Stanford Center for Chicano Research (SCCR) inaugurated the Annual Ernesto Galarza Commemorative Lecture in 1986. The program invites prominent Chicana/o scholars or community leaders to inform the university and larger community about issues of major concern to Chicanas/os and to advance the center's research agenda. The SCCR publishes lecture proceedings and disseminates them at a national level. The inspiration for these lectures is Dr. Ernesto Galarza,* a Stanford alumnus, an intellectual, visionary, and scholar who strived to improve the lot of farmworkers in the 1940s and 1950s, and later addressed the problems affecting Chicanas/os in health, educational, and socioeconomic development. "The Galarza Prize for Excellence in Research" is awarded at this event to an undergraduate and graduate student after a competition that encourages students to work with Stanford faculty on a one-to-one basis. [SOURCE: http://ccsre.stanford.edu/UE_maj_ChicanoGalar.htm]

ANTONIO MACEO BRIGADE

During his administration, President Jimmy Carter publicly declared that his policy toward Cuba would not be hostile, as it had been with previous presidents. Basically, he encouraged rapprochement with the Cuban government. Fidel Castro,* in turn, made overtures of reconciliation with the thousands of Cubans who had fled to the United States since his takeover in 1959. Taking this cue, in 1977 a group of 55 young, idealistic Cuban exiles, calling themselves the Antonio Maceo Brigade, traveled to Cuba to participate in service work and to achieve a degree of rapprochement with the Cuban government. There they met with President Castro and some of his top officials. Back in Florida, many of the exiles branded these young envoys as traitors, and in 1979 militants assassinated one of the *brigadistas*, Carlos Muñíz Varela of Puerto Rico. A clear message was sent out to the rest of the Cuban community that any alleged Castro sympathizers would have to face the wrath of the militants. [SOURCES: Masud-Piloto, *From Welcomed Exiles to Illegal Immigrants*, 73; García, *Havana USA*, 203-204.]

APOLINAR PARTIDA, CLEMENTE (?-1922)

As a boy in San Antonio, Clemente Apolinar Partida was committed to a Texas insane asylum after having his skull cracked by a blow to the head. During the summer of 1921, 14-year-old Theodore Bernhart and a group of boys teased and threw rocks at demented Clemente as he drank from a small spring. The infuriated Clemente retaliated by catching Bernhart and crushing his head with a rock and gouging out his eyes. The San Antonio Mexican community wanted to have Apolinar declared mentally incompetent, but an all-white jury found him guilty of first-degree murder. Clemente Apolinar Partida became the last person to hang legally in Texas, at Huntsville in February 1922. [SOURCE: Rosales, *Pobre Raza!*, 144.]

ARCE, JULIO G. "ULICA" (1870-1926)

Julio G. Arce was a newspaper publisher from Guadalajara who took up exile in San Francisco, vowing never to return to Mexico because of his disillusionment with the Mexican Revolution. Born the son of an eminent physician in Guadalajara in 1870, Arce dedicated himself to journalism by founding a newspaper when he was only fourteen. As a practicing pharmacist in Mazatlán, Sinaloa, in 1911, Arce and his family were forced to abandon the city because he opposed the Maderista rebellion. After he resettled in Guadalajara, Carranza army officials imprisoned the rebellious journalist because of his continued opposition to the revolution. After his release, he and his family took the next boat into exile.

Julio G. Arce

In San Francisco, Arce first worked as a laborer, became editor of *La Crónica* (The Chronicle), and then founded his own newspaper, *Mefistófeles*. He soon bought *La Crónica*, which he re-named *Hispano América*; the newspaper continued publishing until 1934, eight years after Arce's death. A prolific writer, Arce satirized American culture and how it affected Mexican immigrants. However, he was most important in his criticism of the American justice system, particularly how it worked against Mexicans and Mexican Americans. Arce claimed Mexicans were framed often and treated unfairly, such as not being provided interpreters. He criticized the community for not getting involved in the justice process until after a defendant had been sentenced to death, when it was virtually too late to help. Arce invited family and friends to approach the Mexican consul and the press to improve the chances of a fair defense. [SOURCE: Kanellos, *Hispanic Periodicals in the United States*, 86-52.]

AREÍTO

In 1973, a group of young and radical Cuban emigrés, mostly from the New York area, traveled to Cuba at the behest of the Cuban government and returned marveling at what they considered revolutionary accomplishments. In early 1974, they began issuing a magazine entitled *Areíto* in order to celebrate the revolution and dispute U.S. propaganda against the Cuban state. They also criticized emigrés for their "bourgeois lifestyles" and the leaders of the Cuban exile community for encouraging political intolerance, racial bigotry, and sexism.

In 1978, *Areíto* members, many who had left Cuba as children and teenagers, claimed in an anthology, *Contra viento y marea* (Against Wind and Tide), published by Havana's Casa de las Américas, that they had left only because they were following their parents' wishes. In 1978, the anthology received the Casa de las Américas Prize from the Cuban government.

Areíto encountered a great deal of hostility, not only from established exile leaders, but from other Cuban students and intellectuals in the United States. The editorial staff of *Areíto* was constantly harassed by conservative emigrés. *Areíto* survived well into the 1980s, in spite of the opposition it received from fellow Cuban Americans. In keeping with their political beliefs, the editors supported the revolutionary movements of all the Americas, especially the struggles in Chile, Nicaragua, and El Salvador. [SOURCE: García, *Havana USA*, 202-203.]

ARGENTINE, KANSAS

During 1924, Mexican parents, mainly from Guanajuato, and the Mexican consul protested when white parents petitioned to segregate Mexicans students in the Argentine, Kansas, high school. After much protesting, Mexican children were allowed to attend the white high school in Argentine, but segregation was enforced in the elementary schools. This compromise did not sit well with either white or Mexican parents, but at least it did not bar the Mexican children from attending high school, which was the case in many places in Texas. [SOURCE: Laird, "Argentine, Kansas: The Evolution of a Mexican American Community, 1905-1940," 123.]

ARTE PÚBLICO PRESS

From its beginnings in the Hispanic civil rights movement to its current status as the oldest and most accomplished publisher of contemporary and recovered literature by U.S. Hispanic authors, Arte Público Press and its imprint, Piñata Books, have become a showcase for Hispanic literary creativity, arts, and culture. In the early 1970s Hispanic writers were not being published by the mainstream presses even though their production was increasing.

To address this need, Nicolás Kanellos,* a literature professor at Indiana University Northwest founded the *Revista Chicana-Riqueña* in Gary, Indiana, in 1972. This quarterly magazine eventually evolved into *The Americas Review*, which received praise and prestigious awards nationwide. After 25 years of launching the careers of numerous Latino authors, the publication of *The Americas Review* ceased in 1999.

The legacy left by this literary magazine, however, provided the foundation for Arte Público Press, which Kanellos inaugurated in 1979. The press provided an even more important national forum for Hispanic literature. When Kanellos was offered a position at the University of Houston in 1980, he was invited to bring the press with him.

As part of the ongoing efforts to bring Hispanic literature to mainstream audiences, Arte Público Press launched the Recovering the U.S. Hispanic Literary Heritage Project* in 1992. The 15-year Recovery project represents the first nationally coordinated attempt to recover, index, and publish lost Hispanic writings that date from the American colonial period through 1960.

The notion of an imprint dedicated to the publication of literature for children and young adults was planted by an urgent public demand for books that accurately portray U.S. Hispanic culture. In 1994, a grant from the Mellon Foundation allowed Arte Público Press to transform the dream into a reality. With its bilingual books for children and its entertaining novels for young adults, Piñata Books has made giant strides toward filling the void in the literary market created by an increased awareness of diverse cultures. [SOURCE: http://artepublicopress.com]

LA ASAMBLEA GENERAL

As Mexico and the United States verged on war in 1919 because of border raids, Mexican officials and immigrants reacted furiously to a congressional speech by the U.S. Senator from Arizona, Henry Ashurst, who proposed annexing Baja California. E. Medina, an officer in the Mutualista Colonia Hidalgo in Bisbee, Arizona, organized La Asamblea General, to object. The group sent Ashurst a resolution calling his proposition imperialistic and circulated copies to Spanish-language newspapers throughout the United States. From Pueblo, Colorado, three immigrants—Fermín Cortés, Francisco M. Tapia, and Pablo Cárdenas—wrote to *El Imparcial de Texas** newspaper in support of the Bisbee group. This action demonstrated the ability of Mexican immigrants to create networks that transcended their local communities. [SOURCE: Rosales, *Pobre Raza!*, 23.]

LA ASAMBLEA MEXICANA

As Houston's Mexican population increased five-fold from 1910 to the mid-twenties, tension between the legal system and the immigrant community increased. Businessmen led by Fernando Salas and Frank Gibler, a former U.S. consul married to a Mexican, formed the Asamblea Mexicana in 1924 to help immigrants who had been jailed unjustly. The organization forced the suspension of a police sergeant in 1928 for jailing, without medical attention, a young Mexican injured in an auto accident. That same year La Asamblea, through Frank Gibler, an Anglo who probably had more influence than fellow members, helped release at least five Mexicans from jail. Like most other organizations established by Mexican immigrants in this era, its effectiveness was diminished by its inability to survive. [SOURCE: De León, *Ethnicity in the Sunbelt*, 36, 39.]

ASOCIACIÓN BORICUA DE DALLAS, INC.

Founded in 1981, the association became incorporated as a nonprofit organization in the State of Texas in 1985. Since its inception, for Puerto Ricans in the Dallas area, it has served to promote, foster, and celebrate Puerto Rican culture and heritage by sponsoring cultural, educational, and artistic activities, and by honoring Puerto Ricans who stand out in the community for their positive contributions. More importantly, the organization encourages other civic participation, such as involvement in local electoral politics, to assure that the interests of the Dallas Puerto Rican community are protected. [SOURCE: http://www.elboricua.com/Directory.html]

LA ASOCIACIÓN DE JORNALEROS

In Texas, Mexicans formed La Asociación de Jornaleros (The Journeymen's Association) in 1933, which represented everything from hat-makers to farmworkers. The union was too diverse to be effective and it died after Texas Rangers* arrested the leaders of an onion harvester strike in Laredo in 1934. Reasons for the difficulty in organizing in Texas were identified by one historian as: "a tradition of paternalistic labor relations, a comparatively repressive political atmosphere, and the huge distances ethnic Mexicans traveled in the migratory labor stream combined to militate against the level of labor unionism that evolved in California." [SOURCE: Foley, *Mexicans, Blacks and Poor Whites in Texas Cotton Culture*, 199; Gutiérrez, *Walls and Mirrors*, 107.]

ASOCIACIÓN TEPEYAC

The Asociación Tepeyac (Tepeyac Association, named after the mount on which the Virgin of Guadalupe appeared in Mexico City), is the largest organization offering protection to Mexican immigrants in New York City. The organization started in 1997 when parish priests in the South Bronx asked Cardinal O'Connor of the Archdiocese of New York for assistance in ministering to the spiritual and social needs of an increasing Mexican immigrant population in their borough. Cardinal O'Connor acceded to the appeal, and the group formed El Equipo Timón (The Rudder Team), partnered with the Jesuits Order of Mexico, and began to visit locales where Mexicans gathered in the city, inviting them to attend activities organized by the Equipo Timón in South Bronx churches. This led to identifying natural leaders who would continue to organize Mexicans to protect their rights as immigrants and to deal with everyday social issues, such as workplace abuse and police harassment. Now the association not only provides legal immigration counseling and day job coordination but it leads efforts to influence the Mexican government to render assistance in resolving their problems. [SOURCE: http://www.tepeyac.org/ns50.alentus.com/histo.asp]

ASPIRA, Inc.

Since its formation in 1958, ASPIRA has developed from a small nonprofit agency in New York City, specializing in counseling Puerto Rican youth, to a national association with offices in 5 states, Puerto Rico, and the District of Columbia. ASPIRA has greatly influenced education reform in New York City. Central to its founding was the role played by educator and social worker Antonia Pantoja* and other members of the Puerto Rican Forum, Inc., the oldest and largest Puerto Rican social service agency in the country.

A lawsuit initiated against the New York City Board of Education in 1974 by ASPIRA led to a landmark Consent Decree* which assured that Spanish-speaking and other non-English-speaking students in the city would have access to bilingual education until they achieved an English-language proficiency which facilitated equal access to education.

Working closely with the Board of Education and the Latino Roundtable on Educational Reform, ASPIRA has been an effective advocate for the educa-

Antonia Pantoja (far right) at ASPIRA meeting

tional needs of Latino children without compromising the educational success of all children. According to one statistic, 90 percent of high school seniors who undergo ASPIRA orientation graduate and go on to college. In addition, the ASPIRA program has been essential to helping bridge the cultural and linguistic gap between Puerto Rican/Latino parents and the New York City educational facilities. It is now a national organization based in Washington, D.C., and while it still primarily serves the Puerto Rican community, other Latinos now receive the benefits of the ASPIRA programmatic agenda, such as sponsorship of cultural events, school programs, scholarship, and student loan programs. [SOURCE: Tardiff and Mabunda, *Dictionary of Hispanic Biography,* 652-3.]

ASPIRA CONSENT DECREE FOR BILINGUAL EDUCATION

In 1972, ASPIRA, Inc., a national grassroots educational service program brought the first suit against a school district to force it to follow federal guidelines for instituting bilingual education. The suit claimed that tens of thousands of Latino students in the New York City school system were receiving inadequate instruction in their native language. As a consequence, in 1974, Puerto Ricans gained the "ASPIRA Consent Degree," a court-mediated compromise, that mandated the Board of Education to provide Puerto Rican and other Spanish-speaking youngsters transitional bilingual education services. The legal counsel to ASPIRA of New York, Puerto Rican Legal Defense and Education Fund (PRLDEF),* has overseen the implementation of the ASPIRA Consent Decree on behalf of Puerto Rican parents for the remainder of the twentieth century and up to the present period. Bilingual education as a pedagogical prescription has been mired in controversy in recent years. Critics have charged that the approach hinders the learning of English. However, in 2003, the PRLDEF released a study that, although it acknowledged that many mistakes were made in the implementing of bilingual education, also found that critics blaming the bilingual teaching for poor educational progress in the classroom did not consider non-classroom factors. The PRLDEF report called for a new approach which does not abandon the philosophy completely, but which streamlines the process of teaching children who do not speak English in the schools. [SOURCE: http://www.prldef.org/About/aboutus.htm]

ASSOCIATED FARMERS OF CALIFORNIA

In California, following the cantaloupe strike of 1928 there were a series of labor disputes in which Mexicans were the main actors. In 1930, two major outbreaks took place in the Imperial Valley among lettuce packers and trimmers led by an all-Mexican union, the Asociación Mutual del Valle Imperial (The Imperial Valley Mutualist Association). Between 1931 and 1941, Mexican agricultural workers struck at least 32 times in California, all the way from Santa Clara in the north to the Imperial Valley in the south.

Farmers found their own method to combat these efforts. For example, after a major strike of primarily Mexican workers in the San Joaquin cotton strike of 1933, they founded the Associated Farmers of California, to stem the onslaught of Mexican-led strikes. Railroad companies and other agricultural industries backed the association, leading critics to believe that the group served as a front for interlocking agriculture business interests. When the Lafollette Congressional Committee formed in the 1930s to investigate labor abuses by employers, it cited the group for violating the civil rights of workers. [SOURCE: Rosales, *Testimonio*, 243-245; Meier and Rivera, *A Dictionary of Mexican American History*, 25.]

ASSOCIATION FOR PUERTO RICAN-HISPANIC CULTURE

The Association for Puerto Rican-Hispanic Culture was established in New York City during 1965 as a cultural not-for-profit organization. The association's main goal was to bring to New York an awareness of the contributions made by the Hispanic civilization by emphasizing the values, the events, and the great figures constituting Hispanic tradition. In addition, the association has served as a contemporary showcase in greater New York Area for Hispanic contributions in the arts. [SOURCE: http://www.hispaniconline.com/res&res/hisporgs/culture_1.html]

ASSOCIATION OF COMMUNITY ORGANIZATIONS FOR REFORM NOW

The Association of Community Organizations for Reform Now (ACORN) was formed in 1970 by a group of Arkansas welfare mothers in a movement to unify the powerless in pursuit of economic justice for all Americans. With more than 175,000 member families organized into 850 neighborhood chapters in 75 cities across the country, today it is the nation's largest community organization of low- and moderate-income African-American, white, and Latino families. Since 1970, ACORN efforts have resulted in better housing for first-time home buyers and tenants, living wages for low-wage workers, more pubic and private investment, and better public education in communities organized by ACORN. As the organization states in its website: "We achieve these goals by building community organizations that have the power to win changes—through direct action, negotiation, legislation, and voter participation." [SOURCE: http://www.acorn.org/index.pp?id=2703]

ASSOCIATION OF HISPANIC ARTS

Based in New York City, the Association of Hispanic Arts, Inc. (AHA) was founded in 1975 as a not-for-profit organization with the goal of integrating Latino arts, artists, and art organizations into the cultural life of the nation. AHA supports artists and organizations through advocacy and outreach programs and services, as well as through such career-building resources as workshops, grant opportunities, and symposiums. [SOURCE: http: //www.latinoarts.org]

ASSOCIATION OF MEXICAN-AMERICAN EDUCATORS

In 1965, California Mexican-American teachers and administrators banded together to create the Association of Mexican-American Educators. It provided input when state and local boards of education, administrators, and faculties devised policies which affected the educational needs of Mexican-American youth. It also participated in politics, most notably when it worked for the election of a Mexican American running for the Los Angeles School Board in 1965. One of its more mundane activities was to act as a clearing house for research on Mexican-American education. [SOURCE: Samora and Simon, *A History of the Mexican-American People,* 196; http://www.jsri.msu.edu/ museum/pubs/MexAmHist/chapter22.html]

ATENCIO, TOMÁS (1932-)

A native of Dixon, New Mexico and a Korean War veteran who studied philosophy in California and then worked in various organizing efforts in California and Texas, Atencio returned to New Mexico in the late 1960s. By then, he had acquired a great amount of Chicano Movement* influence outside of the state. Once back, he organized La Academia de La Nueva Raza in Santa Fe. This grassroots institute emphasized gathering knowledge from village elders through a process called *La Resolona*—informal discussions held by elders in village plazas warmed by the sun. The knowledge which Atencio and his group collected was called *oro del barrio* (barrio gold). Atencio's project demonstrated that New Mexico Chicano* intellectuals could use grassroots and regional knowledge to promote cultural identity. Atencio is now president of New Mexico's Rio Grande Institute, an organization designed to promote self-awareness among Mexican Americans, as well as to foster and preserve their traditions and culture. Throughout most of his life, Atencio has written about his ideas in numerous books and articles. [SOURCE: Rosales, *Chicano!*, 214-215, 224.]

AUSTIN COLONY

In 1821, Moses Austin received permission to obtain land grants from Spain and settle Anglo-American families in Texas, but he died before the project could materialize. His son, Stephen F., prepared to settle a colony of 300 American families between the Colorado and the Brazos rivers. As the plan unfolded, the Spanish government fell to independence forces and Austin learned that the Mexican government did not want to honor the previous agreement. Mexico underwent a chaotic two years of trying to establish a new government, but Austin managed to obtain the concessions anyway from the newly designated Emperor of Mexico, Augustín Iturbide. Under the provisions, every family received 177 acres, and Austin was given 100,000 acres for overseeing the undertaking. The Mexican government waived the tithe to the newcomers, a donation that Mexicans were obliged to pay the Catholic Church, and they were free of any other taxes for six years and subject only to half payments for another six. In addition, the agreement allowed immigrants to import tools and materials for their own use to the value of $2,000 without having to pay customs duty on these imports. Naturalization was conferred automatically on married and self-supporting settlers after they resided in Mexico for three years. Finally, if they were not already Roman Catholics, they had to covert.

Both the Spanish and later the Mexican officials believed that by providing these generous provisions to the American colonists they would end filibustering expeditions by American adventurers seeking to foment revolution and annex Mexican lands to the United States. On August 18, 1824, the first grantees in the Austin Colony entered Texas. Seven months later, the Mexican government allowed the State of Texas-Coahuila to grant land to future colonists. [SOURCE: Campa, *Hispanic Culture in the Southwest*, 179-180.]

AVANCE

In 1973, the Zale Foundation provided seed funding for a group of community social workers to create AVANCE in San Antonio, Texas under the guidance of Dr. Gloria G. Rodríguez. The founders' goal was to provide tools to the community that would strengthen the family unit in low-income areas of the city. Such a prescription would maximize the personal and economic success of these families and also enhance their parenting skills so that they could learn to optimally nurture their children's development. This was done by providing support and education services to heads of families. AVANCE now operates at the national level through their center, disseminating educational material and offering consulting services to providers and policy-makers who work with high-risk Hispanic families. [SOURCE: http://www.avance.org/]

AYRES REPORT

During the early 1940s in Los Angeles, the gang activity of *pachucos** (zoot-suited Chicano street youth) provoked a severe police crackdown and an onslaught of negative media coverage that inflamed a widespread public backlash against Mexicans. Some observers even linked this youth culture to Mexican *sinarquistas* (Fascists). In the atmosphere of War World War II, this was enough to paint all Mexican Americans, who were either children of immigrants or immigrants themselves, with the brush of disloyalty.

These attitudes were exacerbated by the attitudes held by law enforcement officials. In 1942, a number of *pachuco* youths were accused of killing a teenager at a party at a place called Sleepy Lagoon.* In their hearing before the grand jury, Edward Duran Ayres, the Los Angeles sheriff's department chief of the Foreign Relations Bureau, testified that Mexicans were prone to violence and he blamed this condition on their mixed ancestry. The Spaniards and indigenous peoples, according to this dubious eugenics theory, had a history of violent conflict, and after the two groups had merged genetically, the ensuing offspring inherited the worst characteristics of the two races. Ayres' superior, Sheriff E.W. Biscailuz, fully supported this contention, which became known as the Ayres Report. Once publicized, attitudes toward Mexican-American youth were negatively influenced. [SOURCE: Escobar, *Race, Police, and the Making of a Political Identity*, 168-169.]

BACA-BARRAGÁN, POLLY (1941-)

In the late 1960s, with a degree in political science from Colorado State University, Polly Baca-Barragán became one of the first staffers of the Southwest Council of La Raza in Phoenix, Arizona. This organization was part of the now formidable National Council of La Raza.* Born in LaSalle, Colorado, she returned to her home state and served in the state legislature.

Baca-Barragán served as director of Spanish-Speaking Affairs for the Democratic National Committee from 1971 to 1972. In 1978, she became the first Mexican American to serve in the Colorado legislature. Throughout her career, Baca-Barragán has strived to deal with the problems of the poor, especially to create affordable housing for them. [SOURCE: Meier and Rivera, *A Dictionary of Mexican American History*, 29.]

BADILLO, HERMAN (1929-)

Born in born in Caguas, Puerto Rico, on August 21,1929, Herman Badillo was orphaned in Puerto Rico and was sent in 1940 to New York to live

Herman Badillo

with relatives. He acquired all of his education in city schools, including his bachelor's at City College and his law degree at Brooklyn Law School. Badillo entered politics in 1961, losing in a run for state assembly. He was subsequently elected Bronx Borough President in 1965, 4 years after serving as Commissioner for the Department of Relocation. He later made a strong showing in a race for mayor and in 1968 he was elected to the U.S. Congress, eventually serving four terms.

Largely through the efforts of New York Congressman Herman Badillo, the Congressional Hispanic Caucus* was first organized. This signified that for the first time there were enough Hispanic congressmen to have a caucus: a group of five. The caucus is dedicated to voicing and advancing, through the legislative process, issues affecting Hispanic Americans in the United States and its territories.

Congressman Herman Badillo of New York resigned his congressional seat to become the first Puerto Rican appointed as deputy mayor of New York City, under Mayor Edward Koch in 1978. In the 1960s and 1970s, Badillo and other old-line politicians were challenged by Puerto Rican radicals, who accused them of being outdated and ineffective. They charged that Badillo and others had done little to alleviate poverty, substandard health and living conditions, inadequate daycare programs, and unemployment. [SOURCE: Sánchez Korrol, *From Colonia to Community*, 235.]

BAKKE CASE

Many institutions of higher learning attempted to recruit racial minorities during the 1970s to promote diversity and provide them an opportunity which historically had been denied. But in 1978, Alan Bakke filed a suit against the University of California at Davis for reverse discrimination after his application to medical school had been rejected. Provoking Bakke's litigation was the practice of the medical school of sustaining a permanent number of slots for non-white students. Bakke claimed his rights under the Fourteenth Amendment's Equal Protection Clause had been violated because minority students with lower grades and test scores than his were admitted. The lower federal courts ruled against the University of California, charging that using race as a factor in admission was unconstitutional, but the university appealed to the U.S. Supreme Court, which rendered a decision in the case known as *Regents of the University of California v. Bakke* (1978). Ruling that race and ethnicity could be factors in admission practices, the court also maintained that having quotas solely on the basis of race was unconstitutional; thus the ruling amounted to a compromise.

The Mexican-American community took an interest in this case, particularly because it did not have its own universities, as did African Americans and Native Americans. Generally, the community reacted negatively to the courts' decision. [SOURCE: Leeson and Foster, *Constitutional Law.*]

BALDORIOTY DE CASTRO, ROMÁN (1822-1889)

A native of Guaynabo, Puerto Rico, Román Baldorioty de Castro is regarded as one of the most significant fathers of the movement for Puerto Rican independence from Spain. After studying science and biology in Spain and France, he returned to Puerto Rico in 1853 to become a science teacher in San Juan. He also served as Puerto Rican delegate to the Spanish parliament, where he fought for the abolition of slavery and to guarantee constitutional rights for Puerto Rico. To enhance his political goals, he edited and contributed to various journals and newspapers. In 1887, Baldorioty de Castro founded the Autonomist Party, an organization that promoted home government for Puerto Rico. Because of a swelling sentiment for autonomy, Spanish colonial officials began a campaign of repression against political dissenters, and Baldorioty was singled out and imprisoned. His imprisonment in El Morro Castle affected his health and in 1889 he died, shortly after his release. [SOURCE: http://welcome.topuertorico.org/culture/famouspr.shtml]

BARBOSA, JOSÉ CELSO (1857-1921)

The mulatto José Celso Barbosa, born in Bayamón in 1857, was the first black to attend the prestigious Jesuit Seminary in Puerto Rico. After graduation, he went on to receive a medical degree from the University of Michigan. After returning to Puerto Rico he joined the Autonomist Party led by Román Baldorioty de Castro.* In 1893, Barbosa founded the first Puerto Rican cooperativa, El Ahorro Colectivo (The Collective Savings), and in 1907 published

El Tiempo (Time) newspaper. Just before the Spanish American War,* which resulted in Puerto Rico's independence from Spain, Barbosa formed the Republican Party and, on July 4, 1899, advocated that the island become a state of the United States. After the U.S. occupation, he served as a member of the Executive Cabinet from 1900 to 1917 and a member of the Puerto Rican Senate until his death in San Juan in 1921. [SOURCE: http://www.loc.gov/rr/hispanic/1898/barbosa.html]

BARELA, CASIMIRO (1847-1920)

Born in Embudo, New Mexico, Casimiro Barela's family moved in 1867 to southern Colorado, where Barela became a farmer, cattleman, and politician. Barela in 1875 was the only Hispanic delegate to the state constitutional convention of Colorado. Barela secured a provision in the state constitution protecting the civil rights of the Spanish-speaking citizens in addition to a rule providing for the publication of laws in Spanish, English, and German. The state constitution was written and published in both English and Spanish. Elected to the state senate in 1876, Barela served seven consecutive terms, until 1916. Barela held various other elected posts before becoming a state senator. While serving in politics, he kept up his interests in banking and other businesses and became one of the wealthiest men in the state. [SOURCE: Campa, *Hispanic Culture in the Southwest*, 149-152.]

BATISTA, FULGENCIO (1901-1975)

Born in Oriente Province of Cuba in 1901, Fulgencio Batista as an army sergeant in 1935 led a barracks revolt that overthrew a president installed by the military to replace the banished dictator Antonio Machado. The next year, Batista overthrew the government that he himself had helped come to power, and in 1940, after a series of machinations, he was elected the first president under a new constitution promulgated that same year. Batista had become perhaps the most astute opportunist in the history of Cuba. He returned Cuba to levels of corruption not seen since the Machado years. But, at least in this period, he seemed content to allow democracy to take its course by allowing elections. Two irresolute and corrupt administrations followed Batista's in 1944 and 1948, dashing any hopes that these new leaders would bring political stability and honesty to the troubled island republic. Consequently, many Cubans became disillusioned

Fulgencio Batista

with the promises of democracy. Then in 1952, Batista seized power again. This time he ruled as an arrogant dictator and took Cuba to yet new heights of repression and corruption.

During Batista's last rule in the 1950s, the dictator controlled most of the economy and much of the political process. By the time a young lawyer named Fidel Castro* initiated guerrilla warfare against his regime, the former sergeant's feral methods of running his country began to alienate even the most cynical of American supporters. Thus, when Castro came to power in February, 1959, his 26th of July Movement did not meet much resistance from the United States, and at home, he acquired a wide and popular following. At that point, Batista fled with a coterie of supporters to Florida. He died in 1975. [SOURCE: http://www.historyofcuba.com/history/batista.htm; Rosales, "A Historical Overview," in Kanellos, *Hispanic-American Almanac,* 47-48.]

BATTLE OF FORT SAN CARLOS
In May 1780, during the American Revolution, Spanish militias from villages in present-day Missouri were called to help defend the Mississippi River community of St. Louis from an attack by a British force of 1,200 Canadians and Native Americans. Under the command of Spanish Lt. Governor Fernando de Leyba, the Spanish militia, consisting of 29 regulars and 281 militia men, helped American independence fighters in the battle on May 26, a successful effort which drove the British out of Upper Louisiana and the Upper Mississippi River. [SOURCE: http://www.neta.com/%7 E1stbooks/misso.htm]

BEAR FLAG REVOLT
In March 1846, John Charles Fremont took it upon himself to invade California and liberate it from Mexico. Congress would not declare war against Mexico until April of that year. The Mexican military leader, José Castro, ordered Fremont and his entourage out of California. The Americans, however, remained in the Sacramento Valley.

A band of Anglo settlers, calling themselves the California Battalion of Volunteers, became emboldened by Fremont's presence and raided the home of General Mariano Vallejo* in Sonoma and imprisoned the pioneer Californio. The raiders, led by William Knight and Robert Semple, selected General Vallejo because he was a wealthy landholder and an officer in the Mexican Army; his capture served as a symbolic foothold in the liberation of California from Mexico. The rebels held Vallejo and his family incommunicado for four months. Other Bear Flag rebels in northern California devastated ranches, killed cattle, and destroyed crops as a prelude to the war the Americans were trying to incite. Their most infamous act was the killing of aged José de los Reyes Berreyesa and his two nephews, Francisco and

Ramón de Haro, as they beached their boat after a fishing trip. [SOURCE: Campa, *Hispanic Culture in the Southwest*, 98-99.]

BECAS PARA AZTLÁN PROGRAM

The Becas para Aztlán program was a combined effort beginning in 1979 by La Raza Unida Party,* the Mexican government, and the University of Houston to provide Mexican-American students with an opportunity to study at the Colegio de Mexico, Mexico's premiere liberal arts institution. Eventually, in conjunction with the Committee for Rural Democracy, the Mexican government used this program to train medical professionals in Mexican medical schools to expand medical care-giving in Mexican-American barrios in the United States. Because of the program's success, it was expanded to include scholarships for graduate students of social science and humanities. [SOURCE: http://hrc.utsa.edu/hrc/projects.htm#aagpbl; http://libraries.uta. edu/tejanovoices/interview.asp?CMASNo=066]

BELPRÉ, PURA (1900-1982)

A folklorist and children's librarian, Pura Belpré devoted much of her work to preserving the customs and cultural traditions of the Puerto Rican people. Born in Cidra, Puerto Rico, Belpré became the first Puerto Rican to work as librarian in the New York Public Library. In 1921, Belpré executed Latin community projects in several branches of the library system, while also serving as the chief storyteller at the Seward Park Branch. Outside the library, she helped implement Latino programs at the Union Settlement House, Madison House, and the Educational Alliance, institutions with considerable Puerto Rican clientele. Touched by the concern for cultural traditions among the early migrants, Belpré was especially concerned about edu-

cational and culural programs for children, and thus she established programs emphasizing Puerto Rican traditions, games, and folk tales. She felt that young people's self-esteem and desire to learn could be bolstered through storytelling and the internalization of positive language and cultural values. The greatest contributions in fulfilling community cultural needs took place at the Harlem branch, to which she was assigned. Through her efforts, Hispanic exhibitions and programs focusing on the contributions of Latin writers and artists became an institutional fixture.

Belpré eventually began writing down her stories and published more than a dozen

Pura Belpré

children's books, first with a small press, Warne, and later with many of the mainstream commercial publishers of children's literature. Her full-length young adult novel, *Firefly Summer*, which recreates life and culture in Puerto Rico at the turn of the twentieth century, was not published during her lifetime, due to its having been written during World War II, when there was a shortage of paper and a cutback in publishing; it was first issued some fifty years later, in 1997 by the Recovering the U.S. Hispanic Literary Heritage Project.*

Among her best-known children's books are *Pérez and Martina* (1932), *The Tiger and the Rabbit* (1946), and *Juan Bobo and the Queen's Necklace: A Puerto Rican Folk Tale* (1962). Belpré also had a rewarding career in translating English-language children's books to Spanish for major publishing houses. REFORMA,* the organization of librarians serving Hispanic communities, annually confers an award for children's literature in her honor. Pura Belpré died in 1982. [SOURCE: Sánchez Korrol, *From Colonia to Community*, 69.]

BENAVIDES, SANTOS (1823-1891)

Born in Laredo to a prominent family, Santos Benavides became the mayor of his hometown in 1857. Later, he fought for the Confederacy, attaining the rank of Brigadier General. During the Civil War, he recruited many Tejanos (Texas Mexicans) to the Confederate cause and fought to protect the cotton trade with Mexico; Mexico's trade was essential to the South's success. Following the war, Benavides continued his political activities in Laredo and the legislature. He founded and served as president of the Alianza

Benavides Brothers (left and center) in Confederate Army

Hispano-Americana,* which was established to encourage acculturation while protecting civil rights and cultural identity. [SOURCE: Meier and Rivera, *Dictionary of Mexican American History*, 37.]

BERREYSEA FAMILY

The prominent Berreysea family lost its lands in northern California and much of its wealth following the American acquisition of California in 1848 and the subsequent Gold Rush of 1849. The Berreyseas held the land where the New Almaden mercury mine was located. Mercury, an essential ingredient in the amalgamation of gold, made their holdings even more conspicuous, to vigilantes, squatters, and other usurpers. Persistent lawsuits drained the family's resources. Not only did the Berreyseas lose their lands, but in the 1850s eight members of the family were killed by Americans. The remaining members fled to southern California and Mexico. [SOURCE: Meier and Rivera, *Dictionary of Mexican American History*, 38.]

BERRÍOS MARTÍNEZ, RUBÉN (1930-)

Born in Aibonito, Puerto Rico in1930, Berríos has been a lifelong advocate of Puerto Rican independence from the United States. His beliefs led him to head the Puerto Rican Independence Party from 1970 to 1993. In 1971, as a consequence of his role in a sit-in protesting the U.S. military presence on the island of Culebra, U.S. officials jailed him for three months. Berríos, a firm believer in working through the system to obtain his goals, also served in the Puerto Rican Senate from 1972 to 1973. [SOURCE: http://welcome.topuertorico.org/culture/famouspr.shtml]

BETANCES, SAMUEL (?-)

Samuel Betances was born in the South Bronx. Today he is recognized for his inspirational and motivational presentations on such issues as affirmative action in the job market and in educational institutions. Betances uses his own experience as a motivational source. After his birth, Betances' mother took him to Puerto Rico but he returned to the slums of New York City while still a child and against great odds, overcame poverty, racism, violence, welfare, and illiteracy in two languages to obtain a doctorate from Harvard University. He is a trained sociologist and has taught at various universities during the last thirty years. Betances is Full Professor of Sociology at Northeastern Illinois University in Chicago, where he teaches race relations, the U.S. Latino experience, church and society, education and reform, and gender issues. [http://www.speakersaccess.com/speaker.php?id =5&back=home]

BEXAR COUNTY EQUAL OPPORTUNITIES COUNCIL

Founded in 1967, the Bexar County Equal Opportunities Council worked to improve the occupational welfare of the working man. Basically, the organization strove to provide equal employment opportunities for all employees in Bexar County, Texas, without regard to sex, race, color, religion or national origin. [SOURCE: Lane, *Voluntary Associations among Mexican Americans in San Antonio*, 4.]

BILINGUAL EDUCATION ACT

During the 1960s civil rights struggles, community leaders, and educators charged that the educational needs of children whose native language was not English were not being met. Even before federal funding was provided, educators had implemented specific instructional methods of bilingual education using local resources. Concurrently, they pressed officials of the U.S. Department of Education and the Office for Civil Rights to address the language issues of the classroom. The U.S. Congress, then, through the efforts of Senators Joseph M. Montoya* of New Mexico and Ralph Yarborough of Texas, became sensitive to this public concern and, in 1968, the Bilingual Education Act, sponsored by these two senators, was passed. That same year, President Lyndon B. Johnson* signed it into law; it became known as Title VII of the Elementary and Secondary Education Act.* While the U.S. government made its first commitment to addressing the language problem among national minority school children, many school districts ignored the mandate. In May 1970, Stanley Pottinger, director of the Office for Civil Rights, sent a memorandum to school districts with significant numbers of national-origin minority children to inform them of their responsibility under Title VI of the Civil Rights Act,* which outlawed discrimination in federally supported programs; the memorandum also warned them that by ignoring the bilingual requirements they would be guilty of violating that code. The Bilingual Act was amended and refined in 1973 and again in 1978; eventually the opportunity for federal funding led to its implementation throughout the nation.

Nonetheless, in the last two decades of the twentieth century, critics of bilingual education have eroded Title VII's mandate for native language instruction. In 1984, for example, no more than four percent (known as the 4 percent cap) of total funds which schools received from Title VII were allowed for programs not directly using bilingual pedagogic philosophies. Secretary of Education William Bennett in 1985 argued that this cap was not sufficient, and in 1988 it was increased to 25 percent. In the late 1990s, Congress enacted a "Special Rules" provision, and almost any program serving students with limited English proficiency is eligible for funding whether or not it offers native language instruction. [SOURCE: Baker and Hakuta, "Bilingual Education and Latino Civil Rights" http://www.law.harvard.edu/groups/civilrights/papers/bilingual/bilingual.html]

BILINGUAL EDUCATION AND CUBANS IN DADE COUNTY

The influx of Cuban refugees to Dade County, Florida, where Miami is located, led to Spanish becoming a public form of communication. But the educational system did not reflect the importance of bilingualism. In 1963, the Dade County public school system, recognizing this reality, experimented with bilingual education pedagogy, long before the federal government would provide a bilingual education mandate. The first concrete effort to implement the bilingual experiment started in Miami's Coral Way Elementary School, a project funded by the Ford Foundation.* Teachers at the school adhered to what came to be defined as the true meaning of bilingual education. Instead of using Spanish as a transitional language until the Cuban students learned enough English to be assigned to mainstream classrooms, this pedagogical approach encouraged students to retain Spanish while learning English, and thus become fully bilingual. In classrooms and groups of mixed native speakers of English and native speakers of Spanish, the method also taught Spanish to the native English-speakers. Dade County's innovative approach served as a model for bilingual education programs around the country. [SOURCE: García, *Havana USA,* 41-42, 81-82.]

BILINGUAL EDUCATION IN EARLY CALIFORNIA

Los Angeles city officials enacted the first school ordinance in 1851 supportive of bilingual education. It provided that "all the rudiments of the English and Spanish languages should be taught" in all the schools subsidized by public funds.

In 1856, political leader Antonio Coronel* became the first Hispanic to petition a local school board for bilingual education. Coronel promoted the Spanish language because of the economic interests and the public service that could be rendered through its use. Although the petition failed to have the Los Angeles school board implement bilingual education, his action, along with his considerable political and intellectual leadership as an entrepreneur and newspaper publisher, set an important precedent.[SOURCE: San Miguel, "Education" in Kanellos, *Hispanic-American Almanac,* 297.]

THE BILINGUAL FOUNDATION OF THE ARTS

The Bilingual Foundation of the Arts was founded in 1973 by Latino actors led by Carmen Zapata. Originally it existed as an itinerant theatre company performing in various venues throughout Los Angeles, California, but in 1980, the troupe established a permanent home in Lincoln Heights and has since mounted numerous productions. Since its founding, the foundation has reached more than one million children and teenagers through its touring theatre-in-education programs, while still maintaining a permanent stable of adult patrons. The productions of the foundation, which maintains the only professional bilingual theatre company on the West Coast, are

Carmen Zapata

partially funded by box office receipts, but most of its expenses are met through private donations and grants. [SOURCE: http://www.bfatheatre.org/]

BILINGUAL PRIVATE SCHOOLS ASSOCIATION

Established in 1975 in Miami, Florida, the Bilingual Private Schools Association's (BIPRISA) main goal is to raise community awareness of the advantages offered by bilingual education. BIPRISA is made up of bilingual private schools, and through its organizational efforts, several private schools have been founded throughout the United States. [SOURCE: http://www.hispaniconline.com/res&res/hisporgs/edu_1.html]

BILINGUAL REVIEW/PRESS

Bilingual Review/Press began publishing the works of Hispanic writers in 1973 at a time when few outlets existed in mainstream press for the rising need that was prompted by an artistic renaissance among Latinos in the United States. The press has averaged the publication of eight to ten titles a year and usually keeps about 150 titles on its backlist. Most of its books are in English and are by or about U.S. Hispanics; the press has published bilingual and Spanish-only titles as well. Since its founding by Dr. Gary Keller, then a professor at York College, the press has pursued a publication agenda that foregoes purely commercial entertainment and focuses instead on works that treat serious issues that are socially relevant to the large Hispanic population in the United States. Importantly, while Bilingual Review/Press publishes works by both established and emerging writers, it also keeps alive important Mexican-American works that have gone out-of-print since the 1960s in its Clásicos Chicanos/Chicano Classics series. The press moved to Arizona State University in 1987, when Professor Keller was offered a position at that institution. [SOURCE: http://www.asu.edu/brp/brp.html]

BISBEE "DEPORTATIONS"

Two months after the United States entered the World War I in 1917, copper mine workers went on strike in Bisbee, Arizona. The stoppage was influenced by the Industrial Workers of the World (IWW), or Wobblies, creating anxiety in this southeastern Arizona community. Vigilantes rounded up some 1,200 strikers, many of whom were Mexican, and shipped them out of Arizona in crowded trains without food and water, to Columbus, New Mexico, where most of the deportees remained stranded for two months under the care of federal agencies. Eventually, many of the "deported" workers made their way back to Bisbee on their own. Charges against the illegal vigilante action were filed over the next three years, but no court action followed. [SOURCE: http://digital.library.arizona.edu/bisbee/index.php]

BISHOP'S COMMITTEE FOR HISPANIC AFFAIRS.

In January 1945, Archbishop Robert E. Lucey* helped found the Bishop's Committee for the Spanish Speaking (BCSS) in San Antonio, Texas. Today it is known as the Bishop's Committee for Hispanic Affairs. Lucey, other clergy and Catholic lay leaders considered that improving the social and spiritual welfare of Texas' Mexican Americans was a church responsibility. This commitment was evident as early as 1941, when Lucey helped organize summer programs of "social justice," which instilled in priests a commitment to improving the deplorable conditions of poverty and racism endured by Texas Mexicans.

During the next three years, strategizing meetings led to the founding of the BCSS with a goal of empowering Texas Mexicans politically and in the workplace. The committee established its permanent headquarters in San Antonio, with Archbishop Lucey as its executive director, and planned to expand through a system of regional offices throughout the Southwest. As part of its agenda of obtaining social and economic justice, the BCSS first centered its programs in cities such as San Antonio, El Paso, and Corpus Christi, offering religion classes for children, child-care programs, clinics, community centers, public housing, youth work, and labor organizing campaigns.

In 1950 while Lucey served on President Harry S. Truman's investigative panel looking into the plight of rural workers, the BCSS began championing the cause of migratory farm laborers. Public hearings around Texas provided Lucey with the opportunity to solicit testimonies attesting to the substandard salaries and exploitation endured by farmworkers and *braceros* (Mexican guest workers). The hope that such remonstrance would result in protective legislation for farmworkers was dashed when politicians only showed indifference. Lucey then launched a volunteer project in which Diocese parishioners contributed their time to help poor migrants as they followed crop harvests. However, these efforts only provided temporary relief. The lack of a total commitment from the church resulted in meager funding and the project waned. Nonetheless, throughout the 1950s, the committee continued to fight for farmworkers and oppose the Bracero Program,* which Lucey considered a system of "slave laborers."

When in the 1960s, Texas farmworkers initiated a series of strikes to gain collective bargaining rights, the BCSS provided support. When younger, outspoken priests did not toe the line, the authoritarian Lucey resorted to punitive measures. In 1969, a number of priests demanded his resignation; it was the end of his long association with the BCSS. That same year, the committee became the Bishops' Committee for Hispanic Affairs and broadened its agenda to include a greater national reach. A number of high-ranking Catholic clergy have succeeded Lucey in remaining committed to the initial goals of the organization. In 2002, the Reverand James A. Tamayo, the Bishop of Laredo, was elected director and continues to promote the mission of the committee, which is:

- To ASSIST the Catholic Church in its efforts to serve the large Catholic Hispanic/Latino population in the United States and in the New Evangelization.
- To COORDINATE Hispanic ministry efforts in the Catholic Church through regional and diocesan offices, pastoral institutes, secular and ecclesial organizations, and apostolic movements.
- To PROMOTE the implementation of the National Pastoral Plan for Hispanic Ministry, *Ecclesia in America, Many Faces in God's House: A Catholic Vision for the Third Millennium*, and other church documents, as well as the development of small ecclesial communities.
- To INTEGRATE the Hispanic presence into the life of the Catholic Church and society.

[SOURCE: Acosta, "The Bishops' Committee for Hispanic Affairs," http://www.tsha.utexas.edu/handbook/online/articles/BB/icb5.html; http://www.usccb.org/hispanicaffairs/mission.shtml]

BLACK BERETS

In Albuquerque, New Mexico, the Black Berets were formed in 1969 to work in conjunction with the publishers of *El Grito*, a newspaper loosely associated with La Alianza Federal de Las Mercedes* and the Chicano Youth Association (CYA),* started by José Armas. Alianza director Reies López Tijerina's* renown was one of the reasons that New Mexico attracted so many Chicano* activists from outside of the state. The Black Berets and the CYA, however, were among the few organizations that engaged in urban-style protests, especially against police brutality. One of their most militant acts was to force their way into Governor Bruce King's office to lodge a number of grievances on behalf of Chicanos. Many of the members were arrested in this incident. [SOURCE: Rosales, *Chicano!*, 214.]

BLANC, GIULIO V. (1955-1995)

Born in Havana in 1955, Giulio V. Blanc emigrated to the United States in 1960 and subsequently received degrees from Harvard College and the Institute of Fine Arts in New York City. Because of his numerous articles and catalog essays, Blanc is ranked as one of the leading authorities on Latin American art. In the 1970s and 1980s, Blanc established himself as a promoter of Cuban and Cuban-American artists by opening venues in U.S. galleries and museums. For example, he brought to Miami's Cuban Museum of Art and Culture some of the most significant exhibitions ever mounted by Cubans in the United States, such as the *The Miami Generation* (1983). To the New York's Studio Museum in Harlem, Blanc brought *Amelia Peláez: A Retrospective* (1988) and the celebrated *Wifredo Lam and His Contemporaries* (1991). Blanc was especially proud of the *The Miami Generation* exhibit which featured Cuban-born artists who emigrated to the United States after the Cuban Revolution of 1969 and were raised with bicultural influences. [SOURCE: http://www.aaa.si.edu/collections/findingaids/blangiul.htm#a2]

BLANCO, LUCIO (1879-1922)

During the Mexican Revolution, political exiles in the United States, considered dangerous by the group in power in Mexico were often kidnapped and taken back to Mexico, where they faced reprisals. The most notorious "extradition" of this type was of the land-reform advocate from Coahuila, Lucio Blanco. Like Emiliano Zapata,* Blanco, who was born in Nadadores, Coahuila, in 1879, emerged from the chaos of the Mexican Revolution with an untarnished reputation on both sides of the border as true to his ideals. After Venustiano Carranza's assassination, Blanco fell from favor among the new ruling clique led by Álvaro Obregón. From his South Texas exile, where he had many friends among other exiles and Texas Mexicans, Blanco plotted to overthrow the Mexican government. Mexican agents reported in the Spring of 1922 that Blanco's plan to take over Nuevo Laredo military installations and use the border town as a launching pad for further insurrection was gaining many adherents. A worried President Obregón then instructed Secretary of the Interior Plutarco Elías Calles to extradite Blanco and arrest him. Early on the morning of June 7, 1922, Calles' agents posed as weapons traffickers and lured Blanco to the Laredo, Texas, townsquare and kidnapped him, purportedly to take him across the river to the Mexican side on a raft. The next day, however, his body was found on the Texas bank of the Rio Grande. [SOURCE: Rosales, *Pobre Raza!*, 181.]

BLISS BILL

In 1931, California Assemblyman George R. Bliss, from Carpinteria, introduced a bill designed to segregate students of Native American, Mexican, and Asian descent under "separate but equal" rationale. The bill passed in the California Assembly but was defeated in the Senate. Lawmakers recognized the difficulty of separating Mexicans, who were considered white, after the precedent set by the Lemon Grove decision that same year had established that Mexicans could not be segregated on a racial basis. Still, school boards maintained segregation by relying on the need to provide remedial language instruction. [SOURCE: Alvarez, Jr., "The Lemon Grove Incident: The Nation's First Successful Desegregation Court Case," *The*

Journal of San Diego History, http://www.sandiegohistory.org/journal/86 spring/lemongrove.htm]

BLOODY CHRISTMAS CASE

On Christmas Eve, 1951, police from the Lincoln Heights jail in Los Angeles beat seven young men, most of them of Mexican descent, at intervals of several hours. The jailers, who became drunk while celebrating Christmas, went into the prisoners' cells, wished them a Merry Christmas, beat them, and burned them with lighted cigarettes. When the inmates were finally hospitalized, one prisoner had sustained a severe concussion and had barely enough blood to sustain his life. All of them had injuries of one kind or another. The Community Services Organization (CSO)* demanded a Grand Jury investigation. Five of the policemen involved in the fracas had to serve prison sentences ranging from 1 to 10 years. The CSO acquired national attention because of its successful activist role in this incident. [SOURCE: "Sí Se Puede! César E. Chávez and His Legacy," http://latino.sscnet.ucla. edu/research/chavez/themes/ufw/history2.html]

BLUE RIDGE FARM

During the 1920s, the majority of Mexican prisoners in Texas served their sentences at Blue Ridge Farm, a segregated Texas facility. In December 1929, the Mexican Embassy protested that the 260 prisoners at the farm were serving questionably long sentences, performing extremely hard labor, and were being subjected to floggings and attacks by guard dogs. In one incident, a prisoner, Anastasio Reyna, fell ill on a farm detail and when he asked for assistance the guards forced him to go back to work. Reyna collapsed and died from sunstroke. As in other prisons during this time, only a small number of the Mexican convicts at Blue Ridge understood English—the majority were born in Mexico. [SOURCE: Rosales, *Pobre Raza!*, 166.]

BORDER LIAISON MECHANISM

The rise in violence along the United States-Mexico border in the 1980s and early 1990s led the two countries to establish in 1992 a joint Border Liaison Mechanism (BLM) to treat border problems of mutual concern. To accomplish this, the BLM had under its umbrella a number of units, such as the Council for Public Safety, created in mid-1997. The council was created in part, to respond to shooting incidents in which both U.S. officials and Mexican smugglers were implicated. In addition, the council has sought to establish a cooperative linkage between U.S. and Mexican law enforcement agencies (federal, state, and local) in the San Diego-Tijuana area. [SOURCE: Martin, "Mexico-U.S. Migration," *Immigration in U.S.-Mexican Relations*, http://www.iadialog.org/publications/country_studies/immigrat.html]

Border Patrol

BORDER PATROL

Previous to the restrictive laws of 1917 and 1924, the Immigration and Naturalization Service (INS)* had maintained special inspectors on the border to halt Chinese entries who were barred completely from entering the United States. The Border Patrol, organized in 1924 to augment thinly staffed customs agents, was given primary responsibility for curbing illegal entries from Mexico, because now all immigrants had to fulfill more stringent requirements to enter the United States. But personnel limitations limited its effectiveness. In 1925, for example, only nine men, responsible for some ninety miles of border, operated in the El Paso area.

To upgrade contravention, Secretary of Labor James J. Davis, who oversaw this immigration agency, created three principal immigration districts with headquarters in San Francisco. Harassment by agents of Mexicans heightened in the 1920s, prompting the Mexican Chamber of Deputies to pass a law requiring the government to extend protection to emigrants. In 1940, the INS became part of the Department of Justice and grew to become one of the largest federal agencies. The Border Patrol continues to monitor migration at the international borders and, although its record of excessive harassment and violation of civil rights has improved from its early days, immigration rights activists constantly criticize the agency for often enforcing immigration laws using overzealous methods. [SOURCE: Rosales, *Chicano!*, 37; http://www.cbp.gov/xp/cgov/border_security/border_patrol/history.xml]

EL BORICUA

Founded in 1995, *El Boricua* is an electronic monthly cultural magazine that is solely available on-line. Both the web site where the magazine appears and the publication itself are dedicated to reach Puerto Ricans wherever they might reside, "so that they can remember their culture, learn about their roots and history, and be proud to call themselves Boricuas and Puertorriqueños." Through a variety of articles, written by volunteers, the magazine provides its readers with a glimpse of Puerto Rican "history, historical places, culture, traditions, typical recipes, music, musicians, Boricua heroes of today and yesterday," and promotes a positive image of Puerto Ricans and the island. Based in New York City, the staff continues dedicated to these objectives. [SOURCE: http://www.elboricua.com/aboutus.html]

BORICUA '96, VOTER VISIBILITY CAMPAIGN

Boricua '96, Voter Visibility Campaign was held on Saturday, March 29, 1996, in Washington, D.C., in conjunction with Boricua First! National Puerto Rican Affirmation Day.* At this event, activists discussed the issues facing the Puerto Rican community in the 1996 presidential elections and developed action plans to insure the visibility and political presence of the Puerto Rican community during this election. [SOURCE: http://www.bateylink.org/about.htm]

BORICUA FIRST! NATIONAL PUERTO RICAN AFFIRMATION DAY

Boricua First! was celebrated in Washington, D.C., on March 29, 1996, by Puerto Rican leaders from throughout the United States and Puerto Rico. The event brought attention to the public policy needs of the Puerto Rican community and celebrated the contributions of the Puerto Rican community. A number of strategy sessions developed solutions to the many issues facing the Puerto Rican community in the United States. In addition, the event served to bolster a national Puerto Rican leadership network to implement the political agenda formulated at this meeting.

Special tribute was paid to the Puerto Ricans who have served in the military. In addition, delegations met with various congressional leaders and cabinet agency heads to present public policy agendas. Public policy forums were hosted by Puerto Rican members of Congress in the Capitol Building on the issues of health, education, veterans affairs, and economic development. The Boricua First! activities in Washington, D.C., ended with the presentation of petitions to President Clinton for the pardon of the fifteen Puerto Rican political prisoners who had been convicted and jailed in the 1980s for subversive activities linked to Puerto Rican independence movements. [SOURCE: Gonzales and Rodríguez, "Puerto Ricans—U.S. Citizens in Limbo," http://www.indigenouspeople.net/indios2.htm]

BORINQUEN FEDERAL CREDIT UNION

Philadelphia community volunteers founded the Borinquen Federal Credit Union in 1974 to serve the employees and clients of Casa del Carmen, a social service organization. It was closed in 1986, but because it served such a crucial role in the community, Puerto Rican leaders reopened it a few months later. The credit union, located in the North Fifth Street Latino barrio of Philadelphia, demonstrated just how important such a financial institution can be in serving neighborhood banking needs and encouraging local economic development. [SOURCE: http://www.2.hsp.org/collections/balch %20manuscript_guide/html/puertorican.html]

BOX, JOHN CALVIN (1871-1941)

A prominent Texas politician and member of the House of Representatives from Texas, John C. Box, played a crucial role in congressional hearings during the 1920s that examined the growing threat of the "Mexican problem," that is, the sentiment that Mexican immigrants were unwanted and undesirable. Born near Crockett, Texas, while serving in Congress from 1919 to 1931, he sponsored the most vehement nativist legislation to curb Mexican immigration. Box along with fellow colleagues in Congress had successfully curbed immigration from Southern and Eastern Europe, but he and his fellow restrictionists found curbing Mexican immigration more difficult. A strong southwestern lobby of growers and employers constantly received waivers on provisions which normally excluded Mexicans, particularly those of the laboring class, from admission into the United States. The only partial victory for Box and other restrictionists occurred at the onset of the Depression in 1929, when Congress finally passed the Immigration Act of 1929, which effectively slowed Mexican immigration, even authorizing deportation of undocumented workers. The act also stipulated that any immigrants caught with improper documents could be jailed, fined, and deported without hesitation. [SOURCE: Reisler, *By the Sweat of Their Brow.*]

BRACERO PROGRAM

Mexican president Lázaro Cárdenas hand-picked General Manuel Ávila Camacho to replace him in 1940. Ávila Camacho was a moderate who decided during World War I to curry favor with the United States by supporting the war effort. Negotiating the Bracero Program, which provided badly needed workers during World War II, became the most important manifestation of this support.

In 1943, the Emergency Farm labor Program, also known as Public Law 45, was implemented to meet this wartime need for labor. At first, many growers initially opposed the project because they loathed to comply with federal regulations concerning wages and housing. Texas farmers rejected it

Braceros leaving Mexico for the United States

outright, preferring to use their own methods of recruitment. Then in late 1943, Texas employers discovered that Mexican workers were not as easy to obtain as in previous years and asked to be included in the program. The reputation for mistreatment of Mexicans that Texas subsequently acquired prompted the Mexican government to prevent the entry of guest workers into the Lone Star State.

The Bracero Program, as it was better known, was instrumental in reviving immigration from Mexico during the war years. Starting in 1942, U.S. labor agents actually went into Mexico and recruited thousands of workers, who in turn inspired many others to immigrate without the benefit of the program. Until the program ended in 1964, many of these contract-laborers worked primarily in agricultural communities and in railroad camps, some of them staying in the United States or returning later after they had been returned to their home country. Often the provisions established by the agreement, which would insure the well-being of the *braceros*, were violated by employers.

Employers, in the main, supported continuing the program beyond the war years, while the millions of dollars which the guest workers sent back to Mexico persuaded the Mexican government to agree on a continuance. However, the American labor movement and Mexican-American leaders eventually persuaded Congress to discontinue the program in 1964. [SOURCE: García, *Operation Wetback*, 18-71.]

BRACERO PROGAM FOR PUERTO RICANS

In 1898 after the United States had acquired Puerto Rico, the island remained occupied by the military until 1917, when Puerto Rico obtained limited local autonomy. The same year, the Jones Act* granted U.S. citizenship to Puerto Ricnas. In the meantime, thousands of subsistence farmers on the island lost their land and livelihood, as large sugar plantations financed mainly by Americans came to dominate the countryside. The displaced peasants either entered the rural wage labor force or migrated to urban areas, where many became seasonally unemployed.

When the United States entered World War I, labor shortages plagued many industries on the mainland as the economy boomed because of wartime production and as thousands of young Americans were conscripted into the military. The possibility of Puerto Rico as a labor source loomed large. In October 1917, F.C. Roberts, a special representative of the Labor Department, traveled to Puerto Rico to research the possibilities; he estimated that 75,000 Puerto Ricans could come to the United States as guest workers, a number confirmed by Santiago Iglesias, a member of the Puerto Rico Senate and president of the Free Federation of Labor for Puerto Rico, an affiliation of the American Federation of Labor. In May 1918, the U.S. Labor Department announced that it planned to transport more than 10,000 Puerto Rican laborers to the United States to work on war-related projects in Norfolk and Newport News, Virginia, and Baltimore, Maryland.

The U.S. Employment Service set the wage at 35 cents an hour, with time-and-a-half for overtime work. Guest workers would live in government-arranged housing and would be allowed to eat in the government commissary, each man paying 25 cents per meal. The War Department agreed to transport the islanders on the home trips of transports carrying supplies to the mobilization base at San Juan. [SOURCE: "To increase common labor supply with Porto Ricans," *U.S. Employment Service Bulletin*, Department of Labor, Washington, D.C., May 21, 1918 (Washington, D.C.: National Archives), http://historymatters.gmu.edu/d/5065/]

BRISCOE, DOLPH (1923-)

In the 1972 Texas gubernatorial election, La Raza Unida Party (LRUP)* candidate Ramsey Muñiz* was pitted against rancher Dolph Briscoe, a conservative banker and rancher from Uvalde, Texas, who had won the Democratic primary in a tight race against Frances "Sissy" Farenthold, a liberal. The Republicans were hopeful that in the general election the LRUP would serve as a "spoiler" for Briscoe and the Democrats, allowing their candidate, Henry Grover, to prevail. During his campaign, Muñiz crisscrossed Texas attempting to persuade Mexicans to change their Democratic voting ways and to woo disaffected white liberals and black leaders. The Republican Party appreciated the LRUP, however, because it stood to remove a significant sector of the Mexican-American vote from the ranks of the Democratic Party. In the elections, Muñiz obtained 6 percent of the Texas votes, the vast majority of which had been cast by Mexican Americans. This surprisingly large margin denied Briscoe a majority over his Republican opponent. In the ultimate analysis, the Texan LRUP stood no chance of winning a statewide election; it only functioned as a potential "spoiler" that would benefit Republicans. [SOURCE: Rosales, *Chicano!*, 237-238, 245-246; Acosta, "Raza Unida Party," *The Handbook of Texas Online*, http://dev.tsha.utexas.edu/handbook/online/articles/RR/war1.html]

BRITE RANCH

A by-product of the Mexican Revolution was border banditry, smuggling, and vice. These developments disturbed Anglo Americans to such a degree that a backlash, which the historian Ricardo Romo dubbed the "Brown Scare,"* exacerbated an already existing antipathy. One incident typifying these dynamics occurred when pillagers, allegedly Villistas (followers of Pancho Villa*) crossed the border near Marfa on Christmas day, 1917 and raided the Brite Ranch and general store, taking about $2,000. Guests coming to a party given by ranch foreman Vandel Neill were warned off and allowed to proceed to the house unharmed. But bandits fired on postman Mitchell Welch as he approached in a hackney; they killed two Mexican passengers and hung the mailman when he tried to stop them from stealing his mules. On January 18, 1918, in response to the attack, vigilantes and Texas Rangers,* with U.S. Army troops lying in wait, executed fifteen Mexican immigrants in the Texas town of Porvenir.* [SOURCE: Rosales, *Pobre Raza!*, 19.]

BROWN BERETS

The genesis of the Los Angeles Brown Berets is found at Camp Hess Kramer,* a 400-acre spread in the rolling hills just east of Malibu, California. In April 1966, in an effort to address such problems as gangs, school drop-out rates, access to college education among Mexican-American youths, the Los Angeles County Human Relations Council and community leaders met with some 200 teenagers from various backgrounds in round-table discussions. The next year, many of the same young people attended a follow-up meeting at the camp. There the leadership qualities of David Sánchez, a youth worker for the Episcopalian Church of the Epiphany under Father John Luce, stood out, and he earned a place on the Mayor's Youth Council, which elected him chairman. Aware from first-hand experience of the tension existing between the police and Mexicans in Los Angeles, Sánchez tried to bring up the issue to the youth council, but was rebuffed.

This experience showed him that working through the system was often cumbersome and ineffective.

In the summer of 1967, at age seventeen and still working for Father Luce, Sánchez wrote a successful proposal to the Southern California Council of Churches for funding to start the Piranya coffee house—envisioned as a hangout to keep teens out of trouble. Sánchez invited friends from Camp Hess Kramer to form the Young Citizens for Community Action (YCCA). Initially, the group tried to work within the system, but the social ferment which characterized East Los Angeles during this time radicalized the YCCA. L.A. Police often harassed them because the group criticized law enforcement tactics, and the young Mexican Americans in turn became more alienated from the officials. In March 1968, the group attracted national attention when it helped organize a walkout of East Los Angeles high school students who protested inadequate education conditions. Then in early June, L.A. County officers arrested thirteen persons (The L.A. Thirteen), some of them, members of the YCCA, for organizing the walkouts. By this time the group became known as the Brown Berets, a moniker which stemmed from the color of the headgear which the young Chicanos* began to wear as part of their paramilitary uniform. Many militant organizations, sported berets during this era, the most famous being the Black Panther Party, made up of Marxist-spouting activists whose antics Sánchez and his cohorts saw first-hand in California. After much legal maneuvering, the county dropped charges against the L.A. Thirteen.

By 1971, internal dissension led to erosion of the organization, but later that year Sánchez began La Caravana de la Reconquista, a tour of the Southwest designed to proliferate Brown Beret ideas; this tactic did not ward off their continuing decline. In an attempt to dramatize their cause, 26 Brown Berets occupied Santa Catalina Island in August 1972, arguing that the Channel Islands were not ceded in the Treaty of Guadalupe Hidalgo.* After a 24-hour occupation, the sheriff's department forced the Brown Berets back to the California mainland.

Immediately after this event, Sánchez disbanded the organization. At one point, the Brown Beret leadership exceeded five thousand, but it's collapse probably reflected the inability of the group to create an ideological base, which could resonate among the general Mexican-American community. [SOURCE: Marín, *Social Protest in an Urban Barrio*, 75-76; Escobar, "The Dialectics of Repression," 1495-6.]

BROWN SCARE

Coined by the historian Ricardo Romo, this term referred to the exacerbated tension created by the increasing numbers of Mexicans who immigrated to the United States during the time of the Mexican Revolution, mostly between 1910 and 1930. Like the "Red Scare" of later years, the "Brown Scare" made Anglos paranoid toward Mexican Americans and led to violations of their civil and human rights. Border violence and revolutionary warfare received wide coverage in the popular press, thus adding to the "Brown Scare." Increasing this fear was the apparent failure of American efforts to regulate the border. Thus, the scare played off fears that Mexico and Mexicans might overrun the borderland region. [SOURCE: Romo, *East Los Angeles*, 89-111.]

BUILDING UP LOS ANGELES

Building Up Los Angeles is the largest state-commissioned National Service project in the Los Angeles area. The project, which started in 1992, functions with the collaboration of more than 60 community-based organizations, colleges and universities, and human service agencies. Building Up coordinates 150 AmeriCorps members, who address many critical needs of local Los Angeles neighborhoods. The accomplishments of the project include the establishment of after school programs, neighborhood beautification programs, and youth forums designed to bridge divisions among African-American and Chicano/Latino communities. [SOURCE: http://clnet.sscnet.ucla.edu/community/intercambios/buildla.htm]

CABALLEROS DE LABOR

In 1888, the Caballeros de Labor, one of the first Hispanic labor unions to serve the Southwest, was founded in San Miguel County, New Mexico, under the leadership of Juan José Herrera, a district organizer for the Knights of Labor (a nationwide union founded in Philadelphia in 1869). Although the Caballeros de Labor was a labor union, it had never been chartered by the Knights of Labor, possibly because most of its efforts were directed at fighting Anglo-American land-grabbing. [SOURCE: Meier and Rivera, *Dictionary of Mexican American History*, 60.]

CABEZA DE VACA, EZEQUIEL (1864-1917)

Born near Las Vegas, New Mexico, Ezequiel Cabeza de Vaca received his college degree from Denver's Jesuit St. Regis College. Upon returning to New Mexico, he taught school in rural areas. In 1890, he began his journalistic career with the leading Spanish-language newspaper, *La Voz del Pueblo*,* published by Félix Martínez,* an originator of El Partido del Pueblo Unido, an affiliate of the national Populist Party. After helping organize the party, Cabeza de Vaca became the editor of *La Voz del Pueblo* in 1900, a position that allowed him to enter into the orbit of political power in New Mexico. At the state constitutional convention in 1910, Cabeza de Vaca fought for provisions to protect the rights of Mexicans. Cabeza de Vaca was elected lieutenant governor in the state's first elections in 1911 and governor

Vicente Ximenes being sworn into the EEOC

in 1916. He died only two months after he began his term as governor. Many New Mexicans believe that if he had lived, Cabeza de Vaca would have fought for universal educational and civil rights. [SOURCE: Meier and Rivera, *Dictionary of Mexican American History,* 60-61.]

CABINET COMMITTEE ON OPPORTUNITIES FOR SPANISH-SPEAKING PEOPLE

By the 1960s, traditional Mexican-American civil rights leaders began to reflect the confrontation tactics which were becoming so prevalent in the Black civil rights movement. They showed this militancy when they walked out of the 1966 Equal Employment Opportunity Commission (EEOC)* in Albuquerque; the walkout reverberated among Mexican-American organizations throughout the country. In response to the protests, President Lyndon B. Johnson* named Vicente Ximenes* to the EEOC; subsequently, Ximenes established the Inter-Agency Cabinet Committee on Mexican American Affairs* to advocate for opportunities among the many programs set up under President Johnson's Great Society initiative. With Richard Nixon's election, the committee became the Cabinet Committee on Opportunities for Spanish-Speaking People; its responsibility included representation of Puerto Ricans, Cubans, and other Latinos. Many activists, however, became disenchanted with the committee, which devolved to Nixon appointee Henry Ramirez. According to the critics, the unit ceased to advocate for opportunities for the Spanish-speaking. The Cabinet Committee failed to produce effective programs but instead promoted the administration and the reelection of the president among Spanish-speaking voters. More Latinos were hired at top-level jobs under Nixon than previous presidents, but they did not last long. [SOURCE: Samora and Simon, *A History of the Mexican-American People*, 245.]

CALIFORNIA AGRICULTURAL LABOR RELATIONS ACT

In the 1970s, a labor struggle between the unionists led by César Chávez* and the California agricultural industry threatened the well-being of the state's most important source of revenue. In 1975, to put an end to the turmoil, Governor Jerry Brown pushed the Agricultural Labor Relations Act through the state assembly to provide California farmworkers protection from which they were excluded when the U.S. Congress passed the National Labor Relations Act in 1935. The California act basically created an agency to arbitrate accusations of unfair labor practices by agricultural interests when dealing with farmworkers.

The various offices of the board throughout California were empowered to conduct elections to determine if the majority of the workers sought union representation. Board officials could only act when an election petition was signed by the majority of the workers. Unfortunately for labor organizers, after Jerry Brown's term, a conservative George Deukmajian was elected governor. He appointed Agricultural Labor Relations board members who favored the growers' interests, according to union officials. In 1985, the journalist Jerome R. Waldie charged that David Sterling, a former Republican legislator with an anti-labor voting record, was appointed General Counsel by Deukmajian to deflect from the board the complaints issued by farmworker advocates. According to Waldie, Stirling also allowed agricultural employers charged with unfair practices to bypass regional investigators who found proof of wrongdoing and to deal directly with him. Dolores Huerta,* a prominent organizer, complained that because of this arrangement, "the growers disobey the law and get away with it." As an example, she reeled off a number of instances in which the United Farm Workers (UFW)* had won elections but had waited years to be certified by the board. [SOURCE: Rosales, *Chicano!*, 149-150; http://www.friendsfw.org/Advocates/ALRA_CA/ALRA_CA_25.htm]

CALIFORNIA ANTI-VAGRANCY ACT

The California Anti-vagrancy Act, also known as the "Greaser Law," was passed in 1855, a time in which numerous other codes were implemented to control the activities of Hispanics. Although it contained regulations against vagrancy, the law was explicitly and blatantly anti-Mexican, indicating that persons "commonly known as 'Greasers'" would be targeted. The following year, the legislature removed the objectionable phrase, but the law continued to be used to curb Mexicans more than any other group. [SOURCE: Meier and Rivera, *Dictionary of Mexican American History*, 65-66.]

THE CALIFORNIA CHICANO NEWS MEDIA ASSOCIATION

Founded in 1972 in Los Angeles, the California Chicano News Media Association (CCNMA) is the oldest regional organization of journalists of color in the country. It has become widely respected within the journalism industry for sponsoring educational and professional activities that have helped increase the number of minority journalists in the news media. Latino journalism students received the association's first scholarships in 1976, and its job fair, first held in 1978, has emerged as the largest event of its kind on the West Coast, which directs employment opportunities to journalists of color. In 1979, the association established its executive office at the University of Southern California's Annenberg School for Communication. CCNMA publishes a quarterly newsletter, *El Sol*, which provides news on the activities of its members and signals current journalism issues and upcoming events. [SOURCE: http://www.ccnma.org/]

CALIFORNIA JOINT IMMIGRATION COMMITTEE

Founded in 1905 as the Japanese Exclusion League of California, it reorganized as the California Joint Immigration Committee in 1923. The committee's representatives included James K. Fisk of the American Legion (Committee Chair); Paul Scharrenberg of the State Federation of Labor; John T. Regan, Grand Secretary of the Native Sons of the Golden West; Charles M. Goethe, President of the Immigration Study Commission (Committee Treasurer); Ulysses S. Webb, Attorney General of the State of California; and V.S. McClatchy (Committee Executive Secretary). After the success of Asian exclusion legislation, the committee turned its attention toward excluding both Mexican and Filipino immigrants, who had been exempted from both the quotas and racial exclusion of earlier legislation. The committee soon began working on developing a legal precedent that would apply the exclusionary provisions of the 1924 Immigration Act to Mexican immigration. In 1935, the organization successfully influenced Judge John Knight of the First Federal Circuit Court in Buffalo and Naturalization Examiner to reject the naturalization bid of Timoteo Andrade,* an immigrant from Jalisco, Mexico. The decision was based on the grounds that the 1924 Immigration Act prohibited the naturalization of anyone ineligible for immigration—i.e., non-whites, except for Africans who could immigrate by quota. In this case Judge Knight ruled that Andrade was of non-white Indian stock. After receiving considerable pressure from the Department of State, Knight rescinded his ruling and Andrade became a citizen. Nevertheless, doubt remained about the ability of Mexicans, who were considered to be non-white, to immigrate, a threat that was eradicated when Mexicans were officially declared to be white in 1940 by the census bureau and all federal agencies that used racial classification to conduct their activities among the U.S. population. [SOURCE: Lukens Espinosa, "Mexico, Mexican Americans and the FDR Administration's Racial Classification Policy," 105.]

CALIFORNIA LAND ACT

In 1851, the U.S. Congress passed the California Land Act, a bill sponsored by California Senator, William McKendree Gwin. Ostensibly, Senator McKendree Gwin offered this legislation as a sympathetic gesture to his Hispanic constituents so that they could adjudicate property disputes. The act created a three-person commission to determine whether California grantholders had legitimate claims to lands they had obtained prior to the annexation. The Board of Land Commissioners convened from January 1852 to March 1856, and applied a number of criteria in making its determinations: Spanish and Mexican law, the terms of the Treaty of Guadalupe Hidalgo (1848),* principles of equity, and Supreme Court precedents. Any grants rejected or unclaimed reverted to the public domain, where they would be opened for settlement.

California representatives in Congress were instrumental in gaining the passage of the land act. Before 1851, Californios owned most of the good land. Prompted by pressure from immigrants and their squatting, this law sought to legitimize land claims or open them up. Because of Anglo interests and biases, confusion, and deceitful lawyers, Californios lost probably two-fifths of their lands. [SOURCE: http://www.pbs.org/kpbs/theborder/history/timeline/7.html]

CALIFORNIA LATINO CIVIL RIGHTS NETWORK

Sacramento was the site of a 1994 conference in which two hundred prominent California Latino leaders from around the state met to draft a proactive plan to empower the Latino community in California. The participants concluded that a need existed for an ongoing collaborative effort across the state that would gather and disseminate information critical to the Latino community's well-being. The collaboration, they decided, should also include technical and legal assistance to organizations and individuals who, while in the forefront of promoting the civil and human rights of Latinos in California, often lacked resources and expertise. As a result of this meeting, the California Latino Civil Rights Network was created. [SOURCE: http://www.californiatomorrow.org/resources/friends_and_allies/]

CALIFORNIA LATINO COUNCIL OF THE DEAF AND HARD OF HEARING, INC.

Founded in Los Angeles in 1966 by Mark Apodaca, California Latino Council of the Deaf and Hard of Hearing's mission is to promote leadership, advocacy, education, and to address the needs of the deaf and hard of hearing in the Latino community. The council, which is governed by a twelve-member board, holds a yearly statewide conference for parents of Latino deaf. Funding for the organization came from the Greater Los Angeles Council on Deafness, Inc. [SOURCE: http://www.deafvision.net/clc/]

CALIFORNIA RURAL LEGAL ASSISTANCE

Funded by the Federal Office of Economic Opportunity, an integral part of President Lyndon B. Johnson's Great Society program,* California Rural Legal Assistance (CRLA) was founded in 1966 designed to provide free legal services to Californians near the poverty level. Accordingly, many of CRLA's clients were Mexican Americans. California-state conservatives, including Governor Ronald Reagan, were suspicious and opposed the organ-

César Chávez discussing farmworkers' problems in the Salinas Valley with CRLA community workers Héctor De la Rosa and Enrique Cantú Flores.

ization. However, because the CRLA was effective, it was able to maintain its funding. By the 1980s, it was handling more than 13,000 cases yearly and was studying legal needs in housing, agricultural work, and education. Based in Sacramento, the CRLA's 22 offices throughout the state provide no-cost legal services and a variety of community education and outreach programs to more than 20,000 poor rural Californians on a yearly basis. CRLA workers estimate that their efforts have improved living conditions for millions of farmworkers, new immigrants, welfare mothers, school children, the elderly, the physically challenged, and entire low-income communities. [SOURCE: Meier and Rivera, *Dictionary of Mexican American History*, 66; http://www.crla.org/welcome.htm]

CAMBIO CUBANO

At age 58, Eloy Gutiérrez Menoyo, a veteran anti-Castro crusader, founded Cambio Cubano (Cuban Change). In the 1950s insurgency against Cuban dictator Fulgencio Batista,* Gutiérrez Menoyo commanded the Second Escambray Front, a guerrilla group which was independent of the July 26th Movement of Fidel Castro. Soon after Castro's victory, Gutiérrez Menoyo turned against Castro and helped found the exile paramilitary group Alpha 66 in Florida. In 1965, Gutiérrez Menoya led a mission inside of Cuba, but was caught and spent 22 years in Cuban prisons. After his release in 1987, Gutiérrez Menoyo was exiled to Florida, where instead of continuing his strident and militant path to change Cuba, he advocated the lifting of U.S. sanctions, which he felt were fruitless and harmful; he also called for immediate negotiations with the Cuban government

A proponent of a wide-ranging dialogue between Cuba and the Cuban-American community, Gutiérrez Menoyo put his beliefs into action in September 1994, when he held talks in Madrid with Cuban Foreign Minister Roberto Robaína. In June 1995, he returned for a week-long visit to the Cuba he had not seen since his release from prison. After meeting at length with President Fidel Castro and other high-ranking officials as well as with dissidents on the island, he returned to the United States and published an op-ed in the *Washington Post*, indicating that he found "a greater openness to new ideas on the part of Cuban officials. If the Cuban government is now prepared to show tolerance and respect for the views of those like myself," he wrote, "then indeed a new beginning can be made and we can face the future with renewed hope." [SOURCE: Elliston, "The Myth of the Miami Monolith," http://www.hartford-hwp.com/archives/43b/027.html; García, *Havana USA*, 165.]

CAMEJO, PETER (1941-)

Peter Camejo, chair and cofounder of Progressive Asset Management, which promotes socially responsible investments, was born in New York City in 1941. A descendent of one of Venezuela's wealthiest families, Camejo has devoted his life to progressive politics. In 2003, Camejo became the Green Party candidate for governor of California in that year's infamous recall of the Democratic Party incumbent. In spite of his past as a socialist, Camejo polled five percent of the votes. In the 1960s, University of California-Berkeley officials expelled him for his key role in the Free Speech Movement, along with its leader Mario Savio. The movement was considered to be the beginning of radical 1960s politics on campuses across the nation. While a member of the Socialist Worker Party (SWP), Camejo started a chapter of La Raza Unida Party* in Oakland, California, a move which made him a key player of the Chicano Movement.* In 1976, Camejo ran for president of the SWP. Camejo is one of the founders of the original U.S. Green Party founded in 1991. [SOURCE: Rosales *Chicano!,* 229.]

CAMP HESS KRAMER

Located east of Malibu, Camp Hess Kramer was the site of a meeting of 200 teenagers and community leaders, which was sponsored by the Los Angeles County Human Relations Council. From the meeting, a group of young leaders came together later to form the Young Citizens for Community Action (YCCA). This organization met in the Piranya coffee house and eventually turned into the militant Brown Berets.* [SOURCE: Marín, *Social Protest in an Urban Barrio,* 75.]

CANALES, JOSÉ T. (1877-1976)

José T. Canales was born in Nueces County, Texas, on March 7, 1877. He served in the Texas State Legislature, representing South Texas from 1912 to 1928. In 1910, Canales married Annie Wheeler of Houston. On January 31, 1918, at special hearings motivated by the severity of Texas Ranger* brutality, numerous Texas officials, including State Representative José T. Canales, called for curtailment of their authority. As Canales put it in a letter to C.H. Pease, a legislator who opposed his efforts, "I want to clear out a gang of lawless men and thugs from being placed . . . in the character of peace officers to enforce our laws." Such mounting public criticism tarnished the Ranger's romantic image. Canales was elected county judge in 1914 and served until he returned to state legislature in 1917. His desire to help his people led him to become a civil rights activist. Judge Canales drafted the League of United Latin American Citizens (LULAC)* Constitution in Corpus Christi in 1929, then served one term as the fourth president of LULAC. Elected at the height of the Great Depression, in 1932, Canales saw education as the best hope for Hispanic Americans and promoted the establishment of the LULAC Scholarship Fund, providing young persons an opportunity for higher education. [SOURCE: Larralde, "J.T. Canales and the Texas Rangers."]

CANCEL, HILTON (?-)

Hilton Cancel is President of El Pueblo of North Carolina, a nonprofit state-wide advocacy and policy organization dedicated to strengthening the Latino community in the state. Born in New York City to Puerto Rican parents, he served with the Indianapolis Police Department until he retired in 1985. Mr. Cancel won the Indiana Jefferson Award for advocate work on behalf of Latinos. His activism has been especially directed toward assuring that Latinos have equal representation in law enforcement agencies. [SOURCE: http://www.elpueblo.org/]

CAPETILLO, LUISA (1879-1922)

Born in Arecibo, Puerto Rico, on October 28, 1879, Luisa Capetillo became the first Puerto Rican woman to be a recognized leader in the labor movement, with her participation in a 1907 strike of tobacco factories in Arecibo, Puerto Rico. She joined the Federation of Free Workers and, in 1910, she founded the newspaper *La mujer* (The Woman). For the next two decades she was active as an organizer in New York, Florida, and again in Puerto Rico. She is also known as one of Puerto Rico's first feminists. Capetillo published three books of her essays, plays, and other writings in support of labor, anarchism, and feminism. Overcome by tuberculosis, Capetillo died on October 10, 1922. [SOURCE: Tardiff and Mabunda, *Dictionary of Hispanic Biography,* 166; www.artepublicopress.com]

Luisa Capetillo

CÁRDENAS MARTÍNEZ JR., LEÓN (1895?-1914)

Although Texas law forbade the execution of minors, León Cárdenas Martínez, Jr. said to be 16 at the time of the murder of Emma Brown in Pecos, was executed on May 11, 1914. According to Cárdenas Martínez's father, officers took the boy to the murder site, held a gun to his head, and told him that if he confessed they would protect him from a menacing lynch mob. During the July 1911 trial, incensed townspeople forced León Cárdenas Martínez, Sr. to abandon his butcher shop and take his family out of town. The mob included the Reeves County Sheriff. While the Mexican Protective Association of San Antonio raised money to appeal the sentence in Reeves County, local whites broke up support meetings. At the trial, a jury of Anglos ignored efforts by lawyers to demonstrate that Cárdenas Martínez was under legal age for execution. In addition, the sheriff prevented his lawyers from interviewing the defendant properly, and community pressure intimidated them into not appealing the case. This sentence helped prompt El Primer Congreso Mexicanista (The First Mexicanist Congress)* in Texas that sought to address issues of criminal justice. Since American relations with Mexico were severed, the Spanish ambassador requested in vain that the youth's sentence be commuted. [SOURCE: Rosales, *Pobre Raza!*, 143.]

CARDOZO, BENJAMIN NATHAN (1870-1938)

The first Hispanic named to the Supreme Court of the United States was Benjamin Nathan Cardozo of the famed Sephardic Jewish family which dated back to colonial days. Born in New York City in 1870, Cardozo received his legal training at Columbia University. He was elected judge of the New York Supreme Court in 1914 and, in 1915, became an Associate Justice of the New York Court of Appeals. He became chief justice of that court in 1927. Cardozo was named by President Franklin D. Roosevelt to the U.S. Supreme Court in 1932. Cardozo became known as the most influential liberal justice of his times. Part of his reputation came from his opinions on legal questions, especially those dealing with public welfare and President Roosevelt's New Deal. One of his most noteworthy opinions was that upholding the Social Security Act. Many of Cardozo's ideas were fully expressed in his writings. He was the author of such important books as *The Nature of the Judicial Process* (1921), *The Growth of the Law* (1924), and *The Paradoxes of Legal Science* (1928). [SOURCE: Kanellos, *Hispanic Firsts*, 89.]

CARGO, DAVID (1929-)

Born on January 13, 1929, in Dowagiac, Michigan, David Cargo moved to New Mexico in 1957 after receiving a law degree from the University of Michigan. He practiced law in Albuquerque and, in 1960, he married New Mexico native, Adelaida Josefina Anaya. Cargo served in state legislature from Bernalillo County until his election as New Mexico governor in 1967. At this time, Reies López Tijerina* and his land-grant organization, La Alianza Federal de las Mercedes,* were at the height of their activity. Cargo tried to sympathize with the organization's goals while also maintaining law and order in northern New Mexico. His attempt to steer a middle course displeased both establishment and militant groups. Cargo appealed to the Alianza members to call off their meetings because of the likelihood of their being arrested even though he believed they had the right to convene.

Cargo gave the Aliancistas permission to hold a meeting in the town of Coyote on May of 1967 and then left New Mexico to visit his home-state of Michigan. While the governor was gone, Alfonso Sánchez, the District Attorney of Rio Arriba County where Coyote is located, arrested a number of Tijerina's followers for trying to convene. Consequently, on June 5, Tijerina and other Aliancistas attacked the jail in Rio Arriba to free their comrades arrested in Coyote and wounded two officers in the process. The event received national attention especially after New Mexico national guard troops and other law officers embarked on one of the largest manhunts in New Mexico history. It became a hallmark of audacity for fledgling Chicano Movement* activists. Cargo vocally disapproved of Alfonso Sánchez's actions during his absence. [SOURCE: Rosales, *Chicano!*, 161-164; Nabokov, *Tijerina and the Courthouse Raid.*]

CART WAR

Mexicans and Tejanos (Mexican Texans) by the mid 1850s dominated the transporting of goods from Indianola, a port north of Corpus Christi, to San Antonio and other towns in the interior of Texas. Hispanic carters moved freight more rapidly and cheaply than their Anglo competitors because of the use of oxcarts and intimately knowing the terrain. Anglos had been harassing the Mexican carters since 1855, but it was not until July 1857, that the violence escalated with the destruction of oxcarts by hired thugs and the lynching of Mexican carters. Although the attempt was not completely successful, this and other abuses demonstrated antipathy toward Mexicans and especially showed that Anglo Americans felt Mexicans did not have the constitutional rights which they themselves prized. Appeals to local authorities by Mexican tradesmen were to no avail and the violence continued to increase. Not until the Mexican ambassador in Washington, Manuel Robles y Pezuela, protested to Secretary of State Lewis Cass in October 1857, did Texas officials intervene to put a stop to the violence. Cass appealed to Texas governor Elisha M. Pease, who in turn mobilized the state militia to patrol the trade routes and protect the Mexican carters. By December, the violence subsided. [SOURCE: Weber, "Cart War," *The Handbook of Texas Online*, http://www.tsha. utexas.edu/handbook/online/articles/view/CC/jcc1.html]

CASA CENTRAL

Founded in 1954, Casa Central serves as a social service agency for Chicago's Hispanic community. Casa was funded by a multi-denominational group of churches. Located in the city's northwest side, Casa offers programs for children, women, families, and the elderly. Casa Central estimates that its programs "touch the lives of some 20,000 low-income residents each year through a comprehensive network of 25 bilingual/bicultural social service agencies." It sponsors, for example, El Teatro Juvenil, a youth-based theater group as one of its community outreach projects. Casa has received numerous awards from the City of Chicago and at the national level for its work. [SOURCE: http://www.casacentral.org/History.htm]

CASA CORNELIA LAW CENTER

The Casa Cornelia Law Center in San Diego, California, was established in 1992. The center provides legal services to indigent persons seeking political asylum, victims of domestic violence, and under-age detainees apprehended by the Immigration and Naturalization Service.* [SOURCE: www.casacornelia.org/about_us/History.html]

LA CASA DE LAS MADRES

La Casa de las Madres was founded in 1976 to provide emergency residential shelter to battered women and their children in downtown San Francisco. The center also provides counseling, family-based assistance services, and referrals to other social services. The Emergency Crisis Shelter can house and support thirty-five women and their children per night. Two 24-hour Crisis Phone Lines and a Pop-In Counseling Center are available so that women and children can reach La Casa's facilities at any time of the day or night. Also offered are teen intervention programs through the Community Education & Outreach Program. All services are offered free-of-charge in English and Spanish. [SOURCE: http://www.lacasa.org/]

CASA LATINA (SEATTLE)

Founded in 1994 in Seattle, Washington, as a community-based project, the CASA Latina seeks to educate Latino seasonal workers so they may become economically independent and contributing members of their communities. Migrant workers can obtain information and skills necessary to make decisions and take action to improve their lives through a number of CASA programs. A crucial part of the center's services are classes stressing practical English that will help workers communicate with potential employers, co-workers, and authority figures. CASA provides outreach services to homeless Latinos in Seattle's downtown district, educating them on their rights and responsibilities. Longer termed services include citizenship, literacy, and family literacy classes. Many of CASA's workers are volunteers. [SOURCE: casalatinainc.org/aboutus.html]

LA CASA LATINA (UNIVERSITY OF PENNSYLVANIA)

In 1994, a group of Latino faculty and staff at the University of Pennsylvania established the Latino Faculty and Staff Association. This gave impetus to the students whom two years later formed the Latino Student Coalition. Once established, the two groups in 1998 proposed the creation of the University of Pennsylvania Center for Hispanic Excellence, whose objective was to increase the presence of the Latino community at the university. President Judith Rodin accepted the proposal and on September 21, 1999, the center, also known as La Casa Latina, was inaugurated. Now, La Casa reaches out not just to the Latino Community but also to anyone at the university interested in Latino culture. La Casa has established links of community service to the extensive surrounding Latino community of Philadelphia. The center currently serves as a comprehensive resource center for Latino students of the four undergraduate schools at the University of Pennsylvania and for the community. [SOURCE: http://www.vpul.upenn.edu/lacasa/comserv.html]

CASA LATINA, INC. (NORTHAMPTON, MASSACHUSETTS)

Established in 1968 in Northampton, Massachusetts, the Casa Latina, Inc. provides the Latino community throughout Massachusetts with an opportunity to empower itself. It provides cultural and community education that allows newcomers to develop their full potential and empowers them to participate more successfully in a culturally diverse environment. The center has tutoring, legal aid, health, and family crisis services. [SOURCE: http://www.hispaniconline.com/res&res/hisporgs/regional_1.html]

CASTAÑEDA, CARLOS EDUARDO (1896-1958)

Born on November 11, 1896, in Ciudad Camargo, Tamaulipas, Mexico, Carlos Eduardo Castañeda became one of Texas' foremost historians and professors. He moved to Brownsville, Texas, in 1906 with his parents, Timoteo and Elisa (Leroux), and with his numerous siblings. After distinguishing himself in high school, Castañeda received an A.B. in 1921 from the University of Texas (UT) and taught high school Spanish. After obtaining his M.A. in 1923, also from UT, the College of William and Mary in Virginia hired him as an associate professor. Returning to Austin in 1927, Castañeda became librarian of the García Collection at UT and worked on his Ph.D., which he earned in 1932. He continued in his position as librarian but also served as Associate Professor of History.

Castañeda took a leave of absence during World War II and was the regional director of the President's Committee on Fair Employment Practices* from 1939 to 1946, an executive unit that investigated workplace discrimination. In 1946, he returned to UT as Full Professor of Latin American history, a position he held until he passed away in 1958. As a historian, Castañeda pioneered scholarly research on the Catholic Church in Texas and the Spanish borderlands. Castañeda received many honors for his voluminous contributions in history, but more importantly, his personal perseverance made him a role model for Mexican Americans hungering for professional recognition and status.

As a member of the League of United Latin American Citizens,* Professor Castañeda also became committed to civil rights and worked with the organization to confront such issues as school segregation and workplace discrimination. It is his prominence in this role that led to his appointment to the President's Committee on Fair Employment Practice during World War II. [SOURCE: Almaráz, "Castañeda, Carlos Eduardo (1896-1958)," *The Handbook of Texas Online*, http://www.tsha.utexas.edu/handbook/online/articles/view/CC/fca85.html]

CASTAÑEDA V. PICKARD

After the 1974 *Lau v. Nichols** case, the second major court case that defined the language rights of non-English-speaking children in the schools was the *Castañeda v. Pickard* decision of 1981, which was argued in the Fifth Circuit Court of Appeals at the federal level. This case narrowed the scope of what was considered "affirmative steps" in education of language-minority students. The decision mandated that language programs for minority children with limited English proficiency could conform to three standards: (1) they must be based on a "sound educational theory"; (2) they must be "implemented effectively" with adequate resources and personnel; and (3) after a trial period, they must be evaluated as effective in overcoming language handicaps. The court buttressed its findings by invoking the Equal Educational Opportunity Act (EEOA) of 1974,* which obligated school districts to take "appropriate action to overcome obstacles of language that impeded equal participation by students in instructional programs." The *Castañeda v. Pickard* decision did not mandate specific pedagogical techniques for fulfilling bilingual education, but proponents of native-language instruction have used *Castañeda v. Pickard* to support bilingual education programs. [SOURCE: Baker and Hakuta, "Bilingual Education and Latino Civil Rights."]

CASTILLO, LEONEL (1939-)

Leonel Castillo (1939-) became the first Hispanic to direct the U.S. Immigration and Naturalization Service.* Born in Victoria, Texas, Castillo received his B.A. from St. Mary's University in San Antonio and his Master's in Social Work from the University of Pittsburgh in 1967. After graduating from St. Mary's in 1961, Castillo served in the Peace Corps in the Philippines from 1961 to 1965. After the Peace Corps, Castillo returned to Houston and, in 1970, won a surprise victory in the race for city comptroller against a twenty-five-year incumbent. In 1974, he was named treasurer of the Texas Democratic Party. [SOURCE: Meier and Feliciano, *Dictionary of Mexican American History*, 72.]

CASTRO, RAÚL (1916-1977)

In 1975, voters elected Raúl Castro the first Hispanic governor of Arizona. Born on June 12, 1916, in Cananea, Sonora, Mexico, he moved as a child with his poverty-stricken parents to Pertleville, Arizona, where he became the family's wage earner after his father died. Despite having to work in migrant labor, mining, and ranching, he was able to earn a degree from Arizona State College in 1939, after which he went to Washington, D.C. to work for the State Department. Castro returned to Arizona in 1946 and earned a law degree from the University of Arizona in 1949. He entered politics and served in various elected positions. In 1964, he was appointed ambassador to El Salvador and, in 1968, ambassador to Bolivia. He ran unsuccessfully for governor in 1970 but was victorious in 1974. In 1977, he resigned from his office to serve as ambassador to Argentina. [SOURCE: Meier and Feliciano, *Dictionary of Mexican American History*, 72-73.]

CASTRO, ROSIE (1947-)

Rosie Castro was born in San Antonio, Texas, in 1947 and raised by her single Mother and an older woman on the city's Westside. By her account, Castro rebelled against the traditional role ascribed to Mexican girls while in high school, a trait that led her advocating a greater role for women in the Texas Chicano Movement.* A sympathizer of La Raza Unida Party (The United People Party-LRUP),* in 1971, Rosie Castro ran for the San Antonio City Council on the ticket of the Committee for Barrio Betterment. In 1972, Ms. Castro attended the LRUP convention in El Paso, Texas advocating a larger role for women within the party. Ms. Castro currently works at the San Antonio Housing Authority. [SOURCE: http://www.accd.edu/pac/lrc/chicanaleaders/castro.htm]

CASTRO, SAL (1930-)

Sal Castro who was born in Los Angeles in 1932, played a crucial role in the high school walkouts in East Los Angeles during 1968. Castro graduated from California State University at Los Angeles in 1955 and worked in parks and recreation programs with young children until he became a public school teacher. Repatriated as a child with his Mexican-born parents, he obtained his early education in Mexico but when he was ten years old, he returned with his mother to Los Angeles and began school in an English-speaking environment. His own experiences as a student and later as a teacher convinced him that the Los Angeles school system remained unresponsive to the needs of Mexican-American children.

In 1968, high school students walked out of their classes to dramatize what they considered abysmally poor educational facilities affecting the East Los Angeles schools which were predominantly Mexican American. They demanded more Mexican-American educators, access to bilingual education, and removal of racist educators. The planners were all young people, many not yet out of their teens; none were over thirty. Parents and other community adults supported their efforts. The most prominent of this group was Castro, a Lincoln High School teacher who school officials fired after claiming he violated faculty conduct codes by becoming involved in the planning of the walkouts. After his dismissal, he was not re-instated until five years later, at a reassigned location. Community protests, including a sit-down strike in the chambers of the school board, followed. Subsequently, Castro was arrested. The East Los Angeles walkouts inspired others in the Southwest. [SOURCE: Rosales, *Chicano!,* 190-194; http://www.xispas.com/opinion/sal1.htm]

CASTRO, VICTORIA M. (1949-)

Victoria M. Castro was a pioneer in the Los Angeles Chicano Movement.* While a student at California State University, Los Angeles, in 1968, Castro was one of the organizers of the East Los Angeles high school walkouts. Prior to the walkouts, David Sánchez, one of the founders of the Brown Berets,* recruited Castro, Ralph Ramírez, and other friends from Camp Hess Kramer* and they formed the Young Citizens for Community Action (YCCA). Castro became the first president of the YCCA, later known as the Young Chicanos for Community Action. When David Sánchez changed the name to the Brown Berets, she relinquished her presidency. Ms. Castro received a bachelor's degree from California State Los Angeles, a teacher credential from the University of California at Santa Cruz and a Master of Science degree in Urban Education and Administration from Pepperdine University. Still active in educational issues, Castro presently serves on the Los Angeles Unified School District Board of Education. Prior to her election to the board, Ms. Castro spent 25 years as an employee of the Los Angeles Unified School District. [SOURCE: http://chicano.nlcc.comvcastro.html; http://www.lausd.k12.ca.us/lausd/board/castro; Marín, *Social Protest in an Urban Barrio,* 75-76.]

CATHOLIC LEAGUE

The Catholic League, founded in 1973 by the late Father Virgil C. Blum, S.J., is the nation's largest Catholic civil rights organization. Its main purpose is to assure that Catholics—lay and clergy—can exercise their full civil rights in American public life without defamation or discrimination. The

Catholic League tries to safeguard the rights to religious freedom and freedom of speech of Catholics guaranteed by the First Amendment. [SOURCE: http://www.catholicleague.org/faqs.htm]

CATÓLICOS POR LA RAZA

On Christmas Eve, 1969, a group calling itself Católicos por La Raza (Catholics for the People-CPLR) tried to disrupt midnight Mass at St. Basil's Church in Los Angeles and were beaten up by plainclothes policemen. One demonstrator, Dave Domínguez, almost died. The CPLR explained that in Los Angeles, the church spent $4,000,000 in churches for the wealthy and owned at least one billion dollars in real estate. The CPLR demanded that the church be more responsive to the needs of its Mexican parishioners and use its money to promote not just spiritual aid but material help. A chief target of the CPLR's criticism was Cardinal J. Francis Mcyntire, who oversaw the Los Angeles Catholic Church and allegedly once said, "I was here before there were even any Mexicans. I came to Los Angeles 21 years ago." [SOURCE: Rosales, *Chicano!*, 195; Chávez, *"¡Mi Raza Primero!"*, 6-7.]

CAVAZOS, LAURO F. (1927-)

In 1980, Texas Tech University broke its long tradition and hired one of its own alumnae as president: Lauro F. Cavazos. A medical doctor and researcher, Cavazos assumed the presidency of the university and of its Health Science Center. Then, in 1988, President Ronald Reagan appointed Dr. Cavazos the first Hispanic Secretary of Education. In 1989, President George H.W. Bush reappointed Cavazos to the post. Cavazos was instrumental in having President Bush sign the executive order creating the President's Council on Educational Excellence for Hispanic Americans. Cavazos resigned in December 1990; he could not support many of the president's educational policies. [SOURCE: Carrasco, "Law and Politics," 277.]

CEJA, MANUEL (1920-?)

Manuel Ceja helped organize the Mexican American Movement (MAM),* which emerged in southern California during the 1930s under the auspices of the YMCA. The members were made up of upwardly mobile youth, mostly college students who had committed themselves "to improve our conditions among our Mexican-American and Mexican people living in the United States" and to pursue "citizenship, higher education . . . and a more active participation in civic and cultural activities by those of our national descent." A model of MAM's professed ideals, Ceja was born in Los Angeles in 1920 of immigrant parents. He attended Compton Jr. College and graduated from the Spanish American Institute, a leadership tank for Mexican Americans. He was also a volunteer coach at the local chapter of the

Mexican American Pioneer Club, a boys club within the MAM. In a July 1938 issue of the *Mexican Voice*, a newsletter published by MAM, Manuel Ceja wrote a piece entitled, "Are We Proud of Being Mexicans?" It came very close to the rhetoric of identity used by Chicanos* in the 1960s. [SOURCE: Rosales, *Chicano!*, 100-101.]

CELERY FIELD STRIKE OF SOUTHERN CALIFORNIA

In 1936, Mexican workers struck the celery fields in southern California, which led to police violently attacking and suppressing two thousand strikers with a force of 1,500 armed men. Injured strikers were refused aid at local hospitals, and tax-payer dollars were employed by local authorities in hiring field agents to visit growers to urge them not to settle. The growers themselves spent thousands of dollars in hiring armed guards from a local strikebreaking detective agency. [SOURCE: McWilliams, *North from Mexico,* 192.]

THE CENTRAL AMERICAN REFUGEE CENTER

Formed in 1983 as a nonprofit immigration and human rights organization, the Central American Refugee Center (CARECEN) has served the refugee community on Long Island and throughout southern New York State. Since its founding, CARECEN has worked to protect the civil rights of Central American immigrants, increase understanding between the native-born and newcomer communities, and raise awareness of the interaction of human rights disasters and immigration. The courage of Salvadoran Archbishop Oscar Romero has been the inspiration for CARECEN's work; the center also draws inspiration from Emma Lazarus's poem at the base of the Statue of Liberty. [SOURCE: http://www.icomm.ca/carecen/]

CENTRAL AMERICAN REFUGEE PROJECT

In 1980 with financial support from the Marin Community Foundation in northern California, Jesús Campos, a refugee from El Salvador, started the Central American Refugee Project (CARE) to assist compatriots like himself in surviving in the United States. At that time, many Salvadorans in California had fled government-inspired terror, which was prompted by challenges by Marxist guerillas and Liberation Theology activists. Some of the refugees simply fled the violence without being involved politically, but others like Campos fled because their political involvement made them fear for their lives—he had participated in Christian liberation movements. Working in office space provided by the Marin County Episcopalian Churches, Campos organized festivals at Pickleweed Park Community Center on Salvadoran holidays, as well as a Latin football league; in addition, he collected used furniture and toys from various churches and distributed them to indigent families. Campos organized protests before the San Rafael City Council against the occasional roundups of refugee day laborers. Campos would accompany sick and injured Salvadoran nationals to the hospital, where he often served as translator. In the late 1980s, CARE ran out of funding and saw its functions taken over by larger, better established agencies. Nonetheless, the small effort proved enormously valuable at a time when few other such services existed. [SOURCE: Hutchinson, *When the Dogs Ate Candles,* 66-67.]

CENTRAL AMERICAN REFUGEES

In the 1980s the sources of immigration from Latin America began to expand beyond Cuba, Mexico, and Puerto Rico. More than 500,000 Salvadorans, Guatemalans, and Nicaraguans entered the United States in search of political asylum between 1979 and 1985. While many legitimately sought political asylum from local repression in their countries, just as many probably sought economic security in the United States, since their home countries were extremely poor, a situation which worsened with political turmoil. As a consequence, the Immigration and Naturalization Service* refused them asylum on political grounds and classified them as economic refugees. Salvadoran and Guatemalan refugees (but not Nicaraguans) were escaping countries with governments supported by the United States. As such, admitting large numbers of Salvadoran and Guatemalan political refugees then would contradict U.S. foreign policy.

The political instability that created the diaspora stemmed from civil war in El Salvador, insurgency in Guatemala, and a counterrevolutionary war in Nicaragua backed by the United States. The United States was not the only destination for refugees. To escape these political conditions, refugees went anywhere that would be safer than their homelands. For example, by the end of 1982, 70,000 Salvadorans had fled to Guatemala; 120,000 to Mexico; 30,000 to Honduras; and 22,000 to Nicaragua. Thousands of others found their way to Costa Rica, Panama, and Belize. Moreover, the war prompted internal displacement within El Salvador; one estimate puts this number at more than 200,000.

The primary cause of this monumental outflow of Central American refugees has been the violent repression perpetrated by authoritarian governments backed by the United States. El Salvador and Honduras, for example, have received between 1979 and 1990 more than $2 billion in military aid from the United States. Under the presidency of Ronald Reagan, aid to Guatemala was resumed after President Jimmy Carter had cut it off in 1977, when Amnesty International declared the Guatemalan government as one of the most repressive in the world. In addition, Reagan's administration, with congressional approval, supported the Contras, the rebel army trying to overthrow the Sandinista government of Nicaragua.

Nicaraguans seeking political asylum because they fled persecution from the Sandinistas presented U.S. immigration authorities with a thorny problem. Although the administration had financed the Contras, the Nicaraguan government still had diplomatic relations with the United States and was not a Communist nation—this would have allowed Nicaraguan refugees to more easily claim asylum.

The U.S. Congress in 1985 approved $27 million to continue efforts to overthrow the Sandinista government, but failed to pass immigration reform. As a consequence, more than 500,000 Central American refugees in the United States found themselves in an ambiguous immigration status, a situation that has been clarified over the years. [SOURCE: Masud-Piloto, *From Welcomed Exiles to Illegal Immigrants*, 120-13.]

CENTRAL AMERICAN RESOURCE CENTER

In 1986, Salvadoran refugees established the Central American Resource Center (CARECEN) in San Francisco in response to mounting refugee issues created by the political turmoil in Central America. The center accomplished this by devising strategies and self-help programs that would help to provide the immigrants legal aid, health care, education, social work, employment, and civil rights. The center now has a clinic which provides legal aid, immigrant visa petition, and citizenship classes. Its health clinic offers physical examinations, referrals, health fairs, and a women's clinic; its dental clinic provides dental treatments, cleaning, and x-rays. In addition CARECEN has implemented a tutoring program for both adults and children in math, English, and computers. Many community members also take advantage of the arts and sports offerings at the center. [SOURCE: http://www.carecensf.org/]

EL CENTRO, FLORIDA STATE UNIVERSITY

Started in 1979, El Centro has served as the main advocate of support and services for Hispanic/Latino students at Florida State University (FSU) in Tallahassee. Hispanics and other students freely gather at the El Centro facilities, exchange cultural experiences, and find a sense of belonging. At the center, students celebrate the achievements and contributions of the Hispanic/Latino culture to the United States. El Centro coordinates and supervises a variety of Hispanic student programs and services and cooperates in a student exchange project with the University of Costa Rica. The center became more essential as the Hispanic student population at FSU grew precipitously in the last two decades of the twentieth century. [SOURCE: http://www.fsu.edu/~el centro/]

CENTRO DE ACCIÓN SOCIAL AUTÓNOMA—HERMANDAD GENERAL DE TRABAJADORES

Mexican-American activist Bert Corona,* along with Magdalena Mora, Soledad "Chole" Alatorre, and former members of Católicos Por La Raza (Catholics for the People)* and the United Farm Workers Union* began Centro de Acción Social Autónoma-Hermandad General de Trabajadores (CASA-HGT) in 1968 to help undocumented immigrants obtain social services and/or legal status. It was the first Chicano Movement-era* organization to explore the relationship between immigration, Chicano* ethnicity, and the status of Mexican Americans in the United States. According to CASA-HGT's view, Mexican immigrant laborers were an integral component of the American working-class and could claim the same rights as other workers in the United States. This posture departed significantly from that held by most other Mexican-American and Chicano organizations of the time. Embodying this ideological position was CASA-HGT's organizing slogans, "Somos Un Pueblo Sin Fronteras" (We Are One People without Borders) and "Somos Uno Porque América Es Una" (We Are One Because America Is One).

In 1973, CASA-HGT helped to establish the National Coalition for Fair Immigration Laws and Practices, a coalition of mainly Mexican-American community and labor organizations concerned with an escalating immigration controversy throughout the 1970s. In the mid-1970s, the group was reorganized, Corona lost his preeminence and its members began openly espousing a Marxist-Leninist ideology. CASA-HGT had the largest participation of Chicanas in leadership positions of any other organization. Its newspaper, *Sin Fronteras* (Without Borders), for example, was edited by Kathy Ochoa. According to historian, Juan Gómez-Quiñones, CASA-HGT "achieved a significant record of success. It pushed forward ideological and organizational development by providing militant leadership in a wide set of activities in Los Angeles and throughout the nation." The newspaper *Sin Fronteras* was clearly the best militant print organ of the movement. [SOURCE: Gutiérrez, *Walls and Mirrors,* 191-194; Gómez-Quiñones, *Chicano Politics,* 153.]

EL CENTRO CAMPESINO FARMWORKER CENTER, INC.

Located in Florida City, Florida, the El Centro Campesino Farmworker Center was founded in 1969. Its main mission is to improve the living conditions and self-sufficiency of migrant and seasonal farmworkers, their families, and other low-income residents. The Centro Campesino is a private nonprofit community center, which has seven major goals: affordable housing, housing rehabilitation, employment and training in construction, clerical and other vocational skills, youth development, emergency financial assistance, leadership development, and community organizing. Volunteers spend much of their time on home construction, but also in an after school program with farmworker children. [SOURCE: http://www.commercebankfl.com/spanish/about/press/20021231b.htm]

EL CENTRO DE LA RAZA

In the Fall of 1972, a time of recession in Seattle, protestors occupied the abandoned Beacon Hill School near downtown after the English and Adult Basic Education Program at the Duwamish branch of South Seattle Community College lost its funding. The closing of the program eliminated one of the few programs in the city where people who are "interested in making a better and more just world" could gather. It sparked a vision of establishing a more permanent location with greater capacity to empower many the poor of the city, not just Latinos. The participants of the sit-in were convinced that the Beacon Hill site was the most appropriate because of its centralized location, availability, and potential for expansion and development. Later the protesters occupied the Seattle City Council Chambers to underscore the determination to develop an authentic community center at Beacon Hill. After the arrest of the peaceful protestors, Mayor Charles Royer decided to make the facility available to the social activists, and El Centro was born. Since then, El Centro de la Raza has become one of the largest and most productive community-based organizations in the nation. El Centro de la Raza has employed "cultural, educational and civic activities as vehicles to bring together peoples of all races and refuses to separate economic activities from social and human service." [SOURCE: http://www.elcentrode laraza.com/about_us/history.htm]

EL CENTRO ESPAÑOL DE TAMPA

Cigar-workers established as a patriotic cultural organization the El Centro Español de Tampa in 1891 after a frustrated effort to establish a mutual aid society in 1890. The Centro Español, made up of Spaniards and Cubans, was sympathetic to Cuban nationalism. In spite of tensions that would be inherent in an organization of this particular ethnic composition, it survived during the Spanish American War.* After Cuba acquired its independence, Centro members decided to steer the organization towards mutual aid, and the organization lost some of its political orientation. In 1903, with the formation of other Hispanic organizations, El Centro Español lost its claim to being the sole voice of Tampa's Spanish community. [SOURCE: Varela-Lago, "From Patriotism to Mutualism," 5-23.]

EL CENTRO HISPANOAMERICANO

El Centro Hispanoamericano began in 1984 through the efforts of local churches in response to the increasing number of refugees from war-torn El Salvador who were settling in Plainfield, New Jersey; at that time it was

El Centro Español de Tampa

known as El Centro de Refugiados. Over the years the mission of El Centro Hispanoamericano has expanded to assist immigrants from Latin America and elsewhere, particularly those who do not have access to publicly funded legal and social services, adult education, consumer and civil rights advocacy, and cultural programs. The center also provides an educational program that puts in perspective to both immigrants and non-immigrants the role of immigration in the United States. This is done in such a way as to insure dignity, respect, and justice for all. [SOURCE: http://www.elcentronj.org/english/frames.htm]

EL CENTRO HISPANO CATÓLICO

As Cubans, who were overwhemingly Roman Catholic, fled the 1959 Revolution, the Catholic Church became their only source of assistance during the first few years of exile. To meet this need, in 1959, Bishop Coleman F. Carroll established the El Centro Hispano Católico in a remodeled wing of the Gesu parochial school in downtown Miami. By 1961, the Miami Catholic Diocese had spent $1.5 million in programs designed to assist Cuban refugees. This allowed the Centro to provide a wide array of services; including housing, job referrals, English classes, a day nursery, educational programs for children, an outpatient and dental clinic, home visits to the sick, and small loans to cover miscellaneous expenses, such as eyeglasses and dentures, as well as food, toiletries, and used clothing. [SOURCE: García, *Havana USA*, 19.]

EL CENTRO PRESENTE, INC.

Boston-area immigrant rights activists founded El Centro Presente in 1981 after recognizing that political turmoil in Central America had forced immigrants to seek, in New England, refuge from repression or extreme poverty. The center, located in Cambridge, Massachusetts, which eventually came to be run for and by Central Americans, has provided services to more than 35,000 Central Americans since its inception. It serves as a positive example of the ability of immigrants to provide self-help through perseverance and dedication. El Centro Presente offers important legal and educational services, such as leadership training seminars and citizenship programs. The organization relies on volunteers, especially students with Spanish-speaking skills, to assist with these educational programs. [SOURCE: http://www.alternativebreaks.org]

EL CENTRO RADICAL MEXICANO

In Tucson in the 1880s, Carlos Velasco, editor of *El Fronterizo* newspaper, attempted to establish El Centro Radical Mexicano (Mexican Radical Center) to address problems between Mexicans and the Tucson police. This was one of the first organizations to reflect the broader impulse of Mexicans to organize for their own protection in the United States. [SOURCE: Sheridan, *Los Tucsonenses,* 89-90.]

CENTRO TEPEYAC

Founded in 1990, Centro Tepeyac (named after the mount on which the Virgin of Guadalupe is said to have appeared in Mexico City) offers alternatives to abortion available to women facing crisis pregnancies in the Washington, D.C. area. Operating in Silver Spring, Maryland, the Centro's staff and volunteers train the mainly Hispanic parents before and after birth on such basics as prenatal care and healthy early child rearing practices. In addition, they provide emotional support and friendship to the expectant mothers and fathers. Much of this is accomplished through the "Mentor Mom" program, in which volunteers work with clients through a parenting program where they provide guidance and support and serve as parenting role models. In addition, the center provides teen counseling and babysitting services. Ultimately, Centro Tepayac's centerpiece goal is to promote a lifestyle that reflects religious values, particularly regarding sexual behavior. [SOURCE: www.centrotepeyac.org]

CERRO MARAVILLA CASE

Hearings by the Puerto Rico Senate Judiciary Committee held in 1991 and 1992, investigated the 1978 killing of two young independence activists by

Puerto Rican policemen at Cerro Maravilla and the subsequent alleged cover-up by authorities. According to an internal 1978 White House memorandum introduced at the hearings, the FBI had disrupted the activities of the pro-independence movement by attempting to create dissension, intercepting mail, and illegally inspecting bank records. Witnesses at the hearings told of how policemen on the island had reported terrorist bombings that never occurred, while blaming pro-independence activists for bombings which the police themselves had carried out. According to one testimony, during the 1978 electrical workers strike, a police agent sabotaged equipment in a company, blaming it on unionists. Others accused the government of sponsoring right-wing death squads. FBI director, Louis Freeh, admitted that the bureau had engaged in these activities, but that it was a thing of the past. Activists did not agree and they charged the FBI with continuing to engage in frame-ups and inject agent provocateurs in the independence movement. [SOURCE: Stone, "Files Detail FBI's War on Puerto Rican Independence Fight," http://www.themilitant.com/2000/6423/642351.html]

CÉSPEDES, CARLOS "CARLITOS" MANUEL DE (1840-1915)

By 1875, there were more than one thousand Cubans registered to vote in Monroe County, Florida, where Key West is located. The city's first mayor, who had the same name as his father, was the son of Carlos Manuel de Céspedes, the hero of the Ten Years' War in Cuba (1869-1873). Called Carlitos by his family, he was born in Bayamo on January 3, 1840 and fought with his father in the "Ten Years War." Besides Céspedes, voters elected a Cuban alderman during that decade. Carlos "Carlitos" Manuel de Céspedes died in Manzanillo, Cuba in 1915. [SOURCE: Masud-Piloto, *From Welcomed Exiles to Illegal Immigrants*, 9.]

CHACÓN-MOSCONE BILINGUAL-BICULTURAL EDUCATION

In 1976, California Assemblymen Peter Chacón and George Moscone introduced a bilingual education bill in the state legislature, which passed and came to be known as the Chacón-Moscone Bilingual-Bicultural Education Act. This bill was much more supportive of bilingual education because, unlike federal legislation, it explicitly mandated bilingual education as a right of English-language learners. It was strengthened when it required schools to offer bilingual education when ten or more children of the same language background and limited in English-proficiency were enrolled in the same grade. But conservatives began to dominate both the state assembly and the state house; a retrenchment of the bilingual mandate began. In 1987, Governor George Deukmajian launched the first major attack against California's bilingual education laws when he allowed the Chacón-Moscone Bilingual Bicultural Law to sunset. Technically, the requirements of the law remain in effect, but the governor's failure to support the law weakened the bilingual education mandate in California. Since then, no new bilingual education bills have passed in California. [SOURCE: Baker and Hakuta, "Bilingual Education and Latino Civil Rights."]

CHAPA, FRANCISCO (1870-1924)

Francisco Chapa, the editor of San Antonio's *El Imparcial de Texas** from the early 1900s until his death in 1924, nurtured relationships with Anglos in Texas and helped immigrants settle. The Matamoros-born publisher came to Texas as a young businessman in the 1890s and integrated himself into San Antonio's civic and political life. He became an advisor to Governor Colquitt in 1910 and to Governor Ferguson in 1918. Furthermore, his newspaper encouraged the Mexican vote, prompted readers to involve themselves in civil rights issues, and praised Mexican-American veterans of World War I. Appalled by the negative images of Mexicans in the cinema, Chapa used *El Imparcial de Texas* to voice his concern over the degrading images. He took a delegation to the Texas governor to protest the showing of such films. Texas governor, W.P. Hobby, then banned screening movies that portrayed Mexicans poorly. His association with Anglos helped Chapa accomplish many of his goals. [SOURCE: Christian, "Joining the American Mainstream."]

CHÁVEZ, CÉSAR E. (1927-1993)

César E. Chávez was born in Yuma, Arizona, on March 31, 1927. After his father, Librado, lost a farmstead that his own father had homesteaded in the 1880s, the Chávez family was forced to work in the California migrant stream. In 1938, the family wound up in California's San Joaquin Valley suffering the desperate poverty that was endemic among farmworkers in the area. As the family followed the crops, César, his brothers and sisters attended more than thirty schools. César dropped out after the eighth grade to help support his family, but at the end of World War II in 1945, he joined the Navy and served in the Pacific. Discharged in 1948, he married Helen Fabela and rented a house in "Sal Si Puedes (Get Out if You Can)," a poor Mexican neighborhood in San Jose.

As a young husband with a growing family to support, Chávez had no choice but to pick fruit in area orchards. But in 1952, the idealistic farmworker went to work as an organizer for the Community Services Organization (CSO)* at the behest of Fred Ross,* a recruiter for the organization. Founded on the principles established by Saul Alinsky's Industrial Areas Foundation, the CSO used neighborhood canvassing techniques to persuade families to register to vote and to battle racial and economic discrimination.

Community Services Organization national funding convention with Saul Alinsky at extreme left and César Chávez next to last on the right. Edward Roybal, Fred Ross, and Herman Gallegos are at center (all on first row).

Showing remarkable organizing ability, CSO leaders soon dispatched Chávez throughout Arizona and California, where he spurred local community action.

While still in the CSO, Chávez joined forces with the United Packing House Workers of America in a drive to organize packing shed workers, but remembering his own background, his heart lay in organizing the field workers. By 1958, his talents had earned him the national directorship of the CSO. Now he could fulfill his dream of organizing farmworkers, but other CSO leaders resisted. Chávez then resigned in 1962 and convinced other CSO organizers, Gil Padilla and Dolores Huerta* as well as his wife Helen and brother Manuel, to bring the "dream" to life.

By 1965, the fledgling union called the National Farm Workers Association (NFWA) boasted more than a thousand members. That year, the struggle began against California growers; it would last throughout Chávez's life. Inspired by the methods of African-American civil rights activists in the South, the ex-farmworker injected the strategy into his own movement. In April 1966, Chávez led a march from Delano to the state capital of Sacramento, demanding social justice for farmworkers. The event drew much national attention and sympathy, a development that was not lost on Chávez and his followers. Gaining public support seemed more effective than coercing employers through work stoppages; it became the main weapon for the union. As such, on numerous occasions Chávez called for marches and other publicity efforts that revealed the plight of poor farmworkers. A national boycott against all California grapes, for example, resulted in contracts from farmers who had successfully resisted every other union tactic. On more than one occasion, Chávez fasted to bring attention to the workers' cause.

By the late seventies, the NFWA had become the United Farm Workers Association (UFWA),* its internal dissent had weakened the California-based union, and the rank and file began to challenge the leadership in the decision-making process. Many accused Chávez of becoming too authoritarian. A third grape boycott was issued in 1984, mainly to protest pesticide use as harmful to the workers. By now, Chávez' Gandhi-like approach did not resonate as it had in the 1960s and 1970s. In the 1980s, the farmworker movement lost much of its symbolic appeal for Chicanos,* and indeed until César Chávez's tragic death on April 23, 1993, at age 65, the struggle was not as public as in previous years.

The degree to which the farmworker movement succeeded is not the most important measurement of Chávez' place in history. His legacy transcends a lifework's commitment to organizing at the grassroot level, especially farmworkers. More than any other personality in this century, Mexican Americans evoke the name and memory of this soft-spoken labor organizer when they commemorate past civil rights struggles, when they advocate for contemporary social reform, or when they seek a heroic symbol with which to identify. Truly, few Mexican Americans sacrificed and suffered as much as Chávez to help his people. [SOURCE: Griswold del Castillo and García, *César Chávez;* Rosales, *Testimonio*, 269-275.]

CHÁVEZ, DENNIS (1888-1962)

Dennis Chávez

Dennis Chávez became the first Hispanic elected to the U.S. Senate. Born to a poor family in a village to the west of Albuquerque, New Mexico, Chávez attended school in Albuquerque, but was forced to drop out to work. Chávez continued his education on his own and eventually enrolled in law school; he graduated with a law degree from Georgetown University in 1920. Chávez returned to New Mexico, established a private practice and ran for office. In 1930, he won a seat in the House of Representatives; that was followed by his election to the Senate in 1935, where the Democrat staunchly supported the New Deal politics of President Franklin D. Roosevelt. As a senator, Chávez helped draft the Fair Employment Practices Act* and remained relentless in obtaining support until it was enacted in 1941. Chávez served five terms in the Senate until he died of a heart attack in 1962. [SOURCE: Carrasco, "Law and Politics," 277.]

CHÁVEZ, LINDA (1947-)

Linda Chávez, the first Hispanic to become editor of *American Educator,* the quarterly magazine of the American Federation of Teachers, was born in Albuquerque, New Mexico, 1947. Chávez has dedicated much of her energy to promoting the education of Hispanics; however, she constantly challenges the liberal perspective held by most Hispanic civil rights and political leaders. Through her controversial editorials, she caught the eye of conservative politicians, especially as she attacked affirmative action and bilingual education as detrimental to the progress of Hispanics. President Ronald Reagan in 1981 chose Linda Chávez to become his consultant on minority affairs and, in 1983, the president appointed her to the Civil Rights Commission. Subsequently, she became public liaison for the White House, a position that made her the most visible Hispanic-surnamed person and highest-ranking woman in the Reagan administration. In 2000, the Library of Congress honored Chávez as a "Living Legend" for her contributions to America's cultural and historical legacy. In January 2001, President George W. Bush nominated Chávez for Secretary of Labor; however, she withdrew her name from consideration after a disclosure that she had allowed an undocumented immigrant to reside in her house.

Chávez ran unsuccessfully on the Republican ticket for U.S. senator from Maryland in 1986. In 1992, the United Nations Human Rights Commission selected her to serve a four-year term as U.S. Expert to the U.N. Sub-commission on the Prevention of Discrimination and Protection of Minorities.

Today, Chávez is president of the Center for Equal Opportunity, a public policy research organization in Sterling, Virginia. Her weekly syndicated column appears in newspapers across the country, she hosts a daily radio show in Washington, D.C., and serves as a political analyst for FOX News network. Television journalistic programs, such as "CNN & Co.," "The McLaughlin Group," "Equal Time," and "The Newshour with Jim Lehrer" have featured Chávez as a political and social analyst. Chávez' book, *Out of the Barrio: Toward a New Politics of Hispanic Assimilation*, published in 1991, emphasizes her perception that Hispanics can access the opportunity structure in the United States through persistence and hard work and takes to task what she considers to be a liberal interpretation that the burden of discrimination and racism is too difficult to overcome. Much of her activity is channeled through the Latino Alliance, a federally registered political action committee of the

Republican Party, which she chairs. [SOURCE: Tardiff and Mabunda. *Dictionary of Hispanic Biography,* 223.]

CHAVEZ RAVINE

In the early 1950s, the homes in an area of central Los Angeles, California, known as Chavez Ravine were condemned and its Mexican residents forced to leave. Ironically, the usurpation took place because the L.A. City Housing Authority, equipped with newly appropriated federal money, had planned a massive federal housing project, ostensibly to wipe out poverty conditions, and substandard housing. The design called for converting 315 acres of Chavez Ravine into a high-rise housing project of more than 3,300 units; it was to be called Elysian Park Heights. According to the plan, evicted residents would receive priority when the new units were parceled out. But a maelstrom ensued when private business interests opposed turning all this valuable downtown real estate into public housing, and with the help of the *Los Angeles Times*, waged a campaign against the Authority, charging that the public housing undertaking was an experiment in socialism. In 1952, a new mayor, who opposed the project, was elected, and any hope for its realization ended.

In 1958, the Brooklyn Dodgers forsook New York for Los Angeles; part of their deal with the city was the construction of a new stadium. In a referendum, Los Angeles voters allowed the large former Mexican barrio to be turned over to the ball team. By then, most of the ravine dwellers, who were interspersed in three neighborhoods, La Loma, Bishop, and Palo Verde, had left. But the stragglers had to be forced out—a drama accentuating the powerlessness of Mexican Americans in California. [SOURCE: Boehm, "Requiem for the Ravine."]

CHÁVEZ-THOMPSON, LINDA (1944-)

Linda Chávez-Thompson became the highest-ranking Hispanic ever in the history of the AFL-CIO when she assumed the position of executive vice president of the union. Born to sharecropper parents in Lubbock, Texas, on August 1, 1944, she was one of eight children who worked with her parents in Texas cotton fields, an experience that contributed to her chosen vocation as a labor leader. Chávez-Thompson began her trade union career in 1967, when she joined the Laborers' International Union, and rose to prominence in San Antonio with the American Federation of State, County and Municipal Employees (AFSCME), AFL-CIO. In 1995, she was elected executive director of Texas Council 42, AFSCME. Chávez-Thompson became executive vice president of the AFL-CIO in spite of considerable opposition. The federation's president, John Sweeney helped her election because he felt that Chávez-Thompson would embody the union's need to bridge the considerable gap that existed between the AFL-CIO and Latinos. She is also on the executive committee of the Congressional Hispanic Caucus Institute, the board of trustees for the Labor Heritage Foundation, and President Clinton's Race Advisory Board. [SOURCE: http://www.gale.com/free_resources/chh/bio/chavez_l.htm]

CHICANA LIBERATION IN THE CHICANO MOVEMENT AND ITS LEGACY

The Chicano Movement* of the 1960s and 1970s has left a lasting legacy, which directly and indirectly led to the flourishing of civil rights activism that is extending into the twenty-first century. Chicano* civil rights activism was dominated by males, which often resulted in issues crucial to Chicanas being relegated to the backburner or worse: ignored. At the National Chicano Youth Liberation Conference* held in Denver in 1969, for example, Chicanas in attendance insisted on addressing their oppression by males, many of whom asserted that the priority of the Chicano Movement was to liberate the males first. The women delegates held an impromptu workshop that issued a statement condemning chauvinism within the Chicano Movement. Many Chicanas, needless to say, were not deterred from pursuing the issue and soon Chicana liberation organizations began to multiply and flourish.

For example, in 1970, California Chicanas founded the Comisión Femenil Mexicana Nacional (Mexican National Feminist Commission)* that promoted the formulation of public policies to address the specific needs of Chicanas. This organization's emphasis on developing leadership roles and organizational skills among its members provided a model for subsequent organizing efforts. In the early 1970s, issues of gender equality within La Raza Unida Party (LRUP)* prompted Martha Cotera* and other Chicanas to demand a greater voice in the party and to organize the first Chicano feminist meetings in Houston during 1971 and 1972. These types of initiatives put Chicanas in the forefront of international feminist movements and led to the creation of such groups as the Mexican American Women's National Association (MANA)* in 1974.

MANA succeeded in advancing Chicanas from all socioeconomic backgrounds and political ideologies through leadership training and network communication at the national level. Although MANA emerged in Washington, D.C., soon after its founding its membership extended into sixteen states; by the 1980s, MANA regional chapters existed throughout the United States. MANA continues to sponsor an annual convention in different cities of the United States to discuss issues affecting Mexican-American women. From its Washington, D.C. headquarters, MANA publishes a monthly newsletter devoted to the same issues. The organization now has expanded to include a diverse group of Latinas in all areas of political, social, and professional life and is the single largest pan-Latina organization in the United States.

In the 1970s, pioneer Chicana activist, Francisca Flores,* created the California League of Mexican American Women, a Los Angeles-based organization stroving for women's rights in Southern California. Also in the 1970s, Alicia Escalante founded the Chicana National Welfare Rights Organization and in the same decade joined with Francisca Flores to establish the Chicana Service Action Center. These groups served to develop among Chicanas organizing and leadership skills through workshops, conferences, and community activities with such crucial thematic issues as education, immigration, child care, and reproductive rights.

In 1981, Mujeres Activas en Letras y Cambio Social (Women Active in Letters and Social Change-MALCS)* came into being in Santa Clara, California, through the efforts of Chicana academicians. MALCS sought to restructure the recruitment and retention policies of universities in order to increase the number of Chicana faculty and students. It also provided guidelines on revising the curriculum and in conducting academic research that contributed directly to the advancement of Chicanas in the United States.

Some organizations had the same goals but perhaps advocated with less militancy and more aspiration towards middle-class mobility. Nonetheless, their formation can be seen as an indirect result of the consciousness raised by the Chicana liberation movement. One such organization, the Hispanic Women's Corporation,* was founded in Phoenix, Arizona, in 1985. It emerged to empower Latinas with projects such as its annual "Our Youth Leadership Conference," which invites more than 200 Latina high school students to a summit, where the young women are provided leadership training, access to resources, and a forum on networking. Similarly, the National Council of Hispanic Women (NCHW),* composed of individual women and organizations, such as universities and corporations, exists to empower Hispanic women and assist them in attaining a prominent role in American society.

Groups that deal with health care and the more urgent needs of working-class women have emerged, directly or indirectly, as a result of Chicana movement consciousness. La Casa de las Madres* was founded in 1976 to offer emergency residential shelter to battered women and their children in downtown San Francisco. The same year, eight head start mothers living in Denver's Westside community founded what would become Mi Casa, a place where women could acquire employment skills and where their children could get help and encouragement in school. In 1986, the National Latina Health Organization (NLHO)* was formed in Oakland, California, by health-care givers to raise awareness about how to provide preventive care and to address the most prevalent health problems among Latinas. In 1991, the Sisters of Color* was founded in Denver with the vision of advocating for health equity and improved quality of life predominantly for women of color, their families, and their communities.

In the 1970s, the National Association for Chicano Studies (NACS) began to promote activism in Chicano-applied scholarship, but it underwent a critical transition, motivated primarily by a debate over gender in Chicano society; reflecting this orientation, it is now entitled the National Association for Chicana/Chicano Studies (NACCS).* Gender and sexual orientation has also led to the founding of Lesbianas Unidas (LU)* in 1984 in order to support and address, through grassroots efforts in Los Angeles, the specific needs of politicized, feminist Latina lesbians.

Projects with a definite conservative bent but which can be considered to have emerged as a result of the consciousness raising of the Chicana movement can also be considered here. For example, in 1971, Catholic nuns founded Las Hermanas* in San Antonio, Texas, with the goal of engaging Hispanic women in active ministry among Hispanics. Perhaps a bigger stretch is the Centro Tepeyac* in the Washington D.C. area, which offers young women, mainly of Mexican origin, alternatives to abortion.

Of course, other Latina organizations exist with similar objectives, but whose impetus also came from the movements of the 1960s, such as the National Conference of Puerto Rican Women* in New York City, which seeks to advance the full participation of Puerto Rican women in mainstream activities. Mujeres Unidas en Justicia y Reforma (MUJER)* was founded in Homestead, Florida, in 1996 to provide services, such as family preservation, emergency financial assistance and community integration. The clients of this organization are from various Latino groups. [SOURCE: Rosales, *Chicano!*; García, "Chicana Civil Rights Organizations."]

CHICANO

In the 1960s, the word Chicano was elevated from its 1920s denotation of working-class Mexican immigrant, and from the slang of the 1940s and 1950s when it was substituted for *mexicano*, to symbolize the realization of a newfound and unique identity. Proudly, Chicanos proclaimed an Indo-Hispanic heritage and accused older Mexican Americans of pathologically denying their racial and ethnic reality because of an inferiority complex.

In the 1930s and 1940s, middle class-aspiring Mexican Americans looked with disdain at their brothers and sisters who did not transcend the working-class Mexican identity that persisted beyond the first generation. Significantly, the Mexican-American middle-classes applied the word "Chicano" pejoratively to identify the lower classes.

Some of the lexicon used in the movement has survived to this day, albeit mainly in circles that have an unbroken tie to the movement—university students, artists, intellectuals, scholars, etc. The most apparent legacy is the word Chicano itself. Outside of the intellectual environment, however, the term is met with indifference, and among Mexican immigrants it is scorned. But the struggle over its use no longer draws the same heat that it did when activists first proposed "Chicano" in the 1960s, when the term was associated with militancy.

During this era, both sides constructed elaborate etymologies of "Chicano." To those who wished for the word to represent the movement, Chicano derived from the ancient Nahuatl word *"mexicano"* with the "x" being pronounced as a "shh" sound. Among the many versions that detractors used to disqualify the term was that it came from "chicas patas," an extremely pejorative reference used to denote new arrivals from Mexico.

At the time of the Los Angeles-school walkouts in the Spring of 1968, Lincoln High School teacher Carmen Terrazas, an opponent of the strike, wrote a letter to the *Los Angeles Times* condemning the word "Chicano" as demeaning to Mexican Americans. Soon after, there appeared in *La Raza* newspaper a "La Adelita Letter to La Malinche." La Adelita was a name for female camp followers and soldiers during the Mexican Revolution, and La Malinche was the consort of Hernán Cortés, who betrayed her people. "As for the term Chicano," wrote La Adelita, "I suggest Terrazas do some research into its origin. We have always referred to ourselves as Chicanos. . . . We gave it to ourselves, the Anglo did not. . . . Terrazas insists on referring to herself as an American of Mexican descent . . . she suffers from an inferiority complex for which I pity her." [SOURCE: Rosales, *Chicano!*; García, *Chicanismo,* 34, 55, 60.]

CHICANO ASSOCIATED STUDENTS ORGANIZATION

The Spanish American Students Organization was organized at the New Mexico Highlands University in 1969 with the advent of the Chicano Movement,* student activists changed its name to Chicano Associated Student Organization (CASO) and re-directed the organization to reflect Chicano Movement ideology. CASO achieved several goals, such as developing a Chicano studies program and hiring more Mexican-American professors. Owing much to CASO's prodding, the university eventually hired Dr. John Aragón as president. [SOURCE: Meier and Rivera, *Dictionary of Mexican American History,* 84.]

CHICANO! THE HISTORY OF THE MEXICAN AMERICAN CIVIL RIGHTS MOVEMENT

In 1996, the Public Broadcasting Service (PBS) aired the documentary *Chicano! The History of the Mexican American Civil Rights Movement,* produced by the National Latino Communications Center* in Los Angeles. Consisting of four, one-hour episodes, the documentary is coordinated by José Luis Ruiz and produced and directed by the renowned filmmakers Jesús Salvador Treviño and Hector Galán. The first part, "Quest for a Homeland," chronicles efforts by Reies López Tijerina* to regain ownership of land grants at Tierra Amarilla, New Mexico. The episode then shows a link of this movement to the Chicano Moratorium,* a massive protest march by Mexican Americans against the Vietnam War. The second part, "The Struggle in the Field," examines how farmworker activists under the nonviolent leadership of César Chávez* launched a movement in California to form a national labor union, which sought an end to the extreme exploitation of agricultural workers. Under the leadership of "Taking Back the Schools," the third part documents the struggle to reform an educational system that in East Los Angeles had failed to properly educate Chicano* students. The main focus of this segment is the 1968 walkout by thousands of Mexican-American youth from their high schools. "Fighting for Political Power," the final installment of the series focuses on the emergence of La Raza Unida Party (LRUP),* a Chicano political party in Texas. The party spread throughout the nation and, although it did not survive, remained an inspiration for a generation of political activists who continued voter registration strategies they learned through participation in the LRUP. A companion book of the same title, written by F. Arturo Rosales, was published by Arte Público Press in 1996. [SOURCE: http://www.lib.berkeley.edu/MRC/LatinoVid.html]

CHICANO LIBERATION FRONT

In 1971, the Chicano Liberation Front (CLF) claimed responsibility for a series of bombings in Los Angeles. The bombed sites included City Hall and a U.S. federal building, where one person died. To be sure, CLF was on the fringe of the Chicano Movement* and, to this day, no CLF members have publicly admitted they belonged to the group. [SOURCE: Escobar, "The Dialectics of Repression," 1499.]

CHICANO MOVEMENT

The late 1960s and early 1970s were a time of intellectual ferment and rebellion in the United States. Caught up in the mood, young Mexican Americans throughout the country sought a new identity while struggling for the same civil rights of previous generations. This activism became known as the "Chicano Movement." The word Chicano* was elevated from its use in the 1920s to denote working-classs Mexican immigrants, and from the slang of the 1940s and 1950s when it substituted for *mexicano*, to symbolize the realization of a newfound and unique identity. Proudly, Chicanos proclaimed an

Indo-Hispanic heritage and accused older Mexican Americans of pathologically denying their racial and ethnic reality because of an inferiority complex.

In the Movement, an attempt was made to use some of the same symbols of their immigrant grandfathers, but with a few added touches. Tapping several intellectual traditions, attempts were made to define true ethnic character. Allusions were made to factual and mythical pasts. For example, the concept of Aztlán, the mythical place of origin of the Aztecs, became the Chicano Movement name for the Southwest; many Chicanos aspired to reconquer the Southwest, at least culturally. In addition, participants in the movement differed from the previous Mexican-American generation in that they did not care if they were acceptable to the mainstream and they rejected assimilation. Many of the images they construed reflected their alienation as they blended *pachuco* cultural modes, *pinto* (ex-convict) savvy, pre-Columbian motifs, and myths with a burning conviction that Chicanos were deliberately subordinated by a racist American society. Chicano student organizations sprang up throughout the nation, as did barrio groups such as the Brown Berets.* Thousands of young Chicanos pledged their loyalty and time to such groups as the United Farm Workers Organizing Committee,* which under Cesar Chávez* had been a great inspiration for Chicanos throughout the nation. An offshoot of both impulses, the farmworker and the student movement, was La Raza Unida Party* in Texas, an organization formed in 1968 to obtain control of community governments where Chicanos were in the majority. [SOURCE: Marín, *Social Protest in an Urban Barrio*; Muñoz, *Youth Identity and Power*.]

CHICANO POLICE OFFICERS ASSOCIATION

The Chicano Police Officers Association (CPOA) was founded in Albuquerque, New Mexico, in 1973 to ensure that the rights of Mexican Americans were protected during the hiring and promoting processes in the police department. Because of lawsuits filed by CPOA of alleged discrimination, the city implemented a review of general department procedures. [SOURCE: Meier and Rivera, *Dictionary of Mexican American History*, 84.]

CHICANO PRESS ASSOCIATION

At its apogee, the Chicano Press Association (CPA), established in 1969, had twenty-three members across the country; most were located in California. The publications, almost always printed in rather primitive facilities, even by sixties standards, always contained polemical views of events and issues that affected Chicanos.* For example, during the walkouts of East Los Angeles High schools in 1968, CPA newspapers *La Raza, Inside Eastside* and *The Chicano Student* helped fuel the passions of students and boycott supporters. A few days before the walkouts, *La Raza* blasted the shortcomings of the school system and encouraged students to leave their classes. In 1969, Mexican American Youth Organization (MAYO)* activists started *El Degüello* (the Beheading) in San Antonio, Texas, a newspaper that railed against Gringo injustice. The choice of the term was designed to antagonize Anglos, because this was also the war cry (no quarter) given by Antonio López de Santa Anna when his soldiers killed all the defenders at the Alamo.

Although the publications reflected the unique ideological positions of the organizations that sponsored them, the publishers reached a consensus on what the political purpose of the CPA should be. The CPA'S founding document states the following:

> The CPA is a confederation of community newspapers dedicated to promoting the movement of La Raza for self-determination and unity among our people. The CPA affirms that the time has come for the liberation of the Chicano and other oppressed people. We want the existing social order to dissolve. We want a new social order. The CPA supports the struggle against exploitation and all forms of oppression with the goal of building a new society in which human dignity, justice and brotherhood will prevail.

The publications that belonged to the Chicano Press Association in 1969 were:

El Papel, Albuquerque
El Chicano, San Bernardino
El Degüello, San Antonio
The Forumeer, San Jose
La Voz Mexicana, Wautoma, Wisconsin
Carta Editorial, Los Angeles
La Revolución, Uvalde, Texas
El Grito del Norte, Española, New Mexico
El Yaqui, Houston
Bronze, San Jose
Chicano Student Movement, Los Angeles
Lado, Chicago, Ill.
La Raza, Los Angeles
Infierno, San Antonio
El Malcriado, Delano, Calif
La Raza Nueva, San Antonio
Inside Eastside, Los Angeles
El Gallo, Denver
Compass, Houston
La Verdad, San Diego
Nuestra Lucha, Delray Beach, Florida
Coraje, Tucson, Arizona

[SOURCE: Rosales, *Chicano!*, 210.]

CHICANO YOUTH ASSOCIATION

Formed in 1969 by José Armas in New Mexico, The Chicano Youth Association (CYA) was one of the first organizations in New Mexico to engage in urban-style confrontation politics. It organized walkouts in Albuquerque and Roswell in the early 1970s to protest the lack of courses relating to Mexican-American culture, and it protested against racist educators. The CYA was successful in changing the curriculum and some policies. [SOURCE: Rosales, *Chicano!*, 214.]

CHICANOS POR LA CAUSA

In 1968, students at Arizona State University in Tempe organized the Mexican American Student Organization (MASO)* as part of a growing trend among Latino students in pressing universities and colleges to meet the educational needs of their communities. After making this commitment, some of the students quickly took the movement to the Phoenix barrios. In 1969, the students joined with community activists and incorporated Chicanos Por La Causa (CPLC), a strident civil rights and community development organization. After the fledgling organization obtained a small seed grant from the Ford Foundation,* the ambitious, idealistic young militants that organized it then proceeded to pursue the dream of transforming the Phoenix Chicano* community. The initial activity of the group focused on educational issues and politics. In 1969, for example, the organization ran a slate of barrio residents for an inner city school board election and the following year helped organize walkouts at Phoenix Union High School, a school with a predominantly minority student body to protest inadequate funding and the lack of relevant courses.

By 1970, the Ford Foundation had provided full funding, and within a short time the organization's militant edge gave way to a more programmatic approach. By 1974, CPLC's milder image allowed it to receive federal funding. Thus it could pursue economic development, job training, and housing issues in a more structured fashion and open up service centers in Tucson and Yuma. In 2001, *Hispanic News* selected the organization as the second top Hispanic nonprofit in the country as a result of its "22 years of dedicated service to their community." Today CPLC has 30 offices in 23 Arizona cities. The organization estimates that 45,000 people annually receive CPLC services. Few other organizations that came out of the Chicano Movement* have survived, let alone reached the mammoth proportions of CPLC. [SOURCE: Rosales, *Chicano!*, 210-213.]

CHILDREN AND IMMIGRATION

According to a Harvard longitudinal study done in the late 1990s of 407 immigrant children, 85 percent of them had experienced a separation from one or both parents during the migratory process. Furthermore, 35 percent of immigrant children had experienced separation from their fathers for more than five years. According to the researchers, children accompanied by parents and siblings to the United States and who were not separated in the process of settling down, had experienced fewer depressive symptoms than children whose families had separated during the migratory process. This five-year project followed the 407 recently arrived immigrant youths from Central America (including El Salvador, Guatemala, Honduras, and Nicaragua), China (Hong Kong, Mainland China, and Taiwan), the Dominican Republic, Haiti, and Mexico. The ages of these youths ranged from nine to 14 at the beginning of the study. The research team selected the participants, sorted by gender and country of origin, from seven school districts in the Boston and San Francisco greater metropolitan areas. [SOURCE: Suárez-Orozco, "The Transnationalization of Families," http://www.gse.harvard.edu/news/features/suarez06292001.html]

LOS CINCO

In 1963, five Mexican-American candidates displaced the all-white city council in Crystal City, Texas,* where Mexican Americans made up 85 percent of the population. They came to be known as "Los Cinco." Their election ended an Anglo-dominated city government that had been in power since the town's founding in 1907; it was the first such replacement in the United States. The local Teamsters Union at the Del Monte cannery and the Political Association of Spanish-Speaking Organizations (PASSO)* helped organize the community and elect Los Cinco.

Following the election, the group's inexperience, along with intimidation by Anglos, proved difficult barriers. Visible in-fighting and other troubles obscured the progress Los Cinco made in ameliorating discrimination for Spanish-speakers. After two years, Los Cinco were replaced by a mixed Anglo Mexican-American council.

A more successful challenge came in 1969, when the entire council was again replaced by Chicanos.* As a result of this revolt and a protest against discrimination in the Crystal City schools, a political party was formed, La Raza Unida (The United People's Party-LRUP),* which expanded very fast throughout Texas under the leadership of José Angel Gutiérrez.* Crystal City became the first city in the United States to have a Chicano third party controlling the local government. Subsequently, LRUP gained control of the government of Zavala County and made inroads into other areas. By 1981, however, the party was in decline, especially as the Democratic Party began to make reforms and become more inclusive of Mexican Americans and their issues.

LRUP and Crystal City are important historically for bringing about political change and forcing the two-party system in the United States to take Hispanics into account. [SOURCE: Rosales, *Chicano!*, 220-221.]

CINE ACCIÓN

In 1980, Latino film and video makers organized Cine Acción in the Bay Area to publicize the production of Latino media arts, and provide Latinos access to the film and video industry. The Living Room Festivals programmed on KQED (San Francisco) in the 1992 and 1993 seasons were produced by Cine Acción to air works by members of the organization. The organization publishes a monthly bulletin and quarterly newsletter, provides year-round screening of films and videos through Cineteca de Cine Acción, and sponsors the annual ¡Cine Latino! Media Festival. Cine Acción publishes and distributes *Cineworks*, a catalogue of film and video by members that contains a vast array of works addressing Latino cultural identity, politics, and imagery. [SOURCE: www.nvr.org]

CINTAS FOUNDATION

In 1957, Oscar B. Cintas, the former Cuban ambassador to the United States, established the Cintas Foundation, which provided young artists of Cuban ancestry living outside of the island twelve-month fellowships in painting, sculpture, printmaking, architecture, music composition, and creative writing. [SOURCE: García, *Havana USA*, 195.]

CÍRCULO DE TABAQUEROS

The Círculo de Tabaqueros originated in Brooklyn in the early 1900s and served as a meeting center for Hispanics, mainly Puerto Rican tobaccoworkers and their families. The group consisted of a mixture of social organizations and philosophical forums. Some members favored progressive or radical ideas, such as syndical anarchism, socialism, and other left-wing ideologies.

But just as important was the role the headquarters of this association played in providing members an opportunity for social and recreational activities, such as playing chess and dominoes, discussing current events, and planning forthcoming cultural and intellectual projects. Sunday afternoons, for example, were reserved for theatrical performances, in Spanish, lectures and workshops on the politics of social and economic change.

Like many other immigrant labor organizations, the Círculo de Tabaqueros became a hotbed of radical labor organizing. Many of the Círculo study circles discussed the history of Puerto Rico's labor union movement and, as such, contributed to the founding of the Federación Libre de Trabajadores, one of Puerto Rico's most important trade unions. Part of the workers' education process was employing a reader (*lector*) during their many hours rolling cigars; the *lectores* read from newspapers, fiction and nonfiction books, and political tracts and became an important source of raising the consciousness of their social class and status as laborers. [SOURCE: Sánchez Korrol, *From Colonia to Community*, 139-140.]

CISNEROS, HENRY G. (1947-)

Henry G. Cisneros was elected Mayor of San Antonio in 1981 and as a consequence became the first Mexican-American head of a prominent American city (San Antonio ranked as the ninth largest city). His highest public achievement was as Secretary of the U.S. Department of Housing and Urban Development (HUD) from 1992 through early 1997.

Cisneros was born in San Antonio on June 11, 1947, to a middle-class Hispanic family. After receiving a B.A. from Texas A&M in 1968, he married Mary Alice Pérez, whom he had met in high school. He continued his studies at Texas A&M, obtained an M.A. in urban planning and then moved to Washington, D.C., to work at various government jobs. Cisneros then earned a master's degree in public administration at the John F. Kennedy School of Government at Harvard, and, in 1975, he received his Ph.D. in the same field from George Washington University.

Henry G. Cisneros

Returning to his hometown, he felt prepared to take on the lifelong ambition of playing a leading role in the city's administration and ran successfully for a seat on the San Antonio City Council, where he subsequently served two terms and earned a reputation for strengthening the city in many ways, including obtaining federal funds to improve living conditions in San Antonio's Hispanic neighborhoods.

Cisneros raised his sights in 1981 and ran successfully for mayor. Well-liked by his constituency, he earned three additional two-year terms. His popularity transcended the San Antonio's Hispanic community to citizens of all backgrounds. Cisneros was encouraged to run in 1990 for governor of Texas, but the illness of his son forced him to change his goals.

In 1992, he worked hard on Bill Clinton's presidential campaign and after his election, Clinton invited Cisneros to be the secretary of HUD. Cisneros found this federal agency in disarray and proceeded to streamline the functions of the unit. Homelessness, which had increased dramatically since the 1980s, became one of HUD's top priorities under the San Antonio native. In eighteen months, old and dilapidated housing were torn down across the nation, and tenants were moved to better housing. Cisneros received plaudits from housing experts across the nation for transforming HUD into an agency that worked effectively to end racial segregation and poverty in inner cities.

During his tenure in this high-profile position, a scandal that developed into a full-scale federal investigation derailed Cisneros' promising career. In mid 1994, political fundraiser Lynda Medlar, accused Cisneros of reneging an oral agreement for a monthly maintenance payment in return for keeping secret a lapsed love affair between the two of them. The damage came when she quietly accused Cisneros of lying about the payments to the FBI during his background investigation for the position of secretary of HUD. To avoid a prison sentence, Cisneros agreed to plea guilty and received probation. In January 1997, Cisneros resigned his post, citing his financial needs, and became president of Univisión, the leading Spanish-language television network. After serving at Univision, Cisneros went out on his own to establish American City Vista, a corporation building/housing for low- and moderate-income families. [SOURCE: Tardiff and Mabunda, *Dictionary of Hispanic Biography*, http://www.galegroup.com/free_resources/chh/bio/cisneros_h.htm]

CITIZENS ASSOCIATION SERVING ALL AMERICANS

The Citizens Association Serving all Americans (CASAA) was a group of Anglos and some middle-class Mexican Americans in Crystal City, Texas* that formed to oppose the all-Mexican American La Raza Unida Party (The United People's Party-LRUP)* in 1970. The LRUP, a new independent party made up mainly of young Mexican Americans had targeted city council and school board seats in order to bring about community control. Mexicans predominated in this small Winter Garden area town but they had very little political or economic power. CASAA ran a slate of Mexican Americans in the elections and tried to discredit LRUP's campaign by hinting that José Angel Gutiérrez,* the party's leader was a Communist. Immediately before election day, CASAA hired a plane to drop pamphlets accusing Gutiérrez of being an atheist. The campaign was ineffectual, and LRUP candidates fared well in the election. [SOURCE: Navarro, *La Raza Unida Party,* 34, 51.]

CITIZEN'S COMMITTEE FOR THE DEFENSE OF LATIN AMERICAN YOUTH

During World War II, media coverage of the gang activity of *pachucos* (zoot-suited street youth) inflamed a widespread public and police backlash against Mexicans. The repression of Mexican-American youths threatened the civil rights gains activists had previously obtained. In Los Angeles, California, with a gigantic Mexican-American population, activists led by the lawyer Manuel Ruiz came to the defense of arrested youths by forming the

Citizen's Committee for the Defense of Latin American Youth. The committee provided legal support for the Sleepy Lagoon* defendants, who were accused of killing another Mexican-American teenager at a party in 1942. The committee became especially active during the Zoot Suit Riots* of 1943, when servicemen stationed in the Los Angeles-area commandeered taxi cabs and spilled out into the streets of East Los Angeles to beat up every Mexican teenager that crossed their path. They did this with the tacit support of the press, their superiors, and the police. Significantly, in this process, Ruiz became an early promoter of bilingual education as a "means to teach any curricular subject, whether it be Americanization, hygiene or anything else." He lamented the contradictory policy that "Spanish may be taught, but the Spanish language cannot be used to teach." [SOURCE: Escobar, *Race, Police, and the Making of a Political Identity*, 227.]

CITIZENSHIP EMPOWERMENT PROGRAM

Established in Oakland, California, in 2001, the Citizenship Empowerment Program is designed to assist low-income immigrants in obtaining U.S. citizenship. Program staff also provide them with an orientation that will allow them to become active participants in the civic and political processes. [SOURCE: http://www.sscf.org/citizenship/mainframe.php3]

CIVIC ACTION COMMITTEE

On January 4, 1958, a number of Mexican-American affiliated organizations met to organize a poll tax drive under the auspices of the Civic Action Committee to increase increase the Hispanic electorate in the city of Houston. At the meeting, participants were told that out of 60,000 Spanish-surnamed individuals in Houston, only 1,200 had paid the poll tax, which was necessary to vote in Texas until the practice was abolished for national elections by the 24th Amendment to the U.S. Constitution in 1964 and by *Harper v. Virginia Board of Elections*, the Supreme Court decision for state elections, in 1966. Although Mexican Americans understood the injustice of the poll tax, which was meant to discourage them and African Americans from voting, such was their desire to make their voice heard that they launched campaigns to persuade Mexican Americans to pay the tax. They canvassed neighborhoods and directed citizens to the nearest poll tax deputy.

These efforts were undertaken throughout Texas, and in 1961, Henry B. González* from San Antonio was elected to Congress as a result. In Houston, Civic Action Committee members were often part of the local League of United Latin American Citizens (LULAC),* whose members were prohibited from becoming involved in political campaigns in the name of the organization. Significantly, in Houston, the Civic Action Committee was crucial to forming the Viva Kennedy clubs* to deliver the Mexican-American vote for the Kennedy-Johnson ticket in 1960. Many committee members became an integral part of the Political Association of Spanish-Speaking Organizations* formed to maintain the momentum gained during the Kennedy campaign. The Civic Action Committee lasted until the end of the 1960s. [SOURCE: Civic Action Committee Bulletins, Council 60 of LULAC, Houston, Texas.]

CIVIL PRACTICE ACT

The Civil Practice Act of 1850, passed in the California legislature, excluded Chinese and Indians from testifying against whites. At first, Mexicans were not targeted, but eventually it was extended to Mexicans because they were partially Indian. [SOURCE: Trueba, *Latinos Unidos,* 3.]

CIVIL RIGHTS ACTS (1957, 1960, 1964, 1968)

Within the space of eleven years, Congress passed four Civil Rights Acts in response to increasing pressure from African Americans and other ethnic constituencies arguing that the Constitution did not sufficiently provide protection for minority groups. After President D. Eisenhower broached the need for such protection in two State of the Union addresses in 1956 and 1957, the 1957 Civil Rights Act was enacted. The Civil Rights Commission was then established to examine why voting by minorities, specifically African Americans, was lower than that of whites. The commission also appraised federal legislation dealing with equal rights and attempted to eliminate race restrictions in voting. Finally, it created a new civil rights division in the Justice Department in order to make it easier to procure federal protection for persons who were prevented from voting.

The 1960 Civil Rights Act, also passed during the Eisenhower years, again stressed voting rights and attempted to bolster the Civil Rights Commission. It also declared that violations associated with voting were a federal offense—a move that generally strengthened the ability of the federal government to intervene in cases dealing with civil rights violations.

The Civil Rights Act of 1964 widened the orbit of equal rights protection beyond voting rights. The Equal Employment Opportunity Commission (EEOC)* was created, for example, to prevent discrimination in employment based on gender or race. Provisions in the act prohibited prejudiced practices in public accommodations, in legislation, and in applying federal and state expenditures. The latter provision would make it difficult for segregated schools to obtain funding; thus it promoted school desegregation. After he had steered the 1964 act through Congress, President Lyndon B. Johnson* signed it into law on July 2, 1964, and delivered the idealistic promise of a "Great Society," in which all citizens had an equal chance to realize the American Dream.

The 1968 Civil Rights Act went even further by prohibiting housing discrimination. In addition, it extended rights to Indians in tribal courts. Concerned with riots, the act made promoting riots a federal offense. [SOURCE: Donato, *The Other Struggle for Equal Schools,* 54.]

CLEMENTE, ROBERTO (1934-1972)

Roberto Clemente, born in 1934 in Puerto Rico, excelled as one of the finest all-around baseball players of his era, but admirers also remember him for his dedication to humanitarian issues and for his generosity. Because of this combination, Clemente became one of most idolized figures in the American Latino community. Clemente displayed both a love and a talent for playing baseball from the time he was a boy in Puerto Rico. The Brooklyn Dodgers placed him on a farm team in Montreal in 1953, but he showed so much talent that a year later, the Pittsburgh Pirates drafted him into the sports organization, where he remained for the rest of his career. Clemente's baseball achievements were numerous both as a batter and as a defender.

In 1972, Clemente was still at the top of his form, even though he had played eighteen seasons for the Pirates. He became the eleventh major league player to accumulate 3,000 career hits. On December 31, he died in a plane crash as he traveled to Managua, Nicaragua, to help organize relief operations after the city was ravaged by a severe earthquake. Clemente's death was deeply mourned in his native Puerto Rico, which had been the beneficiary of so much of his unstinting generosity. Not long afterward, baseball paid its own tribute by waiving the normal post-career five-year waiting period to induct Clemente into its Hall of Fame. [SOURCE: http://educate.si.edu/spotlight/olympics.html; http:www.robertoclemente.si.edu/english/index.htm]

CLIFTON-MORENCI STRIKE, 1903

Because of the industrial nature of mining, the most intensive institutional union efforts involving Mexicans took place in Arizona. In 1903, a number of strikes rocked the mining regions of the southeastern part of the state. The most important one took place at Clifton-Morenci involving Mexican and Italian miners, led by William "Wenceslado" Laustenneau,* A.F. Salcido, and an Italian, Frank Colombo. In this stoppage, 3,500 men, angered because their employer would not comply with a state law guaranteeing an eight-hour day, went out; eighty to ninety percent were of Mexican descent. The strike ended when heavy rains and flooding destroyed the section where the homes of the poorer workers were located. This premature termination of the strike probably averted a clash between federal troops, Arizona Rangers and the armed strikers. Laustenneau, Salcido, and Colombo were convicted of inciting a riot in the three-day work stoppage, during which armed workers milled through Morenci, occupying company buildings and making demands. They were sentenced to two years at the infamous Arizona Territorial Prison in Yuma. [SOURCE: Weber, *Foreigners in Their Native Land,* 219; Mellinger, *Race and Labor in Western Copper*, 42-48.]

CLIFTON-MORENCI STRIKE, 1915

In September 1915, Mexican and Anglo mine workers at Clifton and Morenci went out on a strike which lasted nineteen weeks. The main issues were lower pay scales for Mexicans, arbitrary methods of control by foremen, and the low salaries paid during prosperous periods. Ironically, the Western Federation of Miners, a union which in the past had opposed the hiring of Mexicans, became the negotiating agent for the strikers. Governor G.W.P. Hunt and Sheriff James G. Cash called in the National Guard to prevent the importation of strikebreakers, a move which deterred the violence that characterized many other strikes of the era. After four and a half months, the strike came to an end when the company agreed to guarantee equal wage rates for Anglo and Mexican workers. [SOURCE: Samora and Simon, *A History of the Mexican-American People*, 178; http://www.jsri.msu.edu/museum/pubs/MexAmHist/chapter22.html]

CLUB CHAPULTEPEC

In the Mexican-American generation, the clarion call among ambitious young was education and self-improvement. The apotheosis of this formula made it a guiding principle that conceivably could eradicate discrimination and mistreatment in proportion to the degree of education Mexicans achieved. Youth clubs, such as Houston's Club Chapultepec founded in 1937 by young Mexican-American girls, followed this ethos. It strove for education and mobility. When a young Mexican was killed in his Houston city jail cell by his incarcerators, the group protested in writing. Its letter condemned police misconduct, but a major cause of such injustices, the statement read, stemmed from Mexican's difficulty with English. It was crucial for Mexicans to learn to speak and write good English, a goal the club established for itself. [SOURCE: Kreneck, "The Letter From Chapultepec," 268-269.]

CLUB VESTA

Club Vesta, founded in Phoenix, Arizona, in 1954, admitted only Mexican-American college graduates at a time when few Mexican-Americans graduated from high school. The group took its name from the mythical Roman goddess, Vesta, who symbolized purity, exclusivity, and perpetuity. Since its members were middle-class, the organization focused on the obstacles to social and economic mobility, such as racism and segregation, in order to achieve higher status and greater prestige both as individuals and as an ethnic group. As such, its social activity was limited to raising funds for scholarships, which they awarded in annual black-and-white galas that provided its members with a status they found so difficult to obtain from Anglo Americans. Many immigrant organizations pursued similar objectives; the difference is that Club Vesta prized Anglo symbols of success, such as an American college degree, fluency in English, etc. [SOURCE: Rosales, *Chicano!*, 98.]

COHEN, JERRY (1937-)

Educated at Amherst College and the University of California where he received a degree in law, Jerry Cohen served as attorney for the United Farm Workers* under César Chávez* from 1965 to 1975 and was the chief negotiator for the union. After the hard-fought battle during the late 1960s, it was Cohen who John Giumarra, Sr.,* one of the biggest grape growers, called to indicate that the grape boycott was so successful that he arranged for all San Joaquin Valley table grape companies to meet with Chávez and his associates to negotiate a settlement. Cohen is also responsible for writing the 1975 California Agricultural Labor Relations Act to provide California farmworkers protection from which they were excluded when the U.S. Congress passed the National Labor Relations Act in 1935. Cohen continues to practice constitutional and labor law today in California. [SOURCE: Rosales, *Chicano!*, 145-148; http://www.farmworkermovement.org/essays/essays/197%20Jerry %20Cohen.pdf]

COLFAX COUNTY WAR

Mexican Americans in New Mexico became involved in the Colfax County War over control of the Maxwell land grant because they were *vaqueros* and small landowners. This "war" continued throughout the 1870s through a series of skirmishes, as mainly Hispanic settlers and small ranchers attacked enforcers who worked for the Santa Fe Ring and its backers; the Santa Fe Ring systematically usurped the land of less powerful New Mexicans. [SOURCE: Meier and Rivera, *Dictionary of Mexican American History*, 95.]

DE LA COLINA, RAFAEL (1898-1979)

During the Great Depression, Mexican envoys worked diligently, sometimes effectively, to help compatriots in the United States. Consul Rafael de la Colina constantly lodged protests against the raids by the police in Los Angeles, where hundreds of Mexicans were rounded up and jailed before it was decided if they had entered the country illegally. Historian Francisco Balderrama, however, asserts that, de la Colina interpreted his duties narrowly: To keep his superiors informed and to solicit pledges of fair treatment from U.S. officials. He was also handicapped by the lack of support from his superiors in Mexico City. A protest from the secretary of foreign relations might have stopped the massive raids before the immigration agents themselves had halted them.

The Mexican consuls, however, were at their best in assisting Mexicans in the exodus. De la Colina, for example, helped the Comité Mexicano de Beneficencia (Mexican Welfare Committee)* in providing immediate relief to destitute immigrants and in assisting L.A. County officials to repatriate as many Mexicans as possible on railroad trains scheduled specifically for that. Los Angeles County was so enthusiastic about ridding the city of Mexicans that it provided train fare on Mexican railroads so that the immigrants would return all the way to homes in central Mexico and not remain at the border. [SOURCE: Rosales, *Chicano!*, 82-3.; Balderrama and Rodríguez, *Decade of Betrayal*.]

COLÓN, JESÚS (1901-1974)

Jesús Colón was one of the most important Hispanic columnists and intellectuals in the New York Hispanic community for more than fifty years. He was born in Cayey, Puerto Rico, in 1901, shortly after the United States annexed the island as a territory. He stowed away on a ship to New York in 1917, the year U.S. citizenship was granted to Puerto Ricans. Originally from the tobacco growing and manufacturing region of Puerto Rico, where he had already labored among the cigar rollers, he was able to attend the Central Grammar School in San Juan, where he edited the school newspaper, *Adelante* (Forward). Upon his arrival in New York City, he became involved in numerous community and labor organizations, as well as the Puerto Rican Socialist Party.* Colón dedicated himself assiduously to reading and learning as much as he could. After graduating from the Boys' High Evening School in Brooklyn, Colón became the quintessential autodidact and strove

to exercise his learning through journalism and commentary in Spanish-language newspapers. Through the course of his career, it is estimated that he produced more than four hundred published items in some thirty newspapers and periodicals. He also served as an officer for numerous community organizations and even ran for Controller of the City of New York on the Communist Party ticket in 1952 and 1969.

Coming from a modest background and having socialized among tobacco workers and union organizers, Colón became the voice of the working class. His trajectory through labor and Hispanic community

Jesús Colón

newspapers was consistent in its ideological focus, although he did at first assume the guise required by the conventions of Spanish-language *cronista* (columnist). As best can be gleaned from the incomplete historical record, Colón began his formal journalistic career in 1923 as a correspondent for Puerto Rico's *Justicia* (Justice), the official newspaper of the Federación Libre de Trabajadores (Free Federation of Workers). His writings appeared consistently in *Gráfico*,* beginning in 1927 under his own name and the pseudonyms Miquis Tiquis and Pericles Espada. He later made the transition to English commentary as a columnist for the *Daily Worker*, the newspaper of the Communist Party in the United States. Colón also founded and operated a publishing house, Hispanic Publishers (Editorial Hispánica), which issued history and literary books, as well as political information in Spanish.

Colón published a selection of his newspaper columns and essays in 1961 in book form under the title of *A Puerto Rican in New York and Other Sketches*. Two other collections have been published posthumously, *The Way It Was and Other Sketches* (1993) and *Lo que el pueblo me dice* (What the People Tell Me, 2001). In these essays, or sketches, as Colón preferred to call them, his major themes are 1) the creation and development of a political consciousness, 2) the development of Puerto Rican nationalism, 3) advocacy for the working-class poor, and 4) the injustices of capitalist society in which racial and class discrimination are all too frequent and individual worth does not seem to exist. The collections are richly expressive of a socially conscious and humanistic point of view. [SOURCE: Kanellos, *Hispanic Periodicals in the United States,* 111-112.]

COLÓN, MIRIAM (1936-)

Miriam Colón

Born in Ponce, Puerto Rico in 1936, Miriam Colón became a pioneer of the Hispanic theater movement in New York City. Colón, whose mother was a seamstress and father, a salesman, started acting as a teenager in school plays in Puerto Rico. Colón was the first Puerto Rican admitted to the Actors' Studio of Elia Kazan and Lee Strasberg. Colón performed extensively on Broadway, in films and television, and still found time to promote the recognition and opportunities for Hispanics in the performing arts. In 1967, she co-founded the Puerto Rican Traveling Theater, which performed in the open air in neighborhoods for many years. It is still active, however, in an Off Broadway theater house. [SOURCE: Fernández, *Miriam Colón.*]

COLONIZATION LAW OF 1824

In 1824, the newly minted Mexican Congress passed the Nationalization Colonization Law, opening up the North to colonization by Anglo-Americans. Two conditions facilitated this process. In 1823, a predecessor and seemingly successful experiment known as the Austin Colony* allowed immigrants from the United States to settle in Texas. Moses Austin had begun negotiations with Spanish officials while the province still belonged to Spain in 1821. That same year, Mexico achieved its independence and Austin died. The new government was reluctant to honor the agreement, but Moses Austin's son, Stephen F., managed to get the colony concession from Agustín Iturbide, the newly declared emperor of an independent Mexico.

The second condition which facilitated the colononization process was that Mexico became more liberal. After republican forces deposed Iturbide and established a constitutional democracy with elected legislators, the colonization scheme was pushed by Texan Juan José Seguín, who was elected to the national congress from Texas. The legislation basically continued the same agreement negotiated between Iturbide and Stephen F. Austin and, soon, empresarios applied for contracts to bring in American colonists. The colonization law provided opportunities to all nationalities, although mainly Mexicans, Europeans, and Americans profited. More latitude and priority of choice was given to Mexicans in the parceling out of land. They were exempted from the decree that obliged foreign nationals to settle at least ten miles from the coast, a restriction that had not applied to the Austin project. This preferential treatment provoked resentment among the Americans, contributing to a mood that aided to a developing desire for independence from Mexico. [SOURCE: Campa, *Hispanic Culture in the Southwest,* 180; Barker, "Mexican Colonization Laws," *The Handbook of Texas Online,* http://www.tsha.utexas.edu/handbook/online/articles/view/MM.html]

COLORADO INTER-AMERICAN FIELD SERVICE COMMISSION

In 1948, the Colorado Inter-American Field Service Commission sought to develop a more positive attitude toward Spanish-speaking communities in Colorado, a process which could be accomplished, according to its founding principals, through grassroots democracy. Because it was largely ineffective, the commission soon disbanded, but it became a building block for future civil rights organizations in the state. [SOURCE: Meier and Rivera, *Dictionary of Mexican American History*, 95-96.]

COMISIÓN FEMENIL MEXICANA NACIONAL, INC.

Founded in 1970 in Los Angeles, California, the Comisión Femenil Mexicana Nacional (Mexican National Women's Commission) had some 5,000 members in 23 affiliate chapters in the 1980s. The organization advocates His-

panic women's rights and works to advance Hispanic women politically, economically, socially, and educationally. It administers the Chicana Service Center, which provides job skills training; the Centro de Niños (The Children's
Center), which provides bilingual child development programs; and Casa Victoria (Victory House), which is a group home for teens. Its standing committees include Development, Education, Health and Welfare, Legislative, Reproductive Rights, and Teen Pregnancy. The commission publishes *La Mujer* (The
Woman) semiannually. [SOURCE: Kanellos, "Organizations," 390.]

COMISIONES HONORÍFICAS MEXICANAS

In January 1921, President Álvaro Obregón sent Los Angeles consul
Eduardo Ruiz to inspect labor conditions in the Southwest after receiving
numerous requests for assistance from *braceros*. Ruiz found his countrymen
living in deplorable conditions, but had few options for improving their lot.
Although consulates existed in every major city of the Southwest, consular
personnel lacked the resources to provide meaningful aid. Thus, the consuls
decided that the best use of their limited resources would be to direct the
immigrants into self-help efforts.

This decision led to the formation of an exemplary self-help organization: the Comisión Honorífica Mexicana. The numerous *comisiones* that
would be established would also serve as a liaison between the expatriate
community and the consulates as well as vehicles for promoting Mexican
nationalism.

On April 9, 1921, Ruiz and Luis Montes de Oca presented their concept
for the commissions at a San Antonio meeting of consuls from throughout
the country. Ruiz and Montes de Oca asked journalist, Jesús Franco,* from
El Paso to attend because of his recent research trips taken on behalf of the
Mexican government.

The commissions were then conceptualized as an extension of the consulates with the primary function of increasing the level of protection for
Mexicans in the United States and protecting "with total selfishness the
respect and dignity of the Mexican nation." Each commission would act as
the official representative of its community and hold annual elections to
choose its members. Some of the basic responsibilities were to document
cases of abuse, investigate work-related injuries, visit incarcerated Mexicans
to find out if they had any needs, and register all Mexicans in the area with
the consulate. They also promoted loyalty to the Republic of Mexico, com-
memorating national and cultural holidays. The commissions were to avoid
any incidents that might lead to international problems and, instead, promote
positive relations between local authorities and the communities they represented. Each was responsible for raising money to provide for its expenses.

Soon after the conference, the attendees created the first commission in San Marcos, Texas, on April 14, 1921. A large ceremony commemorated its founding and all but three of the conference participants attended the ceremony. [SOURCE: Águila, "Protecting 'México de Afuera'", 61-62; Rosales, *Pobre Raza!*, 24, 42, 108, 114, 140, 151.]

COMITÉ CUBANO PRO DERECHOS HUMANOS

Based in Havana, the Comité Cubano pro Derechos Humanos (Cuban Committee for Human Rights) took on the task of defending Cubans repeatedly persecuted and jailed for their protests against Cuba's state policies. The committee was especially active in 1991, when Cuban officials harassed and imprisoned island intellectuals (many of them members of the state-run writers and artists union) for issuing a declaration calling for democratic reforms. This prompted more than one hundred Cuban intellectuals in exile (and fifty European and Latin American intellectuals) to send letters of support, applauding the attempt by Cuban writers to demand liberty of expression within the system. They also urged "governments, the news media, cultural groups, and human rights groups to monitor their futures." [SOURCE: García, *Havana USA*, 193.]

COMITÉ DE INTELECTUALES POR LA LIBERTAD DE CUBA

The Comité de Intelectuales por la Libertad de Cuba (The Committee of Intellectuals for the Liberty of Cuba), based in New York City, was organized by Cuban exile writers crusading for a more democratic government in Cuba; its long-term goal was the overthrow of Fidel Castro. The group sponsored "dissident congresses" as a vehicle for discussing Cuban political and economic affairs and protesting human rights abuses. In 1979, playwright dramatist Eduardo Manet, a committee member, organized the first congress in Paris. It was succeeded by others in New York (1980), Washington (1982), Madrid (1986), and Caracas (1987). Always in the forefront of congress agendas were the rights of political prisoners in Cuba. The organization always sought to recruit other European and Latin American intellectuals as well as government leaders, celebrities, and international organizations, such as Amnesty International, Americas Watch, and PEN. [SOURCE: García, *Havana USA*, 192-193.]

COMITÉ MEXICANO DE BENEFICENCIA

In 1931, perhaps the most devastating year of the Depression, Mexican consul Rafael de la Colina* organized the Comité Mexicano de Beneficencia (Mexican Welfare Committee) in Los Angeles to promote and coordinate the relief effort for an emigrant community ravaged by the unemployment and the resultant lack of basic necessities. The group was made up of 60 local merchants and professionals. To inaugurate the committee, a variety show was held at the downtown Philharmonic Auditorium, featuring Mexican theater and film stars. Most of the proceeds from the fund-raising event went towards helping Mexicans return home. About one-third of the 150,000 Mexicans in Los Angeles returned to Mexico in the early years of the Depression. [SOURCE: Monroy, *Rebirth*, 95.]

COMITÉ MEXICANO CONTRA EL RACISMO

Mexican intellectuals and activists joined the Mexican-American civil rights campaign to further better treatment. The Comité Mexicano Contra el Racismo (Mexican Comittee Against Racism) was formed in 1943 with the blessing of poet and career diplomat Jaime Torres Bodet, who was also serving as Mexico's Minister of Education. Its purpose was to combat the poor treatment of Mexicans in the United States and to ameliorate prejudice against such groups as Jews at a time when cooperation between the two countries against the fascist threat in Europe was at its peak. News of the group's efforts were published in its own journal, *Fraternidad* (Fraternity). The Comité reflected the Mexican-Americanist perspective on the nature of racism, i.e., that only a minority of racists were responsible for these acts— not the majority of the American people nor the U.S. government. The committee ceased to exist by the end of the 1940s, a sign that it had served the interests of the popular front of world organizations opposed to Fascist and Nazi threats. [SOURCE: Gómez-Quiñones, *Chicano Politics*, 36.]

EL COMITÉ-MOVIMIENTO DE IZQUIERDA NACIONAL PUERTORRIQUEÑO

In 1970, a Vietnam veteran named Federico Lora, who was Dominican, led a group of Puerto Ricans and other Latinos in occupying a Manhattan building on 88th Street and Columbus Avenue. This act of squatting was part of a strategy to resist urban renewal efforts to tear down older residences in order to build high-rise apartments. The group called itself El Comité and became prominent in leading the housing struggle on the West Side of Manhattan. Eventually, El Comité became a multi-issue based organization. For example, it also pressed for bilingual education and community control of the schools. El Comité spread to other areas in New York and to such cities as Boston. It also organized a student and worker sector and sparked the formation of the Latin Women's Collective. *Unidad Latina* (Latin Unity) served as its publication organ in keeping the community abreast of the most salient issues. In January 1975, in a constituent assembly in New York City, the organization adopted a Marxist-Leninist approach and proclaimed as its long-term goal the building of socialism in the United States. With this ideological shift, it changed its name to El Comité-Movimiento de Izquierda Nacional Puertorriqueño (Puerto Rican

National Leftist Movement-MINP). MINP was dissolved in 1981. [SOURCE: Torres and Velázquez, *The Puerto Rican Movement,* 10, 88-89.]

COMITÉ PRO PAZ

In April 1967, the Comité Pro Paz (Pro Peace Committee) of Mexican Americans in East Los Angeles organized a "Mitin al Aire Libre Para Protestar por la Guerra en Viet Nam" (An Open Air Protest Meeting against the War in Vietnam) at Lincoln Park. It represented the sentiment growing among Mexican Americans that draft boards for the war in Vietnam were targeting minorities disproportionately. Later, the committee opened a draft-counseling center to offer guidance to young draftees. [SOURCE: Acuña, *Community Under Siege.*]

COMITÉ PRO-REPATRIACIÓN (HOUSTON)

During the Great Depression unemployment in the Galveston Bay and Ship Channel region around Houston, Texas, became so serious that the three cities of Houston, Galveston, and Pasadena pooled their resources to provide relief for the hungry to form the Tri-City Relief Committee. When resources became so limited that cutbacks were required, committee administrators refused aid to Mexicans and blacks. One result was that Bartolemé Casas organized the Comité Pro-Repatriación (Pro-Repatriation Committee) in 1931. Members of the committee sponsored such events as mock bullfights and dances to raise funds for assisting their countrymen in returning to Mexico with a degree of dignity. [SOURCE: Rosales, *Chicano!,* 71.]

COMITÉ PRO-REPATRIACIÓN (VROMAN)

Unemployed Mexicans stranded in the United States during the Great Depression often made their own efforts to return to Mexico. The Comité Pro-Repatriación in Vroman, Colorado, was organized precisely for this purpose. After the Mexican consul in Denver had rejected the committees request for help, because his office lacked funds, it appealed directly to Mexican President Pascual Ortiz Rubio. In the communiqué to the president, the committee complained of receiving poor treatment by Anglo authorities in Colorado and outlined what they expected from the Mexican government. As a result, between 80 and 100 families eventually returned to the homeland, hoping to settle in land provided by the government; they were also given loans and other aid to begin farming. Such requests were common and prompted subsequent efforts by Ortiz Rubio and his successor, Abelardo Rodríguez, to implement measures that would help the returning emigrants. As it turns out, most efforts were woefully inadequate. [SOURCE: Balderrama and Rodríguez, *Decade of Betrayal,* 162.]

COMMISSION ON SPANISH-SPEAKING AFFAIRS, OHIO

The Commission on Spanish-Speaking Affairs was founded in 1977 as a governmental agency in the state of Ohio. Its purpose is to serve as an advocate for Ohio's Hispanics and to provide recommendations to the governor and general assembly on all affairs affecting Hispanics residing in Ohio. [SOURCE: www.state.oh.us/spa; http://ochla.ohio.gov/ochla/mission.htm]

COMMITTEE OF TEN

In 1969, the Black and Puerto Rican Student Community (BPRSC) at the City University of New York (CUNY) delegated a few of their members to form the Black and Puerto Rican Committee of Ten. That spring the group orchestrated a major strike and campus shut-down but had to withdraw from the occupied buildings on May 5, after the administration secured a court injunction. The committee also worked with students from the Black League of Afro-American Collegians (BLAC) and the Puerto Rican Alliance (PRA) at Brooklyn College at a sit-in at the college president's office. In both sit-ins, the students demanded open admissions, the establishment of Black and Puerto Rican studies, the hiring of minority faculty, and adjustments to the curricula which would be more reflective of changing student demographics. [SOURCE: Torres and Velázquez, *The Puerto Rican Movement*, 126-127.]

COMMITTEE ON RAZA RIGHTS

In July 1995, local community activists in Oxnard, California, called for a community meeting in the oldest and largest Mexican-American community in the city, known as La Colonia. At the meeting, the participants began organizing a community-based organization around the principles of Mexican-American self-determination. The outcome of this meeting was the formation of the Committee on Raza Rights (CRR). Guiding the activism of the CRR were the following principles: "(1) Raza Self-Determination and the liberation of the masses of Raza; (2) Building a Raza Liberation Movement, independent of governmental funding, and non-Raza or multi-national formations; and (3) Defend the human and civil rights of all Raza." From its inception to the present, CRR has organized and participated in more than 200 events (national and local) in what its members refer to as "Occupied Mexico/Aztlán." CRR believes that La Raza must work outside of the two-party system to achieve its goals. [SOURCE: http://www.latinola.com/story. php?story=427]

COMMUNITIES ORGANIZED FOR PUBLIC SERVICE

In San Antonio during 1974, Ernesto Cortés, Jr.* and other young priests created Communities Organized for Public Service (COPS) in order to improve housing and general living conditions for Mexican Americans. Similar to the Community Services Organization (CSO),* the San Antonio group was founded on the principles established by Saul Alinsky's Industrial Areas Foundation, including house-by-house visits to persuade barrio families to join in voter registration drives, as wells as to battle racial and economic discrimination. COPS gained its support from the Catholic Church, civil service employees, especially from Kelly Air Force Base, and the political power of the large Mexican-American community in San Antonio. [SOURCE: Meier and Rivera, *Dictionary of Mexican American History*, 97.]

COMMUNITY PROPERTY

The legislature of the Republic of Texas adopted and subsequently passed on to the state legal code the Spanish legal concept of community property. Husbands and wives were to share equally in the profits and fruits of their marriage. Under Anglo-American law, however, property belonged exclusively to the husband, and on the death of her spouse, the wife was protected only by a life-interest in one-third of the lands of her deceased spouse. The Republic of Texas recognized this inequity and specifically excluded the Anglo-American law of matrimonial property. The previously Hispanic provinces of Texas and Louisiana were the first to protect wives through common-law statues. Today, community property law is prevalent in states that have an Hispanic heritage: Texas, Louisiana, New Mexico, Arizona, Nevada, and California. It has also been pointed out, that even the right to file a joint income tax return derives from the Spanish principle. [SOURCE: Rosales, *Chicano!*, 13-14.]

COMMUNITY REHABILITATION SERVICES, INC.

Community Rehabilitation Services, Inc. (CRS) began in Los Angeles as the "Spanish-Speaking Task Force for the Handicapped" in 1974, when a group of Latinos with disabilities coalesced to develop a self-help organization. The Task Force's vision expanded and, in 1979, it became the Community Rehabilitation Services, Inc. Many of the project's service providers and many of its board members have disabilities themselves. The disabled community received its first opportunity to obtain more equitable treatment with the passing of the Americans with Disabilities Act in 1990. CRS employs some of the federal funding made possible by this act to enact many of its services in the Los Angeles- and San Gabriel Valley-area. The services of CRS now reach every ethnic group in this region. Recently, Mandarin- and Korean-speaking staff members have been added to accommodate the growing populations who speak those languages. [SOURCE: http://clnet.ucr.edu/]

COMMUNITY SERVICES ORGANIZATION

When the Community Services Organization (CSO) was founded in 1947, it became the first predominantly Hispanic civil rights group to adopt the tactics that would characterize American civil rights movements in the post-War period and would form the backbone of the Chicano Movement.* Many of the CSO activists had acquired experience in the Unity Leagues* founded by newspaper-publisher Ignacio I. López. Mainly made up of Mexican Americans, many of its leaders were trained in the dramatic, confrontational tactics developed by Saul Alinsky and his Industrial Areas Foundation: mass demonstrations, picketing, confronting those in the system for its malfunction. Alinsky, in fact, hired César Chávez* and Fred Ross* to organize the CSO. Other important Mexican-American leaders became involved who would also make history in the struggles of the decades to come, notably Dolores Huerta* and Tony Ríos. The CSO also obtained the support of the Catholic Church. The CSO's first major victory came in 1949, when it organized and led the movement to elect Edward Roybal* to the Los Angeles City Council. But beyond the political realm, the CSO concentrated on neighborhood services and community health issues. To effect these ends, the CSO organized by going door-to-door in working-class and lower-middle-class neighborhoods, with many women in leadership positions. César Chávez was later successful in taking many of the tactics and much of the philosophy of the CSO and the Industrial Areas Foundation into the struggle to unionize farmworkers. [SOURCE: García, *Memories of Chicano History: The Life And Narrative of Bert Corona*,163-8.]

COMPEÁN, MARIO (1940-)

Mario Compeán, a core participant in the Mexican American Youth Organization (MAYO)* and the La Raza Unida Party (The United People's Party-LRUP)* was born in San Antonio in 1940 and attended schools there, including Edgewood High, a school which MAYO targeted for a walkout in 1968. Compeán, who had worked as a migrant worker, enrolled at St. Mary's University in San Antonio in the Spring of 1967. There he met four other students—José Angel Gutiérrez*, Nacho Pérez, Willie Velásquez* and Juan Patlán—and began discussing Texas politics, the California Chicano Movement,* and conditions of Mexican Americans. They eventually founded MAYO, the forerunner of the Texas LRUP.

Compeán helped pioneer the strategy of getting attention through shock tactics. For example, amid patriotic speeches at the Fourth of July festivities held at the Alamo Mission in 1967, Gutiérrez and Compeán carried picket signs with the message: "What about Independence for La Raza?" The response from both Mexican Americans and Anglos was mainly apathetic, but the local media did cover the event.

In order to support himself, Compeán became a trainer for the federally funded Volunteers in Service to America (VISTA) and used that position to recruit MAYO members to work in South Texas's poverty-stricken areas. Early in 1968, he and Ignacio Pérez played a leading role in the MAYO-inspired walkouts by students in San Antonio's West Side, who demanded bilingual education and other educational reforms.

After the LRUP was organized out of MAYO and had registered local victories in South Texas in 1970, Compeán urged statewide campaigns, a notion opposed by LRUP leader, José Angel Gutiérrez, who felt local elections were more crucial. Compeán, however, mustered support among the rank and file, arguing that a dramatic state-level campaign would serve as a catylist to Chicanos,* who hungered for representation; it would also rally resources and volunteers faster than regional offensives. Compeán's position won out, and Gutiérrez accepted the outcome in good spirits. Although he did not become a candidate for any of the election slots, Compeán remained a force in the selection of the aspirants. For example, when the less nationalistic, but politically attractive Ramsey Muñiz* was nominated as the gubernatorial candidate, Compeán forced the selection of the more militant Alma Canales as the LRUP hopeful for lieutenant governor. The party slate was unsuccessful, but it drew away enough votes from the Democrat Dolph Briscoe* that a Republican won the state house.

In 1973, the LRUP won a remarkable array of local elections in South Texas, emboldening the LRUP to increase its efforts to gain statewide strength. Compeán was chairman of the Texas LRUP; the statewide effort would now be under his watch. Ramsey Muñiz, still feeling victorious as a spoiler in the 1972 elections and heartened by the 1973 rural triumphs, decided early in 1974 to again seek the governorship. Muñiz insisted on a toned-down campaign to attact the moderate vote, but Compeán insisted pursuing a more nationalistic tact. The two became bitter enemies, and at the 1974 state convention in Houston, Compeán resigned as chairman. The results of the 1974 statewide efforts were more disappointing than ever. By 1978, the LRUP was in its death throes. Mario Compeán collected the remnants of the party and launched himself as candidate for governor. He received less than two percent of the total votes cast. Many former LRUP members had defected to his camp in the course of the year. Like other party leaders, he left politics, but he was certainly one of the core figures in one of the most significant attempts in history to form a third party in the United States. [SOURCE: García, *Rise and Fall of La Raza Unida Pary*; Navarro, *Mexican American Youth Organization*.]

COMUNIDAD ORGANIZADA PARA EDUCACIÓN

In 1968, a small group of Mexican-American parents formed the Comunidad Organizada Para Educación (COPE) in Brownsfield, California. COPE aspired to influence school board decisions on curriculum, pedagogy, and policy that affected the members' children. It mainly sought to influence the application of Title I funds the U.S. Department of Education had assigned for improving the education of "disadvantaged" students in the district. The Mexican-American group challenged school officials on the criteria used to form the Title I advisory committee, which was required by federal guidelines. As a consequence, the district allowed the organization to play a more significant role in the making of policy. After this experience, Mexican-American activism increased in the community, creating an atmosphere in which other local MexicanAmerican organizations began to question more vigorously the educational power structure. [SOURCE: Donato, *The Other Struggle for Equal Schools*, 73.]

LA CONFEDERACIÓN DE SOCIEDADES MEXICANAS

Between 1915 and 1925, Los Angeles experienced the most rapid increase in the Mexican population. As in other areas with large Mexican communities, defense organizations quickly appeared. La Liga Protectora Mexicana (The Mexican Protective League) and La Confederación de Sociedades Mexicanas (The Federation of Mexican Societies), for example, pursued legal rights issues and kept lawyers on retainer for that purpose. In the 1920s, California had the most disproportionate sentencing of Mexicans to the gallows than any other state, and immigrant groups soon manifested intense opposition to capital punishment. An emblematic case was that of Mauricio Trinidad, convicted of murder after a very inadequate defense effort presented by a lawyer who only made a ten-minute defense plea. The president of Confederación, Daniel Venegas,* wrote directly to Governor Richardson to ask for clemency for Trinidad. [SOURCE: Rosales, *Pobre Raza!*, 133-134.]

LA CONFEDERACIÓN DE SOCIEDADES MEXICANAS DE LOS ESTADOS UNIDOS DE AMÉRICA

In Chicago, where the Mexican arrest rate in the 1920s was higher than in southwestern communities, Mexicans launched the most intensive crusades to help compatriots in trouble with the law. An umbrella organization for thirty-five Chicago mutual aid societies, La Confederación de Sociedades Mexicanas de los Estados Unidos de América (The Federation of Mexican Societies in USA) was founded in Chicago on March 30, 1925. It had the following aims, according to José Amaro González in his study of Mexican mutual aid societies: Helping new arrivals in the city find a place to stay, providing job referrals, providing defense funds to help Mexicans before the courts, making emergency loans from the credit union, and combating racial discrimination in public places. La Confederación did not survive long, but cooperation between organizations continued. [SOURCE: González, *Mutual Aid for Survival,* 152.]

CONFEDERACIÓN DE UNIONES OBRERAS MEXICANAS

Formed in 1928 at the urging of the Mexican government and through the auspices of the Los Angeles-based Confederación de Sociedades Mexicanas (CSM),* the Confederación de Uniones Obreras Mexicanas (CUOM) served as an umbrella group for fledgling agricultural unions in southern California made up of Mexican Americans. The organization acquired the largest base of Mexican laborers and worked closely with the Confederación Regional de Obreros Mexicanos (CROM), Mexico's largest umbrella labor organization. In 1928, the CUOM group had more than 3,000 members, representing eight different unions. The Mexican government urged the forming of the group to deal with the problem of increasing unemployment among Mexican immigrants as the U.S. economy began to show signs of weakness, a process that lead to the Depression of the 1930s. As a consequence, CUOM advocated repatriation and immigration restriction as much it did labor organizing. Such equivocal objectives compromised the organization's effectiveness, and its membership dropped. In 1933, new life was breathed into the CUOM again at the urging of the Mexican government. Consul Ricardo Hill joined with militants, such as Guillermo Velarde, to revive the union under a new name, the Confederación de Uniones de Campesinos y Obreros Mexicanos (CUCOM). The union edged out the more radical Cannery and Agricultural Workers Industrial Union (CAWIU), which had been involved in similar organizing. CUCOM then embarked on a series of strikes in southern California, but the more radical wing of the organization soon encountered differences with Hill, a rift interpreted by his critics as a desire to control Mexican workers on behalf of his government. [SOURCE: Weber, *Dark Sweat, White Gold,* 159-60; González, *Mexican Consuls and Labor Organizing,* 65-66.]

EL CONGRESO DEL PUEBLO

El Congreso del Pueblo (the Council of Hometown Clubs) founded in 1956, worked closely with the Migration Division, the Puerto Rican government agency that dealt with the issues of Puerto Ricans on the mainland. It drew its support from a working-class base and sought, more forcefully than the Migration Division, to ameliorate the most pressing socioeconomic problems facing Puerto Ricans. Led by community activist Gilberto Gerena Valentín, El Congreso represented some eighty hometown clubs the year of its incorporation. Individually, these clubs provided shelter, jobs, emergency financial help, and other social benefits to its members, but under the El Congreso umbrella, they took a broader, more confrontational stand when dealing with racism, police brutality, and discrimination. [SOURCE: Sánchez Korrol, *From Colonia to Community,* 226.]

EL CONGRESO DE PUEBLOS DE HABLA ESPAÑOLA

In 1938, a coalition of labor and local Mexican-American and Mexican community activists led by Luisa Moreno,* a Guatemalan, organized the California-based El Congreso del Pueblo de Habla Española (Spanish-Speaking People's Congress). In April 1938, the first meeting of El Congreso was held in Los Angeles. Supporters included Hollywood actors Anthony Quinn, Rita Hayworth, and Bert Corona,* who remained a lifelong civil rights and labor leader. Her co-leader, Josefina Fierro de Bright, a Los Angeles-Mexican American, was the wife of screenwriter John Bright, who was instrumental in politicizing the organization to radical stances.

The Congreso meeting attracted more than 1,000 delegates from 128 organizations, whose combined membership was 70,000 people, including students, union members, teachers, and politicians. In large part, the congress' agenda relied on platforms that had been forged by labor-oriented Mexican-American and Mexican immigrant organizations since the 1920s. Delegates at the meeting confronted problems affecting Latinos, such as education, housing, health, job discrimination, and segregation. Congreso goals, while complementing those of middle-class organizations, such as League of United Latin American Citizens (LULAC),* hesitated in the emphasis on acquisition of American values. The group did demand the civil rights for Mexican Americans guaranteed by the Constitution; in addition, it espoused unity among all Latinos in the United States, including Mexican immigrants, a group that LULAC had distanced from its organizational objectives. A meeting scheduled for March of 1939 never materialized. The first meeting held in Los Angeles had been labeled subversive by local officials, a suspicion that led to FBI investigations. In addition to this type of intimidation, the pressures of supporting the national government during World War II also led to the decline of the organization by the mid-1940s.

During the course of its existence, the Congreso provided political education for a generation of Mexican-American and immigrant political and social combatants, including George I. Sánchez,* Eduardo Quevedo, Luisa Moreno, Josefina Fierro de Bright, and Bert Corona. These activists continued battling for immigrant and civil rights into the 1950s and, in the case of Quevedo and Corona, into the 1960s and beyond. [SOURCE: Gutiérrez, *Walls and Mirrors,* 110-111; García, *Mexican Americans,* 45.]

CONGRESS AGAINST COEXISTENCE

In 1974, representatives from seventy Cuban exile organizations attended the "Congress Against Coexistence" in San Juan, Puerto Rico. The delegates came together to protest the possibility of the Organization of American States (OAS) voting to lift the sanctions against Cuba. Concurrently in Miami, Cuban exiles destroyed the Torch of Friendship, a monument that had been erected at Bayfront Park as a commemoration of hemispheric solidarity. The OAS did lift the sanctions a year later, in 1975, prompting exile organizations to form the "Liberty Caravan," a thousand-car parade to the Orange Bowl, where the participants ended the event by staging a boisterous rally. [SOURCE: García, *Havana USA*, 138.]

CONGRESS OF MEXICAN AMERICAN UNITY

The Congress of Mexican American Unity was formed in Los Angeles in 1966, with Esteban Torres* as its chairperson. A coalition of more than 300 groups, the congress was designed to coordinate the efforts of the numerous community development and civil rights organizations active since the 1950s. The congress still existed during the height of the Chicano Movement,* although few of the participants had adopted the Chicano Movement ideology. Nonetheless, in response to efforts of Chicano Moratorium* leader, Rosalío Muñoz,* the group drew up an anti-war resolution and sent it to President Richard Nixon. Primarily, the letter lamented the burden the war had put on Mexican Americans and the divisions that the struggle had created in the country. After the killing of journalist Rubén Salazar* on August 29, 1970, at the Chicano Moratorium, the Congress of Mexican American Unity established a complaint center so it could document police overreaction as hundreds of people who had been gassed during the protest march charged the police with using anti-crowd control tactics even before some of the demonstrators started resisting. [SOURCE: Marín, *Social Protest in an Urban Barrio*, 202; Gómez-Quiñones, *Roots of Chicano Politics*, 80.]

CONGRESSIONAL HISPANIC CAUCUS

Organized in 1976 by five Hispanic Congressmen: Herman Badillo* (NY), Baltasar Corrada (PR), E. "Kika" de la Garza* (TX), Henry B. González* (TX), and Edward Roybal* (CA), the Congressional Hispanic Caucus (CHC) was originally formed to serve as a legislative organization through which legislative action, as well as executive and judicial actions, could be monitored to ensure that the needs of Hispanics were being met. The founders felt it was necessary to work in cooperation with other groups, both inside and outside Congress, to strengthen the federal government's commitment to Hispanic citizens and to provide the Hispanic community access to the operation and function of the American political system. CHC publishes the *Legislative Review,* a monthly journal. [SOURCE: Kanellos, "Organizations," 390.]

CONGRESSIONAL HISPANIC CAUCUS INSTITUTE

The Congressional Hispanic Caucus Institute (CHCI), based in Washington, D.C., is sponsored by the Congressional Hispanic Caucus (CHC).* The institute's staff offers programs designed to promote leadership development training for talented young Hispanics, as well as the opportunity to enter a wider range of professional areas. In 1976, five Hispanic congressmen—Herman Badillo* (NY), Baltasar Corrada (PR), E. "Kika" de la Garza* (TX), Henry B. González* (TX), and Edward Roybal* (CA)—organized the CHC in order to promote legislative and other government activity that could benefit Hispanics. An additional goal was to strengthen the federal commitment to Hispanic citizens and heighten the Hispanic community's awareness of the operation and function of the American political system, a goal that could be accomplished by the CHC cooperating with other groups, both inside and outside of Congress.

Since its founding the CHC has developed educational programs and other activities that have increased the opportunities for Hispanics to participate in and contribute to the American political system. To facilitate this process, in 1978, CHC members established a 501(c)(3) nonprofit organization. The House Committee on the House Administration, in October, 1981, stipulated that all congressional caucuses must move fund-raising off of government premises. The members of the CHC thus decided to maintain its legislative support organization on Capitol Hill and move into the community its nonprofit, fund-raising organization, naming it the Congressional Hispanic Caucus Institute, Inc. (CHCI).

In 1985, influential Hispanic business persons from the private sector and community leaders from across the country were named to the CHCI Board of Directors, and in conjunction with the Hispanic members of Congress, they began implementing the institute's objectives at the local, state, and national levels. [SOURCE: http://www.chci.org/]

LOS CONQUISTADORES

Just as Chicano Movement* activity in Angeles influenced other areas, the Mexican American Movement (MAM),* also located in Los Angeles, was an important vehicle for spreading the message of Mexican Americanization to New Mexico and Arizona. MAM sought the improvement of conditions among Mexican-American and Mexican people living in the United States and pursuit of citizenship, higher education, and active participation in civic and cultural activities. Its appeal reached especially into Arizona, after members of a club called Los Conquistadores (The Conquistadors) at

Arizona Normal School had attended a conference sponsored by the MAM in Los Angeles. They returned to Tempe, excitedly propagating lessons learned at the conference. The organization existed until the 1950s. Ironically, during World War II, Fernand Cattelain, a professor of Romance Languages at Arizona State Normal, wrote to the Department of State to warn that Los Conqistadores had the potential for becoming a fifth column organization because of the mistreatment of Mexicans in Arizona. [SOURCE: Rosales, *Chicano!*, 99-101.]

CONSORTIUM OF NATIONAL HISPANIC ORGANIZATIONS

Founded in 1976 in Washington, D.C., the Consortium of National Hispanic Organizations has 26 organizational members who have come together to discuss and share information on issues affecting the Hispanic community. The consortium sponsors seminars and symposia. Its committees include civic education, health, housing, immigration, international issues, labor, and press and media. The consortium issues reports and sponsors an annual convention. [SOURCE: Kanellos, *The Hispanic American Almanac*, 391.]

CONSTITUTION OF COLORADO

The constitution of the state of Colorado, approved in 1875, specifically protected the civil rights of Spanish-speaking citizens and called for all laws to be published in both English and Spanish. The constitution itself was drafted in both languages. [SOURCE: Kanellos, *Hispanic American Almanac*, 278.]

CONSTITUTION OF NEW MEXICO

Anticipating statehood, New Mexicans in 1910 held a constitutional convention that created a document that was approved in 1912, when New Mexico became a state. Many of the provisions of the new constitution reflected Hispanos' strong desire for protection. In the previous half century, they had lost much of their land through litigation and fraud, government seizure, and tax delinquencies. Like Hispanics in other parts of the Southwest, New Mexicans experienced racial and ethnic prejudice, but because of their large numbers, they achieved some political self-determination, a degree of power put to good use at the constitutional convention. Articles II and XII, for example, made New Mexico a bilingual state by putting English and Spanish on an equal basis for all state business. These sections of the constitution allowed funding for training programs for bilingual teachers, forbade segregation of Anglo and Hispanic children, and reiterated their rights guaranteed by the Treaty of Guadalupe Hidalgo.* [SOURCE: Forrest, *The Preservation of the Village,* 10.]

CONTADORA PEACE PROCESS

Civil unrest has been a major reason for emigration from Central American countries to the United States. Refugees seeking asylum and migrants seeking better economic conditions came in unprecedented numbers during the 1970s and 1980s. Not surprisingly, conditions in their home areas became a major concern for the newly arrived in the United States. They waited with great hope when in January 1983, representatives from Mexico, Venezuela, Colombia, and Panama met on Contadora Island off the Pacific coast of Panama to discuss a diplomatic initiative that would prevent a regional conflagration among the Central American states of Guatemala, El Salvador, Honduras, Nicaragua, and Costa Rica. A Contadora peace proposal resulted from these year-long meetings in September 1984. The government of Nicaragua approved the draft treaty that resulted, but the other four Central American countries rejected the plan. In 1985, the governments of Peru, Uruguay, Argentina, and Brazil formed a Contadora Support Group in order to resurrect the faltering talks, and offered a revised plan. But in June 1986, the process was suspended unofficially, when the Central American governments refused to sign the new offer. Eventually, the Central American representatives conducted direct negotiations with each other, and the Contadora initiative came to fruition. [SOURCE: Hey and Kuzma, "Anti-U.S. Foreign Policy of Dependent States," 30-62.]

CONTRERAS, MIGUEL (1952-2005)

When in 1996 Miguel Contreras was elected Executive Secretary-Treasurer of the Los Angeles County Federation of Labor, AFL-CIO, he became the first Latino elected leader of the 107-year organization. This federation branch is one of the largest in the nation, comprising 350 local unions, and more than 800,000 union members. Contreras was born on September 17, 1952, and raised in the small Central Valley farm town of Dinuba. As a young man, he joined his father as an activist in the United Farm Workers,* led by César Chávez,* where he worked as a boycott organizer and union negotiator. He became an organizer for Hotel Employees and Restaurant Employees (HERE) in 1977 and for fourteen years led a number of successful strikes. Contreras helped rebuild HERE in Nevada, New York, and Los Angeles. At which time he became director of the L.A. County Federal's political arm and, when the federation's Executive Secretary-Treasurer, Jim Wood, died, AFL-CIO affiliates asked Contreras to replace him in May 1996. Contreras then led a massive union-sponsored grassroots political drive that has succeeded in numerous electoral victories favorable to unions, including the campaign of Antonio R. Villaraigosa* in 2001. Unfortunately, because of his untimely death in 2005, Contreras did not live to see Villaraigosa elected as the first Hispanic mayor of Los Angeles in 133 years. He is survived by his wife María Elena Durazo, president of HERE Local 11 and their two sons. [SOURCE: http://www.csulb.edu/~cfa/contreras.html]

LA COORDINADORA PAZ PARA LA MUJER

La Coordinadora Paz Para la Mujer was founded in 1989 in San Juan, Puerto Rico, as an umbrella for feminist groups concerned with helping victims of domestic violence. Since its inception, the Coordinadora has come to represent 18 organizations that strive to shape a society where women can live in a more just, peaceful world. The umbrella group formed in response to the passage of Public Law 54 for the prevention of domestic violence, key legislation for which individual feminist organizations militated throughout the 1980s. The Coordinadora through its affiliates, provides a watchdog function to assure that legal authorities enforce the provisions of this law. In addition, the organization also coordinates educational programs that sensitize the public to the existence of family violence through the electronic and print media and helps organize workshops that reveal to welfare and health professionals family strategies that prevent conditions leading to violence. The Coordinadora also organizes yearly commemorations for the Día Internacional de la Mujer (International Women's Day) on March 8 and El Día de No Más Violencia contra la Mujer (No More Violence Against Women Day) on November 25. [SOURCE: http://www.pazparalamujer.org/enlaces.html]

COORDINATING COMMITTEE ON JUSTICE AND PEACE IN VIEQUES

The Coordinating Committee on Peace and Justice in Vieques emerged in 1999 during a campaign to persuade the U.S. Navy to cease its training operations on the island of Vieques in Puerto Rico. In the 1940s, the U.S. military took over two-thirds of the island, located off the eastern coast of Puerto Rico. One end is used for a large ammunition dump and the other for a live firing range and amphibious assault training area. Island residents and others have resisted this Navy occupation of their land for decades. The issue exploded in April 19, 1999, when a civilian guard, David Sanes, was killed after a U.S. warplane dropped its bombs miles off target.

Protesters immediately set up civil disobedience camps on the firing range, forcing the Navy to suspend training exercises. Tens of thousands of people joined marches and rallies, demanding the U.S. Navy leave Vieques completely. Under this pressure, a wide range of political figures, including pro-statehood governor Pedro Rosselló, called for Washington to stop using Vieques as a target range and return use of the entire island to the Puerto Rican people. On November 21, 1999, Vieques activists announced the formation of the Coordinating Committee for Justice and Peace in Vieques to rationalize the many protest efforts. [SOURCE: McArthur, "Puerto Rican Protesters Get Ready to Face U.S. Navy".]

CORONA, BERT (1918-2001)

The son of a colonel in Pancho Villa's* army, Bert Corona was born on May 29, 1918, in El Paso, Texas. He attended El Paso city schools and later the University of Southern California and the University of California at Los Angeles, where he graduated in commercial law. His list of contributions to Mexican-American civil rights is lengthy. He played crucial roles in many grassroots organizations, beginning with the Mexican American Youth Movement* in southern California during the 1930s under the auspices of the YMCA. The members were made up of young college students who strove to improve conditions for Mexican-American and Mexican people in the United States. Later, Corona helped establish the National Congress of Spanish-speaking People* in 1939, one of the first organizations in the Southwest to protect the civil rights of Mexican Americans.

A man of diverse social interests, Corona was also involved with union leadership as well and in the 1930s helped organize cannery and warehouse workers for unions that belonged to the Congress of Industrial Organizations. In 1959, Corona and Eduardo Quevedo* called a meeting in Fresno to form the Mexican American Political Association (MAPA),* an organization that showed an assertiveness which eluded other groups, such as League of United Latin American Citizens* or the American G.I. Forum.* It sought to expand Mexican Americans' political interests and to assert their importance in the political process.

During the Chicano Movement,* Corona organized Hermandad General de Trabajadores (General Fraternity of Workers) in the Los Angeles area. His concern with educational issues later led him to assume the presidency of the Association of California School Administrators and to become a professor at California State University, Los Angeles. Corona remained active until his death in 2001. [SOURCE: Meier and Rivera, *Dictionary of Mexican American History*, 102-103; García, *Memories of Chicano History*.]

CORONA, JUAN (1934-)

Arrested in May 1971, for allegedly killing 25 farmworkers found near Yuba City, California, labor contractor, Juan Corona, was found guilty in 1973 and sentenced to 25 consecutive life terms. A court of appeals reversed the conviction in 1978 of the Mexican-born convict and ordered a re-trial, citing insufficient representation and the suppression of evidence. Mexican-American organizations and individual activists claimed racial prejudice pervaded the proceedings. The whole event gained national exposure. Civil rights proponents used the case to demonstrate the pitfalls Mexican Americans faced in acquiring equal protection under the law. [SOURCE: Meier and Rivera, *Dictionary of Mexican American History*, 103.]

CORONEL, ANTONIO F. (1817-1894)

Born in the interior of Mexico, in 1817, Antonio F. Coronel, made a successful transition from being a citizen of Mexico to one of the United States after California was annexed. He served as superintendent of schools for Los Angeles in 1852 and became mayor of the city the following year. Coronel attempted to provide protection of the rights and culture of Hispanics living in the city by promoting bilingual education and monitoring municipal codes that would deny them their civil rights. In addition, Coronel was a cultural figure who owned a theater, wrote poetry, and was involved in the arts. [SOURCE: Weber, *Foreigners in Their Native Land*, 210.]

Antonio F. Coronel

CORTÉS, EDWIN (1956-)

Cortés is considered a political prisoner by his supporters, having been arrested for his activities as a member of the Committee to Stop the Grand Jury and for the freedom of the five Puerto Rican nationalist prisoners who were jailed in the 1950s for subversive activities linked to Puerto Rican independence movements. Born and raised in Chicago, he was one of fifteen children. In 1973, while still in high school, a teacher told him the reason Puerto Rican history was not taught was because the island did not have a history. This prompted him to join the Latinos Unidos student group, which called for a Latino Studies curriculum. After graduating from high school, Edwin entered the University of Illinois in Chicago, where he became involved in a campaign to establish support services and recruitment for Latinos. As a student leader he supported self-determination struggles in the Third World and also participated in the founding of the Puerto Rican Student Union. His social commitment led him to work in community programs that offered recreational and employment opportunities for young people. In 1983, he was convicted of seditious conspiracy and sentenced to 35 years in prison for his effort to free the Puerto Rican political prisoners. [SOURCE: http://www.prisonactivist.org/pps+pows/edwin-cortes.html]

CORTÉS, ERNESTO Jr. (?-)

Ernesto J. Cortés, Jr., a native of San Antonio, Texas, graduated from Central Catholic High School in San Antonio, and received a B.A. from Texas A&M University, where he majored in English and Economics. He left postgraduate work in Economics at the University of Texas at Austin to pursue his vision for community change. Cortés became the first community organizer to receive the MacArthur Fellowship, commonly known as the "genius" fellowship, for his more than twenty years dedicated to organizing grassroots communities to empower themselves and make changes in the structure of power in their schools and communities. After receiving training at the Industrial Areas Foundation in 1973, Cortés went on to organize Communities Organized for Public Service (COPS)* in his native San Antonio. He later created grassroots organizations and movements in Los Angeles, Houston, El Paso, Dallas, Tucson, Phoenix, Albuquerque, New Orleans, and other cities in the Southwest, and built them into a network. Today he is the Southwest Director for the Industrial Areas Foundation. Thanks to his community organizing, government has been more responsive to providing services for poor people and educational access and achievement has improved for low-income neighborhoods. Cortés is a member of the Carnegie Task Force on Learning in the Primary Grades, the Pew Forum for K-12 Education Reform, and the Aspen Institute Domestic Strategy Group. [SOURCE: http://www.salsa.net/peace/faces/cortes.html]

CORTÉS RUBIO, SALVADOR (1911-1931)

In May of 1931, the nephew of Mexican president Pascual Ortiz Rubio, Salvador Cortés Rubio, was motoring with his brother and a friend to Mexico after studying at Saint Benedicts College in Kansas. Near Ardmore, Oklahoma, two deputy sheriffs in plainclothes thought the youths looked suspicious and followed their car from a highway hamburger stand. When his brother Emilio Cortés Rubio, who was driving, stopped so Salvador could urinate, the policemen pulled up behind them. According to Emilio, the youths had bought guns and ammunition to take back to Mexico and at first did not realize that the men in plainclothes were police. Emilio Cortés put a gun on his lap to defend himself, he said, but when a deputy pulled him out of the car, Cortés dropped it. The other officer panicked and fired a number of volleys, killing the unarmed Salvador Cortés and a third student present, Manuel García Gómez. At trial, the two officers were found innocent in spite of vigorous efforts by prosecutors, who came under pressure from the Mexican government to show that the deputies had shot needlessly. [SOURCE: Rosales, *Pobre Raza!*, 85.]

CORTEZ, GREGORIO (1875-1916)

The memory of Gregorio Cortez was preserved as lore in South Texas mainly by Mexican-American border dwellers until the Chicano* folklorist, Américo Paredes,* immortalized his story in *With His Pistol in His Hand* (1958). Since then, Cortez has become a symbol of resistance against the Anglo domination of the Southwest.

The story begins on June 12, 1901, when Sheriff W.T. Morris of Karnes County was killed by Cortez. The sheriff and a deputy went to the Mexican immigrant's ranch to inquire about a stolen horse. Because of a language misunderstanding, Morris pulled his gun to arrest Cortez, and Cortez shot Morris in self-defense. Cortez then began his flight toward the Mexican border, and a ten-day chase became one of the most publicized manhunts in Texas history. The fugitive did not make it to the border, but because of his bravery and his ability to elude capture, he gained legendary status among Mexicans and Anglos alike. It took a number of trials over a period of four years before Cortez was finally hauled off to serve a life sentence at Huntsville prison. Significantly, Cortez was not jailed for the shooting of Morris, which the jury considered self-defense, but for the killing of Sheriff G. Glover, who surprised him hiding out at the house of another Texas rancher in Gonzalez County two days after he had fled the Karnes debacle. Although many Anglos howled for his head—lynching threats abounded—Mexicans launched a massive effort in support of Cortez. During the next few years, thousands of dollars were raised to pay B.R. Abernathy, who with a team of four lawyers mounted a formidable defense. Even after Cortez was sentenced and imprisoned, supporters continued to clamour for clemency, and in 1915, Governor Oscar Colquitt pardoned Cortez. Cortez died a year later. [SOURCE: Rosales, *Pobre Raza!*, 93; Paredes, *"With His Pistol in His Hand."*]

CORTINA, JUAN NEPOMUCENO (1824-1894)

Juan Nepomuceno Cortina was born into a wealthy Mexican family in Camargo, Tamaulipas, a community just south of the Rio Grande River. By 1859, he had witnessed numerous instances of Anglo abuses and mistreatment of fellow Mexicans. Inharmonious race relations already existed throughout the entire Southwest, in particular in California where symbolic figures, such as Joaquín Murrieta* and Tiburcio Vásquez,* had championed the struggle for social justice and civil rights in the eyes of many Mexicans.

On July 13, 1859, Cortina observed one of his former employees being harassed by a law enforcement official in Brownsville, Texas. The marshal had arrested and mistreated the worker with indignation. Cortina shot the officer and declared that war between the Anglos and Los Tejanos (Texans) had begun. On September 28, 1859, Cortina and his men seized control of

Juan Nepomuceno Cortina

Brownsville, seeking the men he considered to be the most notorious persecutors of Mexicans, only to find they had fled. Local officials appealed to Mexican authorities to persuade Cortina to evacuate Brownsville, which he did, leaving for his family ranch in Tamaulipas. On September 30, he issued a proclamation declaring the rights of Mexicans to their heritage, pride, dignity, land, and self-preservation. In the meantime, Brownsville officials captured one of his men, Tomás Cabrera, and sentenced him to hang. Simultaneously, a posse of Americans and Texas Mexicans failed in an attempt to dislodge Cortina from his family estate on the Mexican side of the border. To save Cabrera, Cortina again threatened to invade Brownsville, and on November 23, 1859, he issued a second proclamation, which outlined the complaints of Mexicans against their Anglo oppressors. Finally, in December, Texas Rangers* aided by U.S. Army regulars fought Cortina and his men, forcing a retreat into the Burgos Mountains south of Matamoros, where he remained in hiding for more than a year.

When Texas joined the Confederacy during the American Civil War, Cortina's army, in support of the Union cause, invaded Zapata County in May 1861, starting the Second Cortina War. Defeated by the Texas Mexican, Santos Benavides,* a captain in the Confederacy, Cortina again retreated into Mexico. During the French Intervention, which began in 1862, Cortina fought on the side of the Republican troops of Mexican president, Benito Juárez, declared himself governor of Tamaulipas in 1863 and was promoted to general of the Mexican Army of the North. Eventually Juárez persuaded Cortina to relinquish the governorship post just a few months after he had vanquished the army of the imposed Emperor Ferdinand Maximilian in 1867. Cortina retired to his ranch near Matamoros in 1870, influential citizens in Texas attempted, unsuccessfully, to obtain a reprieve for Cortina in recognition of his services to the Union cause. After the rebuff, Texas ranchers accused the veteran fighter of continuing to raid and steal cattle. The Mexican government caved in to diplomatic pressure from the United States and, in 1875, put Cortina under arrest in Mexico City, where he died on October 30, 1894. Regardless of his checkered career, among border Mexicans, Cortina became a legend in the cause for social justice and civil rights among people of Mexican descent. [SOURCE: Thompson, "Cortina, Juan Nepomuceno," *The Handbook of Texas Online*, http://www.tsha.utexas.edu/

handbook/online/articles/view/CC/fco73.html; Larralde and Jacobo, *Juan N. Cortina and the Struggle for Justice in Texas.*]

EL COSMOPOLITA

Despite its being owned by Anglo-American businessman Jack Danciger, *El Cosmopolita* (The Cosmopolitan, 1914-1919) cultivated an identity of defending the Mexican community. The newspaper provided a vast array of information that the Spanish-speaking immigrants needed to survive in Kansas City, such as housing and employment information, and it did work to defend them against discrimination and exploitation. The newspaper protested against segregation, racial prejudice, police harassment, and brutality, injustice in the judicial system, and mistreatment in the work place. Unlike other commercial newspapers, such as San Antonio's *La Prensa*, Kansas City's *El Cosmopolita* consistently supported the Mexican Revolution and railed against U.S. interventionism. [SOURCE: Kanellos *Hispanic Periodicals in the United States*, 36-37; Rosales, *¡Pobre Raza!*, 35-36.]

COTERA, MARTHA (1938-)

Martha Cotera, born in Mexico, was a core activist for La Raza Unida Party (The United People's Party-LRUP)* in the late 1960s. Along with other Chicano Movement* activists in Texas, she was concerned about the lack of relevant education. Cotera co-founded the Jacinto Trevino College in 1970, an alternative Chicano school in Austin, Texas. In addition, she was a leader in pursuing the issue of gender equality within LRUP. In fact, Cotera organized Chicano feminist meetings in Houston in 1971 and 1972, meetings which today are seen as the pioneering efforts that have resulted in Chicanas* being in the forefront of today's international feminist movement. Cotera continues to be a leading spokesperson for Chicana feminism and politics. Today, she owns a research and data company in Austin, Texas. [SOURCE: http://chicano.nlcc.com/cotera.html; García, *United We Win*, 186, 230; Navarro, *La Raza Unida Party*, 20, 52, 266.]

COUNCIL OF MEXICAN AMERICAN AFFAIRS

Organized in 1954 in Los Angeles to serve as an umbrella organization for all Mexican-American groups in the city, the Council of Mexican American Affairs' (CMAA) objectives included developing leadership skills and coordinating the various activities of the 44 member groups. Mainly a middle-class organization, one of the CMAA's main concerns was to change the images members of mainstream society held of Mexican Americans. The high number organizations represented in the council proved too unwieldy, as did the financial problems that beset the CMAA. It was forced to curtail its programs and lost effectiveness by early 1960s. Nonetheless, some of the conferences sponsored by CMAA in the area of education, drug education, and job training proved very successful. [SOURCE: Samora and Simon, *A History of the Mexican-American People*, 195–196.]

COUNCIL OF SPANISH SPEAKING ORGANIZATIONS, INC.

On October 1, 1962, a group of Latino leaders founded the Council of Spanish Speaking Organizations, commonly known as Concilio to solve the problems that the Philadelphia Latino Community was facing. Since its inception, Concilio's mission has been to foster and make accessible family counseling, educational, health, and cultural services to North Philadelphia Latinos. Its services include GED classes, foster care, education to children in the home, and even helping to organize the Puerto Rican Festival of Philadelphia. In addition to the services given to Philadelphia's poorest communities, Concilio in the 1990s has lead campaigns to raise over $150,000 to help rebuild community infrastructures after catastrophic events and to seed community-owned micro economies. [SOURCE: http://members.tripod.com /phillysalsa/so-cial.htm/]

COURT OF PRIVATE LAND CLAIMS

Congress established the Court of Private Land Claims in 1891 to expedite the confirmation of land grants. Consisting of five judges, the court had jurisdiction over Arizona, Colorado, and New Mexico. While it existed, the court processed about 300 claims over some 35 million acres. The court found several cases of fraud and enlargement of boundaries. It confirmed one-third of the claims. Nonetheless, special rights of the corporate land-holding villages in New Mexico were virtually ignored. The court rejected ninety-five percent of the land claims brought up for litigation. It confirmed fewer than one dozen community grants. However, after commercial use taxes were paid, several of those confirmed were lost, owing to the general lack of cash in the Hispanic economy and because of the difficulty in collecting funds from a large number of villagers to pay this onerous levy; tax indebtedness and foreclosures followed. Often the villagers did not realize their losses for months and, occasionally, even for years, because the process was often so subtle. [SOURCE: Bradfute, *The Court of Private Land Claims.*]

COVENANT HOUSE

Covenant House origins can be traced to a blizzard in 1969, when a Franciscan priest, Father Bruce Ritter, provided shelter to six young runaways in his small Manhattan apartment. This modest gesture grew into Covenant House, the largest shelter program for homeless youths in the Americas. Besides shelter, at Covenant House homeless youths can obtain, food, clothing, education, vocational preparation, drug abuse treatment, legal services, recreation, spiritual care, and assistance in finding permanent housing and aftercare. Covenant House was eventually incorporated in New York City in 1972, but has expanded to Anchorage, Atlantic City, Detroit, Fort Lauderdale, Houston, Los Angeles, Newark, New Orleans, Orlando, Washington, D.C., and, outside the United States, to Toronto, Vancouver, Guatemala, Nicaragua, Honduras, and Mexico. [SOURCE: http://www.casa-alianza.org/EN/about/offices/covenant/]

CRESPO, MANUEL (1903-1989)

Manuel Crespo became an important political and business figure in the Houston Hispanic community throughout most of the twentieth century. He was born on November 12, 1903, in Orense, Spain, immigrated to the United States in 1920, and worked in Texas doing various odd jobs. In Houston, he found work at the Mexican Funeral Home and eventually bought out the owners. He built up a successful business and found common cause with the city's large Mexican population. He was a member of various Mexican fraternal organizations, but in the 1930s, he joined other Hispanics, mainly Mexican Americans, to form the Latin American Club,* a civil rights group which became a forerunner to a local League of United Latin American Citizens* chapter. In the 1960s, he was one of the founders of the Political Association of Spanish-Speaking Organizations* and the Viva Kennedy Clubs* in Houston. [SOURCE: García, "Crespo, Manuel," *The Handbook of Texas Online,* http://www.tsha.utexas.edu/handbook/online/articles/CC/fcr83.html]

CROSS BORDER NETWORK

The Cross Border Network for Justice and Solidarity (CBN) was founded in Kansas City, Missouri, as a nonprofit network in 1997 by labor, religious, environmental, student, and human rights activists. The organization's goal was to work for justice and build solidarity with people affected by the economic dislocations created by the North American Free Trade Agreement (NAFTA). CBN volunteers linked up with Nuevo Laredo's Center for Workers and Communities (CETRAC), a maquiladora worker's organization that provided plant employees with strategies for survival in the border industrial environment. In 2002 CBN volunteers also cooperatively built a primary school with CETRAC and the members of Colonia Santiago M. Belden. [SOURCE: http://www.crossbordernetwork.org/about.html]

CRUSADE FOR JUSTICE

The Crusade for Justice (CFJ) was founded in Denver, Colorado in 1966 and, for a short time, it became the most successful organization in the Chicano Movement.* The CFJ was led by Rodolfo "Corky" Gonzales,* a former professional boxer, bail bondsman, Democratic Party leader, and a major protagonist in Denver's War on Poverty. Gonzales had become disenchanted with mainstream politics by 1966 and, with a group called Los Voluntarios (The Volunteers)* that he had formed in 1963, he began protesting Denver's policy toward its impoverished Mexican-American population.

The name of the organization came from a 1966 speech in which Gonzales declared "on this day a new crusade for justice has been born." The name stuck, and in 1968, Gonzales and his group bought a building and named it the Center for the Crusade for Justice; it became a place where the Mexican-American community could gather for a variety of services. It contained a 500-seat auditorium, a ballroom, a dining room, a kitchen, a Mexican gift shop, a gymnasium, a nursery, an art gallery, a library, and classrooms.

The CFJ became involved in educational reform in the late 1960s, seeking to end discrimination in the Denver Public Schools. In November 1968, the CFJ presented a list of demands at a school board meeting, and the following spring, Gonzales led a walkout at West Side High School, calling for the removal of a teacher who had made racist remarks in the classroom. The walkout lasted three days, during which riots broke out and several confrontations with the police ensued. The police jailed twenty-five protesters, including Gonzales.

The CFJ achieved prominence after Gonzales co-chaired, with Reis López Tijerina,* the Mexican-American contingent of the Poor People's Campaign*

Center for the Crusade for Justice

in the Spring of 1968. Gonzales had been impressed by efforts by blacks to gain civil rights and achieve self-sufficiency during a previous Poor People's March.

The CFJ became so well-known that in 1969 it sponsored the National Chicano Youth Liberation Conference* to bring together and unify Mexican-American young people from around the country. The conference focused on two issues: cultural identity and social revolution, emphasizing ethnic nationalism and cultural pride. An estimated 1,500 youths attended. During the conference, those in attendance drafted El Plan Espiritual de Aztlán. This document articulated the growing feelings of nationalism and a desire for self-determination among the Mexican Americans of the Southwest. It also asserted the need for Mexican Americans to control their communities. In short, the El Plan Espiritual de Aztlán stressed the movement's commitment to developing justice and independence.

The group then took on the issue of police brutality and earned the enmity of Denver's law enforcement establishment; with this came constant police harassment. On March 17, 1973, Denver police clashed with CFJ members and in the fracas, a policeman and Crusade member were wounded, and twenty-year old Louis Martínez* was killed. This outbreak, which led to the almost complete dissolution of the CFJ, was indirectly provoked by an incessant vigilance of the CFJ activities in Denver. [SOURCE: Meier and Rivera, *Dictionary of Mexican American History*, 111-113; Marín, *A Spokesman of the Mexican American Movement*.]

CRUZ AZUL MEXICANA

At a convention of Mexican consuls held in San Antonio on April 9, 1921, the attendees devised a plan to expand government protection and take advantage of the resources in the numerous expatriate communities existing throughout the United States. An important component of this strategy was the formation of the Cruz Azul Mexicana, an organization that would support women in tending to the social well-being of their communities in the United States. The plan called for women to visit the hospitalized and incarcerated and conduct fund-raising campaigns for special causes, such as feeding and clothing the homeless. By the end of 1920s, many of these groups existed throughout the United States and their effectiveness depended on the degree to which local members acquired resources. In El Paso and San Antonio, for example, the organization sponsored extensive clinic services provided by volunteer medical practitioners. [SOURCE: Águila, "Protecting 'México de Afuera,'" 61-62.]

Cruz Azul Handbook

CRYSTAL CITY

In Crystal City, a south Texas town, Mexican Americans challenged the entrenched Anglo establishment on two different occasions in the 1960s; the events transformed the city's politics. In 1963, when the town had a population of 10,000 of which more than 85 percent were Mexican Americans, five working-class Mexican Americans, known as Los Cinco,* ran a successful campaign to unseat the all-white city council. The local Teamsters Union and the Political Association of Spanish-Speaking Organizations (PASSO)* organized the campaign. Los Cinco remained in power for two years, but they proved ineffective, due to political inexperience and Anglo sabotage. Then a mixed Anglo Mexican-American council, backed by the original white council, was elected.

In 1969, a more significant revolt occurred. It stemmed from what began as a protest against school discrimination that led to a school board take over and the recapture of City Hall by a new third party, La Raza Unida (The United People's Party-LRUP).* José Angel Gutiérrez,* a Crystal City-native who had gone to San Antonio to college but came back to lead this movement, became head of the school board.

After the 1969 takeover, the LRUP held a virtual stranglehold on the Crystal City government. In fact, the city became a testing ground for learning how to mobilize a community and gain leadership experience. Federal funding helped establish new programs in bilingual education, housing, and government. Unfortunately, Crystal City became over-dependent on federal assistance. In addition, it had trouble creating enough jobs to satisfy all the residents. Gutiérrez eventually became a county judge and the LRUP came to control the government of Zavala County. However, factionalizing over issues and personalities prevented effective administration. In 1981, Gutiérrez resigned his position and left Crystal City never to come back in any official capacity. [SOURCE: Navarro, *Mexican American Youth Organization*; García, *United We Win.*]

CUBA INDEPENDIENTE Y DEMOCRÁTICA

In 1981, Huber Matos, a former political prisoner, founded Cuba Independiente y Democrática (CID) in Caracas, Venezuela. CID soon established offices in major cities in Latin America and the United States and by combining seven radio stations scattered throughout the Caribbean, the organization beamed news to Cuba twenty-four hours a day. CID relied on *cabildeo*, or lobbying, to promote its political interests through traditional methods such as press conferences, meetings, and dinners. CID distributed *News Cuba* in English to senators and congressmen, the press, colleges and universities, and labor unions. Matos also aired his views on national and international affairs through a Spanish-language newspaper with a circulation of at least fifty thousand issues. CID hoped to end Fidel Castro's rule by encouraging rebellion from within instead of using military action. As such, the organization counted on its propaganda efforts, especially the radio broadcasts, to inform the population on political alternatives and spur them into action. [SOURCE: García, *Havana USA,* 154.]

CUBAN AMERICAN LEGAL DEFENSE AND EDUCATION FUND
Founded in 1980 in Fort Wayne, Indiana, the Cuban American Legal Defense and Education Fund advocates equal treatment for Hispanics in education, employment, housing, politics, and justice. It strives to end negative stereotyping of Hispanics and to educate the public about their plight in the United States. It publishes a monthly *Hispanic Newsletter* (See National League of Cuban American Community-Based Centers). [SOURCE: Kanellos, "Organizations," 390.]

CUBAN AMERICAN NATIONAL COUNCIL
Founded in 1980 by a handful of Cuban Americans who met in Washington, D.C., the Cuban American National Council (CANC) aims to meet the needs of a diverse, fast-growing Hispanic community. As a private non-profit social service agency based in Miami, Florida, CANC researches the economic, social, and educational needs of Cuban Americans and other Hispanics and assists them in their adjustments to American society. The council administers a network of programs in the three above-named areas and also fosters multiethnic cooperation. Although the initial constituent population was Cuban American, in recent years, the CANC has adjusted its service agenda to accommodate the needs of the ethnically changing Latino population in the United States. It publishes a quarterly, the *Council Letter*. [SOURCE: Kanellos, "Organizations," 391; http://www.hispaniconline.com/res&res/hisporgs/regional_2.html]

CUBAN AMERICAN NATIONAL FOUNDATION
A year after the presidential election of Ronald Reagan in 1980, a group of wealthy Cuban businessmen in Miami founded the Cuban American National Foundation (CANF). The organization, which was formed during a conservative mood in the United States, counted among its members many veterans of the Bay of Pigs, who had organized into The Brigade 2506 Veterans Association. CANF, a nonprofit organization, framed its goals around helping the Reagan administration formulate a "realistic" foreign policy towards Cuba.

To influence congressmen, CANF employed a political action committee called the Free Cuba PAC, which was modeled after the American Israel Public Affairs Committee (AIPAC), a Jewish organization with a very successful history of lobbying U.S. policy for Israel. Free Cuba PAC provided substantial donations to the re-election campaigns of senators and congressmen who supported a tougher policy toward Cuba. It is estimated that between 1983 and 1988, the Free Cuba PAC contributed some $385,000 to such congressmen as Democrat Lloyd Bentsen and Republican Dan Quayle, both of whom became vice-presidential candidates in 1988. In addition, through *Boletín Informativo* (Informative Bulletin) and *Cuban Update*, it produced and disseminated research on the economic, political, and social issues affecting Cubans in the United States and in Cuba. [SOURCE: Masud-Piloto, *From Welcomed Exiles to Illegal Immigrants*, 102, 106, 131, 133, 140; Kanellos, "Organizations," 390-391.]

CUBAN AMERICANS AND DIALOGUE WITH CUBA

President Jimmy Carter's reconciliation overtures to Cuba, which verged on opening up diplomatic and economic links, resonated with some Cuban exile organizations during the 1970s. Prominent advocates of *diálogo*, as the notion of reconnecting with the Fidel Castro government became known, were the Cuban Christians for Justice and Freedom, the National Union of Cuban Americans, and the Cuban American Committee. In 1979, President Jimmy Carter received a petition with more than ten thousand signatures requesting normalization of relations from the Cuban American Committee. Reconciliation became particularly associated with individual advocates, such as Reverend Manuel Espinosa, pastor of the Evangelical Church in Hialeah. To the chagrin of conservative emigrés, Espinosa, a former officer in Castro's military and an activist in numerous anti-Castro organizations, preached sermons from the pulpit advocating the normalization of diplomatic relations with Cuba.

The reconciliation lobby in the emigré community never became effective because it never attracted a significant following. Part of the reason for this failure was the fear that joining the effort would result in accusations of being Communists, a stigma that few exiles could afford in the ultra-conservative atmosphere of the Cuban-American community. From past experience, members of the community knew that such an onus could affect careers, businesses, relationships, and even invite violent retribution. For example, militant Cuban exiles severely beat the Reverend Espinosa in 1975, while other advocates of the *diálogo* experienced boycotted businesses, vandalizing of their homes, personal harassment, and ruined reputations. The *diálogo* also acquired international proportions. [SOURCE: Masud-Piloto, *From Welcomed Exiles to Illegal Immigrants*, 75-77.]

CUBAN AMERICANS AND DOMESTIC ISSUES

While Cuban exile political activism in south Florida in the 1970s continued to be dominated by a desire to overthrow Fidel Castro, many increasingly turned to a concern for civil rights, economic development, and cultural maintenance. In this decade, American citizenship was sought out by an increasing number of emigrés. Dade County experienced a surge of Latino businesses transforming the region into one of the most productive economic enclaves in the nation. Domestic politics achieved greater priority in this era. Emigrés accounted for eight percent of registered voters in Dade County in this era and became elected to some of the most important offices in city and county governments. Some Cubans began to identify with other ethnic Hispanics and promoted pan-Latino unity. They became more involved in organizations such as the League of United Latin American Citizens* and the National Council of La Raza.* In addition, they created their own institutions with similar goals such as the Cuban National Planning Council, the Spanish American League Against Discrimination, and the National Coalition of Cuban Americans. While many individuals in these groups shared the anti-Castro views of the exile community, their participation focused on voting rights, employment, housing, education, health, and other domestic concerns. [SOURCE: García, *Havana USA*, 137.]

CUBAN BOATLIFTS AND ARILIFTS

When Lyndon B. Johnson became president after John F. Kennedy's assassination, he also vowed to embrace Cubans who wished to leave their homeland. Cubans qualified for immigration status under special immigration provisions for refugees fleeing repressive governments. But Fidel Castro had announced as early as 1965 that Cubans could leave Cuba if they had

Mariel boatlifter receiving refugees

relatives in the United States. Castro stipulated, however, that Cubans already in Florida had to come and get their relatives at Camarioca Bay. Nautical crafts of all types subsequently left Miami for Camarioca and returned laden with Cubans eager to rejoin their families on the mainland. The spectacle of the motley fleet of boats converging on Miami docks was dramatic, but the trip was also dangerous for the thousands of fleeing Cubans. Many of the boats were not seaworthy and capsized. An airlift was then organized with a great deal of publicity and fanfare. The effort fell far short of the projected goal of transporting 200,000 refugees in the first year, but thousands did make it to the United States before the flights ended in 1973. [SOURCE: Masud-Piloto, *From Welcomed Exiles to Illegal Immigrants,* 57-63.]

CUBAN COMMITTEE FOR DEMOCRACY

Founded in 1993, the Cuban Committee for Democracy (CCD) works in Washington, D.C., to challenge the monopoly on exile political influence that the Cuban American National Foundation* has held for more than twenty years. Noted business and academic figures from the exile community have served in the CCD leadership. One of the founders, and once president of the organization, prominent Miami lawyer Alfredo Durán was captured in the Bay of Pigs invasion and imprisoned in Cuba for more than a year. Today, however, he advocates dialogue, reconciliation, and respect for Cuba's (present and future) sovereignty. Sharing this approach is Marcelino Miyares, who has served as vice president and is a broadcasting executive with Times Square Studios in New York. Prominent academicians, Alejandro Portes, chair of the Sociology Department at Johns Hopkins University, and María Cristina Herrera, founder and director of the Institute for Cuban Studies at Miami-Dade University, have also served on the CCD board.

One of the CCD's agendas is to open up travel to Cuba by U.S. citizens, a position which resonates with exiles who desire more contact with friends and relatives in the homeland. CCD is in the forefront in its opposition to embargo and actively lobbies in Washington to abolish this sanction. [SOURCE: Elliston, "The Myth of the Miami Monolith," *NACLA Report on the Americas* (Sept/Oct 1995), http://www.hartford-hwp.com/archives/43b/027.html]

CUBAN DEMOCRACY ACT

The "official" end of the Cold War, marked by the fall of Communism in eastern Europe in the late 1980s, spelled an end to the so-called "Soviet threat." Many politicians, encouraged by anti-Castro exiles, now paid more attention to the "Cuban threat." Cuba and Fidel Castro were accused of derailing the democratization of Latin America by supporting political subversion, drug-trafficking, and denying human rights on the island itself.

Fidel Castro

During the 1992 presidential election year, the Cuban issue came to the forefront of public discussion. That year a bill designed to tighten the U.S. economic embargo against Cuba and to strengthen the prospects for democracy in the island was introduced by U.S. Representative Robert Torricelli (D-NJ), Chairman of the House Western Hemisphere Subcommittee. Called the "Cuban Democracy Act" (CDA), or the Torricelli bill, the legislation would prohibit U.S. subsidiaries in third countries from trading with Cuba and prevent ships that had recently visited Cuba from docking in U.S. ports. Even President George H.W. Bush refused to support the bill because relations with U.S. allies might be compromised.

Bill Clinton, running on the Democratic ticket against Bush, initially rejected supporting the Torricelli bill but in the midst of the campaign, during the summer months, he decided to embrace it. Because Clinton made this very surprising announcement at a Miami fund-raiser organized by the predominantly Republican and conservative Cuban American National Foundation,* the move seemed an obvious ploy to draw away Cuban-American votes from Bush, who also changed his mind about the legislation. Needless to say, the bill passed and became an even greater obstacle to normalization of relations with Cuba; relations with allies were damaged extensively and the embargo was criticized and ridiculed by foreign nations and even by the international capitalist community. [SOURCE: Masud-Piloto, *From Welcomed Exiles to Illegal Immigrants*, 120-131.]

CUBAN EMIGRÉ JOURNALS

The intellectual diaspora from Cuba provoked by the rise of Fidel Castro's revolution resulted in a core of the intelligentsia being formed in the United States. A rich Spanish-language record of publication was inevitable in the emigré community. Foremost was the production of literary journals. From New York City came *Exilio* (1967–73), edited by Víctor Batista Falla and Raimundo Fernández Bonilla. At the University of Pittsburgh in 1970, scholar Carmelo Mesa Lago founded the *Cuban Studies Newsletter*, which marked the emergence of Cuban Studies as an academic discipline. The Editorial Universal in Miami published *Revista Alacrán Azul* (1970-71). At the University of Hawaii, Matías Montes Huidobro edited *Caribe* (1975–80); *Escandalar*, edited by Octavio Armand, came out of New York (1978–82). This pioneering output was dominated by constant critical, less often sympathetic, reflection on Cuba's revolution, interspersed with nostalgic imagery and pure art productions steeped in the Hispanic tradition. In early 1974, however, the Antonio Maceo Brigade, a leftist organization, issued a magazine entitled *Areíto** in order to celebrate the revolution and to challenge U.S. and conservative emigré propaganda against the Cuban state. In spite of the opposition experienced by the publishers, the magazine managed to survive until the 1980s, longer than some of the earlier publications.

After 1980, Cubans who arrived during the famous Mariel boatlift* produced a new wave of artistic and literary magazines. In 1983, Reinaldo Arenas, Roberto Valero, and Juan Abreu initiated *Revista Mariel* in Miami to publish works by well-known emigré authors as well as those of Latin American and European writers. The magazine moved to New York, where it continued to publish the writings of authors who in Cuba had no literary outlet. Also it challenged the negative stereotypes, which the current weave of exiles, known as *marielitos*, had faced. *Revista Mariel* encountered financial problems and ceased publication in 1985, but Marcia Morgado resuscitated it as *Mariel Magazine*, which survived from 1986 to 1988. [SOURCE: García, *Havana USA*, 196.]

CUBAN EXILE TERRORISM

Militant anti-Castro Cuban exiles resorted to violence against Cubans who advocated a *diálogo* (dialogue) with Fidel Castro's government. One-hundred-and-three bombing attempts and six political assasinations aimed at targeted "collaborators" were investigated by the FBI and Miami law enforcement officials between 1973 and 1976. One of the most notorious of these acts was the assasinations of Luciano Nieves and Ramón Donéstevez in Miami for merely expressing their desires for coexistence with Castro's Cuba.

In 1978, when President Jimmy Carter encouraged rapprochement with the Cuban government, a gesture welcomed by Castro and many exiles, extremist Cuban exiles became angered at this seemingly new turn in American foreign policy. They subsequently escalated the war against Castro. Utilizing extreme methods, they silenced many of their fellow exiles, even the ones who did not agree with their position. The terrorist groups acquired colorful names, such as El Cóndor, Comandante Zero, Movimiento Neo-Revolucionario Cubano-Pragmatista, Coordinación de Organizaciones Revolucionarias Unidas (CORU), Poder Cubano, Acción Cubana, M-17, Frente de Liberación Nacional de Cuba, and Omega 7. Operating on a grand international scale, members of these organizations embarked on a campaign of fear and retribution. They bombed Cuban embassies and consulates, murdered Cuban diplomatic employees, harassed and threatened individuals and institutions suspected of having ties to the Castro government, and placed bombs aboard Cuban-bound commercial flights.

Omega 7, perhaps the most active of these organizations, extended its threats by embarking on a virtual war against anyone who traveled to Cuba; they bombed the Cuban and Soviet missions to the United Nations, travel agencies selling trips to Cuba, an Aeroflot agency, and businesses belonging to Committee-of-75 members, one of the most vocal *diálogo* organizations. Unlike the paramilitary organizations of the 1960s, who had aimed insurgent acts at Cuba or its allies, the militant extremists attacked anyone they perceived to be an enemy, including residents of the exile community abroad. Tragically, they considered injury to innocent victims as a means to a just end. [SOURCE: Masud-Piloto, *From Welcomed Exiles to Illegal Immigrants,* 75-77.]

CUBAN MUSEUM OF ART AND CULTURE

In 1987, a fund-raising auction of Cuban art sponsored by the Cuban Museum of Art and Culture in Miami succeeded to such a degree that the museum announced another sale for the following year. A controversy arose when exile community conservatives discovered that the 1988 effort would include paintings by Cuban artists who critics claimed were still associated with Fidel Castro's Cuba. In spite of enormous pressure from the conservatives, the museum board decided in a very close vote to go through with the event; it also succeeded in terms of sales and attendance. Opponents then engaged in a harassment campaign that included intimidating museum patrons and a bombing of the art building. A board struggle ensued in which the member opponents of the art event resigned in protest and created the Cuban Museum Rescue Committee. This group put pressure on the Miami City Commission to audit the museum, which it did without finding any financial irregularities.

Exile conservatives accused the remaining board members of being *infiltrados* (spies) and threatened them with death. Because of his role as the auction's chief organizer, detractors targeted Ramón Cernuda for special scrutiny. Federal officials, at the instigation of the museum's detractors, launched an investigation of Cernuda, which resulted in his arrest for harassment and a variety of other charges, none which resulted in a conviction. Other board members were subjected to this scrutiny and, by 1992, the museum's future seemed uncertain. An attempt to evict the museum from the city-owned property was blocked by a federal judge for civil rights violation. Subsequently, financial woes tested the museum's ability to survive, as former patrons cancelled their pledges and the Florida state legislature cancelled its funding. Nonetheless, with funding from the Ford Foundation* the museum organized a number of successful exhibitions over the next two years.
[SOURCE: García, *Havana USA,* 198.]

CUBAN REFUGEE ASSISTANCE: A RATIONALE

After the victory over the Cuban dictator Fulgencio Batista,* Fidel Castro increasingly adopted socialistic ideas and turned to the Cuban Communist Party for support, but not before the Eisenhower administration broke off relations with his revolutionary government. Eventually, the Soviet Union pledged its support to Castro, while the American government initiated a plan to welcome refugees. Eisenhower's motives to allow disaffected Cubans to enter the United States unencumbered were largely political. The 1950s were characterized by a Cold War mentality in which the Soviet Union and the United States waged an intense propaganda campaign for world prominence and acceptance. The flight of refugees was correctly anticipated by American officials to be middle-class and essential to Cuba's economic well-being. Thus, their escape would deprive Cuba of technical and professional skills, serve as a propaganda victory against communism, and, by extension, deliver a blow to the Soviet Union's world prestige. But the Eisenhower administration projected another role for the exiles. Considering the history of discontented Cubans using the United States as a mustering point for insurgency against governments on the island, American officials foresaw the potential for a repetition with the latest wave of arrivals.

With the election of John F. Kennedy to the presidency, relations between the two countries did not improve. President Eisenhower had encouraged Cuban refugees to prepare an invasion of Cuba to topple Castro, and Kennedy continued this policy. In April 1961, Cuban exiles who were trained and armed by the United States, but who did not receive direct military support in their invasion, attempted a foray into Cuba that was doomed from the beginning. The failure of the infamous Bay of Pigs invasion embittered the thousands of Cubans who were in exile, but Castro's position at home was strengthened. To many observers throughout the world, especially in the Third World, the United States was clearly taking the side of the usurpers, who attempted to overthrow a legitimately based government.

With the Bay of Pigs fiasco behind him, Kennedy continued to welcome Cuban refugees and to provide more structured military training for Cubans, most of whom still desired another attempt at overthrowing Cuba's communist government. But in 1962, Kennedy redeemed himself from the Bay of Pigs disgrace by backing down the Soviet Union on a Russian plan to establish missile bases in Cuba. After this, the more viable of the two courses inherited from the Eisenhower years was to expand the refugee program.

Increasingly, welcoming refugees became more important to the U.S. policy of destabilizing the Cuban revolutionary government than armed insurrection or outright invasion. Such a course deprived Cuba of the merchants, technicians, and professionals so necessary to the island's struggling economy. In the ten years after the disastrous Bay of Pigs invasion, almost 500,000 Cubans left the island. Because of the heavy influx, a special program was initiated to settle the refugees outside of Florida. Although the majority of the fleeing Cubans stayed in Florida, thousands more went to other regions of the United States, especially to California, New York, and Chicago, areas that already had large populations of Hispanics. An elaborate project ensued that included numerous prerogatives for incoming Cubans. Refugee emergency housing, English-language training, federal educational funds for Cuban children, and medical care became part of a package that facilitated the immigration process.

When Lyndon B. Johnson* became president after Kennedy's assassination, he also vowed to embrace Cubans who wished to leave their homeland. Cubans then qualified for immigration status under special immigration provisions for refugees fleeing repressive governments. But Fidel Castro had announced as early as 1965 that Cubans could leave Cuba if they had relatives in the United States. Castro stipulated, however, that Cubans already in Florida had to come and get their relatives at Camarioca Bay. Nautical crafts of all types systematically left Miami for Camarioca, returning laden with anxious Cubans eager to rejoin their families on the mainland. The spectacle of the motley fleet of boats converging on Miami docks was dramatic, but the trip was also dangerous for the thousands of fleeing Cubans. Many of the boats were not seaworthy and capsized. An airlift was then organized with a great deal of publicity and fanfare. Thousands more arrived in the United States before the flights ended in 1973.

Castro also tapped the refugee issue so that he could gain moral backing from the rest of Latin America and from the millions of Cubans living on the island who still supported him. He charged those who wanted to leave the island with betrayal, branding the emigrants with the epithet *gusano* (worm), which rhymes with *cubano* and is a derogatory name. In addition. he constantly reminded the world that, while Americans welcomed Cubans as displaced persons fleeing political persecution, they would not allow the same considerations to Chileans, Haitians, and other Latin Americans escaping repressive governments.

The final and most dramatic influx of Cubans came in the early 1980s. By that time much of the hard antipathy that Cubans felt toward Castro had become as much ritualistic as real. A generation had grown up in the United States that did not have the same sentiments as their parents. In addition, President Jimmy Carter, determined to depart from the Cold War policies of his predecessors, made advances toward Castro, urging reconciliation with the Cubans in the United States. [SOURCE: Rosales, "A Historical Overview," 47-52.]

CUBAN REFUGEE EMERGENCY CENTER

In 1960, in response to an appeal from the Cuban Refugee Committee, President Eisenhower authorized the Mutual Security Act to allot one million dollars to resettle Cuban refugees fleeing Castro's revolution. The decision qualified the exiles as political refugees because Cuba was now a Communist state. The decision also partially funded the Cuban Refugee Emergency Center known as "Freedom Tower," but most of the burden of relief fell to private groups. The most prominent were the Centro Hispano Católico and the Protestant Latin Refugee Center. The influx of refugees was so large that private organizations were overwhelmed. Undoubtedly President Eisenhower would have provided more help, but his term ended just as the diaspora began to accelerate. The center's initial efforts, even with limited federal assistance, managed to help thousands of refugees. [SOURCE: García, *Havana USA,* 20-21.]

CUBAN REFUGEE PROGRAM

Almost immediately after his inauguration in 1961, President John F. Kennedy declared Cuban exiles a national responsibility and established the Cuban Refugee Program, which involved relief aid from the departments of State, Labor, Defense, and Agriculture, coordinated through the Department of Health, Education, and Welfare. Besides resettlement assistance, Cuban exiles received monthly relief checks, health services, job training, adult educational opportunities, and surplus food distribution. The Dade County public school secured federal help to partially fund the influx of the more than thirty-five hundred Cuban refugee children who had enrolled in public schools by the Spring of 1961. Initially, presidential discretion determined the how and when federal funds for all these programs would be spent, but in 1962 the Migration and Refugee Assistance Act (P.L. 87-510) established permanent authority for the relief program. [SOURCE: Masud-Piloto, *From Welcomed Exiles to Illegal Immigrants*, 49-50.]

CUBAN RESEARCH INSTITUTE

The Cuban Research Institute (CRI) was created in 1991 after the ultra-conservative Cuban American National Foundation,* which received funding from the Florida legislature to establish a Cuban Studies program at Florida International University (FIU), was unable to accomplish its goal. The faculty and administrators including FIU's president, Modesto "Mitch" Maidique* opposed the project, which if funded would have pursued a polemical and extremely politicized research agenda. The FIU community understood, nonetheless, that a Cuban-American Studies project was needed at the university. As the largest university in southern Florida, located in a community which is a gateway between Cuba and the United States and that contains more than 700,000 persons of Cuban origin, FIU is geographically situated for this program. As a consequence, in 1991 the provost, upon the recommendation of a faculty committee, established the CRI, which fulfills the university's three-fold mission of research, teaching, and service. The project has been able to draw on a nucleus of faculty experts on Cuba and the Cuban-American community to form what has become the largest institute of its type of any U.S. university. [SOURCE: http://lacc.fiu.edu/cri/#Mission]

CUBAN STUDIES INSTITUTE AT MIAMI'S FLORIDA INTERNATIONAL UNIVERSITY

In 1989, the ultra-conservative Cuban American National Foundation (CANF)* succeeded in getting a bill introduced in the Florida legislature to appropriate $1 million to help fund the Cuban American National Foundation Institute at Miami's Florida International University (FIU). The legislation caused uproar because this Cuban Studies program would be under the complete control of the CANF. At FIU, the administration and most of the faculty condemned the bill and mounted a campaign to oppose even taking a vote on this bill. FIU's president, Modesto "Mitch" Maidique,* a member of the CANF advisory board, did not support the effort either. The uproar prompted Jorge Más Canosa* to withdraw his proposal for the FIU institute, but the Florida House and Senate allocated $1 million to the CANF so that it could establish an independent research entity on Cuba and the Caribbean. All in all, while the CANF did not succeed in this effort, the event demonstrated the level of power achieved by the anti-Castro lobby in Florida. [SOURCE: García, *Havana USA*, 151.]

CULTURE CLASH

Symbolically, on Cinco de Mayo (May 5), 1984, in San Francisco's Mission District,* a group of Chicano* actors/entertainers, including Richard Montoya, Ric Salinas, and Herbert Sigüenza formed improvisational theater company Culture Clash. Since then, the group has played in such venues as the Kennedy Center, Lincoln Center, the Public Theater, The Mark Taper Forum, La Jolla Playhouse, INTAR, Dallas Theater Center, Berkeley Repertory Theater, South Coast Repertory Theater, and San Diego Repertory Theater. In addition, Culture Clash has been invited to countless universities, colleges, and comedy nightclubs throughout the country. Culture Clash writes and performs its own material, such as the renowned play, "A Bowl of Beings," which premiered on the Public Broadcasting System's Great Performances Series. Culture Clash satirizes many of the political and social issues that confront the Latino community, without being strident or overly polemic, a feat accomplished by injecting humor that is often self-deprecating. [SOURCE: http://www.cultureclash.com/posada.html]

DEAF AZTLÁN

Deaf Aztlán is an online resource for Deaf Latinos/as living in the United States. In addition to its online web site, Deaf Aztlán provides a news and discussion list for deaf Latinos/as and their supporters. [SOURCE: Aztlán for Deaf Latinas/os, http://www.deafvision.net/aztlan/]

D

DEAF HISPANIC STUDENTS AT ROCHESTER INSTITUTE OF TECHNOLOGY

The Hispanic Deaf Club is a social organization for deaf Latinos/as attending the Rochester Institute of Technology. It was founded in September 1995 by Jamie Mariona and a small group because "they wanted to share their struggles and accomplishments" at the National Technical Institute for

La Defensa

the Deaf . The organization is open to all Hispanic and non-Hispanic deaf or hearing-impaired students and encourages them to learn about Hispanic cultural traditions and participate in the Hispanic/non-Hispanic community. [SOURCE: http://www.rit.edu/~hdcwww/project.html]

LA DEFENSA

With the advent of the Depression, New York did not experience the massive repatriation of Hispanics that occurred in the Southwest. Instead, hard economic times on the island brought even more Puerto Ricans to the city, a trend that would intensify during World War II as northeastern industries experienced labor shortages and recruited heavily in Puerto Rico. The massive influx of Puerto Ricans during and just after the war further intensified the community's identity as a native American citizenry. And their local newspapers appealed to them as citizens to organize politically and vote. In 1941, a new newspaper, *La Defensa* (The Defense), appeared in East Harlem specifically to further the interests of Hispanics in the area who were there to stay "no somos aves de paso" (we are not here as temporary birds). [SOURCE: Kanellos, *Hispanic Periodicals in the United States*, 107-108.]

DEGANAWIDAH-QUETZALCOATL UNIVERSITY

Deganawidah-Quetzalcoatl University (DQU), the first Native American and Chicano* university, was founded on April 2, 1971, near Davis, California, after a protracted struggle to have the deed transferred from an old Army communications center. In November 1970, just before dawn, a small group of young Native Americans jumped over a metal fence surrounding a then defunct communications center, surprising the few soldiers left to guard the drab cinder-block Army buildings. They pitched a tepee, fulfilling the main tenets of a carefully planned "occupation," while outside Chicano supporters cheered. Nearly 35 years later, DQU is still there, but it has survived tenuously, at times unable to meet budget requirements. Through funding from the Federal Tribal College Act, DQU is able to maintain a two-million dollar annual budget, providing for a two-year undergraduate degree. Unfortunately, the school does not qualify for state funding but continues in its mission of "providing a quality education, community involvement, and learning opportunities for all Native American Indians in California and all those that have a desire and ability to learn." [SOURCE: Meier and Feliciano, *Dictionary of Mexican American History*, 117; http://www.dqu.cc.ca.us/pages/catalog02-04/general_info/mission.html]

DELGADO, ABELARDO BARRIENTOS (1930-2004)

Abelardo Barrientos Delgado, known to everyone who knew him as "Lalo," is one of the most important pioneers of Chicano* literature. Born in Chihuahua, Mexico, in 1930, Lalo Delgado moved to El Paso, Texas, with his mother when he was twelve years old. Not long thereafter, he began writ-

ing and, when death took him in 2004, he had penned fourteen books, including *Chicano: Twenty Five Pieces of a Chicano Mind* (1969) and *The Chicano Movement: Some Not Too Objective Observations* (1971). His verse alternated from acrimoniously biting and politically charged to gentle and sensitive. Delgado, who received a B.A. in Spanish literature from the University of Texas at El Paso, traveled around the world reading his poetry and was instrumental in creating Chicano Studies programs at the University of Utah, the University of Colorado, and at Denver's Metropolitan College. His political civil rights

Abelardo Barrientos Delgado

activity was extensive, as well, and even included a 30-day fast. His concern for migrant worker rights committed him to march alongside farmworker organizers César Chávez* and Dolores Huerta.* Delgado's best known poem was "Stupid America" (1969), which depicted the alienation of Chicano young people in a society which rejected and neglected them. [SOURCE: Rodriguez, "Abelardo 'Lalo' Delgado."]

DELGADO V. THE BASTROP INDEPENDENT SCHOOL DISTRICT

After World War II, the League of United Latin American Citizens* filed a lawsuit in Texas to eliminate educational segregation of Mexican-American children. In June 1948, the federal court in Austin decided that this kind of segregation was unconstitutional, based on the Fourteenth Amendment. Mexican Americans were officially classified as white, thus they were not subject to the "separate-but-equal" doctrine. Because of Mexican-American children's problems with the English language, however, the court allowed segregation in the first grade only. The Texas State Board of Education issued an accommodating statement of policy and instructed local school districts to abolish segregation of Mexican Americans. Some schools did not comply, and it took further prodding by Mexican-American civil rights activists to enforce the decision. [SOURCE: Meier and Rivera, *Dictionary of Mexican American History*, 118.]

DE OLIVERA ELEMENTARY SCHOOL

In 1929, students, parents, and the Mexican government objected to efforts by the San Bernadino, California, school board to segregate Mexicans with African Americans at the De Olivera Elementary School. The community refused to accept the rationale given by Ida Collins, the County Superintendent of Public Instruction, who claimed the purpose for the separation was to help the children learn English. [SOURCE: Rosales, *Chicano!*, 70.]

Puerto Rican Day Parade, 1964

THE DESFILE PUERTORRIQUEÑO

The Desfile Puertorriqueño, sponsored by the Coordinating Council for the Puerto Rican Day Parade was formed in 1958 to organize the Puerto Rican Day Parade to be held each June 9. The parade has subsequently become the most significant display of Puerto Rican solidarity in New York City. While the organizing motive was a cultural one, the Puerto Rican Day Parade has become a demonstration of the political and economic power held by the Puerto Rican community. [SOURCE: Sánchez Korrol, *From Colonia to Community,* 226.]

DESPERTAR MASSACRE

In the 1970s, Christian liberation movements swept through poverty-stricken areas of El Salvador because they offered relief from economic, social, and personal oppression that defined the lives of many Salvadorans.

This wave of hope, however, also became a threat to government authorities and the established classes. As a consequence, the movement suffered an onslaught of repression in which many of the practitioners of this social philosophy and their followers were murdered, including Archbishop Oscar Romero after he had started supporting the movement.

As part of the strategy to halt the movement, the military targeted Christian centers for destruction. One of these came to a particularly tragic end. On a Sunday morning in January 1979, the First Infantry Brigade and the National Guard rolled their tanks into El Despertar Retreat Center, located in the San Antonio Abad neighborhood of San Salvador. The center's leader, Father Octavio Ortiz, was crushed beneath the treads of a tank; then soldiers killed four youths and carried the rest off to National Police Headquarters. In the ensuing months, the army subjected a string of participants in Christian-base activities to interrogation, torture, assassination, and disappearance. [SOURCE: Hutchinson, *When the Dogs Ate Candles,* 66-67.]

DESPIERTA BORICUA

In 1972, Puerto Rican students organized Despierta Boricua (DB) at Yale University. Its main objectives were to foster a sense of community among Puerto Rican undergraduates at Yale; serve as vehicle for voicing concerns to the Yale administration; and to coordinate and sponsor educational activities dealing with Puerto Rican issues. DB employs forceful advocacy measures to achieve these objectives and coordinates a vast array of cultural, educational, and social events. In addition, DB also encourages Yale Latino undergraduate interaction with the New Haven community through service initiatives. Despierta Boricua sponsors formal discussions and speakers on political and social issues, art exhibits, community service projects, parties, movie nights, and study breaks at La Casa Cultural. In addition, DR publishes *El Boletín*, a bi-weekly newsletter. DB also maintains strong ties with the other Latino organizations through its membership in the Concilio, the coordinating council of La Casa Cultural. [SOURCE: http://www.yale.edu/db/]

DÍAZ, SANTIAGO (1910-?)

In 1975, 65-year-old Santiago Díaz, a resident alien, filed a constitutional challenge as the lead plaintiff to the Social Security Act requirement stipulating that resident aliens must prove five years of uninterrupted residence in the United States before they are eligible for Medicare. The first hearing in the U.S. district court in Florida resulted in a decision finding the requirement unconstitutional. But the Department of Health, Education, and Welfare appealed this ruling to the U.S. Supreme Court, which reversed the lower court ruling, holding that Congress may condition aliens' eligibility for participation in Medicare, or any other federal program, on citizenship or continuous residence in the United States. [SOURCE: http://www.jurisearch.com/default.asp]

DICKERSON MONTEMAYOR, ALICE (1902-1989)

Born on August 6, 1902, in Laredo, Texas, Alice Dickerson Montemayor was elected to a number of national posts in the League of United Latin American Citizens (LULAC).* She was the first woman to achieve such a distinction in an organization that since its founding in 1929 had been dominated by men. In fact, women could not join LULAC as full-fledged members until 1933, when segregated councils were created so they could participate.

Even as a very young woman, Montemayor stood out in South Texas. After graduating from high school in 1924, a rarity for the working-class and for Mexican Americans, let alone a woman, Montemayor attended Laredo Business College for a year. In the 1930s, while her only child, Francisco Jr., was in school, she helped charter the Laredo Ladies LULAC. She was such a vibrant local activist that she soon rose to national prominence. Between 1937 and 1940, Montemayor served in three national posts: second national vice-president general, associate editor of *LULAC News* and director general of Junior LULAC. As a writer in the *LULAC News*, and in general throughout her LULAC activism, Montemayor was a tireless promoter of the right of young people and women to participate fully in the affairs of the organization. Her role in LULAC declined after 1940, but few women have left such a legacy, not only in the organization's history but also in the history of Latina women. [SOURCE: Orozco, "Alice Dickerson Montemayor's Feminist Challenge to LULAC in the 1930s."]

THE DIGIORGIO STRIKE

The seasonal farm labor force in California before and after World War II was composed of dust bowl refugees and Mexican Americans. In 1947, the employees at DiGiorgio farms, one of the largest agri-businesses in Kern County, reflected this ethnic mix. Although there was often tension between white and Mexican workers, they began discussing the necessity of collective bargaining and planned an organization of farmworkers. Bob Whatley, who emerged as one of their leaders, wrote to the president of the National Farm Workers Union (NFWU), H.L. Mitchell, asking for help. Mitchell dispatched two organizers, Henry Hasiwar and Ernesto Galarza,* who began to organize a chapter of the NFWU, Local 218.

By September 1947, the two organizers had signed 858 DiGiorgio employees into Local 218. After corporation officials rebuffed the union's requests for recognition, Local 218 decided to strike on October 1, 1947. After one of the longest strikes in California history, the strike and Local 218 were crushed by the DiGiorgio Fruit Corporation. [SOURCE: Samora and Simon, *A History of the Mexican-American People,* 190.]

DIMAS INCIDENT

During the 1966-67 farmworker strike in the Lower Rio Grande Valley, a Texas Ranger* severely beat a United Farm Workers* organizing committee member named Magdaleno Dimas. On June 1, 1967, Texas Ranger Captain Alfred Y. Allee* broke into a Rio Grande City home, where Dimas was hiding after a warrant was put out for his arrest on charges related to strike activity. Dimas sustained several injuries. Allee admitted hitting Dimas with a shotgun; medical examinations revealed a brain concussion, a serious blow to the lower back, as well as multiple bruises and lacerations. The Texas Rangers denied allegations of brutality and other civil rights violations. State senator Joseph J. Bernal investigated the incident and requested that the Rangers be removed from the Rio Grande Valley. Governor John Connally ignored Bernal's recommendation and did not remove the Rangers. [SOURCE: Meier and Rivera, *Dictionary of Mexican American History*, 120.]

DISLOYALTY ACT

The thirty-fifth legislature of Texas passed the Disloyalty Act during World War I. Subsequently, German Americans and, more prevalently, Mexicans experienced rampant xenophobia, putatively for those expressing anti-American sentiments. To offset this stigmatization, Mexican Americans joined in the war efforts on a number of home fronts. In the El Paso Valley, Mexican-American farmers pledged to increase agricultural production to meet wartime demands. *El Imparcial de Texas* * and *La Prensa* newspapers continued to promote Mexican-American loyalty and support for the war effort with weekly listings of Mexicans killed or wounded in the European theater. [SOURCE: Rosales, *Chicano!*, 92.]

DOE V. PLYER

In 1977, the Mexican American Legal Defense and Education Fund (MALDEF)* filed suit against a Tyler, Texas, school district in an attempt to prevent the school district from charging tuition for children who did not have permanent immigration status. In October 1980, a federal appeals court upheld the district court's ruling that charging tuition was unconstitutional. According to the decision, by treating undocumented children differently, the Tyler school district violated the Equal Protection Clause of the Fourteenth Amendment. [SOURCE: Meier and Rivera, *Dictionary of Mexican American History*, 122.]

DOMÍNGUEZ, ADOLFO (?-?)

The 1931 jailing of Chicago's Mexican vice consul, Adolfo Domínguez, reveals the prejudice that law enforcement officials held towards Mexicans. At this time, Great Depression unemployment exacerbated ethnic hostility toward Mexicans, an enmity manifested by local neighborhood policemen. Domínguez managed the consulate's *atropello* (abuse) division and, as arrests of Mexicans increased in the 1930s, the aggressive official scurried in and out of courtrooms attempting to assure justice for his compatriots. On the morning of July 7, the vice consul entered Judge Thomas Green's courtroom to determine why white assailants of two Mexican girls hurt at a Fourth of July race riot were not charged. Judge Green launched into a tirade upon learning of the vice consul's presence and sent him off to the county jail to serve a six-month sentence for contempt of court. Mexican Ambassador Manuel Téllez then protested the jailing of a presumably immune Mexican diplomat. The Department of State, sensitive to the international implications of Judge Green's action, had already acted. The State Department, consequently, sought to quickly suppress the Chicago incident, cabling Governor Lewis Emmerson in Springfield to request his help in averting any further complications. Over Green's objections, another judge freed Domínguez on his own recognizance. Green remained defiant throughout the whole affair, but Chief Justice Sonseteby of the Illinois Supreme Court, at the behest of Governor Emmerson, persuaded Green to expunge the original sentence and issue a statement admitting his error. The Department of State sent an official apology to Mexico through Ambassador Téllez, and the international imbroglio ended. [SOURCE: Rosales, *Pobre Raza!*, 128-129.]

DOMÍNGUEZ, FRANK E. (?-?)

Frank E. Domínguez, who defended accused murderer Aurelio Pompa,* was one of the many Mexican-American lawyers, i.e., born in the United States, who was very active in helping Mexican immigrants in trouble with the law. His extensive efforts to appeal Pompa's death sentence for the killing of his supervisor at a Los Angeles construction site in 1922 were to no avail, however. Domínguez, who was in partnership with an Anglo attorney, also penned essays opposing capital punishment for *La Opinión* and *El Tucsonense* newspapers. [SOURCE: Rosales, *Chicano!*, 82.]

DOMINICAN AMERICAN NATIONAL ROUNDTABLE

Founded in 1997, the Dominican American National Roundtable (DANR) is based in Washington, D.C. and advocates for the empowerment of Dominicans in the United States and Puerto Rico. Incorporated in 2000 as a 501 (c)(3) not-for-profit organization, the DANR is the first and only national organization addressing issues and concerns of the growing Dominican American community, such as education, health, economic development, and political empowerment. [SOURCE: http://www.danr.org/ip.asp?op=History]

DOMINICAN-AMERICAN STUDENT ASSOCIATION

Organized in 1995 at Florida International University, the Dominican-American Student Association promotes the advancement of students of Dominican heritage on campus. Association members provide information and assistance to new Dominican students, and projects positive images to the general university community of Dominican culture and history. Dominican students are encouraged to contribute to their community outside the university through service projects. [SOURCE: http://www.fiu.edu/~soc/club_dir.htm]

THE DOMINICAN POPULATION

Dominicans have been immigrating to the United States in steadily rising numbers since the 1960s. In the 1990s, they became the second largest group of immigrants to the United States from this hemisphere (after Mexicans). Nonetheless, other than in New York City and a few other places in the Northeast, their presence has gone almost unnoticed. Baseball, a game that is as much a part of the national identity in the homeland as it is for Americans, has shattered the invisibility of Dominicans in the United States. Dominican players have taken their domination of America's favorite pastime to high levels.

Of course, the islanders are making their mark in many other areas of life on the mainland. The 2000 U.S. Census put the Dominican population in the United States at about 1.5 million, surpassing Cubans as the third-largest Hispanic group in the United States (after Mexicans and Puerto Ricans). The Dominicans have immigrated for a variety a reasons, not the least of which is poverty in the homeland. Yet many Dominican immigrants to the United States are middle-class and, while some have tasted success as professionals and entrepreneurs, many more labor in the factories or the immense service sector of northeastern cities. But as has happened with massive immigration from Mexico, Korea, the Philippines, Cuba, and Vietnam, U.S. intervention in the affairs of the Dominican Republic, including invasions in 1916 and 1965, have resulted in a domination that has found a release in immigration.

As their numbers increase, Dominicans are transcending their traditional destinations, largely the Northeast and Puerto Rico, and are now a growing presence in Miami. More recently, the emigré community is discovering that increasing numbers do not translate into the ability to defend their interests. In spite of some setbacks and disputes within the community, Dominican unity and organization is growing, along with commensurate political clout. In addition, community leaders see the value of pan-Latino coalescing with other Latinos. Dominicans along with Salvadorans, Colombians, Hondurans, Nicaraguans, Peruvians, Ecuadorans, and others are forcing an expansion of the traditional scope of Hispanic minority status in the United States. [SOURCE: Castro and Boswell, "The Dominican Diaspora Revisited."]

DOMINICAN STUDIES INSTITUTE

The Dominican Studies Institute began as a pilot program in 1992 and was officially accredited as an organized research unit two years later at City University of New York (CUNY) after Dominicans in New York from both the community and academia urged CUNY Chancellor W. Ann Reynolds to create a research unit devoted to the mission of gathering, producing, and disseminating data on the experience of their people in the United States and elsewhere. Dominicans, they pointed out, represented one of the city's largest ethnic communities. Chancellor Reynolds agreed that such a program was necessary. Despite sizable numbers of Dominicans were enrolled at CUNY, only two Dominicans then held permanent positions on the university faculty, and few classes existed that dealt with the Dominican experience, either in the United States or back in the homeland.

Historian Frank Moya Pons from Hostos Community College was loaned to CUNY to begin organizing the studies program and, in February 1994, the CUNY Board of Trustees formally approved the research unit that would become the Dominican Studies Institute (DSI). Since its inception, the DSI has sponsored a number of well-attended conferences, symposia, and panels on social science and humanities topics. Invited guests have included Haiti's president Jean Bertrand Aristide and former Dominican president Juan Bosch. The institute has been inducted into the Inter-University Program for Latino Research, a nationwide consortium of thirteen major university-based Latino research enterprises, headquartered at the University of Notre Dame. In addition, it serves as a residency site for the Rockefeller Foundation Humanities Fellowships program; through this program, DSI hosted ten resident scholars between 1996 and 1999. In addition, the DSI has initiated a publications program. One of the most notable publications is *Dominican Republic: A National History* (1995), by the leading Dominican historian, Frank Moya Pons. It is the first major Dominican history in English to appear in more than sixty years. [SOURCE:http://www.ccny.cuny.edu/dsi/about.htm]

DOMINICAN WOMEN'S DEVELOPMENT CENTER

The Dominican Women's Development Center began in 1988 in the Washington Heights section of New York City with the goal to improve conditions for Dominican women in that area. According to Rosita Romero, director of center in 2001, "We wanted to have a more equal role with the men in our community." During its inception, the organization operated with nine volunteers and a budget of $30. Today, with 25 paid employees and a budget of $1 million, the center offers women education, empowerment and support programs, English-language classes, a personal development and information technology program, as well as domestic violence programs. Of the four Dominican organizations in Washington Heights, the center is the only one headed by a woman. [SOURCE: *The Brown Daily Herald*, (25 Ap. 2001), http://www.cuny.edu/events/cunymatters/2001_winter/dominicanstudies.htm; http//portal.cuny.edu/portal/site/cuny/?.&epi_menuItemID=879]

DOMINICANS 2000

In 1996, a group of Dominicans met at the City University of New York to discuss forming an organization to formulate strategies to resolve issues and problems facing the Dominican community in the United States. In February 2000, "Dominicans 2000: Building Our National Agenda" was created. In the subsequent months, participants at the summit met in diverse forums to began fulfilling the goals established. Dominicans 2000 has now become a nonprofit organization that creates networks, organizes forums, and forms committees to conduct research and implement programs throughout the Dominican community. [SOURCE: http://dominicans2000.org/d2000/history.html]

DRYING OUT

A program in the 1940s and 1950s, providing documentation and thus legal status to many undocumented immigrants, was referred to as "Drying Out." The program was created out of concerns on both sides of the border about increasing mistreatment of undocumented immigrants as their numbers grew precipitously in this era. United States' authorities returned undocumented workers to Mexico, where they were given contracts that allowed them back into the United States. By the end of 1950, more than 200,000 Mexicans legitimized their status in this way. Opponents criticized the program because they believed it encouraged Mexicans to cross the border illegally in hopes that they would subsequently receive the opportunity to become a legitimate immigrant. Proponents, on the other hand, indicated that the program sought to protect the rights of undocumented workers. [SOURCE: Meier and Rivera, *Dictionary of Mexican American History*, 122.]

DUAL WAGE SYSTEM: THE "MEXICAN RATE"

Wage discrimination in the mining industry, which paid Mexicans a lower "Mexican rate," was finally recognized by the government and abolished. The International Union of Mine, Mill and Smelter Workers-CIO proved its charges before the National War Labor Board that three large mining companies classified employees as "Anglo-American Males" and "Other Employees." Included in the latter classification were all females, Latin Americans,

Negroes, Filipinos, and Indians. When a Mexican with no experience was hired, he was classified as a "common laborer" and paid $5.21 per day; an Anglo with no experience was classified as a "helper" and paid $6.36. In addition, "Other Employees" rarely got wage increases, receiving for as much as ten years their initial rate of pay. The board ordered the elimination of the discriminatory rates. Nevertheless, workers had to strike throughout the Southwest in 1946 because the companies had been stalling in implementing the labor board's orders. [SOURCE: McWilliams, *North from Mexico*, 197-8.]

THE EAST LOS ANGELES COMMUNITY UNION

One of the most well-endowed community initiatives started during the Chicano Movement* was The East Los Angeles Community Union (TELACU), which still exists. After the high school walkouts gained national publicity, the United Auto Workers (UAW) union and some other labor groups financed the formation of TELACU, officially incorporated in 1968. It first provided economic development inside the barrios and assisted self-help groups in obtaining funding. This experiment stemmed from a UAW policy inspired by its long-time president, Walter Reuther, to help stem the deterioration of inner cities. The two UAW officials, Esteban Torres and Glen O'Loane, chosen to administer TELACU were at first met with suspicion by traditional organizations and even new ones, such as the Brown Berets.* But when it became clear that they controlled many of the resources necessary to deal with East Los Angeles' problems, the two union men were accommodated into the fold.

With funding from outside unions, TELACU extended its activities to include crime-prevention, drug-abuse counseling and, at one point, even taking over an ailing mattress factory. Eventually, millions of dollars were dispersed through the organization, and Torres became a political king-maker. Some of the more idealistic radicals never accommodated to what they called "poverty pimping," but more often funds from the group brought it widespread allegiance and it came to dominate East Los Angeles social activism.

Among the TELACU clients was a group called LUCHA, which delivered drug rehabilitation. Many of the participants in this organization were hardened ex-convicts led by Eduardo "Mo" Aguirre, who many activists felt was an unsavory enforcer for TELACU administrators. Over the years, TELACU became involved in political issues, including the 1974-attempt to incorporate East Los Angeles. The organization received large-scale funding from the federal Office of Economic Opportunity, which allowed it to expand its vast empire even further—in 1985 TELACU's assets were valued at eighty million dollars. Today, some of the organization's services include helping small businesses, raising scholarship funds, maintaining senior citizen services, and providing adult education. [SOURCE: Chávez, *Eastside Landmark*; http://www.picced.org/cdc-telacu.php]

EASTSIDE INTERCAMBIOS

East Los Angeles activists, in 1995, formed a committee to address and ameliorate issues and social problems related to children, youth, and families in the community. The committee established a mechanism to fulfill these objectives and called it the "Eastside Intercambios." The strategy employed by Intercambios was to improve networking opportunities for the large number of care-giving projects in Los Angeles. Through the project they could share current information about events and expand resources within the city that were designed to improve service delivery. [SOURCE: http://clnet.sscnet.ucla.edu/community/intercambios]

EL ECO DEL PACÍFICO

After California was annexed by the United States, San Francisco was able to support a number of Spanish-language newspapers, including the two dailies *El Eco del Pacífico* and *El Tecolote* (1875–1879). The ownership and editorship of many of these papers was made up of immigrants from Spain, Chile, Colombia, and Mexico. The largest of these was *El Eco del Pacífico*, which had grown out of a Spanish-language page of the French-language newspaper *L'Echo du Pacifique* and had become independent in 1856 under the editorship of José Marcos Mugarrieta. San Francisco's Spanish-language newspapers covered news of the homeland, which varied from coverage of Spain and Chile to Central America and Mexico, and generally assisted the immigrants in adjusting to the new environment. Very closely reported on was the French Intervention in Mexico, with various of the newspapers supporting fund-raising events for the war effort and aid for widows and orphans, in addition to working with the local Junta Patriótica Mexicana, even printing *in toto* the long speeches made at the Junta's meetings. The newspapers reported on discrimination and persecution of Hispanic miners and generally saw the defense of the Hispanic *colonia* to be a priority, denouncing abuse of Hispanic immigrants and natives. Hispanic readers in the Southwest were acutely aware of racial issues in the United States and sided with the North during the Civil War, which also was extensively covered in the newspapers. [SOURCE Kanellos, *Hispanic Periodicals in the United States*, 33-34.]

ECONOMIC OPPORTUNITY ACT

Pegged to President Lyndon B. Johnson's* "War on Poverty," the Economic Opportunity Act of 1964 created the Volunteers In Service To America (VISTA) and the Job Corps. VISTA assigned volunteers to low-income

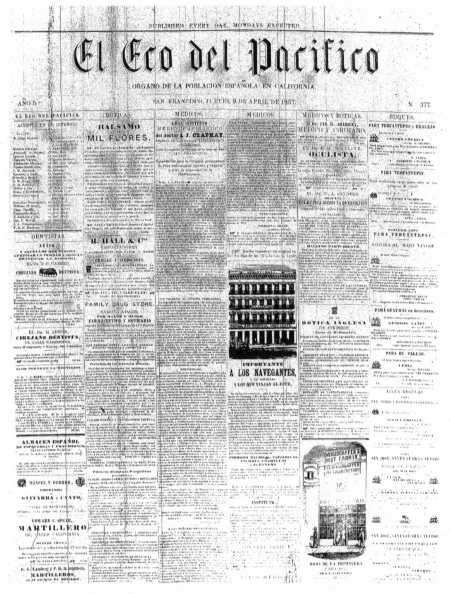

El Eco del Pacífico

areas to engage in community-action projects. The Job Corps recruited young people, native to these areas, to work in public projects. Both programs helped Mexican Americans improve their economic and social position and ironically provided young idealists, often with a bent for leftist politics, to conduct work they might have done anyway. [SOURCE: Meier and Rivera, *Dictionary of Mexican American History*, 123.]

EDICIONES UNIVERSAL

Cuban emigrés arrived in such large numbers after the Cuban Revolution of 1959 that their weight precipitated the establishment of their own publishing houses. Many of the exiles were scholars, poets, novelists, but as cut off as they were from Spanish-language outlets back home, they found the need for a vehicle to circulate their works before a wide audience in the United States and in the rest of the Spanish-speaking world. In 1965, Juan Manuel Salvat, one of the many members of the Cuban intelligentsia now in Miami, founded Ediciones Universal to publish the literary and scholarly works of leading emigré intellectuals, as well as classics of Cuban history, art, and literature. To this day, his bookstore, the Librería Universal on Calle Ocho, serves as a gathering place for artists and writers of the community. [SOURCE: García, *Havana USA,* 195.]

EDUCATIONAL ISSUES COORDINATING COMMITTEE

On March 1, 1968, high school students walked out of their classes to dramatize what they considered the abysmally poor educational facilities of the East Los Angeles schools, which were predominantly Mexican American. A committee of parents and other concerned citizens formed the Emergency Support Committee* to support the students. Less than a month after the first walkout, the Emergency Support Committee became the Educational Issues Coordinating Committee (EICC), led by the Reverend Vahac Mardirosian,* a Baptist minister born in Mexico of Armenian heritage. The EICC brought many groups of activists together to discuss educational issues. The group drafted a list of demands and presented it to the school board. The list asked for a relevant cultural curriculum, the training of teachers in local conditions, and the hiring of more Mexican Americans. After determining that the school board was not doing enough, a group of 800 members of the EICC marched through the school board's offices. Several weeks later, EICC members marched through local schools in protest. Eventually in June, thirteen EICC members were arrested for conspiring to incite riots; they became known as the L.A. Thirteen. The EICC mobilized and protested the arrests. Later, the EICC undertook a sit-in at the school board when the school district would not reinstate Sal Castro,* a teacher indicted as part of the L.A. Thirteen. The EICC launched another sit-in until, finally in September, the school board voted to reinstate Castro. The fate of the L.A. Thirteen was a criminal court matter, but eventually they were all acquitted of any wrongdoing. [SOURCE: Rosales, *Chicano!,* 191-4; Marín, *Social Protest in an Urban Barrio,* 75-80.]

EDUCATIONAL OPPORTUNITY PROGRAM

The University of California system created the Educational Opportunity Program (EOP) in 1964 to accomplish three goals. First, it sought to provide support to students who might not pursue higher education because of socio-economic reasons. Second, the program tried to increase the number of students from underrepresented ethnic and socioeconomic groups. Finally, it attempted to increase the university system's cultural diversity. Ironically, the program recruited hundreds of Chicano* students in the late 1960s, many who provided a foundation for the Chicano Student Movement,* which in turn made even greater demands on California universities. Universities in other states emulated EOP and, in different guises, these programs still exist. In California, EOP still operates, often in conjunction with other minority recruitment and retention programs. [SOURCE: Meier and Rivera, *Dictionary of Mexican American History*, 125; http://chi.ucdavis.edu/Debvargascvr.html]

ELEMENTARY AND SECONDARY EDUCATION ACT

The Elementary and Secondary Education Act (ESEA) of 1965 authorized federal funding as part of the mandate of the 1964 Civil Rights Act. The funds were targeted at school districts striving to raise the achievement level of youths from disadvantaged backgrounds. Throughout the country, Hispanic community groups who represented this target population began to urge local education officials to take advantage of this funding to better the schooling opportunities for Hispanic children. [SOURCE: Donato, *The Other Struggle for Equal Schools*, 54.]

ELEVENTH US-CUBA FRIENDSHIPMENT CARAVAN

Organized by the Interreligious Foundation for Community Organization (IFCO)/Pastors for Peace* on November 2, 2000, the 11th US/Cuba Friendshipment Caravan crossed the border into Mexico. It carried a cargo of humanitarian aid, which was shipped to Cuba via the port city of Tampico, Mexico. According to the Rev. Lucius Walker, founder and director of IFCO/Pastors for Peace, this activity served as a direct challenge to the U.S. blockade of Cuba. Nine brightly decorated vehicles carried 50 people from across the United States. Participants from Quebec, Great Britain, and Germany gave the Friendshipment Caravan an international flavor. Most of these individuals were working in their own countries to change U.S. policy toward Cuba and support the people there. The shipment consisted of medical supplies, medical equipment, solar panels for generating electricity, computers, and educational materials. The vehicles themselves, ambulances and several large and small school buses, were also donated to the Cuban people. [SOURCE: http://www.ifconews.org]

EL MEXICANO PREPARADO, LISTO, EDUCADO Y ORGANIZADO

Founded in 1966, El Mexicano Preparado, Listo, Educado y Organizado (The Prepared, Ready, Educated, and Organized Mexican-EMPLEO) served to prepare San Quentin inmates for post-internment employment. EMPLEO also sought to foster cultural awareness and cultivate an obligation to La Raza. After several attempts, EMPLEO achieved bilingual education within prison to assist in rehabilitating inmates. [SOURCE: Meier and Rivera, *Dictionary of Mexican American History*, 125-126.]

EL MONTE BERRY STRIKE

The El Monte Berry Strike in 1933, possibly the largest agricultural strike up to that point in history, was led by Mexican unions in California. In June, members of the Mexican Farm Labor Union, an affiliate of the Confederación de Uniones Obreras Mexicanas (CUOM),* officially sanctioned the strike and called for a 25-cent per hour minimum wage. The strike spread from Los Angeles County to Orange County, and the union grew rapidly. In June, the strike ended with the concession of a small increase in wages and recognition of the CUOM. That same year, CUOM became the largest and most active agricultural union in California. In 1935, CUOM was responsible for six of the eighteen strikes in California agriculture and also was effective in winning negotiations without striking. In 1936, CUOM was a leader in establishing the Federation of Agricultural Workers Union of America. By the end of the 1930s, however, CUOM's power waned in the face of increased resistance from the growers, legislators, and because of jurisdictional disputes between the AFL and the CIO, as well as a surplus of workers. [SOURCE: McWilliams, *North from Mexico*, 191.]

EL PASO COUNTY JAIL FIRE

In March of 1916, two months after the Santa Ysabel massacre,* a mass execution of Anglo-American engineers by Villistas in Chihuahua, someone lit a cigarette as convicts bathed with gasoline to get rid of lice at the El Paso county jail. The subsequent explosion engulfed the jail in flames and nine convicts died. The El Paso mayor blamed the prisoners for negligence, but the Mexican community suspected that someone intentionally set the fire to avenge the Villista atrocities. [SOURCE: Rosales, *Pobre Raza!*, 158.]

EMERGENCY SUPPORT COMMITTEE

The Emergency Support Committee was formed after Chicano* students in East Los Angeles high schools walked out of their classes in March 1968. Students were demanding a revamping of the educational system, which was not responsive to the needs of the predominantly Mexican-American student body. They demanded more Mexican-American educators, access to bilingual education, and removal of racist educators. The planners were all young people, many not yet out of their teens; none were over thirty. Parents and other community adults supported their efforts and formed the support committee, consisting of about 25 parents of students arrested in the blowouts. They raised bond money for bail and legal defense and later formed the Chicano Legal Defense Fund as a more permanent vehicle to pay for legal fees as the movement gained momentum. Another offshoot of this initiative was the Educational Issues Coordinating Committee (EICC),* which dealt with the issues in a more proactive fashion. By the end of 1968, the EICC had gained several hundred members. [SOURCE: Rosales, *Chicano!*, 191; Marín, *Social Protest in an Urban Barrio*, 86.]

ENVIRONMENTAL RACISM

The intentional placing of hazardous waste sites, landfills, incinerators, and polluting industries in communities inhabited mainly by the most defenseless members of society has been a common policy pursued by private sector and governmental agencies, according to the study *Toxic Wastes and Race in the United States* (Commission for Racial Justice, United Church of Christ 1987). While working-class whites are often affected, the study found that race was the most significant variable associated with the location of hazardous waste sites. As a result, the greatest number of commercial hazardous facilities are located in communities with the highest composition of African Americans, Hispanics, Native Americans, Asians, and migrant farmworkers. Moreover, the study showed that it is twice as likely that ethnic minorities live in the midst of commercial hazardous waste. According to Irwin Weintraub, a bibliographer at Brooklyn College:

The report indicated that three out of every five Black and Hispanic Americans lived in communities with one or more toxic waste sites. Over 15 million African-Americans, over 8 million Hispanics, and about 50 percent of Asian/Pacific Islanders and Native Americans are living in communities with one or more abandoned or uncontrolled toxic waste sites.

According to civil rights activists striving for environmental justice, a reason why the working poor and minorities are particularly vulnerable is that decision makers see them as weak and passive, unwilling or unable to fight back against the poisoning of their neighborhoods for fear of compromising their economic survival if jobs are lost. [SOURCE: Weintraub, "Fighting Enviromental Racism."]

EQUAL EDUCATIONAL OPPORTUNITY ACT

The U.S. Congress passed the Equal Educational Opportunity Act of 1974 to create equality in public schools by making bilingual education available to Hispanic youth. It also expanded bilingual education by financing the preparation of bilingual teachers and the development of curriculum. [SOURCE: Kanellos, *Chronology of Hispanic American History*, 260.]

EQUAL EMPLOYMENT OPPORTUNITY COMMISSION

Founded in 1964 as a corollary to the Civil Rights Act passed by Congress in 1964, the Equal Employment Opportunity Commission (EEOC) was designed to prevent employment discrimination. The act was signed by President Lyndon B. Johnson* as a part of the his "Great Society" effort to correct the large number of social ills that adversely affected poor people and minorities. Since then, the EEOC has been given by Congress the authority to investigate discrimination claims, to create conciliation programs, to file lawsuits, and to create voluntary assistance programs. Still in existence today, the watchdog agency continues to enforce a range of federal statutes prohibiting employment discrimination. In 1966, Mexican-American leaders walked out of an EEOC hearing, claiming that the newly created unit had disregarded employment discrimination that affected their ethnic group. As a consequence, by the late 1970s, all branches of the federal government and most state governments had taken at least some action to fulfill the promise of equal protection under the law. The EEOC has helped minorities and women eliminate some discrimination based on race and sex. At the same time, the EEOC has come under attack by conservatives who feel that the agency is no longer needed and that it promotes reverse discrimination. [SOURCE: http://www.eeoc.gov/abouteeoc/35th/history/index.html; Bovard, "The EEOC's War on Fairness."]

ESCALANTE, JAIME (1931-)

Born in Bolivia in 1931, Jaime Escalante was the first Hispanic teacher to become the subject of a Hollywood feature film: *Stand and Deliver*. The film narrates the story of how Escalante was able to teach advanced mathematics at an impoverished inner-city school in East Los Angeles, Garfield High, and prepare its students so well that they continuously were admitted to some of the most elite universities in the country to major in math and science. Escalante taught at Garfield from 1974 to 1990. Known as one of the nation's top educators, Escalante received the White House Hispanic Heritage Award in 1989 and the American Institute for Public Service Jefferson Award in 1990. In 1988, Escalante was also the subject of a book that classified his excellence on the national level: *Jaime Escalante: The Best Teacher in America*. [SOURCE: Tardiff and Mabunda, *Dictionary of Hispanic Biography*, 308-11.]

Jaime Escalante

ESCOBAR, ELEUTERIO (1894-1970)

Born in Laredo, Texas, Eleuterio Escobar was a prominent San Antonio businessman and president of La Liga Pro-Defensa Escolar (The School Improvement League), a civic organization dedicated to equal education for Mexican-American children. His own education ended at age 13 after the death of his father, when he went to work to help support his family. After a considerable time as salesman, Escobar started his own successful business, but never forgot the plight of Mexican-American children that he saw throughout Texas in his travels. He and other members of La Liga Pro-Defensa Escolar recognized that segregation was detrimental to their children. They often accepted that it was impossible to immediately obtain desegregation, so they strove to improve the existing facilities. [SOURCE: http://www.pbs.org/kpbs/theborder/history/timeline/16.html]

ESCOBAR, ELIZAM (1948-)

Elizam Escobar was arrested in Evanston, Illinois, with eleven other Puerto Ricans on April 2, 1980, and sentenced to 68 years in a federal prison for seditious conspiracy against the United States because of his involvement in the Armed Forces of the Puerto Rican National Liberation (FALN), an avowed anti-imperialist organization which supported independence from the United States. His supporters, however, consider that his only crime was being one of long line of Puerto Ricans resisting U.S.-government control of their nation's sovereignty. Escobar was born in Ponce, Puerto Rico, in 1948. He studied art in both Puerto Rico and New York, where he worked as a teacher at the Museo del Barrio, in public schools, and as a graphic artist with the Hispanic Artists' Association. Escobar has been incarcerated in prisons in Wisconsin and Oklahoma, and efforts to serve his time nearer to his family, in New York and Puerto Rico, consistently have been denied. While in prison, Escobar has continued writing and painting and had exhibits of his paintings in Puerto Rico, the United States, Latin America, and Europe. He also published articles widely on art and politics in magazines in Canada, England, Italy, Latin America, and the United States. Admirers consider Escobar to be one of the most important Puerto Rican revolutionary painters and poets. His release date was to be 2014, but President Bill Clinton released him in 2003 before leaving office. [SOURCE: http://prisonactivist.org/ppstpows/elizam-escobar.html]

ESCOBEDO V. ILLINOIS

In 1964, Chicago police arrested Danny Escobedo and accused him of murdering his sister's husband. At the police station, they questioned him for several hours, despite his repeated requests to see his lawyer, Barry Kroll, who also sought unsuccessfully for hours to consult with his client. Escobedo subsequently confessed to murder. After Escobedo's conviction, Kroll led a team of lawyers in appealing the conviction to the Illinois State Supreme Court. They lost that appeal, but the case reached the U.S. Supreme Court, where his lawyers argued that Escobedo had been denied the right to counsel, as guaranteed by the Sixth Amendment. In the majority opinion, Supreme Court Justice Ruth Bader Goldberg wrote that Escobedo had not been adequately informed of his constitutional right to remain silent and, instead, had been forced to incriminate himself. Over the years, the case lost authority as a precedent. Now the constitutionality of police interrogation and confession cases have shifted from the Sixth Amendment to the Fifth; the emphasis is now on whether the appropriate and correct warnings have been given and whether the right to remain silent has been waived. [SOURCE: http://www.oyez.org/oyez/resource/case/113]

ESCUELITA BORIKÉN

Founded in 1993, Escuelita Borikén provides a multi-cultural and bilingual pre-school program that results in quality early education to 80 children in Boston's Villa Victoria and the surrounding communities. The Escuelita's pedagogical philosophy is to enhance the physical, social, linguistic, cultural, and cognitive development of children. Accredited by the National Association for the Education of Young Children (NAEYC), the Escuelita partners with Child Care Choices of Boston, the South End Health Center and JUMPSTART. The Massachusetts Department of Education in its comprehensive review of the pre-school reported that "Escuelita Borikén is a great example of a high-quality, successful early childhood program that fosters the development of language skills." [SOURCE: http://www.iba-etc.org/pdf/Annual%20Report.pdf]

ESCUELITAS MEXICANAS

Both Mexican immigrant communities and the Mexican government went to great lengths to preserve the language and culture of Mexican immigrants in the United States. In January 1928, Margarita Robles y Mendoza of the Mexican Ministry of Education toured the southwestern United States to promote Mexican community schools, known as *escuelitas*, most of which were established in California and Texas. To promote the effort, Mexican Chamber of Deputies representative from Oaxaca, Alfonso Ramírez, toured various Mexican immigrant settlements in the United States supposedly to investigate immigrant problems, but his visit really was to reinforce the intensive effort by the Mexican Ministry of Education in promoting Mexicaness. In February 1928, he assured immigrants that their children were still considered Mexican citizens and said parents should discourage Americanization.

The intitiative continued into later years. In Phoenix, local immigrant leaders and Mexican consul Manuel Payno inaugurated La Escuela Mexicana in 1930 with much fanfare during the Cinco de Mayo festivities. Payno was so enthusiastic, he obtained certification from the Arizona Department of Education. Thirty children were enrolled during summer vacation and Payno himself taught Mexican Geography and Mexican History, while volunteer Rosendo Serna taught reading and writing in both languages. [SOURCE: Rosales, *Chicano!*, 191.]

ESPARZA, FRANCISCA (1883-1962)

Francisca Esparza, a member of an old Tejano family, pursued a fierce court battle in the 1940s and 1950s to regain Spanish and Mexican land grants in Texas belonging to her family and other families. Her efforts were unsuccessful. [SOURCE: Meier and Rivera, *Dictionary of Mexican American History*, 132.]

EXILE PRESS AND LATIN AMERICAN IMMIGRANTS IN THE UNITED STATES

An exile press is one that utilizes the vantage point and the protection of foreign soil to issue messages unwelcome to authorities in the homeland. The United States, having established itself as the first political democracy in the Western Hemisphere, has served since its independence from the British Empire as a refuge for expatriates from Latin America and Spain. The important tenets in the U.S. Constitution guaranteeing freedom of speech and of the press ensured that editors who could afford paper and printing would see their work in print, ready to be distributed to whichever communities, domestic, and foreign, they could reach. But the *raison d'etre* of the exile press has always been influencing life and politics in the homeland—even if that goal is moved forward only by distributing publications to expatriate communities. These efforts—to provide information and opinion about the homeland, to change or solidify opinion about politics and policy in the *patria*, to assist in raising funds to overthrow the current regime—although mostly discussed within the confines of U.S. communities, nevertheless maintain a foreign point of reference. A purely immigrant or an ethnic press, on the other hand, is more oriented to the needs of immigrants and/or citizens in the United States: to assisting immigrants in adjusting to the new social environment here, understanding or affecting policy here, providing information on the homeland and/or securing and furthering rights and responsibilities here.

To study the Hispanic exile press in the United States is to examine great moments in the political history of the Hispanic world: the Napoleonic intervention in Spain, the struggles of the Spanish-American colonies for independence, the French intervention in Mexico, the Spanish American War,* the Mexican Revolution, the Spanish Civil War, the Cuban Revolution, the recent civil wars in Central America and the numerous struggles in Latin

America to wrest democracy from dictators and foreign interventions, including incursions by the United States. The very act of U.S. partisanship in the internal politics of the Latin American republics often drew the expatriate stream to these shores. All of these struggles contributed thousands of political refugees to the United States over time, not only because of the traditions of democracy and freedom of expression here, but also because through expansion and Hispanic immigration, the United States became home to large communities of Spanish-speakers. Thus, the refugees found societies where they could conduct business and eke out a livelihood while they hoped for and abetted change in the lands that would someday welcome them home.

The flip side of the coin of freedom in exile is the repression that existed in the homelands that forced intellectuals and writers out. The historical record is rife with prison terms served, tortures suffered, and the names of writers, journalists, publishers, and editors executed over the last two centuries in Spain and Spanish America. At home, many newspaper editors devised ingenious stratagems for hiding presses and hiding the identity of the writers while smuggling issues to readers in secret societies and the privacy of their homes. In Cuba, books and newspapers often stated on their title pages and mastheads that they were published in New Orleans, attempting to throw off the censor and the repressive Spanish authorities.

The first newspapers printed in exile were the bilingual *La Gaceta de Texas* and *El Mexicano*, printed in 1813 in the safety of U.S. territory just across the border from New Spain in Natchitoches, Louisiana (just across the Sabine River from Nacogdoches, Texas). Actually written and typeset in Texas by its publishers William Shaler and José Alvarez de Toledo y Dubois, but printed in Louisiana, both papers were part of the independence movement set in motion by Miguel de Hidalgo y Costilla in central Mexico and taken up by José Bernardo Gutiérrez de Lara in Texas. The insurgency in Texas was violently quashed by Spanish royalist troops. [SOURCE: Kanellos, *Hispanic Periodicals in the United States,* 8-27.]

EXPATRIATE MANIFESTO TO THE MEXICAN GOVERNMENT

On March 30, 2005, Asociación Tepeyac,* the largest organization that offers protection to Mexican immigrants in New York City, joined with expatriate Mexican students and workers in an endeavor to obtain a voice in the political process back home. The group sent Mexican president Vicente Fox and the Mexican Congress a manifesto protesting the repressive actions taken against Mexico City mayor and Partido Revolucionario Demócrata (PRD) presidential candidate, Andrés Manuel López Obrador. The mayor faced a jail sentence for malfeasance in public office, which his supporters say is trumped up by opposition politicians. The effort which replicated an ongoing nationwide emigré movement also wants to obtain the vote for Mexicans abroad, a concession they claim is opposed by conservative forces who do not want López Obrador to run for president in 2006. Similar manifestos were proclaimed on the same day by expatriate groups in Chicago, Atlanta, Los Angeles, and Houston. [SOURCE: Brooks, "Desafuero a López Obrador y comicios en el extranjero."]

FAIR EMPLOYMENT PRACTICES COMMITTEE

The federal government recognized the need to protect "minorities" from job discrimination before the advent of affirmative action. America's first federal equal employment agency was President Franklin D. Roosevelt's 1941-45 Fair Employment Practices Committee (FEPC). An executive order created this commission to investigate incidents of discrimination in employment by private companies with federal contracts. President Roosevelt acted in response to a threat by black civil rights leader, A. Philip Randolph, that he would organize a massive march on Washington D.C. to protest the exclusion of African Americans from defense industry jobs.

The committee had the authority to take measures to abolish discriminatory practices. President Roosevelt appointed Carlos Castañeda,* an historian from Texas, to be a special assistant to the FEPC. Although President Harry S. Truman tried to make the committee permanent, the FEPC was dissolved at the end of the World War II. Senator Dennis Chávez* attempted to make employment discrimination illegal in 1944, he introduced the first Fair Employment Practices bill, but the conservative majority in Congress voted it down. Many states organized similar versions of the FEPC. Congress resurrected a similar program with the Equal Employment Opportunity Commission* in the 1960s. The FEPC had a positive impact in improving the plight of minorities in the workforce. [SOURCE: Carrasco, "Law and Politics," 269.]

FALCÓN, RICARDO (1946-1972)

A member of the Denver Crusade for Justice,* Ricardo Falcón was shot on his way to El Paso to attend the first La Raza Unida Convention in 1972. In Oro Grande, New Mexico, Falcón argued with Perry Brunson, a service station attendant, over Falcón's attempt to spray water on an overheated radiator. In the melée, Brunson shot Falcón, who died almost immediately from his wounds. A self-proclaimed segregationist who belonged to George Wallace's American Independent Party, Brunson was acquitted of murder but six years later he was killed by an unknown assailant. [SOURCE: Rosales, *Chicano!*, 205.]

FANTASY HERITAGE

"Fantasy heritage" is a term coined by Carey McWilliams* in his highly regarded book, *North from Mexico*. According to McWilliams, Mexican Americans highlighted the Spanish background of the Southwest and their own identity while ignoring or hiding their Mexican, mestizo, or Amerindian heritage and/or identity, because being Spanish was more socially acceptable in a racist United States. The "fantasy heritage" emphasized that families of the old Southwest were of pure Spanish heritage, unlike the mixed-race people of later immigrant generations. In addition, Anglos perpetuated this myth as a tool for subordinating Hispanic peoples. Critics of nineteenth-century Southwest Hispanics have probably overstated adherence to the "fantasy heritage," confusing class prejudice with the desire to ingratiate themselves with Anglos. Many of the elites who allegedly cow-towed to Anglo whims were also responsible for resisting Anglo cultural domination and continuing Mexican cultural heritage in the Southwest. [SOURCE: Rosales, "'Fantasy Heritage' Re-examined," 83-106; McWilliams, *North from Mexico*, 44.]

THE FEDERAL BUREAU OF INVESTIGATION AND PUERTO RICAN INDEPENDENCE ACTIVISTS

According to activists involved in the campaign for Puerto Rican independence, the Federal Bureau of Investigation (FBI) has for decades targeted unionists and civil rights activists in a campaign of harassment and victimization. This became evident in the 1970s when the FBI released documents from the Puerto Rican Senate investigation of the 1978 Cerro Maravilla Case,* where two young independence activists were killed by Puerto Rican policemen. According to the critics of this law enforcement procedure, local government officials attempted a cover-up with the complicity of the FBI. In May 2000, FBI director Louis Freeh delivered thousands of previously classified documents to the offices of Congressman José Serrano. These files, 8,600 pages worth, were released in response to Serrano's concern over the massive opposition among Puerto Ricans, both on the island and the mainland, to U.S. military target practice in Vieques, Puerto Rico and the campaign for the release of pro-independence political prisoners.

A *New York Daily News* reporter reviewed the papers and discovered that the FBI had been engaged since 1936 in surveillance and repression of the pro-independence elements. The focus of the surveillance was the Puerto Rico Nationalist Party, in particular Pedro Albizu Campos,* the party's central leader. The documents have A. Cecil Snyder, the U.S. District Attorney in Puerto Rico, writing to J. Edgar Hoover, the FBI director, stating that Albizu Campos published "articles insulting the United States" and delivered "speeches in favor of independence." According to Snyder, Albizu Campos was possibly the author of bombings of U.S. government buildings. That year, FBI agents arrested Albizu Campos and Nationalist Party leaders on charges of conspiring to overthrow the U.S. government. Albizu Campos was sentenced to 15 years amid charges that he and his companions had been framed.

The files reveal that the FBI even had Luis Muñoz Marín,* the first elected governor of Puerto Rico, under surveillance for more than twenty years. An early advocate of independence, Muñoz Marín founded the Popular Democratic Party (PPD), which helped Washington push through the present form of colonial rule, known as commonwealth status.

In the 1960s and 1970s, the Puerto Rican independence movement often merged with the civil rights struggle waged by urban activists in such cities as New York, Philadelphia, and Chicago. The FBI's Cointelpro program sought to disrupt struggles against police brutality, the movement against drafting Puerto Ricans into the U.S. Army, the fight against the U.S. naval occupation of the Puerto Rican islands of Culebra and Vieques, and union struggles. [SOURCE: Stone, "Files Detail FBI's War on Puerto Rican Independence Fight."]

FEDERAL MIGRANT HEALTH ACT

Based on the California Migrant Health Act passed in 1962, primarily because of the efforts of social activist Florence Richardson Wyckoff, the Federal Migrant Health Act helped secure some health services for migrant workers, in some measure providing better opportunities and protection of Mexican-American migrant workers. The legislation has provided funding for medical care projects in various states, the most numerous being in California, Arizona, and Texas. The act still allows local governments to administer the programs, a process which has resulted in uneven application of the services. [SOURCE: http://library.ucsc.edu/reg-hist/wyckoff.html]

FEDERATION FOR THE ADVANCEMENT OF MEXICAN-AMERICANS

Founded in 1964, the San Antonio-based Federation for the Advancement of Mexican-Americans (FAMA) has attempted to serve as an umbrella for all individuals and organizations having as their main objectives the fostering of economic, educational, cultural, spiritual, civic, and social betterment of the Mexican-American community. FAMA has been explicit about promoting the image of the Mexican American as a patriotic, first-class American citizen with full constitutional rights and privileges. While it is interested in voting issues, FAMA does not endorse any candidate for political office nor will it endorse any political party. However, it does want to inculcate in Mexican Americans the knowledge that through the ballot box, not only will they exercise individual, political, and religious freedom, but also have a voice in fashioning public policy that will collectively benefit their interests. [SOURCE: Lane, *Voluntary Associations among Mexican Americans in San Antonio*, 72.]

FEDERATION FOR AMERICAN IMMIGRATION REFORM

Founded in 1979, Federation for American Immigration Reform (FAIR) describes its main objective as educating the American people about the tax burden and social consequences caused by mass and poorly regulated immigration. FAIR, a national public interest organization has more than 70,000 members, according to its founders, and is entirely self-supporting. The organization has offices in the nation's capitol, where staffers lobby Congress to end mass immigration and to reduce the number of entries to 200,000 persons a year, based on FAIR's assessment of the national need. FAIR activists contend that unregulated immigration has swollen U.S. population growth to unacceptable levels, has compromised the ability to establish priority goals in education and social spending, threatens to destabilize the American middle-class, and poses a threat to environmental and ecological objectives. [SOURCE: http://www.fairus.org/]

FERGUSON, GOVERNOR JAMES E. (1871-1944)

James E. Ferguson was a formidable opponent of Mexican immigration in the 1920s. He began practicing law in 1897 and was elected as governor in 1914. Impeached and removed from office in 1917 because of alleged corruption, he was banned from holding any state position. Ferguson unsuccessfully ran for federal offices after he had been acquitted of all charges. Unable to run for Texas governor, his wife Miriam Ferguson obtained the post in 1922 but failed to win again amid more charges that the Fergusons were corrupt. In the 1920s, James E. Ferguson often published tirades against Mexicans in the *Ferguson Forum* during a period in which Mexican immigrant leaders routinely objected to racist literature and negative journalism. In a particularly vitriolic issue of November 1920, he charged that Mexicans were inferior to Negroes and that Mexico had contributed nothing to civilization. Provoking this onslaught was an incident in which a Mexican had knifed a number of people on a train and was bludgeoned to death by white passengers. As a consequence, Ferguson asserted, Mexicans had no reason to be upset by segregation. Alonso S. Perales,* a political activist and World War I veteran, wrote to denounce Ferguson's diatribe in defense of Texas Mexicans and immigrants alike. *El Imparcial de Texas*,* in publishing Perales' letter, characterized him as an American who understands and loves Mexican people. "The majority of Mexicans living in Texas are law abiding, thus Ferguson's propaganda will fall on deaf ears (translated by author)," concluded the newspaper. [SOURCE: Rosales, *Pobre Raza!*, 111-112.]

FERRÉ, MAURICE (1935-)

Puerto Rican Maurice Ferré (1935-) became the first Hispanic mayor of Miami. His election in 1993 as mayor was a sign of the emergence of a Latino voting bloc in Miami. Ferré was reelected five times, but ultimately lost in 1985 to a Cuban-born candidate. During his tenure, he presided over the city's growth as an important center of international trade and banking. The wealthy businessman's electoral career had started in the mid 1960s with his election to the Miami City Council; he later served in the state legislature. [SOURCE: Henderson and Mormino, *Spanish Pathways in Florida*, 305, 308, 310-15.]

FERRER, FERNANDO (1950-)

Born in the Bronx on April 30, 1950, Ferrer was raised by his mother and his grandmother, who worked in the kitchen of the Waldorf-Astoria Hotel. After graduating from New York University on a scholarship, Ferrer became a community activist. As city council member and, later, as Bronx Borough President, Ferrer oversaw the borough's revitalization into international models of urban revival. During Ferrer's 14-year tenure as Borough President, Bronx residents saw the construction of over 66,000 affordable small homes and apartments, the addition of over 34,000 new jobs, an infusion of hundreds of new businesses, and a total investment of over $2.5 billion in institutional renewal and growth. He authored legislation that has generated hundreds of millions of dollars of investment in the city. Following his tenure as Borough President, Ferrer went on to serve as president of the Drum Major Institute for Public Policy (DMI), a progressive think tank and community action group founded in 1961 to support the civil rights leadership of Dr. Martin Luther King, Jr. Ferrer has earned wide praise for refocusing the energies of DMI to tackle problems that increasingly squeeze the working poor and the middle-class, two groups that have historically formed the backbone of the city. In 2001, Ferrer ran for the Democratic nomination for mayor. He won the first primary with 34 percent, but failed to win the necessary 40 percent to win the nomination and ultimately lost a divisive runoff election to Mark Green. [SOURCE: http://www.ferrer2005.com/main.cfm? actionId=globalShowStaticContent&screenKey=engProfile]

FESTIVAL LATINO—CUBAN EMIGRÉ PROTEST

In 1984, Joseph Papp's Festival Latino in New York City drew protest from Cuban exile intellectuals because the fete, which included music, films, and art exhibits from Cuba, excluded the contributions of Cubans in the United States. A letter signed by 80 Cuban artists and writers claimed that this was a "dangerous" demonstration of political censure. In the words of the protest, the "Festival does not have the right to use Hispanics and their culture as a shield for ideological manipulations; nor does it have the right to present to the Hispanics of this city a partial view of their own culture." The protest succeeded, and the following year Papp invited emigré actor Manuel Martín to perform at the festival; in 1986, Miami's Teatro Avance was included by Papp. Cuban exile theater was subsequently involved in the festival on a yearly basis. [SOURCE: García, *Havana USA*, 194.]

FIFTH STREET MERCHANTS ASSOCIATION

Formed in 1975, the Fifth Street Merchants Association sought to represent the interests of Latino merchants in North Philadelphia, mainly Puerto Ricans, the largest Spanish-speaking group in the area. The organization sponsored workshops and advertising promotions to foster business in the area. The Fifth Street Merchants Association also fostered measures to link merchants and the surrounding residential community. Frequently, the group lobbied the city government for improvements in municipal services such as better police protection and street repairs. [SOURCE: http://www.balchinstitute.org/manuscript_guide/html/puertorican.html]

FIRST NATIONAL CHICANO CONFERENCE

In October 1967, a convention called by Reies López Tijerina* was the first national meeting of young militants, and it "ended with the strong feeling that a new movement was being born: a movement whose birth, growth, and power is inevitable." Young Mexican-American organizers from Chicago, Colorado, New Mexico, California, and Texas, many of them students, responded to the invitation. Among these were some of the pioneers in the California Chicano Movement:* David Sánchez, Moctezuma Esparza, Carlos Montes, Carlos Muñoz,* Henry Gómez, and Armando Váldez.* At that meeting, Texan José Angel Gutiérrez* asserted that "Raza" was the best term to identify Mexican-American people—Chicano* was not yet that widespread. Also, the idea of holding a mass national meeting of Mexican-American youth was bandied around—this lead to the historical National Chicano Youth Liberation Conference* of March 1969. And finally, the concept of a Chicano political party emerged at this meeting, an idea that came to fruition with the formation of La Raza Unida Party.* Tijerina announced to the young activists that he had signed a treaty with Hopi Pueblo Indians, bonding his movement to their land struggle; the other Chicanos present pledged to do the same. In addition, the Chicano activists also committed to the black civil rights movement in a fraternal gesture to the Student Nonviolent Coordinating Committee members who were also participating. [SOURCE: Rosales, *Chicano!*, 178.]

FIRST NATIONAL CHICANO/LATINO IMMIGRATION CONFERENCE

The First National Chicano/Latino Immigration Conference was held in San Antonio in 1977. Its aim was to oppose an effort initiated by President Jimmy Carter's administration to stem illegal immigration. Unlike a typical Chicano Movement* meeting, this conference attracted every major Mexican-American organization in the country. Beside the La Raza Unida Party* members, who had taken leadership in organizing the conference, representatives from El Centro de Acción Social Autónoma-Hermandad General de Trabajadores (CASA-HGT),* the American G.I Forum,* the League of United Latin American Citizens,* the Mexican American Legal Defense Fund,* and the Southwest Voter Registration Education Project* attended. The odd mix led to extreme sectarian squabbling, however, and adjourned without reaching an accord. [SOURCE: Gutiérrez, *Walls and Mirrors,* 201.]

FLORENCE FIVE

In 1915, of the twelve men awaiting execution on death row at the Arizona State Prison in Florence—seven Americans (one was a black) and five Mexicans—four of the Mexicans were the only ones hanged. Francisco Rodríguez, Eduardo Pérez, N.B. Chávez, Miguel Peralta, and Ramón Villalobos were scheduled to be hanged for unrelated crimes on the same day in May. Juries had convicted Villalobos and Chávez of killing law officers; Rodríguez and Peralta had killed their wives. Preventing this mass execution became one of first issues of the newly organized La Liga Protectora Latina (The Latin Protective League).*

Governor George W.P. Hunt, a progressive and a foe of capital punishment, managed to postpone the executions through legal maneuvering despite his having been stripped of clemency power during the previous year's referendum. La Liga Protectora Latina and Mexican consul Ives Lelevir circulated petitions and personally met with Hunt and the parole board in Phoenix. Nonetheless, four of the condemned men were hanged in 1915 and 1916. Only Pérez, who had killed another Mexican, received a commutation from the State of Arizona Board of Paroles. In contrast, the board commuted the sentences for the seven Americans on death row. To the Mexican expatriate community, this became one of the greatest injustices perpetuated on their people. For the next ten years or so, various community groups engaged in a sustained civil rights campaign to prevent such uneven application of capital punishment. [SOURCE: Rosales, *Pobre Raza!,* 138-139.]

FLORENCE IMMIGRANT AND REFUGEE RIGHTS PROJECT

The Florence Immigrant and Refugee Rights Project is a nonprofit, community-based legal service organization which counsels and represents indigent immigrants and asylum-seekers detained in removal proceedings in local Immigration and Naturalization Service (INS)* custody. The project was created in 1989 in Florence, Arizona, in response to a plea from Immigration Judge John J. McCarrick. Judge McCarrick, concerned that indigent people in removal proceedings were in danger of having their constitutional and statutory rights disregarded, urged Phoenix-area attorneys to fill the gap in representation left by the absence of a public defender system in immigration proceedings. To remedy this crisis in representation, Attorney Christopher Brelje, supported and encouraged by his law firm, Lewis and Roca, spent a year establishing the project and then continued to serve on the Board of Directors. Two thousand people, more than 10 percent of the national detained population, are held at any given time at INS detention facilities in rural Florence and Eloy, Arizona. In addition, the Florence Project maintains a children's attorney to represent undocumented detainees under the age of eighteen in a private facility called Southwest Keys in Phoenix. Without the right to paid counsel in removal proceedings, an estimated 90 percent of people detained by the INS go unrepresented. Responding to this legal emergency, the Florence Project provides legal services to more than 10,000 people from 50 countries who are detained by the INS on a yearly basis. [SOURCE: http://www.firrp.org/about.asp]

FLORES, FRANCISCA (1913-1996)

Activist Francisca Flores was well-known for fighting for the rights of Mexican Americans in Los Angeles. Born in December 1913, in San Diego, she became politicized early in life. Before World War II broke out, she was inspired by Spanish Republicans and their resistance to Adolf Hitler, by the political positions taken by artists Diego Rivera, José Clemente Orozco, David Alfaro Siqueiros, and Pablo Piccaso. She supported Mexican president Lázaro Cárdenas' nationalization of U.S. petroleum interests in Mexico as a symbol of a poor country standing up to powerful international interests.

Flores made her greatest impact after moving to Los Angeles during the war. The roll call of activities in which Francisca was involved is remarkable. She worked on the Sleepy Lagoon case,* helped Carey McWilliams* with *North from Mexico*, edited *Carta Editorial*, which was often red-baited during the McCarthy era, helped to hide and organize underground screenings of the union-organizing movie "Salt of the Earth,"* was a co-founder of the Mexican American Political Association,* served as the editor and publisher of *Regeneración* (Regeneration), was a founder of Comisión Feminil Mexicana Nacional,* and cofounded and served as the first director of the Chicana Social Service Center in Los Angeles. She knew and was greatly respected by journalist Rubén Salazar* who was killed during the Chicano Moratorium.* Flores published a whole issue of *Regeneración* on his death, including republishing some of his key articles. She lived her life fighting for justice and equality. [SOURCE: http://clnet.sscnet.ucla.edu/research/francisca.html]

FLORES, PATRICK F. (1929-)

Born into a farmworker family in 1929 in Ganado, Texas, a small agricultural community 70 miles south of Houston, Patrick F. Flores is the first

Reverand Patrick F. Flores

Mexican American to be named a bishop of the Catholic Church. He was ordained as a priest in 1956 and served in Houston parishes until 1970, when he became auxiliary bishop of the Diocese of San Antonio, Texas; at the time he was already an important leader of the church. In 1978, he was named Bishop of the diocese of El Paso, Texas, and in 1979, he returned to San Antonio as Archbishop. The El Paso Diocese has one of the largest Hispanic-American congregations in the United States. It includes 23 counties and runs the length of the Texas-Mexican border. Bishop Flores' humble background and well-honed bilingual ability has allowed his spiritual and often secular messages to resonate among the one million Catholics in his district. Every Sunday his bilingual Mass from the Cathedral of San Fernando is televised throughout the western United States. Flores has worked for Mexican-American social justice, especially when the issues involved migrant farmworkers; his close relationship with César Chávez* and the farmworkers is an indication of this. In addition, his energies have also been directed at educational problems. In 1975, for example, he helped start the National Hispanic Scholarship Fund. [SOURCE: http://dailycatholic.org/issue/2000Jun/jun30nv1.htm]

FLORES MAGÓN, RICARDO (1874-1922)

By 1900, the most important Mexican revolutionary journalist and ideologue, Ricardo Flores Magón, had launched his newspaper *Regeneración* (Regeneration) in Mexico City and was promptly suppressed. Flores Magón was jailed four times in Mexico for his radical journalism. Following a sentence of eight months (in which the judge prohibited his reading and writing while in jail), Flores Magón went into U.S. exile; in fact, the Mexican government, backed by its supreme court, had prohibited the publication of any newspaper by Flores Magón. In 1904, he began publishing *Regeneración* in San Antonio, then in Saint Louis in 1905, and in Canada in 1906; in 1907, he founded *Revolución* in Los Angeles, and once again in 1908 revived

Regeneración there. Throughout these years, Ricardo and his brothers (Enrique and Jesús) employed any and every subterfuge possible to smuggle the newspapers from the United States into Mexico, even stuffing them into cans or wrapping them in other newspapers sent to San Luis Potosí, where they were then distributed to sympathizers throughout the country.

Along with his brothers, Ricardo Flores Magón emerged as a leader of the movement to overthrow the Porfirio Díaz regime, founding the Liberal Reformist Association in 1901. Flores Magón's approach differed in that he wedded his ideas about revolution in Mexico to the struggle of working people in the United States, and this difference in part accounted for the newspaper's popularity among Mexican and Mexican-American laborers engaged in unionizing efforts in the United States.

Ricardo Flores Magón

Pursued by Díaz's agents in San Antonio, Ricardo and Enrique moved to St. Louis, where they established the Partido Liberal Mexicano (Mexican Liberal Party), dedicated to proletarian social justice in its provision of an ideological base for the revolutionaries. They established a chain of chapters across the Southwest that spread their ideology, largely through meetings, fund-raising events, and the publication of newspapers, pamphlets, and books. By the time he moved to Los Angeles in 1907 to publish *Revolución*, Flores Magón was openly embracing anarchism and losing many of his Mexican and Mexican-American followers, who rejected his extremism.

Flores Magón and *Regeneración* were considered radical by the U.S. government, which during World War I was attempting to suppress radical politics within its borders. The weapon used by the U.S. government against the radical foreign language press was implementation by the post office of the Trading with the Enemy Act and the 1917 Espionage Act; the post office denied second-class mailing privileges to some radical newspapers on the grounds that the government would not function as "an agent in the circulation of printed matter which it regards as injurious to the people" and it otherwise refused its services to persons engaged in enemy propaganda. *Regeneración* was targeted, and Flores Magón indicted on the basis of a manifesto to anarchists and laborers of the world published in the March 16, 1918 edition. The manifesto supposedly contained false statements, interfered with U.S. military operations, incited disloyalty and mutiny, interfered with enlistment and recruiting, and violated the provisions of the Espionage Act; in addition, no English translation had been filed with the U.S. Post Office. In 1918, Ricardo Flores Magón was arrested by federal authorities for breaking the neutrality laws; he was found guilty and sentenced to twenty years in federal prison. He died at Leavenworth federal prison in 1922 of mysterious causes, some of his friends and correspondents allege that he was denied treatment for heart ailments and diabetes. [SOURCE: Kanellos, *Hispanic Periodicals in the United States*, 21-23, 22, 25; Sandos, *Rebellion in the Borderlands*.]

FLOTILLA OF LA VIRGEN DE LA CARIDAD DEL COBRE

The annual flotilla procession in honor of the patron saint of Cuba, the Virgin of Caridad del Cobre, serves the Cuban community in Miami as more than a religious observance. Held since 1960 on September 8, the statue of Mary is temporarily removed from the Ermita Shrine, placed on an elaborately decorated boat and escorted by a procession of festively decorated yachts and sailboats across Biscayne Bay to Miami Marine Stadium. An outdoor mass is then celebrated at the stadium. The pageant is politically charged with the waving of Cuban flags galore, a hymn to the Virgin (to the melody of the Cuban national anthem), and spiritual supplications for Cuba's liberation. The guest of honor list is also laden with political significance. It includes former political prisoners, heads of exile organizations, and local elected officials. The events allow emigrés to reaffirm their faith in God, their faith in themselves, and their hope for a free Cuba. [SOURCE: García, *Havana USA*, 99.]

FORAKER ACT

U.S. President William McKinley, on April 2, 1900, signed the Organic Act of 1900, establishing a civilian government in Puerto Rico, which the United States had acquired after the Spanish American War.* More commonly known as the Foraker Act for its sponsor, Charles Benson Foraker, the legislation provided the president of the United States with power to appoint the governor and an executive council. Puerto Ricans, who did not become citizens of the United States until 1917, could vote and elect the 35 members of the House of Representatives. Also, the act created a judicial system with a Supreme Court and a non-voting Resident Commissioner in the U.S. Congress. With the enactment of the legislation, Puerto Ricans had to abide by the federal laws of the United States. President McKinley appointed Charles H. Allen as the first civilian governor of the island. He was inaugurated on May 1, 1900 in San Juan, Puerto Rico. In 1917, Congress amended the Foraker Act through the Jones Act,* providing U.S. citizenship to Puerto Ricans and a greater measure of self-government. [SOURCE: http://www. loc.gov/rr/hispanic/1898/foraker.html]

FORD FOUNDATION

Founded by automobile industrialists, Henry and Edsel in 1936, to support charitable and educational institutions in their home state of Michigan, in 1950 the foundation from its new New York headquarters began to provide grants on a national and international level. Since 1964, the Ford Foundation, a philanthropic institution, has been the most involved in Latino affairs. In its first year, it provided the University of California at Los Angeles a large grant for a research project on Mexican Americans. The researchers, Leo Grebler, Joan Moore, and Ralph Guzmán, produced eleven advanced reports and one book. The Ford Foundation also helped establish HELP (Home, Education, Livelihood Project), The National Council of La Raza* and the Mexican American Legal Defense and Educational Fund (MALDEF).* The foundation has also funded the Puerto Rican Legal Defense and Education Fund (PRLDEF)* since its inception in 1972; its main goal is to protect the civil and human rights of Puerto Ricans and the wider Latino community. In the field of education, the foundation has until the present supported hundreds of Latino students in graduate schools by providing fellowships to support studies or dissertation research that lead to a doctorate. In these and various other programs, the Ford Foundation has had the most impact of any foundation on the life and culture of minorities on the United States. [SOURCE: http://www.fordfound.org/global/office/index.cfm?office=Cairo#history; Samora and Simon, *A History of the Mexican-American People,* 241; http://www.jsri.msu.edu/museum/pubs/MexAmHist/chapter22.html]

FOREIGN MINERS' LICENSE TAX (1850-51)

During the Gold Rush, anti-Mexican sentiment was so strong in California that in 1850 the state legislature passed the Foreign Miners' License Tax, which levied a charge of 20 dollars a month to non-citizens of the United States in order to be eligible to stake out claims. This became one of the most onerous laws affecting Hispanics. French, Australian, and Irish immigrants were lured to the gold fields, but Mexicans and other Hispanic Americans, who possessed superior mining skills, felt the brunt of this levy. The legislation brought all sorts of trouble. Compelling miners to pay the tax proved difficult and protecting the rights of those who did pay was negligible. Accordingly, most miners avoided payment. The high tax, as well as persecution by vigilantes, encouraged most Mexicans and Mexican Americans to leave the mines. Several Spanish-speaking miners, however, were lynched or murdered by vigilantes.

Even though the tax was repealed the following year, the damage had been done. Moreover, the purpose of the tax was fulfilled, as foreigners left the mines, freeing the opportunity for white Americans. In the immediate wake of the Treaty of Guadalupe Hidalgo,* this tax confirmed many fears that American promises to protect the rights of Mexicans were empty. [SOURCE: Meier and Rivera, *Dictionary of Mexican American History*, 137-138; Weber, *Foreigners in their Native Land*, 151.]

FOREST RESERVE ACT

Between 1893 and 1906, the Forest Service set aside reserves along the Pecos, Jemez, Taos, and Manzano Rivers, but allowed Hispanic sheepmen range privileges based on the principle of "prior use." The grazers had no trouble in filing legitimate claims for this land utilization, but during the harsh winter between 1914 and 1915, many lost as many as 30 percent of their ewes, a disaster that made the rebuilding of their flocks almost impossible. The large ranchers rented sheep to the devastated sheepherders on a share-cropping basis. However, in the process, the sheepmen had to relinquish much of the forest range privileges. In addition, the New Mexico Territory donated four million acres of public land for the support of public education. The withdrawal of so much range land, coupled with the rapid expansion of the commercial livestock business, doomed both the Hispanic and the Indian populations of New Mexico to a land base entirely inadequate to their needs. To make matters worse, the Forest Reserve Act prohibited the colonization of new areas and the founding of new communities, a recourse that would have accommodated the need for land of a growing population. [SOURCE: Forrest, *The Preservation of the Village*, 21.]

FORTO, EMILIO C. (1856-?)

Emilio C. Forto, a long-time resident of Brownsville, Texas, in the late nineteenth and early twentieth centuries became a well-known businessman and political activist in the area. Born in Gerona, Spain, in 1856, Forto moved with his family to New Orleans when he was twelve and then accompanied his older brother, Frederick, to Brownsville, where both became involved in Cameron County machine politics. Typical of the opportunism shown in the politics of this era, Forto served in numerous elected positions both as a Repulican and a Democrat. Often criticized for defending the Texas Rangers,* Forto nevertheless often used his influence to protect Mexicans. During the Texas Ranger retaliation after the Plan de San Diego* uprising, Forto provided legislator José T. Canales* with important information, when the legislator held hearings in January 1918, motivated by the severity of Texas Ranger brutality. Forto joined the numerous Texas officials, including, Canales, in calling for curtailment of their authority. [SOURCE: Preuss, "Forto, Emilio (1856-?)," *The Handbook of Texas Online*, http://www.tsha. utexas.edu/handbook/online/articles/view/FF/ffogu.html]

FORTY-NINERS

While building a sawmill for John Sutter's settlement in the Sacramento Valley in the winter of 1848, James Marshall found some gold nuggets which proved to come from the richest gold-bearing area the world has yet known. Sutter and Marshall tried to keep the discovery a secret lest Mexico, which was in the midst of signing the Treaty of Guadalupe Hidalgo,* would be unwilling to sign away her rights to Alta California. The Mexicans did sign, probably without knowledge of the discovery, but soon afterward in 1849 the news spread like wildfire—the rush of Forty-Niners was on from all over the world.

The first arrivals were Chileans, Peruvians, and Mexicans, but before long, men from Europe and the eastern United States outnumbered the Spanish-speaking miners. Initially, the Anglos had to learn mining skills from the Spanish-speaking miners; their success became directly linked to the knowledge imparted by Mexican and South American miners. Anglo prospectors resented this dependence on Spanish-speaking people, whom they considered undesirable competition.

For a time Spanish-speaking miners had concentrated in the southern part of the mother lode and Anglos in the northern part. But eventually, the Anglos invaded the southern mines, forcing a confrontation. When California passed the discriminatory Foreign Miners' License tax,* compelling all who were not American citizens to pay heavier taxes on their claims, violence erupted. Mexican miners revolted, and Anglos retaliated by lynching and murdering scores of Mexican and Hispanic miners, forcing the survivors to flee. [SOURCE: Samora and Simon, *A History of the Mexican-American People,* 109–112; http://www.jsri.msu.edu/museum/pubs/MexAmHist/chapter22.html]

FRANCO, JESÚS (1898-1972)

Jesús Franco was born in the state of Guanajuato, Mexico, in 1898. After immigrating to El Paso during the Mexican Revolution, he worked to improve his countrymen's living conditions and strengthen their loyalties to the Mexican state. During the 1921 recession, he took various investigative trips throughout the Southwest on behalf of the Mexican government to assess the living conditions of his compatriots. As the Arizona correspondent for El Paso's *La Patria* in the 1920s, Franco also defended Mexicans accused of crimes. He used journalistic forums as well as his position in several Phoenix organizations, such as La Comisión Honorífica

Jesús Franco

Mexicana (Mexican Honorary Commission),* La Brigada Cruz Azul (Blue Cross Brigades),* and Woodsmen of the World. When he started to publish the newspaper *El Sol* in the 1930s, Franco continued his efforts to assure that the civil rights of his people were respected. In the 1940s, he became the Mexican consul in Phoenix, Arizona. His book, *El Alma de la raza,* published in 1929, left behind a treasure of information regarding the efforts made by community activists to protect the civil rights of immigrants and resolve some of their problems. Franco continued publishing *El Sol* until 1962. [SOURCE: Rosales, *Chicano!,* 68.]

G

FREE FEDERATION OF WORKERS

Puerto Rico had an existing labor movement before the United States occupation in 1898, but island unions established direct ties with U.S. labor after the takeover. The first large labor confederation, the Free Federation of Workers (FLT), was established in 1901 and became an affiliation of the American Federation of Labor. The FLT, which had close ties to the Puerto Rican Socialist Party, dominated the island's labor movement until 1940, when a new federation, the General Confederation of Workers, challenged its hegemony. [SOURCE: Figueroa, "NACLA Report on the Americas," (November/December, 1996), http://www.hartford-hwp.com/archives/43/018.html]

FUENTES, FRANK (1921-) AND RAY MARTÍNEZ (1919-2002)

Mexican-American World War II veterans Frank Fuentes and Ray Martínez organized the first American Legion Post for Mexican Americans in Phoenix. There, they successfully overcame protests by white veterans and instituted integrated G.I. housing. This was one way Mexican Americans used the American Legion as a vehicle for civil rights, as well as a social club. [SOURCE: Rosales, *Chicano!,* 97.]

LA GACETA MEXICANA

La Gaceta Mexicana was first published in Houston in 1928. One of the first Spanish-language newspapers in the city, it was issued by the Sarabia brothers, José, Felipe, Socorro, and Jesús, from their family print shop. The newspaper provided publicity for Mexican-American businesses and served as a forum for local immigrant writers to express their views on issues of nationalism and culture. An overriding theme became the desire to maintain Mexican culture in the United States as well as to take pride in their Indian heritage. One essay, for example, entitled "Eduquemos a nuestros hijos" (Let's Educate Our Children), regards the proper education of Mexican children in the United States. Another, "Nosotros los indios" (We the Indians) emphasizes the pride of having Indian blood. An important goal of the newspaper was to promote Houston's growing Mexican business community and to implore Mexican compatriots to take their business to their *paisanos*. [SOURCE: Rosales, *Testimonio*, 107-110; De León, *Ethnicity in the Sunbelt*, 34-37.]

GADSDEN TREATY

Five years after the signing of the Treaty of Guadalupe Hidalgo* in 1848, the United States again acquired territory from Mexico in an agreement that has become known as the Gadsden Purchase. General Antonio López de Santa Anna agreed to this purchase after his return to power in 1853, at that time, the U.S. government had sent James Gadsden to Mexico to settle a boundary dispute with Mexico. The Gadsden Treaty provided the United States with twenty-nine million acres of southern Arizona and New Mexico; from present-day Yuma along the Gila River (25 miles south of Phoenix) all the way to the Mesilla Valley, where Las Cruces, New Mexico, is situated. The United States wished to purchase the area on which to build a secure route for a transcontinental railroad. Mexico received $10 million and relinquished the land in 1854. The treaty respected Mexican land claims with records in Mexican archives. But the treaty addressed new concerns. Under its provisions, Americans could now cross the Isthmus of Tehuantepec as they transported goods to the California coast, and trade between Mexico and the United States, which had been interrupted by the Mexican-American War, was resumed. The question of Indian raids from United States territory into Mexico had always been a sore point with Mexicans, and they attempted to hold the United States responsible through the treaty, but the United States rejected this appeal, and the Mexicans afraid of another invasion did not pursue the issue. [SOURCE: Rosales, *Testimonio*, 16-19.]

GALÁN, NELY (1961-)

Nely Galán was born in Santa Clara, Cuba, emigrated with her family to Teaneck, New Jersey, at the age of two, and grew up in the New York-New Jersey area. In 1978, when only 17, *Seventeen* magazine was so taken by a story Galán had written about the all-girl's Catholic high school she attended that they printed it. The publishers of this popular magazine aimed at young women soon hired her as a teen guest editor. Although she had not graduated from college at age 22, she impressed management at the country's largest Spanish-language TV station, where Norman Lear's WNJU, in New York City, hired her as station manager. Soon she was hosting CBS-TV's "Bravo" and "Salsa Fever" and NBC-TV's "House Party." ESPN then recruited her to sell sports programming to the Hispanic audience. By 1992, HBO had asked her to format programs for Hispanics, and she cofounded HBO en Español. At 31, she formed Galán Entertainment, a venture with 20th Century Fox to produce mass-audience programs for the Latino market. [SOURCE: http://www.geocities.com/Athens/Forum/6517/everything/latinas.html]

GALARZA, ERNESTO (1905-1984)

Born in Jalcocotán, México, Galarza immigrated to Sacramento, California, as a child with his mother and two uncles during the Mexican Revolution, and soon after lost his mother to the influenza epidemic of 1917. Despite poverty and having to work even during his elementary and secondary education, Galarza graduated from Occidental College and later obtained an M.A. from Stanford University in 1929 and a Ph.D. from Colombia University in 1944. Galarza became a renowned expert on labor conditions and practices prevalent in the United States and Latin America, and published pioneering reports for government agencies and books for specialists and the general public in his effort to improve the lives of farmworkers.

Galarza wrote the first exposé of abuse of the Bracero Program* and the inhuman conditions maintained by growers for Mexican farmworkers in his *Strangers in Our Fields*, published by the Joint U.S.-Mexico Trade Union Committee. The report was so successful that it went through two editions for a total of ten thousand copies, and it was condensed in three national magazines, receiving widespread publicity. Galarza's book even spurred the AFL-CIO to begin supporting the unionization of farmworkers by granting $25,000 to Galarza's National Agricultural Workers Union. The book was one of the most damaging documents to the visitor worker program so favored by California agribusiness, and helped to force both the United States and Mexico to allow the program to expire in 1964. The termination of the Bracero Program, in turn, led to the successful unionizing of farmworkers that began in 1965 under the leadership of César Chávez* and what would become the United Farm Workers Union.* [SOURCE: Kanellos, *Hispanic Firsts*, 145; *Rosales, Chicano!*, 286-287.]

GALLUP INCIDENT

Miners in Gallup, New Mexico, rioted in 1935 after Mexicans and Mexican Americans who lived in housing on former property of the Gallup American Coal Company were forced to evict. Authorities tried to coerce miners by stopping relief payments. Tensions rose, and the rioting eventually resulted in three deaths.

A steady stream of outside support came to Gallup, increasing the hostile nature of the situation. One such supporter was Jesús Pallares, the founder of La Liga Obrera de Habla Española (Spanish-Speaking Labor League).* Over one hundred miners, including Pallares, were arrested under the authority of New Mexican anti-syndicalism laws. Pallares was eventually deported. The charges were dropped later, and the workers regained their relief payments. [SOURCE: Meier and Rivera, *Dictionary of Mexican American History*, 142.]

GARCÍA, GREGORIO (1892-1969)

Phoenix attorney, Gregorio "Greg" García, a native of Yuma, was among the most active Arizona criminal lawyers in defending Mexicans. For example, García and Alejandro Martínez, the Mexican consul, led the successful 1926 campaign to obtain a commutation for a deranged Ramón Escobar, who was sentenced to hang for killing his wife in a jealous rage. García was also the main lawyer in Alfredo Grijalva's case,* a southern Arizona rancher accused of killing a customs official in 1926. Grijalva was found guilty but García's defense was vigorous enough to cast some doubt, and the judge sentenced Grijalva to life imprisonment, rather than giving him the death penalty. García was a member of the Alianza Hispano-Americana* and in the 1930s went on to become a founding member of the Latin American Club in Arizona,* an organization that supported the Democratic Party and the New Deal. In the 1940s and 1950s, García worked with attorney Ralph Estrada in desegregation cases in the Phoenix area. [SOURCE: Rosales, *Chicano!*, 82.]

GARCÍA, HECTOR P. (1914-1996)

Hector Pérez García was one of the greatest Hispanic civil rights leaders in history. Born in Llera, Tamaulipas, Mexico, García was educated in the United States after his parents immigrated to Texas. He received his B.A. in 1936 and his M.D. in 1940 both from the University of Texas. During World War II, he served with distinction in the Army Medical Corps, earning the

Hector P. García with Attorney General Robert F. Kennedy and Forumeers

Bronze Star and six Battle Stars. At the end of the war, he opened a medical practice in Corpus Christi and, outraged at the refusal of local authorities to bury a Mexican-American veteran in a city cemetery, he organized the American G.I. Forum,* which is still one of the largest and most influential Hispanic civil rights organizations. In 1967, President Lyndon B. Johnson* named García alternate delegate to the United Nations with the rank of ambassador, and he also appointed him the first Mexican-American member of the U.S. Commission on Civil Rights. In 1965, the president of Panama awarded García the Order of Vasco Núñez de Balboa in recognition of his services to humanity. In 1984, he was awarded the U.S. of America Medal of Freedom. He was also the first Hispanic appointed to the Democratic National Committee. [SOURCE: Ramos, *The American G.I. Forum*; García, *Hector P. García.*]

GARCÍA, MACARIO (1920-1972)

A Medal of Honor recipient from Texas, Macario García was born in Villa de Castaño, Mexico, in 1920. His parents immigrated to Texas in 1923, where he grew up in Sugarland, a small agricultural community near Houston. There he worked as a migrant worker until the Army drafted him in 1942. He received the Medal of Honor for heroism in a Normandy campaign during November of 1944, when he single-handedly destroyed a German machine gun nest. In addition, the U.S. Army awarded García a Bronze Star and two purple hearts for other actions in the campaign against the Germans prior to his heroic stance in November.

García learned firsthand the humiliation that discrimination could bring. After his discharge in the Fall of 1945, he got into an altercation with a restaurant owner in Richmond, Texas, after being denied service. The police arrested García, charging him with criminal assault. The incident earned García celebrity status, and lawyers through the auspices of the League of United Latin American Citizens* defended him until he was acquitted in 1947. As a veteran, García became an outspoken critic against discrimination in the service industry and public housing, particularly that experienced by former Mexican-American soldiers, whom he believed had proved themselves to be loyal Americans. He died in an automobile accident in Alief, Texas, in 1972. [SOURCE: Rosales, *Chicano!*, 96; García,"García, Macario (1920–1972)," *The Handbook of Texas Online,* http:/www.tsha.utexas.edu/handbook/online/articles/print/GG/fga76.html]

GARCÍA, MARIO (?-1924)

In January of 1929, Phoenix police learned that Mario García and two accomplices intended to rob a City Drug Store. Police watched the burglars break a window, enter, and begin to fill their bags. When one patrolman opened fire, the others followed suit. García was shot in the head and killed. Accomplice Leo Bustamante was shot-gunned through the heart. The incident caused an uproar in the Mexican immigrant community of Arizona because of the callous methods used by the officers—the burglars were not armed nor did they ever menace the officers. [SOURCE: Rosales, *Chicano!*, 81.]

GARCÍA, ROBERT (1933-)

Representative Robert García from New York was born in Bronx County, New York, on January 9, 1933. He attended New York public schools, graduating from Haaren High School in 1950, and thereafter attended the City College of New York, the Community College of New York, and RCA Institute. García served in the New York assembly from 1965 to1966 and the New York senate from 1966 to 1978; he was deputy minority leader from 1975 to 1978. He was elected to the Ninety-fifth Congress by special election on February 14, 1978, to fill the vacancy caused by the resignation of Herman Badillo.* García was reelected to the six succeeding Congresses and served until his resignation on January 7, 1990. [SOURCE: Enciso, *Hispanic Americans in Congress, 1822-1995*.]

GARFIAS, MARSHAL ENRIQUE "HENRY" (1851-1896)

Henry Garfias was the highest elected Mexican-American official in Phoenix, Arizona, during the nineteenth century. Garfias, whose father had been a general in the Mexican army, was born in 1851 in Anaheim, California; Spanish was his first language. In 1871, he came to Arizona drawn by a gold rush in Wickenberg, a town 40 miles north of Phoenix. Four years later, he settled in Phoenix, where he operated a freighting business and in 1881 was elected town marshal. After serving eight years, he went on to a number of other city offices: constable, town assessor and tax collector, and street superintendent. In these positions he was able to provide patronage and protection for his constituents. He also published *El Progreso*, a newspaper in Spanish, which helped him garner the Mexican vote.[SOURCE: Rosales, *Testimonio*, 33-36; Luckingham, *Minorities in Phoenix*, 17-18.]

GARZA, BERNARDO F. (1892-1937)

Delegates to the first League of United Latin American Citizens (LULAC)* convention held in Corpus Christi, Texas, in 1929 elected Bernardo F. Garza its first president—he served one term. Born in Rockport, Texas, on June 22, 1892, he had to quit school at age 15 to help his mother María de Jesús Flores de la Garza to support a family of eight. When he was growing up in Rockport, Mexican-American children were segregated to a one-room school away from the fine-brick Anglo school. Garza's dedication to civil rights stemmed from those early experiences of discrimination. At 18, Garza moved to Corpus Christi, Texas, where he worked as a waiter and lived frugally so that he could send money to his family during his high school years and his first two years of college. During World War I, Garza returned to Rockport to work in the shipyards; however, he always had an eye for business. He invested in Corpus Christi real estate, which rose in value and Garza was able to sell it with enough profit to open a restaurant. He remained a businessman until his death in 1937. [SOURCE: http://www.lulac.org/Historical%20Files/Resources/History.html; Orozco, "Garza, Bernardo F. (1892-1937)," *The Handbook of Texas Online,* http://www.tsha.utexas.edu/handbook/online/articles/view/GG/fga85.html]

DE LA GARZA II, ELIGIO "KIKA" (1927-1995)

Eligio de la Garza II has had a long and illustrious career in public service. Born in Mercedes, Hidalgo County, Texas, in 1927, he served in the U.S. Navy at the end of World War II. After attending Edinburg Junior College, de la Garza received a U.S. Army commission as a second lieutenant and served in the Korean Conflict. He earned a law degree from St. Mary's University in 1953, and was then elected to the Texas House of Representatives, where many of the bills he introduced dealing with education and agriculture and water conservation were of great benefit to his constituency in South Texas and for Hispanics throughout the state.

Elected in 1964 to the U.S. House of Representatives from Texas' 15th District, de la Garza became a member of the Committee on Agriculture. From 1981 to 1994, he was the Chairman of the committee, becoming the first Hispanic since 1917 (when Ladislas Lázaro chaired the Enrolled Bills Committee) to chair a standing committee in the U.S. House of Representatives. During de la Garza's thirteen years of leadership as chairman, major agricultural legislation was enacted, which helped struggling farmers with credit, provided important safeguards for soil conservation, and allowed surplus foods to be distributed to the indigent.

In 1976 de la Garza became one of the founding members of the Congressional Hispanic Caucus,* which he chaired from 1989 to 1991. De la Garza stands out among congressmen as a champion of civil rights and for his concern for the less privileged. As a proponent of free trade, de la Garza was an important congressional supporter of the North American Free Trade Agreement (NAFTA) and the General Agreement on Tariffs and Trade (GATT). Throughout his congressional career, de la Garza has been instrumental in improving relations and trade between the Mexico and the United States. In 1978, Mexico's President José López Portillo awarded him the Order of the Aztec Eagle in recognition of his outstanding work. The Aztec medal is the highest honor Mexico can bestow on a foreigner. [SOURCE:

Hispanic Americans in Congress, 1822-1995, Library of Congress, http://www.loc.gov/rr/hispanic/congress/contents.html]

GARZA RODRÍGUEZ, CATARINO ERASMO (1859-1895)

Catarino Erasmo Garza Rodríguez immigrated to South Texas from Tamaulipas, Mexico, in the 1880s and became a firebrand politician who

railed against the treatment of Mexicans on the American side of the border. Born in 1859, he grew up near Matamoros, on his family's hacienda. His early education consisted of home tutoring, and in his late adolescence he took formal schooling in Hualhuises, Nuevo Leon and later at San Juan College in Matamoros. He also served in the Tamaulipas National Guard. Garza married Carolina Connor of Brownsville, Texas, and had two children with her. He held numerous jobs as clothing clerk, sewing machine salesman in Texas, and even Mexican consul in New Orleans. He entered journalism and published two newspapers. In his writing, he criticized Anglo lawmen suspected of lynching Mexicans.

Catarino Erasmo Garza Rodríguez

In 1888, an Anglo American who resented Garza's strident political style shot and wounded Garza in Rio Grande City; the shooting provoked his fellow Tejano citizens to become more vocal in defense of their rights. In 1892, Garza attempted to lead an army of volunteers to unseat the Mexican dictator Porfirio Díaz, but a military force from the United States sabotaged the effort.

Garza continued his insurrection in Duval County, Texas, where U.S. officials attempted to arrest him. With help from his followers, he was able to escape to New Orleans and leave for Central America, where he died on March 28, 1895 in struggles against conservative forces in present-day Panama at Bocas del Toro. Catarino Garza has become a folk hero on both sides of the border, primarily because of his militancy against injustice. [SOURCE: Mendoza, "En el margen del Río Bravo: Catarino Garza's War with the U.S. and Mexico"; Gómez-Quiñones, *The Roots of Chicano Politics,* 291.]

GERRYMANDERING AND LATINOS IN LOS ANGELES

In Spring 2001, lawyers for the Mexican American Legal Defense and Educational Fund (MALDEF)* filed a lawsuit on behalf of 24 registered voters, alleging that Democratic legislators drew congressional districts in Los Angeles and San Diego counties to protect white incumbent representatives Howard Berman, D-North Hollywood; Bob Filner, D-San Diego; and Brad Sherman, D-Sherman Oaks, from potential Latino challengers. Berman's brother, political consultant Michael Berman, was the chief architect of the congressional plan. MALDEF attorney Thomas A. Saenz contended that legislators didn't want Latinos "to have a strong enough vote that could raise a successful primary candidate and oust the incumbent, even though that candidate would almost certainly be a Democrat." MALDEF attorneys sought an immediate order from federal judges barring the congressional primary elections; the judges responded that they would reach a decision as soon as possible. In June 2002, a three-judge panel made up of the two U.S. district court judges and one federal appeals court judge dismissed the lawsuit, to the chagrin of MALDEF staff. [SOURCE: Drouin, "Gerrymandering Suit."]

GIUMARRA, SR., JOHN AND JOHN GIUMARRA, JR.

The Giumarra family owned of one of the largest grape vineyards in the world when the United Farm Workers Union* of César Chávez* went out on strike against California grape growers in the 1960s and 1970s. The family were leaders in the negotiations between farmworkers and growers in Central California after a five-year worldwide grape boycott forced the growers to cave in. Father and son played a prominent role in signing the historic contract of July 1970, that increased wages for farmworkers. According to union lawyer Jerry Cohen,* Giumarra Sr. was "a feisty Sicilian" who swore his farms would never be unionized. Nevertheless, Giumarra approached Cohen to begin negotiations; he was the first one to do so in the San Joaquin Valley. Later, Giumarra told Chávez, "Okay, I give up, you won. . . . I am a tough Italian, but I got to admit you beat us." [SOURCE: Rosales, *Chicano!*, 147.]

GÓMEZ, ANTONIO (1897-1911)

In June 1911, in Thorndale, a small Texas town, a fight ensued after a merchant attempted to eject 14-year-old Antonio Gómez from a store. In the fracas, the boy stabbed and killed a German-American customer. While Gómez was awaiting trial, a mob took the boy from jail, beat him, hanged him, and then dragged his body around town tied to the back of a buggy. A number of Mexican organizations, including La Orden de Caballeros de Honor (The Order of the Knights of Honor), which was established in 1911, protested, but were disappointed when local authorities failed to investigate. Some protestors even accused the Mexican government of inaction. The activist Nicasio Idar, editor of Laredo's *La Crónica*, charged Mexico with neglecting the issue so as not to jeopardize diplomatic relations with the United States. [SOURCE: Rosales, *Pobre Raza!*, 27,119.]

GÓMEZ, ELSA (1939-)

Elsa Gómez, the first Hispanic woman to become president of a four-year liberal arts college, has devoted much of her life to providing educational opportunity to minorities in the nation. Born and raised in New York City, she received a B.A. from the College of St. Elizabeth in New Jersey (1960), an M.A. from Middlebury College in Vermont (1961), and a Ph.D. from the University of Texas at Austin in 1977. Dr. Gómez then started her career at the University of Puerto Rico in 1962. By 1983, she was the dean of the College of Arts and Sciences, but resigned to direct academic programs at the Massachusetts Board of Regents of Higher Education. In 1989, Gómez became president of Kean College in New Jersey. The Latino community has benefited greatly from the commitment Gómez has demonstrated to its educational needs. A major priority has been "to get across to Hispanics that it is important to stay in school, not only for themselves, but to bring the Hispanic perspective higher into businesses." Gómez retired in 2002 but continued to teach part-time at Kean College. [SOURCE:http://www.geocities.com/Athens/Forum/6517/everything/latinas.html]

Elsa Gómez

GÓMEZ, MANUEL N. (1947-)

Born in Santa Ana, California, Dr. Manuel N. Gómez was a pioneer activist in the Chicano Movement,* he participated in the 1969 National Chicano Youth Liberation Conference* and the 1970 Chicano Moratorium* against the Vietnam War. He received a B.A in History from California State University, Hayward (1972), an M.A. in Social Ecology from the University of California, Irvine (1979), and a Ph.D. in Higher Education from the University of Southern California (1998). In 1979, after serving for a number of years in the administration at the University of California, Irvine, he became a program officer with the Fund for the Improvement of Postsecondary Education, a program of the U.S. Department of Education. While there, he designed Project STEP to facilitate a bridge from secondary schools to higher education through a regime of academic preparation, professional development, and community participation. In 1995, Dr. Gómez was appointed Vice Chancellor of Student Affairs at the University of California, Irvine. During 2001-2002 he served for nine months as interim vice president for educational outreach at the University of California System. In addition, he is a published poet and an author of numerous works on higher education. [SOURCE: http://today.uci.edu/Features/profile_detail.asp?Key=106]

GONZALES, ALBERTO R. (1955-)

When Alberto R. Gonzales was sworn in as the nation's 80th Attorney General on February 3, 2005, he became the first Hispanic to be appointed to such a powerful post. Prior to his appointment, he had served President George W. Bush as White House Counsel since January 2001. Gonzales is considered extremely competent and bright; however, his nomination was opposed by liberal Democrats who saw his judicial record as ideologically conservative. Gonzales was born in San Antonio, Texas, in 1955 and raised in Houston, where he graduated from high school. Gonzales enlisted in the U.S. Air Force in 1973 and entered the U.S. Air Force Academy in 1975. In 1977, he transferred to Rice University and two years later earned a degree in political science. In 1982, he earned a law degree from Harvard University, whereupon he returned to Houston to exercise his profession. He eventually became a partner in the law firm of Vinson & Elkins L.L.P. When George W. Bush was governor of Texas, he appointed Gonzales to a series of positions: a senior advisor, chief elections officer, lead liaison on Mexico and border issues, Texas secretary of state, and, finally, a member of the Texas Supreme Court. During Gonzales' meteoric rise, he served on numerous honorary boards and commissions and received a plethora of honors for his leadership activities. [SOURCE: www.usdoj.gov/ag/aggonzalesbio.html]

GONZALES, HELEN (1946-)

Born in San Francisco in 1946, consumer and civil rights advocate, Helen Gonzales, became the hightest ranked Hispanic in the National Gay and Lesbian Task Force, when she assumed the duties of director of public policy in 1995. Gonzales previously had served as staff advocate at the National Consumer Law Center and associate counsel for the Mexican American Legal Defense and Educational Fund.* Gonzales has also been active in women's health issues and served on the board of the Montener National Health Association. She is now director of USAction, a consumer rights policy organization based in San Francisco. Gonzales obtained an A.A. from San Francisco City College in 1970, a B.A. from San Francisco State University in 1972, and in 1975, she graduated from Boalt Hall School of Law at the University of California, Berkeley. [SOURCE: *Hispanic Link Weekly Report* (14 August 1995), 1.]

GONZALES, MANUEL C. (1900-1986)

Prominent among Mexican-American lawyers and civil rights activists in Texas was Manuel C. Gonzales. Born on October 22, 1900, in Hidalgo County, as a boy Gonzales moved with his family to San Antonio, where he graduated from high school and later from Nixon Clay College in Austin. When

World War I broke out, he joined the Army and became secretary to the U.S. military attaché in Madrid. After the war, Gonzales studied law at St. Louis University and the University of Texas. In the 1920s, he participated in fledgling Mexican-American organizations, such as the Order of the Sons of America,* and in 1929, became a founding member of the League of United Latin American Citizens (LULAC),* serving as its third president in 1931. The San Antonio Consul General often asked him to serve as a friend of the court in trials of policemen who killed Mexicans. In 1931, the young attorney represented the Mexican government at the Oklahoma trial of the two deputies who had killed two middle-class students from Mexico, one a nephew of the then president of Mexico. Significantly, Gonzales in addressing the court made sure it knew of his war record. In 1928, he also represented Clemente Rodríguez and Ezequiel Servín, two young Mexicans accused of raping a white girl outside of San Antonio. The defense effort put up by Gonzales failed, and the two were convicted and executed. During his presidency of LULAC, the organization began its crusade to change the banning of Mexican Americans from serving on grand and petit juries in the Texas counties of Sonora, Ozona, Uvalde, and Dimmit. Also during his tenure, LULAC filed a lawsuit against the Del Rio School District to end desegregation. Gonzales became one of the first Mexican Americans to run for political office in Texas with his 1930-unsuccessful attempt at becoming a state legislator. From 1954 to 1978, he served on the Board of Trustees of the San Antonio Union Junior College District. [SOURCE: Oroz-

First LULAC Convention, Corpus Christi, 1929

co, "Gonzales, Manuel C. (1900-1986)," *The Handbook of Texas Online*, http://www.tsha.utexas.edu/handbook/online/articles/view/GG/fgo57.html; Rosales, *Pobre Raza!*, 134-135.]

GONZALES, RODOLFO "CORKY" (1929-2005)

Rodolfo "Corky" Gonzales was born in a Denver barrio to parents who were seasonal farmworkers. Because of the instability of migrant work, Gonzales received both formal and informal education. Gonzales used boxing to get out of the barrio, becoming the third-ranked featherweight in the world. Eventually, he quit boxing and became a successful businessman, political leader, and director of poverty programs. Politics frustrated Gonzales and he soon ended his affiliation with the Democratic Party. As an alternative, he established the Crusade for Justice,* a community service organization. Working with the Crusade for Justice, Gonzales helped organize high school walkouts, demonstrations against police discrimination, legal battles to protect Mexican-American civil rights, and protests against the Vietnam War.

In 1968, Gonzales and Reies López Tijerina* led the Mexican-American component of the Poor People's March* on Washington, DC. At the nation's capital, the efforts by African Americans to gain civil rights and achieve self-sufficiency greatly impressed him. There, Gonzales issued "El Plan del Barrio," a proclamation that mapped out separate public housing for Chicanos,* bilingual education, barrio economic development, and restitution for land

Corky Gonzales and César Chávez

that had been taken from Hispanos in Colorado and New Mexico. To achieve these goals, Gonzales suggested a Congress of Aztlán.

Gonzales also organized annual National Chicano Youth Liberation conferences* that sought to cultivate a national sense of cultural solidarity and to work toward self-determination. The first such conference resulted in El Plan Espiritual de Aztlán (The Spiritual Plan of Aztlán), a document that outlined the concept of ethnic nationalism for liberation. The Chicano National Youth Liberation conferences continued to refine these ideas.

Gonzales authored the famous and influential epic poem, *I Am Joaquín/Yo Soy Joaquín*, which weaves myth, memory, and hope as a basis for a Chicano national identity. He has stated, "Nationalism exists . . . but until now, it hasn't been formed into an image people can see. Until now it has been a dream. . . . [N]ationalism is the key to our people liberating themselves. I am a revolutionary . . . because erecting life amid death is a revolutionary act. . . . We are an awakening people, an emerging nation, a new breed." Gonzales died on April 12, 2005 in Denver, Colorado. [SOURCE: Gonzales, *Message to Aztlán*; Marín, *A Spokesman of the Mexican American Movement*, 1973.]

GONZÁLEZ, ANTONIO (1957-)

Antonio González, who heads the Southwest Voter Registration Education Project (SVREP),* was born in Los Angeles in 1957 to immigrant parents from Mexico. His father supported his family by loading trucks at a Coca Cola plant in Orange, California, during the 1950s. Antonio went on to graduate with a B.A. in U.S. History from the University of Texas-San Antonio in 1981 and worked towards an M.A. in Latin American History at U.C. Berkeley during the 1981-82 academic year. Head of the SVREP since 1994, González also heads the William C. Velásquez Institute,* the policy branch of the project. Endowed with a high level of energy, Gonzaléz's leadership has resulted in increasing the number of Hispanic registered voters from 5 million to 9.3 million in 2005. More than 81 percent of those registered by the project went to the polls in the 2004 presidential election, in comparison to 88 percent of all registered voters. González, who works out of Los Angeles, taps some of the major U.S. foundations and corporations, including State Farm and Telemundo Communications, to meet his $4 million annual budget, which underwrote 300 voter-registration and turnout campaigns in 14 states during 2004. His workers consist of 700 paid personnel and 10,000 volunteers. González is quick to point out that the SVREP is non-partisan, when critics claim it works for the Democratic Party, by demonstrating that in the 2004 presidential race in Florida, an ambitious SVREP effort resulted in a high G.O.P. turnout among Latinos. [SOURCE: http://www.svrep.org/press_room/press_clippings/time_081505.html]

GONZÁLEZ, ELIÁN (1993-)

No other incident brought the rift between Cuban Americans and Fidel Castro's socialist government in Cuba to the forefront as the Elián González drama. Known as "El Niño Milagro," (the miracle child), six-year-old Elián González was plucked from the waters off the Florida coast in November 1999, after a Cuban refugee boat sank; his mother, Elizabeth Brotón Rodríguez, drowned in this desperate escape from Cuba. Back in Cuba, his father, Juan Miguel, demanded that his son be returned, claiming that his ex-wife had taken Elián out of Cuba without his permission. Elián's Miami relatives, on the other hand, wanted to keep him—he had become a hero and a symbol to Cuban Americans. They were supported by a huge groundswell of vocal, anti-Castro Cuban Americans who accused Juan Miguel of being a dupe of Fidel Castro. They argued that if Elián were returned to Cuba, he would be condemned to a life of hell. Juan Miguel accused the Miami relatives of kidnapping the boy, attempting to buy his love with chocolate milk and trips to Disney World. The Immigration and Naturalization Service (INS)* was asked to decide whether Elián should be returned to his family in Cuba. After a long legal battle, the INS decided to return Elián to the island, a determination made by U.S. Attorney General Janet Reno. A predawn raid on April 22, 2000, followed. Photographers captured a terrified Elián cornered in a closet as INS officers wrestled him from his great uncle's home. The same day, however, pictures of a happy boy with his father after their reunion were shown internationally on television. The Cuban-American community, not all who were totally in support of Elián remaining with the Miami relatives, felt frustrated and betrayed. [SOURCE: Time Inc., http://www.time. com/time/poy2000/pwm/elian.html]

GONZÁLEZ, HENRY B. (1916-2000)

Born in San Antonio, Texas, Henry B. González was educated in San Antonio public schools and later earned a law degree from Saint Mary's University. In 1953, he was elected to the San Antonio city council. He championed an ordinance that abolished all segregation laws in the city. Three years later, he was elected to the state senate, the first Mexican American in 110 years. As a senator, González continued to be an advocate for civil rights.

In 1961, González was elected to the U.S. House of Representatives, becoming the first Mexican American from Texas so elected. As a congressman, González introduced bills to improve benefits for farmworkers, housing, training and development for employees, and minimum wage. In 1964, he helped defeat the longterm Bracero Program* that had protected and subsidized temporary workers from Mexico.

When González first served in Congress in the 1960s, his Spanish-speaking constituents found him an important advocate. However, the Texas

Henry B. González

congressman had nothing but disdain for the Chicano Movement,* which gained strength in the late 1960s. He lambasted the Ford Foundation* on the floor of the House of Representatives in April 1969, for funding the Mexican American Youth Organization (MAYO)* because it distributed "literature that I can only describe as hate sheets designed to inflate passions. . . . The practice is defended as one that will build race pride, but I have never heard of pride being built on spleen." Gónzalez was particularly incensed over the metaphoric "Kill the Gringo" speech that José Angel Gutiérrez* had given to gain attention to his cause. González's clout proved decisive in neutralizing and/or alienating support for MAYO from liberal funding sources and political leaders throughout Texas. [SOURCE: Rosales, *Chicano!*, 107, 219, 234, 244.]

GONZÁLEZ, JOSÉ AND SALVADOR ORTIZ (?-1919)

During September 1919, in the midst of a steel strike in Pueblo, Colorado, railroad section hands José González and Salvador Ortiz were jailed on suspicion of killing a patrolman named Jeff Evans. Incensed whites, many of them workers who resented Mexican strikebreakers working in the mills, distracted the police by calling in a riot at the steel mill. Night captain, John Sinclair responded with all of his men, leaving only the deskman to mind the police station. An armed mob marched to the jailhouse, held the official at gun-point and forcibly took the Mexicans in a caravan of automobiles to the edge of town and hanged them twenty-four feet apart from the girders of Fourth Street bridge. [SOURCE: Rosales, *Pobre Raza!*, 119.]

GONZÁLEZ, YSIDRO AND FRANCISCO SÁNCHEZ (?-?)

In December 1914, Ysidro González and Francisco Sánchez killed jailer Henry Hinton in an escape from the Oakville, Texas, jail. A posse immediately captured González who was tried and found guilty. San Antonio judge, W.W. Walling, sentenced him to death. Sánchez, captured later, had to be transported back to Oakville under heavy guard because of lynching threats. As a consequence, Mexicans from Oakville and neighboring communities unsuccessfully attacked the courthouse to obtain González's freedom. Sánchez was saved from the lynch mob, but authorities executed him legally in the Spring of 1915. González, in spite of extraordinary efforts to keep him out of the mob's hands was lynched. A mob took him from jail and fired three shots into his body. A third Mexican in the Oakville jail charged with complicity in the Hinton killing avoided lynching because the jail security was increased. [SOURCE: Rosales, *Chicano!*, 61.]

GONZÁLEZ PARSONS, LUCÍA C. (1852-1942)

Born near Fort Worth, Lucía González married Albert R. Parsons in the 1870s and moved to Chicago. There, Parsons, a journalist, became involved in the labor movement, and he and Lucía became socialists leaders in the Workingmen's and Socialist parties. During the 1880s, Lucía, or Lucy, joined the Chicago Working Women's Union. As a member, Lucy led women's marches in favor of eight-hour workdays and women's rights.

Lucía González Parsons

After authorities executed her husband for his part in the Haymarket Square riot in Chicago, Lucy continued as a labor leader, spokesperson, writer, and publisher. In 1905, she cofounded the International Labor Defense and Industrial Workers of the World. At her urging, the Wobblies stood strong with embattled Russian workers, who were on the verge of their first revolution and pledged non-discrimination against workers of other races or immigrants to the United States; the Wobblies' stance was different from that of other unions, which actively discriminated. [SOURCE: Gómez-Quiñones, *Roots of Chicano Politics*, 287.]

GOOD NEIGHBOR COMMISSION

With racial discrimination in Texas particularly rife, Mexico refused to send *braceros* to that state during the late 1930s and early 1940s. In September 1943, the Good Neighbor Commission was formed under the authority of Texas Governor Coke Stevenson. In January 1945, the commission set out to make farm labor appear more attractive by improving working and housing conditions, as well as the overall treatment of Mexicans. Despite the commission having improved understanding between Anglos and Mexicans, Mexico did not reverse its decision to allow *braceros* into Texas. In 1947, the commission became a permanent state agency. The intention of the commission changed by the 1950s, when it began to serve as a diplomatic agency to coordinate visits by Mexican dignitaries. [SOURCE: Meier and Rivera, *Dictionary of Mexican American History*, 149-50.]

GOOD NEIGHBOR POLICY

The Good Neighbor policy was primarily designed by the Department of State to build good relations with Latin American allies, but the department also attempted to improve the image of Americans among Hispanics living in the Southwest and vice-versa. To accomplish this, Good Neighbor representatives held large conferences in Denver, Colorado, in June and July 1943, and then in August of the same year in Santa Fe, New Mexico, and Phoenix, Arizona. Participants at these conferences attended workshops and meetings, where they tried to reach an understanding of each other's cultures. [SOURCE: Samora and Simon, *A History of the Mexican-American People,* 193.]

LAS GORRAS BLANCAS

In the mid-nineteenth century, many New Mexicans lost great amounts of land to railroad developers, in particular to the Santa Fe, Atchison, and Topeka Railroad. Despite having proper and legal land grants and rights, land speculators organized the "Santa Fe Ring"* in the 1890s. A native vigilante group called Las Gorras Blancas, because they wore white caps, formed in reaction to this usurpation. Formed by a group of disgruntled Mexican residents of the territory in Mora, Santa Fe, and San Miguel counties, these insurgents were determined to drive out the Anglo speculators, usually by force. They tore down fences, destroyed railroad tracks, and even derailed trains. By the early twentieth century, Las Gorras Blancas went into decline, but their struggles to protect or regain stolen or usurped lands resonated in many organizations and political parties to come in the twentieth century. [SOURCE: Rosales, *Chicano!,* 8-9, 90; Rosenbaum, *Mexicano Resistance in the Southwest,* 111-124.]

GOVEA, JESSICA (1947-2005)

Born in Kern County, California, Jessica Govea began working with her farmworker family in California when she was only four. When César Chávez* began organizing the United Farm Workers* in the 1960s, she volunteered as an organizer. Govea then became instrumental in planning and directing boycotts in the United States and Canada. Govea has taught at Rutgers University in New Jersey in the Labor Studies Department and works with the Union Leadership Academy, an organization that provides continuing education opportunities for farmworkers. She was a member of the Extension Division faculty with Cornell University's School of Industrial and Labor Relations in New York City. Ms. Govea died on January 22, 2005 in West Orange, New Jersey. [SOURCE: http://complit.rutgers.edu/swarner/sal/bios.html]

Despues del baile....... gratos recuerdos

Gráfico

GRÁFICO

Since the late nineteenth century, New York, as a port of entry for immigrants from Europe and the Caribbean has spawned numerous immigrant newspapers, whose function, besides providing news and advertising, served to allow newcomers to make a transition to their new homes. In some of those newspapers, the awareness of their communities' evolution towards citizenship status or American naturalization was reflected, and the demand for the rights of citizenship became more pronounced. Even *Gráfico*, which in most respects was a typical immigrant newspaper, began to recognize the American citizenship of its readers (mostly Puerto Ricans and Cubans residing in East Harlem) in order to demand rights guaranteed under the U.S. Constitution. Often the editors penned English-language opinion pieces that balked at being considered foreigners in the United States and the subjects of discrimination.

And while the editors of *Gráfico* often made comparisons of their community with that of other immigrant groups, it is obvious that they were aware of the differences between Puerto Ricans and the other groups; because of the Jones Act of 1917,* for example, Puerto Ricans did not have to take steps to become citizens—it was automatic. [SOURCE: Kanellos, *Hispanic Periodicals in the United States*, 53-57, 106-107.]

"GREASER LAW," *see* **CALIFORNIA ANTI-VAGRANCY ACT**

THE GREAT DEPRESSION AND VIOLENCE AGAINST MEXICANS
Unemployment during the Great Depression encouraged threats and violence towards Mexicans. Typical of the sentiments and organizing against Mexican immigrants was the letter received in June 1930, by the *San Angelo Evening Standard* from the a group that called itself "Darts and Others:" "We are forming a club known as the darts and our aim is to clean up this city making working conditions better for Americans. You will hear from us from time to time as our good work progresses each member will work separately not knowing any other member. All Mexicans must leave."

In May, disgruntled workers in Malakoff, an oil company town near Dallas, took more concrete action. On May 19, unknown persons dynamited the Mexican Hall, a gathering place for Mexicans who worked for the Malakoff Fuel Company, an act of retaliation that the *Dallas Dispatch* attributed to the hiring of Mexicans during the economic crisis. After the blast, placards attached to the wrecked hall read, "LEAVE TOWN, DAMN PRONTO." When County Sheriff C.G. Pharris ignored a request from Dallas consul Juan E. Anchondo that he protect Mexican workers, the consul appealed to the Malakoff Fuel Company. The company's director, who came personally to Malakoff from Dallas, assured the consul that the company would protect Mexicans. He then called Governor Ross Sterling, who dispatched Texas Rangers* to the troubled town. Soon after that, Governor Sterling announced that Rangers had already arrested an individual for the bombing. This satisfied Mexican president Pascual Ortiz Rubio's government, which was under pressure to act decisively in this latest outrage.

Officers of the Unión General de Trabajadores Mexicanos en Los Estados Unidos de América in Dallas, owners of the bombed hall, were not as satisfied. They telegraphed President Ortiz Rubio to thank him for his efforts, but warned that danger still loomed in Malakoff. Once the Rangers left, whites again became aggressive, and local officials refused to act. This message prompted Ortiz Rubio to personally press consular officials to pursue the matter further. The Rangers returned and local officials purportedly arraigned an accused bomber in Tubbleville, a neighboring town.

White worker attacks on Mexicans continued throughout the Depression. In Newport, Arkansas, in June 1931, Tránsito Velásquez, a foreman for a vegetable packing company, complained that twenty-five to thirty Anglo Americans went on a rampage looking for Mexicans to shoot, but that the police dispersed the mob. Velásquez said he was then arrested and jailed for no reason. His wife bailed him out, and Velásquez's boss, Allen Mayer, came to his house and told him and the other Mexicans to leave town immediately. Mayer paid him $38.50 as part of his salary, but did not allow him to pack. Velásquez fled with his family, leaving their belongings behind—furniture, clothing, a stove, and other items.

In response to an inquiry from Oklahoma City consul Joaquín Amador, the Newport police chief blamed Mexicans for the riot. They claimed that when two of his officers quelled a disturbance on June 30 in "Mexican Town", they arrested eight persons of both races. Velásquez was described as the Mexican ringleader who made death threats against the Newport populace. According to the chief, "Those Mexicans had not worked but thirty days and they were causing considerable trouble among the inhabitants of that part of town and were mainly responsible for the affray that took place."

In Chicago, continuous attacks on Mexicans by other ethnic groups seemed endemic in 1931. In its May 20 issue, *El Nacional* warned about the danger of walking the streets because Italian youth gangs robbed Mexicans with impunity. A few days earlier, according to the newspaper, a gang had attacked two Mexicans, beating one up severely and chasing the other back to his neighborhood. "There is an assumption that some Italian politicians protect them [gang members]; when one is caught by the police he is freed . . . with this procedure the neighborhood is terrorized." [SOURCE: Rosales, *Pobre Raza!*, 116.]

GRIJALVA, ALFREDO (1894-?)

In April 1926, Pima County (Tucson) officials charged Alfredo Grijalva, with the killing of U.S. Customs Officer W.W. McKee in an ambush, when he and other agents confiscated a cache of liquor allegedly abandoned by Grijalva and his confederates. Officials freed Grijalva right after his arrest for lack of evidence. They rearrested him only after a witness, who later retracted his story claiming coercion from Pima County deputies, identified him as one of the smugglers.

Alfredo Grijalva

As a consequence, the Comité Pro Grijalva, organized by sympathetic members of Tucson's Mexican community, raised money for an appeal. By December 1927, the group had collected $1,223 for his defense. However, the Arizona Supreme Court affirmed the original judgment, and Grijalva had to serve out his life sentence. Because Grijalva was a naturalized U.S. citizen, Nogales consul C. Palacios Roji initially only pledged support for Antonio Padilla, who was also accused of the murder. Influential relatives of Grijalva in Sonora intervened, however, and the Mexican government finally joined in the efforts for clemency. The state pardoned Grijalva in 1935 after extensive Mexican government and community efforts. Grijalva was then deported. [SOURCE: Rosales, *Pobre Raza!*, 98, 135, 171.]

GRILLO, EVELIO (1919-)

In his book *Black Cuban, Black American*, a memoir based on the first twenty-six years of his life, Evelio Grillo captures the dilemma of Afro-Latinos growing up in the United States. In it, he tells the story of his simultaneous rearing as a Black Cuban and a Black American. Born in Tampa, Florida, in 1919, he lived until he was fifteen in Ybor City, the Latin settlement within the city. Reared bilingually and biculturally, he learned Spanish and Cuban culture in his home. He learned English and black American culture in his neighborhood, in the segregated schools, the segregated church, and in the larger Black-American community into which he was integrated.

As a young man in the 1930s, he attended Dunbar High School in Washington, D.C., a historically African-American institution that graduated a large number of young people who became influential leaders. He then went to Xavier University, an historically black university in New Orleans, Louisiana, and received a B.A. in 1941. During World War II, Grillo served in a segregated Army unit, an experience that demonstrated that the United States did not deliver on its promises of equality. After the war, Grillo received a Master of Social Work degree from the University of California, Berkeley, in

Evelio Grillo

1953, and practiced as a social group worker and community organizer. In the 1950s and 1960s, he organized for the Community Services Organization* in the Bay Area of California.

Black Cubans had a dual identity, especially in the Jim Crow South. They lived largely isolated from the white Cuban community, except in the cigar factories, where they worked with white Cubans, Italians, and Spaniards. Like all blacks, they were totally isolated from the white American community.

Black Cubans were considered black. That was the overwhelming reality of their existence and if they became successful in the United States, it was by taking the same difficult road traveled by non-Latino African Americans. [SOURCE: www.artepublicopress.com; Grillo, *Black Cuban, Black American.*]

GRUPO NACIONAL MEXICANO

During the Depression, immigrants from Colton, California, wishing to repatriate themselves to Mexico organized into the Grupo Nacional Mexicano. Unlike many other poverty-stricken Mexicans in the United States, who could not even afford to pay for the simple transportation cost back to the homeland, this group pooled enough resources to buy land in Mexico. Led by Isaac López, they negotiated for over three years with an American land company to buy Hacienda La Gloria, a property which straddled the boundaries of the adjacent states of Chihuahua and Durango. Obtaining this land, which totaled approximately sixty-five thousand acres, proved complicated because of its dual location, despite the Mexican consular corps in southern California attempting to help them. The hacienda belonged to Loftus, Dysart Development Company of Los Angeles, which was willing to sell, but at a price above market value. The company, however, did provide the colonists with extensive incentives, such as donated farm equipment and the promise to donate part of the land. The group was elated at this and took up the offer. Nevertheless, upon attempting to settle, the group discovered that another landowner had claimed half of property. [SOURCE: Balderrama and Rodríguez, *Decade of Betrayal,* 171-174.]

GUADALUPE HIDALGO, TREATY OF

The Treaty of Guadalupe Hidalgo signified the end of the Mexico-U.S. War in February 1848. The treaty was negotiated by Nicholas Trist, President James Polk's emissary, and was signed in the small town of Guadalupe Hidalgo, outside Mexico City. Within a year of the treaty, Mexicans living in the ceded areas had to declare their intention to remain Mexican citizens or they would become American citizens automatically. Either way, the treaty promised to protect their rights. Their property rights were guaranteed, including claims to land grants under Spanish and Mexican law.

In New Mexico, especially, determining exact boundaries became difficult, since most of the Spanish grants had been awarded either to families or to villages as *ejidos* (communal land grants), a concept unfamiliar to Anglo-American law, which emphasized individual rights and private property. Prominent landmarks, such as rivers, mesas, and geologic outcroppings, often defined property boundaries, and distances were measured in meters and bounds. In addition, before takeover by the United States, Hispanics had the custom of accepting verbal contracts when land exchanged hands or they had lost written agreements. Unfortunately, after annexation, few Hispanic communities or individuals possessed the kind of documentation of their land rights that would stand up in an Anglo court of law.

Although the treaty protected their legal rights, Mexicans had no assurance that their culture would be protected. Only two thousand Mexicans kept their citizenship and moved to a now shrunken Mexico. [SOURCE: Forrest, *The Preservation of the Village,* 19-20.]

GUERRA, CARLOS (1947-)

A pioneer activist in Texas' La Raza Unida Party (The United People Party-LRUP),* Carlos Guerra was born on May 27, 1947, in Robstown, Texas. He was the first and only national president of the Mexican American Youth Organization (MAYO).* Under his leadership, the group implemented the Winter Garden Project, a multi-faceted effort that led to the LRUP being formed in four counties of Texas' Winter Garden area (Frio, Dimmit, La Salle, Zavala). The difficulties encountered in organizing county-by-county led to the creation of a statewide party in 1972. In the early 1970s, Guerra was director of the Texas Institute for Educational Development in San Antonio and in 1974 served as campaign manager for Ramsey Muñiz's* second gubernatorial race. Muñiz chose Guerra to chair his campaign to counter the more stridently nationalistic wing of the LRUP, led by Mario Compeán.* While Guerra shared many of the ideological ideals espoused by Compeán, he was more willing to yield to what appeared to be the political realities of the time; he concurred with Muñiz that a traditional campaign should be waged, which included wooing groups and individuals outside of the party. Mr. Guerra currently writes op-ed columns in English for the *San Antonio Express and News* and in Spanish for *Conexión,* a bilingual San Antonio weekly. [SOURCE: Rosales, *Chicano!,* 216, 246.]

GUTIÉRREZ, ALFREDO (1944-)

Born in Miami, Arizona, Alfredo Gutiérrez became one of Arizona's most successful politicians and civil rights activists during the 1960s and

1970s. In 1974, he was the youngest person ever elected to the state legislature and, by the end of the decade, had emerged as one of its most distinguished leaders. His considerable political skills led him to being selected as majority whip and minority whip in both houses for the Democratic Party. Gutiérrez was born and raised in Miami, Arizona, a small mining town in rural Arizona. His parents and extended family members were involved in union organizing and held fast as a unity providing the values that still guide his life today. When Gutiérrez attended Arizona State University in Tempe, he became one the most colorful leaders in the Mexican American Student Organization,* a group that militantly pressed the university to include in its mission the welfare of the Chicano* community. With other activists, he took the cause out of the university into the community and helped organize Chicanos Por La Causa,* an organization that still exists today—Gutiérrez organized a chapter of the Brown Berets* as part of this process. In 2002, Gutiérrez ran for governor of Arizona in the Democratic Primary. Today, Gutiérrez runs a very successful community development consulting firm. [SOURCE: Rosales, *Chicano!*, 212-213.]

GUTIÉRREZ, JOSÉ ANGEL (1944-)

A key figure in the Chicano Movement,* José Angel Gutiérrez began his career in 1963 by helping to elect Los Cinco,* five Mexican Americans, to the city council of Crystal City, Texas.* The inexperienced Mexican council members were beleaguered and discredited. At the next election, the Anglo

José Angel Gutiérrez

old guard, with its Mexican-American minions, returned to power and established a municipal government with an all-Anglo majority. For Gutiérrez, this failure was probably the most important single event leading to developing his particular brand of politics. As a student at St. Mary's University in San Antonio in 1967, Gutiérrez and four other young Chicanos*— Mario Compeán,* Nacho Pérez, Willie Velásquez* and Juan Patlán—met regularly at the Fountain Room, a bar near St. Mary's, to discuss Texas politics and the Chicano Movement. They eventually founded the Mexican American Youth Organization (MAYO),* the forerunner of the La Raza Unida Party (The United People's Party-LRUP).* MAYO, sought to effect social change for the Mexican-American community and to train young Chicanos* for leadership positions.

A political science professor at St. Mary's, Charles Cotrell, guided their politicization and provided them with non-mainstream ideas. It was under

Cotrell's direction that Gutiérrez produced a Master's thesis entitled, "La Raza and Revolution: The Empirical Conditions of Revolution in Four South Texas Counties," which became the basis for the Winter Garden Project (WGP), an initiative that led to the founding of LRUP in later years.

MAYO members led by Gutiérrez held to the belief that confrontational tactics could convince cowed Texas Mexicans that the Gringo (Anglo) was vulnerable. For example, by engaging in public confrontations with the feared Texas Rangers,* they demonstrated that at least some Mexicans were willing to stand up to those often despised law officials. But MAYO's highly publicized antics also provoked the ire of established Anglo liberals and Mexican-American politicos. San Antonio's Congressman Henry B. González,* for example, almost single-handedly eradicated most of the funding sources for the young militants.

After being stymied in their community development efforts, in 1968 the young activists turned to gaining electoral power. Naming their effort the Winter Garden Project, they chose to start in Crystal City, the hometown of José Angel Gutiérrez and his wife Luz. Although the population of this agricultural town in South Texas was more than eighty percent Mexican, the power structure in both local government and private business was Anglo-American. Gutiérrez and his MAYO cohorts returned to Crystal City to reestablish a Mexican-American majority on the city council. But unfolding local dissatisfaction with the school system prompted the organizers to put gaining electoral goals on hold temporarily.

When Mexican-American students led by Severity Lara* at Crystal City High School led a walkout in 1969, the WGP, led by Gutiérrez, joined high school students and their parents to form the Ciudadanos Unidos (CU). In December, when the school board acted equivocally to their demands, practically all of the Chicano students walked out of their classes. The strike ended on January 6, 1970, when the school board acceded to the reforms demanded by strikers. The next move for Gutiérrez and the group was to gain political power in Crystal City. After the successful school boycotts, Gutiérrez and other MAYO members formed an LRUP chapter and won five positions on the city council and school board in 1970.

Many LRUP delegates at the San Antonio convention in October 1971, aspired to run for state-level races, such as the governorship, but Gutiérrez wanted to organize region by region and opposed this escalation. Nevertheless, delegates led by Mario Compeán* succeeded in targeting state offices for LRUP. The party fielded candidates in the next three state elections, but really only made a dent in 1972, when the LRUP aspirant Ramsey Muñiz* drew away enough votes from the Democratic candidate that a Republican won.

LRUP spread to other regions in the United States, exerting particular strength in Colorado, where the popular Chicano leader Rodolfo "Corky" Gonzales* headed the effort and also called for a national political party. Although Gutiérrez was reluctant to begin a national effort at this point, arguing it could jeopardize his regional strategy, he decided to accede to the national focus and was elected chairman of LRUP at its 1972 convention in El Paso, Texas. The most important issue at the meeting became whether the pragmatic Gutiérrez or the ideological Gonzales would be elected party chairman. Colorado LRUP leaders encouraged rumors that had Gutiérrez making deals with the Republicans in order to obtain funding for LRUP programs in Texas. Nonetheless, Gutiérrez won, provoking a bitter split that could not be bridged by any number of overtures for unity; the national Chicano party initiative was stillborn. Ramsey Muñiz ran for governor in 1974, but attracted fewer votes than in 1972. Then in 1976 he was arrested on federal charges of narcotics trafficking, an incident that destroyed LRUP credibility. In 1978, Mario Compeán ran for governor and received less than two percent of the total votes cast.

In the meantime, disaffected LRUP members in Zavala County formed a breakaway faction and voted José Angel Gutiérrez out of power. In 1982, he left electoral politics for good and earned a Ph.D. in political science at the University of Texas at Austin and later graduated from law school at the University of Houston. Dr. Gutiérrez has served as executive director of the Greater Texas Legal Foundation, a nonprofit organization that seeks justice for poor people, and currently is a lawyer in Dallas and a professor of Chicano Studies at the University of Texas at Arlington. He continues to research and publish on the Chicano Movement. [SOURCE: Rosales, *Chicano!;* Gutiérrez, *The Making of a Chicano Militant.*]

GUTIÉRREZ, LUIS (1953-)

The first Hispanic Representative from Illinois, Luis Gutiérrez, was born in Chicago, Illinois, on December 10, 1953. After graduating from Northeastern Illinois University in 1975, Gutiérrez taught in the public schools of Puerto Rico and Chicago, and worked for the Illinois State Department as a social worker in Children and Family Services. Later, after working for the mayor's office, he was elected an alderman to the Chicago City Council in 1986 and served until 1993.

Gutiérrez learned in the interim the necessity of mainstreaming Latino politics in Chicago by working with other Latino leaders. His major tactic was to coordinate who runs so that office seekers will not compete for the same vote and risk giving away the election to non-Latino candidates. In Chicago, Latino politicians can be divided by their party alliances or their Latino ethnic origin, Mexican American or Puerto Rican. To reach consensus on issues, they now caucus, thereby conserving resources for really important battles, such as whom to support for governor and senator. But this does not mean that they will always agree; the objective is to try to reach agreement before they run against each other.

Gutiérrez's approach has paid off for him personally. In 1992, he won a seat in the U.S. House of Representatives from Chicago's Fourth District and was reelected in 1994, both times garnering more than seventy-five percent of the votes. Because of Gutiérrez's considerable experience in Chicago urban politics, he has made positive contributions in House of Representative committees that affect, among other issues, urban affairs, banking, housing, veterans' benefits, and consumer affairs. Congressman Gutiérrez also attends to the problems of minorities and issues related to Puerto Rico.

Gutiérrez has mastered the art of consolidating political power by sharing power, building effective electoral coalitions, and bringing the community and its leaders together to speak with one voice. [SOURCE: Andrade, "Gutiérrez Unites, Strengthens Latino Vote," *Chicago Sun-Times* (March 29, 2002), www.puertorico-herald.org; Hispanic Americans in Congress, 1822-1995, http://lcweb.loc.gov/rr/hispanic/congress/gutierrez.html]

GUTIÉRREZ, REBECCA MUÑOZ (1917–2000)

Rebecca Muñoz Gutiérrez was an important Mexican-American student leader in the 1930s and 1940s. In 1937, with her siblings, Rosalío and Josephine Muñoz, she helped found Los Conquistadores,* the first Mexican-American student organization at Arizona State Teachers College (now Arizona State University, ASU). Rosalío Muñoz, Sr. was the first Mexican American to obtain a Master of Arts degree at ASU. Conquistadores members were influenced by the activity of California's Mexican American Movement (MAM)* in Los Angeles, which became an important vehicle for the Americanization of children of Mexican immigrants. On a trip to Arizona, Félix Gutiérrez met Rebecca Muñoz; through his influence she and other Arizona students attended a conference sponsored by MAM in Los Angeles. They returned to Tempe, excitedly propagating lessons learned at the conference. The Muñoz family left a crucial legacy for Mexican Americans in Arizona and established the lesson of the importance of student organizations at the university level. [SOURCE: Rosales, *Chicano!*, 101; Christine Marín, Department of Archives & Manuscripts, Arizona State University, Email Obituary, 16 March 2000.]

HARLEM RIOTS

In July 1926, Puerto Ricans were attacked by non-Hispanics as their numbers were becoming larger in Manhattan neighborhoods. The "riots," as they were dubbed by the *New York Times,* took place in the intense heat when

Harlem residents literally lived in the streets to escape their suffocating dwellings. The influx of Puerto Ricans, the most recent arrivals in the area of Manhattan called Spanish Harlem, provoked racist hostility among non-Hispanic neighbors, who were mainly of Italian and Irish stock. The older residents feared competition from these newcomers in housing and jobs. The overwhelming heat exacerbated this already smoldering resentment, a tension which led to the attacks. As Puerto Ricans united to defend themselves, symbols of the homeland became a powerful bond. Adversity and rejection continued to provide impetus to Puerto Ricans as they sought to protect civil rights during the rest of the twentieth century. [SOURCE: Sánchez Korrol, *From Colonia to Community,* 151-152.]

HARTFORD RIOTS

Beginning on Labor Day, 1969, Puerto Ricans in Hartford, Connecticut,* staged a series of riots that lasted two days. The causes of the upheaval can be traced to frustrations caused by years of poverty, second-class status, under-representation, and police brutality suffered by the twenty thousand Puerto Rican residents of Hartford. Police officers arrested more than five hundred people in the melée, and property damage was estimated at $1.17 million. A consequence was that activists organized around the issues that provoked the violence and created organizations to demand rights for the city's Latinos. [SOURCE: Cruz, "A Decade of Change."]

THE HARVARD JOURNAL OF HISPANIC POLICY

The Harvard Journal of Hispanic Policy is the nation's foremost student-operated policy journal dealing with U.S. Latino community issues. Founded in 1985 by Henry A.J. Ramos, the journal features scholarly articles, political commentaries, book reviews, and opinion-leader interviews. The journal was the first student publication established at the Harvard John F. Kennedy School of Government (the nation's leading graduate public policy school). It has inspired the creation of comparable student journals dealing with African-American, Asian-American, and women's policy issues. The journal serves as an important vehicle for public education about Latino community concerns within the broader Harvard and national communities and is a significant magnet for Latino leadership engagement with Kennedy School faculty and administration, as well as national and international policy makers. [SOURCE: http://www.ksg.harvard.edu/hjhp/]

HATE CRIMES

Coined in the United States during the 1980s, the term "hate crime" fulfilled the need for a descriptive term that could be used by journalists and policy makers to describe bigoted violence directed at a wide array of different groups, including Jews, blacks, homosexuals, and other minorities. A hate crime came to mean not just acts of violence, but incidents involving destruction of property, harassment, and trespassing. Thus, synagogue desecrations, graffiti with hateful language, and cross burnings are all considered hate crimes. While such behavior has existed in the United States much longer than the term has been in use, in the 1980s much of this abuse could be attributed to followers of white supremacy groups, such as "skinheads" and pro-Nazi organizations. [SOURCE: Jacobs and Potter, *Hate Crimes.*]

HEALTH CONCERNS

Health Concerns, the sole national organization focusing on the health, mental health, and human service needs of diverse Hispanic communities, was founded in Los Angeles in 1973 as the Coalition of Spanish-Speaking Mental Health Organizations (SSMHO). SSMHO's membership consisted of thousands of health and human services providers and organizations serving Hispanic communities. The organization advocates for the mental health needs of Mexican-American, Puerto Rican, Cuban-American, Central American, and South American communities in the United States. [SOURCE: http://www.hispanichealth.org/aboutus2.lasso]

EL HERALDO DE MÉXICO

El Heraldo de México, founded in Los Angeles in 1915 by owner Juan de Heras and publisher Cesar F. Marburg, has been called a "people's newspaper" because of its focus on and importance to the Mexican immigrant worker in Los Angeles. It often proclaimed its working-class identity, as well as its promotion of Mexican nationalism. Through its publishing house, it issued the first novel narrated from the perspective of a "Chicano," i.e., a Mexican-working class immigrant: Daniel Venegas'* *Las aventuras de Don Chipote; o cuando los pericos mamen.* The most popular Mexican newspaper at this time, its circulation extended beyond 4,000.

Like many other Hispanic immigrant newspapers, *El Heraldo de México* devoted the largest proportion of its coverage to news of the homeland, followed by news directly affecting Mexican immigrants in the United States, as well as news and advertisements that would be of interest to working-class immigrants. Among the social roles played by *El Heraldo de México*, the most important was the defense of the Mexican immigrant, by publishing editorials and devoting considerable space to combating discrimination and the exploitation of immigrant labor; it particularly brought attention to the role played by labor contractors and American employers in mistreating the immigrant workers. *El Heraldo de México* even went a step further in 1919 by attempting to organize Mexican laborers into an association, the Liga Protectora Mexicana* de California (Mexican Protective League of California), to protect their rights and further their interests. [SOURCE: Kanellos, *Hispanic Periodicals in the United States,* 35-36; Romo, *East Los Angeles,* 150-159.]

LAS HERMANAS-UNITED STATES OF AMERICA

Founded in 1971 in San Antonio, Texas, Las Hermanas (The Sisters) has 1,000 members, mostly Catholic nuns, in twelve regional chapters and forty affiliate groups. Las Hermanas advocates for the needs of Hispanics in the church and society, with the specific goal of engaging Hispanic women in active ministry among Hispanics. It conducts leadership training, workshops, and retreats. It publishes *Informes*, a quarterly newsletter. [SOURCE: Kanellos, "Organizations," 391.]

LA HERMANDAD MEXICANA NACIONAL

La Hermandad Mexicana Nacional (The Mexican National Brotherhood), the first union of Mexican undocumented immigrant workers was founded in California in 1951, when Phil and Alberto Usquiano took the lead in organizing a quasi union made up of a large membership of undocumented workers. The first brothers were principally members of the Carpenters Union and the Laborers Union. The Hermandad was organized in response to the Immigration and Naturalization Service's* program to cancel work visas of Mexican nationals. [SOURCE: García, *Memories of Chicano History,* 290-91.]

HERNÁNDEZ, ALFRED J. (1924-)

Born in Mexico City in 1924, Alfred J. Hernández's family brought him to the United States at the age of four. Enlisting in the Army after graduating from high school, Hernández saw military action in Africa and Europe during World War II. It was while soldiering in Italy that he became a naturalized citizen in 1944. He returned home with the rank of technical sergeant and after his discharge, he enrolled at the University of Houston on the G.I. Bill and received his law degree from South Texas College of Law in 1953.

Hernández joined the League of United Latin American Citizens (LULAC)* in 1944 and held many LULAC offices as the years went by. Elected president in 1965, he served two terms. As president, Hernández injected tactics of militancy and confrontation into LULAC politics. He was a major supporter of the much-publicized labor strike in Selma, Texas, which turned into a protest march and ended in a confrontation with Texas governor John Connally on a highway near New Braunfels. He also played a key role in the Albuquerque Walkout of 1966,* when leaders from organizations such as LULAC, the Mexican American Political Association,* La Alianza Hispano-Americana,* and the Political Association of Spanish-Speaking Organizations* walked out of the 1966 Equal Employment Opportunity Commission.*

Triggering the action was the perception that President Johnson, who had promised in his 1965 "Great Society" inaugural address a "War on Poverty," did not follow through when it came to Mexican Americans. [SOURCE: http://www.lulac.org/about/history/history.html]

HERNÁNDEZ, ANTONIA (1948-)

Since Antonia Hernández began working for the Mexican American Legal Defense and Education Fund (MALDEF)* in 1981 as a staff attorney in Washington, D.C., she was heavily involved in most of the issues that MALDEF took on in defense of the civil and educational rights of Latinos. In 1983, Hernández became employment litigation director in the Los Angeles office, seeking greater opportunities for Hispanics in federal employment and promoting affirmative action in private and public sector jobs. In 1985, Hernández became president and general counsel of MALDEF, but in 1987, an executive committee of the MALDEF Board of Directors abruptly terminated her, citing questionable administrative and leadership abilities. They then proceeded to appoint former New Mexico governor Toney Anaya to the post, giving him a $100,000 salary—$40,000 more than Hernández had been making. When Hernández appealed, the board voted 18 to 14 to retain her. Since that time until her retirement from MALDEF, Hernández was the organization's most public spokesperson and the leader responsible for its outstanding record of successful negotiation and litigation.

One of her most intense campaigns was her leadership in defeating the Simpson-Mazzoli immigration bill, which would have required Latinos to carry identification cards. This was just one area of immigrant rights that Hernández and MALDEF were able to make great progress in. Other success stories include the creation of single-member election districts, favorable public school equity court decisions in Texas, and successful challenges to district boundaries in Los Angeles County. Hernández's leadership was crucial in safeguarding bilingual education in the Southwest. MALDEF took the lead in battling against Proposition 187,* which would have denied a free public education and other benefits for the children of undocumented immigrants. Proposition 187 was struck down by a federal court that held unconstitutional provisions involving the determination of legal immigration status, including language which denied immigrants' access to state education services

Under her leadership, MALDEF was active in redistricting efforts, to assure the creation of electoral districts that give the Latino community a fair chance of political representation.

Born in the state of Coahuila, Mexico, Hernández immigrated to Los Angeles, California, with her working-class parents when she was eight years old. Hernández graduated from the University of California at Los

Angeles Law School in 1974, and went on to practice law in the public interest, including doing public defender work. Since leaving MALDEF in 2004, Hernández became the president and CEO of the California Community Foundation. [SOURCE: http://www.gale.com/free_resources/chh/bio/hernandez_a.htm]

HERNÁNDEZ, MARÍA L. DE (1896-1986)

Born in 1896 in Garza García, a village near Monterrey, Nuevo Leon, María L. de Hernández became an important civic, political, and social leader in Texas. Throughout her life, she wrote and spoke about educational opportunities and the civil rights of Mexican Americans, all while raising a family of ten children. Before immigrating to Texas, Hernández taught elementary school in Monterrey and, in 1915, married Pedro Hernández Barrera in Hebbronville. Her political activism began after moving with her husband and growing family to San Antonio in 1918. Throughout the 1920s, Hernández and her husband were involved in various political issues and, in 1929, they helped found the Orden de Caballeros de América (the Order of Knights of America),* an organization which strove to improve the subordinate position of Mexicans in Texas, especially in the educational arena. In 1933, Hernández and Dr. A.I. Mena organized the Asociación Protectora de Madres (Protective Association of Mothers), which provided financial assistance to expectant mothers. Also in the 1930s, the Hernándezes joined Eleuterio Escobar* and other San Antonio activists to found La Liga de Defensa Pro-Escolar (The Pre-School Defense League), whose objectives included improving educational facilities in San Antonio's predominantly Mexican West Side. In the same decade, Hernández also became a stalwart in early League of United Latin American Citizens* activities as a radio spokesperson for local Council 16. From the 1940s to the 1960s, Hernández continued her advocacy on behalf of women through her extensive writings, public speaking engagements, and by helping organize such feminist groups as the Club Liberal Pro-Cultura de la Mujer (Liberal Club for Women's Culture) and El Círculo Social Damas de América (The Social Circle of Ladies of America).

Her interest in electoral parties prompted her to support Henry B. González's* bids for congressional office during the 1960s and, in 1970, she became active in the La Raza Unida Party (LRUP).* A keynote speaker at the LRUP statewide convention of 1972, accompanied by her husband, she toured Texas with Ramsey Muñiz,* who had been nominated at the gathering as the gubernatorial candidate. [SOURCE: Orozco, "Hernández, María de (1896-1986)", *The Handbook of Texas Online,* http://www.tsha.utexas.edu/handbook/online/articles/view/HH/fhe75.html]

HERNÁNDEZ V. NEW YORK

In 1991, Dionisio Hernández appealed to the U.S. Supreme Court a murder conviction in a New York State court, charging that the prosecutor used peremptory challenges to disqualify two prospective Spanish-speaking jurors because of doubts that the jurors could disregard anticipated Spanish-language testimony and consider only the English translation of the court interpreter. The defense lawyer protested the jurors dismissal, claiming this was an attempt to prevent Latinos from jury selection because they might be sympathetic to Hernández. The trial judge, nonetheless, accepted a "race-neutral" explanation offered by the prosecutor. In a six-to-three decision, Supreme Court justices affirmed the lower-court ruling, indicating that the relationship between national origin and language did not merit assigning "suspect class" protection in a court of law. [SOURCE: http://ourworld.compuserve.com/homepages/JWCRAWFORD/hernan.htm]

HERNANDEZ V. TEXAS

The *Hernandez v. Texas* case demanding a white status backfired on Mexican Americans. In Texas, demands for a jury of peers, when the defendant was Mexican, had previously been met with retorts that seating all Anglo juries did not exclude the Mexican race, since Mexicans were supposedly white. But lawyer Juan Carlos Cadena, later a judge in San Antonio, with partner Gus García, successfully argued in 1953 before the U.S. Supreme Court that Pete Hernandez' rights to a jury of peers were violated because no Mexican Americans were on the panel that convicted him of murder. In 1954, the Supreme Court agreed that Hernández, a convicted murderer, had been denied equal protection under that law. The jury that convicted him in Jackson County, Texas, included no Mexican Americans. In addition, the court discovered that in the previous twenty-five years, no Mexican American had ever served on a jury, despite Mexican Americans making up fourteen percent of the county's population.

The case was the first discrimination case concerning Mexican Americans to reach the Supreme Court. The attorneys were also the first Mexican Americans to argue a case in front of the nation's highest court. [SOURCE: García, *Mexican Americans,* 49-50; Olivas, *Colored Men and Hombres Aquí;* www.artepublicopress.com]

HERRERA, JOHN J. (1910-1986)

John J. Herrera, a lawyer and civil rights leader, was born on April 12, 1910, in Cravens, Louisiana. One of the founders of the Latin American Club in Houston,* he led a campaign to obtain equal status for Hispanic municipal employees in the 1930s. Herrera revived the dormant League of United Latin American Citizens (LULAC)* Council 60 in Houston in 1939. He was elected national president of LULAC in 1952. An early proponent of affirmative action, in 1943 he successfully petitioned the President's Employment Practice Commission to oblige Gulf Coast war-industries in Texas to hire minorities in skilled jobs. After obtaining his law degree in 1951, Herrera, along with Gustavo C. García, argued major civil rights cases with history-setting precedence: the 1948 *Delgado v. Bastrop Independent School District*,* which declared the school segregation of Mexican-Americans illegal, and the *Pete Hernández v. Texas** in 1954, the first case argued before the U.S. Supreme Court that concerned Mexican-American civil rights. In the latter case, the practice of systematically excluding Mexican Americans from juries was declared unconstitutional. An early proponent of obtaining power through the ballot box, Herrera ran unsuccessfully four times for the Texas legislature from his home base of Harris County between 1947 and 1958. Herrera was more successful as a union organizer, successfully bringing into existence twelve unions. Herrera died in Houston on October 12, 1986. [SOURCE: Christian, "Herrera, John J. (1910-1986)," *The Handbook of Texas Online,* http://www.tsha.utexas.edu/handbook/online/articles/HH/fhe63.html]

HILL, RICARDO (?-?)

In the 1930s, Mexican consul Ricardo Hill was the central figure in the development of Mexican agricultural labor unions in southern California. Hill, the son of the Mexican revolutionary general, Benjamín Hill, opposed the capitalistic system, a view he often expressed while serving as a consul in southern California. Hill also felt his role as a consul compelled him to protect the interests of Mexican nationals and to represent them whenever and wherever their human and constitutional rights were compromised. Thus, when Mexican farmworkers began to organize into unions, Hill took a leading role in the 1933 convention that founded the Confederación de Uniones de Obreros y Campesinos Mexicanos (CUCOM)* and became an honorary but permanent member of the union's governing board. CUCOM embarked in a series of strikes throughout southern California. When the intransigent growers refused to even negotiate with the new union, an angry Hill publicly made the following vow: "If the Mexicans [sic] workers of Los Angeles County are not organized now, I'll see that they are before winter is over." Hill was not without his critics, however. Many organizers within the union resented the interference of the Mexican government in their affairs and accused him of red-baiting and cooperating with anti-radical California officials and employers. [SOURCE: Escobar, *Race, Police, and the Making of a Political Identity,* 88.]

HISPANIC ACADEMY OF MEDIA ARTS AND SCIENCE

The Hispanic Academy of Media Arts and Science, located in Los Angeles, California, advocates for the fair and equal representation of Hispanics in film and television, monitors how they are portrayed, and works for access to employment at all levels in television and film. The organization sponsors an annual awards event that highlights the contributions of Hispanics to the industry. [SOURCE: Kanellos, "Organizations," 391.]

HISPANIC AMERICAN POLICE COMMAND OFFICERS ASSOCIATION

By 1973 there were sufficient numbers of Mexican Americans in command executive positions in police forces to merit the founding of the Mexican American Police Command Officers Association. Based in San Antonio, Texas, in 1984, the organization became national and changed its name to Hispanic American Police Command Officers Association (HAPCOA) in order to incorporate officers from Latino groups other than Mexican Americans. It is now the oldest advocacy group for Hispanic executives in law enforcement and criminal justice. The chiefs of police, sheriffs, and police superintendents from around the country, through HAPCOA, attempt to foster an atmosphere that results in the promotion and retention of Hispanic-American men and women in professional law enforcement and the criminal justice system. [SOURCE: http://www.hapcoa.org/info/]

HISPANIC ASSOCIATION OF COLLEGES AND UNIVERSITIES

Founded in 1986 and based in San Antonio, the Hispanic Association of Colleges and Universities (HACU) has 34 institutional members, whose purpose is to bring together colleges and universities with corporations, government agencies, and individuals to promote the development of member institutions and improve the quality and accessibility of postsecondary education for Hispanics. HACU promotes nonprofit, accredited colleges and universities whose Hispanic enrollments are at least 25 percent of the enrollment at either the graduate or undergraduate level. Such institutions are eligible for grants as a result of the 1992 Re-authorization of the Higher Education Act. [SOURCE: Kanellos, "Organizations," 391.]

HISPANIC ASSOCIATION OF CORPORATE RESPONSIBILITY

Headquartered in Washington D.C., the Hispanic Association of Corporate Responsibility (HACR) was founded in 1986 as a coalition of the most prominent national Hispanic organizations in the United States. A nonprofit, tax-exempt organization, HACR's mission is to ensure that Hispanics are equitably represented in Corporate America commensurate with Hispanic purchasing power. HACR holds corporations responsible for their inclusion of Hispanics in employment, procurement, philanthropy, and corporate governance. Today, such a posture is even more crucial, according to HACR leaders, because Hispanics constitute the largest minority group and the fastest-growing consumer segment in the nation. To achieve its objectives, HACR provides guidance to Corporate America as it sets out to recruit a multicultural workforce. [SOURCE: http://www.hacr.org/about/]

HISPANIC BUSINESS INITIATIVE FUND OF GREATER ORLANDO, INC.

In 1995, former Orange County Chairman Linda Chapin, Orlando Mayor Glenda Hood, Orange County Commissioner Mary I. Johnson and the Central Florida Hispanic Chamber of Commerce established the Hispanic Business Initiative Fund of Greater Orlando (HBIF) as a community-based nonprofit organization to provide the Hispanic business community with bilingual technical assistance and the necessary tools to build successful enterprises. To function effectively, HBIF relies on four staff members and fifty dedicated volunteers. By emphasizing the power of economic opportunity, HBIF has served as a catalyst for positive community change by contributing to the growth and success of Hispanic-owned businesses. [SOURCE: http://hbiforlando.org/about_us.php]

HISPANIC CIVIL RIGHTS SERIES

Because the accomplishments of Hispanics in their struggle for civil rights have been significant, although they remain largely unknown, Arte Público Press at the University of Houston began commissioning in 1998 a series of books to address the lack of information accessible to students and the general public. The series documents the many contributions to public policy, education, and community affairs by Hispanic civil rights activism. Highlighted are the topics of women's activism, immigration reform, educational equity, the participation of citizens in a democratic society, civic culture and racial/cultural relations. Included in the series are biographies and autobiographies of such important personalities as César Chávez,* Hector P. García,* Evelio Grillo,* José Angel Gutiérrez,* Reies López Tijerina,* Julian Nava,* and Antonia Pantoja.* Through the publication of these timely books, this truly American story of struggle to safeguard the rights that all Americans hold dear will be made a part of the national narrative and brought to the forefront of our national memory.

The Hispanic Civil Rights Series is made possible with the financial support of The Charles Stewart Mott Foundation, The California Wellness Foundation, The Carnegie Corporation, The James Irvine Foundation, The Rockefeller Foundation, and The Ewing Marion Kauffman Foundation. [SOURCE: http://www.artepublicopress.com]

HISPANIC CHURCHES IN AMERICAN PUBLIC LIFE

In 2001, the initiation of the Hispanic Churches in American Public Life research project was announced by the Pew Charitable Trusts, the Hispanic Alianza de Ministerios Evangélicos Nacionales (National Alliance of Evangelical Ministries-AMEN) and the Mexican American Cultural Center (MACC),* in San Antonio, Texas. Coordinated by Dr. Jesse Miranda from AMEN and Dr. Virgilio Elizondo of MACC, the survey has a nationwide agenda scheduled to last three years and is expected to result in the most comprehensive study ever conducted on the impact of religion on politics and civic engagement among Latinos. The project, conducted under the auspices of the Tomás Rivera Policy Institute, which carried out national surveys and community profiles, is directed by Dr. Gastón Espinosa. [SOURCE: Espinosa, "Hispanic Churches in American Public Life."]

HISPANIC COLLEGE FUND, INC.

In 1993, a highly committed group of Hispanic business leaders joined together to establish the Hispanic College Fund, Inc. (HCF), a private nonprofit organization based in Washington, D.C. Its main objective is to develop the next generation of Hispanic business leaders in America by awarding scholarships to deserving Hispanic students. Prompting the forming of the organization was that the number of Hispanic students enrolling in college had been decreasing. HCF organizers recognized that one of the main reasons fewer Hispanic students attended college was lack of financial resources, and without a college education, many Hispanic students faced limited opportunities. This would negatively affect the Hispanic business community, which requires skilled, educated professionals in business management, finance, marketing, sales, information systems, and other areas to be successful. [SOURCE: http://www.hispanicfund.org/]

HISPANIC COMMUNITY CENTER

Founded in Lincoln, Nebraska, the Hispanic Community Center is a social service center that serves Latinos in Lincoln and the surrounding area. The very rapid influx of immigrants from Mexico and Central America prompted the founding of the center in 1982. The main services provided are English- and Spanish-language classes, the sponsoring of cultural groups such as Los Zapatos Alegres (The Happy Shoes) dancers, and celebrating the holidays that are relevant to the diverse Hispanic community. In addition, the center provides mental health outreach, substance abuse counseling, and advocacy in the judicial system. [SOURCE: http://www.nebraskahistory.org/lib-arch/whadoin/mexampub/resource.htm]

THE HISPANIC FEDERATION

The Hispanic Federation (HF) was created in 1990 to provide Latino health and human services agencies serving New York, New Jersey, and other neighboring areas with umbrella assistance in obtaining funds and resources. Through participation in the HF, member organizations strengthened their services in the areas of immigration, legal aid, health care, economic development, job training, AIDS prevention, youth services, leadership development, and housing. One of HF's flagship projects is the Child Health Insurance Program (CHIP) Facilitated Enrollment Project, in conjunction with the New York State Department of Health. In the winter of 1999, CHIP began providing free or low-cost health insurance coverage to all children and teens living in New York State, regardless of the child's immigration status or the family's employment status. CHIP also conducts a referral service to pregnant women to centers which provide the Prenatal Care Assistance Program. [SOURCE: http://www.hispanicfederation.org/about/index.html]

HISPANIC IMMIGRANT NEWSPAPERS IN THE UNITED STATES

The mission of newspapers serving newly arrived communities of Hispanic immigrants, in the second half of the nineteenth century and throughout the twentieth, differed from the exile publications. The latter, concerned themselves almost exclusively with opposing the regimes back home and contributing to their overthrow. Also, the publications differed from those published by Hispanics native to the Southwest, which did not concentrate on issues in Mexico or other Latin American nations. Instead, they mainly covered local and national United States news. Hispanic immigrant newspapers, especially large dailies, such as San Antonio's *La Prensa,* Los Angeles' *La Opinión,* New York's *La Prensa* and *El Diario de Nueva York* served diverse publics of exiles, immigrants, and U.S. minority citizens. But their largest readership was—and, for those that still exist, continues to be—Spanish-speaking immigrants.

In the second half of the nineteenth century when Hispanic immigrant communities began to form in the United States, Spanish-language newspapers were founded to serve immigrant populations and functioned somewhat as described above. Among these were San Francisco's *Sud Americano* (1855), *El Eco del Pacífico* (1856),* *La Voz de Méjico* (1862), and *El Nuevo Mundo* (1864), which served a burgeoning community of immigrants from northern Mexico and from throughout the Hispanic world, as far away as Chile, all drawn to the Bay Area during the Gold Rush and collateral industrial and commercial development. From the 1850s through the 1870s, San Francisco supported the largest, longest-running and most financially successful Spanish-language newspapers in the United States. *El Eco del Pacífico,* the largest of the two, and *El Tecolote* (1875–1879) were both San Francisco dailies owned by immigrants from Spain, Chile, Colombia, and Mexico. These newspapers covered news of the homeland, which varied from coverage of Spain and Chile to Central America and Mexico, and generally assisted the immigrants in adjusting to the new environment. Very closely reported on was the French Intervention in Mexico, with various of the newspapers supporting fund-raising events for the war effort and aid for widows and orphans, in addition to working with the local Junta Patriótica Mexicana, even printing *in toto* the long speeches made at the Junta's meetings. The newspapers reported on discrimination and persecution of Hispanic miners and generally saw the defense of the Hispanic community to be a priority, denouncing abuse of Hispanic immigrants and natives. Hispanic readers in the Southwest were acutely aware of racial issues in the United States and generally sided with the North during the Civil War, which also was extensively covered in the newspapers.

While San Francisco's Hispanic population was the state's largest in the nineteenth century, it was Los Angeles that received the largest number of Mexican immigrants throughout the twentieth century and, along with San Antonio and New York, supported some of the most important Spanish-language daily newspapers, periodicals that began as immigrant newspapers. Between 1910 and 1924, some half million Mexican immigrants settled in the United States; Los Angeles and San Antonio were their settlements of choice. Into these two cities an entrepreneurial class of refugees came with cultural and financial capital sufficient to establish businesses of all types, including newspapers and publishing houses, to serve the rapidly growing Mexican enclaves. Through their publications, they reinforced a nationalistic ideology that ensured the solidarity and insularity of their community, or their businesses, which included the newspapers.

El Heraldo de México,* founded in Los Angeles in 1915 by owner Juan de Heras and publisher Cesar F. Marburg, has been called a "people's newspaper" because of its focus on and importance to the Mexican immigrant worker in Los Angeles. It often proclaimed its working-class identity, as well as its promotion of Mexican nationalism; through its publishing house it issued one of the first novels narrated from the perspective of a "Chicano," i.e., a Mexican-working class immigrant: Daniel Venegas' *Las aventuras de Don Chipote, o cuando los pericos mamen*. Its circulation extended beyond 4,000, *El Heraldo de México* devoted the largest proportion of its coverage to news of the homeland, followed by news directly affecting the immigrants in the United States, followed by news and advertisements that would be of interest to working-class immigrants. The most important role played by the newspaper was the defense of the Mexican immigrant, by publishing editorials and devoting considerable space to combating discrimination and the exploitation of immigrant labor; it particularly brought attention to the role played by labor contractors and American employers in mistreating the immigrant workers. *El Heraldo de México* even went a step further in 1919 by attempting to organize Mexican laborers into an association, the Liga Protectora Mexicana de California.*

The defense of the Hispanic community, perceived by the larger society as alien and hostile, was a mission shared by similar newspapers throughout the Southwest, the Midwest, Florida, and the Northeast. A Midwestern Spanish-language newspaper, *El Cosmopolita* (The Cosmopolitan, 1914–1919),* despite its being owned by Jack Danciger, an Anglo-American businessman intent on selling alcoholic beverages and other products imported from Mexico to the Mexican colony in Kansas City, also served to provide some form of protection to immigrants in that city. Danciger, to further his business interests on both sides of the border, forged extensive relations with the Constitutionalist government of Venustiano Carranza, who used the organ to promote his political agenda in Mexico. Nonetheless, Danciger's Mexican editors provided information that the Spanish-speaking immigrants needed for survival in Kansas City—such as housing and employment information—as well as for defending themselves from discrimination and exploitation. Moreover, the newspaper protested against segregation, racial prejudice, police harassment and brutality, injustice in the judicial system and mistreatment in the work place.

For the Mexican immigrant communities in the Southwest, defense of the civil and human rights also extended to protecting Mexican immigrants from the influence of Anglo-American culture and Protestantism. The publishers, editorialists, and columnists were almost unanimous in developing and promoting the idea of a "México de afuera"—a Mexican colony existing outside of Mexico, in which it was the duty of the individual to maintain the Spanish language, keep the Catholic faith, and insulate their children from what community leaders perceived as the low moral standards practiced by Anglo Americans.

Inherent in the ideology of "México de afuera" as it was expressed by many cultural elites was an upper-class and bourgeois mentality that ironically tended to resent association with the Mexican immigrant working class. To them, the poor *braceros* and former *peones* were an uneducated mass whose ignorant habits only gave Anglo Americans the wrong impression of Mexican and Hispanic culture. To such self-exiled elites, many Mexican Americans and other Hispanics long residing within the United States were little better than Anglos themselves, having abandoned their language and many cultural traits in exchange for the almighty dollar. It was, therefore, important that *la gente de bien*, this educated and refined class, grasp the leadership of the community, down to the grassroots, if need be, in the holy crusade of preserving Hispanic identity in the face of the Anglo onslaught.

Among the most powerful of the political, business, and intellectual figures in the Mexican immigrant community was Ignacio E. Lozano, founder and operator of the two most powerful and well-distributed daily newspapers: San Antonio's *La Prensa,* founded in 1913, and Los Angeles' *La Opinión,* founded in 1926 and still publishing today. Lozano, from a successful business family in northern Mexico, relocated to San Antonio in 1908 with his mother and sister in search of business opportunities; there he opened a bookstore and gradually learned the newspaper business through on-the-job experiences while working first for San Antonio's *El Noticiero* and later for *El Imparcial de Texas.** With the business training and experience that he received in Mexico, Lozano was able to contribute professionalism and business acumen to Hispanic journalism in the United States, resulting in his successfully publishing two of the longest-running Spanish-language daily papers. His sound journalistic policies and emphasis on professionalism resulted in *La Prensa* reaching thousands not only in San Antonio but throughout the Southwest, Midwest and northern Mexico through a vast distribution system that included newsstand sales, home delivery and mail. *La Prensa* also set up a network of correspondents in the United States who were able to report on current events and cultural activities of Mexican communities as far away as Chicago, Detroit, and New York. Unlike the publishers of many other Hispanic immigrant newspapers, Lozano also set about serving the long-standing Mexican-American population in San Antonio and the Southwest, reaching broader segments and all classes, in part by not being overtly political or partisan of any political faction in Mexico and by recognizing the importance of the Mexicans who had long resided in the United States. He and his staff sought to bring Mexican Americans within the "México de afuera" ideology.

Unfortunately, *La Prensa* did not survive long enough to see the Chicano Movement* of the 1960s, the civil rights movement that promoted a cultural nationalism of its own. *La Prensa* suffered a slow death beginning in 1957, when it reverted to a weekly and then was sold repeatedly to various interests until it shut down forever in 1963. Unlike Los Angeles, where *La Opinión* still thrives today, San Antonio did not continue to attract a steady or large enough stream of immigrants to sustain the newspaper as the children of the immigrants became English-dominant. (SOURCE: Kanellos, *Hispanic Periodicals in the United States,* 15-23.)

HISPANIC LEADERSHIP INSTITUTE

Chartered in May 1982, in Chicago, as a voter-registration project, the United States Hispanic Leadership Institute (USHLI) was known as the

Midwest-Northeast Voter Registration until it acquired its present title in 1996. While the organization still emphasizes voter registration, it has expanded its mandate to provide leadership training. As of 2005, more than 185,000 participants have been through the institute leadership programs. These include high school and college students, grassroots community leaders, local public officials, and candidates for public office. The institute also sponsors an annual conference, which has become the largest Hispanic gathering in the nation. At these meetings, the participants, mainly young men and women, receive a number of leadership awards and college scholarships. Dr. Juan Andrade, the institute's founder and director, is committed to USHLI's mission statement: "to fulfill the promises and principles of democracy by empowering minorities and similarly disenfranchised groups and by maximizing civic awareness and participation in the electoral process." [SOURCE: http://www.ushli.com]

THE HISPANIC NATIONAL BAR ASSOCIATION

Founded in California in 1972 as La Raza National Lawyers Association, the Hispanic National Bar Association (HNBA) is an incorporated, non-profit, national association representing the interest of over 25,000 Hispanic American attorneys, judges, law professors, and law students in the United States and Puerto Rico. Since its inception, it has grown to represent thousands of Puerto Rican, Cuban-American, Mexican-American, South and Central American attorneys, as well as any others within the profession. Attorneys affiliated with the HNBA are provided with assistance that can enhance their own professional advancement and are informed about issues affecting the Hispanic community. Ultimately, a primary objective of the HNBA is to educate the American public on the workings of the legal system and to promote confidence in its ability to deliver equitable results. HNBA sponsors annual national conventions, where participants attend educational seminars, continuing legal education classes, and social functions. These meetings have attracted thousands of members, prominent speakers, and guests from the political, social, and economic leadership of the Americas. [SOURCE: http://www.larazalawyers.com/]

HISPANIC RADIO NETWORK

Based in Washington, D.C., the Hispanic Radio Network was created in 1982 in Santa Fe, New Mexico, to inform Hispanics about health, environment, education, social justice, and how to obtain resources. The network accomplishes this through nine Spanish-language radio programs that broadcast on more than 100 popular Spanish-language radio stations throughout the United States. Among the network's programs are "Bienvenidos a América" (Welcome to America), "Mundo 2000" (World 2000), "Sexo y Algo

Más" (Sex and Something Else), "Buscando el Bienestar" (Looking for Well-Being), "Planeta Azul" (Blue Planet), "Consuelo Comenta" (Consuelo Comments), "Camino al Éxito" (Road to Success), "Fuente de Salud" (Fountain of Health), and "Saber es Poder" (Knowledge Is Power). Programs produced by Hispanic Radio Network are designed to inspire and motivate listeners by airing interviews with Hispanic role models who are leaders in health, education, science, the environment, and social justice. [SOURCE: http://www.hrn.org]

HISPANIC SCHOLARSHIP WEB SITE

In November 2002, the National Education Association (NEA) and the National Hispanic Press Foundation created a web site that made available more than 1,000 sources of financial aid to Hispanic students around the country and world. Students can access application guidelines, an alumni section, and a database of scholarships arranged by a variety of categories, including state, college, and field of interest. The site, according to its creators, exists primarily because most Hispanics do not know about the full range of opportunities available for securing an education and financial aid. [SOURCE: www.scholarshipsforhispanics.org]

HISPANIC SOCIETY

The Hispanic Society, also known as the Hispanic Foundation, was founded in San Antonio, Texas, in 1963. Composed mainly of descendants of the Spanish Canary Islanders who settled in San Antonio in 1731, the organization's main objective is to preserve the heritage of San Antonio. In the 1960s, the society petitioned the National University of Mexico City to establish an extension in San Antonio. After an agreement was made, the city provided the buildings, and the university provided a staff that established a program leading to a degree. Hundreds of students, half of them Anglo Americans specializing in Spanish, took courses in language, literature, and other subjects related to Hispanic culture. The society also obtained funding from the Texas legislature for a bilingual educational program for San Antonio schools, in which more than half of the population is Spanish-speaking. The society also promotes projects dealing with the literature and philosophy of Spain. Courses on Spanish philosopher Ortega y Gasset and the poet Miguel de Unamuno have been an integral part of the curriculum. The society's annual social affairs include San Antonio's leading citizens, as well as dignitaries from Spain and Mexico. [SOURCE: Campa, *Hispanic Culture in the Southwest*, 188.]

HISPANIC WOMEN'S CORPORATION

Founded in 1985 in Phoenix, Arizona, the Hispanic Women's Corporation's most important mission has been to empower Latinas. Its members actively seek successful strategies and information that will benefit Latinas in a changing global society. One of its most important projects is its annual Our Youth Leadership Conference, which invites more than 200 Latina high school students to a summit, where the young women are provided leadership training, access to resources, and a forum on networking. Yearly, some 1,000 Latinas from across the country attend the National Hispanic Women's Conference, also sponsored by the corporation in Phoenix, where they obtain professional leadership development and community involvement training and orientation. [SOURCE: http://www.hispanicwomen.org/]

HISPANIC YOUNG ADULT ASSOCIATION

The Hispanic Young Adult Association (HYAA), founded in 1953, was among the first of organizations to base reformist activities on the culture and ideology of Puerto Ricans living in the New York metropolitan area. HYAA, made up primarily of college-trained social workers, advanced assimilation to benefit the careers of young professionals and college students, a notion the organization embraced because it had worked so well for other ethnic groups. HYAA subscribed to the notion that "science and effective social intervention would eventually solve society's ills." The association also aspired to create a leadership committed to integration, rather than to the concerns of the island of Puerto Rico. In the mid 1950s, as HYAA became more involved with issues of identity, it rejected assimilation and defined itself culturally as Puerto Rican, renaming itself the Puerto Rican Association for Community Affairs (PRACA).* As PRACA, however, the group remained committed to creating leadership gains, from the grassroots up, for the Puerto Rican community in the United States. [SOURCE: Sánchez Korrol, *From Colonia to Community*, 225-26.]

HISPANICS IN PHILANTHROPY

Hispanics in Philanthropy (HIP) was founded in 1983 to promote stronger links between philanthropic organizations and Latino communities. HIP has more than 450 members representing corporate, public, and private philanthropies, nonprofit leadership and academia. Based in California, HIP sponsors regional, national, and international conferences and briefings. It also conducts research on potential funding for Hispanic-related projects and the possibility of employment for Hispanics in philanthropy, information is made available to its constituency through HIP publications. In 2000, HIP initiated the Funders' Collaborative Project to offer technical assistance and coordinate the efforts of local, national, and transnational funders and corporations to build capacity among small- and medium-sized Latino nonprofit organizations in the United States and Latin America. [SOURCE: http://www.hiponline.org/home/About+HIP/]

THE HOMESTEAD ACT

In 1862, Congress passed the Homestead Act after seventy years of controversy over the disposition of public lands. Since the founding of the United States, many Americans embraced a free soil ideology, but slaveowners opposed such tenets. Since the 1830s, liberal groups, usually in the North, had been clamoring for free distribution of such lands without slavery. The Republican Party adopted this posture in its 1860 platform and, when the southern states seceded with the beginning of the Civil War, opposition to this policy was removed. With the way cleared, the Homestead Act took effect on January 1, 1863. It allowed any American to file for a quarter-section of free land (160 acres) if it demonstrated the family would live on the land by making specified improvements. Thousands of homesteaders rushed west to claim land. By 1900, some 600,000 farmers received approximately 80 million acres. In California, thousands converged on lands claimed by Mexicans, creating legal entanglements which were many times settled in favor of the squatters. Many of homesteaders were front men for speculators, who took these free lands and held them for future use or sale. [SOURCE: Pence, "The Homestead Act of 1862."]

HOMIES UNIDOS

In 1996, rival gang members in El Salvador created Homies Unidos to stem the warfare, the drug use, and sexually transmitted diseases such as HIV/AIDs that were devastating urban youth. The goal of the organization was to provide meaningful educational and employment opportunities for young men and women as an alternative to a violent lifestyle. Many gang members had lived in the United States, principally in California cities, and had brought the gang lifestyle to El Salvador. In most cases, their parents had been part of a massive migration to the United States caused by the twelve-year war in El Salvador. Poverty, discrimination, and lack of parental control in the United States had alienated the young boys and girls from school and their own families; they were, thus, prime recruits for gangs. In gangs, they found instant substitutes for friends and family. After the war ended, the U.S. Immigration and Naturalization Service* deported many young Salvadorans to El Salvador, a country they hardly knew and where they experienced poverty and alienation, which increased gang activity. The founders of Homies Unidos knew that they could not provide solutions using traditional persuasion, so they recruited the gang members themselves in an attempt to provide alternatives. The experiment has met with success, although the organization has not been in existence long. Homies Unidos now has chapters in major cities of the United States with large El Salvadoran populations. [SOURCE: Rose-Ávila, "Homies Unidos, El Salvador Peer Education with Gang Members," http://www.fhi.org]

HOPWOOD V. TEXAS

The *Hopwood v. Texas* case is named after Cheryl Hopwood, the lead plaintiff who along with three other white students filed a lawsuit in 1992 in the U.S. Western Federal District against the University of Texas Law School. The suit claimed that less qualified students were admitted to the school because of their race. The district court ruled in favor of the plaintiffs but the university appealed and in 1996, a Fifth U.S. Circuit Court of Appeals affirmed the decision from the lower court. The decision prevented Texas colleges and universities from considering race or ethnic origin in admissions or financial aid decisions. Soon after the ruling, the number of Latinos who applied and were admitted to many of the most selective publicly funded Texas universities decreased. The number of Latino students receiving financial aid also decreased drastically. The Texas Higher Education Coordinating Board, the Texas Legislature and university administrators attempted to compensate for these losses by using alternative policies to increase Latino enrollments, despite the *Hopwood* decision. To counterbalance the lack of access to publicly funded universities using SAT scores as the main criterion for admission, the Texas legislature subsequently passed a law requiring admission for all students graduating in the top ten percent of their high school class. Ironically, the *Hopwood* decision created even more opportunity for minority students, many of whom would have been passed over because of low SAT scores and because their high schools were previously considered low-achieving. In 2001, the University of Texas appealed the case to the U.S. Supreme Court, which refused to hear it. However, in June 2003, the U.S. Supreme Court in *Grutter v. Bollinger* ruled against Barbara Grutter, a plaintiff who had filed a similar suit in 1997 against the University of Michigan School of Law. This invalidated the *Hopwood* decision, and Texas could return to the affirmative action policies of the past. [SOURCE: http://www.aaup.org/Issues/AffirmativeAction/aalegal.htm]

HUERTA, DOLORES (1930-)

Dolores Huerta is one of the most significant Latina leaders in the twentieth century, making a mark in many areas but primarily in civil rights and farmworker organizing. Born in the mining town of Dawson, New Mexico, Dolores Huerta was the second child and only daughter of Juan Fernández and Alicia Chaves Fernández. Huerta's ancestry on her mother's side is from New

Dolores Huerta

Mexico; her father's parents came from Mexico. After her parents divorced while she was only a toddler, her mother took her and her two brothers to northern California, where she became a businesswoman. Unlike most farmworker leaders, Huerta had no experience laboring in the fields; instead, she inherited her mother's business skills and, after being an active organizer in Girl Scouts and Catholic youth groups in her youth, Huerta dedicated her life to service, first in the Community Services Organization (CSO)* and then in the farmworkers union.

Huerta's father, a one-time migrant farmworker who received a college degree and was elected to the New Mexico State Legislature, also served to inspire her political and social activism. One of his main concerns as a legislator was labor reform. Unlike Hispanic women of her generation, Huerta attended college and received a teaching certificate, but instead of going into the classroom, she turned to social activism. In the mid-1950s, she began to work for the CSO, a Mexican-American self-help association founded in Los Angeles. Once in, she became one the most successful organizers in registering people to vote and persuading immigrants to attend citizenship classes; she also led grassroots campaigns pressing local governments to make improvements in the Mexican barrios. Recognizing her considerable skills, the CSO sent her to Sacramento to lobby for legislation that would benefit Hispanics. One of her major accomplishment as a lobbyist was persuading the legislature to eliminate the citizenship requirement for public assistance programs. Before serving as a lobbyist, the CSO had assigned her in 1957 to help organize the Agricultural Workers Association in Stockton, an experience that injected in her a lifelong concern about the living and working conditions of farmworkers.

In 1962, Huerta caught the attention of César Chávez,* the director of the CSO in California and Arizona, who resigned to organize farmworkers fulltime. Compatible because of their mutual training, Huerta shared with Chávez the CSO will to win. Huerta became second-in-command to Chávez, helping to shape and guide the nascent National Farm Workers Association (NFWA) which became the United Farm Workers of America.* In the ensuing years, the union had many successes, but an equal number of disappointments. Through it all, she remained faithful to Chávez, but she also spoke out on behalf of women within the union.

Chávez assigned Dolores Huerta to negotiate all union contracts in the early 1970s. Her skills in lobbying and organizing were crucial when the

California legislature passed the California Labor Relations Act, which provided farmworkers the same rights as other workers. After Chávez died, she continued to serve in leadership positions. Huerta sacrificed much in her endeavors, including eschewing financial rewards, going to jail, and even being beaten by policemen and being hospitalized in 1988. [SOURCE: http://www.galegroup.com/free_resources/chh/bio/huerta_d.htm; Rosales, *Chicano!*, 132-135, 147, 150.]

HUMAN RIGHTS FIRST

Since the late 1970s, Human Rights First has been in the forefront of protecting refugee rights in the United States. Based in Washington, D.C., the organization has established two operational venues to fulfill this objective. One is a network of pro bono attorneys who provide legal services to asylum-seekers who ask for protection in the United States but are unable to pay for private representation. The second is developing a reserve of legal knowledge based on the numerous cases handled by the organization in order to advocate for legislative and administrative measures that provide asylum-seekers in the United States with access to fair procedures. Human Rights First led efforts in 1980 to influence the passage of the first refugee legislation in the United States. The organization's efforts to provide relief to asylum-seekers dates to the late 1970s, when its representatives reported on the mistreatment of Haitian asylum-seekers by the Immigration and Naturalization Service* in South Florida. Since these early efforts, Human Rights First has continued to be a forceful voice in Washington for the rights of refugees. [SOURCE: http://www.humanrightsfirst.org/about_us/about_us.htm]

HUMANE BORDERS

Humane Borders was founded on June 11, 2001, by religious activists who wanted to create a just and humane border environment. Members have responded with humanitarian assistance to immigrants risking their lives and safety crossing the U.S. border with Mexico. One of main activities of Humane Borders members is to provide water stations that can be used by the undocumented migrants who are crossing the Sonoran Desert to get to urban areas of Arizona. The group encourages the formation of public policies for a humane, non-militarized border with legalized work opportunities for migrants in the United States and legitimate economic opportunities in the migrants' countries of origin. [SOURCE: http://www.humaneborders.org]

HURRICANE MITCH, EFFECTS OF

In October of 1998, Hurricane Mitch devastated much of Central America, especially Honduras and El Salvador. Apart from the large number of deaths caused primarily by flooding and disease, living quarters were destroyed, employment sources dried up, and food became almost impossible to obtain. Aid was soon forthcoming, especially from the United States, Canada, and Mexico—millions of Latino immigrants in these countries organized gargantuan efforts to gather aid. But thousands of refugees fled to Mexico and the United States. Most of these immigrants were from Honduras, followed by Nicaragua, Guatemala, and El Salvador. Immigration authorities in the United States and Mexico braced themselves for the onslaught.

The Honduran authorities announced the creation of a frontier patrol to supposedly stop illegal immigrants heading north, a move that was probably done under pressure from the United States—Honduran authorities usually do not discourage emigration since Honduras suffers from large unemployment and the country depends on money sent home by Honduran workers in the United States and Canada. Guatemala also passed emigration laws restricting Central Americans crossing the border into Mexico and heading north. Mexican border officials stepped up the apprehension of Central Americans as a way of defusing the problem before it appeared on the much longer 1,700 mile border between Mexico and the United States.

Seeing this hardship, immigrant advocates asked the Clinton Administration to grant either Temporary Protected Status (TPS) or Deferred Enforced Departure (DED) for a period of at least 18 months to Hondurans, Nicaraguans, Salvadorans, and Guatemalans who had arrived in the United States before November 1, 1998. The Clinton Administration did halt deportations for six months and released a small number of Central Americans from detention centers. Some Central Americans were able to avoid deportation because of provisions in legislation that allowed for permanent status for war refugees, but that took time and money for lawyers to prove that deportation could result in "extreme hardship" back home. [SOURCE: Sharry, "After the Hurricane: How U.S. Immigration Policy Can Help," 23-25.]

IBÁÑEZ, DORA VIOLETA (1918-?)

Dora Violeta Ibáñez was born in Ciudad Juárez, Chihuahua, Mexico in 1918, and educated in Texas. She migrated to Arizona with her parents José M. Ibáñez and Eva Sánchez de Ibáñez. Her father, a Presbyterian minister, had a church in Bisbee, Arizona. While there, Dora Violeta Ibáñez received a degree from Arizona Normal School (now Arizona State University). Her father then took a post in Los Angeles, where Dora became active in the Mexican American Movement (MAM).* In 1939, she published an essay in *Mexican Voice* entitled "A Challenge to the American Girl of Mexican Parentage." The essay praised MAM for its work toward education and Americanization. However, Ibáñez criticized the group for targeting men only. She urged Mexican-American women to obtain an education and pursue professional careers. A good place to begin, she stated, was participating in MAM. [SOURCE: Rosales, *Chicano!*, 101.]

IDAR, JOVITA (1885-1946)

Jovita Idar was a member of a very politically active family in South Texas. Her father, Nicasio Idar, the influential editor of Laredo's *La Crónica*, played a key role in 1911 in organizing El Primer Congreso Mexicanista (The First Mexicanist Congress),* the first major convention of Mexicans from throughout the state of Texas. Her brother, Eduardo Idar, was a labor organizer and a founder of the League of United Latin American Citizens.*

Born in Laredo, Texas, in 1885, Jovita Idar was one of eight children in the family of Nicasio Clemente and Jovita Vivero. She earned a teaching certificate from the Holding Institute in Laredo at 18 and taught Mexican children in a small school. She left the classroom, however, to write for *La Crónica*, believing that as a journalist and an activist she could expose the deplorable conditions that existed in the segregated and isolated public schools attended by Mexican children. Idar's pen turned also to revealing the atrocities committed by the Texas Rangers* against Mexicans. When her father and brothers helped organize the Primer Congreso Mexicanista, she was instrumental in organizing the group's auxiliary, called La Liga Femenil Mexicanista (The Female Mexicanist League), which allowed Jovita Idar and other women to form tuition-free schools for Mexican children called *escuelitas*. La Liga, which met at Jovita Idar's parents' home and *La Crónica*, also provided free food and clothing for the needy in the community and published news about its activities.

From left to right: Unidentified man, Rev. Neftalí Ávila, Leonor Villegas de Magnón, María Alegría, Jovita Idar, Rosa Chávez, and Elvira Idar

The Mexican Revolution spilled across the border and provoked massive repression against Mexicans by Texas Rangers and other law officials, and Jovita Idar in 1913 crossed into Mexico and supported the efforts of Venustiano Carranza and his main general, Pancho Villa,* serving as a nurse in the Cruz Blanca, a medical support group of the revolutionaries. During Woodrow Wilson's invasion of Veracruz* in 1914, the border became more militarized than ever, a process deplored by Jovita Idar in her writing. The Texas Rangers, as a result, came to Laredo to destroy her printing press, but she physically blocked them at the door and forced them to back down. Nonetheless, they came back later in the middle of night, broke into the newspaper building, and destroyed the press.

At 32, Jovita Idar married Bartolo Juárez and moved with her husband to San Antonio, where she continued her activism as an active member of the Democratic Party; she hoped to politically empower the Mexican-American community. She also continued her desire to improve educational conditions and, in 1920, founded a free bilingual kindergarten school for Mexicans. She also continued to write about social and educational problems until she died at age 61, in 1946. [SOURCE: La Voz de Aztlán Communications Network, "Heroes and Heroines of La Raza Series."]

ILLEGAL IMMIGRATION REFORM AND IMMIGRANT RESPONSIBILITY ACT

An immigration increase from Mexico and large numbers of refugees from Cuba, Haiti, and Central America (Nicaragua, Salvador, and Guatemala) concerned the American public and lawmakers in the 1980s and early 1990s. As a result in 1996, Congress passed the Illegal Immigration Reform and Immigrant Responsibility Act which was designed to limit assistance to legal immigrants, reduce illegal immigration, and improve the efficiency of the political asylum process. The act also revised the Immigration and Naturalization Service's* procedures, resulting in new guidelines on deportation and detention that have made it easier to deport aliens. [SOURCE: McBride, "Migrants and Asylum Seekers," 289-317.]

IMMIGRATION AND NATURALIZATION SERVICE

The Immigration and Naturalization Service (INS) was created by the U.S. Congress in 1891 and assigned to the Department of Labor. Its tasks included admitting and excluding immigrants, naturalizing, and deporting aliens, as well as guarding the border to make sure illegal activities such as drug smuggling did not occur. The INS and its enforcement agency, the Border Patrol, have been important targets for Mexican-American civil rights activists. The Border Patrol, organized in 1924 to augment thinly staffed customs agents, was given primary responsibility for curbing illegal entries, but personnel limitations restricted its effectiveness. In 1925, for example, only nine men, responsible for some 90 miles of border, operated in the El Paso area. Previous to restrictive immigration laws passed in 1917 and 1924, the INS had maintained special inspectors on the border to halt Chinese entries, who were barred completely from entering the United States.

The INS was often under severe political scrutiny because the entry of foreigners into the United States has been a politically divisive issue. The INS has often been attacked for its inability to stem undocumented entries. After the World Trade Center terrorist attack, critics of the INS became so numerous and vocal that the service was reorganized. On March 1, 2003, INS functions were separated into three divisions and assigned to the Department of Homeland Security (DHS): the Bureau of Citizenship and Immigration Services (BCIS), the Bureau of Immigration and Customs Enforcement (BICE), and the Bureau of Customs and Border Protection (BCBP). Immigration services and benefits, including adjudications, issuance of employment authorization documents, and naturalization now falls under the rubric of the BCIS. President George W. Bush appointed Eduardo Aguirre, Jr., a former Vice-Chair of the Export-Import Bank of the United States to head the BCIS. Michael García, Acting Commissioner of the INS, was appointed by Bush to head BICE, the unit responsible for investigative and interior enforcement duties formerly addressed by INS, the U.S. Customs Service and the Federal Protective Service. The BCBP, charged with border enforcement, immigration investigations, and border policing is headed by Robert Donner, former Commissioner of the INS. This unit now administers Border Patrol activities. [SOURCE: Rosales, *Pobre Raza!*, 87-96, 97-98; http://uscis.gov/graphics/aboutus/history]

IMMIGRATION LAW OF 1830

Perhaps the most vexing development for Anglos who had settled in Mexican Texas was the Immigration Law of April 6, 1830. In 1827, Manuel Mier y Terán, a military officer charged with assessing general conditions in Texas, concluded that Anglos posed a threat to the sovereignty of Mexico. Then in 1830, a coup d'état by Vicente Guerrero's vice president, Anastasio Bustamante, installed a conservative government that was intent on closing off the borders of Mexico to outsiders. The suggestions by Terán found enthusiastically receptive ears among the newly installed conservatives, especially Bustamante's minister, Lucas Alamán, who became an aggressive proponent of legal codification of Terán's views. The law voided land contracts that had not been consummated and only allowed immigration of groups containing one hundred families, such as Stephen F. Austin's colony.* Any Anglo-American immigrants arriving after the law was enacted were forbidden to settle near U.S. borders. In addition, to prevent illegal immigration, the borders with the United States were fortified. Significantly, the law also banned the additional importation of slaves into Texas and began taxing imports. [SOURCE: http://www.tamu.edu/ccbn/dewitt/consultations1.htm]

IMMIGRATION REFORM AND CONTROL ACT OF 1986

In 1986, the U.S. Congress passed the Immigration Reform and Control Act (IRCA), which established a legalization program that would affect hundreds of thousands of Hispanic undocumented workers. To a degree, legalizing their immigration status allowed these immigrants to be less vulnerable to the abuses of employers and provided relief from the threat of arrest by immigration officials. Under this law, undocumented workers could obtain legal status if they had been in the United States before January 1, 1982, and had not left the United States after that date. The bill included sanctions against employers who hired undocumented workers.

It is estimated that IRCA's amnesty and its added provision, the Special Agricultural Worker program (SAW) for seasonal workers, provided two million Mexicans with legal immigration status. Although many immigrants used fraudulent documents to qualify for amnesty or to receive special status as agricultural workers, the vast majority of those who benefited did it through legitimate means. Millions of others, however, have entered without documents after the amnesty date, a process that continues to this date. The amnesty part of IRCA proved to be much more successful than the enforcement measures taken to deter future illegal movements. Employer sanctions were adopted without an effective verification system. A proliferation of fraudulent documents, inadequate border controls, and work day enforcement permitted millions of unauthorized Mexicans to come to the United States despite IRCA's controls. [SOURCE: Martin, "Mexico-U.S. Migration."]

EL IMPARCIAL DE TEXAS

Founded by San Antonio-pharmacist Francisco Chapa* in 1913, *El Imparcial de Texas*, a Spanish-language daily newspaper, often denounced defamation in the English-language public media. Chapa became one of the most effective defenders of civil rights because he successfully developed connections with Anglo-American businessmen and authorities. Through his help, for example, at least three Mexicans condemned to the gallows received clemency. He also promoted naturalization for Mexicans and urged them to vote for politicians whom he himself supported. During World War I, every week, he published the names of Hispanic casualties, as a reminder of the sacrifices Mexicans were making for the cause of democracy. [SOURCE: Rosales, *Pobre Raza!*, 30, 145-146.]

El Imparcial de Texas

INDEPENDENT SCHOOL DISTRICT V. SALVATIERRA

In 1930, Mexican-American parents, with support from the League of United Latin American Citizens,* won their first discrimination suit, attacking segregation in the Texas schools in the case of *Independent School District v. Salvatierra*, brought by Jesús Salvatierra against the Del Rio school district. The courts found that Mexican-American children had been segregated without regard to individual ability; the only legitimate use of segregation should be for special education. The case put an end to the practice of labeling certain schools "Mexican," but, in most instances, segregation did not end, just the naming of the school. [SOURCE: Kanellos, *Chronology of Hispanic American History*, 196.]

INLAND EMPIRE LATINO LAWYERS ASSOCIATION

Since 1985, the Inland Empire Latino Lawyers Association (IELLA) volunteer attorneys have provided free legal services for the poor and underprivileged via legal aid clinics located in the Riverside and San Bernardino counties. Members of the Inland Empire's bar founded IELLA because thousands of residents of limited financial resources and language barriers did not have access to adequate legal counsel. With the help of the United Way,

IELLA has stayed on course in providing access to legal help. [SOURCE: http://www.iellaaid.org]

INQUILINOS BORICUAS EN ACCIÓN

Inquilinos Boricuas en Acción (Puerto Rican Renters in Action) grew out of a 1968 confrontation between predominantly Puerto Rican community activists in Boston and developers who attempted to tear down a Latino neighborhood in order to gain control of the area under the guise of urban renewal. The activists literally turned back the bulldozers, a dramatic maneuver that became a seminal moment in progressive Boston politics. Because of this grassroots effort, affordable housing was provided, and the civil rights of poor, working Latinos in Boston were protected. Standing today where this confrontation took place is Villa Victoria, the 435-unit housing community of 3,000 multicultural residents, right in the middle of the gentrified and affluent South End. [SOURCE: "Acción (IBA)," http://www.elboricua. com/Directory.html]

INSTITUTO DE ESTUDIOS CUBANOS

In 1972, a core of Cuban-American scholars in Miami, Florida, established the Instituto de Estudios Cubanos (IEC) under the direction of María Cristina Herrera. Until the late 1980s, IEC members met every year in such cities as Caracas, Miami, San Juan, Cambridge, and Orlando in an academic forum to study Cuba "in a serious and responsible fashion, with no regards to their political orientation." The organization was made up of moderates, conservatives, and Marxists. Most members did not support Fidel Castro's communist government, but unlike other exile organizations, the IEC was willing to enter into dialogue with Cuban scholars on the island and to study Cuban revolutionary processes from an objective perspective. In 1980, the IEC held a seminar in Havana and, in spite of U.S. State Department opposition, Cuban scholars also participated in the meeting held in the United States. Because of this rather lax attitude towards Cuba, exile hardliners often harassed IEC activists and María Cristina Herrera. [SOURCE: García, *Havana USA,* 206.]

INTER-AGENCY CABINET COMMITTEE ON MEXICAN AMERICAN AFFAIRS

President Lyndon B. Johnson (LBJ)* established the first Inter-Agency Cabinet Committee on Mexican American Affairs and appointed Vicente Treviño Ximenes,* a research economist and politician, as its chair. The committee was established to coordinate programs in federal departments that affected Mexican Americans. As a result, more Mexican Americans were recruited for government positions and more agencies were set up to provide services to the Hispanic community than ever before in history. The committee was the result of Mexicans having registered their largest vote in history in the 1964 presidential elections, voting solidly for LBJ. The establishment of the committee was more specifically a result of the first meeting in the White House of any president with a committee of Mexican-American representatives, in 1966. The committee expanded in December 1969, to become the Cabinet Committee on Opportunities for Spanish-Speaking People,* headed by Henry A. Quevedo. [SOURCE: García, *Memories of Chicano History*, 218-21.]

LA INTERNACIONAL AND LA RESISTENCIA: PIONEER PUERTO RICAN LABOR ORGANIZATIONS IN THE UNITED STATES

Soon after their arrival in the early twentieth century, many Puerto Rican workers in New York City joined La Internacional, a union that fell under the umbrella of the American Federation of Labor. Spanish-speaking tobacco workers, including Puerto Ricans, Spaniards, Cubans, and Mexicans, patronized the more radical La Resistencia. The leadership of La Internacional followed North American trade union "bread & butter" dictums, such as collective bargaining, better working conditions, and wages while avoiding the rhetoric of social revolution or the establishing of a political party dominated by workers' interests. In contrast, La Resistencia, followed more revolutionary principles, popular among Latin American anarcho-syndicalist organizations. These unions also advocated mutual aid and Hispanic cultural activity. Examples of mutual aid organizations which existed alongside the unions are La Aurora, La Razón, and El Ejemplo. [SOURCE: Sánchez Korrol, *From Colonia to Community*, 138-139.]

INTERNATIONAL CONFERENCE ON CENTRAL AMERICAN REFUGEES

On December 16, 1992, the United Nations held the International Conference on Central American Refugees. At this plenary meeting, a number of resolutions were issued to encourage nations to deal with the Central American migration crisis. The most fundamental need, peace in their homelands, could only be met through the cooperation among leaders of Central America. The conference called upon the nations receiving these migrants as they traveled to the United States, mainly Mexico and Belize, to implement humane immigration and repatriation policies. [SOURCE: http://www.un.org/documents/ga/res/43/a43r118.htm]

INTERNATIONAL INSTITUTE OF RHODE ISLAND

In 1921, the Young Women's Christian Association established the International Institute of Rhode Island to assist foreign-born women in acclimating to their new American surroundings. The staff and volunteers of the institute served as translators and brokered functional relations between immigrants and their landlords, employers, and government officials. They also offered assistance in whatever capacity was needed. The institute also created separate "nationality" clubs and teas for Polish, Italian, Armenian, Russian, and Portuguese women and established English classes for them. As the ethnic groups from the turn of the century became second- and third-generation, the institute almost went out of existence, but Vietnamese refugees in the 1970s and Hispanic immigrants in the 1980s again required support for the institute. Today, it continues to help reunite families, provide English classes and citizenship lessons to an increasingly Hispanic clientele. [SOURCE: Retsinas, "The International Institute of Rhode Island," 122-140.]

INTERNATIONAL LADIES GARMENT WORKERS UNION

Mexican working women as a group became very active for the first time in organizing workers in the garment industry during the 1930s. Rose Pesotta, an organizer for International Ladies Garment Workers Union, from New York, recruited heavily among Mexican women in Los Angeles and, in 1933, the union launched a massive strike that brought garment production to a halt in Los Angeles. The strike prevailed despite harassment by city officials spurred on by the sweatshop owners. As a consequence, a contract was signed with a number of shops for an increase in wages. Pesotta continued organizing in Los Angeles through World War II, and Latina workers responded enthusiastically, belying the warning Pesotta had received upon embarking on unionization efforts in Los Angeles that Mexicans would not respond to organizing efforts. The union, primarily in Local 266, earned pension plans and other benefits for Latina workers throughout the 1950s and 1960s. The union has persisted to this day and continues to organize among garment industry centers that employ Latinas, such as Los Angeles, El Paso, and cities on the East Coast. It has been in the forefront of recognizing that undocumented workers should be organized in spite of numerous raids by the Immigration and Naturalization Service* on factories employing Mexican and Central American women. [SOURCE: Rosales, *Chicano!*, 119; http://www.usc.edu/isd/archives/la/pubart/Downtown/HiddenLabor/]

INTERRELIGIOUS FOUNDATION FOR COMMUNITY ORGANIZATION/PASTORS FOR PEACE

Founded in 1967, the Interreligious Foundation for Community Organization/Pastors for Peace (IFCO) has worked consistently in the United States to end the U.S. economic blockade of Cuba. Since its founding, and through the leadership of Rev. Lucius Walker, Jr., IFCO has organized five campaigns to send humanitarian aid to Cuba in a process called "friendshipments." The first Friendship Caravan in 1993 consisted of 103 participants in 43 vehicles, who after visiting 90 U.S. cities collected 12.5 tons of unlicensed humanitarian aid to Cuba.

Since then, the cargoes have included school supplies, medicine, and computers. The humanitarian projects, however, have directly challenged U.S. policy, which regards such aid as "trading with the enemy." The blockade does not allow Americans to sell or provide Cuba with food, medicine, or any other goods that originate in the United States. For example, in 1994, the Department of the Treasury froze $43,000 in the organization's bank account to prevent it from operating. In 1996, after San Diego policemen and border officials attacked Friendship Caravan members attempting to cross a shipment destined for Cuba into Mexico, the federal government issued a federal subpoena demanding all the records of the group in order to conduct a Grand Jury probe of its activities, a manuever IFCO activists interpreted as harassment to slow their progress. IFCO has also organized humanitarian aid shipments to Haiti, Iraq, and other nations affected by scarcity of medicine, food, and other non-military goods. [SOURCE: http://www.ifconews.org/]

INTER-UNIVERSITY PROGRAM FOR LATINO RESEARCH, UNIVERSITY OF NOTRE DAME

Leading Latino scholars founded the Inter-University Program for Latino Research (IUPLR) in 1983 to employ the expanding body of knowledge on the Latino community in local, state, regional, national, and international levels in order to effect social change. IUPLR established as its mission the sharing of resources and the advancement of scholarship that would identify and help solve problems and influence social policy affecting Latinos in the United States. The consortium, made up of 16 Latino research centers based at major universities across the breadth of the nation, has expanded the pool of Latino scholars and strengthened the capacity of Latino research centers to conduct and make available Latino-focused research. [SOURCE: http://www.nd.edu/~iuplr/]

INVASION OF VERACRUZ

In April 1914, President Woodrow Wilson ordered the invasion of Veracruz, Mexico, ostensibly as a punitive action against Mexico for three minor incidents for which the White House held General Victoriano Huerta's government responsible. Huerta came to power after he ordered the assassination of Mexican president, Francisco I. Madero, the founder of the Revolution of 1910. The incident which received the most publicity was the arrest of several American sailors as they docked in Tampico to load up on supplies. In addition, Mexican officials detained a mail courier which delayed an official Department of State dispatch. In reality, the American president did not approve of the method used by Huerta to take over Mexico. To get support from the American people for the invasion, however, Mexicans were cast as undisciplined and violent. The ensuing backlash led to anti-Mexican demonstrations, sometimes marked by violence against immigrants. This was simply one of the incidents during this period of turmoil that led to the negative opinion that United States' citizens had of Mexicans. [SOURCE: Quirk, *An Affair of Honor*.]

JAPANESE EXCLUSION LEAGUE OF CALIFORNIA, *see* CALIFORNIA JOINT IMMIGRATION COMMITTEE

JIMÉNEZ, MARÍA (1950-)

For thirty-five years, María Jiménez has devoted her time and energy to organizing unions and farmworkers in Mexico, and more recently she has directed the Immigration Law Committee of the Enforcement Monitoring Project (LEMP), founded in 1987 and sponsored by the American Friends Service. Under the project's mission of documenting human rights violations in the U.S-Mexican border region, Jiménez has worked with community-based groups in four border areas: San Diego, southern Arizona, the El Paso/New Mexico area, and the Rio Grande Valley in Texas. Born in Mexico in 1951, Jiménez came to Texas with her family while still a child and attended schools in Houston. At the University of Houston (UH), where she enrolled in 1968, she discovered a political-activist orientation that has continued to guide her commitment to social reform. As a Political Science major, in the 1960s and early 1970s she became involved in the Chicano Movement,* confronting such issues as segregation in the local public schools and the necessity to make UH relevant and accountable to the Mexican-American community. While still a young student leader, she became involved in laying the groundwork for the creation of the Mexican American studies program. Jiménez graduated from UH in 1975, moved to Mexico, and devoted her time to union- and community-organizing for ten years. After returning to Houston in 1985, the American Friends Service Committee made her director of LEMP. The Mexican American Studies program at the university often asks her to teach classes so that students can learn firsthand from her experiences. [SOURCE: Markley, "Understanding Latino Activism."]

JIMÉNEZ, RICARDO (1956-)

Ricardo Jiménez is one of 11 Puerto Rican nationalists arrested in the 1980s, convicted of seditious conspiracy and sentenced to a 98-year prison sentence. His crime was an alleged membership in the Armed Forces of Puerto Rican National Liberation (FALN). Born in Puerto Rico in 1956, Jiménez moved with his family to the U.S. mainland when he was still an infant. While attending Tuley High School in Chicago, he joined ASPIRA* because of the school's failure to provide a relevant curriculum for Puerto Rican students. As a student leader, Jiménez was active in the struggles that ultimately led to the creation of the Roberto Clemente* High School. Jiménez was and exemplary honor student and the 1974 recipient of the city of Chicago's Senior High School Student of the Year award. In the community, he worked on projects dealing with drug prevention and housing. Later a student at Loyola University and then at the Illinois Institute of Technology in Chicago, he continued as a student leader, promoting a Latino Studies curriculum and affirmative action in the corporate world of technology. In 1999, President Bill Clinton issued a clemency order releasing political prisoners, after years of efforts by Puerto Rican civil rights groups to effect their release. Jiménez was included in that clemency. [SOURCE: http://www.hartford-hwp.com/archives/43/003.html]

JOB TRAINING PARTNERSHIP ACT

After Congress passed the Job Training Partnership Act (JTPA) in the Spring of 1982, the Reagan administration inaugurated the project on October 13. The JTPA has established programs to prepare youth and unskilled adults for entry into the American work force and to provide job training to economically disadvantaged individuals facing serious employment obstacles. Individuals who qualify for the program are retrained, they upgrade their job skills, receive job placements, referrals, development, and work experience. The project also provides funding for youth work programs in the summer. The services are specifically directed at underdeveloped communities with high unemployment profiles. [SOURCE: http://www.redlakenation.org/jtpa/jtpa.html]

JOHNSON, LYNDON BAINES (1908-1973)

Lyndon B. Johnson was born in Texas in 1908. Following the 1963 assassination of President John F. Kennedy, he became the 36th president of the United States. Before embarking on his very successful political career, Johnson taught elementary school in an all-Mexican school in Cotulla, Texas. In 1949, immediately after his election as U.S. Senator from Texas, Johnson helped secure the burial for Felix Longoria* in Arlington National Cemetery with full honors, after Longoria was denied burial in his hometown's segregated cemetery. This incident was but one episode in the ambiguous relationship the president would have with the Mexican-American community. As a Senator in 1957, he helped pass the first national civil rights legislation since the Civil War. At the 1960 convention, the Democratic Party nominated Johnson for the vice presidency, a politician who early on recognized the importance of the emerging Mexican-American vote in his home state and who urged presidential nominee John F. Kennedy to be responsive to this constituency. President Johnson is remembered for his "War on Poverty" program, the passage of many civil rights bills, and the increased involvement of U.S. troops in the Vietnam War. In 1967, President Johnson established the Inter-Agency Committee on Mexican American Affairs* after Mexican-American organizations that had supported his presidency protested that their communities had not been compensated. Because of the tremendous pressures brought on by the decisions he made during the Vietnam conflict, he chose not to run for a second term in 1968. [SOURCE: Rosales, *Chicano!*, 97; Pycior, *LBJ & Mexican Americans.*]

JONES ACT

Congress passed the Jones-Shafroth Act, more popularly known as the Jones Act in 1917, and President Woodrow Wilson signed it into law on March 2, 1917. The act granted Puerto Ricans U.S. citizenship, even if they were born on the island. Although they had citizenship, Puerto Rican islanders could not vote for the president. Neither could they elect congressmen and senators to Congress. Instead, Puerto Rico could have representation in Congress through a Commissioner in the House of Representatives to advise on issues pertaining to Puerto Rico, but could not vote. Migration out of Puerto Rico was a defined trend several years before the Spanish American War,* however, it established a pattern that would be repeated and accelerated in the twentieth century. Skillful diplomacy by island politicians resulted in the passage of this congressional bill that created two Puerto Rican houses of a legislature whose representatives were elected by the people. Moroeever, the U.S. Congress had the power to stop any action taken by the legislature in Puerto Rico. The United States maintained control over fiscal and economic matters and exercised authority over mail services, immigration, defense, and other basic governmental matters. Puerto Ricans living on the mainland, however, could enjoy the full benefits and privileges of citizenship, including the right to elect congressmen and senators from their home districts and states on the mainland. [SOURCE: http://www.loc.gov/rr/hispanic/1898/jonesact.html]

JUANITA, LYNCHING OF

The lynching of Juanita, or Josefa (probably her real name), was one of the most infamous anti-Mexican incidents during the Gold Rush of California. On the evening of July 4, 1851, in Downieville, California, Joseph Cannon celebrated Independence Day by breaking down the door of the cabin shared by Juanita and her lover, José. The next day José and Cannon got into an argument over the broken door, and as the quarrel started to become physical, Juanita intervened. Cannon reportedly called Juanita a whore. Enraged, Juanita purportedly stabbed Cannon, who died from the wounds. Vigilantes immediately put Juanita on trial. Some townspeople attempted to defend her, including a doctor who claimed she was pregnant. Another doctor, however, disputed the diagnosis, and that was enough for the mob to decide to hang her. The hanging is considered a lynching because of the impromptu trial that had no legal sanction. Most importantly, it reflected how strong anti-Mexican sentiment was in California during the Gold Rush. [SOURCE: http://www.cr. nps.gov/history/online_books/5views/5views5h31.htm]

JUDICIAL WATCH, INC.

Established in 1994, Judicial Watch, Inc.'s mission is to serve as an ethical and legal "watchdog" over governmental, legal, and judicial systems and to promote ethical values and morality in the public life of the United States. Based in Washington, D.C., Judicial Watch is a non-partisan, nonprofit foundation that has established branch offices throughout the country. The organization receives its support from private individuals who share Judicial Watch's commitment to rooting out public corruption in government and public institutions and to make sure offenders are brought to justice. [SOURCE: http://www.judicialwatch.org/about.shtml]

KANELLOS, NICOLÁS (1945-)

Since the 1970s, Nicolás Kanellos, who was born on January 31, 1945 in New York City, has been the driving force in making Arte Público Press* one of the nation's most important presses and the main public outlet for Hispanic literary creativity. In the early 1970s, Kanellos co-founded, with Luis Dávila, the *Revista Chicana-Riqueña*, which later became *The Americas Review*, a journal that published and promoted some of the most important Latino literature, art, and thought in the United States. In 1979, Kanellos founded Arte Público Press to further the creation of a national forum for Hispanic literature. The following year, he left Indiana University Northwest, his academic base since 1971, for the University of Houston and was invited to bring Arte Público Press with him.

Author of numerous articles and several major books on Hispanic literature and theater, Kanellos received his Ph.D. from the University of Texas in 1974 and is currently Brown Foundation Professor in the Department of Modern and Classical Languages at the University of Houston. He has continued his mission of bringing Hispanic literature to mainstream audiences through the Recovering the U.S. Hispanic Literary Heritage Project,* founded in 1992. The undertaking is the first coordinated, national attempt to recover, index, and publish lost Latino writings that date from the American colonial period through 1960. A recipient of numerous awards, in 1988 President Ronald Reagan presented Kanellos with the White House Hispanic Heritage Award for Literature. He was honored in 1989 with an American Book Award in the publisher-editor category and in 1994, President Bill Clinton appointed Kanellos to a six-year term on the National Council for the Humanities. He has also served as a fellow of the Ford, Lilly, and Gulbenkian Foundations. [SOURCE: http://coh.arizona.edu/newandnotable/honordegree/]

KENNEDY, ROBERT F. (1925-1968)

Robert F. Kennedy was born in Brookline, Massachusetts, in 1925. His adult life, after graduating from Harvard Law School, in 1955, was immersed in political and public service. During the Eisenhower administration, he served as an attorney for the U.S. Department of Justice and was chief counsel to the Senate Permanent Investigations Subcommittee. When his brother, John F. Kennedy, ran for the presidency in 1960, Robert F. Kennedy ran the campaign and then was appointed U.S. Attorney General. In this capacity and after 1964 as a U.S. Senator, Kennedy expressed his concern for the plight and for the enforcement of civil rights. Perhaps more than any other politician in the twentieth century, Kennedy mobilized support from racial minorities, such as African Americans and Hispanics. In 1968, Kennedy was assassinated while campaigning in Los Angeles for the presidential nomination during the California Democratic Primary. That same year, Kennedy had visited East Los Angeles to lend support to the actions of Chicano* high school students who had walked out of classes to protest educational conditions; he had also promoted the efforts of the United Farm Workers (UFW).* On the night of his assassination, Dolores Huerta,* Vice President of the UFW, was at his side moments before he was killed. [SOURCE: http://en.wikipedia.org/wiki/Robert_F._Kennedy]

KNOW-NOTHING PARTY

The American Party, nicknamed the Know-Nothing Party, was founded in 1852 in order to stem political inroads made by Irish immigrants in East Coast cities. Its predecessor was the secretive Order of the Star-Spangled Banner, founded in New York City in 1849 just after Irish immigration inundated such cities as Boston and New York. The party captured city hall in New York and gained control of the Massachusetts and Delaware legislatures. The organization spread to other parts of the country, including Texas, where members of this group were blamed for denying Mexican Catholics their rights and for perpetrating crimes against them. In its 1856 nominating convention, members disagreed over the slavery issue, causing the party's northern members to withdraw. The Know-Nothing Party candidate for the presidency, Millard Fillmore, only polled a small vote and won only in Maryland. The party disappeared soon afterwards. The informal moniker resulted from the party members replying, "I know nothing," to questions about their activities. [SOURCE: http://www.infoplease.com/ce6/history/A0827946.html]

KU KLUX KLAN

In 1865, Confederate Army veterans organized the Ku Klux Klan (KKK) as a social club in Pulaski, Tennessee. Nathan Bedford Forrest, a Confederate general, became the Klan's first Grand Wizard. The name Ku Klux Klan was crafted from the Greek word *kuklos* (circle) and the English word *clan*. Using black robes and hoods, KKK members soon practiced terrorism against freed slaves of African background in order to intimidate their entry into politics and stem any attempts to provide them with civil rights. In 1871, the Force Bill was passed in Congress, authorizing the president of the United States to use federal force to suppress KKK activities, an act that led to its demise. In the beginning of the twentieth century, the organization was revived in Alabama with a wider agenda of repression. The KKK now became anti-Catholic, anti-Semitic, and nativist; by the 1920s, estimates of its membership were as high as 2 million; it had acquired considerable political power throughout the American South and in some Midwestern states.

In the Southwest, the KKK during this era became a force along the border violently repressing Mexican immigration as well as lobbying for its restriction. Because of its incessant threats against border vice, in 1921 an El Paso judge declared that KKK members who took the law into their own hands would be prosecuted. In 1926, the Calexico Ku Klux Klan was among many lobbyist groups militating against border smuggling and in favor of prohibiting access to illicit border businesses.

Mexicans did not suffer the same degree of KKK terrorism as did African Americans, but a number of incidents against Hispanics did occur. In 1923, a number of cross burnings around the mining communities of Globe and Miami alarmed many Arizona Mexicans. During that same year, there were reports of Ku Klux Klan cross burnings aimed at intimidating Mexicans in Santa Barbara, Ventura, and Richmond, California. In the latter community, the burnings coincided with a concerted effort to segregate Mexicans in black neighborhoods.

In Texas, KKK activity was more violent against Mexicans. During the Depression of 1921, at a time of KKK-inspired violence, Texas Rangers* secured the safety of Mexicans assaulted by masked men in the towns of Ranger, Eastland, and Breckenridge, among others. Anti-Mexican violence subsided with the end of the recession, but the agricultural economy again faltered in 1926, and outbreaks returned, especially in Texas. The Houston consul complained that in December, hooded KKK members attacked about 50 Mexicans and 30 Blacks in Sugarland, forcing them to leave town. Most of the Mexicans were humble peons, the consul said. Then as Depression-related unemployment took a toll among American workers in 1931, Anglos blew up a Mexican mutual aid society building in Malankoff, Texas, in what some observers believe was Klan-inspired violence. The Texas governor again sent Rangers to protect Mexican workers because they accepted low wages. Wracked with internal divisions and intimidated by public backlash, the Klan's influence declined in the 1930s. But after World War II, and as the African-American civil rights movement picked up strength, small pockets of uncoordinated violence against African Americans emerged. Latinos were no longer as prominent in the KKK's agenda of repression in this era. [SOURCE: Rosales, *Pobre Raza!*, 72-73, 91, 112, 114, 115; http://www.pbs. org/wnet/jimcrow/stories_org_kkk.html]

LABOR UNIONS AND LATINO WORKERS

In recent years, the AFL-CIO and other labor organizations have met the challenge of immigration with new optimistic rhetoric and corresponding innovative policy. Historically, labor unions in the United States, convinced that immigrant labor depressed wages and robbed their members of a livelihood, allied themselves with immigration restrictionist lobbies. Now, they hope that newcomers to this country will supplant the dwindling rank-and-file that was once comprised of largely white male natives. In 1995, AFL-CIO President John Sweeney and Treasurer Richard Trumka tapped Linda Chávez-Thompson* to become the highest-ranking Hispanic ever in the history of the AFL-CIO by designating her as executive vice president of the giant labor federation. The direction was obviously made because, in the words of Chávez-Thompson, "The unions need to look like the people they're trying to organize."

Since Chávez-Thompson's ascendancy, many Latinos have been promoted to key positions in AFL-CIO affiliated organizations. For example in 1996, Eliseo Medina* a former official of United Farm Workers of America* became head of the Service Employees International Union. In 1996, the late Miguel Contreras* was elected the first Latino Executive Secretary-Treasurer of the Los Angeles County Federation of Labor, AFL-CIO, and his wife Maria Elena Durazo rose to head Los Angeles' hotel employees union local. In New York, Dennis Rivera has led an Independent Hospital Workers Union since 1999, while the hotel employee's local in Las Vegas is lead by Geoconda Argüello. Latino ranks in unions have grown from 1.2 million members in 1992 to 1.6 million in 2002. In part, this growth can be attributed to membership among low-wage workers, who are largely undocumented Hispanics: poultry workers, carpet makers, janitors, and construction tradesmen.

While these gains in real numbers are impressive, however, the percentage of Hispanics who are union members has not kept up with the growth of their overall population. One reason for this is that the sectors where most Latinos work—tourism, manufacturing, and the apparel industry—have been affected by an economic slowdown since the mid 1990s. In addition, this new labor initiative might be hurt further by the plan President George W. Bush unveiled in 2004, which would allow foreign residents and undocumented workers, who can prove they have a job or a job offer from a U.S. employer, to qualify for a three-year temporary work visa. The unions fear that approved workers would be even more vulnerable to punitive measures that would allow employers to bust union efforts in the sectors where organizers are the most active, and workers would receive frozen sub-standard wages. [SOURCE: Radelat, "Wall Street and Business Wednesdays."]

LA FOLLETTE CIVIL LIBERTIES COMMITTEE

Beginning in 1936, the La Folette Civil Liberties Committee, a U.S. Senate subcommittee, investigated impediments to the right of labor to organize and associated denial of civil liberties. Senator Robert La Follette, Jr. headed the committee and began examining labor organizing issues in the steel, auto, and mining industries.

In June 1937, the committee held hearings to investigate the "Republic Steel Massacre," which had occurred in Chicago on May 30, 1937, when striking workers at Republic Steel held a rally at a commons next to the plant and the police ruthlessly shot into the crowd, killing 10 workers. The "Republic Steel Massacre" became union lore, but not until the 1970s did people know the extent to which Mexican laborers had been involved. The La Follette hearings, in fact, interviewed a number of Mexican participants in regard to the atrocity.

The publication of both John Steinbeck's *Grapes of Wrath* and Carey McWilliams' *Factories in the Fields** in 1939 prompted the committee to turn its attention to California agriculture. In the winter 1939-40, the committee held a month of public hearings in San Francisco and Los Angeles.

In October 1942, the La Follette Committee issued its report, but World War II news kept the findings from becoming widely known. The committee concluded that growers used violence and that workers lived in misery. The Associated Farmers were found to practice espionage, blacklisting, and vigilante justice against workers trying to organize. It recommended laws to stabilize agricultural employment, to help recruitment, to improve labor standards and relations, and to establish a wage board to determine fair wages. The conjunction of wartime distractions and high production demands prevented any effective action. [SOURCE: Rosales, *Testimonio,* 249-257.]

LA LUZ, JOSÉ (?-)

Born in Ciales, Puerto Rico, José La Luz moved with his parents to Bridgeport, Connecticut, in 1964, where he became an activist with the Partido Socialista Puertorriqueño (Puerto Rican Socialist Party-PSP). In 1972, he and other civil rights activists joined in a campaign to pressure local newspapers, the *Hartford Courant* and the *Hartford Times*, to hire Puerto Ricans and feature the community in its pages. La Luz became the top socialist leader and organizer in Hartford, and in 1973, the PSP named him regional secretary for New England. One year later, the party appointed him to the U.S. branch secretariat. In the 1990s La Luz worked as an organizer for the American Federation of State, County and Municipal Employees in Puerto Rico. [SOURCE: Torres and Velázquez, *The Puerto Rican Movement*, 73-74; http://www.hartford-hwp.com/archives/43/010.html]

DE LA LAMA, PEDRO (?-?)

Pedro de la Lama became one of Arizona's most active crusading journalists. He helped found a La Liga Protectora Latina,* one of Arizona's first civil rights organization and published numerous newspapers in Phoenix including the vitriolic *Justicia*. He came from Veracruz during the late nineteenth century, first to Solomnville, a mining community and then to Phoenix. By his own account because he opposed the War with Spain, "he was almost lynched." During the Mexican Revolution, he sided with the reaction—first with the opportunistic Pascual Orozco when he turned against Francisco I. Madero in 1913 and then with various exiled malcontents in the 1920s. Nonetheless, in spite of his seemingly conservative alignments, few activists in this era were as strident as they sought to protect the rights of Latinos. However, his political skills were often questioned because he was quick-tempered and extremely contentious. [SOURCE: Rosales, *Chicano!*, 68; McBride, "The Liga Protectora Latina," 82-90.]

LAMBDA SIGMA UPSILON LATINO FRATERNITY

Established in 1979 at the Livingston Campus of Rutgers University by 20 men, the Lambda Sigma Upsilon Latino Fraternity's main mission was to provide Latinos with representation on campus. Although the fraternity was founded as a Latino organization, it now has members from multi-ethnic backgrounds: Italian, Chinese, Egyptian, Arabian, Indian, Russian, Polish, Portuguese, Jewish, African American, and Palestinian. Lambda Sigma Upsilon Latino Fraternity members strongly believe that individual and collective success can be achieved through a culturally diverse brotherhood of college and university men who, through close association with each other, maintain honesty, commitment, respect, and trust. [SOURCE: http://users.aol.com/lsup4 joe/LSU-PIONEROS/HISTORY.HTM]

LAND GRANTS

In much of the Southwest, the property-owning system was originally based on Spanish land law. The Crown issued *mercedes* (land grants) to colonizing groups, who divided them among themselves. The petitioners then lived in villages and walked or rode out to their assigned plots to plant, irrigate, and harvest. Land use was governed collectively, utilizing a system called *ejidos*. The villages were organized around a plaza, where inhabitants gathered to establish policy and settle disputes.

With the changeover after the United States acquired New Mexico, villagers continued using "public domain" lands as they had for centuries, but in the twentieth century the U.S. Forest Service* took control of these grounds. Soon, economic growth fostered land antagonisms, and although the villagers participated in the new ventures and competed with newcomers, lack of capital prevented their full integration. According to some interpretations, the collective approach that evolved among the small farmers did not engender the keen competitive spirit that was common among Anglos and their rich Hispanic collaborators. This notion also holds that Hispanos pursued a traditional way of life that put less emphasis on profits and more emphasis on family. This assumption can be put to debate, but if true, such fealty must have blunted their competitive edge.

The Spanish and Mexican land grants have been contentious issues in the Mexican-American struggle for civil rights. In the Treaty of Guadalupe Hidalgo (1848),* the United States promised to honor the grants and the property rights of the Mexican residents in the lands being annexed after the U.S. Mexican War. Article X of the treaty declared that "all grants of land made by the Mexican government or by competent authorities in territories previously appertaining to Mexico . . . shall be respected as valid, to the same extent . . . . as if the said territories had remained within the limits of Mexico." Although the U.S. Senate eliminated Article X before it ratified the treaty, a protocol appended to the treaty assured Mexico that the rights of Mexican Americans would be fully guaranteed because "these invaluable blessings, under our form of Government, do not result from Treaty stipulations, but from the very nature and character of our institutions." For many villagers in the remote regions of the new territory of the United States, the promises of the agreement were not honored. The United States did not adequately implement the treaty's provisions. Mexican Americans seeking to prove legitimate ownership of their lands were forced to appear in front of legal committees or engage in lengthy and expensive litigation. The judges or council members often were ignorant of Spanish and the legal system under which the land grants had been administered. Consequently, Mexican Americans often had their land taken from them by an alien American judicial system and through outright fraud. This alienation from their land encouraged and exacerbated impoverishment. The federal government has refused to take an active role in restoring these land grants. [SOURCE: Rosales, *Chicano!*, 155-157; Forrest, *The Preservation of the Village,* 7-8.]

LARA, SEVERITA (1952-)

Born in 1952 in Texas, Severita Lara was one of the student leaders of the 1969 high school walkouts in Crystal City, Texas.* Participants in the walkouts and ensuing school boycott called for more equitable consideration of Mexican-American students in school activities and curriculum design. Chicano* students, frustrated with a policy that put a grade ceiling on the students eligible to be candidates for cheerleading positions, decided to protest after Lara wrote a pamphlet criticizing the process. School officials suspended her for three days. In an interview taken in 1992, Lara

recalled the feelings that provoked her and her student companions to walk out of Crystal City High School:

Eighty-five percent of the [student] population was Mexican American, yet in all of our activities, like for example, cheerleaders . . . there's always three Anglos and one mexicana. . . . We started questioning. Why should it be like that?

In the early 1970s, Lara became one of the founding members of La Raza Unida Party.* As an adult, Lara served on the Crystal City council and as mayor. She is now a librarian at Crystal City High School. [SOURCE: Gutiérrez, *We Won't Back Down*; Rosales, *Chicano!*, 221; Tejano Voices, http://libraries.uta.edu/tejanovoices/interview.asp?CMASNo=013]

Severita Lara

LARRAZOLO, OCTAVIANO (1859-1930)

Octaviano Larrazolo was the first Hispanic to become a U.S. senator. The native of Allende, Chihuahua, Mexico, was elected to complete the term of a New Mexico senator who died in office, A.A. Jones. Larrazolo graduated from St. Michael's College in Arizona and served as a teacher and principal of an elementary school in Texas, when he was appointed in 1885 as Clerk of the U.S. District and Circuit Courts in El Paso. In Texas, he was also elected district attorney twice and served on a school board. After moving to New Mexico in 1895, Larrazolo became governor of the state in 1918 and a U.S. congressman in 1927. Larrazolo is said to have

Octaviano Larrazolo

been a gifted orator in both English and Spanish. Larrazolo was elected to the U.S. Senate again in 1929, but did not complete the term due to poor health.

Larrazolo was an early, strong advocate for Mexican-American civil rights. A little known aspect of his political career is his pardon of seventeen Mexicans in 1920 who were indicted for their role in the Villista raid on Columbus, New Mexico. The alleged raiders were brought to New Mexico during the Pershing Expedition and convicted on flimsy evidence. Larrazolo was denied the Republican nomination for governor as a result of this controversial move. [SOURCE: Campa, *Hispanic Culture in the Southwest*, 51-52.]

LATIN AMERICAN CLUB, ARIZONA, INC.

In 1933, Mexican-American leaders, mainly the sons of immigrant leaders who came from Mexico before 1920, started the Latin American Club of Arizona, Inc. In the forefront of this effort were attorneys Gregorio "Greg" García, Ralph Estrada, Val Córdova, William Fellows, among others. Most belonged to the Alianza Hispano-Americana,* an organization started by previous generations but which did not entirely embody the aspirations of these young English-speaking leaders. Their prescription for successfully defeating the debilitating discrimination suffered by Arizona Mexicans called for integration into the American political system. The group supported non-Mexican political candidates who seemed responsive to the needs of Mexican Americans. Typically, the organization supported the Democratic Party and the New Deal. The group published *El Latino Americano,* a bilingual newsletter which publicized their activities and expressed, often eloquently and plaintively, their desire to full participantion in the workings of the American system. The organization lasted into the 1950s and its leaders, such as Ralph Estrada and Greg García, worked to end school segregation in Arizona. [Rosales, *Chicano!*, 105.]

LATIN AMERICAN CLUB, HOUSTON, TEXAS

Convincing the Houston city council to put Mexican-American employees on permanent status rather than being "temporary" became one of the first issues of Houston's Latin American Club (LAC), which was founded in 1935 by Leonard J. Lewis, George Dreary, Félix Tijerina,* and John Henry Duhig. Although Tijerina was the only founder with a Spanish name, the other officers had Mexican-American backgrounds. In reality, the Mexican-American employees worked full-time for the city; they just did not get the fringe benefits. The dispute came to the forefront during May 1938, after the city did not pay its Mexican workers for taking off on April 22, the commemoration of the Battle of San Jacinto (where General Antonio López de Santa Anna was defeated in 1836). LAC, then became a League of United

Latin American Citizens (LULAC)* chapter and forced the issue. In response, city councilman S.A. Starsky retorted that he did not understand why Mexicans should get a paid day off to celebrate their own defeat. This insensitive retort further incensed the LULAC council, which doggedly pursued the issue until Starsky apologized. More importantly, the Mexican workers were given permanent status. The organization lasted until 1941 but other issues pursued by the LAC included registering Mexican-American voters, supporting efforts to get Mexicans classified as "White," and supporting aspirants for political office in Texas if they showed sensitivity to issues pertaining to La Raza. [SOURCE: Kreneck, *Mexican American Odyssey,* 68-71, 78-79; De León, *Ethnicity in the Sunbelt,* 85-89.]

LATIN BUSINESS ASSOCIATION

Established in 1976 as a private nonprofit organization, the Latin Business Association (LBA) is one of the nation's largest organizations representing the issues and concerns of Latino business owners. Based in Los Angeles, California, the LBA promotes the growth of Latino-owned businesses by generating development opportunities, by providing educational workshops, and by actively advocating in the mainstream economy on behalf of its constituency. Much of this networking is accomplished through its annual events: the Sol Business Awards and the National Latino Business Expo. At these gala events, the LBA, which represents the business interests of more than 440,000 Latin businesses in Southern California, members receive special annual awards for achievements in specific categories of social and business endeavors. [SOURCE: http://www.lbausa.com/about-us/default.asp]

LATINO CIVIL RIGHTS TASK FORCE

In 1991, community leaders in Washington, D.C. established the Latino Civil Rights Task Force in response to several nights of civil disturbances in the Mount Pleasant area of the nation's capital. With help from the Washington Lawyer's Project, the group recruited a team of leading law firms and prepared a comprehensive report and testimony on the status of Latinos in D.C. The resulting study documented the difficulty the Latino community encountered in gaining access to local government services, housing, employment, education, and recreation. Another crucial finding concerned the degree to which police misconduct and lack of communication affected the Latino community. In January 1992, the task force presented these reports at hearings of the U.S. Commission on Civil Rights. As a result, the Commission issued its 1993 report, adopting most of the recommendations presented in the task force's testimony. The significant outcomes of these efforts included stemming attempts to reduce bilingual and English-as-a-Second-Language programs in the D.C. public schools, as well as improving channels of communication with law enforcement officials. [SOURCE: http://www.washlaw.org/index.html]

LATINO COALITION

Public Advocates, Inc. in 1992 provided a small staff and seed money to start the Latino Coalition as a vehicle for addressing Latino health issues in southern California and to formulate policy that would bring about social change for the uninsured, the immigrant, and under-served people of color. After receiving support from a variety of foundations, the Latino Coalition hired additional staff to design a program that would mobilize leading Latino health experts and communities of color around health policy. The Latino Coalition board of advisors now identifies issues of concern that require advocacy, after obtaining input from the community. The Latino Coalition has forged crucial links with state and national health care organizations and has often testified as expert witness in the California State Legislature on health issues. [SOURCE: http://www.lchc.org/]

LATINO COLLABORATIVE

Created in 1987 as a grassroots network, the Latino Collaborative represents Latino media artists based in New York. In the 1990s, its membership expanded to more than 200 affiliates across the United States. Its main function is to promote the financing, production, distribution, and exhibition of films and videos made by and about Latinos in the United States. The Latino Collaborative also publishes a monthly newsletter and a catalogue describing members' work and offers occasional curated series, such as the recent "Otras Cosas del Querer" (Other Things of Love) lesbian and gay Latino film and video series and a 1988 collaboration with Deep Dish Television entitled "Latino Images." [SOURCE: National Video Resources, www.nvr.org]

LATINO FEDERATION NETWORK

The Los Angeles riots in April of 1992, precipitated by the acquittal of the police who asaulted Rodney King, left Los Angeles County in a state of disarray. But Latinos suffered disproportionally from the resultant lack of jobs, housing, education, and social services. As community groups attempted to deal with this aftermath, it became apparent that Latinos lacked a united front and the ability to organize. On March 19, 1994, several Latino coalitions and grassroots organizations attended the Latino Federation Conference at California State University-Los Angeles to establish the Latino Federation Network, which would provide comprehensive communication among the vast array of organizations so that the community could confront major issues and concerns more effectively. [SOURCE: http://clnet.sscnet.ucla.edu/community/unity.html]

THE LATINO GERONTOLOGICAL CENTER

The Latino Gerontological Center (LGC) was established in 1991 in New York City, with a mission of improving the lives of Latino seniors through advocacy and by preparing them for the hardships which they would face. Additionally, the LGC has assisted in the creation of new programs that are more tailored to the needs of Latino senior citizens. The founding of the LGC was prompted by the demographic data showing that the Latino elderly population in the Americas is increasing five-fold in the first half of the twenty-first century. This growth curve will create unprecedented demands on service providers for the elderly, a process that makes the mission of the LGC even more urgent. Since its founding, the project has coordinated community seminars and organized national and international conferences that reflect the core goal of caring for the elderly. [SOURCE: http://www.gerolatino.org/organize.html]

LATINO IDENTITY IN THE UNITED STATES

Today, an uneasy ethnic solidarity exists among Latino groups in the United States. At the political level, there is much rhetoric that attempts to bring them all under one rubric, and indeed the term "Latino" has been fostered as an agent of this process. While most Cubans are conservative on issues dealing with Cuba and Communism, they share the same ideology with Mexican Americans and Puerto Ricans when it comes to cultural maintenance and resistance to what many consider debasing American values. Another bond is language, an issue that has been forced into the political arena by the "English Only" movements. All Latinos resent the onus placed on them because they speak Spanish, a language that is despised in many quarters of the Anglo-American community.

The development of a rubric "Latinidad" has been facilitated by two Spanish-language television networks, not to mention hundreds of radio stations that indirectly pound the message of ethnic bonding into millions of Latino homes. Variety entertainment programs, soap operas, and talk shows that air nationally are many times crafted to bring a balanced appeal to the varied Spanish-speaking peoples taking their turn at the American opportunity structure. A plethora of slick cover magazines have appeared in the last twenty years, all aimed at the Latino groups. Some use English, others Spanish, or they contain bilingual renditions. This Latinization process alone, perhaps unwittingly, is bound to evolve a pan-Latinism strikingly unique to the United States.

In large cities, such as Los Angeles, Chicago, Houston, and Miami, Latinos of all kinds are thrown together and, many times, common ties result in an affinity and collaboration. Where they have been together for a longer time as in Chicago, Mexicans and Puerto Ricans who have lived together since the 1940s have merged into political coalitions, and interethnic marriages have produced thousands of Chicano-Riqueños. The melding of Salvadorens, Puerto Ricans, Mexicans, and Spaniards in San Francisco has also been transpiring for a long time and there, during the heady sixties movements, a strong Latino consciousness emerged, as in the Mission District.* In Los Angeles and Houston, entrepreneurs have tapped the Latino market, creating chains of enormous food stores called El Tianguis and Fiesta. These outlets cater to the food tastes of every imaginable Latino group.

The other scenario is that differences will make for a separate evolution in the respective communities. As each Latino group evolves in the United States, with separate identities, they will become ensconced and comfortable in their own elaborated ethnicity. Indeed, this is true of the older and larger Latino groupings who see themselves as Mexican Americans, Cuban Americans, and mainland Puerto Ricans. Hispanos in northern New Mexico, who are, for all intents and purposes, Mexican Americans, at times even remain insular from this group. So what can be expected from them when it comes to identification with a larger national denomination?

Furthermore, inter-ethnic prejudices still persist at the community level along Latinos. For example, at times Latin Americans or Spaniards living in the United States distance themselves from Mexican Americans or Puerto Ricans so they will not be mistaken for them by non-Latinos, who have prejudices towards those groups. Or they might buy into Anglo-American prejudices and unwarranted stereotypes against certain groups in an unconscious effort to ingratiate themselves with the mainstream population. This is true, even if back home they might have never dreamed of having these misgivings toward other Latinos.

Another common source of inter-Latino antipathy is based on class origins. If the majority of one group is working-class, as is the case of Mexicans, Puerto Ricans, Dominicans, and Central Americans, middle-class immigrants who come from South America often find it difficult to relate to what they consider a lower-class culture. They demonstrate this attitude, of course, towards the lower classes back in their homelands, as well. That phenomenon is even borne out among upper-class Mexicans in the United States, who look with disdain at compatriots who come from the "clases populares."

There is even opposition to amalgamation among some Latino intellectuals, who see the whole trend towards Latinization as a tool of consumerism, especially when the term "Hispanic" is used as a referent term. Obviously it would be easier to aim at a large market, rather than disparate groups. There is also a residue of resentment within some in the Latino community toward Cuban exiles because of that group's persistent support of a conservative foreign policy towards Latin America. But the ultimate fear is that a bland, malleable ethnic group will emerge.

Regardless of the destructive prejudices that exist between Latino groups or the well-intended admonitions of the intelligentsia, common roots exist between Latinos, regardless of national or class origin. These will eventually make crucial links that no one can foresee so that Latinos can take a rightful place in the American mosaic. [SOURCE: Rosales, "A Historical Overview," 52-53.]

LATINO INSTITUTE

Created in 1974, the Latino Institute began as a bold experiment to address the concerns of the three major Latino groups in Chicago —Mexicans, Puerto Ricans, and to a lesser degree, Cubans—and to apply socioeconomic prescriptions for removing obstacles that hindered the improvement of their quality of life. At that time, Chicago was the only city that housed the three dominant groups in large numbers. Significantly, the Latino Institute chose the word "Latino" to signify that a pan-Latino consciousness had emerged among Chicago's Spanish-speaking population. After growing to become one of the largest political advocates for Latinos in the nation, the institute encountered problems with financing and ended its operations in 1994. In its heyday, the institute provided leadership training, applied research to solving community problems, and developed advocacy strategies for influencing public policy. The institute pioneered advocacy programs to confront gender specific problems and taught social service providers how to deal with the specific problems Latinas encountered. Eventually, many organizations sought the solution-oriented strategies the institute had pioneered. [SOURCE: Cárdenas, *La Causa,* 55-79.]

LATINO ISSUES FORUM

The Latino Issues Forum (LIF) was established in 1987 as a nonprofit public policy and advocacy institute dedicated to broadening access for Latinos to higher education, economic development, health care, citizenship, regional development, and telecommunications. From its San Francisco office, the LIF serves as a clearinghouse providing the news media with accurate information and sources that will result in fair and effective coverage of issues that deal with the Latino community. [SOURCE: http://www.lif.org/]

LATINO MEDICAL STUDENT ASSOCIATION

In 1982, Latino students in California, mindful of the need to increase the number of Hispanic students that were recruited, prepared, admitted, and trained in medicine and other health professions, began establishing a network of medical students throughout the entire state. Two years later at a statewide meeting, the Chicano/Latino Medical Student Association (CMSA) was formed. In 2002, while headquartered in Garden Grove, California, CMSA changed its name to the Latino Medical Student Association (LMSA) to reflect a more diverse Latino constituency. Since 1982, the LMSA has spearheaded the efforts of increasing the numbers of qualified Chicano/Latino students gaining acceptance into medical school, and endeavors to be a strong voice in advocating for programs, services, and equity for Latino students committed to obtaining higher education. [SOURCE: www.lsma.net]

LATINO MIDWEST VIDEO COLLECTIVE

In 1986, Latinos attending the film school at the University of Iowa founded the Latino Midwest Video Collective (LMC). Now based in Chicago, the collective has affiliates in Mérida, Yucatán, Mexico, and Antofagasta, Chile. Through the LMC, members of the organization have found a more effective way of promoting the production and distribution of their works, whose main focus is the Latino experience in the Midwest, gay sexuality, women's issues, cultural identity, and racism. [SOURCE: National Video Resources, www.nvr.org]

LATINO POLICY FORUM SERIES

The Latino Policy Forum Series, a public affairs television program that first aired in September 2004, provides a forum for the discussion of the most pertinent issues facing Latinos throughout the United States. Produced by Myra Estepa and hosted by Carlos Perales, the program is televised in Manhattan and reaches out to one of the largest Hispanic markets in the United States: the New York-New Jersey area. Guests include community activists, artists, and academicians. It is sponsored by the Policy Division of the Puerto Rican Legal Defense and Education Fund* and by the City College Center for Workers Education, the Program in Latin American and Hispanic Caribbean Studies at the City College, and the National Association of Hispanic Journalists.* [SOURCE: PRLDEF Reports, September 2, 2004.]

LATINO PROFESSIONAL NETWORK

Organized in 1987 as a tax-exempt organization, the Latino Professional Network (LPN) provides career, educational, and social opportunities for Latinos in Massachusetts and throughout the nation. LPN members obtain a wide variety of resources with their LPN affiliation; monthly networking meetings with major corporations; scholarship opportunities from educational partners, such as Harvard University and Bentley College; as well as access to employment opportunities throughout the country and abroad. LPN continues to increase the visibility of Latinos and promote an image of diverse professionalism. [SOURCE: http://www.lpn.org/content/home/home.cfm]

LATINOS & LATINAS FOR HEALTH JUSTICE

Latinos & Latinas for Health Justice (LLHJ) was started in 1999 by leaders of the California Latino Alcohol and Drug Coalition (CAL-LADCO) after that organization closed its doors. LLHJ now continues the work CAL-LADCO had been doing since the early 1990s, which is to pursue prevention policy and provide unique approaches to Latino alcoholism. LLHJ has developed a more extensive statewide network in providing for Latinos in the substance abuse prevention field because it has the ability to reach a larger constituency and a greater pool of resources. [SOURCE: http://www.cal-lluhc.org/]

LATINOS FOR POSITIVE IMAGES

Founded in 1995 in New York City, Latinos for Positive Images (LPI) is composed of individuals and organizations who are concerned with fair images of Latinos in the media. The LPI attempts to empower the community by providing information relating to media and the images of Latinos in the media. The organization has established a network of contacts in order to provide support for Latino artists currently involved in the media and for those striving to get into the field. [SOURCE: http://www.columbia.edu/~rmg36/ncprr_ny/ncprrny6.html]

LATINOS IN HARTFORD

The 2000 Census revealed that Hartford, Connecticut, was the seat of the largest Latino community of any major city north of Florida and east of the Mississippi, in proportion to the overall city's population. Founded by a Dutchman and settled by Puritans, until the 1960s Hartford was the hub of an insurance empire with a predominantly white-collar population of "bankers and brokers, hairdressers, and haberdashers." The city's population has risen above 40 percent Hispanic—one of the largest concentration among major cities outside California, Texas, Colorado, and Florida. Already more than half of the school children are Latino, a demographic trend that is expected to continue in the twenty-first century.

City politics have been transformed in parallel to the demographic change. In 2002, Eddie A. Perez,* who was born in Corozal, Puerto Rico, but who in 1969, at age 12, settled with his family in Hartford, was elected mayor. Much of the city government staff and two city council members are all native speakers of Spanish. Moreover, Hartford's web page is bilingual, as is the after-hours telephone voice messaging system.

The Hispanization of Hartford dates back to the 1940's, when Connecticut's tobacco farmers recruited Puerto Ricans, mainly from the island's small towns and rural villages, to harvest their crops. In the 1960s, Puerto Ricans began settling in Hartford between black neighborhoods on the North End and dwindling white residential areas on the South End; Blacks make up 38 percent of the city's population. In recent years, Cuban, Portuguese, Dominican, Colombian, Peruvian, Brazilian, and Mexican immigrants have joined Puerto Ricans in their neighborhoods. Many of the Latino migrants have arrived in Hartford from New York City and other Eastern seaboard metropolitan areas, attracted by an atmosphere of less competitiveness and lower housing costs.

Consumers can now choose from a variety of options for Latino goods and services. Puerto Rican *bodegas* (grocery stores) and bakeries sit side by side Central and South American restaurants and shops. Peruvians have obtained such a significant presence that, in 2002, their consulate in Boston opened an office in downtown Hartford. And in June 2003, a $6.5 million improvement project designed to renovate central Hartford's roads, sidewalks, street lights, and bus shelters was begun by the Spanish-American Merchants Association. The program, which as of 2005 is still in effect, is intended to transform Little Puerto Rico into the New England hub of Hispanic commerce.

Nonetheless, in spite of their demographic superiority within the city limits, Latinos only make up 10 percent of the 1.1 million residents of the greater metropolitan area. Many suburban whites view Hartford as a former bastion of New England culture and prosperity, blemished by a dark cloud of poverty and "foreignness." Indeed, the influx of mostly Puerto Rican Hispanics has tested Hartford's ability to accommodate the influx. A study on the city's Puerto Rican community by José Cruz, an associate professor of Political Science at the State University of New York at Albany, indicates that new arrivals relocated here without an employment promise and with few other options for making a living. Beginning on Labor Day, 1969, Puerto Rican neighborhoods were rocked by a series of riots that lasted two days. The causes of the upheaval can be traced to frustration from years of poverty, second-class status, under-representation, and police brutality suffered by the twenty thousand Puerto Rican residents that then lived in Hartford. Job growth, according to Mayor Perez, can be created by bringing in Hispanic-led corporations to complement, or compete with the city's financial services and fading manufacturing sectors. In 2002, Perez traveled to Puerto Rico to persuade bank and retail executives to begin operations in the city.

All of these formidable barriers need addressing in Hartford before Latino leaders can provide a liveable environment, free from the malaise of poverty and all of the attendant social ills. [SOURCE: Zielbauer, "Hartford Bids a Bilingual Goodbye to a White-Collar Past."]

LAU V. NICHOLS

In *Lau v. Nichols*, the U.S. Supreme Court held that the San Francisco Unified School District discriminated against a non-English-speaking student, Kinney Lau, by not providing a program to deal with his language problem, thereby depriving him of meaningful participation in school. This decision has served as a cornerstone for the creation and maintenance of bilingual education programs across the country. The *Lau* decision laid the basis for a new interpretation of equal education opportunity, an opportunity that takes into consideration the linguistic differences of students, when compared to the opportunities given to all English-speaking students.

California became one of the first states in the nation to mandate bilingual education in 1976 when it enacted Assembly Bill AB–1329, requiring bilingual education in school districts serving limited English-proficiency (LEP) children. While the ruling was made as a result of an Asian-American initiative in San Francisco, this decision provided the Mexican American Legal Defense and Education Fund (MALDEF)* with a rationale for pursuing bilingual education efforts after a major court battle defeat in Denver to implement such education. [SOURCE: Donato, *The Other Struggle for Equal Schools,* 106; Rosales, *Testimonio,* 400-403.]

LAUSTENEAU, WILLIAM "WENCESLAO" (1870-1906)

William "Wenceslao" Lausteneau was born in Chihuahua, Mexico, in 1870. With A.F. Salcido and the Italian, Frank Colombo, Lausteneau led the Morenci Copper strike of 1903. He was subsequently convicted of inciting a riot in the three-day work stoppage where armed workers milled through Morenci making demands, and sentenced to two years at the Arizona Territorial Prison. After serving four months, Lausteneau and four Mexican convicts attempted an escape on April 28, 1904, by taking hostages. Guards fired into the group, nonetheless, foiling the escape. Lausteneau received an additional 10 years and became an Arizona folk hero among Mexicans and unionists alike. Lausteneau died from an illness at the Yuma Territorial Prison on August 20, 1906. [SOURCE: Rosales, *Pobre Raza!,* 174-175; McElroy, "William H. Lausteneau: Menace or Martyr."]

LEADING FOR LIFE/UNIDOS PARA LA VIDA SUMMIT

On May 4, 1998, at the Leading for Life/Unidos para la Vida summit sponsored by the Harvard AIDS Institute, the actress Rosie Pérez joined Latino community leaders in calling for confronting the rapidly growing problem of Latinos and the AIDS epidemic. The urgency was prompted by new statistics released by the Centers for Disease Control showing that Latinos suffered from a disproportionate AIDS infection rate. The center projected that by 2003, Latino AIDS cases, on an annual basis, would surpass those of non-Latino whites. Besides Pérez, in attendance were leaders from academia, business, entertainment, law, the media, medicine, politics, religion, and sports. Leaders at the summit adopted a call for action outlining concrete action steps to address the epidemic. First, it would be necessary to raise awareness nationally and to develop a national follow-up. Joining the Harvard AIDS Institute in co-sponsoring the summit was the Latino Commission on AIDS, the American Red Cross Hispanic HIV/AIDS Education Program, the U.S.-Mexico Border Health Association, and the Mauricio Gastón Institute. Primary funding for the campaign came from the Henry J. Kaiser Family Foundation and the Centers for Disease Control and Prevention. [SOURCE: http://www.hsph.harvard.edu/press/releases/press05041998.html]

LEAGUE OF UNITED LATIN AMERICAN CITIZENS

The League of United Latin American Citizens (LULAC) was and still is one of the largest Mexican-American organizations. LULAC's original objectives emphasized the social, political, and economic rights and duties of Mexican Americans; it was not initially interested in direct political action. Established in 1929 in Corpus Christi, Texas, LULAC merged three other organizations: Order of the Sons of America,* Knights of America, and League of Latin American Citizens. In the 1930s, the first class-action lawsuit against segregated public schools was filed by LULAC. That same decade, LULAC took the lead in changing the classification of Mexican Americans from "Mexican" to "White" in the 1940 U.S. Census. Although largely middle-class in membership, LULAC became more active after World War II, pursuing the end of inequality in American legal, education, and political systems. For instance, it took a lead role in the passage of the New Mexico state fair employment practice law of 1949. Today, LULAC is one of the most influential Mexican-American organizations in the Southwest and remains a strong advocate for Mexican-American civil rights and liberties. LULAC has 110,000 members in 12 regional and 43 state groups.

LULAC Convention, Houston, 1937

Embracing other Latino groups now, LULAC is concerned with seeking full social, political, economic, and educational rights for Hispanics in the United States. LULAC supports the 15 LULAC National Education Service Centers, offers employment and training programs, conducts research on post-secondary education, and sponsors Hispanics Organized for Political Education, which encourages voter registration and political awareness. LULAC publishes the *HOPE Voter's Guide* reports, and the monthly *LULAC National Reporter.* [SOURCE: Kanellos, "Organizations," 391-392.]

LEAGUE OF UNITED LATIN AMERICAN CITIZENS WOMEN

The League of United Latin American Citizens (LULAC)* extended full membership privileges to women in 1933, and Mexican-American women enthusiastically began to organize gender-segregated councils, which they called "Ladies LULAC." Although this segregation continued until the1960s, the women-only chapters demonstrated that women could make significant contributions to the national civil rights struggle. The most vital Ladies LULAC were mainly founded in Texas and New Mexico. Alice, Texas, had the first ladies council in 1933 and then in 1934, council #9 was founded in El Paso, Texas. That year, the office of Ladies

LULAC Women's Auxiliary

Organizer General (LOG) was created by LULAC in order to provide a national impetus to continue organizing. The LOG effort resulted in 26 councils by 1940, while the men had 100. By the end of the century, women had integrated with men, constituting more than 50 percent of LULAC's membership. In 1994, LULAC women helped elect Belén Robles, the first female national president of LULAC. [SOURCE: Orozco, "League of United Latin American Citizens (LULAC)," http://college.hmco.com/history/readerscomp/women/html/wh_020400_leagueofunit.htm]

LEHMAN COLLEGE

The first department of Puerto Rican Studies was started in 1969 at Lehman College of the City University of New York by student activists who felt that the university did not provide enough history or curriculum that was relevant to the experience of Puerto Ricans. Now called the Department of Latin American and Puerto Rican Studies, it offers a Bachelor of Arts degree in Puerto Rican Studies and an interdisciplinary Bachelor of Arts degree in Latin American and Caribbean Studies. The department also participates in the interdisciplinary Comparative Literature Program and the Women's Studies option. [SOURCE: Torres and Velázquez, *The Puerto Rican Movement*, 138.]

LEÓN, DANIEL DE (1852-1914)

Born on the island of Curaçao of Spanish-America/Sephardic Jewish parents, Daniel de León became one of the most important labor leaders and socialist theorists in the United States during the last two decades of the nineteenth and the first decade of the twentieth centuries. His numerous writings were published and circulated widely, as the rights of workers became more and more the concern of intellectuals in the United States. After an education in Germany and the Netherlands, he moved with his Venezuelan-born wife to New York City in 1872, where he became involved with the Cuban independence movement and wrote for Spanish-language newspapers. He studied law at Columbia and later became a lecturer, hoping to become part of the permanent faculty of that institution. As his involvement with the labor movement intensified, he was severed from Columbia and decided to dedicate himself completely to the cause of the working class. By 1891, De León was the Socialist Labor Party candidate for governor of New York. For many years he was the editor of the Socialist Labor weekly *The People*. In addition to his editing and his prolific writing—he also translated the works of Karl Marx—De León helped to found in 1905 one of the most important labor organizations in history, the Industrial Workers of the World (Wobblies), but as a radical, he was expelled from that organization shortly after its founding. He then organized a competing institution, the Workers' International Industrial Union. As a theorist and writer, de León developed many advanced views on such topics as women's suffrage, the power of the vote among working people, war, and politics. [SOURCE: Reeve, *The Life and Times of Daniel De León.*]

LESBIANAS UNIDAS

Founded in 1984 as a committee of the Gay and Lesbian Latinos Unidos (GLLU), the Lesbianas Unidas (LU) was formed to support and address, through grassroots efforts in Los Angeles, the specific needs of politicized, feminist Latina lesbians. The LU has grown from an initial membership of five women to close to 1,000 by the end of the twentieth century. A major issue among LU members is the debate over whether the organization should pursue political issues versus a social agenda. Nonetheless since its inception, the LU has fulfilled both goals. For example, LU sponsors an annual retreat, participates in grassroots mass demonstrations, such as protests against anti-immigration initiatives, has supported Connexxus Women's Center/Centro de Mujeres Latinas Outreach Program in Los Angeles, has participated in the Lesbians of Color National Conference, in Día de La Mujer/International Women's Day annual celebration, and the Latina Lesbian Encuentros.

In 1994, LU became independent of GLLU and agreed upon the following mission statement: "LU is committed to struggle against racism, sexism, classism, ageism, homophobia, biphobia and all other forms of oppression. Our strength lies in the unity we foster by honoring the richness of our diversity." [SOURCE: http://www-lib.us.edu/~retter/luweb.html]

LIGA OBRERA DE HABLA ESPAÑOLA

The Liga Obrera de Habla Española (Spanish-Speaking Labor League) was organized in Gallup, New Mexico, in 1934, among coal miners in an effort to save miners arrested and/or charged with a variety of offenses stemming from their long-lasting strike against the Gallup-American Company (a subsidiary of Kennecott Copper Company). Jesús Pallares, a miner originally from Chihuahua, Mexico, was the main organizer. With some 8,000 members, the league succeeded in forcing the authorities to abandon criminal syndicalism proceedings and won relief for the strikers. The personal price for this victory was the one paid by Pallares—one often meted out to Mexican-origin organizers—when he was arrested and deported. [SOURCE: McWilliams, *North from Mexico*, 195.]

LIGA PROTECTIVA MEXICANA

Formed in Kansas City, Missouri, after World War I, one of the main objectives of the Liga Protectiva Mexicana was helping countrymen from Mexico cope with the ravages of the recession of 1921, which provoked much unemployment and rumors of general deportations. The protective association lasted only until 1923, by which time the threat of mass deportation had passed. [SOURCE: Meier and Rivera, *Dictionary of Mexican American History,* 193-4.]

LIGA PROTECTORA LATINA

The goals of La Liga Protectora Latina (The Latin Protective League), formed in Arizona in 1915 by Mexicans with long U.S. residence, was not as oriented towards the old country as groups started by more recently arrived immigrants in newer *colonias*. Article IV of its incorporation papers also demonstrates that besides providing traditional mutual aid benefits, protecting civil rights figured as a crucial objective. By 1917, it had established an extensive network of 30 lodges throughout the state. It played a significant role in the copper mine strikes of 1917 by uniting Mexican and Mexican-American miners and opposing the activities of the Industrial Workers of the

World. Like other organizations, the Liga foundered during the Great Depression.

One of the first actions of the Liga was averting the hanging of five Mexicans for unrelated crimes in May 1915. In the ensuing years, the group led protests against proposed legislation to prohibit non-English speakers from working in Arizona mines. [SOURCE: Rosales, *Pobre Raza!*, 138-139.]

LA LIGA PROTECTORA DE REFUGIADOS

During the Mexican Revolution, U.S. officials regularly arrested political refugees for violating neutrality laws, for border banditry, for smuggling arms into Mexico, and for labor union activity. The experience gained by helping defend imprisoned exiles was important to immigrants who also had to learn to defend themselves and their communities in the U.S. legal system and attempt to protect their civil and human rights. The most persecuted activists were Partido Liberal Mexicano (PLM) members, whom authorities, pursued even before the Mexican Revolution of 1910. In the Spring of 1912, Dr. J.B. Ruffo, chief surgeon in Francisco I. Madero's army, defected to Pascual Orozco in the anti-Madero rebellion. When Orozco's fortunes declined, Ruffo fled to the United States and, in October of 1912, was recruiting support for the rebels in Phoenix, Arizona. At the behest of Phoenix consul Francisco Olivares, Ruffo was arrested in Tucson and jailed. Ruffo's imprisonment prompted the founding in Phoenix of La Liga Protectora de Refugiados (The Refugee Protection League) by Pedro de la Lama* and other Mexican activists, who two years later started La Liga Protectora Latina (The Latin Protective League),* an organization that took on job discrimination and criminal justice issues in Arizona. [SOURCE: Rosales, *Chicano!*, 64-65.]

LIGA PUERTORRIQUEÑA E HISPANA

In 1927, a league was formed in New York to increase the power of the city's Hispanic community through unification of its diverse organizations. Among the very specific goals of the La Liga Puertorriqueña e Hispana (The Puerto Rican and Hispanic League) were representing the community to the "authorities," working for the economic and social betterment of Puerto Ricans, and propagating the vote among Puerto Ricans. That same year, the Liga founded a periodical, *Boletín Oficial de la Liga Puertorriqueña e Hispana*, to keep its member organizations and their constituents informed of community concerns. However, the *Boletín* evolved into much more than a newsletter, functioning more like a community newspaper, including essays and cultural items as well as news items in its pages. [SOURCE: Kanellos, *Hispanic Periodicals in the United States,* 108-109.]

La Liga Puertorriqueña e Hispana

LITTLE HAVANA

As thousands of exiles fled the Cuban Revolution in the 1960s, many came to Miami, Florida, and settled in a four-square-mile area southwest of the central business district that became known as "Little Havana." The new influx dramatically expanded an already existing Cuban neighborhood, housing Cuban and Latino-owned drugstores, *bodegas* (grocery stores), and other businesses where the new arrivals could obtain familiar goods. In addition, the newcomers had access to low-cost housing and public transportation, allowing convenient commuting to their jobs in the central business district of the city. Moreover, the main refugee assistance centers were located there: the Centro Hispano Católico* and the Cuban Refugee Emergency Center.* Central Miami, like a lot of American cities in the 1960s, was expiring with the advent of suburban development, but Cubans established their own businesses and renovated old buildings on what became the main thoroughfares of Little Havana along Flagler Street and southwest 8th Street (Calle Ocho).

Essentially, the influx of Cubans transformed what was becoming a dilapidated and decaying inner city into a lucrative commercial and residential district. Fourteen percent of the total Cuban population in the United States resided in Little Havana by 1970. Nonetheless, social mobility and overcrowding prompted many Cuban Americans to move west and south into other residential areas or to adjoining cities in Dade County. Little Havana residents moved mainly to Hialeah, because many of the exiles found jobs at Miami International Airport and the Hialeah race tracks. The town's population was 74 percent Latino by 1980. It became the first city in South Florida to elect a Cuban-born mayor. Higher income Cubans moved in large numbers to Coral Gables and Miami Beach, but Little Havana remains to this day the symbolic center of the Cuban exile community in the United States. Many celebrations, organizations, and political activities of the Cuban-American community are based in this section of Miami. [SOURCE: García, *Havana USA,* 86.]

LITTLE SCHOOL OF 400

Under the leadership of Houston's Felix Tijerina,* the League of United Latin American Citizens* initiated the Little School of 400 in the 1950s. The pilot project began in Ganado, Texas, during the summer of 1957, teaching pre-school Mexican Americans 400 English words before they began regular school. At first Tijerina attempted to raise private funds for this effort but could not muster the support. Eventually, the Texas legislature passed a bill to fund a similar project in 1959. Many observers believe that this project was the precusor of the federally funded headstart programs. [SOURCE: Rosales, *Chicano!*, 99; Kreneck, "Little School of the 400," *The Handbook of Texas Online,* http://www.tsha.utexas.edu/handbook/online/articles/view/LL/kdl2.html]

LOBBYING FOR MEXICAN IMMIGRANT LABOR—EARLY 20th CENTURY

After 1880, because of the railroad, dramatic changes in the southwestern economy greatly stimulated Mexican immigration. During the two decades before 1900, 127,000 Mexicans entered the United States from Mexico. Radical economic transformations that occurred not only in the Southwest, but in Mexico as well, accounted for this trend. By 1900, a railroad network integrated Texas, New Mexico, Arizona, and California with northern Mexico and parts of central and southern Mexico. The economic impact of the railroads soon drew Mexicans into the United States in a movement that dwarfed the influx of previous years. Emigration from Mexico really accelerated with the outbreak of the Mexican Revolution of 1910. It is estimated that between 1900 and 1930, more than a million Mexicans crossed the border.

The influx was facilitated by the active recruitment of Mexicans by southwestern extractive, agricultural, and transportation corporations, such as the American Smelting and Refining Corporation of El Paso, the Phelps-Dodge Corporation, the Amalgamated Sugar Company, and the Southern Pacific Railroad. But the need for Mexicans coincided with a restrictionist mood perpetuated by nativist organizations, such as the The California Joint Immigration Committee, which led the campaign to hinder Asian immigration and made it difficult for Chinese and Japanese farmers to operate in the Golden State. But assuring that immigration laws would not restrict Mexicans was taken on by lobby groups, such as the U.S. Chamber of Commerce, the U.S. Sugar Manufacturers' Association, the Farm Bureau Federations of California and Texas, and the Arizona Wool Growers Association, to name a few.

To offset the notion that Mexicans in any way would threaten Americans, southwestern employers and their associations concocted a stereotype of Mexicans as child-like, inoffensive creatures who were satisfied with very little and did not want to stay in the United States. Charles Teague, a large landowner in California and an activist in agricultural and booster associations, published numerous articles portraying Mexicans in this manner. Ironically, restrictionists put forth negative stereotypes that saw Mexicans as menacing and threatening, while supporters of Mexican immigration posited stereotypes with benign but negative characteristics.

During World War I, the *New York Times* printed a 1918 editorial praising the salutary affects that Mexican labor had in southwestern agriculture, and John B. Carrington, the head of the San Antonio Chamber of Commerce, declared that "Mexican labor had put Texas on the map." Indeed, Americans appeared to Mexican officials to lust after their workers. The U.S. federal government participated in the recruitment efforts. In a move designed to improve strained relations between the two countries during the war, the Department of State invited a group of Mexican newspaper editors and publishers to Washington. Once there, government representatives implored the Mexican journalists to persuade their government to be more cooperative in allowing laborers to enter the United States. On June 16, the same day that the journalists were meeting with U.S. government officials, waivers to the literacy requirements of the 1917 immigration act, which had been provided to Mexicans who worked in agriculture, became applicable to all industries that needed Mexican labor, and automatic renewals continued as they were needed for the duration of the war.

A report written by Howard C. Hopkins, a Department of Labor official, charged that Mexicans entering the country illegally and captured by Texas Rangers* were treated with "more brutality than any other service." According to Hopkins, this played into the hands of pro-German Mexicans who wanted to prevent emigration in order to sabotage U.S. agriculture. The Mexican government attempted to parley the need for Mexican labor in the United States during World War I into a diplomatic advantage in order to insure better treatment of Mexican workers, especially in Texas. In 1918, after the massacre of 15 Mexicans by Texas Rangers in Porvenir, Texas,* the Mexican government and Mexican-American leaders began to pressure Texas officials to curb such violence. Andrés G. García, Inspector General of Consulates in El Paso, wrote to Tom Bell, Deputy Labor Commissioner in Texas, indicating that Mexico would limit the flow of Mexican workers into Texas unless Texas Ranger abuse and the drafting of Mexican citizens into the military was curtailed. Bell apparently took this to heart and wrote to the governor's office asking that García's protests be given serious consideration.

Restrictionists again turned their attention to Mexicans in the 1920s, when they were excluded from the most restrictive laws thus far, the immigration quota acts of 1921 and 1924—Mexicans escaped their limitations because the law did not apply to the Western Hemisphere—which were aimed at Asians and southern and eastern Europeans. The restrictionists had one main ally in Congress, Representative John C. Box (D-Texas),* who served on the House Immigration Committee. Box introduced the first of many restrictionist bills in 1926. This first bill sought to apply quotas to the entire Western Hemisphere. This led to four years of debates, in which several lobbying groups testified in favor of the restriction of Mexican immigration. The debates eventually got past the committee and onto the floor of the Congress in 1930. The primary group seeking such restrictions was the American Federation of Labor. Its argument was simple: Mexicans were depriving Americans of jobs because they worked for lower wages and were often used by employers as strike breakers. In addition, Mexicans were demonized by such proponents of eugenics as Roy Garis, an economist from Vanderbilt University. Despite all of this lobbying, very little was done to restrain immigration from Mexico. More than anything else, the vigilant and sustained lobbying of the southwestern employers thwarted the efforts of the nativists. [SOURCE: Lukens Espinosa, "Mexico, Mexican Americans and the FDR Administration's Racial Classification Policy," 19-35; Rosales, *Chicano!*, 69-70.]

LONGORIA, FELIX (1919-1945)

Felix Longoria, a young Mexican-American soldier, was killed in action on June 16, 1945, at Luzon in the Philippines. His remains were initially buried in the Philippines, but eventually the Army returned them to the United States in January of 1949. Late in 1948, the U.S. Army had informed Felix Longoria's widow that her husband's remains would be returned to Texas. While the family knew of Felix's fate, the military immediately sent them the medals earned by the soldier, including the Bronze Star; the news came as a surprise. The widow, Beatrice Moreno de Longoria, hurriedly arranged for funeral services in Three Rivers, Longoria's hometown. Thomas Kennedy, also a veteran but a newcomer to Texas who had recently purchased the town's only funeral home, agreed to bury the soldier in the Mexican cemetery. He denied the family, however, the use of his chapel for the wake, assessing correctly that local whites would be offended. Instead he offered to conduct a private wake at a family member's home.

Beatrice Longoria, hurt and confused, turned to other family members, who in turn contacted Dr. Héctor P. García,* a former Army medical officer who also served in the war. García had recently helped found the American G.I. Forum* in Corpus Christi, precisely to deal with the many humiliating experiences returning Mexican-American veterans faced in Texas. After energetically publicizing the incident, García obtained support from Lyndon B. Johnson,* then newly elected to the Senate from Texas. With much fanfare, the Senator arranged to have Longoria's remains buried at Arlington National Cemetery on February 16, 1949.

In the meantime, public opinion, even at the international level, turned against Three Rivers because of the degrading treatment afforded the family of a decorated veteran. Kennedy then claimed his actions stemmed from the possibility of violence at the wake; Beatrice and her deceased husband's family were estranged. Eventually, Kennedy and political leaders in Three Rivers relented and offered to provide full services. By then, Dr. García and Senator Johnson were intent on going through with the plans for the Arlington burial. [SOURCE: Carroll, *Felix Longoria's Wake;* Ramos, *The American G.I. Forum,* 9-17.]

LÓPEZ, JOE EDDIE (1939-)

A pioneer participant and leader in Arizona politics, Joe Eddie López was born in Duran, New Mexico, in 1939. As a boy, he and his family moved around the Southwest in the migrant stream, but in 1949 they settled in Maricopa County, Arizona, where Phoenix is located. After graduating from high school in 1957, López attended Arizona State University (ASU), but after his marriage, he entered the housing industry, achieved a highly skilled status as steam fitter, and worked to unionize construction workers. As the Chicano Movement* came to Phoenix, López became intractably linked to the goals of this social and political movement. He joined with the United Farm Workers* in Arizona and Chicano* activist students from ASU—his wife was one of them—to organize Chicanos Por La Causa,* a civil rights and community development organization.

López soon turned to using the ballot box to bring about change. In 1972, he was elected to the Maricopa County Board of Supervisors and served until 1976. He also served for six years as a member of the Phoenix Union High School District Governing Board from 1990 to 1996. In 1991, he began his career as a legislator, first in the Arizona House of Representatives, from 1991 to 1992, and then in 1996 as a state senator. López is currently a member of numerous community civic organizations. With his wife

Rosie, he is a founding member and current activist in the Arizona Hispanic Community Forum. More than any other legislator, López has supported progressive issues dealing with educational reform, civil rights, and consumer protection. [SOURCE: http://www.azleg.state.az.us/members/=jlopez.htm]

LÓPEZ, LINO (1910-1978)

Mexican-born civic leader, lecturer, educator, and social worker, Lino López financed his education as a youth by working in agriculture. After completing his A.B. at the University of Chicago and some graduate work at the University of Tennessee, López worked shortly in the grocery business. Over time, he became engrossed in creating social change in the Mexican-American community and went to work for the Illinois Welfare Department. Later, he served on the Bishops Committee for the Spanish-speaking* in Chicago. He then went on to work as a counselor, primarily for Chicano* youth in Texas and Colorado.

Between 1953 and 1978, López worked with several organizations that focused on the development of Mexican-American youth, including the Denver Commission on Human Relations and the Latin American Research and Service Agency, which he had helped to organize. He also was instrumental in the establishment of a dozen chapters of the American G.I. Forum.* A considerable amount of his work took place with students in San Jose and Redlands, California. He helped organized the Mexican American Youth Organization* in several high schools in Northern California and continued to promote youth awareness as an instructor at Redlands University. His death did not bring his work to an end; rather, his memory still survives as he has received posthumous awards from groups such as the Latin American Educational Foundation. [SOURCE: Meier and Rivera, *Dictionary of Mexican American History,* 201-202.]

LÓPEZ RIVERA, OSCAR (1943-)

Oscar López Rivera was one of the 11 political prisoners given clemency by President Bill Clinton because of concerted appeals to him by civil rights organizations and sympathetic politicians before he left office in 2000. Born in San Sebastián, Puerto Rico, in 1943, López moved to Chicago with his family as a young boy. As he grew to adulthood, he became a prominent community activist and an intractable independence proponent. López's activities in the Chicago area led to the founding of the Dr. Pedro Albizu Campos High School and the Juan Antonio Corretjer Puerto Rican Cultural Center. His social activism also included work on behalf of health care, employment training, drug use prevention, and eradicating police brutality. In addition, he was active in the Committee to Free the Five Puerto Rican Nationalists.* This led to his being forced underground in 1975. Despite his being the subject of a five-year manhunt by the FBI, López was arrested in 1981. López was tried and sentenced to a term of 55 years for seditious conspiracy and other charges. While imprisoned, López Rivera published many short stories and political essays. [SOURCE: www.prisonactivist.org]

LÓPEZ TIJERINA, REIES (1926-)

Chicano* activists had no greater symbol of defying the establishment than Reies López Tijerina, who achieved fame in a dramatic struggle for the restitution of Spanish and Mexican land grants in northen New Mexico. Born in Fall City, Texas, on September 21, 1926, to a family of seasonal farmworkers, in the 1960s he began leading the movement to regain the lands lost at the end of the Mexican-American War to developers, both wealthy Anglos and Hispanics, and the federal parks system.

Tijerina had spent the better part of his youth migrating with his farmworker family and, upon reaching adulthood, became a traveling Pentecostal preacher. After a failed attempt at establishing a religious commune in Arizona, he took his retinue to northern New Mexico, his wife's Patsy home area, and preached among the predominantly Catholic Hispanos in the mountain valleys of Rio Arriba County. In the early 1960s, as the U.S. Forest Service* began restricting Hispanos' grazing and water rights on federal lands, Tijerina became attracted to the land-grant cause and helped form the Corporation of Abiquiu.

As the Abiquiu movement grew, its headquarters was moved from Tierra Amarilla in 1963 to Albuquerque, and the membership changed its name from the Corporation of Abiquiu to La Alianza Federal de las Mercedes.* The Alianza members became hopeful when Tijerina announced that his research in Mexico City archives revealed that the United States had violated the terms of the Treaty of Guadalupe Hidalgo* by not respecting the legality of land grants.

To persuade officials to investigate their claims, Alianza members marched from Albuquerque to the steps of the state capital in Santa Fe in July 1966. Frustrated because Governor Jack Campbell rebuffed the group's request, in October of 1966 the Alianza occupied Echo Amphitheater, a campground in the Kit Carson National Forest, which had been an original *merced* (land grant). The group established the Republic of San Joaquín del Río Chama and evicted the forest rangers assigned to the area. Government officials arrested Tijerina and five others but eventually released them on bond.

By the Spring of 1967, a more sympathetic governor, David Cargo,* replaced Governor Campbell and gave the Alianza permission to convene a meeting in the town of Coyote in May 1966. When district attorney Alfonso Sánchez of Rio Arriba County discovered that the land-grant crusaders intended to formulate plans to again occupy the Echo Amphitheater campground, he tried to prevent the meeting by blocking the road to the village and making a number of arrests. Governor Cargo was out of the state and could not intervene. Consequently, Tijerina and other Alianza members on June 5 attacked the jail in Rio Arriba to free their comrades arrested in Coyote, wounding two officers in the process. They discovered, too late, that their comrades had already been freed on bail. Within hours, acting governor L.C. Francis mobilized the National Guard and embarked on one of the most massive manhunt's in New Mexico history. The state police, without warrants, searched the homes of Alianza members and their sympathizers.

When Governor Cargo returned, he demobilized the National Guard, but Tijerina and the other fugitives were quickly arrested. After the courthouse incident, the raiders were charged with second-degree kidnaping, assault to commit murder, an unlawful assault on a jail, and a number of more minor infractions. Nonetheless, a state judge freed the Alianza members on bail and dropped many of the charges against them. In his trial, Tijerina fired his lawyer and defended himself brilliantly. The jury, made up of Hispanics, found all of the defendants not guilty.

The federal government then put Tijerina and four others present at the Echo Amphitheater confrontation on trial in southern New Mexico for an array of federal violations. The jury, made up primarily of Anglos, found Tijerina guilty on two counts of assault against forest rangers, and a federal judge sentenced him to two years in prison.

Tijerina's nationally publicized exploits earned him a heroic reputation among Chicano Movement* participants. They exalted him as a national leader in the struggle against the Establishment and against old-guard Mexican Americans, who were considered *vendidos* (sell outs). Tijerina, did not disappoint them. He invited Chicano Movement activists to New Mexico to plan Movement strategy and then took a lead in protesting against a conference held in El Paso in the Fall of 1967 where President Lyndon B. Johnson* decided to appoint Vicente Ximenes* as director of the Inter-Agency Committee on Mexican American Affairs.* Ximenes and other Mexican-American leaders who attended this meeting were considered too tame for Chicano militants.

After the courthouse raid, however, extreme violence characterized all activities surrounding the land-grant movement, both by and against the Alianza, a situation that began to erode Tijerina's hold on leadership. Bombings of the Alianza headquarters and the murder of Eulogio Salazar, one of the deputies wounded at the courthouse raid and who was scheduled to testify against the Alianza members, distracted Tijerina and his followers from day-to-day organizing activity.

Nonetheless, in February of 1968, Tijerina, surrounded by a coterie of the faithful, joined the Poor People's March* on Washington organized by the civil rights leader Dr. Martin Luther King, Jr. Although King was assassinated during this period, the Alianza contingent still marched and spent 60 days at the nation's capital, making friends among civil rights leaders from the Native-American and African-American communities.

While in Washington, Tijerina announced his intention to conduct a citizen's arrest of a number of federal and state officials back in New Mexico, an action that by now was a routine of his political-theater tactics. A side of affect of these unconventional antics, however, was that law enforcement agencies kept Tijerina and the group under constant surveillance. On June 6, 1969, the Alianza again converged on Coyote and set up a tent city on private land to camp out while they held their annual conference. Tijerina was now at the height of his fame and prestige among Chicano Movement activists, who attended this conference from different parts of the United States.

At the end of the conference the participants watched in awe as Patsy Tijerina set fire to a National Forest Park sign. When a Forest Service employee tried to stop her, Tijerina came to her aid, was beaten and almost shot. The police dispersed the crowd, but arrested both husband and wife. Eventually, all of the accumulated federal charges against Tijerina earned him a five-year sentence. For her part in the sign burning, Patsy Tijerina received probation.

Tijerina was granted an early release from prison on July 26, 1971, contingent on his not associating with the militant stance of the Alianza. But New Mexico authorities in June 1974, incarcerated Tijerina, this time for charges stemming from the courthouse raid. He had served only a few months, when Governor Bruce King released him in response to constant pressure from New Mexico influentials.

Throughout the 1970s, Tijerina devoted only token attention to land-grant issues. He emerged from federal prison with a new philosophy: to work towards brotherly love among all races and ethnic groups and to better relations between the police and minorities. He also became obsessed with achieving heroic recognition. In 1972, he lead a caravan of adherents to Mexico City and ingratiated himself with Mexican government officials, including President Luis Echeverría, himself bent on projecting a populist image among his people.

By the mid seventies, the much strained relationship with state officials had eased. The city of Albuquerque funded his Brotherhood Awareness Center, the new name for the Alianza. But Tijerina still had a few antics up his sleeve. During his trip to Mexico, he asked President Echeverría to investigate the New Mexico land grants. The Mexican leader responded by establishing an agency charged with helping protect Mexican Americans in the United States and a commission to investigate land claims. This latest gambit again alienated Tijerina from the New Mexico establishment. After press outcry, Albuquerque officials revoked funding for his project.

Eventually, Tijerina lost even his most avid supporters, but the Alianza continued to function until the 1980s, when the weakened organization finally collapsed. Although the Alianza movement had divided many New Mexicans, it had also brought attention to the plight of the poor in one of the most impoverished areas of the United States. In addition, Alianza activity also energized other Hispanics in New Mexico and throughout the country into civil rights activities and educational reform. [SOURCE: Rosales, *Chicano!*, 154-170.]

LOS ANGELES COMMITTEE FOR THE PROTECTION OF THE FOREIGN BORN

The Los Angeles Committee for the Protection of the Foreign Born (LACPFB) was founded in 1950 in reaction to passage of the Internal Security Act, a law that provided authorities with sweeping powers to arrest or intimidate activists suspected of harboring subversive foreigners. Although the organization was not specifically Mexican American, it worked closely with such California groups as the Community Services Organization (CSO)* and the El Congreso del Pueblo de Habla Española.* The LACPFB established a branch in East Los Angeles that focused on protecting Mexican immigrants, including CSO members Josephine Yáñez and Eliseo Carrillo, Jr., from accusations that they had violated provisions of the Internal Security Act. The organization also vigorously protested neighborhood sweeps and raids on factories and fields, part of the Operation Wetback effort to rid the United States of undocumented immigrants. LACPFB also supported other Mexican organizations, such as the left-leaning Asociación Nacional México-Americana, a coalition labor group, and the Comité Defensor del Pueblo Mexicano, which defended compatriots in union and/or community activists. Mexican-American activists accused the government of using deportation campaigns as thinly veiled actions of a "strike-breaking, union busting force in the fields, shops, and factories." These charges were borne out by the deportation of union activists, Luisa Moreno,* Josefina Fierro de Bright, and Frank Dávila, on grounds ranging from violating immigration statutes to affiliation with Communists or Communist-front organizations. [SOURCE: Gutiérrez, *Walls and Mirrors*, 172-173.]

LOS ANGELES TEAM MENTORING, INC.

Los Angeles Team Mentoring, Inc. was founded in South Central Los Angeles after the civil unrest in 1992. Funded by the Amelior Foundation as a pilot program at Horace Mann Middle School, the program employed innovative methods to reach more young people, such as assigning adult mentors who would serve as positive role models. Team mentors work primarily with middle school students in an effort to help them as they grow up in challenging urban environments. The goal of the project is to help them recognize and reach their potential as young people and students, and to succeed as parents, workers, and citizens. [SOURCE: http://clnet.sscnet.ucla.edu/community/intercambios/latm/]

LOUISIANA PURCHASE

During the late eighteenth century, Spain's most vulnerable area threatened by the land aggrandizement aspirations of the newly formed United States was the far northern frontier of New Spain (Mexico). One reason is that Spain had difficulty in peopling this vast territory on the empire's periphery. To augment its forces in the interior of New Spain, which were busy squelching the independence movement that had started on September 16, 1810, with the insurrection of Father Miguel Hidalgo y Costilla, the Spaniards withdrew their troops from the frontier presidios. This further weakened the lines of defense in the North, inviting incursions from the newly independent but aggressive North Americans. The danger of Yankee encroachment was apparent to the Spaniards much earlier, however. In 1803, a powerful France under Napoleon Bonaparte acquired from Spain the Louisiana Territory, which she had ceded during the Seven Years War in the previous century. Napoleon, who was vying for dominance in Europe and needed revenue quickly, sold the vast territory to the United States by the secret Treaty of San Ildefonso, thus violating an understanding that it was not to be alienated. After the sale, the borders of the dangerous infant nation now connected directly with New Spain. [SOURCE: Weber, *Foreigners in Their Native Land*, 53; Rosales, "A Historical Overview," 19-20.]

LUCEY, ROBERT E. (1819-1977)

Born in Los Angeles, California, Robert E. Lucey entered the Catholic priesthood in 1916, rose in the church to be appointed in 1934, Bishop of the Amarillo Diocese in Texas and then Archbishop of San Antonio in 1942. Bishop Lucey dedicated many of his pastoral duties to the promotion of rights for agricultural workers and was subsequently appointed to the President's Commission on Migratory Labor in 1950. He also helped found the Bishops' Committee for the Spanish Speaking,* a national organization that provided the Catholic laity both a vehicle and incentive to deal with the many social problems affecting Latino Catholics in the United States. Although he was conservative in the ecclesiastical sphere, Bishop Lucey proved to be a liberal in socioeconomic matters. As a result, he gained a national reputation as a champion of social justice and civil rights and as being especially concerned with the plight of poverty-stricken Mexican Americans in southwest Texas. He fought for child-labor legislation and for inclusion of migrant agricultural workers in the protection of federal labor laws. In his own diocese, he insisted on employing only union labor and he supported farmworker strikes for union recognition and better wages. During the 1966 march of the Rio Grande City melon strikers to Austin, Lucey urged them stand up and defend themselves against discrimination and oppression. He retired in 1969 due to hostile pressures and died in 1977. [SOURCE: Meier and Rivera, *Dictionary of Mexican American History*, 205.]

LUNA, SOLOMÓN (1858-1912)

Born in Los Lunas, New Mexico, to a wealthy and prominent family, Solomón Luna became a politician, rancher, and businessmen. He attended St. Louis University and entered politics as a Republican in Valencia County, where he eventually dominated the scene. Luna took an active role in New Mexico's statehood and appealed to the Hispano-American community for support of his actions in state politics. More importantly, Luna actively sought to include the Spanish language and *nuevomexicano* culture within the state's constitutional guarantees upon statehood. He succeeded in his efforts to sustain rights of the Hispanic population through a series of safeguard clauses in the state's constitution. Luna lived to see New Mexico enter the Union as the 47th state in 1912. [SOURCE: Meier and Rivera, *Dictionary of Mexican American History*, 203-4.]

THE LUTHERAN IMMIGRANT AND REFUGEE SERVICES

The Lutheran Immigrant and Refugee Services (LIRS) provides some of the most comprehensive assistance to refugees and immigrants who come to the United States. Its antecedents go back to 1918, when the National Lutheran Council (NLC), from its offices in New York, responded to an immigration and refugee crisis created by the destruction during War I; it set up a Welfare Department with an office for "the rehabilitation and placement of Lutheran refugees." The project continued to provide services to refugees during World War II by establishing refugee camps in Germany, Austria, and Italy for displaced persons (DPs) from Eastern Europe in an effort to help those who wanted to immigrate to the United States. After the war, the Lutherans continued providing refugee services, primarily to immigrants from East Germany, but increasingly to help other newcomers to the United

States. Refugees from Indochina and Chile in the 1970s, *marielitos** from Cuba and Haitians in the 1980s, Central Americans in the 1980s and 1990s, fleeing political repression, war, famine, natural disasters, all came within the purview of LIRS programs. Crucially, the LIRS also provides funding for smaller, local projects providing legal aid and/or social services to immigrants. [SOURCE: http://www.lirs.org/who/history.htm]

LYNCHING

Lynching, that is, taking a prisoner out of a jail cell or simply arresting suspects to execute them without due process, dramatically affected Mexicans in California, Arizona, New Mexico, and Texas during the nineteenth century. It is estimated that between 1848 and 1928, mobs lynched at least 597 Mexicans, a statistic that varies because the definition of lynching has altered so much over time. Despite oral lore, only two discernible lynchings of Mexicans can be documented for southwestern states other than Texas during the early part of the twentieth century—one in Arizona and the other in New Mexico. Outside of the Southwest, seven Mexicans are known to have been lynched, two in Colorado, two in Oklahoma, two in Nebraska, and one in Kansas. In Texas, however, perhaps as many as thirty lynchings of Mexicans, depending on how the practice is defined, took place after 1900. However, this tally does not include all illegal executions. [SOURCE: Rosales, *Pobre Raza!*, 118-121; Carrigan and Webb, "The Lynching of Persons of Mexican Origin or Descent in the United States, 1848 to 1928," *Journal of Social History,* Winter 2003, http://www.findarticles.com/p/articles/mi_m2005/is_2_37/ai_111897839/pg_2]

M

MAGÓN, RICARDO FLORES, *see* FLORES MAGÓN, RICARDO

MAIDIQUE, MODESTO A. (1940-)

Modesto A. Maidique became the first Cuban-American president of a major university: Florida International University in Miami. The Cuban-born immigrant received his Ph.D. in Engineering from the Massachusetts Institute of Technology in 1970. [SOURCE: Kanellos, "Prominent Hispanics," *Hispanic-American Almanac*, 729.]

Modesto A. Maidique

MAMMOTH TANK STRIKE

One of the most violent reactions to Mexican efforts to organize and obtain higher wages took place during November 1897, at Mammoth Tank, a coaling and water depot near Yuma, Arizona. In the midst of a "wildcat strike" against the Southern Pacific, José Rodríguez killed strikebreaker Francisco Cuevas. San Diego County deputies and Arizona officers were called to the scene because, although Rodríguez had fled, the atmosphere remained explosive. When the deputies arrived in a railroad car, they arrested a number of protesting Mexicans and detained them with their hands tied behind their backs. The other workers, who were unarmed, threw rocks at the officers, who then fell back to the train, from where they fired at the mob, killing six of the angry workers. The strikers managed to confiscate a gun from the retreating officers and wounded a deputy. Officers arrested eighteen of the Mexicans, but the rest, about 250, fled. [SOURCE: Rosales, *Chicano!*, 116.]

MANIFEST DESTINY

The doctrine of Manifest Destiny was an expression of American nationalism used to justify, rationalize, and explain U.S. expansionist efforts during the nineteenth century. In essence, Anglo Americans wanted to fulfill a "manifest destiny" of expanding their country all the way to the Pacific coast. Indeed many Americans believed that God had provided signs that these lands could be taken from Mexico with impunity. After the annexation of Texas in 1845, President James K. Polk sent John Slidell to Mexico with an offer of twenty-five million dollars for Mexico and California, but Mexican officials refused to even see him. Polk then sent General Zachary Taylor across the Nueces River to blockade the mouth of the Rio Grande River at Port Isabel. On April 25, 1846, Mexicans retaliated by crossing the river and attacking U.S. troops, inflicting casualties. Now able to justify war immediately, Polk went to Congress and obtained a declaration of war against Mexico.

John L. O'Sullivan, the journalist who had coined the term "Manifest Destiny," felt that Mexicans in the northern provinces would welcome U.S. rule because they had come to despise the neglect by Mexico's centralized rule and because "'an irresistible army of Anglo-Saxon[s]' would bring with them 'the plough and the rifle . . . schools and colleges, courts and representative halls, mills and meeting houses." Some scholars see adherence to this ideology by Anglo Americans as a reflection of their religious traditions, including "predestination," the notion that God only selected successful, enterprising individuals to go to heaven. [SOURCE: Gutiérrez, *Walls and Mirrors,* 15; Weber, *Foreigners in Their Native Land,* 56, 66, 96.]

MANO NEGRA

The Mano Negra (Black Hand) was a secret organization that developed in New Mexico in the early 1900s. Made up of mostly Hispano small landowners, the Mano Negra used terrorist tactics to frighten Anglo homesteaders moving into and fencing off land in the Rio Arriba area of northwestern New Mexico. [SOURCE: Meier and Rivera, *A Dictionary of Mexican American History,* 210.]

MAQUILADORAS

The *maquiladoras* (assembly plants) first appeared on the Mexican border in 1963. The Mexican government, in a program known as the Border Industrializaton Program (BIP),* allowed American companies to install plants to assemble manufactured goods in Mexico. The parts for these products, at first mainly clothing and electronic equipment, came from the United States and were exempted from tariffs. Such a program was in contravention of Mexico's industrial policy established in the late 1940s to foment what is known as Industrial Substitution, a project that would make Mexico self-sufficient in manufacturing. As such, this exception obliged the foreign manufacturers to install the plants only at the border and immediately export their products out of Mexico for sale on the world market. In this way, they would not compete with local manufactures. Eventually, *maquiladoras* spread to various parts of Mexico, and the franchises were given to manufactures from other countries—but with the same stipulations that had been established originally. Mexico allowed this because immigration to the United States had created vast bottlenecks of unemployed workers in border towns. The *maquiladoras,* it was believed, would provide needed jobs.

While employment in these plants provided needed benefits and wages, superior to what could be obtained in the rest of Mexico, the jobs went mainly to women. This created social dislocation, as men still had to migrate to the United States for jobs. In addition, the assembly-line work offered very little chance for advancement and often left women with little defense against employer whims. Moreover, because of Mexico's more relaxed environmental protection policy, *maquiladoras* have become a major source of industrial pollution affecting both sides of the border. [SOURCE: Lorey, *The U.S.-Mexican Border in the Twentieth Century,* 104-105.]

MARDIROSIAN, VAHAC (1925-)

The Reverend Vahac Mardirosian, a Baptist minister in Los Angeles, became one of the most articulate leaders supporting high school students who had walked out of East Los Angeles schools in April 1968. Popularly known as "blow outs," the protests demanded a revamping of the educational system, which was considered as unresponsive to the needs of the predominantly Mexican-American student body. Born in Alepo, Syria, of Armenian heritage, Reverend Mardirosian immigrated with his family to Mexico City when he was only two and then to Tijuana, where Mardirosian grew up and received his early schooling. Upon turning nineteen, he left home for California, where he worked and graduated from a Baptist seminary as an ordained minister in 1946. In 1948, he married Eunice and then was sent to Topeka and Chicago to minister to Mexican communities in those cities. In 1952, he returned to Los Angeles, where he continued his religious work as a pastor and the Baptist director of Hispanic ministries of the American Baptist Churches of the Pacific Southwest.

On the morning of March 1, 1968, an event catapulted Rev. Mardirosian to the forefront of the civil rights struggle in East Los Angeles. While at a breakfast meeting with other Baptist ministers, he heard that students had left their classes at Garfield High and were milling around in the streets. Fearing for their safety, the minister drove to the school and sought out the leaders. After about three hours, he gained their confidence and they allowed him to mediate with school administrators. Mardirosian did not think twice about joining a small group called the Emergency Support Committee (ESC),* consisting of about 25 parents. Less than a month after the first walkout, the ESC changed its name to the Educational Issues Coordinating Committee (EICC)* and the group formally elected Mardirosian chairman, but not by acclamation—many of the younger militants opposed him because they feared he was too moderate. Nonetheless, in the ensuing confrontations with the school board, the Baptist minister managed to provide leadership and a degree of cohesion.

Rev. Mardirosian has been tireless in advancing educational reform for Hispanics in California. He was the founder and executive director of the Hispanic Urban Center in Los Angeles, a project that provided teachers with in-service training about the culture and heritage of Mexican Americans. Through the auspices of the American Baptist Churches, he founded the ABC Project Head Start Program. Mainly through his efforts, the Parent Institute for Quality Education was created. The Institute offers, in coordination with school districts throughout California, training classes for parents on becoming informed and vigilante advocates for their children's education. In May 1998, California State University conferred an Honorary Doctorate Degree to Rev. Mardirosian in recognition of the significant contributions he has made to the children of California. He is now retired and lives in Solana Beach, California. [SOURCE: Rosales, *Chicano!*, 191-194.]

MARIELITOS

In April 1980, a dramatic incident in Havana, Cuba, received worldwide attention: a bus carrying a load of discontented Cubans crashed through the gates of the Peruvian embassy in Havana, and the passengers received political asylum from Peru. When it became apparent that what the gate-crashers really wanted was to leave Cuba, Fidel Castro began to revise his policy of gradually allowing Cubans to leave. In a calculated move, the Castro government announced that whoever wanted to leave Cuba should go to the Peruvian embassy. Immediately, ten thousand people crowded in. The Cuban government then processed and gave exit documents to those who came forth. Cuban exiles who happened to be on the island at the time of the embassy gate-crashing, returned to Miami and organized a flotilla of 42 boats. With Castro's blessing, they began round-the-clock evacuation of the "Havana Ten Thousand." President Jimmy Carter, as did presidents before him, welcomed the new influx of Cuban exiles.

Since the flotilla converged at Mariel Harbor to pick up passengers, which totaled over 125,000 by the time the Cuban boatlifts* ended in 1980, the refugees became known as *marielitos*. The explanation given by Castro for this whole phenomenon was rather simplistic. He charged that his policy of allowing exiles to visit the island had contaminated many erstwhile revolutionaries with the glitter of consumerism. It is probably true that travelers from the United States to the island did tempt Cubans with their abundance of consumer products, convincing many that life in a capitalist society was easier than life in Cuba. Nonetheless, Castro had to accept that socialism was at this point experiencing many difficulties and not delivering on many of the promises made some twenty years earlier.

The new refugees differed significantly from the earlier waves of displaced Cubans. Few were from the middle- and upper-classes of pre-Castro Cuba, as were most exiles then living in the United States. There were also racial differences: the new arrivals were more reflective of the general racial composition of Cuba, with many blacks and mulattoes in the *marielito* ranks. Furthermore, in a crafty move, Castro had deliberately cast out many political and social misfits during the boatlift, an act that unfairly stigmatized the majority of 1980 emigrés, who were in the main normal, hardworking Cubans.

During the *marielito* exit, Castro and President Carter became entangled in a now familiar struggle over which country would get more political capital from the refugee issue. Thousands of new arrivals crowded into processing centers, living in tent cities, and even a football stadium in Miami. Many of the refugees became frustrated over the delay in being able to leave the camps. For many, the stay in these "temporary camps" stretched out into months, even years. The Castro government was quick to imply that the United States was not really that anxious to provide refuge to Cubans who were poor, uneducated, and racially not as white as the previous influx.

[SOURCE: Rosales, "A Historical Overview," 49-51; Masud-Piloto, *From Welcomed Exiles to Illegal Immigrants,* 95-97.]

MARIELITOS AND RESENTMENT TOWARDS CUBANS

During the Marielito boatlift in 1980, when thousands of Cubans, poorer and more racially mixed than previous exiles, fled the island, local non-Cuban residents in Florida complained of losing jobs to the newcomers, who purportedly worked for lower salaries and thus depressed wages for Miamians as a whole. While most Miamians sympathized with the *marielito* plight, they were not as willing to carry a burden they felt had been created by transnational conditions not of their making. Some state leaders also feared the worsening of ethnic and racial relations because of the burden posed by renewed immigration from Cuba. As it was, antagonism over the presence of Cubans was evident even before the *marielito* influx. In November 1980, voters in Dade County repealed the Bilingual-Bicultural Ordinance, which had been passed in 1973, making it unlawful to use county funds "for the purpose of utilizing any language other than English, or promoting any culture other than that of the United States." The anti-Cuban sentiment subsided, however, when in May 1985, the Cuban government, angry over the Reagan administration's installation of Radio Martí, suddenly ended the sanctioned emigration from the island. [SOURCE: Masud-Piloto, *From Welcomed Exiles to Illegal Immigrants,* 95-97.]

MARQUEZ, JESSE (1950-)

Born in 1950 in Wilmington, California, Jesse Marquez is a pre-eminent Chicano environmentalist in southern California. A union electrician by day and an environmentalist by night and weekends, Marquez somehow has found time to work towards a healthier environment for his community. He diligently attends local community meetings and public hearings, as well as state forums, and he provides key written and verbal testimony that has prompted the public and officials to maintain a vigilance on pollution violations. Marquez's activism dates back to his high school days, when in 1968 he attended a UCLA summer youth leadership program. The investment paid off because the young leader became involved in numerous activist civil rights projects, from stopping police brutality to promoting bilingual education. When he recognized that one of the biggest issues was the environmentally hazardous Los Angeles Harbor area, where he grew up, Marquez became a key organizer, in the 1980s, of the Coalition For a Safe Environment. The group, which began with 15 members in 2005, grew to more than 300. His interest in environmental issues has prompted Marquez to work towards a professional certificate in UCLA's Archaeology program. [SOURCE: Ruiz, "The Marquez Equation: Knowledge x People = Power."]

MARTÍ, JOSÉ (1853-1895)

Through tireless organizational efforts in New York, Tampa, Key West, and New Orleans, through fund-raising and lobbying of tobacco workers, through penning and delivering eloquent political speeches and publishing a variety of essays in Spanish and English, José Martí was the Latin American quintessential intellectual "man of action," while at the same time becoming a pioneer of Spanish-American literary Modernism. Martí, a native of Havana, Cuba, invested his freedom and his life in the cause of Cuban independence from Spain, ultimately losing his life on a Cuban battlefield in 1895 at the young age of 42. Before his death, however, Martí was a key figure in the revolutionary press movement, especially in New York, where he was the founder of the important newspaper of the last phase of the revolution: *Patria* (Country 1892–19?).

Martí's experience as a revolutionary journalist dated back to his youth in Cuba, where he had been imprisoned for ideas contained in an essay and in a play he had published in the newspaper *La Patria Libre* (The Free Country). He later was sent to study in Spain, where he obtained his law degree and published a political pamphlet, *El presidio político en Cuba* (Political Imprisonment in Cuba). In 1873, Martí moved to Mexico, where he edited *Revista Universal* (Universal Review); in 1877 he served as a professor in Guatemala and edited the official state newspaper there. In 1879, he returned to Cuba and was promptly exiled to Spain. From 1880 on, he began the first of his various residencies in New York. In Caracas in 1881, Martí founded and edited the *Revista Venezolana*, which only lasted for two numbers, and then he promptly returned to New York. In the grand metropolis, Martí maintained an active life as a writer, publishing books of poetry and numerous essays and speeches. The most curious of his publishing feats was the founding and editing of *La Edad de Oro* (The Golden Age) in 1889, a monthly magazine for children—he had earlier published a book of verse, *Ismaelillo* (1881?), written for his son.

In all his organizing and countering of annexationist impulses with demands for independence and self-determination for Cuba, Martí warned of the imperialist tendencies of the United States. He did not live to see his fears become reality: the United States declared war on Spain, and, after signing the peace with Spain, unilaterally forced a constitution on the Republic of Cuba that depended on U.S. intervention, as called for in the Platt Amendment.

José Martí

One of Martí's greatest virtues was his ability to bring the various classes and factions together in the revolutionary cause; this virtue included extending open arms to Puerto Rican intellectuals to unite their efforts with those of Cubans. [SOURCE: Kanellos, *Hispanic Periodicals in the United States*, 12, 17-20, 62, 67.]

MARTÍNEZ, ELIZABETH "BETITA" (1925-)

Born in Washington, D.C. to Manuel Guillermo and Ruth Phillips Martínez, Elizabeth "Betita" Martínez has been an author and activist for almost 50 years. In her writing, she has documented the Chicano* struggle for social justice since the 1960s. She received a B.A. with Honors from Swarthmore College in Pennsylvania (the only student of color at the time) in 1946 and an honorary doctorate from Swarthmore in 2000. In the 1960s she worked in the civil rights movement with the Student Nonviolent Coordinating Committee (SNCC), where she was one of two Latino staff members. Her first book, *Letters from Mississippi* (1965, re-issued in 2003) came out of that experience. In 1968, Martínez was asked to move to New Mexico to support the land-grant movement being led by Reies López Tijerina.* Putting her considerable writing talent to good use, she soon began publishing the Chicano Movement* newspaper *El Grito del Norte*; the newspaper was published until 1975. While an activist in New Mexico, Martínez attended the first Chicano Youth Liberation Conference* in Denver in 1969 and La Raza Unida Party's (The United People's Party)* national convention in El Paso, Texas, in 1972. Martínez has written numerous articles and books, including *500 Years of Chicano History*, a bilingual, pictorial history. Since moving to San Francisco in 1976, where she lives in the Mission District,* Martínez has worked on community issues, such as health care, immigrant rights, and anti-racist training, and has served as a consultant and mentor to Latino youth groups. In 1997, she co-founded—and now directs—the Institute for MultiRacial Justice, a resource center to help build alliances among peoples of color. She has received 18 awards for leadership, scholarship, and service from professional organizations, and many more from student and community groups. She has also been an adjunct professor of Ethnic Studies and Women's Studies in the California State University system; she has been a guest lecturer on more than 200 campuses. [SOURCE: Rosales, *Chicano!*, 214; http://www.infoshop.org/texts/crass_martinez.html]

MARTÍNEZ, JR., FÉLIX (1857-1916)

Félix Martínez, Jr. founded the first Hispanic third party in United States history. Born at Penasco, Taos County, New Mexico, on March 29, 1857, Martínez studied for five years at St. Mary's College in Mora, New Mexico. After working as an employee partner in various retail businesses in Colorado, he moved to Las Vegas, New Mexico, where he continued in mercantile ventures and eventually turned to newspaper publishing and politics. After breaking with the Democratic Party, he ran in 1890 and 1892 as a candidate of El Partido del Pueblo Unido (The United People's Party) and won a seat on the territorial council in the second election. In addition, the party swept all offices in San Miguel County in 1890. The principal issues of the party were land tenure and the common people's mistreatment by the dominant political leaders, both Anglos and Mexicans. In 1899, Martínez moved to El Paso, Texas, where he furthered his business and publishing interests and was later appointed by President William Howard Taft as U.S. Commissioner General to South America. [SOURCE: Gómez-Quiñones, *Roots of Chicano Politics,* 281.]

MARTÍNEZ, LOUIS (1953–1973)

On March 17, 1973, Crusade for Justice (CFJ)* members in Denver clashed with police after officers who tried to break up a party. In the process, Louis Martínez fired and wounded a police officer and was promptly shot and killed. Martínez was twenty years old. At the same time, Ernest Vigil, a major leader in the CFJ, was shot in the back, and a bomb exploded in a CFJ-owned building. The clashes of the Crusade for Justice with police represented one of the most violent phases of the Chicano Movement.* [SOURCE: Rosales, *Chicano!,* 247.]

MARTÍNEZ, MARÍA ELENA (1940-)

Born in Wiley, Texas, in 1940, María Elena Martínez was the first Mexican-American woman to head a political party in Texas. She received a degree in Spanish from North Texas University in 1964. In the late 1960s as a student at the University of Texas, Martínez joined the Mexican American Youth Organization (MAYO)* and participated in numerous activities, such as the 1969 Del Rio civil rights march and the labor strikes involving Chicanos.* After receiving her M.A. in education in Austin, she traveled to Cuba with the Venceremos Brigade, an experience that energized her commitment for social change. After holding numerous leading positions within the La Raza Unida Party (LRUP),* in 1978, Martínez was elected chairperson of the party pursuant to protests that women were kept out of prominent positions within LRUP. [SOURCE: http://libraries.uta.edu/tejanovoices/interview.asp?CMAS-No=133#]

MARTÍNEZ, VILMA S. (1943-)

Born in San Antonio, Texas, the daughter of a carpenter, Vilma Martínez graduated from the University of Texas in 1965 and obtained her law degree from Columbia Law School in 1967. By 1973, she headed the Mexican

Vilma S. Martínez

American Legal Defense and Education Fund (MALDEF).* As President and General Counsel of the organization, Martínez moved towards broadening its goals to include wider funding sources and intense activities in areas of concern for Chicanos,* such as education, employment, and political access. In 1974, she successfully defended the right to bilingual education for non-English-speaking children and consequently was appointed by Governor Jerry Brown in 1976 to the University of California Board of Regents. During her presidency of MALDEF, one of Martínez's major accomplishments was her campaign toward expanding the U.S. Voting Rights Act, which since its passage in 1965 had only applied to blacks and Puerto Ricans. Attorney Vilma Martínez was the first Hispanic to win the Jefferson Award for public service from the American Institute in recognition of her pioneering work in civil rights as director of MALDEF. [SOURCE: Telgin and Kamp, *Latinas! Women of Achievement.*]

MÁS CANOSA, JORGE (1939-1997)

Born in Cuba in 1939, the wealthy Cuban businessmen Más Canosa immigrated to South Florida in 1960 and built a thriving business in telecommunications. He also used his wealth and standing to oppose Fidel Castro. In 1981, Más Canosa formed, in Washington, D.C., the first organization to influence U.S. policy through lobbying and financial contributions to campaigns: the Cuban American National Foundation (CANF).* It established its center in Washington, D.C. With the zealous and energetic Más Canosa at the helm, CANF began influencing U.S. policy toward Cuba principally through its political action committee, Free Cuba PAC, which donated to the campaign funds of congressmen and senators maintaining a hard line towards Fidel Castro's Cuba. The CANF also became a principal lobbyist for the establishment by the U.S. Government of Radio Martí, a radio station founded to broadcast news and features to Cuba and serve as a supplement to the censored or ideologically biased transmissions that characterized the Cuban broadcast media. [SOURCE: García, *Havana USA*, 147-148.]

MASSACHUSETTS LATINO CONFERENCE

In May 2002, hundreds of Latino activists and academics from across Massachusetts met in Boston at a conference sponsored by the Mauricio Gastón Institute at the University of Massachusetts to discuss politics, health, immigration, and other issues facing their communities. The turnout was made up of Puerto Ricans, Dominicans, Mexicans, Central and South Americans, a reflection of the increasing diversity of Latinos in Massachusetts. Much of the discussion centered not just on what should be done but on the unity that could be achieved among such a diverse array of ethnic groups. The group also identified pertinent issues common to most Latino and Caribbean groups: immigration, bilingual education, health care access, and community organizing. The conference discussed race differences among the Latinos themselves and the tension and divisions that these differences can create. [SOURCE: Miller, "Latinos Debate Race, Identity Questions," 3; Abreu, "Second Latino Public Policy Conference Draws 600," http://www.gaston.umb. edu/publications/gr/9xxnl/articles/latpubpolcon.html]

Jesús Colón in front of the McCarran Commission

MCCARRAN-WALTER IMMIGRATION AND NATIONALITY ACT

Congress passed the McCarran-Walter Immigration and Nationality Act of 1952 in order to continue the quota system that was integral to the immigration acts of 1921 and 1924. The law placed greater restrictions on immigration from Western Hemisphere countries and was seen as a potential threat to immigrants' civil rights by President Harry S. Truman, who subsequently vetoed it. Congress overrode his veto, and since that time the law has been interpreted and used in the deportation and restriction of Mexican immigrants. Regardless, the naturalization and citizenship clauses proved a viable option in legalizing the status of Mexicans coming into and residing in the United States. On the other hand, that part of the legislation which set up machinery for the investigation and deportation of alleged subversive groups resulted in the silencing Mexican-American unionists and civil rights leaders in their fight for equality. Several prominent leaders were deported under this act. [SOURCE: Gutiérrez, *Walls and Mirrors*; Samora and Simon, *A History of the Mexican-American People,* 195; http://www.jsri.msu.edu/museum/pubs/MexAmHist/chapter19.html]

MCWILLIAMS, CAREY (1905-1980)

Carey Mcwilliams was born in Northern Colorado and raised on the family cattle ranch. After moving to Los Angeles, McWilliams became interested in journalism and at various points in his life, worked as a lawyer, author, and editor. While at the University of Southern California, McWilliams studied labor law, in particular farm labor policy, and published *Factories in the Field* (1929). He also served on several state agency boards, becoming president of the Division of Immigration and Housing in California. Both his academic and political experiences aroused his interest in racism and its particular affect on Mexican Americans. He explored this issue to considerable depth in his book *North From Mexico,* which was first published in 1949. His vigorous and outspoken involvement on behalf of the civil rights of Mexican Americans situated him as a key figure in the Sleepy Lagoon murder case* in 1943. The reversal in the convictions of seventeen Mexican-American youths in this case is partially credited to the dedication that he and Mexican-American leaders put into this effort. McWilliams injected and circulated his views on civil liberties in *The Nation* magazine, which he edited between 1955 and 1975. Carey McWilliams stands out as a giant in the struggle for social justice and civil rights for minorities and the foreign born. [SOURCE: Meier and Rivera, *A Dictionary of Mexican American History,* 207.]

MEDINA, ELISEO (1946-)

Eliseo Medina was one of the first organizers for the United Farm Workers (UFW)* in the 1960s. Born in Mexico, in 1958 he and his family joined his father in California's San Joaquin Valley. His father, a former *bracero* who had worked in agriculture since the 1940s, continued to follow California crops with the family. While living in Delano, the incipient farmworker movement led by César Chávez* drew Medina into union activity at age nineteen. The union asked him to head the grape boycott in Chicago in 1968, when he was hardly out of his teens. He was supposed to be there for a few weeks, but he wound up staying a year. After that, he traveled widely to garner support for union boycotts. In the early 1970s, Medina directed the UFW field offices in Imperial Valley, California, and in Florida. In 1977, he was selected to serve as the union's second vice president. Medina has remained in various labor organizing endeavors and today is executive vice president of the Service Employees International Union. [SOURCE: http://www.seiv.org/about/officers_bios/me-dina-bio.cfm]

MÉNDEZ ET AL V. WESTMINSTER SCHOOL DISTRICT ET AL

In 1945, a group of Mexican-American parents in California filed suits against four Orange County elementary school districts in what became the landmark *Méndez v. Westminster* case. Supporting the parents were the League of United Latin American Citizens* and attorneys from the Lawyer's Guild, who argued that segregation violated the constitutional rights of Mexican children guaranteed by the Fourteenth Amendment. Circuit Court Judge B. McCormick found that school board members had segregated Mexican-American children on the basis of their "Latinized" appearance and had gerrymandered district boundaries in order to ensure that Mexican Americans attended separate schools. At least 5,000 Mexican-American children were affected. As expected, the *Westminster* decision had an important impact on the future efforts to desegregate Mexican children. [SOURCE: Donato, *The Other Struggle for Equal Schools*, 2.]

MERCADO, J.J. (?-?)

A Mexican school teacher in Houston, J.J. Mercado, established a chapter of La Agrupación Protectora Mexicana (The Mexican Protective League)* in 1913. The league worked with the Mexican consul to mediate between discriminated Mexicans and their employers, especially for not receiving benefits after injuries. [SOURCE: Rosales, *Chicano!*, 62; De León, *Ethnicity in the Sunbelt*, 9, 10, 13, 17.]

MERCEDES, see LAND GRANTS

MEXICAN AMERICAN AFFAIRS UNIT

In 1969, the U.S. Office of Education created a Mexican American Affairs Unit to find out how Mexican-American children were faring in U.S.

public schools. This federal education agency had already acknowledged that public schools were not serving Mexican-American children as well as they did whites. The creation of the Mexican American Affairs Unit was the direct outcome of Mexican-American leaders demanding their fair share of President Lyndon B. Johnson's Great Society programs.* In 1970, it became the Office for Spanish-Speaking American Affairs and was placed under the auspices of the Office of Special Concerns of the Commissioner of Education. This agency coordinated such educational programs as Project Head Start, Upward Bound, and Follow Through, all of which primarily focused on minority and socioeconomically disadvantaged youth. [SOURCE: Donato, *The Other Struggle for Equal Schools*, 61.]

MEXICAN AMERICAN COMMUNITY SERVICES AGENCY, INC.

The Mexican American Community Services Agency, Inc. (MACSA) began in 1964 when a group of community activists in Santa Clara County, California, began to identify strategies to help the growing Latino community find solutions to injustices, such as discrimination, racism, poverty, police brutality, educational inequity, and inadequate access to public services. Since that time, MACSA has been committed to programs for young Latinos at three youth centers, fifteen schools, and a number of library and community sites. In addition, MACSA began one of the few Health Care Senior Centers in the county, a program that provides the Latino elderly an opportunity to age with dignity. In response to the lack of affordable housing in the community, MACSA has erected two subsidized housing centers for seniors and families. Although the Latino community has made great strides since MACSA's founding, many challenges still exist, and MACSA continues to provide services and solutions for many of the issues that affect the Latino community of Santa Clara County. [SOURCE: http://www.macsa.org/body_frame.html]

MEXICAN AMERICAN CULTURAL CENTER OF SAN ANTONIO

One of the main goals of the Mexican American Cultural Center (MACC), when it was founded in 1972 in San Antonio, was "to help raise the consciousness of a positive image of Hispanos in the United States." MACC became a place, where members of Padres Asociados para Derechos Religiosos, Educativos y Sociales (Fathers Associated for Religious, Educational, and Social Rights), or Los P.A.D.R.E.S.,* could conduct workshops on how religious objectives overarched with social concerns benefit Hispanic Americans. Over the years, staff and volunteers used television appearances to expand their work throughout the Southwest while MACC's resources have increased and come to include an extensive library and a bookstore with a large selection of Spanish-language publications, and an extensive video and DVD-rental collection. From its inception, Bishop

Patrick F. Flores* was active in helping maintain a strong program of folk culture activities in order to sustain the cultural identity of Hispanics. Still in existence, MACC has been building bridges between cultures among Latinos and other Americans with little deviation from its original trajectory. In addition, because of the changing demographics of the Latin American population in the United States, the orbit of influence extends to Mexico and Central America. Classes are held in San Antonio and Guadalajara, Mexico, and MACC's mobile teams make presentations across the country. Some of the topics include multiculturalism, border immigration issues, and the roots of racism. In order to ensure such a cosmopolitan aspect to MACC's educational objectives, the staff is not only from the United States, but also from Central and South America, and Puerto Rico. Moreover, MACC's students come from South America, Canada, Australia, and many European countries. After training, they leave MACC to serve all over the world as chaplains, missionaries, and teachers. [SOURCE: http://www.maccsa.org/; Campa, *Hispanic Culture in the Southwest*, 185-186.]

MEXICAN AMERICAN EDUCATION COMMISSION

When Mexican-American high school students walked out of their classes on March 1, 1968, to dramatize what they considered poor educational facilities in East Los Angeles, a committee of parents and other concerned citizens formed to support the students. Called the Emergency Support Committee, then the Educational Issues Coordinating Committee,* the group only meant to provide urgent and emergency assistance to the student strikers. However, this effort evolved into the formation of the Mexican American Education Commission (MAEC), which for almost forty years has established inroads within the Los Angeles Unified School District (LAUSD) for equitable educational opportunity for Chicano/Latino students. MAEC continues to provide an informed community perspective to the Board of Education about programs and issues related to the more than 600,000 Chicano/Latino students who comprise over 75 percent of LAUSD students. The commission conducts surveys, participates in LAUSD committees, and meets with school and community groups before making these recommendations. [SOURCE: http://thomas.loc.gov/cgi-bin/query/z?r105:E10MR8-405]

MEXICAN AMERICAN JOINT COUNCIL

The Mexican American Joint Council was founded in 1967 in Texas to serve as an umbrella group for several Mexican-American political and civil rights organizations. Its first president was the pioneer educator, George I. Sánchez,* who pursued an aggressive political agenda. Among the council's major objectives was the dissolution of the Texas Rangers* and the promotion of Mexican American involvement in local, state, and national politics in order to obtain more social and economic benefits. [SOURCE: Meier and Rivera, *A Dictionary of Mexican American History,* 221.]

MEXICAN AMERICAN LEGAL DEFENSE AND EDUCATION FUND

The Mexican American Legal Defense and Education Fund (MALDEF) was founded in 1968 by Chicano Movement* activists in order to maintain a fund for any litigation dealing with civil rights. Headquartered in Los Angeles, it currently has six affiliate offices, in San Francisco, Los Angeles, Sacramento, San Antonio, Chicago, and Washington, D.C. Litigation departments are maintained in the areas of education, employment, immigration, and voting rights. MALDEF maintains a law school scholarship and other programs to assist students in entering the legal profession. It publishes two triquarterly newsletters, *Leadership Program Newsletter* and *MALDEF Newsletter.*

In the early 1970s the Southwest Council of La Raza (SWCLR) gave the organization its main impetus when it provided it funding along with the Southwest Voter Education Registration Project (SVREP).* Although an outgrowth of the Chicano Movement activity, the organization strove to bring about change through the system. Over the years and until the present-day, MALDEF has pursued numerous cases affecting Mexican Americans collectively, such as those dealing with educational neglect, bilingual education, affirmative action and the rights of undocumented workers. Its first director was lawyer Pete Tijerina. Mario Obledo, who in the 1980s went on to become LULAC's* most strident president, was the organization's first general consul. In 1973, the MALDEF board hired Vilma S. Martínez,* a native of San Antonio, who oversaw the organization's rise to prominence. One of the most publicized MALDEF achievements was the 1982 *Plyer v. Doe* case; the organization successfully argued before the U.S. Supreme Court to force a Houston school district to educate the children of undocumented workers. [SOURCE: Rosales, *Chicano!,* 219, 264-265; Gutiérrez, *Walls and Mirrors,* 201-209.]

MEXICAN AMERICAN LIBERATION COMMITTEE

Organized in Tucson, Arizona, by Salomón "Sal" Baldenegro, Raúl Grijalva, Lupe Castillo, and other University of Arizona students, the Mexican American Liberation Committee (MALC) sought to organize walkouts at Pueblo and Tucson high schools. The walkouts did not have the impact that those in Los Angeles did, but they did help to bring attention to issues of overcrowding and the need for bilingual education and Mexican culure classes. Later in 1970, MALC tried to convince city officials to turn the Del Rio golf course into a people's park, which led to the building of a community center. [SOURCE: Rosales, *Chicano!,* 211-2; Navarro, *La Raza Unida,* 205-207.]

MEXICAN AMERICAN MOVEMENT

The quintessential Mexican youth organization emerged in southern California during the 1930s under the auspices of the YMCA. It was called the Mexican American Movement (MAM). The members were made up of upwardly mobile youth, mostly college students who had committed themselves "to improve our conditions among our Mexican American and Mexican people living in the United States" and to pursue "citizenship, higher education . . . and a more active participation in civic and cultural activities by those of our national descent."

The organization propagated these views through its newsletter, the *Mexican Voice*. The newsletter bombarded its readers with the ideal of progress through education and hard work. It minimized racism as a major detriment to success. In a July 1938 issue, Manuel Ceja* wrote a piece entitled, "Are We Proud of Being Mexicans?" It came very close to the rhetoric of identity used by Chicanos* in the 1960s. An exemplar of MAM's professed ideals, Ceja was born in Los Angeles in 1920 to immigrant parents. He attended Compton Junior College and graduated from the Spanish American Institute, a leadership tank for Mexican Americans. He was also a volunteer coach at the local chapter of the Mexican American Pioneer Club, a boys club within the MAM.

In the article, Ceja claimed to have overheard a boy respond to a query about his ethnicity by saying he was Spanish. Ceja asked, "Why are we so afraid to tell people that we are Mexicans? Are we ashamed of the color of our skin, and the shape and build of our bodies, or the background from which we have descended?" He emphasized that the bilingual and bicultural attributes of Mexican Americans could open up innumerable doors and added, "Then why is it that we as Mexicans do not command respect as a nation? Are we doing justice to our race when we do not endeavor to change this attitude?" While they extolled the virtues of being Mexican, when confronted with a situation where they had to choose between Mexicaness and being American, they chose the latter. MAM ideology equated with Americanism.

The *Mexican Voice* continuously posited the belief that Mexicans needed to improve themselves in order to be accepted and to succeed in the United States. Paul Coronel, in an "Analysis of Our People," an article he wrote for the newspaper, stated that Mexico's poverty and its corrupt and weak political leadership created a deficient culture, but education was the solution to this problem. In another article, Coronel observed that Mexican girls married whites who had better jobs and could provide a better life. He then chided a friend who angrily derided the women for turning their backs on fellow Mexicans and saying, "We are not good enough for them." Coronel continued that he did not blame the women, because Mexican Americans needed to wake up and work harder so that they could also make good husbands.

Some of MAM's most dynamic leadership came from its female members. Like their male counterparts, they also held strong beliefs of progress through self-improvement. Importantly, they also advised this for women. Particularly active was Dora Ibáñez.* Born in Mexico, she attended public schools in Texas, worked her way through college in Iowa and Arizona, where she received a teacher's certificate from the Arizona Normal School (now Arizona State University) in Tempe. In a 1939 *Mexican Voice* essay entitled, "A challenge to the American Girl of Mexican Parentage," she praised the direction MAM males took towards education and Americanization. But she feared that the group aimed this message mainly at men. She also encouraged Mexican-American females to strive for education and professional careers; that was why they should be more active in MAM. [SOURCE: Rosales, *Chicano!*, 99-101.]

MEXICAN AMERICAN OPPORTUNITY FOUNDATION

Founded in 1963 by Dionicio Morales,* the Mexican American Opportunity Foundation (MAOF) provides educational and charitable assistance to the general public. The foundation, located in Montebello, California, provides career training classes in office management, computer science, and other job skills that usually lead to white collar employment. In addition, numerous day care centers for children and senior citizen centers are operated by the foundation. A United Way member agency since 1970, MAOF has become the largest Hispanic community-based organization west of the Mississippi, with a budget in excess of $60 million a year. [SOURCE: http://www.maof.org/maof.htm]

MEXICAN AMERICAN POLITICAL ASSOCIATION

By the late 1950s, Mexican Americans, more than ever impressed with the success of the black civil rights movement, consciously or unconsciously emulated many of its strategies. Determined to obtain political agency, in 1959 Edward Roybal,* Bert Corona, and Eduardo Quevedo met in Fresno and formed the Mexican American Political Association (MAPA). MAPA's goals varied because militant and moderate members differed on strategies. But the group's loose organizational structure allowed it to function effectively in spite of divisions. Soon the organization spread throughout the Southwest. Although nonpartisan, the group always supported Democratic Party candidates whose orientation was progressive or liberal on issues concerning Chicanos.* MAPA supported Chicano candidates at all levels and continued assisting the community in dealing with the state and federal bureaucracies. Although headed by charismatic leaders, the group suffered internal breakdowns, which led to its decline by the early 1970s. [SOURCE: Rosales, *Chicano!*, 108-109, 167, 192, 200; Gómez-Quiñones, *Chicano Politics,* 67-68, 92-93.]

MEXICAN AMERICAN STUDENT ORGANIZATION

In the Spring of 1968, Arizona State University (ASU) students who had been to California or heard Chicano Movement* speakers from that state decided to create their own version of this movement in the Phoenix area. After a summer of planning and organizing, the core group formed the Mexican American Student Organization (MASO), which later became Movimiento Estudiantil Chicano de Aztlán (MEChA).* In its first militant action, the MASO students were joined by white radical students from the Young Socialist Alliance (YSA) and Students for a Democratic Society (SDS) in occupying the president's office at ASU to demand that the university sever a contract with a linen service that employed Mexicans only in menial positions. Not one Mexican-American worker at this laundry was in management or in clerical jobs, but all the shop-floor workers were Mexicans, blacks, or native Americans. After two days of the sit-in, university officials promised not to renew the contract. MASO became an overnight sensation after this event because no one expected such militant action from ASU students. This initial activity provided the first experiences for many activists, who today form the core of Chicano* political and civil rights leadership in Maricopa County. [SOURCE: Rosales, *Chicano!*, 212-213.]

MEXICAN AMERICAN WOMEN'S NATIONAL ASSOCIATION

The Mexican American Women's National Association (MANA) was founded in 1974 with the goals of expanding leadership and developing Mexican-American women's equality with men and non-Mexican Americans of both genders. The organization sponsors an annual convention in different cities of the United States to discuss issues affecting Mexican-American women. From its Washington, D.C. headquarters, MANA publishes a monthly newsletter devoted to the same issues. The organization now has expanded to include a diverse group of Latinas in all areas of political, social, and professional life and is the single largest pan-Latina organization in the United States. [SOURCE: http://www.hermana.org/Orgfrm.htm]

MEXICAN AMERICAN YOUTH ADELANTE

The Mexican American Youth Adelante (MAYA) was a federation formed by Chicano* gangs in south El Paso. Organized in the late 1960s with the objective of counteracting juvenile delinquency, it attempted to guide its members into positive activities by employing Chicano cultural nationalism; it hoped to assist its members in escaping the trap of poverty and discrimination. MAYA included in its arena of social concerns, education, employment, better housing, and equal opportunity. While MAYA relied on radical, confrontation-conscious ideology, its board of directors felt that more could be achieved by accommodation and cooperation with establishment institutions without losing sight of maintaining cultural goals. [SOURCE: Meier and Rivera, *A Dictionary of Mexican American History,* 223.]

MEXICAN AMERICAN YOUTH ORGANIZATION

In the Spring of 1967, José Angel Gutiérrez,* Mario Compeán,* Nacho Pérez, Willie Velásquez* and Juan Patlán met regularly at the Fountain Room, a bar near St. Mary's University in San Antonio to discuss Texas politics and the emerging Chicano Movement.* They eventually founded the the Mexican American Youth Organization (MAYO), the forerunner of the La Raza Unida Party (LRUP).* During this time, organizers from César Chávez's* United Farm Workers* were unionizing farmworkers in South Texas, which instantly attracted the soon-to-be MAYO activists. But the farmworker struggle served more as a source of inspiration than a permanent objective, and the group turned to other issues. MAYO deliberately used militancy and confrontation tactics against the Anglo establishment to demonstrate to Texas Mexicans, whom MAYO members considered cowed, that the Gringo was vulnerable. They held demonstrations to demythologize some of Texas' most sacred symbols, such as the Alamo and the Texas Rangers.* The limelight which MAYO so assiduously sought, however, also made the group a highly visible target. The Anglo establishment responded to the challenge posed by the new radicals by eradicating their financial base and by accusing them of threatening security.

MAYO's highly publicized activities also provoked the ire of established Mexican-American politicos whose support the activists did not particularly court. San Antonio's Congressman Henry B. González,* a highly successful Texas politician, lambasted the Ford Foundation* on the floor of Congress in April 1969, for funding "militant groups like MAYO."

From 1967 to 1969, MAYO played a crucial role in various school walkouts and in 1970 its members formed the LRUP, the catalyst for Chicano* success in the Crystal City* school board elections. [SOURCE: Rosales, *Chicano!,* 215-222; Navarro, *Mexican American Youth Organization.*]

MEXICAN CIVIC COMMITTEE

After World War II, many returning Mexican-American veterans in Chicago came back more assertive, ready to take their place in a society which by any reckoning they had fought to preserve. As they became politically active, especially in Cook County Democratic politics, the new emerging leaders saw in Mexican-American war-time involvement an embodiment of their hopes and aspirations, and they formed new community organizations, such as the Mexican Civic Committee. One of the founders, Frank M. Paz,* became the most well-known spokesmen for this generation, articulating the objectives of the committee as promoting economic opportunity and ending discrimination towards Mexican Americans in the Chicago area. The Mexican Civic Committee served as one of the first Mexican-American civil rights groups in the Midwest. [SOURCE: Kerr, "The Mexicans in Chicago," http://www.lib.niu.edu/ipo/1999/iht629962.htm]

MEXICAN FINE ARTS CENTER MUSEUM

The Mexican Fine Arts Center Museum, located in the Pilsen neighborhood, south of the Loop in Chicago, has become the largest museum in the United States dedicated to promoting Mexican art and culture. The Center Museum came into existence in 1987, when a group of public school teachers pooled $900 to begin the project. The museum has attracted numerous exhibitions to its seven well-preserved galleries. For example, in 2004 it mounted the works of Frida Kahlo and Diego Rivera. In 2005, it hosted the Gunther Gerzso show. In addition, the museum conducts community-oriented workshops, theatrical, and musical events. The museum's core mission is to demonstrate that Mexican culture can exist on both sides of the United States' demarcation line without borders, "sin fronteras." [SOURCE: http://www.frommers.com/destinations/chicago/A19423.html]

MEXICAN MINISTRY OF FOREIGN RELATIONS REPORT ON IMMIGRATION

In 1928, the Secretaría de Relaciones Exteriores, Mexico's Foreign Ministry, issued a report describing the treatment of Mexicans in the United States. The 52-page study detailed the travails facing immigrants, such as abuse by employers, segregation, physical attacks by prejudiced whites, police brutality, and inequities in the justice system. Immigration issues had always served to create tension between the two countries and, in the past, Mexico had delivered a plethora of diplomatic notes protesting mistreatment of its compatriots to Department of State officials. But this document, which was formally published and distributed widely in diplomatic circles in both the United States and Mexico, served as a vehicle to publicly air these grievances primarily in Mexico. [SOURCE: Rosales, *Testimonio*, 149-150.]

THE MEXICAN MUSEUM

The Mexican Museum was founded in 1975 in the heart of San Francisco's Mission District,* to exhibit the aesthetic expression of the Mexican and Mexican-American people. Today this vision has expanded to reflect the current demographics of the very large Latino population in the country. In 1982, the museum was moved to San Francisco's Fort Mason where it has a permanent collection of more than 12,000 pieces. This unique array includes Pre-Conquest, Colonial, Popular, Modern and Contemporary Mexican and Latino, and Chicano Art. The museum is now in San Francisco's Yerba Buena Arts District. [SOURCE: http://www.mexicanmuseum.org]

MEXICAN MUTUAL AID SOCIETY OF THE IMPERIAL VALLEY

The first union to organize farmworkers in the Imperial Valley, California, was one formed under the leadership of Mexican vice consul Carlos Ariza in Calexico. Originally known as La Unión de Trabajadores del Valle Imperial (The Union of Imperial Valley Workers), which was built upon the foundation of two Mexican mutual aid societies: La Sociedad Mutualista Benito Juárez, El Centro (1919) and La Sociedad Mutualista Hidalgo, Brawley (1921); the organization changed its name to Mexican Mutual Aid Society (MMAS) of the Imperial Valley in 1928. That year, the Imperial Valley Cantaloupe Workers' Strike was the first attempt at work stoppage by Mexican farmworkers in modern California. Ariza had been called upon so often to intervene in labor disputes that he thought establishing a union might be a solution. The strike was broken easily, primarily through threats and violence. However, most growers agreed to pay the fifteen cents per crate wage requested by the workers although they did not recognize the union as a bargaining agent. [SOURCE: González, *Mexican Consuls and Labor Organizing*, 166.]

MEXICAN REVOLUTION

The Mexican Revolution of 1910 played an important role for Chicano Movement* activists. The memory of the Revolution left a legacy for all Mexicans and Mexican Americans. Heroes of the Revolution, such as Emiliano Zapata and Francisco "Pancho" Villa,* became icons for Chicano Movement activists. These activists called on the Mexican Revolution's legacies to remind Chicanos* that theirs was a revolutionary heritage. Aside from the ideological or artistic, the Revolution and its symbols were used by Chicanos widely in art and literature, the Revolution was responsible for many Mexican refugees and immigrants making their homes in the United States and fathering the generations that would give rise to modern-day Chicanos. [SOURCE: Rosales, *Chicano!*, 26.]

MEXICAN VOICE, see MEXICAN AMERICAN MOVEMENT

MEXICAN YOUTH CONFERENCE *also see* MEXICAN AMERICAN MOVEMENT

On January 10, 1943, the Mexican American Movement in Southern California held it's annual meeting at the downtown YMCA in Los Angeles. The gathering, which promoted education and self-improvement, attracted young

Mexican Americans from New Mexico and Arizona. [SOURCE: Rosales, *Chicano!*, 101-102.]

MI CASA RESOURCE CENTER FOR WOMEN

Mi Casa began in 1976, when eight head-start mothers living in Denver's Westside community felt they needed a place for women who wanted more for themselves and their families. At first, they did not have a name for the concept, but as they met and articulated their goals, "Mi casa" embodied what they wanted. By 1978, they called their vision Mi Casa Resource Center for Women. As the center grew, it became a safe and supportive place where women could complete their education, acquire employment skills, and where their children could get help and encouragement in school. In the years since its founding, thousands of low-income women, primarily Latinas and youth have arrived at Mi Casa with little more than hope and dreams for a brighter tomorrow, a good job, a home of their own, and a positive future for their children. Social welfare activists consider Mi Casa a national model for welfare reform. [SOURCE: http://www.micasadenver.org/]

MIDWEST COUNCIL OF LA RAZA

Established in 1970 as part of the Institute for Urban Studies, University of Notre Dame, with Olga Villa as the first director, the Midwest Council of La Raza concerned itself with a variety of issues that Mexican Americans in the Midwest encountered, such as migrant worker problems, education, and civil rights. The council represented ten Midwestern states, worked closely with Mexico's Centro de Estudios Chicanos e Investigaciones Sociales, and published *Los Desarraigados* (The Uprooted), a study of Mexicans in the Midwest. In addition, during its existence, the council sponsored numerous conferences, such as Mi Raza Primero Conference, the Awareness Conference, the Mexican American Midwest Conference, and the Symposium on Perspectives of Catholic Bishops on Church and Human Rights. The organization ceased to exist by the end of the 1970s, but it paved the way for other projects at Notre Dame, such as the Julian Samora Research Institute. [SOURCE: Meier and Rivera, *A Dictionary of Mexican American History*, 229.]

MIGRANT MINISTRY

The Migrant Ministry, an interdenominational Protestant group of church women founded in 1920, established as its first projects, four migrant day care centers in New Jersey and Maryland, and within two decades, similar programs existed in several other states. By the 1950s, migrant ministry programs, now with formal support and sponsorship from the National Council of Churches (NCC), existed in thirty-eight states. Its initial goal was to confront poor housing, inadequate sanitation, low literacy levels, and moral laxity among migrant farmworkers. In the 1960s, the ministry turned more to union organizing, was very important in the California grape strike, and in unionizing efforts in Texas. The Migrant Ministry strongly supported César Chávez's* efforts to organize Mexican-American migrant farmworkers in the Central Valley of California. In 1971, the National Migrant Ministry became the National Farm Worker Ministry (NFWM), and "the emphasis shifted from social services to servanthood, in which the church worked with farmworkers in their self-determination through organizing, boycotts, strikes, protest actions, and political advocacy." Jim Drake, a newly ordained minister in 1965, joined the union full time, representing the Migrant Ministry, and devoted his energies to helping to organize workers. Not all members of the NCC agreed with this emphasis; they felt that the organization should have remained concerned with charity works. Often, bitter debates divided members within the organization. The NCC today is still influential in numerous social issues, albeit many of the more conservative critics have withdrawn for membership. [SOURCE: Berkowitz, "Freedom Fighter: Remembering the National Farm Worker Ministry's Jim Drake," http://www.workingforchange.com/article.cfm?ItemID=12221]

MIGRATION DIVISION OF THE DEPARTMENT OF LABOR OF PUERTO RICO

In 1947, the Puerto Rican legislature established the Bureau of Employment and Migration to provide protection to the thousands of migrants moving to the mainland during and after World War II. The department was renamed the Migration Division of the Department of Labor of Puerto Rico in 1951, and assigned to the Puerto Rican Secretary of Labor. From 1951 to 1960, the sociologist, Clarence Senior, headed the division and on the mainland, Puerto Rican activist Joseph Monserrat directed the division's activities in New York City in the 1950s. In 1960, Monserrat was named national director, a position he held until 1969. Under Monserrat, the Migration Division attempted to control and monitor the general migratory stream from Puerto Rico, including seasonal agricultural migration. At the height of the Civil Rights Movement in the 1960s, Puerto Rican activists charged that the division did little to foster efforts toward self-determination and that it defined adjustment as the adoption of mainstream U.S. mores and middle-class values. [SOURCE: Sánchez Korrol, *From Colonia to Community*, 224.]

MIRANDA V. THE STATE OF ARIZONA

The *Miranda v. the State of Arizona* case became a turning point in determining the civil rights of persons accused of a crime. It resulted from the 1963-arrest of Ernesto Miranda for armed robbery of a bank worker, in Phoenix, Arizona. Miranda's record was extensive, including armed robbery as an adult and a juvenile record of attempted rape, assault, and burglary. After taken into custody, he signed a written confession to the robbery and also to a crime committed eleven days before the robbery: kidnapping and raping a slightly retarded 18-year-old woman. His lawyers appealed the case to the Arizona Supreme Court after his conviction, arguing that Miranda did not know he was protected from self-incrimination. The lawyers, Bill Flynn and John Frank, lost, but on appeal to the U.S. Supreme Court, the conviction was overthrown in 1966. Chief Justice Earl Warren wrote the majority opinion in this landmark ruling, indicating that at the point of arrest, the accused has the right to remain silent. The decision put the burden on arresting officers to inform an arrested person of that right; if that does not take place, prosecutors may not use statements made by defendants while in police custody. This procedure has come to be called "Reading the Miranda Rights." Prosecutors re-tried Miranda, who was convicted on the basis of other evidence, and he received an eleven-year sentence. In 1972, Miranda was stabbed to death in a bar fight. [SOURCE: http://www.thecapras.org/mcapra/miranda/rights.html#MirandaVsArizona]

THE MISSION DISTRICT

After World War II the Irish middle-class which had inhabited the Mission District of San Francisco moved to the suburbs in large numbers. This flight made way for a wave of Central Americans who arrived to work in the factories that supported the war effort. Starting in the 1960s, even more Central Americans continued to arrive into this historic area of the city seeking political refuge from increasing political and economic instability in their home countries. Gradually the face of the Mission District changed once again and it became a barrio composed of Mexican, Cuban, Salvadoran, Bolivian, Chilean, Guatemalan, and Nicaraguan dwellers; truly a rich blend of many Latino cultures. As the district began to assume a Latin profile in the 1960s, imbued by residences and businesses, urban redevelopment schemes which did not take into account the organic formation of the barrio, threatened the jobs and homes of Spanish-speaking immigrants. The district became a hotbed of radical political activity and protest. In 1967, seven children of Central American immigrants were accused of killing an Irish-American police officer. This event polarized the neighborhood along racial lines as barrio residents were convinced the boys were scapegoats. The arrest of "Los Siete de la Raza" (The Raza Seven) and their subsequent trial became a cause celebre. This along with other such issues politicized many young Latinos who began to participate in progressive organizations such as the United Farm Workers Movement.* The political mood of the era also spawned an artistic renaissance. The political theater of the San Francisco Mime Troupe, for example, made the Mission District home as did other highly politicized artists who began Galería de la Raza and painted stunning murals on barrio walls which portrayed the often distressful history of the Latino immigrants who came to the Mission District in the sixties, seventies and eighties. Gentrification and the arrival of Asian and Arab families who bought businesses, apartment buildings, and homes began to threaten barrio identity in the late seventies. Nonetheless, amidst a diverse community of nationalities, cultures, and classes the barrio has been able to retain much of its rich and colorful Latin American identity. [SOURCE: http://www.kqed.org/w/hood/mission/index.html]

MOLINA, GLORIA (?-)

Gloria Molina became the first Hispanic woman ever to be elected to the California State Assembly in 1982. She continued her political career in 1987 by being elected to the Los Angeles city council, on which she served until she was elected to the Los Angeles County Board of Supervisors in 1991, the first Hispanic since 1875 to serve in that position. The daughter of Mexican immigrants, she grew up in Pico Rivera, an area of greater Los Angeles. In her capacity as a community worker and elected official, Ms. Molina's energies have been devoted to working on urban problems facing young people. Accordingly, many recreation and park improvements in Los Angeles have come through her efforts. [SOURCE: http://molina.co.la.ca.us/scripts/gmbio.htm]

MONTES, CARLOS (1947-)

Carlos Montes was born in Mexico in 1947 and, in 1956, his parents brought him to Los Angeles, California. Montes helped found a number of historic organizations in Los Angeles during the Chicano Movement,* including the Mexican American Student Association (MASA)* at East L.A. College in 1967, the Brown Berets* in 1967, and the National Chicano Moratorium Committee* in 1970. In an interview from 1992, he remembered how events outside of his home area inspired him to continue his activism. In a 1968 trip to New Mexico, he observed that Reies López Tijerina,* the land-grant activist, seemed to be trying to establish a separate state: "The whole concept of an alliance of Free City States . . . we had a meeting with them, they had their own mayor . . . their own sheriff . . . apart from the so-called U.S. government. . . . We tripped out . . . the grazing rights, communal lands, we want our land back . . . We said, 'Shit, these people want their own land, they all got their own government structure.'" During his activist period, he also was a core organizer of the 1968 East Los Angeles high school walkouts. Today, Montes works as a community organizer. [SOURCE: Rosales, *Chicano!*, 178, 188, 193, 194.]

MONTOYA, JOSEPH M. (1915-1974)

Joseph M. Montoya was one of New Mexico's most active and successful politicians. The hallmark of his career was maintaining a seat in the U.S. Senate from 1964 until his death in 1974. Born on September 24, 1915, in Peña Blanca, New Mexico, Montoya attended Regis College in Denver and received a law degree from Georgetown University in 1938. In 1936, Montoya was elected to the New Mexico House of Representatives while he was still a student at Georgetown; he became the youngest representative in the state's history. After his election to the U.S. Senate, Montoya served as Democratic floor leader. Senator Montoya was one of the authors of a new Bilingual Education Act in 1974,* which expanded bilingual education by financing the preparation of bilingual teachers and the development of curriculum. Senator Montoya's voting record provided support for farmers and labor unions. He was also one of the early senate opponents of American involvement in Vietnam, primarily because of the large number of casualties sustained by Mexican Americans. In addition, he introduced legislation to protect consumers, the poor, Indians, and the elderly. His defeat in 1976 by lunar astronaut Harrison Schmitt marked the end of the Anglo-Hispanic Senate balance in New Mexico, i.e. one Anglo and one Hispanic Senator. Rumors regarding the use of his office to influence business dealing helped unseat the heretofore popular senator. This balance arrangement had existed since Dennis Chávez* had been appointed U.S. Senator to replace Bronson M. Cutting. Chávez had served twenty-seven years when Montoya succeeded him in 1964. [SOURCE: http://en.wikipedia.org/wiki/Joseph_M._Montoya]

MORALES, DIONICIO (1919-?)

Born in Arizona in 1919 and raised in Ventura County, California, by migrant farmworker parents, Dionicio Morales' life is marked by his dedica-

tion to securing equality of employment and economic opportunity for persons of Mexican decent. Overcoming many obstacles to attain an education, Morales graduated from Moorpark High School in 1937 and attended Santa Barbara State College. He majored in sociology and continued his university studies at the University of Southern California for a year-and-a-half in 1943-1944.

In 1963 he founded the Mexican American Opportunity Foundation (MAOF)* in East Los Angeles, a project that developed skill-training programs, child care centers, a nutrition program for elders, child care referral services, legal aid

Dionicio Morales

for immigrants, innovative preschool education, and food banks. Eventually, MAOF outreach offices were created in Bakersfield, San Diego, Oxnard, Salinas, Downey, Pico Rivera, and Santa Ana.

Prior to his MAOF work, Morales worked for the Amalgamated Clothing Workers Union as an inspector of working conditions in the garment industry. This experience influenced him in recognizing the importance in creating employment opportunities at the entry level for working-class Mexican Americans. Morales' influence grew at both the state and national levels, a clout that enabled him to secure policy-making positions in government and in the private sector for Hispanics. [SOURCE: Morales, *Dionicio Morales: A Life in Two Cultures*.]

MORENO, LUISA (1907-1992)

Luisa Moreno, a Guatemalan immigrant who came to the United States as a child and was educated at the College of the Holy Names in Oakland, California, became the first Hispanic vice-president of a major labor union: the United Cannery, Agricultural, Packing and Allied Workers of America (UCAPAWA). Moreno had broad experience organizing tobacco workers in Florida, factory workers in New York City, cane workers in Louisiana, cotton pickers in Texas, and sugar beet workers in Colorado. Moreno was organizing cannery workers in California when she developed the idea to create a national congress of Hispanic workers and communities, which she was able to accomplish under the auspices of the CIO and with the assistance of many other union organizers, especially women. Moreno was a leader in bringing the UCAPAWA to giant canneries in California, such as Calpak, Del Monte, Campbell's, and Libby's. During the McCarthy era, she was persecuted severely for her politics and her labor activities. For example, Moreno was ordered to face a deportation hearing and, rather than let the authorities create bad publicity for the unions, she went voluntarily into exile in Guatemala. In Guatemala, she supported the democratic government of Jacobo Arbenz before he was overthrown by the CIA. After the triumph of the Communist revolution in Cuba, she went there to work in the educational system. Moreno died in Guatemala in 1992. [SOURCE: García, *Memories of Chicano History*, 116-20.]

MORÍN, RAÚL R. (1913-1967)

Raúl Morín was born in Lockhart, Texas, but grew up in San Antonio. Before World War II, Morín served in the Civilian Conservation Corps and when the war started, he joined the U.S. Army as an officer. He was injured in combat. Like many other Mexican-American war veterans, he was concerned about the continued discrimination that greeted them after the war; in many places in the Southwest, Mexicans were still subjected to segregation and barred from public facilities in schools, theaters, swimming pools, restaurants, and housing tracts. As did others of his generation, Morín strove to achieve political power and social status by making good use of his war record. His book, *Among the Valiant*, chronicles the feats of Mexicans in World War II and the Korean War, making the much-accepted claim that Mexican Americans were the most decorated ethnic group because of heroic action. After his discharge, Morín participated in many Mexican-American organizations as a civil rights activist and as a member of the Los Angeles Mayor's Advisory Committee. The city of Los Angeles erected a Raúl R. Morín Memorial in East Los Angeles in honor of Hispanic war veterans. [SOURCE: Rosales, *Testimonio*, 183-184.]

MOTHERS OF EAST LOS ANGELES-SANTA ISABEL

The impetus for the creation of the Mothers of East Los Angeles-Santa Isabel (MELA-SI) came in 1984 when community parents opposed the construction of a proposed state prison in East Los Angeles. After succeeding in this campaign, the organization has since been the leading opponent of environmentally hazardous ventures proposed for East Los Angeles, such as a municipal waste incinerator, an oil pipeline, and other such projects that pose a danger to the community. A major victory for MELA-SI was when it forged an alliance with Huntington High School students to stop a toxic plant that would have treated 60,000 gallons of cyanide and other hazardous chemicals across the street from the high school. MELA-SI has engaged in other campaigns to assure environmentally sound neighborhoods in other parts of California. It cooperates with city officials to design and promote programs and projects in which the community participates to stem environmental deterioration in their immediate living areas. [SOURCE: http://latino.ssc-net.ucla.edu/community/intercambios/melasi/history.html]

MOVEMENT FOR NATIONAL LIBERATION

The Movement for National Liberation (MLN) was organized in 1977 by activists who had been the core of at least a decade of community efforts in Chicago to confront educational issues and problems affecting the Puerto Rican community. Finding its inspiration in the Puerto Rican independence movement, MLN adopted the concept of "internal colony" to describe the socioeconomic position of the Puerto Rican community in the United States. The group embraced the use of armed struggle to achieve the liberation of Puerto Ricans, both on the island and on the mainland. MLN also believed that other Puerto Rican leftist movements had erroneously disregarded this option. To achieve its objectives, MLN used the strategy of providing services to meet the day-to-day needs of the community. In this way, its members felt, a community-base could be established to eventually spread their political ideology. As such, they attempted to provide medical services and other social programs to Puerto Ricans in Chicago. [SOURCE: Torres and Velázquez, *Puerto Rican Movement*, 9-10.]

MOVIMIENTO ESTUDIANTIL CHICANO DE AZTLÁN

Movimiento Estudiantil Chicano de Aztlán (Chicano Student Movement of Aztlán-MEChA) is the most widespread and largest Chicano* student organization. There are literally hundreds of MEChA chapters in universities scattered across the United States. MEChA was born in 1969, when California Chicano students met at the University of California, Santa Barbara, in a conference that became one of the most crucial events in the Chicano Movement.* It was sponsored by the Coordinating Council on Higher Education, a network of students and professors who earlier had attended the Chicano Youth Conference in Denver* and had returned full of enthusiasm and energy. By now, the Chicano student community was ready to implement a higher education plan that would go beyond previous pronouncements. A major objective was to create college curriculum that was relevant and useful to the community. Higher education, the students reasoned, was a publicly funded infrastructure that enhanced the business community and other white bastions of power, but very little was expended on the needs of the tax-paying Chicano communtity.

The students at the Santa Barbara meeting wrote El Plan de Santa Barbara (The Plan of Santa Barbara),* a cultural political message articulating their ideology that would be used by future Chicano studies programs and students. A major tenet of the document emphasized a mildly separatist nationalism that members of MEChA had to embrace. This meant a rejection of assimilation into American culture. Mechistas (members) still strove to better the Chicano community through education and through collective efforts, not just individual success that came from rejecting the roots of Chicanos. As such, the group decided to bring all California Chicano student groups under one standard, called El Movimiento Estudiantil Chicano de Aztlán. Prior to the creation of this symbolic nomenclature, most student groups employed the term "Mexican American" when naming their organizations. For example, in southern California, a number of United Mexican American Students (UMAS) chapters existed on university campuses. On Bay-area campuses, there were various chapters of the Mexican American Student Confederation (MASC), and there were many other such groups in Arizona, New Mexico, and Texas. By the late 1970s, most of these organizations had folded and were replaced by MEChAs or had changed their name to MEChA.

Chicano student organizations, before and after they appropriated the name MEChA, succeeded in bringing about numerous and significant changes in institutions of higher education. Since the 1960s, most Chicano/Mexican American studies programs were initiated after pressure was brought to bear by these groups. Cultural awareness projects and events, the promotion of multiculturalism on and off campuses, remaining vigilant so that these gains were maintained, often fell under the purview of Mechistas. Today, although MEChAs still exist in most colleges and even high schools and they hold national conferences, their influence has waned. Hundreds of Mexican-American student groups still celebrate cultural pride, but just as zealously promote the political and economic success of Hispanics through education and integration into mainstream society. Indeed, the ideological stance taken by early organizations has been diminished somewhat, and often the MEChA chapters are very similar to their more tame counterparts. Perhaps one of the most significant accomplishments of the earlier militant groups is that they served as a training ground for a generation of politicians who, after the zeal of the Chicano Movement* began to wane, succeeded in entering mainstream electoral politics. [Rosales, *Chicano!*, 183, 200, 212, 267.]

MOVIMIENTO FAMILIAR CRISTIANO

Founded in 1969 in Houston, Texas, the Movimiento Familiar Cristiano (MFC) has 5,000 members in 42 regional groups. The organization is made up of husbands and wives working together to improve the quality of life in the Spanish-speaking communities of the United States. The program involves a cycle of four years of study of family life. The organization also sponsors retreats and publishes manuals, brochures, and the monthly *MFC-USA Bulletin.* [SOURCE: Kanellos, "Organizations," 392.]

MOVIMIENTO PARA LA INDEPENDENCIA

The Movimiento para la Independencia (Movement for Independence-MPI) was established in Puerto Rico in 1959 and its representatives organized the Vito Marcantonio Mission in 1964 in East Harlem and the Lower East Side of New York City. During the 1960s, MPI's main mission was to mobilize people for Puerto Rican independence, sponsoring parades and local community struggles. First-generation Puerto Ricans dominated the group, many with ties to the nationalist movements of Puerto Rico in the 1950s. MPI's main stateside mission was to provide financial and propagandistic support for the independence movement on the island. During the 1960s, MPI expanded from New York City to New Jersey, Pennsylvania, Connecticut, Massachusets, and the Midwest, becoming especially active in Chicago. It continued as a broad-based organization involved in local issues at the same time that it expressed demands for Puerto Rican independence. In the late 1960s, at the prodding of the Young Lords Party,* MPI began reconceptualizing its mission on the mainland, paying more attention to the day-to-day concerns of Puerto Ricans. [SOURCE: Torres and Velázquez, *The Puerto Rican Movement*, 49-51.]

MUJERES ACTIVAS EN LETRAS Y CAMBIO SOCIAL

Founded in 1982, in Santa Clara, California, Mujeres Activas en Letras y Cambio Social (Women Active in Literature and Social Change-MALCS) has 90 members in its seven regional groups. Made up of Hispanic women in higher education who foster research and writing on Hispanic women, MALCS seeks to fight race, class, and gender oppression at universities and to develop strategies for social changes. It publishes a tri-quarterly newsletter, *Noticiera de MALCS*. [SOURCE: Kanellos, "Organizations," 392.]

MUJERES UNIDAS EN JUSTICIA, EDUCACIÓN Y REFORMA

Mujeres Unidas en Justicia, Educación y Reforma (MUJER) was founded in Homestead, Florida, in 1996 as a private, nonprofit organization by grassroots Hispanic women. Susan Reyna, the organization's primary founder, recognized the special needs of poor Hispanics after her husband abandoned her in 1975 and left her a single mother with two children. Living in Florida at the time, she turned to Organized Migrants in Community Action, which provided help and then a job, as well as meetings with other single mothers in a support group. Later, she resigned her job as deputy director at Homestead's Centro Campesino Farmworker Center* to devote herself fulltime to MUJER's development. Since its founding, the program's services, which include family preservation, emergency financial assistance, and community integration projects, have reached more than 50,000 people. More recently, MUJER has instituted an outreach program that brings HIV/AIDS prevention education to the farm labor fields of Dade County. Although the organization reaches mainly Hispanic women, MUJER provides services to all women who desire them. MUJER staffers believe that the empowerment of Hispanic women of all ages can be obtained by promoting awareness of issues that affect the community and by providing strategies that can bring about change to help resolve these issues. One of its flagship projects is the Mana program, which is designed to promote leadership and self-esteem in young Hispanic women. [SOURCE: http://www.mujerfla.org/movies/index3m.swf]

MU SIGMA UPSILON SORORITY

Founded by five women of Latino descent on November 21, 1981, at Rutgers University, Mu Sigma Upsilon Sorority was the first multicultural minority sorority at the university. The founders were determined to bring together women from different parts of the world, break down cultural and racial barriers, and build the permanent bridges that would connect all Rutgers women. Hence, its motto became "Mujeres Siempre Unidas," or "Women Always United." Mu Sigma Upsilon develops cultural programs, provides social services to its surrounding communities, and tutors high school students. Its members also volunteer in a variety of community projects, including providing shelter and aid to the homeless, health care, and domestic violence prevention. [SOURCE: http://www.blackgirl.org/sororities.html]

EL MULATO

Issues of race and slavery were central to the Cuban independence movement and were interrelated with the politics of race in the United States. One

El Mulato

of the more interesting Cuban revolutionary newspapers was *El Mulato* (The Mulato, 1854-?), which was published in New York before the U.S. Civil War and had as its mission to unite the Cuban revolutionary movement with the movement to abolish slavery. Founded by Carlos de Colins, Lorenzo Alló, and Juan Clemente Zenea, it sounded a contrary note to the Cuban annexationist movement and its newspapers. The reaction to *El Mulato* among the Creole elite leaders of the annexationist movement was bitter. Editorials attacked *El Mulato* and mass meetings were called to condemn the newspaper for promoting social unrest. Proudly proclaiming the paper's Afro-Cuban identity, *El Mulato* editor, Carlos de Colins, challenged the leadership of the revolution to consider Cuba's Africans (he did not permit the euphemism "colored classes") as citizens worthy of freedom, just as their country was worthy of liberty. [SOURCE: Kanellos, *Hispanic Periodicals in the United States,* 13-14.]

MUÑIZ, RAMSEY (1939-)

Ramsey Muñiz was born in Waco, Texas, in 1939. He obtained a law degree from Baylor University in 1969 and practiced in Waco, Texas. While only peripherally involved in the Mexican American Youth Organization (MAYO)* as a student, in 1972, delegates at the convention of the fledgling Chicano* political party in Texas, La Raza Unida Party (LRUP),* chose him to run for governor. To the surprise of the LRUP insiders, the tall, muscled, and good-looking Muñiz, a former starter of the Baylor University football team, projected an attractive and imposing figure. The well-dressed Muñiz did not alienate the more conservative Mexican-American voters in Texas, as might other more militant-looking Chicanos.*

During his campaign, Muñiz crisscrossed Texas, accompanied by his wife Albina, attempting to persuade Mexican Americans to change their Democratic voting ways and to woo disaffected white liberals and black leaders. Indeed, the Reverend Ralph Abernathy, who inherited the helm of the Southern Christian Leadership Conference from Martin Luther King, endorsed Muñiz for governor. Most Texas liberals shied away from the LRUP, but as election day approached, some chose to support Muñiz over the conservative Dolph Briscoe,* who had supported the segregationist George Wallace at the Democratic Convention in Miami that summer. Muñiz garnered six percent of the final vote, nearly overturning Democrat Dolph Briscoe's slim victory over Republican Henry Grover.

Muñiz, still feeling victorious as a spoiler in the 1972 elections and heartened by the rural triumphs in 1973, decided early in 1974 to again seek the governorship. He made it clear from the start, however, that the campaign would reach out to all possible constituencies, not just the Texas Mexican population. He even explained that La Raza Unida meant "the people united," in order to steer away from appearing to use the race card. More militant nationalists within the party opposed him, but José Angel Gutiérrez,* the erstwhile leader of the LRUP, supported him, and Muñiz again was chosen as candidate. To Muñiz's frustration, and in spite of repeating the ardent campaigning he showed in 1972, he received even fewer votes. Muñiz did not even duplicate the 1972-role of spoiler, as Briscoe, running against a weak Republican candidate, won handily. Since party leaders deemed the 1974 Muñiz bid a failure, the former gubernatorial contender saw his influence wane within the party. Muñiz moved to Robstown, Texas, and started a law practice, but fell in with bad company. In July 1976, he was arrested on federal charges of narcotics trafficking. [SOURCE: Rosales, *Chicano!*, 237-247; García, *United We Win.*]

MUÑOZ JR., CARLOS (1938-)

While a graduate student at California State University at Los Angeles, Carlos Muñoz Jr. was one of the founders of the United Mexican American Students (UMAS), an organization that played an important role in the 1968-East Los Angeles high school walkouts. The group devoted numerous hours to discussing educational inadequacies and how they could be remedied. Perhaps influenced by the black cultural movement, UMAS members agreed that the education of Mexican Americans lacked cultural relevancy. Soon the planners favored the idea of a walkout as a means of dramatizing their issues. Because of his involvement in the walkouts, Muñoz was arrested for conspiracy to disturb the peace and became one of the "L.A. 13," along with other students and community leaders charged with conspiracy to disturb the peace. Today, Dr. Muñoz is professor emeritus at the University of California, Berkeley, where he was instrumental in the formation of Chicano studies programs from the 1960s until his retirement at the end of the twentieth century. He is the author of *Youth Identity and Power: The Chicano Movement.* [SOURCE: http://chicano.nlcc.com/]

MUÑOZ MARÍN, LUIS (1898-1980)

Luis Muñoz Marín was the first island-born governor of Puerto Rico under American rule. After receiving his early education in Puerto Rico, Muñoz began his college education at Georgetown University in 1918. Muñoz earned degrees in journalism and law while developing a career in politics. He also published the *Revista de Indias* (Review of the Indies) and served as the editor of various newspapers. As a student at Georgetown, Muñoz served as secretary to the resident commissioner for Puerto Rico in Washington, D.C., but upon returning to the island, he became a labor organizer while working for the Secretariat of the Pan American Union. In 1932, after being elected to the Puerto Rican Senate for eight years, he founded the Popular Democratic Party. In 1941, his colleagues elected him president of

Luis Muñoz Marín

the Senate, and in 1949, Muñoz became the first governor of Puerto Rico, serving until 1965. As governor, he was one of the principal architects of the Commonwealth of Puerto Rico, a political status that established Puerto Rico as a "Free Associated State" of the United States. To many Puerto Ricans, this status was a contradiction in terms, in reality a euphemism for colony. Also while governor, Muñoz helped define "Operation Bootstrap,"* an industrial development scheme that offered American industries tax incentives for locating plants in Puerto Rico in order to help the economic development of the island. In addition, under Muñoz a number of other programs were instituted to help improve the Puerto Rican economy, the transportation infrastructure, and the educational and health delivery systems. An unfortunate outcome of the capital-intensive transformation of the economy was the migration of rural dwellers to urban centers of the United States, most notably New York City. Luis Muñoz Marín died of a heart attack on April 30, 1980. [SOURCE: Tardiff and Mabunda, *Dictionary of Hispanic Biography*, 592-94.]

MUÑOZ, ROSALÍO (1949-)

The Brown Berets* and Rosalío Muñoz, a former University of California at Los Angeles (UCLA) student body president, played a pivotal role in steering the Chicano Movement* in the direction of anti-war protest. Born in Los Angeles, California, in 1949, Muñoz became politicized into the Chicano Movement by other Chicano students at UCLA in 1968. After graduation in 1969, Muñoz's anti-war stance had become more defined, and when he received a notice to appear at the Army induction center, Muñoz decided to become a symbol against the war and to provide a message for Chicanos.* With his friend Ramses Noriega, he trekked across California and the Southwest in an effort to attract community people and students to a demonstration in California, which became known as the Chicano Moratorium* against the war. Joining with the Brown Berets of Los Angeles and other Chicano activists, Muñoz formed the National Chicano Moratorium Committee and slated a national day of protest for August 29, 1970. The event became one of the largest mass protests ever by Mexican Americans. But unfortunately, a series of mishaps provoked law enforcement officials to violently put an end to the mainly peaceful rally, a police riot that resulted in the death of three participants, including that of the well-known journalist, Rubén Salazar.* [SOURCE: Rosales, *Chicano!*, 202-207.]

MURRIETA, JOAQUÍN

One of California's most enduring legends is that of Joaquín Murrieta. He has served as a symbol of resistance to Anglo-American dominance among Mexican Americans and South Americans alike. According to one version of Murrieta lore, he joined thousands of his compatriots who poured into California from the state of Sonora during the Gold Rush of the 1850s. Chileans, on the other hand, see Murrieta as one of theirs—the Gold Rush also attracted thousands of Chileans and Peruvians. Whatever his nationality, according to legend, Murrieta had mined gold peacefully until Anglos jumped his claim, killed his brother, and raped his wife. In his attempts to avenge himself on the "gringos," Murrieta became the scourge of the mining country in northern California. Any crime committed by a Mexican seemed to be attributed to Murrieta; often, this included deeds that were committed on the same day in opposite sides of the state. The California legislature in the Spring of 1853 posted a $1,000.00 reward for his capture and sent an organized force of California Rangers to track him down. The rangers killed a Mexican who was thought to be Joaquín Murrieta after months of chasing bandits across the

Joaquín Murrieta

mining country. The Rangers brought back a head preserved in whisky and, to collect their reward, they obtained the testimony of numerous individuals who swore that the head belonged to Joaquín Murrieta. This legend, which has remained vital until this day, was given its modern-day contours by the publication in 1854 of a semi-fictional biography by John Rollin Ridge. Ridge, who was a Cherokee Indian, probably empathized with the repression of Latin Americans and presented Murrieta as a Robin Hood, driven to crime by an evil Anglo society. [SOURCE: Weber, *Foreigners in their Native Land*, 205-206; www.artepublicopress.com]

MUSEO DE LAS AMÉRICAS

The Museo de las Américas was incorporated on April 29, 1991, in Denver, Colorado. It is the first museum in the area with a mission of educating the public about the artistic and cultural achievements of Latinos. The concept emerged from a concern shown by Latino educators, artists, professionals, business owners, and community volunteers with regard to the necessity of fostering an understanding of and appreciation for the achievements of Latino people. Since its inception, staff and volunteers have been collecting, preserving, and interpreting the diverse art, history, and cultures of this region from ancient times to the present. The museum is located in an area of Denver that is rapidly becoming the commercial and cultural center of the Latino community. [SOURCE: http://www.museo.org]

EL MUSEO DEL BARRIO

In 1969, a group of East Harlem's Spanish-speaking parents, educators, artists, and community activists founded El Museo del Barrio in a school classroom as an adjunct to the local school district. The founding of the museum reflected the rise of the Puerto Rican civil rights movement as well as a campaign in the New York City art world that called for major art institutions to have greater represention of non-European cultures in their collections and programs. El Museo's main goal was to become for the Puerto Rican community an educational institution and a place of cultural pride and self-discovery. Soon, El Museo became a founding member of the Museum Mile Association, along with some of the city's most distinguished cultural institutions, including The Metropolitan Museum of Art, the Guggenheim Museum, the Jewish Museum, and The Museum of the City of New York. Today, the original educational mission of El Museo still guides its collections and programs, but it has also broadened its mission, collections, and programs in response to substantial growth in the Mexican, Central and South American, and Caribbean communities, both in New York and at the national level. [SOURCE: http://www.elmuseo.org]

EL MUSEO LATINO

Founded in Omaha, Nebraska, in 1993, El Museo Latino is dedicated to Latino arts (local, regional, national, and international). The first Latino museum in Nebraska, it serves local youth by providing school tours and sponsoring a performing dance group. It also features exhibits, family activities, art and cultural classes, and special events, such as the celebration of Hispanic holidays. Mindful of the need to document local history, the Museo serves as a local repository for copies of the Omaha-related materials collected through the "Mexican American Traditions in Nebraska" project. [SOURCE: http://www.nebraskahistory.org/lib-arch/whadoin/mexampub/resource.htm]

MUTUAL AID SOCIETIES—MEXICAN

Mexican mutual aid societies have existed in northern Mexico and the American Southwest since the late nineteenth century. These organizations provided workers with life insurance for a premium of a few dollars or pesos a month so that upon their death, a dignified funeral would be provided. These societies also provided a modicum of workplace protection, but over time expanded their concerns to include the cultural, political, social, and economic well-being of their members in both countries. For example, the founding statement of La Sociedad Mutualista "Benito Juárez" in Houston, Texas, issued on May 25, 1919, took pride in naming the organization after the Indian, Benito Juárez, Mexico's most revered political leader. It illustrated an emphasis on expatriate nationalism as well as a pride in their Amerindian past. In Tucson, the Alianza Hispano-Americana (The Hispanic American Alliance)* did not adhere to Mexican nationalism as closely. Established in 1894 as a political and mutual aid organization, by the 1920s it evolved into a protector of civil rights for Mexicans. The effort was based in Tolleson, a town that became a base for unionization as late as the 1960s and the 1970s. Mexican workers also organized societies with the stated purpose of providing insurance and to confront labor problems. Pedro de la Lama,* one of the founders of La Liga Protectora Latina,* tried to organize a pseudo-union, Los Agricultores Mexicanos (Mexican Agriculturalists) in the Phoenix area during 1930.

Sometimes the societies formed larger umbrella groups in order to address issues of protection. For instance, at El Primer Congreso Mexicanista (The First Mexicanist Congress)* convened in 1911 under the leadership of Nicasio Idar, the editor of *La Crónica*, four hundred Mexican leaders, mostly from the middle-class, came together and developed strategies to deal with segregation, lynching, land ownership, police brutality, and unusual punishment of Mexican people in the Southwest. The death sentence of one youth, León Cárdenas Martínez,* and the earlier lynching of Antonio Gómez, Jr.* had incited the meeting. An umbrella organization for thirty-five Chicago mutual aid societies, La Confederación de Sociedades Mexicanas de los Estados Unidos de América (The Federation of Mexican Societies in USA),* was founded in Chicago on March 30, 1925. Finding jobs, temporary shelter, and offering protection from the police emerged as the core objectives of this ambitious undertaking by this and other mutual aid societies. [SOURCE: Rosales, *Chicano!*, 62-65.]

MUTUAL AID SOCIETIES—PUERTO RICAN

Puerto Ricans in New York City organized mutual aid societies in the early 1900s. Tobacco workers in Manhattan's Lower East Side and Chelsea districts organized themselves into *Cofradías* and *Hermandades* of urban workers and artisans of Puerto Rico extraction. Artisan organizations on the island of Puerto Rico had existed since the mid-nineteenth century. The founders patterned these early self-help organizations, called *gremios*, on the Spanish guild system. By 1900, at least fifteen *gremios* regulated artisan markets, controlled conditions of employment, and provided fairs for the exchange of merchandise. These organizations also provided medical and hospital aid, and other forms of aid, such as burial insurance and family dowries. The *gremios* competed with each other when celebrating the anniversary of their patron saints, trying to outshine each other in the grandiosity of the event. Islanders instinctively took this organizing tradition when they migrated to the mainland, a factor which helped foster unionization to significant degrees of self-help. In 1926, the Porto Rican Brotherhood of America,* a Manhattan-based community association, was formed with basically the same objectives as the *gremios*, and soon Brotherhood chapters sprang up in various eastern seaboard cities with large Puerto Rican populations. [SOURCE: Sánchez Korrol, *From Colonia to Community,* 136.]

NATIONAL ASSOCIATION FOR BILINGUAL EDUCATION

Founded in 1975 in Dallas, Texas, the National Association for Bilingual Education (NABE) is made up of educators, community people, and students. Organized at a time when the federal government had recently authorized funding for bilingual education, the group aggressively promoted and publicized bilingual education and compiled statistics on regional needs in this area. NABE provided a placement service, which benefited the members as well as school districts and bilingual training programs. Now based in Washington, D.C., NABE also publishes the *Journal of Research and Practice,* a quarterly journal and holds annual meetings devoted to representing both the interests of language-minority students and the bilingual education professionals who serve them. Since the mid 1980s, bilingual education acceptance among the public and among politicians has waned, and the organization has faced an uphill battle for a decreasing share of federal funding in the area of education. Nonetheless, NABE still continues to pursue its goals of:

1. Improving instructional practice for linguistically and culturally diverse students
2. Expanding professional development programs for teachers serving language-minority students
3. Securing adequate funding for the federal Bilingual Education Act and other programs serving limited-English-proficient students
4. Defending the rights of language-minority Americans
5. Keeping language-minority Americans clearly in focus as states and communities move forward with educational reforms.

[SOURCE: http://www.nabe.org]

NATIONAL ASSOCIATION FOR CHICANA/CHICANO STUDIES

In 1972, the National Association of Chicano Social Scientists (NACSS) was formed by an emerging cadre of Chicano* graduate students and entry-level professors. Later, the group became the National Association for Chicano Studies (NACS) in order to accommodate a broader base of academic disciplines. Eventually, its main framework of analysis, the internal colony model, lost favor. More recently NACS, has reflected post-modernist trends, which radically reconstruct European intellectual thought, including Marxism (from which the internal colony model acquired its analytic tools). Postmodernism has revived interest in the cultural positioning of the 1960s, especially among intellectuals in literature and the arts. NACS still exists today, although it is undergoing a critical transition, motivated primarily by a debate over gender in Chicano society; reflecting this orientation, it is now entitled the National Association for Chicana/Chicano Studies (NACCS). [SOURCE: Rosales, *Chicano!*, 255; http://clnet.ucr.edu/research/NACCS]

NATIONAL ASSOCIATION OF HISPANIC JOURNALISTS

The National Association of Hispanic Journalists (NAHJ) has approximately 1,500 members, including working journalists, journalism students, other media-related professionals, and academic scholars in a network of various state and regional affiliates. NAHJ seeks to enhance opportunities for Hispanic journalists and works to seek balanced and fair portrayal of Hispanics by the media. It supports Hispanic journalists maintaining their identity as they work within the non-Hispanic media. The organization has various programs to encourage Hispanic students to go into journalism, including its annual essay contest, whose winners are awarded scholarships. NAHJ publishes a newsletter and is governed by a 16-member board of directors that consists of executive officers and regional directors who represent geographic areas of the United States and the Caribbean, NAHJ's national office is located in the National Press Building in Washington, D.C. [SOURCE: Kanellos, "Organizations," 392; http://www.nahj.org/mission.html]

NATIONAL ASSOCIATION OF HISPANIC PUBLICATIONS

Founded in 1982 in Orlando, Florida, the National Association of Hispanic Publications has 25 chapters made up of senior-level staff from more than 100 Hispanic newspapers, magazines, and newsletters from throughout the United States. The organization functions to research Hispanic media, to promote Hispanic publications, to encourage advertisers to use these publications, and to encourage Hispanics to enter the field. It publishes the *Hispanic Media Directory* and the quarterly *Hispanic Print*. [SOURCE: Kanellos, "Organizations," 392-393.]

NATIONAL ASSOCIATION OF LATINO ARTS AND CULTURE

Based in San Antonio, Texas, the National Association of Latino Arts and Culture (NALAC) was founded in 1989 to provide the national Latino cultural and art community with promotional services and opportunities, needs which neither public nor private mainstream arts service organizations addressed. NALAC operated with part-time or temporary staff, but in 1998, after becoming fully staffed, the organization greatly expanded its activities and programs. More than 300 Latino arts organizations in the United States are now served by NALAC in the Mexican-American, Puerto Rican, Cuban, Dominican, Central-American, and South-American communities. NALAC provides direct services to its constituency through regional meetings, publications, and programs. Representatives of these organizations meet biennially at a NALAC-sponsored national conference to discuss current issues that affect Latino Arts and attend workshops on technical assistance and capacity building. [SOURCE: http://www.nalac.org.]

NATIONAL ASSOCIATION OF LATINO ELECTED AND APPOINTED OFFICIALS EDUCATIONAL FUND

Established in 1975, the National Association of Latino Elected and Appointed Officials Educational Fund is based in Los Angeles, California. It is one of the foremost organizations consistently providing Latinos the tools to participate fully in the American political process by developing and implementing programs that promote the integration of Latino immigrants into American society. A crucial strategy of the Educational Fund is to provide assistance and training to Latino youth to assure the formation of a critical core of future leaders. It also maintains a clearinghouse of research information that will keep Latino elected and appointed officials informed on the most important issues affecting the Latino population. [SOURCE: http://www.naleo.org/]

NATIONAL ASSOCIATION OF LATINO INDEPENDENT PRODUCERS

The National Association of Latino Independent Producers (NALIP) was founded in 1999 by a group of Latino producers, educators, and media activists in order to promote the advancement, development, and funding of Latino and Latina film and media arts in all genres. Based in Los Angeles, through its yearly conferences featuring issue-oriented panels, workshops, a digital center, keynote speakers, and networking sessions, the organization provides access and opportunities for Latino/as at all points in the media production pipeline. In addition, NALIP develops projects that train aspiring young media enthusiasts to ensure the next generation of media makers. NALIP also regularly updates its Latino Media Resource Guide, an essential directory that includes credits and contacts for Latino film, television, and documentary makers, production companies, film schools, diversity opportunities and distributors. [SOURCE: http://www.athensecolatino.com/v2n10/producers.html]

NATIONAL CATHOLIC WELFARE CONFERENCE—THE SPANISH-SPEAKING PEOPLE'S DIVISION

In July 1943, the Office of Inter-American Affairs* provided funds to the National Catholic Welfare Conference to hold its first seminar on the Spanish-speaking, which took place in San Antonio, Texas. In December 1945, the "First Regional Conference on Education of the Spanish-Speaking People in the South West" took place in Austin and focused on school segregation and bilingual education. The project attracted stalwart civil rights leaders and educators, such as professors George I. Sánchez,* Carlos E. Castañeda,* and San Antonio attorney Alonso S. Perales.* Buoyed by the success of this meeting, similar conferences were sponsored in Denver, Santa Fe, and Los Angeles. In the fall of 1944, the office also helped begin the Colorado Inter-American Field Service Commission,* which established service clubs throughout Colorado, registered voters, provided scholarships, made health surveys, promoted better recreational facilities, and strove to end discrimination and secure the rights of Spanish-speaking people. The individual clubs formed the Community Service Clubs, Inc., an umbrella vehicle in Denver, Colorado, which published the *Pan American News*. In Texas, these meetings led to the establishment of the Good Neighbor Commission* by Texas governor, Coke Robert Stevenson in 1943. The commission recommended legislative measures to end discrimination but these were never implemented. [SOURCE: Samora and Simon, *A History of the Mexican-American People*, 193–194; http://www.jsri.msu.edu/museum/pubs/MexAmHist/chapter19.html]

NATIONAL CAUCUS OF HISPANIC SCHOOL BOARD MEMBERS

Founded in 1975, the membership of the National Caucus of Hispanic School Board Members is made up of board members and others interested in the education of Hispanic students. The organization, located in Phoenix, Arizona, is an educational advocacy group as well as a caucus of the National School Boards Association. [SOURCE: Kanellos, "Organizations," 393.]

NATIONAL CHICANO COUNCIL ON HIGHER EDUCATION

In 1975, the National Chicano Council on Higher Education (NCCHE) was founded in Los Angeles as a result of a meeting of representatives of the Chicano academic community who felt that institutions of higher learning needed to pay more attention to needs of the Mexican-American community, both in and outside of academia. Funded by a Ford Foundation* grant, the organization recognized that there existed a compelling need for Chicanos to begin pressing universities and colleges to deal with the multitude of problems that Chicano students and faculty were facing in these institutions. NCCHE's strategy to achieve theses objectives was two-fold: to foster a national dialogue regarding positions on educational issues affecting Chicanos, and to develop and sponsor research and other academic activities among Chicanos. [SOURCE: Meier and Rivera, *A Dictionary of Mexican American History*, 245.]

NATIONAL CHICANO MORATORIUM COMMITTEE

On December 19, 1969, the National Chicano Moratorium Committee organized a rally of 2,000 anti-war demonstrators at Obregon Park in East Los Angeles to help Chicanos* protest the Vietnam War, because the mainstream anti-war movement had alienated the Mexican-American community. The committee continued organizing moratoriums under Rosalío Muñoz,* and held a second rally at Salazar Park in February 1970, bringing out 5,000 people. The committee eventually changed its name to the National Chicano Moratorium Committee (NCMC) and organized a national day of protest for August 29, 1970. Thousands of Mexican Americans arrived to march on Laguna Park in the East Los Angeles business district. By 3:00 in the afternoon, 30,000 people had crowded into the park.

Near the park, some demonstrators had stolen liquor from the nearby Green Mill Liquor store. Police arrived, and soon demonstrators were resisting. After the battle ended, three were dead, including Rúben Salazar,* a *Los Angeles Times* columnist and local TV station manager. The deaths and arrests outraged the community. In response some months later, the NCMC demonstrated against the Los Angeles Police Department. Unfortunately, all the incidents ended in violence. The worst of these occurred on January 31, 1971, when the Los Angeles policemen fired into a group of rioting Chicanos, killing one and wounding 35. This incident ended the NCMC activities. [SOURCE: Rosales, *Chicano!*, 198-203, 206.]

NATIONAL CHICANO YOUTH LIBERATION CONFERENCE

When Rodolfo "Corky" Gonzales* called the National Chicano Youth Liberation Conference for March 1969, in Denver, Chicanos* throughout the country learned who he was. More than one thousand young people attended and engaged in the most intense celebration of Chicanismo to date—most were from California. The most enduring concept that came out of this meeting was El Plan Espiritual de Aztlán (The Spiritual Plan of Aztlán), which proposed Chicano separatism, a position justified because of "brutal Gringo invasion of our territories."

The conference, held in the headquarters of the Crusade for Justice,* was an ambitious attempt to achieve self-determination for Chicanos, but it was more a celebration than a strategic planning meeting. However, no other event had so energized Chicanos for continued commitment. The idea of a national protest day against the Vietnam War emerged from the conference and, indeed, it became a reality in the National Chicano Moratorium* Against the

War. In addition, the assembly also provided one
of the earliest attempts to deal with the role of
women in Chicano society. Chicanas in attendance insisted on addressing their oppression by
males. The Chicano Movement* had been dominated by males, many who asserted that the priority of the Chicano Movement was to liberate
the males first. The women delegates held an
impromptu workshop that issued a statement
condemning chauvinism within the *movimiento*.
Unfortunately, when workshop leaders read the
results of their particular sessions, Crusade for
Justice women hushed up the complaints and
concurred with the prevailing male idea: that
women were not ready for liberation. Many Chi-

Rodolfo "Corky" Gonzales

canas, needless to say, were not deterred from pursuing the issue. [SOURCE:
Rosales, *Chicano!*, 178, 181, 183, 199, 210, 228, 230.]

NATIONAL COALITION OF HISPANIC HEALTH & HUMAN SERVICES ORGANIZATIONS

As it became apparent that the mental health system responded poorly to
the needs of Hispanics, a small group of Hispanic mental health professionals from throughout the nation gathered in Los Angeles in 1973 to establish
strategies for confronting this issue. Paramount among the problems facing
Hispanics were open hostility from health institutions, having medical services denied for speaking Spanish, and being subjected to misdiagnoses and
unnecessary institutionalization. The response was to establish the Coalition
of Spanish Speaking Mental Health Organizations (COSSMHO) known
today as the National Alliance for Hispanic Health (the Alliance). Today, the
National Coalition of Hispanic Health & Human Services Organizations
(COSSHMO) has 507 members. From its base in Washington, D.C., the
organization coordinates research and functions as an advocate for Hispanic
health and social services needs. COSSHMO pursues its mission by conducting national demonstration programs, coordinating research, and serving
as a source of information, technical assistance, and policy analysis for
community-based organizations. COSSHMO responds to the health needs of
Mexican American, Puerto Rican, Cuban American, Central American, and
Latin American populations by targeting difficult and sometimes controversial problems, such as juvenile delinquency, child and sexual abuse, adoles-
cent pregnancy, diabetes, and AIDS. Through its publications *Roadrunner*
and *Reporter*, which are issued six times a year, and the monthly, *COSSMHO*

Aids Update, the organization provides a constant and comprehensive barrage of useful and relevant information to its large constituency. [SOURCE: Kanellos, "Organizations," 393; http://www.hispanichealth.org/]

NATIONAL CONCILIO OF AMERICA

Founded in 1977, the National Concilio of America (NCA) is based in San Francisco, California. It has 13 member organizations representing a network of over 100 community-based organizations. Its purposes include cultivating leaders that will interact with local voluntary and philanthropic institutions, train staff in the technical skills required for administration, conduct needs assessments, review demographic and marketing data, develop long-range plans for Hispanic communities, and identify existing financial resources. Many of these goals are accomplished through local "concilios," which address the needs of Hispanic communities at the grassroots level. The NCA publishes two quarterlies, *Executive Brief* and *Horizontes* (Horizons), a newsletter. [SOURCE: Kanellos, "Organizations," 393.]

NATIONAL CONFERENCE OF PUERTO RICAN WOMEN

Established in 1972 in Washington, DC, the National Conference of Puerto Rican Women has 4,500 members in 12 chapters in the United States: Washington, D.C.; Miami, Florida; Orlando, Florida; Chicago, Illinois; East Chicago, Northern Illinois; Indiana; Tri-County Chapters, Maryland; Nassau-Suffolk (Long Island) and New York City, New York; Philadelphia, Pennsylvania; California; and Northern Virginia. The organization sponsors an annual conference that serves as its main education and networking. The organization coalesces with other women's groups and national Hispanic organizations, therefore extending its visibility and outreach throughout the United States and Puerto Rico. The organization strives to ensure the participation of Puerto Rican women in the mainstream of social, political, and economic life of the United States, works for equal rights for all Hispanic women, and offers leadership development. It publishes the quarterly *Ecos Nacionales* (National Echoes). [SOURCE: Kanellos, "Organizations," 393]

NATIONAL CONGRESS FOR PUERTO RICAN RIGHTS

Organized in the Bronx, New York, in 1981, the National Congress for Puerto Rican Rights is a grassroots organization dedicated to securing full civil rights for Puerto Ricans and ending discrimination against them. The group has a national membership of four to five thousand members. In the 1980s, the organization led a campaign which lobbied Congress to pass legislation that would provide Puerto Rico with more independence. Congressman Ron Dellums of California responded and, in 1988, he introduced a bill calling for Puerto Rico's right to self-determination and a plebiscite on Puerto Rico's status. By not insisting on independence as the only venue for activist groups, the National Congress for Puerto Rican Rights felt that it could unite people with different positions on Puerto Rico's political status. Such a position could avoid the bitter divisions obstructing the common goal of achieving civil rights for all Puerto Ricans. [SOURCE: Torres and Velázquez, *The Puerto Rican Movement*, 339.]

NATIONAL CONGRESS OF PUERTO RICAN VETERANS

Founded in 1967 in New York City, the National Congress of Puerto Rican Veterans has 8,000 members. It functions as a support group for Puerto Rican veterans by assisting them in obtaining equal treatment and fair access to services provided to all veterans. The organization has established a direct link to the U.S. Veteran's Service Administration and provides counselling on how to apply for benefits from the Veteran's Service Organization. [SOURCE: Kanellos, "Organizations," 393.]

NATIONAL COUNCIL OF HISPANIC WOMEN

Founded in 1985, The National Council of Hispanic Women (NCHW) is composed of individual women and organizations, such as universities and corporations. The main goal of the council is to empower Hispanic women and provide them with a prominent role in American society. The strategy used is to develop more direct representation for its members by placing Hispanic women in positions of leadership in business and government that will influence policy-making. These efforts by the NCHW have resulted in greater opportunities for Hispanics as general economic and social disadvantages have been ameliorated. Organization members are involved in lobbying for Hispanic interests at national conferences and in public policy debates. To keep its members informed about public policy issues affecting the Hispanic community, the NCHW holds an annual conference and publishes the quarterly *NCHW Newsletter.* [SOURCE: Kanellos, "Organizations," 394; http://www.britannica.com/eb/article?tocId=9125022]

NATIONAL COUNCIL OF LA RAZA

Founded in 1968 in Arizona as the Southwest Council of La Raza, the group was renamed the National Council of La Raza (NCLR) and relocated to Washington, D.C. in 1972. Since its inception, the NCLR through its community-based affiliates network has reached more than four million Hispanics. These include more than 300 Hispanic community-based organizations located in 41 states, Puerto Rico, and the District of Columbia. In addition, NCLR serves an informal but broader network of more than 35,000 groups and individuals nationwide. It conducts research and serves as an advocate for Hispanic causes. It also offers private sector resource development training, board of directors training, and proposal writing training. While headquartered in the capital, NCLR has field offices in Los Angeles, Chicago, Phoenix, and McAllen, Texas. It publishes a variety of newsletters and reports. The NCLR sponsors an annual conference, which is one of the premier national Hispanic events. At this annual meeting, more than 6,000 participants attend extensive information and training workshops while representatives of Hispanic community-based organizations take advantage of the opportunity to interact with private-sector representatives, public officials, and community leaders. [SOURCE: Kanellos, "Organizations," 394; http://www.nclr.org/]

NATIONAL DAY OF SOLIDARITY

On October 27, 1974, the Puerto Rican Socialist Party* mobilized twenty thousand people, filling up Madison Square Garden in solidarity for the independence of Puerto Rico. Not only did this represent the largest political assembly of Puerto Ricans in the United States, but it also demonstrated the strong support that independence organizations had obtained during the decade. [SOURCE: Torres and Velázquez, *The Puerto Rican Movement*, 54.]

NATIONAL EDUCATIONAL TASK FORCE OF LA RAZA

In 1970, a group of Mexican-American academicians organized the National Educational Task Force of La Raza to increase educational opportunities for Chicanos.* Once formed, the task force conducted training institutes to instill in young people the desire and preparation for higher education. Functioning through a number of regional offices, primarily in the Southwest, it was also involved in developing more effective community relations. Although the organization no longer exists, its activity served to provide future orientation to similar efforts in higher education. [SOURCE: Meier and Rivera, *A Dictionary of Mexican American History*, 248.]

NATIONAL HISPANIC CORPORATE COUNCIL

Founded in 1985, the National Hispanic Corporate Council, which is based in Phoenix, Arizona, is made up of 43 executives of Fortune 500 companies. Its goals include exchanging information, ideas, and research that will assist corporate America in focusing on the Hispanic community and the market it represents. [SOURCE: Kanellos, "Organizations," 394.]

NATIONAL HISPANIC COUNCIL ON AGING

Founded in 1980, with its headquarters in Washington, D.C., the National Hispanic Council on Aging has 3,000 members in 4 chapters. The council is an advocate for Hispanic senior citizens and develops and disseminates information, educational materials, research, and policy analysis regarding the Hispanic elderly. The council is affiliated with the American Society on Aging and the Gerontological Society of America. It publishes a quarterly newsletter, *Noticias.* [SOURCE: Kanellos, "Organizations," 394.]

NATIONAL HISPANIC INSTITUTE

The National Hispanic Institute (NHI) was founded in 1979 and it works with educated Latino youth who want to channel their skill and talent to community development. NHI, which is based in Maxwell, Texas, develops training strategies to enhance critical/analytical thinking, writing, networking, team work, problem-solving, and public speaking. These services are provided annually to 3,000 Latino high school and college students in Texas, New Mexico, Colorado, Illinois, California, and Nevada. In addition, 1,000 parents and professionals also receive training. A centerpiece program of the NHI is the Lorenzo de Zavala Youth Legislative Session in which students learn network-building, constituency development, and coalition-building in an eight-day legislative session held in Maxwell. [SOURCE: www.nhi-net.org]

NATIONAL HISPANIC LEADERSHIP AGENDA

The National Hispanic Leadership Agenda (NHLA) was founded in 1991 and serves as a coalition of 41 national Hispanic organizations and civic leaders from throughout the United States and Puerto Rico. Based in Washington, D.C. the NHLA attempts to influence public policy affecting the Hispanic community. With this mission in mind, in October 2000, the NHLA distributed "An Agenda for the Advancement of Hispanic Americans," a national public policy document addressing social and economic issues affecting all Latinos. In 2001, in response to the tragic events of September 11th, the NHLA established "Unidos for America," a call for solidarity and unity with all Americans. [SOURCE: http://www.bateylink.org/nhlboard.htm]

NATIONAL HISPANIC UNIVERSITY

Troubled by the lack of Latinos he saw enrolled in colleges, Roberto Cruz, a professor at Stanford University who graduated with a Ph.D. in education from the University of California, Berkeley, founded the National Hispanic University (NHU) in 1981 in Oakland, California. Ten years later, NHU moved to San Jose where Cruz forged relationships with community colleges, San Jose State University, and NASA. NHU's mission is "To enable Hispanics, other minorities, women, and others to acquire an undergraduate degree or certificate using a multicultural educational experience to obtain a professional career in business, education, or technology." The four-year,

300-student institution offers some five majors, including international business and computer science. Graduates of NHU have a higher-than-average job placement rate and a higher rate of going on to graduate school. [SOURCE: http://www.nhu.edu/about_nhu/history.htm]

NATIONAL LATINA HEALTH ORGANIZATION

In 1986, the National Latina Health Organization (NLHO) was formed by healthcare givers to raise awareness about how to provide preventive care and to address the most prevalent health problems among Latinas. Based in Oakland, California, NLHO has identified self-help methods and self-empowerment processes, knowledge that is disseminated so that the community can take greater control of its health practices and lifestyles. In addition, NLHO is committed to providing these services within a bilingual setting. Significantly, the organization considers traditional *curanderismo* (folk healing) as an important component of dealing with health issues. [SOURCE: http://www.latinahealth.org/]

THE NATIONAL LATINA/O LESBIAN, GAY, BISEXUAL & TRANSGENDER ORGANIZATION

Founded in 1987, the National Latina/o Lesbian, Gay, Bisexual & Transgender Organization (LLEGÓ), has become the only national nonprofit organization rendering services to organize Latina/o lesbian, gay, bisexual and transgender communities at all levels. Based in Washington, D.C., LLEGÓ promotes an educational goal of persuading the Latino and mainstream communities to overcome social, health, and political obstacles due to sexual orientation, gender identity, and ethnic background.

The mission of LLEGÓ includes:

- Forming a national organization to effectively address issues of concern to lesbian, gay, bisexual, and transgender Latinas/os at local, state, regional, national, and international levels.
- Creating a forum of awareness, understanding, and recognition of lesbian, gay, bisexual, and transgender Latina/o identities, legal rights, relationships, and roles.
- Formulating and sustaining a national health agenda that includes the impact of HIV/AIDS, breast cancer, and other health-related issues.
- Developing a supportive network for sharing information and resources. Educating and sensitizing Latina/o and non-Latina/o communities by actively working against internalized issues that

divide and oppress them, such as sexism, racism, homophobia, and discrimination.

[SOURCE: http://www.llego.org/]

NATIONAL LATINO CHILDREN'S INSTITUTE

Incorporated in 1997 in San Antonio, Texas, the National Latino Children's Institute (NLCI) focuses exclusively on children. Its primary mission is to serve as the voice for young Latinos. This mandate is fulfilled by staffers promoting and implementing NCLI's Agenda. By assembling focus groups and public forums, NLCI gathers information about policies and programs affecting Latino children. Data compiled in these work groups result in tool kits that are then passed along to community organizations and national partners to help build healthy communities for young people. [SOURCE: http://www.nlci.org]

NATIONAL LATINO COMMUNICATIONS CENTER

Established in 1975 at Los Angeles public television station KCET as the Latino Consortium, in 1991 it was incorporated as the National Latino Communications Center, a media arts production resource center that supported, produced, and syndicated Latino programming for public television. Although it is no longer in existence, the NLCC played an important role in the ability of Latinos in the United States to participate in the broadcast communications media. The project also provided grants to Latino media artists and technical support. One of the centers important services was a quarterly newsletter that discussed issues facing Latino producers and included updates on the center's work, such as the establishment of a National Latino Film and Video Archive, a project that attempted to stem the loss of pioneer television programs and documentaries dealing with Latinos. One of the NLCC's crowning achievements was the airing of *Chicano!* on the Public Television Service, a four-part series on Mexican civil rights history. [SOURCE: http://latino.sscnet.ucla.edu/community/nlcc/]

NATIONAL LEAGUE OF CUBAN AMERICAN COMMUNITY-BASED CENTERS

The National League of Cuban American Community-Based Centers was founded in 1978 in Fort Wayne, Indiana, to establish linkages among Cuban American community centers and to open new centers wherever needed. The league assesses the needs of minority communities in relation to education, training, manpower development, and health care. In recent years the league, with funding from the U.S. Department of Education TRIO program, has expanded its offerings to all first-generation college aspirants. It also promotes awareness among Hispanics of employment opportunities. [SOURCE: Kanellos, "Organizations," 394; http://www.fwtrio.com/]

THE NATIONAL NETWORK FOR IMMIGRANT AND REFUGEE RIGHTS

Founded in 1996, the National Network for Immigrant and Refugee Rights (NNIRR) is a national umbrella group that coordinates activities for immigrant, refugee, community, religious, civil rights, and labor organizations. Based in Oakland, California, the NNIRR provides a forum for sharing immigrant-related information and analysis, as well as community education. In addition, the network promotes the implementation a just immigration and refugee policy in the United States that facilitates defense of the rights of all immigrants and refugees, regardless of their immigration status. The NNIRR also seeks to educate the public and policy framers about the global, political, and economic conditions exacerbating international patterns of migration. According to its mission statement, this is a necessary step in establishing an international base of support "and cooperation that will strengthen the rights, welfare and safety of migrants and refugees." [SOURCE: http://www.nnirr.org]

NATIONAL ORIGINS QUOTA ACT

The National Origins Quota Act of 1924 created new restrictions on the immigration of southern and eastern Europeans and banned immigration from Asia. When enforced, the law set a quota for immigrants entering the United States at two percent of the total number of immigrants residing in the United States, according to the 1890 census. However, shortly after its passage, Congress voted to replace the two percent regulation, starting on July 1, 1927, by an overall cap of 150,000 immigrants annually and established quotas for each sending country by a "national origins" determination, as revealed in the 1920 census. Asian immigrants were totally banned as were Canadian Native Americans. Lobbyists representing agricultural and mining interests managed to persuade Congress not to include the Western Hemisphere. This ensured that the Mexican labor source would be protected. [SOURCE: http://www.u-s-history.com/pages/h1398.html]

NATIONAL PUERTO RICAN COALITION, INC.

In 1977, the U.S. Commission on Civil Rights assembled a group of 40 community leaders and representatives from the Puerto Rican community in Washington, D.C. to discuss the future of the stateside Puerto Rican community. The group mainly discussed how to confront issues and problems identified by the Commission on Civil Rights in a 1976 report entitled *Puerto Ricans in the Continental United States: An Uncertain Future*. The result was the creation of the National Puerto Rican Coalition, Inc. (NPRC), to represent the interests of the community before national policy makers. Today, the NPRC continues to function as an umbrella for community-based organizations and individuals throughout the United States and the island of Puerto Rico. It has become one of the leading Puerto Rican advocacy organizations and an important voice in the national Hispanic policy arena as the Chair Organization of the National Hispanic Leadership Agenda.* [SOURCE: http://www.bateylink.org/about.htm]

NATIONAL PUERTO RICAN FORUM

Founded in 1957 in New York City, the National Puerto Rican Forum is concerned with the overall improvement of Puerto Rican and Hispanic communities throughout the United States and it designs and implements programs in job counseling, training and placement, and the teaching of English. It sponsors career services and a job placement program at the national level. It publishes occasional reports. Antonia Pantoja* led Puerto Rican social activists in organizing the forum in order to become more independent of the NAACP and the American Jewish Committee, which had served as power brokers for the Puerto Rican community with city officials. Pantoja and her cohort of community activists felt it was important for Puerto Ricans to pursue their own agenda by promoting community enterprises and finding their own funding for their programs. [SOURCE: Kanellos, "Organizations," 394-395; Sánchez Korrol, *From Colonia to Community*, 226-227.]

NATIONAL REPATRIATION COMMITTEE

During the Great Depression, thousands of Mexicans returned to Mexico either because they were deported or were coerced by relief authorities or because they voluntarily desired repatriation. The Mexican government, scarce on resources, sometimes provided transportation from the border to their homes in the interior of Mexico, but other than that did little to alleviate the problems faced by those who returned. When Abelardo Rodríguez assumed the presidency of Mexico from Ortiz Rubio after the latter resigned in 1932, he formed a Comité Nacional de Repatración (National Repatriation Committee) to raise half a million pesos in order to found special colonies for the repatriates in the Pacific coast areas of Oaxaca, Guerrero, Jalisco, Colima, and Baja California. However, this effort failed miserably. In spite of a great amount of planning, which included preparing for sanitation, housing, farming techniques, and other issues, the funding was insufficient and the land was either jungle-infested or barren. [SOURCE: Balderrama and Rodríguez, *Decade of Betrayal*, 175-177.]

MEXICANS BEING SHIPPED TO HOMELAND

Houston Chronicle photo of Repatriation

NATIVISM AND LATINOS

In the United States, large-scale outbursts against immigration began in the nineteenth century when Anglo-American nativists reacted first to the influx of Catholic Irish and German newcomers and then to Asians and southern and eastern Europeans. Nativists feared that these foreigners posed a threat to Anglo-American culture and values. The Know-Nothing Party* emerged in the 1850s to curtail political inroads being made by Catholics. In Texas, members of this group were blamed for denying Mexicans their rights and for perpetrating crimes against them.

The Civil War and internal divisions put an end to the Know-Nothings at the same time that many Irish and German Catholics slowly achieved a degree of acceptance. But with the rise of industrialism, a large influx of eastern and southern European laborers revived nativist sentiment against immigrants who did not speak English, were not Protestants, and possessed an array of customs and values that seemed diametrically opposed to Anglo-American culture. In addition, low wages and underemployment kept the newcomers in a constant state of poverty, a condition which provoked attendant social problems and made them even more undesirable. As a consequence, organized labor made up of nativists sought immigration restrictions. Employer lobbying efforts proved more formidable than those of restrictionists, however, and immigration policy of the United States throughout most of the nineteenth century remained among the most liberal in the world. The Chinese Exclusion Act of 1882 became the only victory that nativists and their allies could achieve.

The twentieth century brought a more opportune climate for restrictionists. Because World War I had stalled immigration from Europe, employers became less vigilant about protecting a source which seemed in decline. In addition, a war-time fear that foreigners could be disloyal and dangerous provided the ideal climate for pushing legislation that would at last curtail the influx of unpalatable newcomers. Federal legislation in 1917 required literacy as a prerequisite for legal entry into the United States, a restriction designed to keep out eastern and southern Europeans, who had higher illiteracy rates than the more desirable immigrants from Northern Europe. In 1921, a quota act was passed that favored Northern Europe and then, in 1924, another act lowered the quota even further for the undesirable "New Immigrants." Asian immigrants were totally banned. Curiously, Mexicans received special treatment during this era. For example, Congress waived the 1917 literacy requirements for Mexican immigrants, and the quota acts of 1921 and 1924 excluded the Western Hemisphere; Mexicans and a fewer number of Canadians and Cubans were the only immigrants entering from these areas in the 1920s. The Jones Act of 1917,* which tightened the control that the United States had over Puerto Rico, provided citizenship to all Puerto Ricans.

On the surface it appeared that nativists did not target Latinos on their list of undesirable immigrants. The main thrust of anti-immigrant fervor was centered in the urban Northeast and the Midwest. Although nativists did not want Puerto Ricans, they could not be banned. Cubans migrated primarily to Florida, while Mexicans who worked primarily in the Southwest and West did not enter into the nativist field of vision.

Nonetheless, many groups and individuals who saw foreigners as a threat to the American way of life did cast Mexicans as undesirables. In the 1920s, such nativists as Roy Garis, a professor at Vanderbilt University, and John C. Box,* a Congressman from Texas, led campaigns to restrict the immigration of Mexicans, claiming this group was the most reprehensible new arrival. But powerful employers, who now used Mexican labor as a replacement for the vanishing European immigrant, blocked restrictions. Besides, because Mexico bordered the United States, Mexicans returned home more regularly than other immigrants, thus easing the threat they posed to to the "natives." Also, most nativists saw the Chinese and Japanese immigrants as the greatest problem in the West. As a consequence, Mexicans received a reprieve.

During the Great Depression of the 1930s, production in all sectors of the American economy almost came to a standstill, and Mexican labor so assiduously recruited in the past, became unwanted. Because they were no longer needed, Mexicans lost the support of employers, who in the past had provided the only protection from those wishing to halt their influx. A massive repatri-ation program, funded by local municipalities, employers, and private chari-ties, resulted in almost half of the one-and-one-half million Mexicans return-ing to Mexico, including many who had been born in the United States. During the 1930s, nativist groups almost succeeded in halting immigration from Mex-ico, a ban they had successfully imposed on Asians a century earlier.

But Mexican Americans managed to prove their loyalty to the United States during War World II and achieved significant social mobility, as well. Anti-Mexican sentiment based on the influx of new arrivals would have probably faded, as it did for the descendants of such groups as the Italians, Jews and Polish, the so-called New Immigrants. But the return of American prosperity after the war resulted in a need for Mexican labor. An influx of unassimilated Hispanic newcomers, not just from Mexico but from Central America and the Caribbean as well, entered in increasing numbers, reaching a crescendo in the 1990s. Again nativism seems to have risen. English-only campaigns, public referendums that try to ban social services to immigrants without documents, have proliferated in the last decades. [SOURCE: Reisler, *By the Sweat of Their Brow,* 127-150.]

NAVA, JULIAN (1927-)

Julian Nava has been a diplomat, historian, author, and educator whose roots go back to the Mexican Revolution. He is one of eight children who were raised in East Los Angeles. Like many other Chicanos,* he served in the U.S. Navy and used his service time to finance his college education. After receiving an A.B. from Pomona College in 1951 and a doctorate in History from Harvard University in 1955, Nava taught at the University of Puerto Rico and later at California State College at Northridge. Dr. Nava's commit-ment to solving problems confronted by Chicanos in contemporary American society prompted him to run and finally be elected to the Los Angeles school board. He was also a member of the board of the Plaza de la Raza and the Hispanic Urban Center, as well as an advisory committee mem-ber of the Mexican American Legal Defense and Education Fund.* Much of Nava's research and writing has focused on and advo-cated for bilingualism.

Julian Nava

Ironically, Dr. Nava, whose election to the school board earned accolades from the Mex-ican-American community in Los Angeles, became suspect in 1968 among Chicano Movement* activists who confronted the school board in a sit-in to reform the East Los

Angeles schools. Militants ritualistically hurled the *vendido* (sell out) epithet at Mexicans in power, such as Dr. Nava, to force them into compliance. Like other "Establishment" Mexicans, Dr. Nava was astute enough to co-opt the militants or move sufficiently towards their position to effect a silent compromise.

In 1980, President Jimmy Carter named Julian Nava United States ambassador to Mexico, the first Mexican American to serve in that position. [SOURCE: Nava, *Julian Nava: My Mexican-American Journey.*]

NEW AMERICA ALLIANCE

In 1999, a group of Latino business leaders formed the New America Alliance in order to empower Latinos through strategic philanthropy and public policy advocacy. The organization, led by a 23-member founding board of directors, vowed to commit their time, expertise, and resources to the organization and its goals. Based in Virginia, the project works to provide new capital investments in order to accelerate Latino business expansion, to support public policies, and solicit private commitments that will make it possible for every Latino student in America to graduate from high school, and to support both Latino and non-Latino leaders who are committed to serving the best interest of the Latino community. [SOURCE: http://www.naaonline.org/]

NEW MEXICO ALLIANCE FOR HISPANIC EDUCATION
NEW MEXICO CONSTITUTION

Anticipating statehood, New Mexicans in 1910 held a convention to create a constitution, which was finally ratified in 1912, when New Mexico became a state. Many of the provisions of the new constitution reflected the Hispanos' strong desire for protection. In the previous half century, they had lost much of their land through litigation and fraud, government seizure, and tax delinquencies. Like Hispanics in other parts of the Southwest, New Mexicans experienced racial and ethnic prejudice, but because of their large numbers, compared to inmigrating Anglos, they were able to achieve some political self-determination, a degree of power which was put to good use at the constitutional convention. Articles II and XII, for example, allowed New Mexico to become a bilingual state, putting English and Spanish on an equal basis for all state business. These sections of the constitution allowed funding for training programs for bilingual teachers, forbade segregation of Anglo and Hispano children, and reiterated that rights guaranteed by the Treaty of Guadalupe Hidalgo* would be respected. [SOURCE: Forrest, *The Preservation of the Village,* 10.]

NICARAGUAN ADJUSTMENT AND CENTRAL AMERICAN RELIEF ACT

On November 19, 1997, President Bill Clinton signed the Nicaraguan Adjustment and Central American Relief Act (NACARA), which was enacted by Congress that same year. Congress passed NACARA to provide immigration benefits and relief from deportation to certain Nicaraguans, Cubans, Salvadorans, Guatemalans, nationals of the former Soviet bloc countries and their dependents. The Act, however, is considered by immigration justice advocates a "classic example of legislative sausage-making." While NACARA provided permanent residence to Cubans and Nicaraguans in the United States prior to December 1995, Salvadorans and Guatemalans in the United States since 1990 could only obtain permanent residence if they demonstrated that their deportation would result in "extreme hardship." According to critics, the more lenient treatment of Cubans and Nicaraguans was due to their having fled from nations with socialist governments. The other refugees from Central America came from countries the United States supported, no matter how repressive their governments might have been. Partially in response to this dissent, the Trafficking and Violence Protection Act of 2000 was signed into law on October 28, 2000 adding two more categories of individuals from other nations eligible to apply for relief from removal under NACARA. [SOURCE: http://uscis.gov/graphics/services/residency/nacara203_main.htm]

NOSOTROS

Founded in 1970 by actor Ricardo Montalbán in Los Angeles, California, the main purpose of Nosotros was to improve the portrayal of Latinos/Hispanics in the entertainment industry. Unlike Montalbán, not all members were actors. The organization also wanted to expand employment opportunities in the industry for Latinos, regardless of whether they worked in front or behind the camera. Also, Nosotros fostered training programs so that its members could become better actors and industry professionals. In addition, to insure that the entertainment industry would have a steady source of Latino professionals, the organization established a recruitment policy to seek creative youngsters and encourage them to enter the entertainment industry. Today, Nosotros is the premier organization in this field, but it has also left a lasting legacy in the many established pro-

Ricardo Montalbán

fessionals who were helped out by this pioneering group. [SOURCE: http://www.nosotros.org/]

NOVELLO, ANTONIA (1944-)

Born in Fajardo, Puerto Rico, Antonia Novello was the first woman and the first Hispanic to be appointed Surgeon General of the United States (1990-1993). She received a B.A. (1965) and an M.D. (1970) degrees from the University of Puerto Rico and an M.A. in Public Health from Johns Hopkins University in 1982. In 1986, Novello left a private practice to became a clinical professor of pediatrics at Georgetown University Hospital. In 1987, the National Institute of Child Health and Human Development named her coordinator for AIDS research and then Deputy Director. As Surgeon General, Dr. Novello used her influence to promote the need to focus on women with AIDS, neonatal transmission of HIV, and the rising domestic violence epidemic in the United States. In addition, she broadened the participation of Latinos in health organizations and convened national and regional meetings to discuss community health needs. [SOURCE: http://www.greatwomen.org/women.php?action=viewone&id=1]

NUEVAS VISTAS CONFERENCE

The Nuevas Vistas Conference was convened in April 1969, to discuss pedagogy for teaching Mexican Americans. During the keynote address by Governor Ronald Reagan, Brown Berets* and other Chicano Movement* activists disrupted the speech and fires were started throughout the Biltmore hotel, where the conference was held. The police arrested ten participants, but the fires had been set by a police infiltrator, Fernando Sumaya. [SOURCE: Rosales, *Chicano!*, 194.]

OCHOA, ESTEVAN (1831-1888)

Four years after Tucson was incorporated as a city in 1871, its first Hispanic mayor was elected: Estevan Ochoa, a wealthy freighter. He was the only Mexican mayor of Tucson ever elected following the Gadsden Purchase.* From a wealthy Chihuahua family, Ochoa became a loyal American, so loyal in fact that he fiercely opposed the Confederacy. He grew up learning the freighting business and developing bilingual-bicultural skills that allowed him to both prosper in business in the United States and Mexico as well as to win the confidence of both the Anglo and Mexican electorates in Tucson. During the 1860s through the 1870s, he served in the territorial legislature and on the city council. [SOURCE: Gómez-Quiñones, *Roots of Chicano Politics*, 268.]

OCCUPIED AMERICA

In 1972, Professor Rodolfo Acuña* of California State University at Northridge wrote and published the first comprehensive history of the Chicano people. The text, *Occupied America,* which presented the model of Mexican Americans as an internal colony of the United States, became the most used Chicano history book in colleges and went through subsequent editions in 1981 and 1988. [SOURCE: Tardiff and Mabunda, *Dictionary of Hispanic Biography,* 4.]

OFFICE OF ECONOMIC OPPORTUNITY

The Economic Opportunity Act of 1964 (EOA) was a major accomplishment of the "War on Poverty," a campaign waged during President Lyndon Johnson's* administration as part of the "Great Society."* Congress passed the act in August 1964, after Sergeant Shriver, who had a strong connection to the previous Kennedy administration, had drafted the plan. Shriver became director of the Office of Economic Opportunity (OEO), which originally administered EOA, and served until 1969. The funding from the OEO underwrote job training, adult education, and loans to small businesses; the latter a strategy designed to attack the underlying causes of unemployment and poverty. The OEO no longer exists and, while many of its programs have been rescinded, other units within the federal government still implement former OEO projects. A core component of the OEO became the Community Action Agencies (CAA's), organized at the local level throughout the nation. More than one thousand existed by the end of the 1960s with the responsibility of implementing Great Society programs. The character of the CAAs varied greatly. OEO funds were channeled through nonprofit organizations, city agencies, and community-controlled groups. Hallmark projects of the EOA included VISTA (Volunteers In Service To America); the Job Corps; the Neighborhood Youth Corps; Head Start; Adult Basic Education; Family Planning; Community Health Centers; Congregate Meal Preparation; Economic Development; Foster Grandparents; Legal Services; Neighborhood Centers; Summer Youth Programs; Senior Centers; among others. Many future community activists and leaders came out of these centers. [SOURCE: http://www.blackseek.com/bh/2001/33_EOA.htm]

OFFICE OF INTER-AMERICAN AFFAIRS

The Office of Inter-American Affairs was created in Franklin D. Roosevelt's administration on July 30, 1941, to solidify alliances with Latin American countries during World War II. Nelson Rockefeller was its first director. In April 1942, journalist and civil rights activist Carey McWilliams* became the director of the Spanish-Speaking Peoples Division within the Office of Inter-American Affairs. This special division was organized with the goal of reducing discrimination against Mexican Americans. To accomplish this, McWilliams set up conferences and workshops, and provided fellowships to integrate Mexican Americans more fully into the American way of life. After the war, Harry Truman eliminated the office and assigned some of its functions to the State Department. [SOURCE: Meier and Rivera, *A Dictionary of Mexican American History*, 262.]

OLIVÁREZ GRACIELA (1928-1987)

Graciela Olivárez, born and raised in Sonora, a mining town in eastern Arizona, became one of the most outstanding citizens in the state's short history. She obtained a lasting life orientation as she grew up in a mining environment, where workers struggled for social and economic justice through labor organizing. During War World II, family economic difficulties forced her to leave school without finishing the eighth grade and move to Phoenix, where she worked in clerical positions. In the late 1950s while a bilingual secretary for an advertising agency, she became a radio disk jockey. At this time in Arizona, the Hispanic public rarely heard people like themselves on the radio. "Action Line," a popular program in the 1960s featuring civil rights discussions provided her visibility in the growing Phoenix metropolis. She also came to the attention of officials in President Lyndon B. Johnson's* War on Poverty and was named director of the newly formed Office of Economic Opportunity branch in Arizona. But the limitations inherent in the federal bureaucracy frustrated her desire to realize more widespread social objectives. Deciding that she needed educational credentials to be more effective, in 1965 Olivárez enrolled at the University of Notre Dame law school. Although she lacked a high school education, she became the first woman law graduate of that institution.

After her graduation, Olivárez returned to Arizona to continue her work in confronting issues of poverty and racism as consultant to the Urban Coalition in Phoenix and as director of Food for All, a food stamp program. But her commitment to civil rights continued, along with involvement in the women's liberation struggle. Olivárez became a charter member of the National Organization for Women; she considered herself a "pro-life" feminist, one of the few in the women's rights movement to hold such a belief.

In 1978, the University of New Mexico hired her as director of the Institute for Social Research and Development and then Governor Jerry Apodaca selected her to head the New Mexico State Planning Office, thus making her the highest-ranking woman government official in New Mexico and perhaps the entire Southwest. In spite of her busy schedule, Olivárez still found time, along with Vilma S. Martínez,* to serve on the board of the Mexican American Legal Defense and Education Fund.* In 1977, she became director of the federal government's Community Service Administration and, consequently, the highest-ranking Hispanic female in the Carter administration.

In 1980, she started the Olivárez Television Company, Inc. She continued her work in broadcasting and philanthropy until her death in 1987. [SOURCE: Chicano Research Collection, Hayden Library, Arizona State University, Tempe.]

OPERATION BOOTSTRAP

Operation Bootstrap, or as it was called in Spanish, "Manos a la Obra", was a campaign created in 1948 for the economic development of Puerto Rico. The campaign included rapid industrialization on the island, achieved in part by creating tax shelters for Amerian industries that re-located to Puerto Rico. A brainchild of the popular governor Luis Muñoz Marín,* the plan emphasized investment, primarily American, in light industry and manufacturing. The official assessment made by the United States government and planners in Muñoz Marín's administration of this program is that in a little more than four decades, much of the island's crushing poverty was eliminated. To a large degree, the process did provide more technical employment for some Puerto Ricans. But as investors turned away from sugar production, agricultural employment declined, and Operation Bootstrap did not adequately provide replacement jobs. Thus even more Puerto Ricans were forced to migrate to the continent in search of work. In the 1960s, petrochemical plants and refineries, industries that required even less labor than light industry, pervaded much of the economy. The net result was as inevitable: more migration. [SOURCE: Rosales, "A Historical Overview," 44-45.]

OPERATION PETER PAN

Operation Peter Pan was a children's program designed to bring thousands of Cuban children to the United States, supposedly to escape forced indoctrination by Fidel Castro's* government after the triumph of the Cuban Revolution in 1959. Wild rumors, abetted by American officials, circulated in Cuba and the refugee community in the United States that children were forcibly taken from their homes and sent to the Soviet Union to receive a Communist education. Within three years, 14,048 mostly male children left Cuba and were fostered in this country by various groups, including the Catholic Church. Most of these youngsters were scions of the middle and upper classes, and because many were nurtured further in this country, they became fairly well educated. As a consequence, today there are countless middle-aged Cuban professionals who were not rejoined with parents and other family members until their adult years, if at all. [SOURCE: Rosales, "A Historical Overview," 48.]

"OPERATION WETBACK"

After World War II, the influx of Mexican immigrant workers entering the United States both legally and illegally increased dramatically. By June 1954, the increase in illegal immigration outdistanced the use of Mexican contract labor, inciting governmental enforcement of immigration legislation. "Operation Wetback" was an Immigration and Naturalization Service (INS)* program to round up and deport Mexican undocumented workers en masse. In 1953, the INS deported 865,318 Mexican undocumented immigrants. In the immediate years after implementation, large numbers were expelled; 1,075,168 in 1954; 242,608 in 1955; and 72,442 in 1956. Some observers assessed that "Operation Wetback" benefited union organizers attempting to establish unions among Mexican Americans because the deportation campaign removed undocumented workers from competing in labor sectors where they worked. But the campaign often harmed native, naturalized or permanent residents of Mexican descent. Often, the basic civil rights and liberties of Mexican Americans were either denied or abused beyond tolerance as authorities apprehended them or employers shunned them, thinking they were "wetbacks." Many Mexican aliens suffered physical and emotional abuse as they were sometimes separated from and not allowed to communicate with their families after the workers had been apprehended. The programs success is questionable as it did very little to curb the increasing flow of undocumented workers into the United States, mostly because it lacked sanctions for violations committed by employers. [SOURCE: Samora and Simon, *A History of the Mexican-American People,* 195; http://www.jsri.msu.edu/museum/pubs/MexAmHist/chapter19.html#ten]

ORANGE COUNTY CITRUS STRIKE

Some 2500 Mexican farmworkers tied up a $20 million citrus crop in Orange County for several weeks with a strike in 1936. More than 400 special armed guards were recruited. Some 200 arrested strikers were formally arraigned in an outdoor bull-pen, which served as a courtroom. Orange County remained in a state of virtual siege for several weeks as local newspapers celebrated the vigilantism used against the farmworkers on strike. [SOURCE: McWilliams, *North from Mexico,* 192-3.]

ORDEN DE CABALLEROS DE AMÉRICA

In 1929, Mexican Americans María L. and Pedro Hernández* founded one of the earliest Hispanic civil rights organizations, Orden de Caballeros de América (Order of the Knights of America), an organization which continued to pioneer civil rights and educational opportunity for Mexican Americans. This was an offshoot of the Order of the Sons of America, which had split by 1929 into three groups. The chapter in Harlingen became the League of Latin American Citizens. Nonetheless, the Sons continued in other cities, but eventually all the organizations merged into the League of United Latin American Citizens (LULAC)* at a meeting in Corpus Christ in 1929. LULAC has survived to this day. María Hernández' viewpoints assured that the Caballeros would be the first Hispanic civil rights organization with a specifically feminist viewpoint. [SOURCE: Tardiff and Mabunda, *Dictionary of Hispanic Biography*, 422.]

ORDER OF THE SONS OF AMERICA

One of the first Mexican-American civil rights organizations founded in Texas was the Order of the Sons of America (OSA), which existed in the early 1920s, and had been organized in San Antonio by Luz Sáenz, a teacher and World War I veteran in 1921. The organization, made up mostly of U.S.-born members, concentrated on encouraging naturalization and participation in U.S. institutions and to achieve civil rights in general for all Mexicans. Among the OSA's main objectives were the encouragement of Mexican Americans to register and vote and to attempt to serve within the jury system, from which they were excluded. The group's tenure came to an end in 1929 after internal divisions created dissention. The San Antonio chapter

Order of the Sons of America

became the Order of the Knights of America, while the members in Harlingen became the League of Latin American Citizens as early as 1927 and attempted to form a statewide organization. The OSA eventually joined with all of the splinter groups to form the League of United Latin American Citizens* during a historical meeting in Corpus Christi in 1929. [SOURCE: Rosales, *Chicano!*, 90-91.]

OXNARD AGRICULTURAL STRIKE

In February 1903, in Oxnard, California, more than 1200 Mexican and Japanese farmworkers organized the first farmworker union, the Japanese-Mexican Labor Association (JMLA). It was also the firs union to win a strike against the already very strong agricultural industry in California. The rapid development of the sugar beet industry in Ventura County and its dependence on cheap seasonal labor amid the highly racist European American society that had moved into the area resulted in unfair as well as racist labor practices by the contractors and the association of farmers and refiners. The banding together of the Japanese and Mexican farmworkers marked the first time in history that two racialized ethnic groups united when faced with Anglo-American discrimination and extremely unfair labor exploitation. Their founding of the union was not an easy task, given the enormous linguistic and cultural barriers that the organizers had to overcome. The JMLA press release on calling the history-making strike eloquently spoke to the relationship of the workers to the industry owners and managers: "Many of us have families, were born in the country, and are lawfully seeking to protect the only property that we have—our labor. It is just as necessary for the welfare of the valley that we get a decent living wage, as it is that the machines in the great sugar factory be properly oiled—if the machine stops, the wealth of the valley stops, and likewise if the laborers are not given a decent wage, they too, must stop work and the whole people of the country will suffer with them." By the first week in March, the JMLA had recruited more than 1200 workers, over ninety percent of the entire sugar beet work force. Despite strike-breaking efforts, violence, and repression by the industry owners, who were supported by the judicial system, the JMLA won an overwhelming victory and ended the strike on March 30. Due to the success of the JMLA, labor unions began to rethink their policy of not organizing non-white labor and of not organizing farm labor. One of the important benefits for Mexican workers was that they had learned some doctrines and techniques from the Wobblies who were involved and were able to apply them in their own Mexican unions. [SOURCE: Almaguer, *Racial Fault Lines*, 183-203; McWilliams, *North from Mexico*, 190.]

PACHUCO

The term *pachuco* was applied in the 1940s and 1950s to Mexican-American youths in the urban Southwest who adopted a certain lifestyle that included the wearing of zoot suits, the tattooing of a cross on one hand, the use of a Spanish-English argot called *caló*, and membership, in gangs. The etymology of the term is unclear, but it is thought to have derived from the smuggler's argot of El Paso, the city that was known to them as *el pachuco*. For their odd, "foreign" customs, pachuco youths were scapegoated during World War II, especially in Los Angeles, by Anglo Americans who saw them as criminal threats. Some observers even linked this youth culture to Mexican *sinarquistas* (Fascists). Although they deplored the violence and harassment sometimes inflicted on these youths by police and servicemen, especially during the infamous "Zoot Suit Riots," parents and Mexican-American leaders did not approve of pachucos. The phenomenon elicited a great amount of hand-wringing among Mexican-American leaders, who saw deteriorating Anglo attitudes as a setback to gains they thought they had made during the 1940s. The scholar George I. Sánchez* saw *pachuquismo* as "A breakdown in family structure", but he blamed economic exploitation, and blatant racial and ethnic discrimination against Mexican Americans for its rise. [SOURCE: Mazón, *Zoot Suit Riots.*]

Youth stripped of zoot suit by servicemen

Hispanic Secretariat Meeting with Catholic Bishops

LOS P.A.D.R.E.S.

Founded in 1969, Los P.A.D.R.E.S. has 500 members, mostly Hispanic Catholic priests, brothers, and deacons. The acronym stands for Padres Asociados para Derechos Religiosos, Educativos y Sociales (Fathers Associated for Religious, Educational, and Social Rights). Its purpose is to develop the critical conscience whereby poor people see themselves as masters of their own destiny and capable of bringing about structural change. It promotes a supportive ministry and advocates on behalf of Hispanic issues and rights in the Church. Los P.A.D.R.E.S. publishes a quarterly newsletter, *Los P.A.D.R.E.S.* [SOURCE: Kanellos, "Organizations," 392.]

PALACIOS, DIANE (1952-)

Born in 1952, Diane Palacios, a high school student in Crystal City, Texas, led classmates in protest of the school's policies concerning extracurricular activities during 1959 and 1970. She protested to the principal over the cheerleading selection process. Summer came and the protest stood still. The next year, similar protests over homecoming queen elections occurred, led by Severita Lara. Eventually, Crystal City students confronted the school board and gained concessions. The school board, however, reneged on the concessions and so the Mexican American Youth Organization (MAYO)* recruited students for a walkout. [SOURCE: Rosales, *Chicano!*, 221-22.]

PAN AMERICAN POLITICAL COUNCIL

Organized in July 1948, with Lisandro Gómez as president, the Pan American Political Council was created by members of LULAC* Council 60 in Houston to educate Mexican-American voters on political issues and to promote a voting block to give Houston Mexicans political clout. It is likely that the founders used the organization to circumvent national LULAC's reluctance to engage directly in political elections. [SOURCE: Archives, Council 60 of League of United Latin American Citizens, Houston, Texas.]

PAN AMERICAN ROUND TABLE

On October 16, 1916, Mrs. Florence Terry Griswold assembled a group of women at a luncheon in San Antonio "to provide mutual knowledge and understanding and friendship among the peoples of the Western Hemisphere, and to foster all movements affecting the women and children of the Americas." As the group continued meeting, it came to be known as the Pan American Round Table, a name taken from the medieval round table as a symbol of unity, perpetuity, equal representation, and opportunity. The group based its guiding principle on the belief that women could develop an understanding of hemispheric issues not available to men, who operated mainly commerce and politics. Round table participants believed that understanding and friendship could only flourish through education and communication, not legislation. Importantly, Mrs. Griswold's project provided refugees from the Mexican Revolution the resources to adapt materially and culturally in San Antonio, often after a traumatic trek across the border. From its San Antonio base, the movement grew throughout Texas. The first Table in a Latin American country was organized in Mexico City in 1928. By 1944, there were so many chapters throughout the United States and Latin America that the Alliance of Pan American Round Tables was founded in Mexico City.

Today, the Round Tables has 1400 chapters. Each group operates autonomously with its own constitution and membership, by invitation only all the cultures of the hemisphere are represented in the membership. Projects sponsored by the chapters include educational programs, libraries, scholarships and financial aid for Latin American students, as well as children's programs in art, music, and dance. The Florence Terry Griswold Endowment Fund was created in 1991 to ensure perpetual scholarship awards for Latin American students accepted in graduate programs at Texas public universities. [SOURCE: Marchbanks, *The Pan American Round Table*.]

PANTÍN, SANTIAGO YGLESIAS (1870-1939)

Yglesias Pantín was born in 1870 in La Coruña, Spain, where he received an elementary education and became a carpenter. He relocated to Cuba, where he became active in organizing labor through the Círculo de

Trabajadores de la Habana (Havana Workers' Circle) from 1889 to 1896. In 1899 he moved to Puerto Rico, where he was instrumental in organizing the Partido Obrero Social (Workers' Social Party) and later became an organizer for the American Federation of Labor for Puerto Rico and Cuba. In 1917, Yglesias Pantín founded the Federación Libre de Trabajadores de Puerto Rico (Free Federation of Puerto Rican Workers) and the Socialist Party. From 1917 to 1933, Yglesias Patín served as a legislator in the Puerto Rican Senate. From 1925 to 1933, he served as Secretary of the Federación Panamericana de Trabajo (Panamerican Federation of Labor). In 1932 and 1936, he was elected Resident Commissioner to represent Puerto Rico in Washington, D.C. During his years as a labor organizer, Yglesias Patín also founded and directed three newspapers: *El Porvenir Social* (The Future of Society, 1898), *La Unión Obrera* (Worker Unity, 1903), and *Justicia* (Justice). He died on December 16, 1939, in Washington, D.C. [SOURCE: Kanellos, *Chronology of Hispanic American History,* 140.]

PANTOJA, ANTONIA (1922 -2002)

Antonia Pantoja was one of the major leaders of the Puerto Rican community in the United States. Born in San Juan, Puerto Rico in 1922, she came to New York City in 1944 after working as rural teacher for two years following her graduation from the University of Puerto Rico's Normal School. It was while working as a welder in a furniture factory that she first encountered the depressed economic conditions of New York Puerto Ricans. This experience motivated Pantoja to dedicate her life to community organizing in order to strengthen the ability of Puerto Ricans to deal with their own problems. Pantoja realized that racism and discrimination, political powerlessness, and limited access to education and economic opportunity combined to keep the community poor. She began her reform work in the factory, providing information to other workers about their rights and how to organize a union. In the meantime, understanding that a formal education would make her more effective, she earned a bachelor's degree from Hunter College on a scholarship in 1952 and later received a Master's in Social work from the same institution in 1954. She later received a Ph.D. from Union Graduate School in Yellow Springs, Ohio in 1973.

While in New York in the early 1950s, she attended graduate school at Columbia University and joined with other Latino students and formed the Hispanic Youth Adult Association, which later became the Puerto Rican Association for Community Affairs (PRACA).* As an assistant professor at Columbia University, Pantoja was appointed to the Bundy Panel, a group that oversaw the decentralization of the New York public schools. Pantoja also organized the Puerto Rican Forum, and in 1961, created and directed ASPIRA,* a community organization devoted to the education and leadership

Antonia Pantoja receives award from President Clinton

development of youth in the city of New York. In 1968 ASPIRA became a national organization. Essentially by the mid 1960s, Pantoja had been a crucial catalyst in establishing the most influential Puerto Rican organizations in New York City. Pantoja also instituted the Universidad Boricua* in 1970, a research and resource center in Washington, D.C., and Producir, an economic development project in Puerto Rico. In 1973, after receiving her Ph.D., she became Chancellor of the Universidad Boricua. Then, in the late 1970s, while an associate Professor at San Diego State University, the University Graduate School for Community Development was created largely through her efforts. In 1996, President Bill Clinton bestowed on Pantoja the Presidential Medal of Freedom, the highest honor a civilian can receive from the United States government. Without a doubt, she can be described as the quintessential foe of poverty and racial discrimination. Pantoja died in New York City of cancer in April 2002. [SOURCE: Pantoja, *Memoir of a Visionary;* Sánchez Korrol, *From Colonia to Community*, 227.]

PARDO ZAMORA, RUBÉN C. (1911-1931)

In February 1931 immigration officials deported Rubén C. Pardo Zamora for illegal entry, but he returned to work at the Monserrat ranch near San Diego, California, where officers Joseph P. Byrne and Harry W. Cunningham arrested him again. When Pardo Zamora tried to escape, Cunningham fired at him at a distance of fifty feet, missed, but downed him with a second shot. Cunningham then handcuffed the mortally wounded Mexican as he lay on the ground. C. Kuykendall, district chief of the immigration office, justified the officer's actions because the young Mexican was an "incorrigible" whose deportation had stemmed from having smuggled in 14 pints of tequila. The San Diego District Attorney agreed. On the other hand, E.F. Pearson, Pardo Zamora's boss for five years, said that he was among the most industrious workers. An article in the *San Diego Union* deplored the killing and said it was difficult to accept the accidental shooting explanation because the coroner's report revealed that Pardo Zamora was beaten, either before or after the shooting. District Attorney Tom Whelan of San Diego County reopened the case, but the officers were again exonerated. [SOURCE: Rosales, *Pobre Raza!*, 87.]

PAREDES, AMÉRICO (1915-1999)

Américo Paredes was born in Brownsville, Texas, a border town located at the place where the Rio Grande River empties into the Gulf of Mexico. The experiences acquired while growing up on the border between Texas and Mexico provided Paredes with the intellectual material that was articulated during a lifetime of writing about the complicated, bicultural society that characterized this region. Paredes' early educational experience was shaped by Brownsville's public schools and at the local community college. He produced his first pieces of poetry and fiction in the late 1930s. Paredes served overseas in the U.S. Army during World War II, working as a reporter for *The Stars and Stripes.* After the war, Paredes enrolled at the University of Texas at Austin and became the first Mexican American to receive a doctoral degree from that institution (Ph.D. in Folklore and Spanish in 1956). Paredes' dissertation dealt with the story of Gregorio Cortez,* a Mexican-American folk hero from South Texas who, after killing a white sheriff during a botched up attempt to arrest him, attempted to flee to Mexico. The ensuing ten-day chase became one of the most publicized manhunts in Texas history. The fugitive did not make it to the border, but he gained enduring legendary status among Mexicans and Anglos alike. It took a number of trials over a period of four years before Cortez was finally hauled off to serve a life sentence at Huntsville. Due to Paredes' book, *With a Pistol in His Hand: A Border Ballad and Its Hero*, the story that Paredes heard sung as a *corrido* when he was growing up was enshrined as a symbol of resistance during the Chicano Movement* of the 1960s; the dissertation was published in 1958.

Paredes taught English, Folklore, and Anthropology at the University of Texas from 1951 until his retirement, more than thirty years later. He was instrumental in the development of the field of Folklore in academia as well as in the field of Mexican American studies. Paredes served as president of the American Folklore Society and was recognized for his leadership internationally. In the United States, he was awarded one of the nation's highest awards for a humanist, the Charles Frankel Prize given by the National Endowment for the Humanities (1989), and in Mexico, the highest award given a foreigner by the Mexican government, the Águila Azteca (the Aztec Eagle) medal in 1991.

Besides publishing numerous research articles, Paredes is the author of *Folktales of Mexico* (1970), *A Texas Mexican Cancionero* (1976),

Américo Paredes

and *Uncle Remus con chile* (Uncle Remus with Chile, 1992). He is also the author of two novels, *George Washington Gómez* (1990) and *The Shadow* (1998), both of which were written decades before their publication. The former is today considered a forerunner of Chicano literature for its analysis of the protagonist as being caught between two cultures and forced to Americanize. The latter won a national award for novel-writing in 1954, but Paredes was unable to find a publisher at that time. He is also the author of numerous stories published in newspapers and magazines, some of which were collected in his *The Hammon and the Beans* (1994). Likewise, *Between Two Worlds*, a selection of poetry in Spanish and English that was published in newspapers in the Southwest from the 1930s to the 1960s, was issued in book form in 1991. [SOURCE: Kanellos, *Hispanic Literature of the United States.*]

PARENT INSTITUTE FOR QUALITY EDUCATION

The seed for the Parent Institute for Quality Education (PIQE) was planted in 1987, when a few community activists in San Diego decided to change the confrontational approach used in the previous 20-30 years to effect educational reform in predominantly Latino school districts of southern California. One of the most serious challenges to the education of Latinos, they concluded, was the growing "achievement gap" and high dropout rate of students. Instead of the walkouts, lawsuits, protests, and countless educational advisory committees, the Reverend Vahac Mardirosian,* a retired pastor, and Dr. Alberto Ochoa, an education professor at San Diego State University, attempted a new approach. To this end, they chose the predominantly Latino Sherman Elementary School in San Diego County, whose academic achievement ranked last among the 109 elementary schools in the county. The new strategy involved assembling the parents of Sherman students to discuss the gamut of issues creating educational problems. The expected two-hour dialogue with a dozen parents expanded into eight weekly meetings in which ninety parents participated. The sessions were so successful that the concept was taken to other schools; PIQE was born.

Dr. Ochoa transformed the knowledge obtained in these gatherings to a nine-week workshop for parents. Since 1987, 300,000 parents have graduated from PIQE classes throughout California. Another PIQE component is the "Coaches" program, a more advanced initiative designed to develop parent leaders to take the project forward. Today, half of the costs of these programs are paid by the school districts with Title I, Title VII, or GEAR UP funds. PIQE covers the other half of the cost through fund-raising efforts involving grants and private donations. [SOURCE: http://www.castategearup.org]

PARLIER, CALIFORNIA

In 1972, the small town of Parlier located in central California, achieved fame when an all-Mexican-American city council replaced an all-Anglo council. This had never occurred in the state's history. Many factors provoked the Mexican-American community to challenge the Anglo establishment, including land ownership, discriminatory practices within the political system, and strained relations between Hispanics and the police. The political revolt arose when the city council did not appoint a Chicano,* as many people had expected, to succeed the town's police chief, who had died in office. Instead, the Anglo council hired an individual from outside the community. The success of this revolt is attributed to massive voter registration and education drives. [SOURCE: Meier and Rivera, *A Dictionary of Mexican American History,* 270.]

PASTOR, EDWARD (1943-)

Edward Pastor became Arizona's first Mexican-American Congressman in October 1991. Born in 1943 in Claypool, a copper-mining community in central Arizona, he and his two youngest siblings attended public schools in Miami, Arizona. He later became the first mem-ber of his family to attend college. In 1966, Pastor graduated from Arizona State University (ASU) with a B.A. in Chemistry, taught high school in Phoenix, and then returned to ASU and received a law degree in 1974. But instead of practicing law, he became the Deputy Director of the Guadalupe Organization, Inc. in Guadalupe, Arizona, an impoverished community of Yaquis and Mexicans south of Tempe. Pastor then decided to enter politics, a path paved by other Chicano Movement* activists, and in 1976 voters elected him to the Maricopa County Board of Supervisors, a position he held until he ran for Congress in 1991. Voters have continued to elect

Edward Pastor

Pastor to represent Arizona's 2nd District in the House of Representatives until the present time. [SOURCE: http://www.house.gov/pastor/NewBiography.htm]

PAZ, FRANK X. (?-?)

Frank X. Paz (or Pax, as he sometimes spelled it) served as the first president of the Mexican Civic Committee* in Chicago in the 1940s. He came to Illinois during his youth from Morelia, Michoacán, and attended the University of Illinois, earning a degree in engineering. In 1930, he married Chicago-born, Sarah Sayad Paz, the first baby of Assyrian descent born in Chicago. Through the Mexican Civic Committee* and his writings, Paz strove to improve the conditions under which Mexicans lived in Chicago. He asserted that in the 20 years that Mexicans had lived in Chicago, they had made few gains—even in the unions. Paz often evoked the failure of the United States to provide equal opportunity to Mexicans and make good the promise of the "American way of life." His wife also worked on campaigns to help Assyrian refugees and to promote Assyrian cultural events in Chicago. [SOURCE: Valdés, "Region, Nation, and World-System: Perspectives on Midwestern Chicana/o History," http://www.jsri.msu.edu/RandS/research/ops/oc20.html]

PEÑA, FEDERICO (1947-)

Federico Peña became the first Hispanic mayor of Denver, Colorado, one of the nation's major cities. At age 36, Peña was elected Denver's 37th mayor and was re-elected to a second term in 1987. At the time he entered office, he was among the youngest chief executives in Denver history. Mayor Peña's efforts to strengthen Denver's economy placed the city in the national spotlight. The U.S. Conference of Mayors selected Denver over 100 other cities as the winner of its prestigious "City Livability Award." Peña later went on to serve as Secretary of Transportation in the Clinton administration. [SOURCE: Kanellos, *Chronology of Hispanic American History*, 226.]

PEOPLE'S CHURCH

In the fall of 1969, in New York the Young Lords* needed more space to continue projects aiding welfare mothers, providing free breakfasts for children and free clothing for the poor. They needed more space, but the pastor of the First Spanish Methodist Church on 111th Street refused their request to use the church building when it was vacant during the week. The Young Lords took the dispute to the congregation, but were arrested and beaten by police. Three weeks later, the Lords occupied the building and renamed it the "People's Church," and set up "Serve the People" programs: free breakfast and clothing programs, health services, community dinners, and a liberation school. [SOURCE: Torres and Velázquez, *The Puerto Rican Movement*, 214.]

PERALES, ALONSO S. (1898-1960)

Alonso S. Perales played one of the most important roles in protecting the civil rights of Mexican Americans during the twentieth century. Born in Alice, Texas, on October 17, 1898, his parents Susana (Sandoval) and Nicolás died when Perales was only six. Having to work at a very young age, Perales nevertheless finished public school in Alice. After marrying Marta Pérez, he went to business college in Corpus Christi and was later drafted when the United States entered World War I. After his discharge, he obtained a civil service position with the Department of Commerce in Washington, D.C. While there, he continued his education and received a B.A. and, in 1926, a law degree at the National University. Perales then worked for the Department of State and served on thirteen diplomatic missions to the Dominican Republic, Cuba, Nicaragua, Mexico, Chile, and the West Indies. After returning to Texas to practice law, in 1945 he again worked in the diplomatic service in the United Nations conference as legal counsel to the Nicaraguan delegation. In the 1950s, he also worked with the Department of State under Dwight D. Eisenhower's administration.

But Perales, who became one of the most influential Mexican Americans of his time, will best be remembered for his work in defending "la raza," a term he used in the title of one his books, *En defensa de mi raza*. This two-volume anthology contains his own essays, letters, and speeches, as well as those of his contemporary activists; the articles focused on dispelling charges that Mexicans were an inferior people and a social problem. In his own writings, Perales responded to a series of civil rights abuses in the 1920s, such as lynching. He urged Mexican Americans to demand their constitutional rights as United States citizens. To do this, Perales insisted, Mexicans in the United States did not have to reject their cultural background.

Perales was also a founder of the League of United Latin American Citizens (LULAC)* in 1929. With José Tomás Canales* and Eduardo Idar, he helped write the LULAC constitution. In 1930, he served one term as second president of the organization and then went on to organize LULAC Council 16 in San Antonio. In his role as defender of La Raza, Perales testified before a United States Congressional hearing on Mexican immigration, which was an effort by immigration restrictionists to stop immigration from Mexico. Despite being a stalwart of the Democratic party, Perales helped found the Independent Voters Association, a Mexican-American political club in San Antonio in the early 1930s, which supported New Dealers, mainly from the Democratic Party. In the 1940s, he worked to introduce the Spears Bill* in the Texas legislature prohibiting discrimination based on race. Also in the 1940s, Perales worked on a State Department survey of the extent of discrimination that Mexicans Americans faced during a time when the United States could not afford to be accused of not combating racism by Fascist and Nazi propaganda. A firm believer in integration, he joined mainstream organizations, such as the American Legion and the San Antonio Chamber of Commerce. Considering that he was born in the United States, his command of the Spanish language was impeccable, and he delivered many speeches in that language and wrote numerous columns in *La Prensa* of San Antonio and other Spanish-language newspapers. Perales passed away in San Antonio on October 21, 1960. [SOURCE: Orozco, "Perales, Alonso S. (1898-1960)," *The Handbook of Texas*

Online, http://www.tsha.utexas.edu/handbook/online; Rosales, *Testimonio,* 167.]

PEREZ, EDDIE ALBERTO (1957-)

Eddie Alberto Perez was elected the first Hispanic mayor of Hartford Connecticut in 2001, then re-elected in 2003. Born in Corozal, Puerto Rico, Perez first migrated with his family to New York City. Then in 1969, with his mother and his seven siblings, he moved to Hartford.* Substandard housing and limited opportunities for Latinos contributed to an instability, which forced the Perez' to move frequently, making for an unstable and difficult environment for the family. Nonetheless, after graduating from Hartford Public High School in 1976, and receiving an Associate's Degree from Capital Community Technical College in 1978, Eddie Perez rose to become a community leader by working in advocacy organizations for better housing and educational opportunity. In 1989, Trinity College hired him as its first Director of Community Relations, and in 1994 he earned an economics degree while working full time at the school. As he rose through the administrative ranks, he came to head two comprehensive community revitalization programs with $322 million in investment from Trinity College and Hartford Hospital. After his election, Perez was successful in reducing crime, raising the expectations of public school education, increasing home ownership, and creating more neighborhood economic development. [SOURCE: www.hartford.gov/government/mayor/biography.htm]

PICO, PÍO DE JESÚS (1801-1894)

Pío de Jesús Pico became the first governor of African heritage in North America. Born on May 5, 1801, at San Gabriel Mission, Pico, who was a

mulatto, also had the distinction of being the last governor of California under Mexican rule. As a young man, he became a successful businessman in Los Angeles. In 1828, he was elected to the territorial legislature and assumed a grand stature as a southern Californio political leader. From January to February 1832, he was governor briefly, but then became the civilian administrator of the San Luis Rey Mission. In 1845, he once again became governor, this time at the seat in Los Angeles instead of Monterey. He was attacked on various occasion for land grants that he made and for his sale of mission lands. When the Americans invaded, Pico at

Pío de Jesús Pico

first offered some resistance, but soon fled to Baja California. After the signing of the peace treaty, Pico returned to California and assumed the peaceful life of a rancher. Like many other Californios, he lost all of his lands to mortgage companies when he had to raise funds to defend the titles to the properties from squatters and other usurpers. Under American rule, Pico continued his interest in politics, serving on the Los Angeles City Council and as the Los Angeles County Tax Assessor. He also owned a large hotel, the Pico House, which still stands in downtown Los Angeles. Pico died penniless on September 11, 1894. [SOURCE: Kanellos, *Chronology of Hispanic American History*, 65-66.]

PLAN DE SAN DIEGO

The origins of the Plan de San Diego (San Diego Plan)—named after the town of San Diego, Texas—remain unclear. Purportedly concocted by Texas Mexicans, the plan called upon all racial minorities, Blacks, Native Americans, Asians, and Mexicans, to rise up in arms and drive Anglo Americans out of the Southwest in order to create a separate republic. The planned rebellion, which called for the execution of all Anglo males over sixteen years of age, was scheduled for February 20, 1915, irreverently designed to coincide with George Washington's birthday. Retaliation to the Plan de San Diego was unparalleled in the degree of anti-Mexican violence committed by Anglos, starting when Texas officials released news of the proposed insurrection as soon as Basilio Ramos, Antonio González, and Manuel Flores were caught smuggling the document across the border in January 1915.

During the months of violent reaction to the plan, Texas Rangers* and volunteers summarily executed hundreds of Mexicans in the Rio Grande Valley and forced thousands across the border. The Plan de San Diego also caused urban unrest. In July, wary federal officers arrested 20 Mexicans who were recruiting adherents for revolutionary activity in San Antonio. In August, 28 San Antonio men, identified as supporters of the plan, were arrested after rioting against police.

The Plan de San Diego has been ascribed to all kinds of motives, ranging from machinations by Mexican revolutionary General Venustiano Carranza attempting to increase his power at a time when he was struggling with Pancho Villa, to claims that German provocateurs were working among Mexicans. This last charge, of course linked Mexicans to Germany during World War I. Although the United States was not officially at war with the Axis powers, most Americans sympathized with England at the start of the war. [SOURCE: Sandos, *Rebellion in the Borderlands;* Rosales, *Pobre Raza!*, 15-17, 88-89.]

PLAN DE SAN LUIS POTOSÍ

The Plan de San Luis Potosí called for a general uprising to begin on November 20, 1910 to overthrow the dictator Porfirio Díaz. As the architect of the plan, Francisco I. Madero crossed the border into Mexico, but the uprising failed so that he quickly returned to Texas. This type of bellicose action on the border and others like it prompted a harsh reaction by Anglo Americans. Madero received assistance from some Texans, but most Americans resented actions of the Mexican Revolution being planned or carried out on American soil. By January of 1911, Pascual Orozco, a Madero follower, implemented the plan and Porfirio Díaz was ousted by May. [SOURCE: Rosales, *Chicano!*, 26.]

PLAN DE SANTA BARBARA

In April 1969, one month after the National Chicano Youth Liberation Conference* adjourned at the Crusade for Justice Center* in Denver, Colorado, Chicano* students met at the University of California, Santa Barbara, in a conference that became one of the most crucial Chicano events in California. It was sponsored by the Coordinating Council on Higher Education, a network of students and professors who had returned from Denver full of enthusiasm and energy. By now, the Chicano student community was ready to implement a higher education plan that would go beyond previous pronouncements. A major objective was to create college curriculum that was relevant and useful to the community. Higher education, the students reasoned, was a publicly funded infrastructure that enhanced the business community and other white bastions of power; very little was expended on the needs of the tax-paying Chicano community.

The students incorporated El Plan Espiritual de Aztlán (The Spiritual Plan of Aztlán),* the ultimate ideological expression of Chicanismo, formulated at the Denver meeting, into the design so that it would be used by future Chicano studies programs and students. As such, the group decided to bring all California Chicano student groups under one standard called El Movimiento Estudiantil de Aztlán (MECHA—The Aztlán Student Movement).* The term "Chicano" became canonized after this meeting, especially among the Mexican-origin intelligentsia. Curiously, while the term has at times almost disappeared as a self-reference term, it is as strong as ever at universities. More importantly, at the conference, El Plan de Santa Barbara (The Santa Barbara Plan) was formulated, a design for implementing Chicano studies programs throughout the California university system. The plan eschewed assimilation and produced the most resounding rejection of Mexican-American ideology to date. According to the plan,

Chicanismo involves a crucial distinction in political consciousness between a Mexican American and a Chicano mentality. The Mexican American is a person who lacks respect for his culture and ethnic heritage. Unsure of himself, he seeks assimilation as a way out of his "degraded" social status. Consequently, he remains politically ineffective. In contrast, Chicanismo reflects self-respect and pride in one's ethnic and cultural background. . . . [T]he Chicano acts with confidence and with a range of alternatives in the political world.

These programs contained a curriculum intended to train a vanguard of future Chicano leaders that demonstrated how American capitalism and racism had colonized their people. These same future leaders had to know that:

[T]he liberation of his people from prejudice and oppression is in his hand and this responsibility is greater than personal achievement and more meaningful than degrees, especially if they are earned at the expense of this identity and cultural integrity.

The plan did not ask for specific commitment to physical action—e.g., to unionize or to strive for a separate country. Nor did it ask students to drop out of school. The Mexican-American emphasis on getting a good education remained integral to the Chicano Movement,* but a good education did not mean one had to become an Anglo and had to forget about the community. The plan also asked that students control Chicano studies programs—e.g., the power to select and fire professors in accordance with criteria established by Chicanos, not by the university administration.

After the meeting at Santa Barbara, a spate of programs was pushed into existence through student militancy. The largest and the most intellectually dynamic was the UCLA Chicano Studies Center, founded primarily to conduct research. Most of these centers and teaching programs—practically all of the California state colleges and universities instituted then—remained traditional and did not adhere to a radical departure from academics-as-usual in order to teach liberation, impart cultural nationalist interpretations, and train activist cadres to organize in the community. Perhaps the program that came the closest to these ideals was the one directed by the activist-scholar, Rodolfo Acuña,* at San Fernando Valley State College (now California State University, Northridge). Nonetheless, its fame depended more on Acuña's national recognition than on following the radical precepts demanded by students. Acuña published in 1972 the most widely read survey of Chicano history, *Occupied America*,* containing the radical interpretation expected by Chicano students. [SOURCE: Rosales, *Chicano!*, 183.]

PLAN DEL BARRIO

Rudolfo "Corky" Gonzales* issued El Plan del Barrio in Washington, D.C. during the 1968 Poor People's March.* The proclamation mapped out separate public housing for Chicanos, bilingual education, barrio economic development, and restitution for land that had been taken from Hispanos in Colorado and New Mexico. After the Washington trip, the energized members of his Crusade for Justice* bought an old church building in downtown Denver and converted it into the Crusade headquarters. From there, Gonzales engaged in a series of actions that inspired militancy in the Chicano Movement.* More importantly, as the Black Muslims had done, Gonzales envisioned an array of self-sufficient barrio businesses controlled by his organization. [SOURCE: Marín, *A Spokesman of the Mexican American Movement.*]

EL PLAN ESPIRITUAL DE AZTLÁN *see* NATIONAL CHICANO YOUTH LIBERATION CONFERENCE

PLATT AMENDMENT

After the Spanish American War, Cuba and Puerto Rico came under United States jurisdiction and political control. Cuba was allowed to steer a more independent course, but when Cubans wrote their new constitution in 1901, American officials forced the framers at the constitutional convention to include an amendment drafted in the U.S. Congress by Senator Orville H. Platt which allowed the United States to intervene in Cuban affairs at will. Essentially, both Puerto Rico and Cuba remained under United States hegemony, and almost overnight an intimate, albeit antagonistic, relationship began with the United States. The Platt Amendment allowed for U.S. troops to occupy Cuba three times before 1920. Although the hated measure was abrogated in 1934, Americans continued to control the economy and had an inordinate influence on internal political affairs until the revolution of Fidel Castro* in 1959. [SOURCE: Rosales, "A Historical Overview," 25-26.]

POLITICAL ASSOCIATION OF SPANISH-SPEAKING ORGANIZATIONS

In the 1960 presidential election, John F. Kennedy narrowly edged out Richard M. Nixon; the first Irish Catholic to have ever won the presidency. Mexican-American leaders across the nation took some of the credit for the victory. Kennedy, they claimed, had won the electoral votes in the swing state of Texas with a margin made possible by the Mexican-American vote, which had been mobilized by Viva Kennedy-Viva Johnson Clubs,* a booster group organized by a coalition of Mexican-American organizations from across the country. Never had such a coalition been put together at the national level, and the group did not want to lose the momentum of such a potentially strong force. To institutionalize a national initiative, leaders of the Mexican American Political Association,* the Community Services Organization,* the League of United Latin American Citizens (LULAC),* and Mexican American Political Action, a new group from Texas, came together in Phoenix, Arizona, to develop a strategy. Out of this historic meeting came the Political Association of Spanish-Speaking Organizations (PASSO). George I. Sánchez,* the veteran civil rights leader, proposed that PASSO adopt as its mission the enactment of social and economic measures to advance the position of Mexican Americans, including strict regulation of the Texas-Mexico border; a minimum wage for farmworkers; welfare for the elderly, the widowed, and the orphaned; educational opportunities; and federal aid to education. Despite the participants at the Phoenix meeting coming from diverse regions, PASSO took root mainly in Texas

In 1963, a slate of five Mexican Americans under the auspices of the Teamster's Union and PASSO ran for council seats In Crystal City, Texas,* and won in a history-making campaign. The Anglo establishment had underestimated the ability of Mexicans to organize and was shocked. The Anglo leaders fought back, however, first by threatening the jobs of the newly elected council members and then by hindering day-to-day city government business. Soon, the inexperienced Mexican council members were beleaguered and discredited. At the next election, the Anglo old guard, with its Mexican-American minions, returned to power and established a municipal government with an all-Anglo majority.

PASSO also introduced militancy and confrontation as tactics. At an Equal Employment Opportunity Commission (EEOOC)* meeting in Albuquerque, New Mexico, in March of 1966, the watchdog group heard grievances from members of such organizations as PASSO and LULAC. PASSO and other organizational representatives walked out after demanding that EEOC put Mexican Americans on the commission's board and punish large southwestern corporate employers who discriminated in not hiring Mexican Americans. Judge Albert Peña, a San Antonio politician, explained after the walkout why Mexican Americans were now using these tactics. Government officials told them, he said, "The trouble with you [Mexicans] is you don't make enough noise, you don't demonstrate, you don't raise Cain enough." After the Albuquerque walkout, Joan Moore and Ralph Guzmán, scholars from the Mexican American Study Project at UCLA, observed in an article in the *Nation*, "The new Mexican leader studies Negro civil rights technique with a degree of attention approaching the Pentagon's study of Chinese guerillas." Indeed, the militancy shown by Mexican Americans when they walked out of an EEOC meeting in Albuquerque in 1966 to draw attention to discrimination served as a model for future Chicano Movement* activists. [SOURCE: Palomo Acosta, "Political Association of Spanish-Speaking Organizations (PASSO)," *The Handbook of Texas Online*, http://www.tsha.utexas.edu/handbook/online/; Rosales, *Chicano!*, 108, 216, 220, 267.]

POLL TAXES IN TEXAS

Ostensibly, through poll taxes voters paid for the expenses incurred by entities that fielded elections. The poll tax was used in various southern states to discourage African Americans and poor whites from voting, but it was in Texas that Mexican Americans were the most affected. Adopted in Texas in 1902, the poll tax obliged voters to pay between $1.50 and $1.75 to register to vote. Obviously, this was an inordinate expense and an obstacle to voting among the working classes and poor. Poll taxes affected African Americans and Mexican Americans disproportionately, and civil rights activists from both minority groups joined efforts to outlaw the practice wherever it was applied. Eventually, Congress passed the 24th Amendment to the United States Constitution to prohibit poll taxes; the law went into effect in 1964. In 1966, in *Harper v. Virginia Board of Elections*, the U.S. Supreme Court ruled that poll taxes in state elections were unconstitutional which, became a boon for Mexican Texans and to some degree accounts for the ephemeral success of La Raza Unida Party,* a party made up of Chicano Movement* activists. [SOURCE: http://texaspolitics.laits.utexas.edu/html/vce/0503.html]

POMPA, AURELIO (1901-1924)

On the morning of October 19, 1922, at the site of the new Los Angeles post office, Aurelio Pompa, then 21, killed William McCue, the carpenter for whom Pompa served as a laborer. The prosecution contended that Pompa used tools against McCue's wishes; in an ensuing argument McCue struck the ambitious young Mexican with his fist and the side of a saw blade. Pompa went home, returned with a revolver and shot McCue twice without warning, once in the heart. Mexican witnesses, however, swore that a second argument ensued before Pompa took out a gun and shot McCue. Police arrived just in time to prevent white workmen from lynching Pompa. In April of 1923, Pompa was convicted of first degree murder and given the death sentence. In November, Attorney Frank E. Domínguez* appealed the sentence, citing errors and stating that the verdict was contrary to law, but Superior Court Judge Russ Avery affirmed the original judgment. The Mexican community perceived the slaying as self-defense. An editorial appearing in *Hispano América* captured the highly charged pro-Pompa sentiment:

> The threat of the gallows is being brandished in the case of another Mexican whose name is Aurelio Pompa. Never mind that he had to

kill to protect his own life and, on top of that, half of the jury was in favor of finding him innocent. For the sake of humanity and love of justice, we must mobilize in order to save that unfortunate man.

This sentiment prompted a campaign that netted $3,000 even before the Mexican consul decided to help coordinate fund raising. Jesús Heras, editor of *El Heraldo de México*,* was among the most ardent supporters. The California Mexican community, Pompa's mother, and even Mexican president Álvaro Obregón's mother pressured the Mexican president to intercede. President Obregón then sent an appeal to governor friend William Richardson, and supporters gathered 12,915 signatures petitioning for clemency, but Richardson did not commute the sentence. Pompa's execution on March 3, 1924, shocked and grieved the Mexican community, and he became an instant folk martyr.

The Cruz Azul Mexicana* of San Francisco arranged for the remains to be taken on a Friday night to an Italian-American mortuary, where hundreds of Mexican people who filed past Pompa's casket also saw Pompa's mother grieving at her son's side the whole night. In Los Angeles, hundreds more viewed the corpse for two nights at the Mexican Undertaking Company. On Monday, Pompa's remains were sent on to Sonora, where he was buried in an elaborate funeral at his home town of Caborca. [SOURCE: Rosales, *Pobre Raza!*, 30, 109, 150-151.]

POOR PEOPLE'S CAMPAIGN

The Reverend Ralph Abernathy and Dr. Martin Luther King organized a march on Washington, D.C. in May-June 1968, to dramatize the persistence of poverty in America in spite of the grandiose "War on Poverty" projects initiated by President Lyndon B. Johnson.* Dr. King invited Reies López Tijerina,* the champion of recovering lost lands in New Mexico, and a contingent of his Alianza Federal de las Mercedes* to join the Poor People's March on Washington. This invitation so angered Alianza enemies that, to prevent Tijerina from going had him arrested. Pressure from Mexican-American and Native-American civil rights leaders, nevertheless, convinced state police chief, Captain Joe Black, to intercede with local authorities to release Tijerina. By the time the *aliancistas* joined the Poor People's March as it came through Albuquerque, the Reverend King had been assassinated. The *aliancistas* spent sixty days at the nation's capital, making friends among civil rights leaders from the Native American and African American communities. Tijerina decided to make cause with New Mexico's Native Americans. Today he claims that his movement influenced President Richard Nixon to decree in 1970 the repartition of 18,000 acres among the Taos Pueblo Indians.

Rodolfo "Corky" Gonzales,* leader of Denver's Crusade for Justice,* was also invited to participate, and as a consequence his organization

López Tijerina with Ralph Abernathy during Poor People's March

achieved prominence. While in the Poor People's March, the efforts by the blacks to gain civil rights and achieve self-sufficiency greatly impressed Gonzales, who returned to Denver with many new ideas for implementation. [SOURCE: Rosales, *Chicano!*, 167, 179, 192.]

PORTO RICAN BROTHERHOOD

After its founding in 1923, the Porto Rican Brotherhood in New York City became one of the most significant stateside organizations of the decade. Its purpose was to promote sociability and friendship among its members while attending to their social and intellectual advancement. During the 1920s, the Brotherhood advanced these concerns by enticing Puerto Rican migrants in New York City to join by offering mutual aid and cultural identity. In addition, the organization carried out charitable works and asked its members to volunteer their time for the benefit of the community. A basic tenet followed by the leaders was an acceptance of the working-class origins of its members. [SOURCE: Sánchez Korrol, *From Colonia to Community*.]

PORVENIR MASSACRE

January 28, 1918, Texas Rangers* and Anglo ranchers went to a ranch near Porvenir, Texas, an isolated community of less than 200 Mexicans, and took 15 Mexican small farmers and stock owners a mile out of town, where they executed them and mutilated their bodies with knives. The rest of the village, mainly old men, women, and children, about 150 of them, fled to Mexico leaving behind their farms and stock.

U.S. Army Adjutant General James Harley ordered the disbanding of Company B of the Rangers, who were responsible for the massacre, and the resignation of its commander, Captain J.M. Fox. In a letter to Fox, the general wrote, "Your forced resignation came in the interest of humanity, decency, law and order and hereafter the laws and constitution of this state must be superior to the autocratic will of any peace office . . . vandalism across the border can be best suppressed by suppressing it on the Texas side first."

Less humane reasons propelled the curtailment on Ranger power, however. General Harley also referred to the trouble the incident would bring to international relations, including conducting the war in Europe. Moreover, as early as June of the previous year, Mexican officials had warned that unless Texas prohibited Ranger attacks, such as the Porvenir Massacre, *braceros* (workers) would not be allowed into the state during the labor-scarce period of World War I. The threat greatly concerned both Texas and federal officials, who agreed to find a solution to the problem. [SOURCE: Rosales, *Pobre Raza!*, 90; Justice, *Revolution on the Rio Grande*.]

POZ PAPI

Located in Los Angeles, POZ PAPI was organized by HIV positive Latinos in 2001 to serve as a social and educational organization, where HIV-positive Latinos can come and feel free of the social isolation they experience in the rest of the community. At social gatherings and therapy sessions, they find others who share their condition and concerns. The organization also provides information about HIV to those newly testing positive for HIV, as well as those already living with HIV. Significantly, POZ PAPI also educates people and family members about the misconceptions surrounding HIV. This aspect of the program is designed to reduce the stigma and prejudice towards those infected with HIV. In the words of Juan Antonio Dominion, one of the founders, "Most Latinos don't have that information, mainly because the Latino community is so silent about HIV due to social oppressions such as machismo and homophobia." [SOURCE: http://www.qvmagazine.com/gay-latinolinks.html; http://www.pozpapi.com/]

PREGONES THEATER

Founded in 1979, Pregones Theater is a Puerto Rican producing and presenting company. Based in the Bronx, New York, its main mission is to create and perform contemporary theatre, rooted in Puerto Rican and Latino artistic and musical expressions. Through its major programs—Main Stage, Summer Tour, Residency/Touring, and Visiting Artist Series—Pregones offers Latino communities an artistic venue to challenge and enhance their participative roles in society. The Pregones artistic team plans out its season on a yearly basis and invites visiting artists who are compatible with the theater's mission. [SOURCE: http://www.npnweb.org/index.php3?action=DisplayPage&page=pregones_theater]

PRESIDENT'S COMMISSION ON MIGRATORY LABOR

President Harry S. Truman created the President's Commission on Migratory Labor in June 1950. After convening twelve regional public hearings, the commission recommended in 1951 that Congress pass legislation making employment of undocumented workers unlawful, and that the contracting of workers under the Bracero Program* be streamlined. The commission also recommended that the government facilitate the utilization of domestic labor in areas where *braceros* and undocumented workers were employed. [SOURCE: Meier and Rivera, *A Dictionary of Mexican American History,* 288.]

PRESIDENT'S COMMITTEE ON GOVERNMENT CONTRACTS

Established during Dwight D. Eisenhower's administration, the President's Committee on Government Contracts (PCGC) was one of the first governmental projects to identify "official minorities" as part of a civil rights agenda. Vice President Richard M. Nixon was put in charge of the PCGC when it began in 1956, and the committee's mandate was to assure that employers who had government contracts would hire "Negros" and "other minorities." The latter classification included "Spanish-Americans, Orientals, Indians, Jews, Puerto Ricans, etc." Sensing that Hispanics being placed in the "other minority" category that African Americans would have greater priority, such Mexican-American groups as the League of United Latin American Citizens,* the American G.I. Forum,* the Mexican-American Political Action Committee,* and the Alianza Hispano-Americana* demanded that Spanish Americans be promoted from the "other minorities" categories and placed alongside blacks, arguing that Mexican Americans had suffered as much discrimination as blacks. With the help of Mexican-American congressmen Edward R. Roybal,* Henry B. González,* and Joseph M. Montoya,* they were able to get the elevation that they wanted. [SOURCE: Kotlowski, "Richard Nixon and the Origins of Affirmative Action."]

EL PRIMER CONGRESO MEXICANISTA

The first large convention of Mexicans for action against social injustice, El Primer Congreso Mexicanista (The First Mexicanist Congress) was held in Laredo, Texas from September 14 through 20, 1910. Led by Nicasio Idar, editor and publisher of *La Crónica* newspaper, the program created both an agenda for labor organizing and for protection of civil rights of Mexicans and Mexican Americans in the United States. Through strategies such as organizing and joining trade unions, soliciting the support of the Mexican consular system, having schools that would teach in Spanish and that would teach Mexican culture, improving the plight of Mexican women in the United States, and other strategies to protect Mexican lives and economic interests the congress sought to prevent social injustice. The congress concluded by establishing an on-going organization, La Liga Mexicanista (The Mexicanist League). [SOURCE: Gómez-Quiñones, *Roots of Chicano Politics*, 314-23.]

PROJECT FOR LESBIAN, GAY, BISEXUAL, AND TRANSGENDER HUMAN RIGHTS

In November 1997, the Project for Lesbian, Gay, Bisexual, and Transgender Human Rights (LGBT) submitted a draft bill to the Puerto Rican legislature to amend Article 103 of the Puerto Rican Penal code, a law which criminalized consensual sexual relationships between persons of the same sex. The opponents of this law argued that it encouraged discrimination and violence against gays and lesbians and violated their right to privacy. At the same time, the activists launched Action Alert, a campaign to attract international support for their efforts to amend Article 103. During this period, the LGBT had to contend with a campaign by the religious right to further curtail human rights for the LGBT. At legislative hearings in August of 1997 to review a pending anti-gay code, members of the LGBT community demonstrated their opposition, only to be harassed by some legislators for their gay orientation. One of the protesters, Margarita Sánchez de León of the Movimiento Ecuménico Nacional de Puerto Rico (the National Ecumenical Movement of Puerto Rico) was threatened with arrest by legislators for violating Article 103. [SOURCE: International Gay and Human Rights Commission, http://www.iglhrc.org/site/iglhrc/]

PROPOSITION 187

In November 1994, 60 percent of the California voters approved Proposition 187, the so-called "Save our State"(SOS) initiative. The proposition sought to deny public, social, educational, and health services to aliens who were in California illegally. Governor Pete Wilson, who made immigration restriction an important plank in his campaign for the governorship, endorsed SOS and promised to campaign for its passage. Wilson claimed that if SOS were passed, the U.S. Supreme Court would be obliged to reconsider a 1982 decision in *Plyer v. Doe* that "Undocumented immigrant students are obligated, as are all other students, to attend school until they reach the age mandated by state law." Immediately after the proposition passed, the Mexican American Legal Defense and Education Fund (MALDEF)* and other civil rights organizations challenged its constitutionality and successfully curtailed the implementation of this voter referendum. A similar effort was launched in 2000, but was unable to qualify for the ballot. [SOURCE: Chávez, *Shadowed Lives.*]

PROPOSITION 209

Proposition 209 was passed by the California electorate with 54 percent of the vote on November 5, 1996, as a constitutional amendment. The initiative overturned all state affirmative action programs in California. Civil rights groups quickly filed lawsuits to block the implementation of the initiative at the same time that Governor Pete Wilson directed state agencies to begin phasing out race and gender preference programs. However, institutions of higher education were not hampered by the passage of the initiative, and they found other ways of recruiting minorities. [SOURCE: *News Update*, http://www.ajdj.com/noccri/new.html]

PROYECTO VISIÓN

The World Institute on Disability (WID), based in Oakland, California, started Proyecto Visión (Project Vision) in 2000 to help Latinos with disablities. The U.S. Department of Education's Rehabilitation Services Administration (RSA) awarded WID a five-year grant to work with government agencies and private organizations focusing on employment, education, and technology in order to increase their outreach to disabled Latinos. Recognizing that the population of Latinos with disabilities is one of the fastest growing in the United States, WID's Proyecto Visión established as a primary goal providing Latino organizations with technical services and training so they could better serve their disabled community members. To accomplish this, the project has instituted bilingual technical assistance via a toll-free hotline, a bilingual website, a newsletter and a listserv, annual employment-centered trainings, and leadership development activities. In addition, Proyecto Visión has partnered with such national entities as Telemundo, the Hispanic Radio Network,* the National Council of La Raza,* and the Hispanic Chamber of Commerce in the project. [SOURCE: http://www.proyectovision.net/english/about/index.html]

PUBLIC LAW 78

Opponents of the Bracero Program* were able to reduce the scale of *bracero* employment in the late 1940s by demonstrating sufficient domestic worker availability. However, the outbreak of the Korean War in 1950 thwarted their efforts. In response to labor demands stemming from the war, agricultural employers convinced Congress in 1951 to pass Public Law 78, which renewed and expanded the program. On behalf of organized farm employers, the Congress enacted the law, but its extensions had to be renewed by vote every two years; these extensions were granted until 1964. [SOURCE: http://sunsite.berkeley.edu/calheritage/latinos/pl78nav.html]

EL PUEBLO, INC.

El Pueblo, Inc. was founded in North Carolina in 1992 as a nonprofit statewide advocacy and policy organization to strengthen the Latino community in the area. This goal is achieved through leadership development, education, and promotion of cross-cultural understanding in collaboration with other organizations at the local, state, and national levels. El Pueblo, Inc.'s 15 board members are carefully chosen to include a wide and diverse base of interests, knowledge, skills, and experience in the community. [SOURCE: http://www.elpueblo.org/]

PUERTO RICAN ASSOCIATION FOR COMMUNITY AFFAIRS (PRACA), *see* HISPANIC YOUNG ADULT ASSOCIATION

PUERTO RICAN BUSINESSMEN ASSOCIATION

Founded in 1973 by María C. Sánchez and other activists in West Hartford, Connecticut, the Puerto Rican Businessmen Association (PRBA) served to engage the Latino community in local economic development. The efforts to organize the association came in the wake of militant confrontations led by the Puerto Rican Socialist Party* against the mayor of West Hartford as it strove to end police abuse and other violations of the civil rights of Puerto Ricans in the city. The PRBA supported the efforts but took advantage of this "softening" by more militant activists to seek business opportunities for minorities. The PBRA conducted numerous negotiations with city officials and mainstream economic institutions. [SOURCE: Torres and Velázquez, *The Puerto Rican Movement*, 80; http://www.cwhf.org/hall/sanchez/sanchez.htm]

PUERTO RICO CULTURAL CENTER OF SOUTH FLORIDA

Founded in 1999, the Puerto Rico Cultural Center of South Florida (PRCC) has as its main objective "the study, presentation, enrichment, preservation, and promotion of the values, traditions, and heritage of Puerto

Rican culture." Based in Miami, the PRCC serves the cultural interests of the Puerto Rican community in Miami-Dade, Broward, and Palm Beach Counties. The PRCC serves as the representative of the Institute of Puerto Rican Culture in South Florida. The Miami center is one of four projects established in the United States by the institute; eighty exist throughout Puerto Rico. As a consequence of this arrangement, a continuous cultural bridge exists between Puerto Rico and South Florida, enabling the PRCC to showcase Puerto Rican music, dance, cuisine, arts and crafts, and all other aspects of life in Puerto Rico. [SOURCE: http://www.centroculturalsfl.com/]

THE PUERTO RICAN FAMILY INSTITUTE, INC.
The Puerto Rican Family Institute, Inc. was founded in 1960 for the preservation of the health, well-being, and integrity of Puerto Rican and Hispanic families in the United States. Based in New York City, the Puerto Rican Family Institute's program includes social work and educational services to migrants and newly arrived immigrants, child-placement, prevention programs, and health clinics. Its services are also administered by a branch office in Rio Piedras, Puerto Rico. [SOURCE: Kanellos, "Organizations," 395.]

PUERTO RICAN FESTIVAL, INC.
The Puerto Rican Festival, Inc. in Rochester, New York, is a nonprofit organization established in 1968. The mission of the Puerto Rican Festival, the oldest and largest ethnic Latino festival in upstate New York, is to foster unity and sharing among all Americans in the Rochester area by celebrating the culture, arts, and language of the Latino community. [SOURCE: http://www.elboricua.com/Directory.html#NewYork]

PUERTO RICAN INDEPENDENCE ACTIVISTS UNDER FBI SURVEILLANCE
According to activists involved in the campaign for Puerto Rican independence, the Federal Bureau of Investigation (FBI) has for decades targeted them, as well as unionists and civil right activists, in a campaign of harassment and victimization. This became evident in the 1970s, when the FBI released documents from the Puerto Rican Senate investigation of the 1978 Cerro Maravilla* incident, in which two young independence activists were killed by Puerto Rican policemen. According to the critics of this law enforcement procedure, local government officials attempted a cover-up with the complicity of the FBI. In May 2000, FBI director Louis Freeh delivered thousands of previously classified documents to the offices of Congressman José Serrano. These 8,600 pages of files were released in response to Serrano's concern over the massive opposition among Puerto Ricans, both on the island and the mainland, to U.S. military target practice in Vieques, Puerto

Rico, and the campaign for the release of pro-independence political prisoners. The documents also revealed Washington's war against the independence movement.

Also in May 2000, the FBI released to Congressman José Serrano previously classified files dealing with law enforcement malfeasance. A *New York Daily News* reporter reviewed the papers and discovered that the FBI had been engaged since 1936 in surveillance and repression of pro-independence elements. The focus of the surveillance was the Puerto Rico Nationalist Party, and in particular Pedro Albizu Campos,* the party's central leader. The documents show A. Cecil Snyder, the U.S. District Attorney in Puerto Rico, writing to inform J. Edgar Hoover, the FBI director, that Albizu Campos had published "articles insulting the United States" and delivered "speeches in favor of independence." According to Snyder, Albizu Campos might have been the author of bombings of U.S. government buildings. That same year, FBI agents arrested Albizu Campos and other Nationalist Party leaders on charges of conspiring to overthrow the U.S. government. Albizu Campos was sentenced to 15 years amid counter charges that he and his companions had been framed.

The files reveal that the FBI even had Luis Muñoz Marín,* the first elected governor of Puerto Rico, under surveillance for more than 20 years. An early advocate of independence, Muñoz Marín founded the Popular Democratic Party, which helped Washington push through the present form of colonial rule, known as commonwealth status.

In the 1960s and 1970s, the Puerto Rican independence movement often merged with the civil rights struggle waged by urban activists in such cities as New York, Philadelphia, and Chicago. The FBI's Cointelpro program, launched in this period, sought to disrupt struggles against police brutality, the movement against drafting Puerto Ricans into the U.S. Army, the fight against the U.S. Navy's occupation of the Puerto Rican islands of Culebra and Vieques, and union struggles. [SOURCE: Stone, "Files Detail FBI's War on Puerto Rican Independence Fight," *The Militant,* 64/23 (12 June 2000), www.themilitant.com/2000/6423/642351.html]

PUERTO RICAN LEGAL DEFENSE AND EDUCATION FUND

Incorporated in February 1972 in New York City, the Puerto Rican Legal Defense and Education Fund (PRLDEF) has emerged as a major advocate for the Puerto Rican Community of the United States in securing the protection of its civil rights throughout the United States. The effectiveness of the PRLDEF ranks with that of the NAACP's Legal Defense and Educational Fund (NAACPLDEF) and the Mexican American Legal Defense and Educational Fund (MALDEF).* PRLDEF remains committed to its original objectives, shown below, that were established in the 1972-1973 era of its founding.

- To provide high quality legal representation for the Puerto Rican community at large in order to secure fair an equal protection of the law and of the civil rights of Puerto Ricans.
- To promote legal education and information among Puerto Ricans in order to increase the number of Puerto Rican lawyers serving the community, and to make Puerto Ricans aware of their legal rights.

PRLDEF has not established regional offices outside of New York, but since its founding the fund has litigated landmark cases with profound ramifications for Latinos in Chicago, Pennsylvania, Connecticut, and New Jersey. The first suit initiated by PRLDEF came in the *ASPIRA v. Board of Education*,* which forced the New York City Board of Education to recognize and address the special needs of non-English-speaking students in 1974. PRLDEF joined MALDEF and other litigants by offering amicus curiae (friend of the court) briefs in opposing the *Bakke v. University of California* (1978),* which claimed reverse discrimination suits and endangered affirmative action gains made since the 1960s. The fund also engages in advocacy for improving conditions critical to the situation of Puerto Ricans in education, employment, voting rights, housing, and leadership development. The innovative efforts of the legal education division have produced increasing numbers of Puerto Rican public interest lawyers. Developing a base of committed legal professionals will ensure that the work of defending Puerto Ricans against discriminatory practices will continue. PRLDEF publishes the *Civil Rights Litigation* newsletter. [SOURCE: http://www.prldef.org; Kanellos, "Organizations," 395.]

PUERTO RICAN NATIONALIST ATTACK ON CONGRESS

Puerto Rican nationalists, frustrated at their inability to gain recognition and support for the movement for Puerto Rican independence from the United States, committed one of the first acts of political terrorism when they attacked the U.S. Congress on March 1, 1954. The nationalists, headed by Lolita Lebrón, attacked the U.S. House of Representatives in order to bring national attention to the colonial status of Puerto Rico. Five congressmen were shot. Lebrón and her followers, including Ramón Cancel Miranda, Irving Flores, and Oscar Collazo, were arrested, tried, and convicted. Lebrón subsequently spent 25 years in federal prison without recanting and became a heroine and martyr of the independence movement to the present. [SOURCE: Kanellos, *Hispanic Firsts*, 122.]

PUERTO RICAN PARADE IN FLORIDA

The first Puerto Rican parade in Florida was held in the Tampa area in April 1988. The event, now held every fourth Sunday of April, is organized by an incorporated group headquartered in Lutz. The committee considers the annual Parade and Folklore Festival, which is celebrated in the National Historic District of Ybor City, to be a crucial activity that develops and promotes awareness of Puerto Rican culture, identity, and national pride. The one-day event attracts thousands of people every year and continues to provide a forum for practitioners of Puerto Rican art and culture. [SOURCE: http://www.puertoricoculturalparade.com]

PUERTO RICAN PARADE OF FAIRFIELD COUNTY

Puerto Rican community leaders organized the first Puerto Rican Parade of Fairfield County, Connecticut, in 1995. Forming a committee in Bridgeport to continue this important event, the group, in addition to fielding the annual parade in July, is also committed to the conservation of Puerto Rican culture and to providing outlets for community youth to express Puerto Rican pride though activities such as the Mr. and Miss Puerto Rico pageants. Moreover, the group also sponsors art contests and other cultural activities. [SOURCE: www.prparadeffldcty.org]

PUERTO RICAN POLITICAL PRISONERS

On September 11, 1999, President Bill Clinton gave clemency to 11 members of a Puerto Rican nationalist group after they vowed to renounce terrorism. The act sparked a political backlash in Washington and threatened the bid of first lady, Hillary Clinton, for a U.S. Senate seat from New York. The president offered to release five others, but they rejected the offer. Instead, two were offered reduced prison terms and the remaining three had their fines reduced. The 16 nationalists had been in prison since the early 1980s, when they were convicted of seditious conspiracy in connection with the activities of the Puerto Rican independence organization, Fuerzas Armadas para la Liberación Nacional (Armed Forces for National Liberation), which was allegedly responsible for 130 bombings in the late 1970s and early 1980s. Eight of the released nationalists were also convicted of weapons charges after they were arrested in a stolen van in Evanston, Illinois in 1980. They were charged with the armed robbery of a car rental agency in Evanston and with plotting yet another robbery. Other than the charges of sedition, none of those granted clemency had been convicted of crimes that resulted in death or injuries. In Chicago, where most of the freed prisoners had lived before their incarceration, a celebration was held, to the consternation of Mayor Richard M. Daley and police officials who had been highly critical of the president's act of clemency. After public protests from New

York City Mayor Rudolph W. Giuliani, who also had designs on the Senate as a Republican opponent of Mrs. Clinton, the First Lady called the president to rescind his clemency offer. The move infuriated some Hispanic leaders in New York, inlcuding U.S. Representative José E. Serrano, Democrat from the Bronx. Some activists who had militated for the prisoners' freedom, while happy they were released, nonetheless criticized the harsh terms imposed by the clemency. The 11 were barred from associating with anyone with a criminal record, had their travel restricted, and were prohibited from participating in political movements advocating Puerto Rican independence. The 11 released were:

- Edwin Cortés, 44, arrested in 1983 at the age of 28, sentenced to 35 years in prison
- Elizam Escobar, 51, arrested in 1980 at the age of 32, sentenced to 68 years, a renowned artist
- Ricardo Jimenez, 43, arrested in 1980 at the age of 24, sentenced to 98 years
- Adolfo Matos, 48, arrested in 1980 at the age of 29, sentenced to 78 years, related to a Puerto Rican nationalist who assassinated a U.S. military governor after the 1937 massacre of independence supporters in Ponce
- Dylcia Pagán, 52, arrested in 1980 at the age of 33, sentenced to 63 years, a television producer and editor of *El Tiempo* newspaper.
- Alberto Rodríguez, 46, arrested in 1983 at the age of 30, sentenced to 35 years
- Alicia Rodríguez, 44, arrested in 1980 at the age of 26, sentenced to 85 years
- Ida Luz Rodríguez, her sister, 49, arrested in 1980 at the age of 30, sentenced to 83 years
- Luis Rosa, 39, arrested in 1980 at the age of 19, sentenced to 105 years
- Alejandrina Torres, 60, arrested in 1983 at the age of 44, mother of five children, sentenced to 35 years
- Carmen Valentín, 53, arrested in 1980 at the age of 34, sentenced to 98 years

[SOURCE: Johnson, "Puerto Ricans Clinton Freed Leave Prisons," *The New York Times* (11 September 1999), www.jonathanpollard.org/1999/091199.html; Nebbia and McLaughlin, "Puerto Rican Nationalists to Be Released after Two Decades in Prison," World Socialist Web Site (9 September 1999), http://www.wsws.org]

PUERTO RICAN RIOTS OF 1966

As Puerto Ricans in Chicago celebrated the Puerto Rican Parade on June 12, 1966, a police incident occurred that provoked hundreds of Puerto Rican youths to go on a rampage, breaking windows and burning down many of the businesses in their neighborhoods. Setting off the upheaval was the shooting of a young Puerto Rican man by Chicago police. The rioting, which continued until June 14, became a crucial event in the history of Chicago's Puerto Ricans, drawing attention to strained relations between Puerto Ricans and Chicago's police and the urban blight and poverty that characterized their life in Chicago. A month later, the meaning of the riot was taken up by the Chicago Commission on Human Relations, an open forum for Puerto Rican and other Spanish-speaking residents of Chicago to discuss issues such as housing discrimination, employment practices by the police and fire departments, and inadequate education in public schools. Because of the disturbances, Puerto Rican leaders recognized the urgency of confronting these problems and creating such organizations as the Spanish Action Committee of Chicago, the Latin American Defense Organization and, in the early 1970s, ASPIRA* and the Ruiz Belvis Cultural Center. [SOURCE: http://www.encyclopedia.chicagohistory.org/pages/1027.html]

PUERTO RICAN SELF DETERMINATION UNITED NATIONS RESOLUTION

The right of the Puerto Rican people to decide their own future as a nation was approved by the United Nations. In 1973, the United Nations officially recognized Puerto Rico as a colony of the United States. This finding by the United Nations was of great support to the independence movement on the island and in the United States. [SOURCE: Kanellos, *Chronology of Hispanic American History*, 259.]

PUERTO RICAN SOCIALIST PARTY

The Puerto Rican Socialist Party (PSP) was formed in New York City in the 1960s as the stateside extension of Movimiento para la Independencia,* a group established in Puerto Rico in 1959. Although PSP leadership was comprised mainly of former student and youth activists, the party acquired an extensive working-class membership. PSP's primary objective was to attract Puerto Ricans on the mainland to support the independence of Puerto Rico. By the mid-1970s, the party saw that the key to party growth was increasing its activity in promoting the civil rights of Puerto Ricans in the United States and not solely limiting itself to gaining adherents to the cause of independence for Puerto Rico. As consequence, the PSP turned to the issues of migrant workers, police brutality, housing, welfare rights, student struggles, environmental racism, and trade union democracy. [SOURCE: To-rres and Velázquez, *The Puerto Rican Movement*, 49-53.]

PUERTO RICAN SOCIALIST PARTY CONGRESS

In April 1973, the first meeting of the U.S. branch of the Puerto Rican Socialist Party (PSP), was inaugurated in New York City and attended by three thousand people. At the congress, the PSP announced its intention to become a part of U.S. political history. With the formation of a franchise on the mainland, the PSP had departed from other island independence movements by addressing the social and political struggles of Puerto Ricans in the United States. [SOURCE: Torres and Velázquez, *The Puerto Rican Movement*, 126-127.]

PUERTO RICAN STUDENT ACTIVITIES

In the late 1960s members of Puerto Rican Student Activities (PRISA) emerged as key players in the struggle for open admissions and Puerto Rican Studies at City College, then considered the flagship of the City University of New York. The group entered into coalitions with Black students of the Onyx Society in order to achieve wider objectives for racial minorities on the campus. [SOURCE: Torres and Velázquez, *The Puerto Rican Movement*, 126.]

PUERTO RICAN STUDENT UNION

The Puerto Rican Student Union (PRSU) was the most vital Puerto Rican student group of the1960s and early 1970s. It branched out from New York City to campuses throughout the Northeast. In 1970, the PRSU established community offices in the South Bronx and in East Harlem in an effort to expand its activism beyond student concerns. In 1970, the group joined the Young Lords and sponsored the the first national conference of Puerto Rican students. The PRSU became a forceful influence among all U.S. student movements and promoted the cause of Puerto Rican independence. In the arena of higher education, the PRSU promoted a culturally relevant curriculum as well as admission and retention services for Puerto Ricans and other Latinos. Ultimately, the organization served as a catalyst in the creation of Puerto Rican Studies departments. The group began to decline, some say because of its very close relationship with the Young Lords Party. Despite substantial opposition from some members, PRSU merged with the Young Lords in 1972. [SOURCE: Torres and Velázquez, *The Puerto Rican Movement*, 137-139.]

PUERTO RICAN WEEK FESTIVAL

Philadelphia's annual Puerto Rican Week Festival (Festival Puertorriqueño de Filadelfia) was held for the first time in 1964. Sponsored by the city's Council of Spanish Speaking Organizations, the festival has since grown to include a full week of activities surrounding the celebration of Puerto Rican Day (the last Sunday of September). Among the festivities are a grand parade, banquet, Miss Puerto Rico-Philadelphia pageant, a mini-Olympics, Latino music and dance programs, and speeches focusing on the goals and needs of Philadelphia's Hispanic community. [SOURCE: http://www.balchinstitute.org/manuscript_guide/html/puertoricanwkfest.html]

QUE NADA NOS DETENGA (LET NOTHING STOP US)

The Puerto Rico Federal Affairs Administration's non-partisan registration project, Que Nada Nos Detenga (Let Nothing Stop Us) expected to register 300,000 new voters before September 30, 2005. The initiative was started by Puerto Rican Governor Sila M. Calderón's administration to empower a Puerto Rican population that has grown four times faster in the United States than in Puerto Rico between 1991 and 2004. The project, which operates with 400 workers, has as a primary objective to educate Puerto Ricans on how to impact elections on the local and national level. The success of this project would provide Puerto Ricans with a greater voice in such states as Florida, where their impact has not been felt as much as that of other Latinos. An essential advantage that Puerto Ricans have over other Latinos is that they are all citizens, both on the island and on the mainland and are eligible to vote as soon as they arrive from the Island. [SOURCE: Ortiz, "Puerto Rican Factor."]

RACIAL CONFLICT—UNITED STATES/MEXICO BORDER

Mexico's proximity to the United States has obliged Anglo Americans to live close to an often incompatible culture along one of the longest borders between any two nations. This closeness has bred some affinity, but offensive and defensive forms of contempt have at times characterized relations between the two peoples. Historians have pointed to numerous examples in which Mexicans were cast as undesirables because of their Indian features.

Beginning with the initial contacts with Mexicans in the nineteenth century along the U.S.-Mexico frontiers, Anglo Americans reacted negatively. A primary reason for the reaction was the race contempt that Anglo Americans held for the mixed race Mexicans. During the process of annexation of northern Mexican territories after the War of 1846, these original misgivings exacerbated. In addition, Anglo Americans arriving in what became the U.S. Southwest claimed a "Manifest Destiny"* to live in the conquered territories and saw native Mexicans as foreigners.

The relationship between Anglos and Mexicans continued to evolve within a competitive milieu in trade, mining, and land tenure. Control of Mexican labor by Anglos, while not having the priority of later years, also propagated discord. A major justice issue for U.S. Hispanic citizens was their inability to understand court proceedings conducted in English. Albeit not as tragic as lynching and police brutality, lack of interpreters was more common and as unfortunate. In California courts, Hispanics found justice difficult to come by because there were few Spanish-speaking lawyers. It was not until 1872 that the first Mexican-American lawyer started practicing in Los Angeles. Some communities in Texas during the 1880s still allowed court proceedings to be conducted in Spanish and impaneled Mexican-American jurors who did not speak English. Such privileges were limited, however, to border areas, where Mexicans managed a modicum of political control. In the rest of Texas, an 1856 law prohibiting Spanish in the courts was vigorously enforced.

During the late nineteenth century, border smuggling and banditry engendered a perception that Mexicans were lawless. Although Anglo outlaws were plentiful, Mexican outlaws provoked the greatest indignation. Vigilante committees administered summary justice to all criminals, regardless of race or ethnic background but to a disproportionate number of Mexicans. In nineteenth-century Arizona, few Mexicans served on juries. They were disproportionately sentenced to jail and given longer sentences than Anglos.

Legal mistreatment affected Mexicans more in central Arizona, where they settled at the same time as Anglos in the 1860s after the U.S. acquired the Southwest. The population of the Salt River Valley (the Phoenix area) increased five-fold during the 1870s, and many Anglo newcomers did not share the more benign view of Mexicans held by white settlers in the previous decade. A depression stalling the Arizona economy coincided with the influx of newcomers, making for acute competition. The slightest hint of Mexican wrongdoing was met with severe punishment. Vigilante committees sprang up to deal with Mexican banditry and a number of Mexicans were lynched.

Arizona also experienced border problems, leading to the formation of its own version of the better known Texas Rangers.* The Arizona Rangers were organized at the turn of the century, like their Texas counterparts, to curtail smugglers and cattle rustlers, most of whom were Mexicans.

California also experienced ethnic violence between Anglos and Latin Americans, especially during the intense competition of the Gold Rush. A rash of lynchings, murders, and expulsions sparked legends of Mexican bandits who only preyed on Anglo-American oppressors. Competition for land and trade precipitated other struggles that account for the disproportionate number of lynching of minorities in both Arizona and California during the Depression of the 1870s.

Anglo-motivated economic changes in New Mexico resulted in small wars, fueled by land disputes where Hispanics tried to stem encroaching development by sabotaging such symbols of change as railroads, farm machinery, ranch fences, and Anglo farmsteads. Ethnic antagonism, however, was not as intense as in other southwestern communities, where Hispanics wielded significant legal and economic influence. When clashes occurred, they were motivated as much by class differences among Mexicans as by ethnic cleavages.

Nineteenth-century Texas, with the largest Mexican population and the longest border with Mexico, experienced the greatest ethnic discord, stemming mainly from border conflict and property competition. The region between the Nueces and the Rio Grande rivers was plagued by warfare after Texas won independence in 1836. For example, the Cart War of 1857* started when Anglo freighters, frustrated because Tejanos (Texas-born Mexicans) dominated trade routes in central Texas, hired gunslingers to drive out the Mexicans. Mexican banditry angered Anglos more than anything else. Brigands easily crossed the Rio Grande to Mexico if conditions became "too hot" because of retaliatory Anglo rampages. Texas Rangers zealously suppressed local bandits and Mexicans who struck from across the Rio Grande. In Texas, the lynching of Mexicans increased during and immediately after the Civil War, primarily in South and West Texas, and did not abate until the end of the century. Mexicans and blacks were singled out for the most abusive treatment.

In spite of resistance to Anglo domination and a marked reluctance on the part of Anglo Americans to incorporate Mexicans into daily life and culture, an uneasy symbiosis evolved in which the two groups cooperated at different social and economic levels. Upper-class Mexicans in the Southwest, for example, often intermarried with Anglo newcomers. Moreover, throughout the Southwest, Mexicans served in all law enforcement capacities wherever Mexicans voters retained majorities. Southwest Mexicans also managed to obtain key positions in local governments, which benefitted Mexicans dealing with the mainstream Anglo society.

As a consequence, the racial animosity that began early in the nineteenth century, while showing some signs of abatement as the century came to an end, was resurrected as more and more Anglos settled along the long contiguous border with Mexico.

The arrangement between Mexican and Anglos eroded in the twentieth century after modernization reduced the jobs available for Mexican immigrants to the lowest types of manual labor. Generally, the only white Americans desiring immigrants were employers who tolerated Mexicans as a necessary evil, to be manipulated, and persuaded to return to their country when their labor was unnecessary. The flood of Mexican immigration, however, caught Anglo Americans and their institutions off guard. The rapport with Southwest Hispanics was not adequate for interacting with landless laborers from Mexico who engulfed southwestern *barrios* by the turn of the century. The newcomers were not only extremely poor but often illiterate and perceived as darker than Hispanic natives of the Southwest. Moreover, to the chagrin of immigrant elites, many Anglo Americans did not discern that some immigrants were also middle-class and white. [SOURCE: Rosales, *Pobre Raza!* 1-8; Gutiérrez, *Walls and Mirrors.*]

RACIAL CONSTRUCTION OF LATINOS

As the study of anthropology became formalized in the late nineteenth century, scholars began to stipulate racial categories by phenotype and body shape. As a consequence, all human beings were placed into three main races: Mongoloid, Caucasoid, and Negro. These classifications alone did not espouse racism; i.e., the belief that some races have less desirable physical and intellectual traits than others. The study of eugenics, an early examination of human heredity, attributed superior or inferior characteristics to the genes of the racial groups. Since the eugenicists were European, they concluded that Caucasoid people possessed the most positive attributes. However, some scholars today view racism as a social construction, where the dominant society can racialize undesirable groups, not only because of their physical attributes. For example, in the late nineteenth century, "new immigrants" (southern and eastern Europeans) and their descendants were looked upon with racist disdain, as John Higham pointed out in his classic book on immigration, *Strangers in the Land*. Nonetheless, this racialization changed considerably in the post-World War II period, when the descendants of the "new immigrants" assimilated and acquired economic parity.

This phenomenon has led to another type of analysis, usually described as "Whiteness" studies. Noel Ignatiev in his book, *How the Irish Became White*, describes how the Irish, after being colonized and repressed unmercifully by English imperialism, were racially stereotyped as backward, primitive, savage, barbarian, and papist. In the United States, this continued, but the Irish survived tenaciously by gaining political ground and by organizing unions. Once Irish immigrants and their children captured municipal posts and union leadership, they tried to exclude southern and eastern Europeans from union jobs, from public service positions, and government jobs, a strategy that was at best, a holding pattern. As the other groups, who at one time had been left behind attained economic and class mobility, then phenotype and body shape allowed these formerly despised groups to achieve the preferred racial status. By claiming whiteness, the Irish and the new immigrants could permanently relegate black people to a racial apartheid and concurrently remove a significant competitive group from the avenues of working-class mobility.

So is the construction of Hispanics as a race apart very much different from that of other ethnic groups who were also not very well received? Indeed, antipathy in the United States towards Hispanics has a longer history than is the case for "new immigrants," who have largely assimilated and acquired economic parity. An early source of antipathy towards Hispanics is found in the "Spanish Black Legend."* In order to discredit the reputation of the rival Spanish Empire in the sixteenth-century, English and Dutch propagandists maintained centuries-long campaigns discrediting the Spanish, including such strategies as translating Bartolomé de las Casas' writings that detailed the atrocities visited by conquering Spaniards on the Native Americans. Consequently, Anglo Americans held predisposed negative views of Hispanics in the nineteenth century during imperialistic forays into Mexico's frontiers or into Central America and the Caribbean.

During the process of annexation and conquest of what became the U.S. Southwest, Anglo Americans competed with Mexicans, who owned vast tracts of land, mined expertly for precious metals, and dominated much of the transportation systems. In addition, Anglos despised the "racial" mixture of northern Mexicans, deeming it a mongrelization of the lowest order. After the takeover, many Americans wanted to annex even more territory, but not everyone relished the thought of having to rule over such a large number of non-white peoples. After thoroughly discrediting the Mexican racial pedigree, Anglos justified the often violent methods used to dislodge them from their holdings.

In the Caribbean, thousands of African slaves were imported to work the large sugar plantations, a process that assured Americans would eventually view most Caribbean people as racially different. The United States supported anti-slavery movements in both Cuba and Puerto Rico, but looming darkly behind the whole liberation cause were North American economic and political interests. Before the Civil War, southerners wanted to annex Cuba, but anti-slavery interests in the United States thwarted any such plans. Significantly, opposition to annexation existed among Americans who did not want to add a large number of blacks to those already living in the country. In Cuba, Puerto Rico, and the Dominican Republic, persons with a strong African racial heritage endured racism from those with a Spanish background or from lighter mulattos (mixed Spanish and African). As shall be seen below, when Caribbeans migrated the United States, being lighter did not protect mulattos from extreme prejudice.

Hispanics have also taken their turn at attempting to become white. In the early twentieth century, Cuban whites, blacks, and mulattos sailed the short distance from their island home to Tampa, Florida, mainly to work in the cigar industry. While they made racial distinctions among themselves, Jim Crow laws of Florida forced them to live separately. The descendants of these immigrants either became part of Black America or achieved whiteness and more acceptance. Similarly, the first wave of Cuban migrants who fled the 1959 revolution was largely white, middle, and upper class, professional, and educated, traits making them more acceptable than other Latin American immigrants. In time, many Cuban Americans integrated themselves into south Florida socially, economically, and politically. This changed in 1980, when Fidel Castro* allowed 125,000 immigrants known as *marielitos** to leave the island from Mariel Harbor. The new arrivals reflected more the general racial and class composition of Cuba than those already in the United States: many more were blacks and mulattos. Unfortunately, adding to the racial stigma, Americans and even some Cuban Americans uncritically believed that most of these refugees were political and social misfits. Such a notion stigmatized the *marielitos*, who were in the main normal, hardworking Cubans. Moreover, the new arrivals were not welcomed as warmly as previous arrivals. Thousands were put in "temporary camps," where their stay stretched out into months, even years.

Modern immigration from Mexico, which constitutes the longest sustained influx (1890s-present) into the United States of any group, brought a racially mixed cohort. The majority of Mexicans, perhaps 60 percent, are mestizos (mixed European and Indian, with some African). Twenty percent are European, and the remainder are indigenous natives. Mainly mestizos came to the United States during this elongated influx, but sprinkled among the 40 million who have entered during the twentieth century are a few white Mexicans. Unlike Cubans, few Mexicans were accepted as white throughout all of this period. However, southwest Hispanic natives were by degree more acceptable racially than Mexicans who immigrated to modern labor sectors after 1890. Southwest Mexicans, who traced their roots to before the Anglo takeover, in the late nineteenth century attempted to distance themselves from Mexican immigrants, a process aided by Anglo American attitudes. A November 1926, editorial in the *New York Times* warned about dangers of an unregulated inflow from Mexico. It stated that there were two kinds of Mexicans in the United States: the old stock with more Spanish blood, thus desirable by American standards, and newer immigrants, more visibly Indian. Fortunately, said the *Times*, these latter tended to return to Mexico. As a consequence, the southwestern Mexicans attempted to claim whiteness by separating themselves from the newcomers.

Mexican immigrants and their descendants also attempted to be classified as white or at least to separate themselves from blacks. It became obvious to U.S. Mexicans, even in the immigrant era, that if they were to be classified as colored, it could result in *de jure* segregation and exclusion from the opportunity structure. Mexican Americans successfully obtained official white status in the 1940 census, but that did not end their non-whiteness in the eyes of most Americans.

The majority of Puerto Rican inhabitants are mainly a mixture of African and Spanish. As in Cuba, lighter skin accompanied by higher class status allowed mulattos to mix on a fairly equal basis with the smaller number of more European Puerto Ricans. Poor blacks were marginalized, to be sure, but so were some poor whites known as *jíbaros*. On the U.S. mainland, however, black Puerto Ricans and mulattos found it even more difficult to achieve white status than mestizo Mexicans. Similarly, light Puerto Ricans—some with no African or Indian genes—have been able to distinguish themselves from their darker brethren. This has been a point of great contention among Puerto Ricans in the United States with strong African racial characteristics, who suffer a great deal more discrimination than their lighter counterparts.

But all Latinos in the United States have been racialized, so that other marginalized groups can progress. In Texas, poor whites who worked alongside Mexicans in agriculture became their most ardent persecutors and attempted to gain favor with employers by promoting their whiteness. In California, Asian, and Mexican farmworkers, two racialized ethnic groups, united when faced with Anglo-American discrimination and extremely unfair labor exploitation during the early twentieth century. During the 1930s, Mexicans competed with Dust Bowl refugees, known as "Okies," a despised group of white Americans, who attempted to employ their whiteness to gain advantage.

In Eastern seaboard cities, the children of the new immigrants subjected Puerto Ricans to a non-white status and excluded them from attaining the lean working-class privileges they themselves had attained. This often occurred through violence, as happened in the Harlem Riots* of 1926, when Puerto Ricans were attacked by their neighbors, mainly of Italian and Irish stock. The massive influx of Puerto Ricans intensified during and after World War II, a phenomenon that was also met with racist hostility by the white working class. In Chicago and Hartford in the 1960s, the frustrations caused by years of poverty, second-class status, under-representation, and police brutality led to intensive rioting in the Puerto Rican communities.

A final question is can any of these Latino groups become white as did "new immigrants" and their offspring? The case of Cubans has already been addressed; if *marielitos* had not arrived, Cubans would have successfully reached the precipice of whiteness. Perhaps it is unnecessarily heuristic to speculate what would have happened if Mexican immigration had halted, as it did for new immigrants. Would they have succeeded in becoming white? As has been stated above, theorists of whiteness proclaim that it is not necessary to possess a Caucasian phenotype to achieve that status. For example, because of the inordinate success of many Asians, some scholars are proclaiming that they have achieved whiteness. But considering the great hostility shown recent immigrants from Mexico, it is difficult to imagine that Mexicans will not continue to be racialized. In fact, because of massive immigration, most Latin Americans in the United States, regardless of their origin, will be stigmatized as a colored race. [SOURCE: Almaguer, *Racial Fault Lines;* Horsman, *Race and Manifest Destiny*; Gutiérrez, *Walls and Mirrors*; Sánchez Korrol, *From Colonia to Community*; Masud-Piloto, *From Welcomed Exiles to Illegal Immigrants.*]

RAMÍREZ, FRANCISCO P. (1837-1908)

Born in Los Angeles in 1837, publisher-editorialist Francisco P. Ramírez created a landmark in awareness that Hispanics in California were being treated as a race apart from Euro-Americans. In 1855, when only seventeen years old, he took the Spanish section from the *Los Angeles Star* and founded a separate newspaper. Ramírez is credited with proposing that Mexican people in California be referred to with the term "La Raza." Ramírez was from the outset a partisan of Mexicans' learning the English language, of California statehood, and of the United States Constitution; however, his indignation grew as the civil and property rights of Californios were not protected by the Constitution that he loved so much. He became a consistent and assiduous critic, attempting to inspire Hispanics to unite in their own defense and to spur the authorities to protect the Hispanic residents of California. Ramírez became more bitter as time progressed, at times calling democracy a "lynchocracy" and advising Hispanics to aban-don California; in 1859, he took his own advice and closed his newspaper, *El Clamor Público* (The Public Outcry), down. Ramírez emigrated to Ures, Sonora, Mexico, where he continued working as a journalist and publisher. But in 1862, he returned to California to work as a journalist and editor in San Francisco and Los Angeles, where he espoused a pan-Hispanism, to reflect the increasing diversity of California's Latin American population. After experiencing some difficulties with his employers, he turned to the law and then to politics. He ran unsuccessfully for the state legislature on the Republican ticket. Ramírez fled Los Angeles after

Francisco P. Ramírez

being charged with fraud and returned to Sonora. He lived out his final years in Ensenada, Baja California, where he worked as a lawyer until his death in 1908. [SOURCE: Kanellos, *Hispanic Periodicals in the United States*, 88-89, 99, 165; Gutiérrez, "Francisco P. Ramírez: Californio Editor and Yanqui Conquest," http://www.freedomforum.org/publications/msj/courage.summer2000/y03.html]

RAMOS ÁVALOS, JORGE (1958-)

Born in Mexico City, Jorge Ramos Ávalos is today one of the United States' most noted television reporters and syndicated columnists. Presently, he serves as the main anchor for Noticias Univisión, a program produced through the auspices of Univisión television network, which has numerous outlets throughout the United States and Latin America. After finishing his first degree at the Universidad Iberoamericana in Mexico City in 1981, Ramos worked as a journalist in his native Mexico, but in 1983 he immigrated to Los Angeles, where he worked in menial jobs until obtaining his first news position with station KMEX, the Los Angeles affiliate of Univisión. Continuing with the network, he moved to Miami, Florida, in 1986, where he eventually rose to anchor the main news at the national level. While in Los Angeles, he attended the University of California Los Angeles and in 1987 received an M.A. in International Studies from the University of Miami. In the course of his career, Ramos, has interviewed some of the world's most salient leaders: Fidel Castro,* Bill Clinton, George H.W. Bush and George W. Bush, Vicente Fox, Hugo Chávez, Octavio Paz, Ernesto Zedillo, Sub-commander Marcos, and many others. Univisión has assigned him to cover the most crucial historical events of the last few years. Ramos has published six books in both Spanish and English, in which he posits his support for the rights of Latinos and immigrants. Presently he lives in Miami. [SOURCE: http://en.wikipedia.org/wiki/Jorge_Ramos]

LA RAZA SEVEN see MISSION DISTRICT

LA RAZA LAWYERS OF CALIFORNIA

La Raza Lawyers of California was organized in 1977 as a nonprofit association to support Chicano and Latino Lawyers in California by providing umbrella services to a statewide network of 16 different local affiliates. The organization holds quarterly meetings at various locations around the state and provides more than 2,000 attorneys with professional development programs and legal intelligence that will enhance their ability to function effectively in the legal arena. The coalescing of this large core of legal talent generates a political energy that allows the organization to advocate for Latinos and promote greater equality for them in the justice system. [SOURCE: http://www.larazalawyers.net]

LA RAZA UNIDA PARTY

One of the most significant third-party movements in the history of the United States began in Texas. After José Angel Gutiérrez* and other Mexican American Youth Organization (MAYO)* members led a strike at the Crystal City High School in South Texas, protesting discrimination towards Mexican-American students, the group formed La Raza Unida Party (LRUP) and won five positions on the city council and school board in the April election of 1970. That same year, voters put LRUP candidates in Hidalgo, Zavala, Dimmit, and La Salle county offices. By the Spring of 1970, Chicano activists from outside Texas were greatly impressed with the achievements they saw in Texas, a factor catapulting the LRUP, MAYO, and Gutiérrez into national prominence.

At the LRUP convention in October of 1971 in San Antonio, delegates decided to field candidates in state-level races, such as the governorship. The party selected as gubernatorial candidate in 1972 Ramsey Muñiz,* a Waco lawyer. Because of pressure from the LRUP woman's caucus, Alma Canales

José Angel Gutiérrez at La Raza Unida Party meeting in Chicago

from Edingburg was asked to run for lieutenant governor. In the primary elections, the LRUP drew away enough Mexican-American voters from the Democrats that conservative Dolph Briscoe* defeated Frances "Sissy" Farenthold, a liberal.

By now, the LRUP concept had spread to other areas in such states as Arizona, California, New Mexico, Illinois, Wisconsin, and Nebraska. But Corky Gonzales* and the Crusade for Justice* in Colorado showed the greatest amount of enthusiasm. His vision of the LRUP was to take it nationwide and not to cooperate with either the Democratic nor Republican parties. The Colorado LRUP in 1970 ran candidates for state offices, but they all lost by huge margins. In 1971, Raúl Ruiz, publisher of *La Raza* in Los Angeles, lost his race as a LRUP candidate for the California Assembly but forced the Mexican American Democrat, Richard Altorre, into run-off election with the Republican candidate, which Altorre lost. In 1972, Corky Gonzales finalized plans for El Congreso de Aztlán, a LRUP national convention, to be held in El Paso in September. The most important issue at the Congreso became whether the pragmatic José Angel Gutiérrez from Texas and one of the first Chicanos to run under the party banner, or the ideological Gonzales would be elected party chairman. Gutiérrez won, provoking a bitter split that could not be bridged by any number of overtures for unity; the national Chicano party initiative was stillborn.

The convention was held while LRUP candidates were campaigning for office in their respective states. Raúl Ruiz and his LRUP cohorts returned to Los Angeles from El Paso, hoping to derail the election of another Mexican-American Democrat, Alex García, to the state assembly. But García defeated him resoundingly in the predominantly Mexican-American district. In 1974, a LRUP candidate tried to enter the gubernatorial race but failed to get enough signatures to qualify. That same year, the LRUP led a failed attempt to incorporate East Los Angeles as a separate city.

In Texas in 1972, the LRUP returned to the statewide campaign of Ramsey Muñiz for governor. Muñiz received six percent of the vote, giving Dolph Briscoe's Republican opponent a victory. LRUP activists then returned to organizing in South Texas and the Winter Garden area, where the party won a record number of local elections. These triumphs encouraged the LRUP to again run Ramsey Muñiz as the gubernatorial candidate in 1974, but he did not even duplicate the 1972 role of spoiler in the general election because Briscoe, who ran again as a Democrat, won handily.

After this defeat, Muñiz was arrested in 1976 on charges of narcotics trafficking—an incident that dealt a severe blow to the prestige of the LRUP. Regional leaders tried to maintain local power bases but only Gutiérrez succeeded in remaining a political boss in Zavala County. In 1978, Mario Compeán ran for governor and received less than two percent of the total votes cast. The Republican Bill Clements won against a Democratic liberal, John Hill. In the meantime, disaffected LRUP members in Zavala County formed a breakaway faction and voted José Angel Gutiérrez out of power; in 1982, he left electoral politics for good.

In the rest of the country, the LRUP also died a slow, painful death. After violent clashes with the Denver police department, Crusade for Justice membership declined so precipitously that the organization almost folded. In California, former members turned to Marxist politics or returned to the traditional parties. After 1978, Juan José Peña from New Mexico attempted to keep the fires burning, at times almost alone. [SOURCE: Navarro, *La Raza Unida*.]

REDONDO, ANTONIO (1875-1937)

Antonio Redondo was one of the most active Mexican-American newspapermen in the first half of the twentieth century in both Arizona and California. Born in Altar, Sonora, in 1875, he immigrated to Tucson in 1887. There, he worked as an apprentice in *El Fronterizo,* one of Arizona's first Spanish-language newspapers, published by the Sonoran-born Carlos Y. Velásquez, one of the founders of the Alianza Hispano-Americana (The Hispanic American Alliance).* He also worked for the *Tucson Citizen* as a printer and editor. In 1899, he launched his own newspaper, *El Siglo XX*. He later moved to Phoenix, where he married Luisa Parra and wrote for *El Mensajero*. In 1920, he moved to Los Angeles and took charge of the Spanish section of the *Los Angeles Record* and concurrently served as the Los Angeles correspondent for *El Tucsonense*, Arizona's premier Spanish-language daily, published between 1915 and 1957. In his columns, Redondo advocated political and civil rights activism for Mexicans in the United States. Dismayed by the disproportionate numbers of Mexicans executed in the 1920s, Antonio Redondo became an ardent spokesperson against capital punishment, often using classic arguments of French and English writers of the previous two centuries to argue against this ultimate punishment. In the 1920s, he helped found a chapter of the Alianza Hispano-Americana in Los Angeles and served as leader in other organizations, such as the Woodmen of the World. [SOURCE: Rosales, *Chicano!* 69.]

REDONDO, JOSÉ MARÍA (1830-1878)

José María Redondo became one of Arizona's most prominent politicians and businessmen of the nineteenth century. He was born in Altar, Sonora. Redondo, with his brother Jesús, both from a family of large landowners, established a cattle ranch near Yuma, Arizona in 1854 after the Gadsden Purchase.* Encountering difficulties with Apache Indians, Redondo moved to

Calaveras County, California, with his father and brother, where they had operated mining and merchandizing. In 1859, the family returned to the Yuma area and amassed a small fortune from gold mining during the 1860s. After establishing a 1,000 acre ranch near Yuma (then Arizona City), Redondo built 27 miles of irrigation canals after damming the Colorado River and went on to establish a highly successful farming enterprise, supplying grain and feed for U.S. Army posts in southern Arizona. Despite that his application for citizenship was incomplete, Redondo served three terms in the Arizona legislature, between 1873 and 1878. At the local level, he was county supervisor for seven years and a member of the Yuma City Council. In 1878 he became the Mayor of Yuma. [SOURCE: Marín, "Arizona's Latinos/Latinas: A Who's Who," Chicano Research Collection, Hayden Library, Arizona State University, Tempe.]

REFORMA: THE NATIONAL ASSOCIATION TO PROMOTE LIBRARY SERVICES TO THE SPANISH-SPEAKING

Founded in 1971, REFORMA: The National Association to Promote Library Services to the Spanish-Speaking has 700 members in eight affiliates. Based in Chicago, Illinois, REFORMA works for the improvement of the full range of library services to Hispanics of the United States. REFORMA advocates for the creation of library collections in Spanish, the recruitment of bilingual and bicultural library personnel, and the development of specialized services for the Hispanic community. REFORMA offers scholarships for graduate library study. It is affiliated with the American Library Association. REFORMA publishes the quarterly *Reforma Newsletter.* [SOURCE: Kanellos, "Organizations," 395.]

THE REFUGEE/IMMIGRANT RIGHTS COALITION OF THE RIO GRANDE VALLEY *see* THE VALLEY COALITION FOR JUSTICE

REGIONAL NETWORK OF CIVIC ORGANIZATIONS FOR MIGRATION

In March 2000, 33 representatives of human rights, immigrants' rights, development, and religious organizations from eleven countries gathered in Washington, D.C. at a conference to discuss migration issues. At the meeting, participants compared national perspectives on increased, often repressive, enforcement by immigration authorities in their respective regions and reached a consensus on shared common values and concerns. Representatives presented national reports from their respective countries on the situation of migrants. These individual reports revealed the emergence of regional patterns, as well as the unique situation confronting advocates in each country. The group established the Regional Network of Civic Organizations for

Migration (RNCOM) to establish human rights standards to be carried out over the next year. Attending the RNCOM meeting were representatives from the United States, Mexico, Canada, Guatemala, El Salvador, Nicaragua, Costa Rica, Honduras, Belize, and the Dominican Republic. Attendance was supported by the Ford Foundation,* the MacArthur Foundation, the General Service Foundation, Catholic Relief Services, and the U.S. Department of State. [SOURCE: http://www.mexicousadvocates.org/rcm.htm]

REPATRIATION DURING THE GREAT DEPRESSION

When it became obvious that the economy in the United States was failing and did not have a chance of recovery, Congress passed the 1929 Immigration Act. It served as a partial victory for Texas Congressman John C. Box* and other nativists, who had pressed for a specific Mexican immigration ban throughout the 1920s. Although it was not aimed specifically at Mexico, it became the most restrictive legislation affecting Mexicans up to this point. Its provisions called for imprisonment of one year for those caught without documents a second time and a one-thousand dollar fine. When William Doak was named Secretary of Labor in 1930 by President Herbert Hoover, he decided to use this new law against Mexicans. Throughout the country, Department of Labor agents zealously pursued Mexican undocumented immigrants, working hand in hand with local law enforcement officials.

The Great Depression of the 1930s, which dislocated the lives of all Americans, presented the greatest challenge to Mexican immigrants as the collapsed economy left millions homeless or without jobs. During the worse of the crisis, industrial cities like Detroit were plagued with 75 percent unemployment. By 1932, transient camps ringed every city in the country. In order to eat, the inhabitants depended on soup kitchens, if they were lucky, or on foraging among garbage dumps. This terrible ordeal obviously changed the evolution of the Mexican *colonias* (Mexican immigrant communities) as well. Mexicans, so desirable as workers in the previous decade, were now discharged from their jobs by the thousands and then pressured to leave by community authorities. Between 1929 and 1936, at least 600,000 Mexican nationals and their children, many of whom were born in the United States, returned to Mexico—this represented about one third of the U.S. Mexican population. Economic downturns had been a constant factor in their lives, but nothing compared to the suffering created by this crisis.

Out of work and unable to acquire adequate shelter and food, most Mexican immigrants wanted to return home. But they resented the attitude shown by Americans that they had no right to be in the United States. In the past, opposition to Mexicans living in the United States—from nativists and white workers—had not been transformed into successful campaigns to expel them. This was mainly due to powerful employers who were anxious to protect the Mexican influx. But now nativists could do their worst.

The movement to repatriate Mexicans was the most intense in large industrial cities ravaged by unemployment, such as Los Angeles, Chicago, and Detroit. Similar conditions existed in Texas and Arizona mining communities, where the collapsed market for raw materials forced a drastic curtailment of production. In the industrial Calumet region of Indiana southeast of Chicago, the steel mills in tandem with local governments systematically coerced unemployed Mexican workers and their families to take free train rides back to the border. Relief to the needy in the cities of East Chicago and Gary, both located in Lake County, Indiana, came from various sources, but much of it was controlled by the local government.

The most zealous repatriation campaigns took place in Los Angeles. Even before the passage of the 1929 act, Los Angeles law enforcement officers conducted vagrancy sweeps to clear Los Angeles streets of unemployed workers, of which Mexicans figured disproportionately. The 1929 restrictions provided Los Angeles officials with another weapon to get rid of Mexicans. Charles P. Visel, Los Angeles County coordinator for unemployment relief, worked hand-in-hand with federal agents sent to Los Angeles by Secretary of Labor Doak and local Los Angeles police to arrest as many undocumented Mexicans as possible.

Officials knew that even with beefed up police manpower, it would be impossible to corral all of the undocumented Mexicans. A strategy was devised to intimidate aliens into leaving on their own by publicizing raids where hundreds of Mexicans were rounded up, regardless of whether or not they carried documents. On February 26, 1931, Los Angeles County Deputies and Department of Labor agents took a number of newspapermen on a raid which netted 400 Mexicans at *La Placita*, the historic central plaza of Los Angeles. The next day, photographs of manacled Mexican men being led into paddy wagons appeared on the front pages of Los Angeles dailies. It turned out that only a small percentage of the Mexicans harassed in this manner were undocumented.

In 1931, President Hoover implemented the President's Emergency Committee for Employment (PECE), his solution to unemployment. It was no more than a public relations ploy to make people feel good about providing a marginal number of jobs through the private sector. But the PECE in Los Angeles, of which Charles Visel was a member, worked closely with county officials to coordinate the voluntary repatriation of Southern California Mexicans—i.e. those who were not deportable under the 1929 act. In 1931, Visel traveled to Mexico, hoping to arrange a program to settle in the thousands of Mexicans whom county officials and Visel hoped to repatriate.

The Mexican government did cooperate with various groups in the United States, including Visel's program in Los Angeles County, that raised funds to send Mexicans to the border by promising to take responsibility for the repatriates once they crossed the border. Unfortunately, the engine of repatriation on the American side was more efficient than the one south of the border, resulting in bottlenecks that left thousands of the discarded Mexicans marooned in border towns with little to eat and nowhere to sleep. [SOURCE: Balderrama and Rodríguez, *Decade of Betrayal.*]

REPRESENTACIÓN CUBANA DEL EXILIO

The formation of Representación Cubana del Exilio (RECE) in 1964 originated with a referendum that allowed Cuban exiles in the United States to choose the leaders of a new exile front. This ambitious attempt to unite the community and coordinate propaganda and paramilitary activities was funded by the rum millionaire José "Pepín" Bosch of the Bacardí Company. More than 75 thousand exiles in the United States and abroad who registered with a Comité Pro-Referendum (Pro-Fererendum Commottee) reportedly were polled. Elected to head RECE were civic, political, military, and labor leaders. The exile front traveled throughout Latin America and the United States rallying support for its cause, which consisted of forming an exiled military force and establishing a revolutionary bank to collect funds for its campaigns. Fifty exile organizations had lent their support to RECE by 1967 and embarked on fundraising campaigns. This provided RECE with the ability to finance paramilitary operations and forays along the Cuban coast and harass Cubans on the mainland. The efforts of the group ended before the end of the decade when the FBI and U.S. Coast Guard combined to prevent the group from continuing any further operations. [SOURCE: García, *Havana USA*, 136.]

REPUBLIC OF SAN JOAQUÍN DEL RÍO CHAMA

On October 16, 1966, the Alianza Federal de las Mercedes* activists (*aliancistas*) and their leader, Reies López Tijerina,* occupied Echo Amphitheater, a New Mexico campground in the Kit Carson National Forest. The tract of land they occupied had been an original *merced* (land grant) called San Joaquín del Río Chama, which had been granted by the Spanish Crown in the eighteenth century. Tijerina declared this federal reserve area the "Republic of San Joaquín del Río Chama" and served eviction papers on William D. Hurst, the forest ranger supervisor for Kit Carson.

After making this symbolic gesture, the group quietly vacated the campground, but vowed to come back. To prevent this, Hurst sealed off the entrance with two rangers, reinforced by state police, and announced that anyone entering would have to register and buy a one-dollar permit. Tijerina and a large body of armed *aliancistas* broke through the barricade, captured the rangers and escorted them out of the park. Tijerina then held a press conference, proclaiming that now it was the federal government's turn to defend its claim. Tijerina and five other *aliancistas* were arrested for conspiring to prevent forest rangers from conducting their duties. The group was arraigned and released on bond. This was the beginning of the more militant phase of Alianza politics in the following years. [SOURCE: Nabokov, *Tijerina and the Courthouse Raid.*]

REYES, FEDERICO (1959-)

Since 1996, Federico Reyes, who was born in Mexico in 1959, has been one of the busiest and most dedicated organizers in U.S. labor unions. Today, he is considered the top organizer for the Hotel Employees and Restaurant Employees International Union and a leader of Local 86 in Reno, Nevada. Reyes is representative of the rising number of Hispanic leaders in a labor movement that increasingly looks at the Latino workforce as a sector that needs organizing. In Reyes' words, "Now 60 to 70 percent of the nation's hotel workers are Latinos and they, just like everybody else, know that organizing gives you respect as well as economic benefits."

After immigrating from Mexico in 1976, Reyes worked as a farmworker in California. One year later, he moved to Las Vegas, where word of mouth indicated that the gambling center provided better opportunities for employment. After working as a dishwasher and kitchen helper for a number of years, Reyes then led a bitter struggle to organize employees at the Hilton, one of Las Vegas' largest hotels. [SOURCE: Radelat, "Wall Street and Business Wednesdays."]

REUNIÓN DE ESTUDIOS CUBANOS

In 1969, Cuban emigré intellectuals in the United States joined with other scholars from the United States, Puerto Rico, and Latin America in Washington, D.C. for the first Reunión de Estudios Cubanos, a series of workshops, presentations, and roundtable discussions on Cuba. The assembly represented various institutions and academic disciplines within a diverse ideological spectrum. Open to nonacademics, the Reunión became the first attempt to gather a heterogeneous intelligentsia for a scholarly discussion about Cuba. The papers presented at this meeting appeared in the 1969/1970 edition of the journal *Exilio*. In 1971, a second reunion was convened, and out of this meeting was born the idea of creating an Instituto de Estudios Cubanos (IEC)* to oversee future meetings. The following year under the leadership of María Cristina Herrera, a key organizer of the first Reunión, the IEC was officially incorporated. IEC gatherings have taken place since then in cities such as Caracas, Miami, San Juan, Cambridge, and Orlando. [SOURCE: García, *Havana USA*, 205.]

RICHARDSON, WILLIAM BLAINE (1947-)

William Blaine Richardson was born on November 15, 1947 in Pasadena, California. His mother was Mexican, and his father was an American businessman from Boston who worked in Mexico. Richardson lived in Mexico City from age one to his thirteenth birthday, and Spanish became his first language. He attended high school in Concord, Massachusetts, where his family moved in 1961, then received a B.A. from Tufts University in 1970 and an M.A. from The Fletcher School of Law and Diplomacy in 1971. Richardson moved to Albuquerque in 1978, where he practiced law. In 1982, New Mexico voters elected him to the House of Representatives from the 3rd Congressional District. He served in the House until 1997, when he was appointed by President Bill Clinton to serve as U.S. Ambassador to the United Nations. In 1998, the U.S. Senate unanimously confirmed him as Secretary of the U.S. Department of Energy. In 2002, Richardson ran as the Democratic Party candidate for New Mexico governor and won by the largest margin of any candidate since 1964. At the end of his first term in 2004, Governor Richardson, by most accounts, had made good on his campaign promises to bring about a myriad of fiscal and social reforms. Governor Richardson is the only Hispanic in the United States who has been nominated on three occasions for the Nobel Peace Prize. He lives in Albuquerque with his wife Barbara. [SOURCE: http://www.governor.state.nm.us/governor.php]

RINCÓN DE GAUTIER, FELISA (1897-1994)

Felisa Rincón de Gautier, who along with Luis Muñoz Marín,* was a founder of the Popular Democratic Party in the 1930s. Born in Ceiba, Puerto Rico, on January 9, 1897, she became the first woman to serve as mayor of San Juan, the capital of Puerto Rico. If Puerto Rico, which was under American rule, may be considered part of the United States, then she was the first female mayor of a major American city. As mayor, Rincón de Gautier was a populist who opened the doors of city government to the people. In 1953 the League of American Women gave her its Woman of the Year Award. She was so beloved that she served until 1969 and was named one of the 100 outstanding women of the world. A woman endowed with a great amount of energy, Rincón de Gautier continued as source of inspiration until her death in 1994. [SOURCE: Kanellos, *Hispanics in American History*, 46; http://www.preb.com/biog/felisar.htm.]

RISCO, ELEAZAR (?-?)

Eleazar Risco came to Kansas from Cuba in the 1960s as a ministry student and eventually studied at Sacramento State University. From there he enrolled at Stanford University, where he studied under Ronald Hilton, a self-styled radical who published the *Hispanic American Report*, a journal that exposed CIA ties to anti-Castro Cubans training in the United States before the Bay of Pigs invasion. Luis Valdez,* a Chicano Movement* pioneer and founder of El Teatro Campesino, whom Risco met in the Bay Area, convinced him to go to Delano. Risco dropped out of Stanford to help publish the National farmworkers Association's newspaper, *El Malcriado.* Sent by César Chávez* to East Los Angeles in 1967 to help organize the grape boycott, Risco soon ventured into other activities. At first, he worked on U.S. Department of Justice-financed project to prevent juvenile delinquency. While working on this and other issues, he became one of the founders of the Barrio Communications Project, which published *La Raza* newspaper. [SOURCE: Rosales, *Chicano!,* 187-189.]

RIVERA, TOMÁS (1935-1984)

The son of Mexican citizens who migrated to Texas in the 1920s, Tomás Rivera as chancellor of the University of California, Riverside became one of the highest ranking Latino University administrators in the United States. A gifted writer, Rivera was born in Crystal City, Texas.* Rivera's childhood in the 1930s and 1940s was spent accompanying his parents in the migrant stream that took Mexican workers from south Texas into Oklahoma and Missouri and then into the vegetable fields of Michigan and Minnesota. Rivera worked as a migrant farm laborer through the 1950s, even during his junior college years in Texas, an experience that greatly influenced his writing. After graduating from Southwest Texas State University with a degree in English, Rivera found it difficult to find work as an English teacher because of his Mexican background. He then enrolled again in Southwest Texas State and earned a master's degree in English and administration. In 1969, he received a doctorate in Spanish literature from the University of Oklahoma and began

a career of college teaching, but after a few years, Rivera became administrative vice president at the University of Texas at San Antonio. In 1975, the University of Texas at El Paso named him executive vice president and, in 1979, he was named chancellor of the University of California. He died four years later. But Rivera was also renowned as a foundational writer of Chicano* literature. His most famous book, . . . *y no se lo tragó la tierra/And the Earth Did Not Devour Him*, published in 1971, is considered a classic in American literary history. [SOURCE: Saldívar, "Tomás Rivera—Author. A Biography,"

Tomás Rivera

http://college.hmco.com/english/lauter/heath/4e/students/author_pages/con-
temporary/rivera_to.html]

RODINO BILL

Congressman Peter Rodino of New Jersey introduced legislation in the House of Representatives early in 1973 that would criminalize knowingly hiring illegal aliens. The sanctions consisted of a $500 fine for a first-time conviction for each undocumented worker employed and $1000 and/or imprisonment for one year if the employers were convicted a second time. César Chávez* and other Mexican-American leaders supported the bill and, in fact, had lobbied for these sanctions many times earlier—undocumented immigrants were considered a scourge for organizers because employers often used them to break strikes. Most Mexican-Americans civil rights leaders opposed the "Rodino Bill" because of its potential for application to legal Mexican residents and Mexican Americans, violating their right to obtain jobs without having to prove their legal residency. After much lobbying and demonstrations by civil rights and Latin organizations, Congress defeated this bill. [SOURCE: Meier and Rivera, *A Dictionary of Mexican American History*, 305.]

RODRÍGUEZ, CHIPITA (?-1863)

Chipita Rodríguez became the only woman legally hanged in Texas history. Found guilty of having murdered a horse trader, John Savage in 1863, Rodríguez was hanged, despite the jury's recommendation for mercy because the evidence against her was weak. In California, the first and only woman lynched in that state was Josefa Segovia, who during the Gold Rush had killed an Anglo man who had made advances that she rejected; she was hanged in spite of being pregnant. [SOURCE: Gómez-Quiñones, *Roots of Chicano Politics*, 246.]

RODRÍGUEZ DE TIÓ, LOLA (1843-1924)

Puerto Rican patriot and poet Lola Rodríguez de Tió became the first Hispanic woman to be sent into political exile for her leadership in the Puerto Rican independence movement from Spain. Born on September 14, 1843, in San Germán, Rodríguez de Tió received an education at religious schools and from private tutors. In 1865, she married Bonocio Tió, a journalist who shared Rodríguez de Tió's desire for Puerto Rican independence, and they held literary and political meetings regularly at their home in Mayagüez. In 1868, she wrote the nationalist lyrics that would become the Puerto Rican national hymn, "La Borinqueña." In 1877, the government exiled Rodríguez de Tió; she and her family took refuge in Venezuela for three years and then returned to Puerto Rico. In 1889, she was exiled once again, this time to Cuba, where she continued her revolutionary activities until 1895, when she was exiled again. This

time she took up residence in New York and
again continued to conspire with the leading
revolutionaries for Puerto Rican and Cuban
independence. In 1899, after the Spanish
American War,* she returned to a hero's recep-
tion in Cuba. She remained in Cuba and began
to work on fashioning a new society, one in
which women would have greater liberty and
opportunity. In 1910, she was elected a member of the Cuban Academy of Arts and Letters.
Lola Rodríguez de Tió was a romantic poet, as
her three books of poems readily attest: *Mis
cantares* (My Songs, 1876), *Claros y nieblas*
(Clarities and Cloudiness, 1885), and *Mi libro
de Cuba* (My Cuban Book). Rodríguez de Tió

Lola Rodríguez de Tió

is a beloved patriotic and literary figure, as well as an early feminist, in both
Puerto Rico and Cuba. She died on November 10, 1924 in Cuba. [SOURCE:
Kanellos, *Chronology of Hispanic American History*, 93.]

ROMANO-V., OCTAVIO (1923-2005)

Octavio Romano-V., an anthropologist on the faculty of the School of
Public Health at the University of California, Berkeley served as one of the
most important catalysts to Chicano* scholarship. Romano was born in Mexico City, Mexico, in 1923, and raised in Tecate, Mexico, and later in National City, California. He was the youngest child of María and Manuel Romano.
Living in Berkeley, in 1967 he co-founded with Herminio Ríos *El Grito: A
Journal of Contemporary Mexican American Thought*, an independent publication which served as a forum for a variety of themes, graphic arts, and literature. Through this venue, he published a series of articles scrutinizing traditional scholarship on Mexican Americans, concluding that it was
ahistorical, distorted, and biased. He encouraged young Chicano intellectuals, who also published in the journal, to develop a new paradigm by view-
ing the total experience of Chicanos in the United States. Nonetheless,
although the main purpose of the journal was to polemically attack previous
Anglo-researched social science studies of Mexican Americans, it was
unable to consistently offer alternative approaches.

With Herminio Ríos, Romano also founded Quinto Sol Publications,
which published the first significant Chicano novels of the 1970s after running a competition for a $1000-prize for the best novel. The publications pro-
gram provided a forum to several young aspiring fiction writers who went on
to become successful and well-known writers. A World War II veteran, who
participated in the Normandy campaign, Romano attended college on the

G.I. Bill and obtained a degree in Anthropology from the University of New Mexico in 1952. Continuing his studies at the University of California, Berkeley, he received an M.A. in Cultural Anthropology and then worked for the Public Health Department in Santa Fe, New Mexico. He returned to U.C. Berkeley and received a Ph.D. in Anthropology in 1965. He taught at U.C. Berkeley until his retirement in 1989 and passed away on February 26, 2005. [SOURCE: Rosales, *Chicano!*, 254, 258.]

ROMERO, ANTHONY D. (1966-)

Stanford Law-graduate Anthony D. Romero became the director of the American Civil Liberties Union (ACLU) in September 2001. With a history of public-interest activism, Romero had presided over the most successful membership drive in the ACLU's 82-year history. In his first year, 75,000 individuals became card-carrying members of the organization for the first time. Romero is the first Latino and openly gay man to serve as leader of this preeminent defender of American civil rights. Having previously served in the Ford Foundation's Human Rights and International Cooperation Program, transforming it into Ford's largest and most dynamic grant-making unit, he channeled approximately $90 million in grants to civil rights, human rights, and peace projects in 2000, and launched groundbreaking initiatives in affirmative action, voting rights and redistricting, immigrants' rights, women's rights, reproductive freedom, and lesbian/gay rights. Romero also served for nearly five years as a Ford Foundation* Program Officer for Civil Rights and Racial Justice; and for two years at the Rockefeller Foundation, where he led a foundation review that helped to determine future directions in civil-rights advocacy. Born in New York City to immigrant parents from Puerto Rico, Romero was the first in his family to graduate from high school. He sits on several not-for-profit boards and is a member of the Council on Foreign Relations and the New York State Bar Association. [SOURCE: http://www.aclu.org]

ADOLFO ROMO V. LAIRD, ET AL

The first successful desegregation court case involving Mexican Americans, *Romo v. Laird*, occurred in Tempe, Arizona, in 1925. The suit was brought by Adolfo Romo on behalf of his four children, who were attending the Eighth Street Elementary School, a training laboratory for Tempe Normal School, the forerunner of present-day Arizona State University. Anglo or white children had attended the Eighth Street facility since Tempe was settled in the late nineteenth century because it was the only school in the town. However, in the early twentieth century, rapid population growth resulted as agricultural sectors in central Arizona modernized. Trustees of the Tempe School District #3 then built the Tenth Street School in 1915 but did not allow Mexican children to attend, citing their lack of English proficiency. Romo, whose wife was half Anglo, felt that his English-speaking children did not belong in a segregated facility and attempted to enroll them in the new school, but was refused. He then sued the school district in Maricopa County Superior Court, and Judge Joseph S. Jenckes ordered the Romo children be allowed to enroll and attend. Despite the Romos and other Mexican Americans being considered white for census purposes, Jenckes ruled against segregation because the district, which used students as teachers in the Eighth Street School, violated the 1913 Arizona Civil Code that required school districts to provide all school children in the state an equal education. The judge found that "the defendants [had] failed in their duty to the plaintiff in not providing teachers of as high a standard of ability and qualifications to teach the children of the plaintiff in the said Eighth Street School. . . ." The Romo children and other Mexican Americans enrolled in the new school as a result, but Tempe school officials continued to segregate other Mexican-American children whose parents did not complain. [SOURCE: García, "The Romo Decision and Desegregation in Tempe"; Muñoz, "Separate But Equal? A Case Study of *Romo v. Laird* and Mexican American Education," Reprinted from the *OAH Magazine of History* 15 (Winter 2001), http://www.oah.org/pubs/magazine/deseg/documenta.html]

ROSS, SR., FRED (1910-2002)

Fred Ross became one of the most influential and well-known community organizers of the twentieth century. He is best known for training the United Farm Worker Union* founder César Chávez,* when the unionist worked with the Community Services Organization (CSO)* in northern California during the 1950s. Ross, who the started the CSO, also trained Dolores Huerta,* another organizer during this same era, who helped Chávez found the union. Born in San Francisco in 1910, Ross worked his way through the University of Southern California in the 1930s and earned a degree in education. The country was steeped in the Great Depression, and Ross was unable to find a teaching position, but he did find a job with the State of California in rural relief projects. During World War II, he administered a Japanese internment camp in Idaho. At the end of the war, he returned to California to work with the American Council on Race Relations. Through this organization, he helped organized Unity Leagues,* community action programs designed to stimulate political action that support the election of officials favorable to the social concerns of working-class people and racial minorities. In the 1940s, Ross met Saul Alinsky, and founded the CSO, relying on Alinsky's Industrial Areas Foundation tactic of using community leaders rather than outside organizers. After both Chávez and Huerta separated from the CSO, Ross continued to support United Farm Workers Union efforts. [SOURCE: Griswold del Castillo and García, *César Chávez.*]

ROSS-LEHTINEN, ILEANA (1952-)

Born in Havana, Cuba on July 15, 1952, Miami's Ileana Ross-Lehtinen was the first Cuban American elected to the United States Congress. Following the death of Congressman Claude Pepper in 1989, she beat 10 opponents to represent South Miami Beach, Little Havana, Westchester, Coral Gables, Key Biscayne, parts of Kendall and Homestead, and suburban Miami. In addition, she was also the first Hispanic woman to become a U.S. representative. Ross-Lehtinen came to the United States at the age of 7, when her parents fled the rise of communism in Cuba. She received bachelor's and master's degrees from Florida International University in Miami and went on to teach in her own private school. In 1982, she was elected to the Florida legislature as a Republican. She was elected to the Florida state senate in 1986. [SOURCE: Kamp and Telgin, *Latinas!*, 327-31.]

Ileana Ross-Lehtinen

ROYBAL, EDWARD R. (1915-2005)

In 1949, Edward R. Roybal became the first Mexican American to be elected to the Los Angeles City Council since 1876. A representative from East Los Angeles, his election was very much a part of the effort by returning Mexican-American war veterans to get political representation. Born into a middle-class Mexican-American family in Albuquerque, New Mexico, Roybal began his education in the Los Angeles public schools after his parents had moved there. After attending the University of California and Southwestern University, Roybal became a health care educator in the late 1930s with the California Tuberculosis Association. He served in World War II, returned to Los Angeles and became Director for Health Education in the Los Angeles County Tuberculosis and Health Association. A group of Mexican Americans, many of them frustrated veterans who still faced discrimination in spite of their sacrifices, recognized his political potential, and in 1947, approached him about running for city council. The bid failed, but after a major voter registration drive by the Community Services Organization (CSO)* in Los Angeles that had enrolled 15,000 Mexican Americans, Edward Roybal won a seat on the city council in 1949. He was successful on his second attempt.

In 1954, Roybal raised his sights from representing his community on the Los Angeles city council and unsuccessfully sought the Democratic nomination for Lieutenant Governor. Four years later, he ran for a slot in the Los Angeles County Board of Supervisors and lost. His political fortunes changed when he won a seat in the U.S. House of Representatives in 1962, the first Hispanic elected to Congress since Romualdo Pacheco in 1876. Edward R. Roybal then became the first Mexican American from the twenty-fifth district elected to the United States Congress, where he served for more than three decades. During his tenure in Congress, Roybal worked for social and economic reform. In 1967, he introduced legislation that became the first bilingual education act. In 1982, as chairman of the Congressional Hispanic Caucus, he led the opposition to employer sanctions for hiring undocumented workers, which ultimately was enacted as the Immigration Reform and Control Act of 1986.* [SOURCE: Kanellos, *Chronology of Hispanic American History*, 174, 245.]

Edward R. Roybal

RUIZ, JUAN B. (1896-?)

Juan B. Ruiz was a pharmacist in the 1920s and 1930s in Los Angeles, where he was known as the "Mayor of Little Mexico." Born in 1896 in Sinaloa to a wealthy family who lost everything during the Mexican Revolution, Ruiz prepared for a chemistry career. But by 1920, weary of violence and instability in Mexico, he crossed the border. After enduring many hardships, he finally entered the drugstore business. During the Great Depression, Ruiz was involved in the Comité de Beneficencia Mexicana, which tried to help in the repatriation of destitute Mexicans in Los Angeles. Ruiz was also a writer who researched Mexican folkloric traditions, but unfortunately, his manuscripts have not yet been recovered. [SOURCE: Rosales, "'Fantasy Heritage' Reexamined", 83-106.]

RUMFORD ACT

In 1963, Byron Rumford sponsored a bill in the California Assembly to establish open housing and prohibit discrimination in the sale of real estate. Enacted into law that same year as an amendment to the California state constitution, its passage provoked an electoral reaction in the form of Proposition 14, revoking the legislation. In 1967, however, the U.S. Supreme Court struck down Proposition 14 as unconstitutional, and the open housing code prevailed, a development celebrated by Mexican-American civil rights activists, who had championed Rumford's initiative and opposed Proposition 14. [SOURCE: Meier and Rivera, *A Dictionary of Mexican American History,* 310.]

SALAZAR, RUBÉN (1928-1970)

During the Chicano Movement,* one of the issues that most angered the community was the unnecessary killing of the popular journalist Rubén Salazar as he covered the Chicano Moratorium,* an anti-Vietnam War rally, when a deputy sheriff, Thomas Wilson,* shot a tear gas projectile into the Silver Dollar Cafe, where the journalist was sipping a beer. Born in the border town of Ciudad Juárez on March 3, 1928, Salazar's family crossed the border into El Paso, where he was raised. After serving in the military, Salazar used his G.I. Bill benefits to pursue a journalism degree at Texas Western College, today's University of Texas at El Paso. Throughout his early journalistic career, which spanned about 15 years, he worked competently and quietly, remaining a dedicated husband and father to his Anglo wife and three children. Except for his journalistic subjects, he stayed aloof from direct political or civil rights commitments.

Salazar's forte became investigative reporting. During his first job with the *El Paso Herald Post*, for example, he had himself arrested and then wrote an exposé of drug trafficking and substandard conditions in the El Paso County Jail. Then he wrote a series of articles on border drug trade outlets known as "shooting galleries," after pretending to be a customer. In 1956, he moved to the California Bay Area and reported for the *Santa Rosa Press Democrat*, next with the *San Francisco News* until he was laid off when the newspaper merged with another daily. However, Salazar soon landed a job with the *Los Angeles Times,* where in 1959 he started covering events in the Los Angeles Mexican-American community.

Salazar's growing prestige within the *L.A. Times* earned him a position as a foreign correspondent in Latin America, where he covered the 1965 invasion of the Dominican Republic. His reporting was conventional and not critical of American involvement. Certainly, his writing did not demonstrate the anti-imperialistic tinge which was an important part of the Chicano Moratorium, where he perished. His next assignment was in Vietnam. The dispatches he sent home revealed that he felt the U.S. presence could bring peace, despite the little respect he had for the South Vietnamese leaders.

Next, the *L.A. Times* sent him to Mexico City as bureau chief for Central America, Mexico, and the Caribbean, where he was somewhat critical of the anti-democratic character of Castro's Cuba and the one-party system in Mexico. Salazar finally returned to Los Angeles in January 1969, and started covering the activism of Chicanos* that had blossomed during his absence. Salazar covered the Mexican community dispassionately without incurring the wrath of unforgiving militants nor alienating them, mainly because he sympathized with the goals of the activist, even when he did not condone their tactics. Salazar left the *L.A. Times* to manage the Spanish-language station KMEX in February of 1970, but continued writing a weekly editorial for the newspaper, in which he expressed more subjective opinions.

Increasingly, law enforcement abuses came to dominate the bulk of his commentary. He concentrated on exposing illegal procedures and police brutality, the absence of Mexicans on juries and unwarranted spying on legitimate social service organizations. Such a stance certainly antagonized the law enforcement establishment and, understandably, many of his mourners felt a conspiracy to silence him was what led to his death. Chicanos hoped the investigation would reveal their worst suspicions, that the Los Angeles Police Department had conspired to murder Salazar and end the attacks on the department. The Coroner's Jury, however, decided that there was no cause for criminal action against the deputy who fired into the Silver Dollar Cafe. The decision outraged not only the community, but also many Anglos who saw Salazar as a mediating force between angry militants and a recalcitrant establishment. Rubén Salazar's death transformed him into the most powerful martyr of the Chicano Movement. [SOURCE: Rosales, *Chicano!*, 202-207; Salazar, *Border Correspondent.*]

SALT OF THE EARTH STRIKE

The Salt of the Earth Strike was the first major strike conducted by women and children. From October 1950 until January 1952, the predominantly Mexican Mine-Mill Workers Union struck the mines in southern New Mexico. A local judge issued an injunction prohibiting the mine workers from picketing the mines, which led to the women's auxiliary of the union continuing to picket and organize, quite often with their children at their sides and in their arms, and suffering abuse, violence, and arrest. The strike ended when the union was able to obtain minor concessions. In addition to the importance of the leadership role taken by women, the strike was historically important because it focused on the pattern of discrimination against Mexican workers that prevailed throughout the Southwest. [SOURCE: García, *Memories of Chicano History*, 174-5.]

SAMANIEGO, MARIANO G. (1844-1907)

Arizona political leader and businessman Mariano G. Samaniego became an American citizen after the United States acquired southern Arizona through the Gadsen Purchase* in 1853. After graduating from St. Louis University, Samaniego moved to Tucson in the 1860s and became one of the most important businessmen and public officials. His cattle ranch and freighting business provided much of the impetus for Arizona's growth. Southern Arizona voters elected him to four terms in the territorial legislature from the mid-1870s to the mid-1890s. Samaniego's civic and public commitments led him to champion public education. He played a decisive role in the founding of the state university in 1891 and served on the first board of trustees. Conscious of the Hispanic heritage of southern Arizona, he helped found the Arizona Pioneers Historical Society. Samaniego's concerns included the problems that Mexican Americans increasingly experienced as the territory became more Anglo; Samaniego helped establish the Alianza Hispano-Americana* to protect Mexican-American civil rights and cultural identity. [SOURCE: Meier and Rivera, *A Dictionary of Mexican American History,* 314.]

SAN ANTONIO HISPANIC CHAMBER OF COMMERCE

The San Antonio Hispanic Chamber of Commerce, the oldest such organizations of its kind, serves as a leading advocate of Hispanic, minority, and woman-owned businesses by providing individual business advice, networking, and advocacy. The Mexican Consul, Enrique Santibáñez, chartered the chamber in 1929 as the Mexican Chamber of Commerce, a center for improving political and economic ties between the United States and Mexico; in 1987, the organization changed its title to its present name. Today, it is widely respected for positive contributions to the business life of San Antonio. While an integral goal is to continue the tradition of molding Hispanic community leaders and advancing minority business interests, the original mission articulated in 1929 remains central to its objectives for the twenty-first century. [SOURCE: http://www.sahcc.org/default.asp?main.asp&2]

SAN JOAQUIN VALLEY COTTON STRIKE

In October 1933, Mexican farmworkers struck the cotton industry in the counties of the Central Valley, California. The San Joaquin Cotton Strike was the largest and best organized of labor actions initiated by the radical Cannery and Agricultural Workers Industrial Union in the 1930s. Some 12,000 to 18,000 pickers walked out demanding a raise from 60 cents to one dollar a pound for picked cotton. Growers and vigilante groups attempted to repress the strike violently and, in fact, killed two strikers and wounded various others. California Governor James Rolf called in the National Guard and established a fact-finding board, which eventually created the basis for a compromise: 75 cents per pound and a condemnation of the growers for violation of the strikers' civil rights. [SOURCE: Kushner, *Long Road to Delano*, 57-70; Jamieson, *Labor Unionism in American Agriculture*, 100-105.]

SÁNCHEZ, GEORGE I. (1906-1972)

Born on October 4, 1906 in Albuquerque, New Mexico, into a family with a long history in the state and region, George I. Sánchez was probably one of the most effective social activist-scholars of Mexican-American descent. He grew up in in Jerome, Arizona, where his father worked as a copper miner, but he returned to New Mexico and graduated from high school. Later, he earned a B.A. in Education from the University of New Mexico (1930), then an Ed.D. in Educational Administration, and an M.S. in Educational Psychology from the University of Texas (1931), and a Doctor of Education degree from the University of California, Berkeley (1934). In 1935, the Julius Rosenwald Fund in Chicago employed him as a research associate developing educational models that would effectively serve the needs of Spanish-speaking groups in the United States. Much of the theory and applicative aspects that he pioneered are still emulated as modern-day educators develop bilingual, bicultural education strategies.

Sánchez's research findings were published in countless books and articles, but his most important research, work funded by a grant from the Carnegie Foundation in 1938, was published in *Forgotten People*, a book that studies the economic, social, and political conditions of his fellow New Mexicans. As in much of his other studies on Southwest Mexican Americans, *Forgotten Americans* argues that the poverty and seeming lack of achievement of New Mexican Hispanos is caused more by external forces, such as an impoverished economy and lack of opportunity, than intrinsic defects in their culture. Apart from his considerable contributions in education, throughout all of his life Sánchez engaged in battles against social and educational segregation. A stalwart of the pioneering civil rights League of United Latin American Citizens (LULAC),* he became the organization's thirteenth president in 1941. While leading LULAC, he explored ways by which the federal government could guarantee Mexican Americans full civil rights.

By any standard, Sánchez deserves the sobriquet of being the "most distinguished Mexican American scholar of the time." His contributions as a scholar, writer, editor, social philosopher, civil rights leader, international administrator, and consultant on Inter-American affairs, migrant education, and Indian affairs have few parallels. Before he passed away in 1972, he also supported the efforts of the Chicano Movement* in providing solutions to the problems he confronted for over forty years. [SOURCE: http://www.lib.utexas.edu/taro/utlac/00069/lac-00069.html]

SÁNCHEZ, MARÍA C. (1926-1989)

When voters elected María C. Sánchez to the Connecticut General Assembly in 1988, she became the first Hispanic woman to achieve this post. Sánchez served in the Assembly until her death on November 25, 1989. Born in Comerío, Puerto Rico, in 1926, Sánchez came to Connecticut in 1953, where she became an integral part of the Puerto Rican community in Hartford. Many Hispanic organizations owe their existence to her activism: the

Puerto Rican Parade Committee in 1964,* La Casa de Puerto Rico, the Society of Legal Services, the Spanish American Merchants Association, the Puerto Rican Businessmen's Association, and the Community Renewal Team. As member of the Hartford Board of Education, where she served for 16 programs that put the educational system in closer contact to the community. The intimacy and concern she demonstrated to so many people earned her the moniker "Godmother" of the Hispanic Community. [SOURCE: http://www.cwhf.org/hall/sanchez/sanchez.htm]

THE SANCTUARY MOVEMENT

The Sanctuary Movement began on March 24, 1982, Presbyterian Pastor John Fife declared that his church in Tucson was a sanctuary for Central Americans seeking refuge from government-sponsored violence in their home countries. In a pre-arranged gesture, other Protestant churches with progressive agendas—in Los Angeles, San Francisco, Washington, D.C., and Long Island, New York—followed suit on the same day. The leaders of his loosely organized movement were outraged by the rising death toll of civilians in El Salvador and Guatemala, and by U.S. government deportation campaigns in 1981 that ousted more than 50,000 Salvadorans, many of whom faced danger at home. Sanctuary workers considered these deportations illegal, given that the Refugee Act of 1980 allowed asylum to immigrants who faced a "well-founded fear of persecution" if they returned to their country of origin. The Geneva Convention also obliged governments to allow private humanitarian agencies or individuals to protect refugees from untimely repatriation. Sanctuary Movement activists encountered a U.S. government crackdown against their most active members. John Fife and 15 other activists were arraigned in Tucson, Arizona, on January 23, 1985, charged with conspiracy and harboring and transporting illegal aliens. Religious convictions motivated these activists, but the Reagan administration's support of some of the repressive governments added to their zeal for involvement. [SOURCE: Masud-Piloto, *From Welcomed Exiles to Illegal Immigrants,* 120-131.]

SANTA FE RING

In the 1870s, land speculators organized the "Santa Fe Ring" and engineered schemes in which hundreds of Hispanic landowners lost their farms and ranches over a period of thirty years. Two lawyers, Thomas Benton Catron and his partner, Steven Benton Elkins (later a Senator from New Mexico) became the kingpins in the ring. Operating out of the territorial capital of Santa Fe, the leaders chose other "Ring" members on the basis of the political or financial influence they could wield in the widespread land-grabbing schemes: judges, lawyers, politicians, businessmen, newspaper editors and government bureaucrats.

As an attorney, Catron handled the land title cases of Hispanics that were supposedly guaranteed by the Treaty of Guadalupe Hidalgo of 1848;* he acquired for himself more than 2,000,000 acres in the process. Some well-to-do Hispanics collaborated with Catron and his cronies and, as a consequence, they also acquired land from their less powerful compatriots. The Ring also victimized Anglo and European landowners, who were divested of large landholdings; however, in real numbers, more Hispanos lost mostly smaller pieces of property. When the Santa Fe, Atchison, and Topeka railroad was built from Kansas through the northern part of the New Mexico territory in the 1880s, land became even more valuable, and the Santa Fe Ring's efforts intensified. But affected landowners, both Hispanic and non-Hispanics, fought back in such episodes as the Lincoln County Land War.

In the 1890s, Hispanos also organized themselves into bands of hooded night riders, known as Las Gorras Blancas (The White Caps),* and set out in forays to tear down fences and derail trains, hoping to frighten Anglo land developers and railroad companies into abandoning New Mexico. [SOURCE: Rosenbaum, *Mexicano Resistance in the Southwest.*]

SANTA PAULA AGRICULTURAL STRIKE, 1917

On March 25, 1917, 100 Mexican citrus pickers walked out of the orchards at the Limoneria Ranch in Santa Paula, California. They wanted higher wages but the ranch owners, operators of the biggest source of employment in the district, were threatened by the prospect of unpicked citrus and called in the police, who arrested the strike leaders. This act ended the strike and most of the disillusioned workers returned to the harvest. [SOURCE: Menchaca, *The Mexican Outsiders,* 80.]

SANTA PAULA AGRICULTURAL STRIKE, 1941

With the help of the American Federation of Labor (AFL) in January 1941, agricultural unions called for a county-wide strike, which became known as the "Ventura County Six Month Strike," a stoppage of both harvesters and packers that crippled the county's lemon industry. The strikers demanded the right to collective bargaining, official recognition of their unions, a wage increase from 30 to 40 cents per hour, and payment for time spent in the fields while waiting for the weather to improve before starting to harvest (wet time).

Charles C. Teague, the president and co-owner of Santa Paula's Limoneria Ranch who represented the growers, rejected the AFL claim to representing the strikers and refused to meet with any of the leaders, an impasse that continued for six months. Teague contended that growers would be ruined if they had to meet the wage demands. Nonetheless, in the six months that workers stayed out of the fields, the growers lost thousands of dollars and the workers' poverty increased. The workers and their families established striker camp-grounds in county parks, and the state government provided food for the families. As some of the families lost hope and departed, those who remained lost heart and, after six months, many left to seek employment elsewhere, a gesture which admitted the strike had failed. However, in July, the National Labor Relations Board (NLRB) decided to intervene, a move that uplifted the expectations of the strikers. The NLRB decided to mediate the dispute because some of the strikers worked in packing; thus they were considered industrial workers (NLRB did not represent farmworkers). Ultimately, the board decided that the majority of the strikers were agricultural laborers, ineligible for NLRB coverage. The strike ended, without the workers obtaining their goals; the growers took substantial losses, but that was of little consolation to the workers. Eventually, many of the strikers were rehired, except for the leaders, who were blacklisted. Many workers simply left the area and migrated to urban areas in northern California. [SOURCE: Menchaca, *The Mexican Outsiders,* 84-89.]

SANTA PAULA, FIRST LABOR UNION

The first Mexican labor union in Santa Paula, California, was formed in the mid-1930s after workers refused to harvest citrus fruit. In what came to be known as the Santa Paula Orange and Mupu Citrus Strike, the Mexican workers took matters into their own hands and formed their own union because they received little support from national labor unions, such as the American Federation of Labor (AFL). Nonetheless, when AFL organizers arrived in Santa Paula to provide advice, the growers became more adamant about breaking the strike and began to replace strikers with "dust bowl" refugees, known as Okies. The strike continued, however, and after five days, farmers began to intimidate the workers by bringing in sympathetic police officers, who threatened to arrest the strikers and deport those who were undocumented. Ultimately, Santa Paula Orange and Mupu Citrus strikers returned to work and abandoned the union movement because of the arrest risks and because they would have lost their jobs. Agricultural workers remained more vulnerable because the National Labor Relations Act, passed in 1935, provided a modicum of support for union organizing that did not include the agricultural sector. [SOURCE: Menchaca, *The Mexican Outsiders,* 82-83.]

SANTA PAULA NEW YEAR'S DAY STRIKE

On New Year's Day, 1915, thirteen Mexican farmworkers went out on strike at the Corbett Ranch. In spite of the small size of this stoppage, it demonstrated that Mexicans were beginning to resort to organizing to confront low wages and poor working conditions. Owners of Corbett Ranch, perplexed that Mexicans refused to work on New Year's Day, attributed their action as an example of the Mexicans' lazy nature. Corbett Ranch owners retaliated by firing the strikers and by asking the city government to deny the families of the strikers charity relief, a harsh measure intended to serve as an example to other employees so that they would not strike.

For the Mexican workers, the stoppage ended in disaster, an outcome that could have been averted if the strikers had received assistance from the national labor movement, but Mexican farmworkers were excluded from joining the American Federation of Labor or any other national labor union during this time. [SOURCE: Menchaca, *The Mexican Outsiders,* 80.]

SANTA YSABEL MASSACRE

In January 1916, Villistas (followers of Pancho Villa) dragged 17 American mining engineers from a train at Santa Ysabel, Chihuahua, and killed them. The bodies were brought back from Chihuahua through El Paso in coffins draped with American flags. The killings whipped El Paso Anglos into a frenzy of revenge, and they went on a rampage, attacking every Mexican man they encountered. [SOURCE: Rosales, *Pobre Raza!,* 86, 85, 109.]

SCHOMBURG, ARTURO (ARTHUR) ALFONSO (1874-1938)

Born in Puerto Rico on January 24, 1874, Arturo Alfonso Schomburg began his education in San Juan, where a fifth-grade teacher told him that "Black people have no history, no heroes, no great moments." Being of African descent, such disregard provoked in Schomburg a thirst for knowledge about his people, and he spent the rest of his life studying the history and collecting the books and artifacts that resulted in one of the most extensive collections on African history in the Americas. At seventeen, he migrat-

ed to New York in 1891 and became involved in the independence movements of Cubans and Puerto Ricans. He attended night school at Manhattan Central High School and worked at odd jobs to support himself. Schomburg met the journalist John Edward Bruce, who introduced him to the New York African-American intelligentsia and supported his interest in African and world history.

Arturo Schomburg's quest for historical and literary materials by and about African people resulted in a collection of letters, manuscripts, prints, playbills, and paintings from all over the world, albeit the strength of his materials concerned the United States, the Caribbean and Latin

Arturo Alfonso Schomburg

America and the lives of heroic people in that region. The New York Public Library's Division of Negro Literature, History, and Prints owes much of its collection to materials sold or bequeathed by Schomburg. As a consequence of such treasures, the New York Public Library became a center of intellectual and cultural activity in Harlem. As a curator in the library, Schomberg became a core participant in the social and literary movement known as the "Harlem Renaissance." [SOURCE: Hoffnung-Garskof, "The Migrations of Arturo Schomburg: On Being Antillano, Negro, and Puerto Rican in New York 1891-1938."]

SECRETARIAT FOR HISPANIC AFFAIRS

Based in Washington, D.C., the Secretariat was founded in 1945 and has 140 diocesan directors as members. It offers consultation services operated by the Catholic Bishops of the United States to assist those dioceses with large Hispanic populations in developing a far-reaching and effective response to the pastoral needs of Hispanics in the United States. It conducts and disseminates research and provides liaisons with other institutions and agencies. It publishes the quarterly *En Marcha* (On the March). [SOURCE: Kanellos, "Organizations," 395.]

SECULARIZATION OF MISSION LANDS

Frontier soldiers and civilians had both resented the extensive landholdings belonging to the Franciscan missionaries in California. As a consequence, as soon as Mexico became independent from Spain, they began to pressure the new liberal government in Mexico to secularize the missions, which should have been under control of such regular orders as the Franciscans only temporarily. According to the dictums of secularization, former mission lands would be allotted to the Indian neophytes. The process began with decrees issued in 1826, 1830, and 1831 by Governor Echeandía. Opposition from Mexico's conservatives delayed implementation until 1833. Unfortunately for the natives, machinations by well-placed Californios, many of them former frontier soldiers, resulted in more land winding up in the hands of non-Indians. The Secularization Proclamation ended the California mission system and gave birth to the "Ranchos Era." [SOURCE: Ryan and Breschini, "Secularization and the Ranchos, 1826-1846," http://www. mchsmu-seum.com/secularization.html]

SEGREGATION AND MEXICAN AMERICANS

The separation of Mexican school children from Anglo-American children existed since the U.S. incorporation of the lands that became the Southwestern United States. However, segregation became more intense as Mexican immigration in the late nineteenth and early twentieth centuries resulted in larger numbers of students in Southwestern schools. Even then, segregation was not uniform and was not justified by the "separate but equal doctrine," which affected African Americans, Native Americans, and Asians. To some degree, Mexicans in the United States accepted the rational that Mexican children were separated because they did not know English. But when bilingual children were still being separated in the 1920s, that argument wore thin. It took stability and permanency, however, before the community was ready to mount formal desegregation efforts. A quality education for their children became more important the longer the Mexican immigrants lived in the United States. Challenges to school segregation, either through the courts or through confrontation of school boards and administrators, were mounted by Mexican immigrant leaders as early as the 1920s.

One of the first successful desegregation courts cases took place in Tempe, Arizona, in 1928. Mexican families, many whose ancestors helped settle the city since its 1870s founding, challenged and succeeded in overturning a segregation policy in effect since 1915. One reason for this success is that Tempe Mexicans had a well-developed family network with roots in the Mexican state of Sonora and had acquired the legal ability and capital to make the challenge. Unfortunately, segregation continued for children of the recently arrived or from poorer families until the 1940s. Only some of the offspring of well-established Mexican-American families were able to integrate Anglo schools. More successful was the 1930 undertaking in Lemon Grove, California, a community near San Diego, where Mexican parents successfully sued the school board for placing their children in separate facilities. The community in Lemon Grove had a tight-knit group of immigrants from Baja California who had been in the United States a great number of years, working in the local citrus fruit industry. In San Bernardino, in 1929, students, parents, and the Mexican government objected to efforts by the school board to segregate Mexicans with Negroes at the De Olivera Elementary School. The community refused to accept the rationale given by Ida Collins, the County Superintendent of Public Instruction, who claimed the purpose for the separation was to help the children learn English.

During 1924, Mexican parents, mainly from Guanajuato, and the consul protested to the school board when white parents petitioned to segregate Mexicans students in the Argentine, Kansas, high school. The Argentine community had greater cohesion than the larger but newer Midwest Mexican *colonias* in Chicago and Detroit during this same period because it had about a decade's headstart in its development. As a result of the protest, Mexican students were integrated into the high school, but segregation continued in elementary schools, a practice that neither parents nor the consul questioned. This compromise, which was not to the white parents liking, at least did not bar Mexicans from attending high school, which was the case in many places in Texas.

Through a League of United Latin American Citizens (LULAC)*-sponsored initiative in 1946, attorneys from the Lawyer's Guild succeeded in desegregating a number of southern California schools in the landmark *Westminster v. Méndez* case by arguing that segregation violated constitutional rights of Mexican children guaranteed by the Fourteenth Amendment. At least 5,000 Mexican-American children were affected. The *Westminster* decision had a momentous affect on the future of segregation of Mexican children.

Texas Mexican-American leaders waged the most intense efforts to desegregate schools. LULAC was in the forefront of this campaign and achieved successes even before World War II. During the 1930s, schools in Del Rio, Goliad, and Beeville were integrated, but the bulk of the battle remained for later years. In 1948, lawyers commissioned by LULAC used the historic *Westminster* decision as precedence for challenging segregation policy in the Bastrop, Texas, schools. The court ruled in favor of prohibiting segregation either in separate schools or in separate rooms within the same school.

In 1952, through *Sheely v. González** segregation was abolished in Tolleson, Arizona, a town in Maricopa County where Phoenix is located. The successful integration decision came about because of the resolve Tolleson parents demonstrated in organizing into a civic group to pursue this suit. Also essential in this endeavor was Ralph Estrada, a lawyer and president of the Alianza Hispano-Americana.* Two years later in nearby Peoria, the school board voluntarily ended segregation of Mexicans in local schools—this was the last hold-out in the state. The initiative foiled the desires of school officials who stubbornly clung to the idea that Mexican Americans required separate and different teaching methods. As in the Texas cases, the *Westminster* decision also played a crucial part in the Tolleson case.

But these court victories were only as good as the desire of school administrators to carry out the judicial mandates. In Texas, officials were not very prompt in issuing desegregation orders, and it took the continuous prodding of community people to bring about true integration.

An example of community pressure was applied in Hondo, Texas in 1950, when the American G.I. Forum* asked brand new lawyer Albert Peña to help end segregation in the Hondo schools. Peña requested that the superintendent persuade the board to end segregation because it was unconstitutional. Mexican children could only go up to seventh grade, and then there was no school for them. Peña's request was turned down by the school board and the Department of Education at the state level, Peña and members of the G.I. Forum successfully persuaded all of the Mexican-American parents in

Hondo to attend the school board meeting and complain. Eventually the board capitulated.

Segregation in housing and the use of public facilities, including funeral homes and cemeteries, was likewise de facto and de jure in many areas of the Southwest. Mexican and Mexican American opposition to segregation in public places arose because separate facilities were always inferior, but also because Mexicans found the practice humiliating. Often it was the newspapers and the Mexican consulates who led the protests. For example, in San Francisco, in August 1919, Mexican Consul Gerónimo S. Seguín protested that 113 Mexicans were forced to live in the Negro section and that they had to sit with Negroes in cinemas and other public places. Chicago's *El Nacional* in 1935 inveighed against Mexicans being forced to use Negro undertakers. It urged its readers to use white funeral parlors because intimacy with blacks only brought them down to that level in the eyes of white society,

But prejudice and rejection has persisted to this date, even if official segregation no longer exists. Mexican Americans, now more integrated into mainstream society, display stronger capabilities in their efforts to break down obstacles to economic and social mobility. [SOURCE: Rosales, *Chicano!*]

SELF-HELP GRAPHICS & ART

Since its founding in 1973, Self-Help Graphics & Art (SHG) has become the leading visual arts center in the predominantly Chicano East Los Angeles. The center fosters and encourages creations by Chicano artists and assists in presenting their works to all audiences through SHG's numerous programs and services. The center provides such key support as the Print-making Atelier, which allows artists to create and produce unique serigraphs. The Exhibition Print Program takes SHG-produced print exhibitions to local, regional, national and international audiences. The Professional Artists Workshop Program enhances the professional experience of artists through experimentation with a variety of techniques and mediums. SHG does not charge for its services, this policy has permitted local artists to obtain exposure and resources and has allowed them to be self-supporting. [SOURCE: http://www.selfhelpgraphics.com]

SER-JOBS FOR PROGRESS

Founded in 1964, SER-Jobs for Progress is a voluntary community-based organization based in Dallas, Texas, with 111 affiliate programs in 83 cities. SER has obtained the bulk of its funding through federal contracts. First started in Texas through the efforts of LULAC* and the American G.I. Forum,* it is now a national network of organizations that develops programs for the full utilization of Hispanics in the economy. Its extensive range of activities include a wide array of job-training and educational programs with special emphasis on local job needs. In addition, SER also conducts English language and adult education courses, and provides counseling, and a job placement service. It publishes the quarterly *SER America.* [SOURCE: Kanellos, "Organizations," 395.]

SERRANO, JOSÉ E. (1943-)

As a member of the U.S. House of Representatives, José Serrano is one of the highest ranking elected officials in New York. When he was seven years old, his family moved to New York City from Mayagüez, Puerto Rico, where he was born in 1943. After graduating from high school in the Bronx and attending Lehman College of the City University of New York, he served in the U.S. Army Medical Corps for two years and was discharged honorably in 1966. He worked with the New York City Board of Education and also served as chairman of the South Bronx Community Corporation during this same time. In 1974, he was elected to the New York State Assembly. During his 15 years of service he was chairman of the Education Committee and he sponsored several pieces of landmark legislation, including revamping the process of electing local school boards.

During his tenure in the Assembly, Serrano entered the inner circle of the Democratic Party and, in 1990, Serrano won a seat in the U.S. House of Representatives in a special election called in March 1990, to fill the unexpired term of Robert García.* In November of that year, the voters in the Bronx elected him to a full term. As a congressman, Serrano has worked on legislative issues dealing with labor, education, voting rights, health, immigration, and foreign relations. In the 103rd Congress, Serrano was elected to a two-year term as Chairman of the Congressional Hispanic Caucus* and the Congressional Hispanic Caucus Institute.* [SOURCE: *Hispanic Americans in Congress, 1822-1995.*]

SERRANO V. PRIEST

In 1968 John Serrano, Jr. filed a suit against the California State Treasurer charging that funding schools with local property taxes resulted in an inferior education for his son in the East Los Angeles schools. The case lingered in the adjudication system and it took three decisions by the California Supreme Court, in August 1971, April 1974, and December 1977, to decide that relying solely on local property taxes to fund schools failed to protect the right of all students to receive equal education, as required by the U.S. Constitution. As a consequence, state income taxes are now dispersed to correct disparities in school funding within distinct school districts. [SOURCE: Meier and Rivera, *A Dictionary of Mexican American History,* 326.]

SERVICIOS DE LA RAZA, INC.

In 1972, Servicios de La Raza, Inc. was formed in Denver, Colorado, with a mission of providing and advocating comprehensive, culturally relevant human services to the Mexicano/Chicano, urban, working-class, primarily Spanish-speaking communities of the greater metropolitan area of the city. Today, the facility provides these services with a staff of some 40 trained professionals and is state-licensed to provide mental health and substance abuse treatment. In accordance with its mission statement, assistance is given primarily, but not limited to, the Spanish-speaking population. [SOURCE: www.serviciosdelaraza.org]

SHEELY V. GONZÁLEZ

In 1952, the *Sheely v. González* court decision abolished segregation in Tolleson, a town in Maricopa County where Phoenix is located. The successful integration decision came about because Tolleson parents organized into the Tolleson Civic League. Also essential in this endeavor was Ralph Estrada,* a lawyer and president of the Alianza Hispano-Americana.* Two years later in nearby Peoria, the school board voluntarily ended segregation of Mexicans in local schools—this was the last hold-out in the state. The initiative foiled the desires of school officials, who stubbornly clung to the idea that Mexican Americans required separate and different teaching methods. As in the Texas cases, the *Westminster* decision played a crucial part in the Tolleson case. [SOURCE: Rosales, *Chicano!*, 105.]

SISTERS OF COLOR UNITED FOR EDUCATION

In 1991, Belinda García and Bernadette Berzoza co-founded Sisters of Color United for Education in Denver, Colorado, as a nonprofit project advocating for health equity and improved quality of life predominantly for women of color, their families, and their communities. Among the activities of the Sisters are programs that confront the ravages of drug addiction, the spread of HIV/AIDS infection, education about reproductive health, and domestic violence. Ultimately, the extensive staff of experts at Sisters prepares their clients, mainly Hispanic women, to deal with their most pressing individual problems and enables them to fulfill their potential for a healthier, safer lifestyle. [SOURCE: http://www.sistersofcolorunited.org/who.html]

SLEEPY LAGOON (1942-1944)

In the Los Angeles of the 1940s, gang activity of Mexican-American *pachucos* (zoot-suited street youth) provoked police crackdowns and negative media coverage, which in turn created a widespread public backlash against Mexicans. The issue came to a head with the famous Sleepy Lagoon trial in

1942. A young teenager, José Díaz, was killed at a party in Sleepy Lagoon, a favorite water hole for Mexican-American teenagers.

Twenty-four members of the 38th street gang were arrested and charged, despite flimsy evidence against them. Throughout the trial the judge, the prosecutors, and some of the witnesses for the state engaged in an orgy of anti-Mexican bashing. As if the judge wanted them to appear sinister and unkempt, the defendants were not allowed to bathe throughout most of the proceedings. All except for two were found guilty of murder in varying degrees. A committee was formed to provide legal support for the defendants, whose members included journalist-crusader Carey McWilliams,* labor organizer Bert Corona,* Josefina Fierro de Bright from the Congress of Spanish Speaking People,* Anthony Quinn and an array of other Hollywood actors and movie-makers. Through these efforts, the verdicts were overturned. Curiously, because the activist group contained well-known socialists—McWilliams, Fierro de Bright, and Corona—the effort tried not to be seen as un-American. Nonetheless, committee members were harassed by the Tenney Committee for un-American activities,* which had been set up by the California legislature. [SOURCE: Escobar, *Race, Police, and the Making of a Political Identity.*]

THE SOCIAL SECURITY BOARD AND WHITENESS OF MEXICANS

Following the establishment of the Social Security Act in 1935, the board distributed federal retirement plans. It assigned Mexicans to a non-white racial status. The League of United Latin American Citizens* protested this assignment and initiated a campaign to instate Mexicans in a white category. This incident illustrates the ambiguous and problematic racial identity of Mexican Americans, as well as their own prejudices against African Americans. [SOURCE: Rosales, *Chicano!*, 95-96.]

SOCIEDAD DE AGRICULTORES MEXICANOS DE ARIZONA

During 1930, Pedro de la Lama,* a Mexican immigrant newspaper publisher and businessman, tried to organize Los Agricultores Mexicanos (Mexican Agriculturalists) in Tolleson, an agricultural town in the Phoenix, Arizona, area. The Mexican consul, who opposed de la Lama's leadership because he was a major critic of the Mexican government, accused him of defrauding the members of the union. This triggered an investigation by postal inspectors that led to the group's demise. It served as one of the first attempts to organize Mexican workers and establish Tolleson as the main staging ground for other similar efforts all the way into the 1960s, when the United Farm Workers Union,* which César Chávez* had founded in California, began a movement in that community. [SOURCE: Rosales, *Testimonio*, 238.]

SOUTHWEST NETWORK FOR ENVIRONMENTAL AND ECONOMIC JUSTICE

In April 1990, the People of Color Regional Activist Dialogue on Environmental Justice held a first-time meeting of 80 environmental and economic justice activists from 32 organizations. At its meeting in Albuquerque, New Mexico, the group decided that a coalition umbrella was needed to empower people of color in the Southwest and along the border region of Mexico to influence local, state, regional, national, and international policy on environmental and economic justice. Thus the Southwest Network for Environmental and Economic Justice was born. The network's primary purpose is guided by the unifying principles and strategies that came out of the Albuquerque meeting, basically to give direction to "building a movement" from the perspective of people of color. These include opposing the placement of dangerous incinerators and landfills in immigrant communities, supporting farmworkers striving for a pesticide-free workplace and garment workers impacted by plant closings, as well as assisting communities poisoned by industrial pollution, Native Americans threatened with uranium mining and militarism, and Chicano and African American communities suffering from severe lead poisoning. Today, the network serves representatives of more than 75 grassroots organizations from Texas, New Mexico, Colorado, Arizona, Nevada, and California, as well as citizen organizations from native nations in the region and border states of Mexico. [SOURCE: http://www.sneej.org/history.htm]

SOUTHWEST VOTER REGISTRATION EDUCATION PROJECT

In 1974, the Southwest Council of La Raza (SWCLR)—a creation of the Ford Foundation* in its attempts to bring about social change—provided funding for the Southwest Voter Registration Education Project (SVREP). The SVREP became one of the most important projects funded by the Southwest Council of La Raza. The founder and director, Willie Velásquez,* an original member of the Mexican American Youth Organization (MAYO),* a militant organization which began in San Antonio, opted for the project against the wishes of his fellow members, who went on to found La Raza Unida Party (LRUP),* a third party for Mexican Americans. Velásquez concluded that the LRUP's polarization of the white and Mexican communities could backfire in the form of a backlash. As a consequence, he decided to join the Democratic Party, concluding that "ethnic movements and third parties were ill-fitted to survive in American politics." After resigning under pressure from MAYO, Velásquez "described himself as a Jeffersonian Democrat who believed in the system," and in 1971, began working for the National Council of La Raza,* running the organization's Citizens' Voter Research and Education Project, the forerunner of the SVREP.

During Velásquez's tenure, the SVREP grew into a separate, fully staffed organization with a board of directors and a mission that included voter-registration drives, education, litigation, and research. The registration efforts were by far the most important of the SVREP objectives and, at the time of Velásquez's death in 1988, it had completed one thousand such drives. The project was responsible for increasing the number of Mexican Americans registered to vote in Texas, from about 400,000 in 1980 to 1.2 million during this period. The organization has often joined with the Mexican American Legal Defense and Educational Fund (MALDEF)* to litigate such issues as gerrymandering to prevent minority voting districts to emerge and, by 2000, the SVREP had won one hundred lawsuits against local jurisdictions attempting to block effective minority voting.

Throughout the 1990s, the SVREP committed itself to the most ambitious registration goal in history: one million new Latino voters for the general elections in November 1996, a goal which was almost fulfilled. It continues expanding Latino electorate. The SVREP conducts a Latino Academy yearly in its five regional headquarters in major cities throughout the country. The academy specializes in fostering leadership skills as they pertain to the electoral process. [SOURCE: Rosales, *Chicano!*, 264, 266; Palomo Acosta, "Southwest Voter Registration Project."]

SPANISH AMERICAN WAR

The U.S. war waged against Spain grew directly out of the decades-long struggle of Cuban and Puerto Rican patriots to become free from Spain, a war that had lasted the better part of a century. When in the 1890s, leaders such as José Martí* waged intensive campaigns to bring about independence, Spain's retaliation was characteristically harsh. José Martí was killed four months after the struggle began. One year after the insurrection started, Madrid sent General Valeriano Weyler, a hardened veteran who launched the brutal "war with war" campaign to wipe out the rebel movement. In a highly successful campaign, Cuban propagandists in the United States worked hand-in-hand with the English-language press to evoke sympathy for the Cuban cause against Spain. General Weyler was then pulled out of Cuba to quell the intensity of world public opinion, which had turned against Spain, especially among Americans.

But American support quickly turned into outright confiscation of the Cuban and Puerto Rican rebel cause. When the American battleship, USS Maine, blew up mysteriously in Havana Harbor in April, 1898, "yellow press" newspapers in the United States clamored for war against Spain. President William McKinley, reflecting an American longing for a maritime empire, seized the opportunity and declared war against Spain on April 28. Five months later, Spain capitulated and signed the Treaty of Paris, transferring Cuba, Puerto Rico, the Philippines, and Guam to the United States. President McKinley quickly achieved the overseas realm that he wanted. [SOURCE: Rosales, "A Historical Overview," 25-26.]

SPANISH BLACK LEGEND

An early source of Anglo-American antipathy towards Hispanics is found in the Spanish Black Legend. This anti-Hispanic legend has roots in the sixteenth-century English propagandists' translation of Bartolomé de las Casas' writings detailing the atrocities visited by Spaniards on the Native Americans during the conquest and colonization of the Americas. The English and Dutch translators and elaborators sought to discredit the reputation of the rival Spanish Empire in the New World. As a consequence, Anglo Americans have held negative views of Hispanics even before confronting Mexicans on New Spain's frontiers, where the encounter itself deepened prejudices and provided a least one important rationale for "Manifest Destiny."* The violence of the Texas Rebellion and the Mexican-American War* further fueled the antipathy. [SOURCE: Weber, *The Spanish American Frontier in North America, 336-341.*]

SPANISH REPUBLICAN REFUGEES IN THE UNITED STATES

In the 1930s, Spanish political refugees reached U.S. shores from across the Atlantic: they were fleeing the Spanish fascism of the Flanges led by Francisco Franco. Hispanic communities across the United States embraced the refugees and sympathized with their cause; many Cuban, Mexican, and Puerto Rican organizations had fundraisers for the Republican cause during the Spanish Civil War. Expatriates were fast to establish their own exile press. Their efforts hit fertile soil in Depression-era communities that were already hotbeds for union and socialist organizing. Manhattan and Brooklyn were the centers of Hispanic anti-fascist fervor and contributed to numerous newspapers and publications which maintained socialist or anarchist tendencies. Such newspapers as *España Libre* (Free Spain, 1939–1977) lasted a considerable amount of time. In addition, many Hispanic labor and socialist organizations, made up of Spanish immigrant workers who were not necessarily exiles, also published newspapers that came to support the Republican cause: the long-running anarchist paper *Cultura Proletaria* (Proletarian Culture, 1910–1959) was one. The Hispanic labor press in Tampa, Chicago, and the Southwest also felt solidarity with the Spanish expatriates, supporting the Republican cause in their pages and raising funds for refugees and victims of the Spanish Civil War. [SOURCE: Kanellos, *Hispanic Periodical in the United States, 27-28.*]

SPEARS LAW

In 1945, a Texas state legislator named J. Franklin Spears lent his name to a bill that would make it illegal to discriminate and segregate Mexican Americans. Mexican-American civil rights activists heartened by this gesture, rallied to support the politician's efforts, which to their disappointment was not put to a vote. The Caucasian Resolution, an earlier legislative act, passed in 1943 at the urging of Governor Coke Stevenson; it declared that Anglo Americans should not discriminate against Mexican Americans, who were also Caucasian. The resolution, however, did not have any enforcement provisions, an issue that activists hoped would be remedied with the Spears effort. [SOURCE: Rosales, *Testimonio*, 192-193.]

ST. AUGUSTINE COMMUNITY GARDEN

A community garden was established in Chicago after St. Augustine's Church was torn down in 1990. Church leaders did not foresee that the demolition would erase a significant source of comfort for parishioners and neighborhood dwellers, most of whom were Central American immigrants and refugees. In 1994, Brother Denis, the director of Su Casa, a refugee center which was housed at the church, applied for a Community Development Block Grant from the City of Chicago Department of Environment to help in planting a community garden on the vacant lot at 5043 S. Laflin, where the old church once stood. Thanks to the grant and hundreds of volunteers from the community and from the University of Illinois, the lot is now blooming with flowers and vegetables that are donated to the Women, Infants and Children (WIC) food centers in Chicago. His Eminence Joseph Cardinal Bernardin dedicated and blessed the garden on March 13, 1995, at a dedication that attracted more than 200 people. [SOURCE: Urban Programs Resource Network, http://www.urbanext.uiuc.edu/programs/sucasa.html]

STOP THE OUT-OF-CONTROL PROBLEMS OF IMMIGRATION TODAY

Founded in 1994, in Marin County, California, Stop the Out of Control Problems of Immigration Today (STOPIT) was an early and key organization founded on behalf of Proposition 187,* the initiative that passed in that year to ban illegal immigrants from public social services, non emergency health care and public education. The mission of STOPIT is summed up by Bette Hammond, a founder and director of the orgnization: "We've got to take back our country." [SOURCE: Chávez, *Shadowed Lives*, 193.]

STUDENT NETWORKING COMMITTEE

Organized in 1998 as a corollary of the New York City chapter of the National Congress for Puerto Rican Rights,* the Student Networking Committee invokes Boricua student power as a catalyst for persuading Latino students to become involved in social and political issues that confront the Puerto Rican community in New York City. Its mission is to foster student networking and to provide a forum and support group for student activists. The student networking committee also encourages community and campus activism and has developed networks of student activists between New York City-area college campuses and the local Puerto Rican grassroots communities. The network has sponsored collaborative workshops where campus activists interact with community leaders on such issues as police brutality and racism in local communities and on college campuses. In addition, the network supports a "Student Think Tank" for exchanging ideas, for training, and to devise effective strategies. [SOURCE: National Congress for Puerto Rican Rights, http://ncprr.8k.com/]

SUÁREZ, XAVIER (1948-)

Miami elected its first Cuban-born mayor, Xavier Suárez, in 1985. By then, Hispanics controlled three of five seats on the city commission, and held many of the city's most important administrative and patronage positions. Born in Las Villas, Cuba, the son of a university professor, Suárez moved as an exile to Washington, D.C. with his family in 1961. After studying law and public policy at Harvard University, Suárez made a conscious move to Miami to become involved in politics. After unsuccessfully challenging Maurice Ferré for mayor in 1983, he was finally successful by creating coalitions of Blacks, Anglos, and Hispanics. [SOURCE: Tardiff and Mabunda, *Dictionary of Hispanic Biography*, 368-9.]

EL TEATRO CAMPESINO, *see* VALDEZ, LUIS

TELLES, RAYMOND (1915-)

The most encouraging electoral gain for Mexican Americans in the 1950s was the 1957 election to mayor of Raymond Telles, who was born in El Paso in 1915. After graduating from parochial schools, he obtained a degree from El Paso's International Business College in 1933 and then worked as an accountant for the U.S. Department of Justice for eight years. To further his career, Telles enrolled in the Texas College of Mines in 1940 but had to withdraw when the Army drafted him. He entered the military as a private and rose to the rank of mayor. During his service career, Telles served as a military aide to high level Latin American and Mexican dignitaries when they visited the United States. He also served in a similar capacity when President Truman visited Mexico City. After his discharge, he returned to his hometown and ran for and was elected as the El Paso County Clerk in 1948. Telles' victory demonstrated that Mexican Americans would vote in bloc if the candidate was one of their own. Half of El Paso's population of 250,000 was of Mexican-origin but was always outnumbered by non-Mexican registered voters. To win, Telles needed to carry a sizable percentage of the white vote, which he did by waging a campaign minimizing ethnic and race differences. In addition, Telles did not dwell on the impoverishment affecting a large portion of El Paso's Mexican working class. Instead, Telles struck a more general populist note, that emphasized curbing the power of the professional politicians who had run city hall for years.

Owing to this strategy, he did not scare away potential white supporters, who wanted to see city politics cleaned up. At the same time, he did not appear too tame to a large Mexican electorate that was predisposed to support him because of his ethnic appeal. Moreover, Telles' tenure as an efficient county clerk completed his image as a tested and trusted official. Telles won a second term as mayor and planned a third, but President Kennedy, appointed him Ambassador to Costa Rica in 1961. After serving in various federal positions in the Lyndon B. Johnson administration, Telles returned to El Paso following the election of Richard Nixon to the presidency. In 1969, Telles attempted another campaign for mayor of El Paso but was defeated. President Richard Nixon in 1971 appointed him chairman of the Equal Employment Opportunity Commission;* President Carter appointed him head of the Inter-American Development Bank in El Salvador, again with the rank of ambassador. He continued in this position until he retired in El Paso in 1982. [SOURCE: García, *Mexican Americans,* 84-112.]

TENAYUCA, EMMA (1916-1999)

In the 1930s, Texas produced one of the most well-known labor crusaders in Emma Tenayuca. Born in 1916 in San Antonio, Texas, she was an activist in unionism since her days in high school. After joining the American Communist Party in 1937, she brought to her work a fervor born out of her dedication to the class struggle. In "The Mexican Question in the Southwest," an essay which she co-authored with her husband, Homer Brooks, she provided a vivid demonstration that Mexican workers in the Southwest were part of this conflict. Tenayuca helped organize the well-known San Antonio Pecan Shellers Strike when El Nogal (The Pecan Tree), a syndicate affiliated with the Congress of Industrial Organizations (CIO), packing house union struck against the Southern Pecan Shelling Company in 1938.

In San Antonio, the pecan processors were influential, and the police quickly embarked on a harassment campaign to break the strike. At this point, Tenayuca became a strike leader, but had to resign because of her communist party affiliation. Nonetheless, she continued to support the effort and remained dedicated to the cause. Tenayuca gave such fiery speeches to animate the striking workers that she earned the nickname of *la pasionaria* (The Passionate One). The strike, which lasted one month, succeeded in obtaining higher wages for the pecan shellers, although soon after that, the industry mechanized and laid off workers. When the dispute began in 1938, 10,000 shellers toiled in the Southern Pecan-Shelling Company; by 1941, the company employed only 600 workers. [SOURCE: Rosales, *Chicano!*, 121-123.]

TENNEY COMMITTEE

The Tenney Committee, established in 1941 by the California legislature, served as a fact-finding committee on un-American activities. Headed by Assemblyman Jack B. Tenney, the committee reflected a federal initiative by conducting legislative trials of organizations on individuals suspected of having radical ties. Several members of the Sleepy Lagoon Defense Committee were subpoenaed, for example, during 1943 and 1944, and grilled in an effort to prove their Communist connections. Brushed with this air of disloyalty, the funders withdrew their support of the Sleepy Lagoon Committee in its efforts to defend young Mexican Americans who were probably accused falsely of a murder. The same tactics were again applied by Tenney in 1947 in an attempt to discredit Ernesto Galarza* and the National Farm Labor Union in its strike at DiGiorgio farms. The Tenney Committee did connect the union to the American Communist Party, but only after a large number of people were harassed. The loyalty oath controversy of California in 1949, in which Tenney falsely accused fellow legislature members of communist sympathies, led to Tenney being forced off the committee. [SOURCE: Barrett, *The Tenney Committee*.]

TEURBE TOLÓN, MIGUEL (1820-1857)

Born in Matanzas, Cuba, Miguel Teurbe Tolón in the 1850s worked as an editor for Latin American affairs on the New York *Herald*. He had been had been an editor of Cuba's *La Guirnalda*, where he also launched his literary career as a poet. In the United States, besides working for the *Herald*, he published poems and commentary in both Spanish- and English-language periodicals, and translated into Spanish Paine's *Common Sense* and Emma Willard's *History of the United States*. Teurbe Tolón was one of the most important pioneers of Hispanic journalism in the United States. But it is not only as a journalist that Teurbe Tolón must be remembered. He is one of the founders of the literature of Hispanic exile, not only because of the exile theme in the many poems he published, but also because he was seen as a leader of the literary exile. His work figures most prominently in the first anthology of exile literature ever published in the United States, *El laúd del desterrado* (1856), issued a year after his death. Since the writings of Teurbe Tolón and his colleagues, exile literature has been a continuing current in

Hispanic letters of the United States. [SOURCE: Kanellos, *Hispanic Period-icals in the United States*, 167, 175.]

TEXAS RANGERS

The Texas Rangers have existed in various guises since the Texas Rebellion of 1836. Immediately before the uprising, Texas rebels instituted this organization with a complement of 56 men in three companies. Initially, the rangers participated in the rebellion only peripherally. But during the nine-year period of the Texas Republic, the organization grew to close to two hundred men in twelve companies and acquired a more important role by quelling Indian rebellions, by discouraging law breakers, and keeping Mexicans in a web of control. By the time the United States annexed the Lone Star Republic as a state in 1845, the rangers had become thoroughly institutionalized. Their disdain for Mexicans had become abundantly clear as well. The attitude of W.A. "Big Foot" Wallace is a good example. He came to Texas and joined the rangers to kill "greasers" and avenge the execution of his brother and cousin at the 1836 Goliad Massacre. In 1846 during the Mexican-American War, the rangers had participated in the invasion of northern Mexico led by General Zachary Taylor and achieved worldwide fame as a fighting force. But their waging of war was so ruthless and lethal that among Mexicans they earned the sobriquet "los diablos Tejanos" (Texas devils).

Under United States-annexed Texas, the rangers' role as a militia almost disappeared because the federal government assumed these responsibilities. But with the advent of the ongoing wars begun in 1859 with Juan Nepomuceno Cortina,* the rangers under Captain John S. "Rip" Ford temporarily restored their former glory. After the quelling of Cortina in the 1860s, however, they passed into obscurity, especially during Reconstruction. After northern control over Texas ended in the 1870s, the local white Democrats again dominated Texas politics and restored the rangers' power under Capt. Leander H. McNelly. It is in this era when the lawmen fought with Indian raiders and Mexican bandits that the Texas Rangers acquired their most fearsome and romantic reputation. Along with U.S. Army troops, rangers regularly chased Indians and Mexicans who drove Texas cattle across the Rio Grande, a maneuver which clearly violated Mexican sovereignty. Mexico consistently protested these extralegal pursuits, but eventually the Porfirio Díaz government in the 1880s gave permission for American soldiers and Texas Rangers to make arrests in Mexico only if apprehension came in "hot pursuit." In the course of the century, it became a tradition for Texas Rangers to zealously suppress local bandits and Mexicans who struck from across the Rio Grande. In the process, they harassed local Mexican Americans, maliciously breaking up fandangos and raiding homes of citizens not involved in illegal activity. Anglos had long memories and continued to harbor ill-will

Texas Rangers showing off dead bodies of "bandits" killed

because of atrocities committed against their people during the Texas Rebellion. While held in high regard by most Texans and by Americans in general, among Mexicans they were considered a nemesis known as the "rinches." Even the historian Walter Prescott Webb, who lavished praise on the officers, estimated that they killed anywhere from one thousand to five thousand Mexicans over the years.

The Mexican Revolution, which began in 1910 and lasted almost ten years, whose hostilities overlapped into U.S. border areas, served as an Anglo backlash against Mexicans in the United States and Mexico. This phenomenon, dubbed the "Brown Scare" by historian Ricardo Romo, affected relationships between Anglos and U.S. Mexicans not involved in political intrigue nor in revolutionary activity. In Texas, where border unrest was the most intense, Anglo Americans turned to the Texas Rangers for comfort and safety. On November 20, 1911, Governor Colquitt ordered all Mexican rebels to leave Texas within 48 hours and sent Texas Rangers to the border. Then Pascual Orozco, a player in dictator Porfirio Díaz's ouster, turned against his successor, Francisco I. Madero, in February 1912, and his forces lay siege to Ciudad Juárez. As a result, El Paso residents demanded protection, prompting Governor Colquitt to again deploy the Texas Rangers.

Madero became president in December 1911, and Mexican immigrants came to expect consular protection from Ranger brutality, but the Mexican government remained powerless to provide such security throughout most of the early twentieth century. The printed media painted the Texas lawmen with heroic strokes, fulfilling the public demand for romantic western lore.

An article in the *New York Times* during March 1914, introduced the rangers with the headline, "Texas Rangers, Who Ride Shoot and Dare." They made up, "One of the World's Most Efficient Armed Organizations," whose motto was "Get Them When You Go for Them," said the piece, swelled with admiration for the "derring-do of these men." But events surrounding the Plan de San Diego* in 1915 provoked an orgy of killings by the rangers, unmatched in the history of Texas Anglo-Mexican relations. Dispatches from the Rio Grande City Consul Leoncio Reveles provide detailed information on the atrocities as they intensified in the fall of 1915. His grisly reports tell of the wholesale slaughter by rangers of numerous seemingly non-participants of the plan. By October 1915, calm returned to south Texas, and the rangers were ordered to halt operations, but at least five hundred persons were killed in this period, according to Reveles.

Peace did not return to the border for some time, however. Raids by the followers of Pancho Villa* early in 1916—the January Santa Ysabel massacre* and the Columbus raid* in March—further inflamed feelings towards Texas Mexicans. This antagonism was exacerbated when General Jack Pershing's expedition, sent to find and punish Pancho Villa, sustained numerous casualties at the El Carrizal clash with the Venustiano Carranza* faction of the revolution in June. During this period in El Paso, rangers arrested Mexicans for openly harboring anti-American feelings. In one case, they shot and wounded an eighteen-year-old Pancho Villa after trying to arrest him for recruiting.

Even after border tensions cooled from the white-hot intensity reached during the Plan de San Diego* and the Villa raids, rangers continued to earn Mexican and Mexican American hatred. After bandits, identified in conflicting reports as either *carrancistas* or *villistas*, attacked the Brite Ranch* on December 25, 1917, in the Big Bend area, brutally killing or wounding guests celebrating Christmas, rangers and U.S. troops pursued them into Mexico and allegedly killed several of their number. Then on January 28, 1918, about 30 Texas Rangers, accompanied by Anglo ranchers and 12 U.S. Army soldiers went to Porvenir, an isolated community in the Big Bend region of Texas to arrest supposed participants in the Brite raid. The soldiers stayed on the outskirts, but the others took 15 Mexican small farmers and stock owners a mile out of town and vigilantes executed them and mutilated their bodies with knives

U.S. Army Adjutant General Jame Harley ordered the disbanding of Company B of the rangers, who were responsible for the massacre, and the resignation of its commander, Captain J.M. Fox. In 1919, at special hearings motivated by the severity of ranger brutality, numerous Texas officials, including Legislator José T. Canales,* called for curtailment of their authority. As Canales put it in a letter to C.H. Pease, a legislator who opposed his efforts, "All I want is to clear out a gang of lawless men and thugs from being placed . . . in the character of peace officers to enforce our laws." Nonetheless, this increasing public criticism tarnished the ranger's romantic image and resulted in the disbanding of the most offensive members of the force.

The Texas Rangers even influenced the Border Patrol,* a federal agency of the Immigration and Naturalization Service* which was organized in 1924, to stem undocumented entry into the United States. Clifford Perkins, a high-ranking official of the Border Patrol who was charged with instilling professionalism into the service in Texas, indicated that because many Laredo patrol members were former Texas Rangers, they continued ranger habits and dealt with immigrants as criminals But in the 1920s, reports of ranger atrocities decreased significantly; in fact, authorities at the behest of employers used Texas Rangers on more than one occasion to quell anti-Mexican riots because they interfered with economic stability. Ironically, rangers at times emerged as protectors of Mexicans. During the Depression of 1921, at a time of Klu Klux Klan-inspired violence, rangers secured the safety of Mexicans assaulted by masked men in such towns as Ranger and Breckenridge. Then as Depression-related unemployment took a toll among American workers in 1931, Anglos blew up a Mexican mutual aid society building in Malankoff, Texas. The governor again sent rangers to protect Mexican workers. White workers also attacked Mexicans in Cisco, Texas, and Governor Pat Neff finally sent Captain Hickman and a group of Texas Rangers to protect Mexicans in the afflicted areas, a maneuver that apparently quelled the violence. White workers later retaliated after the rangers had left, which prompted the governor to again deploy the rangers, who arrested an accused bomber in Tubbleville, a neighboring town, and turned him over to local officials for arraignment.

During the Great Depression, the Texas legislature reduced the rangers' budget, and the force was cut down to 45 or less. In the 1930s, also because many of the rangers became involved in partisan politics backing a losing candidate for governor, their fortunes waned further and their budget was slashed again. But when Depression-related crime waves engulfed Texas, creating folk legends such as those of Raymond Hamilton, George "Machine Gun" Kelly, and Clyde Barrow and Bonnie Parker, Texans demanded law and order. In 1935, the new-elected governor, James Allred, heeded these desires and, with the help of the legislature, established the Texas Department of Public Safety (DPS) with three basic units: the Texas Rangers, the Highway Patrol, and a forensics center known as the Headquarters Division. Since the 1930s, the rangers have acquired a more important role in overall law enforcement. With the appointment of Colonel Homer Garrison, Jr. as the new director in 1938, the rangers expanded their numbers and acquired an even higher status by becoming the investigative plain-clothes division, while the Highway Patrol officers were the uniformed state police.

Garrison headed the rangers until he died in 1968, and the DPS-appointed Col. Wilson E. Speir further professionalized and expanded the force, which is now the most advanced police force in Texas. While the evil reputation Texas Rangers acquired among the Mexican population has diminished in recent years, during the Chicano Movement* activists still took them to task and accused them of wrongdoing. Texas Rangers suppressed a farmworker strike in 1967, organized by the Texas contingent of the United Farm Workers Organizing Committee,* in which a young boy was inadvertently killed. The U.S. Commission on Civil Rights investigated the charges in hearings in San Antonio on Texas Ranger behavior and subpoenaed Ranger Captain Y. Allee* to account for charges of brutality. Nonetheless, the most atrocious police tactics attributed to the Texas Rangers by Mexicans in the state can hopefully be considered more history than contemporary behavior. [SOURCE: Rosales, *Chicano!*; Ben H. Proctor, "Texas Rangers."]

TIERRA AMARILLA COURTHOUSE RAID

Reies López Tijerina* and his Alianza Federal de Mercedes (Federal Land Grant Alliance)* members raided and took over the Rio Arriba County court house in Tierra Amarilla, New Mexico on June 6, 1967, to dramatize the plight of New Mexican small farmers attempting to recover their families' Spanish-Mexican land grants. The event became a landmark in the development of the Chicano* civil rights movement and Tijerina a symbol of the civil disobedience that would force authorities to react to demands. Eventually the Alianza waned as Tijerina and some of its followers were arrested and sentenced to prison terms for their illegal acts, which were among the most militant of the Chicano Movement.* [SOURCE: Rosales, *Chicano!*, 267-77.]

TIJERINA, FELIX (1905-1965)

Houston's Felix Tijerina was a salient Mexican-American figure who embodied the kind of leadership that greatly influenced the Mexican-American Generation. He came from a family of farm workers and grew up in the agricultural community of Sugarland, Texas. He was actually arrested for being undocumented upon returning from a trip from Mexico in the 1950s—immigration officials claimed he was born in Mexico. Nonetheless, he straightened out the imbroglio and did not allow the incident to spoil his ability to continue fulfilling the Horatio Alger ideal which so inspired his Mexican-American cohorts with its emphasis on self improvement. As a boy, he moved to Houston where he worked in restaurants and, by his own account, learned to read English from menus. He opened up his own restaurant with his wife, Janie (Juanita) González de Tijerina, who he married in 1933. The restaurant went broke during the Great Depression. In 1937, however, after the economy improved in Houston, Tijerina and his wife modified Mexican food to make it palatable to Anglos and opened a Mexican restaurant in the stylish Montrose area of Houston. Its success led eventually to establishing a chain of four eateries all displaying the familiar "Felix's" throughout the city. He kept his business going in spite of serving in the U.S. Air Corp during World War II. But apart from his business success, Tijerina made one of the greatest impacts on Mexican-American civil rights in Texas. His early involvement came as early as 1935 when he, Leonard J. Lewis, and George Dreary (Hispanics with Anglo names) cofounded Houston's Latin American Club (LAC).* Convincing the Houston city council to put Mexican-American employees on permanent status rather than being "temporary" became one of the first issues of the organization. In the process, LAC became Local Council 60 of the League of United Latin American Citizens (LULAC)* with Tijerina as vice president and later as president. He also served as national president of LULAC in the 1950s for four terms. Under his watch, the influential "Little School of 400,"* which sought to teach preschool Mexican Americans 400 English words was established in Texas. The concept was later adopted by the federal Head Start Program. At first, Tijerina financed the project and then LULAC provided the financial support but Texas Governor Price Daniel was so impressed with the program that he persuaded the Texas Legislature to provide state funding. Felix Tijerina died in his Houston home on September 4, 1965, of heart disease. [SOURCE: Kreneck, *Mexican American Odyssey.*]

TIJERINA, PATSY REIES (1948-)

Born in Tierra Amarilla, New Mexico, Patsy Tijerina married the land grant crusader, Reies López Tijerina in 1965 after his first marriage broke up. In 1969, Patsy Tijerina took up the land grant cause by burning national forest signs, an act which Reies himself could not commit because he would have violated his probation. While he was in jail, Patsy allegedly was sexually assaulted by men associated with the Albuquerque police department. Later, their son was also molested by a state policeman. [SOURCE: Rosales, *Chicano!,* 168-9.]

TIJERINA, REIES LÓPEZ, see LÓPEZ TIJERINA, REIES

TORRES, ESTEBAN E. (1930-)

Esteban Torres is an Hispanic congressmen from the State of California. He was born in Miami, Arizona, in 1930 but at age six moved to East Los Angeles with his family. After graduating from high school, he joined the U.S. Army and served during the Korean conflict. Discharged in 1953 as a sergeant first-class, he worked as an assembly-line welder and became active in the United Auto Workers (UAW). After holding a variety of posts, by 1963 Torres had become the union's director for the Inter-American Bureau for

Caribbean and Latin American Affairs. In the meantime, he attended East Los Angeles College and California State University on the G.I. Bill. Under the auspices of the UAW and its leader, Walter Ruether, in 1968 Torres founded the East Los Angeles Community Union (TELACU)* and, until 1974, directed this community action program that became one of the nation's largest anti-poverty agencies.

After an unsuccessful attempt to win the Democratic nomination to the U.S. House of Representatives in 1974, he returned as an official of the UAW in Washington, D.C. and, in 1977, President Jimmy Carter appointed Torres as a representative to the United Nations Educa-

Esteban E. Torres

tional, Scientific, and Cultural Organization (UNESCO). In 1979, President Carter appointed him Director of the White House Office of Hispanic Affairs.

In 1982, Torres again ran for the U.S. House of Representatives, this time successfully. He represented the newly created 34th District in East Los Angeles County, an area with 60 percent Hispanic population; he has been reelected seven times, with at least 60 percent of the vote. In Congress, Torres' has concentrated on legislation dealing with urban and environmental issues, labor, small businesses, immigration, and consumer rights. Torres has been an active member of the Congressional Hispanic Caucus* and, in the 100th Congress, served as its chairman. [SOURCE: *Hispanic Americans in Congress, 1822-1995.*]

TORRES BODET, JAIME (1903- 1974)

Born in Mexico City in 1903, Torres Bodet's career as a poet, diplomat, and high government official remains one of the most distinguished in Mexican history. Among his many positions was that of Minister of the Secretariat of Foreign Relations and Minister of Education. He was also ambassador to France. In the 1940s, Torres Bodet helped organize the Comité

Mexicano Contra el Racismo (Mexican Committee Against Racism).* With a membership from both Mexico and the United States, the committee strove to pressure the U.S. government to guarantee the human rights of Mexican nationals and Mexican Americans in the United States. The group felt that cooperation between Mexico and the United States, a necessary posture during World War II, provided leverage in ameliorating prejudice. [SOURCE: Rosales, *Chicano!*, 84; Gómez-Quiñones, *Chicano Politics*, 36.]

TRINIDAD, MAURICIO (?-1926)

During the 1920s, the California trial and execution of Mauricio Trinidad at San Quentin symbolized important aspects of the Mexican community and its fight against injustice in the legal system. Trinidad killed Luis Hernández in Colton during 1925, but a witness who disappeared supposedly could have corroborated Trinidad's claim of self-defense. At the trial, his lawyer addressed the jury for only ten minutes and did not call a single witness to testify, nor did he question any of the prosecution's witnesses. Immediately, fundraising began to hire a competent lawyer. In northern California, El Comité de Defensa de Mauricio Trinidad (Mauricio Trinidad Defense Committee) in Richmond, the Sociedad Cruz Azul Mexicana (Mexican Blue Cross Society), the Club Chapultepec,* and the Comisión Honorífica Mexicana (Mexican Honorific Commission)* of San Francisco joined the effort. In Los Angeles, such organizations as La Liga Protectora Mexicana (The Mexican Protection League) and La Confederación de Sociedades Mexicanas (The Federation of Mexican Societies) raised funds as well. The newspapers *Hispano América* of San Francisco and *El Heraldo de México** and *La Opinión* of Los Angeles enthusiastically provided support publicity. Trinidad's new lawyer was hired too late for an appeal, but countless petitions descended on Governor William Friend Richardson, who remained oblivious to the supplications. Trinidad hanged as scheduled on October 14, 1926. Nonetheless, the efforts to save Trinidad demonstrated that by the mid-1920s, a significant network of Mexican ethnic solidarity now spanned the states. [SOURCE: Rosales, *Chicano!*, 70.]

TUCSON EDUCATION COMMITTEE

Francisco Solano León was one of a committee of three (along with two Anglos) to organize Tucson's first public school district in 1867. The Mexican community supported the establishment and funding of public education in Arizona. The community believed that education was indispensable for Mexicans in the United States, and first and foremost for them was the learning of English. They felt that only through mastering English could they compete with Anglos in U.S. society. Three years later, Solano León was one of a committee of seventeen Mexicans who lobbied the governor of Arizona,

Richard McCormick, to establish a public school system. The committee included wealthy Mexican entrepreneurs, such as Estevan Ochoa,* who supported McCormick. Governor McCormick, in turn, pushed for public education and other legislation against discrimination. [SOURCE: Sheridan, *Los Tucsonenses,* 46-47.]

ULICA, JORGE, *see* ARCE, JULIO G.

UNIDAD LATINA

In the early 1970s, Unidad Latina served as the first political publication of the Manhattan Puerto Rican/Dominican civil rights group, El Comité. It began as a bilingual, local community paper and grew into a citywide publication. Through the newspaper, the group activists provided the community information on the day-to-day struggles experienced by Manhattan Latinos and also provided a view of the history of Latinos. The editor, Federico Lora, did most of the writing in the beginning, but eventually all El Comité members turned their hand to producing articles, a process that helped them develop skills and better understand their political mission. [SOURCE: Torres and Velázquez, *The Puerto Rican Movement,* 180.]

UNITED FARM WORKERS OF AMERICA

In the late 1950s, the Community Services Organization (CSO)* sent César Chávez* to Oxnard, California, to help unionize packing shed workers, but the organization did not support the organizing of workers actually working in the fields. When Chávez became National Director of the CSO in 1960, the CSO board would not authorize farmworker organizing, so he resigned to pursue his ambition on his own and he took a fellow CSO worker, Dolores Huerta,* with him.

Chávez and his organizers canvassed each town and camp, signing up small groups in each community. By 1965, the union, now called the National Farm Workers Association (NFWA), had signed up a thousand members and had won some small disputes. But in September, Chávez's fledgling union joined the Agricultural Workers Organizing Committee (AWOC), a union made up mainly of Filipino farmworkers, in a major strike against grape growers in the Delano area. But even this combined strike effort could not force the growers to capitulate. To put pressure on the farmers from another angle, in April of 1966, the union organized a march from Delano to the state capital of Sacramento, emphasizing the lack of social justice for farmworkers. The effort brought national attention to the plight of farmworkers.

These efforts did not persuade the grape producers to negotiate, so the NFWA resorted to boycotting the Schenley Liquor Company, which owned

Picketing for the United Farm Workers national boycott

extensive vineyards in the San Joaquin Valley. The ban succeeded, and Schenley granted all of the union's requests.

In April of 1966, the giant table grape-producing DiGiorgio* Corporation tried to sabotage NFWA gains by allowing the Teamsters Union to represent its workers, but the farmworker union defeated the trucker's union in an election and obtained a contract from the DiGiorgio company.

The union then directed its boycott against the grapes of the Giumarra Vineyards Corporation. When union leaders discovered that companies with union contracts lent labels to the Giumarras,* it asked the American public to boycott all table grapes. The national boycott required so much attention, however, that strike activity was neglected. Moreover, farmers recruited thousands of strike-breakers from Mexico. Some frustrated union members engaged in sabotage against the growers, but Chávez, who was committed to nonviolence, decided in March of 1968 to use a hunger strike to bring his people into line. Chávez's fast captured public imagination and helped promote the boycott and force California grape growers to relent and sign contracts.

Next, failing to achieve negotiations with Salinas Valley lettuce farmers, the union initiated a strike during the summer harvest season of 1970. Thousands of workers honored the strike called by the United Farm Workers

(UFW), as the union was now called, but the crop was harvested. The lettuce farmers obtained workers by signing "sweetheart" contracts with the Teamsters. Again the UFW turned to the boycott but did not experience the same success as with the grape ban.

Grape growers then decided to turn to the Teamsters when contracts expired with the UFW and launched a California-state initiative to outlaw the secondary boycott, Chávez's most potent weapon. The UFW successfully campaigned to defeat the bill, but the effort drained the union's resources. In 1975, Chávez announced a national boycott against Julio Gallo Wineries, the biggest business to sign a Teamster's contract, and led about 3,000 marchers from San Francisco to Gallo's headquarters in Modesto.

California's crucial agricultural industry suffered from these battles, and politicians, led by Governor Jerry Brown, passed a bill called the Agricultural Labor Relations Act to provide California farmworkers protection from which they were excluded when the Congress passed the National Labor Relations Act in 1935. When Jerry Brown's term ended, his successor, the conservative George Deukmajian, appointed Agricultural Labor Relations Board members who favored the growers' interests.

The union experience in California inspired farmworker union movements in Arizona, Texas, Florida, and the Midwest; these met with only modest success. Internal dissent weakened the UFW by the 1970s, as the rank and file began to challenge the leadership in the decision-making process. A third grape boycott was issued in 1984, mainly to protest pesticide use as harmful to workers. The boycott was a far cry from the dynamic effort made in the 1960s.

In the meantime, the union lost many contracts signed in the 1960s and 1970s. The ability of agricultural interests to use undocumented workers has weakened the ability of farmworkers to organize. As consequence, Chávez and many of the UFW organizers have supported restrictive immigration policies; however, this has changed in more recent years. [SOURCE; Griswold del Castillo and García, *César Chávez*; Rosales, *Testimonio*, 269-275; www.ufw.org]

UNITED MEXICAN AMERICAN STUDENTS CONFERENCE

One of the pivotal student meetings which helped launch the Chicano Movement* was sponsored by the University of Southern California's United Mexican American Students (UMAS). Held in 1967, the summit attracted 200 Mexican-American students from throughout southern California on December 16 and 17. This was one of the first occasions that Chicano* students from both southern and northern California met within a movement context. A contingent from the Mexican American Student Confederation (MASC), a group with chapters in the San Francisco Bay Area, and staff from Berkeley's Quinto Sol Publications drove down in a bus. Generally, students from northern California expressed a third world alignment. They adhered to a sketchy form of socialism and identified their cause, not just with oppressed Chicanos, but with other racial minorities in the United States and colonized peoples throughout the world; Communist Cuba, and China served as inspirations.

In session after session, forceful speakers exposed the dire conditions affecting ther communities. The students mapped out a "leadership revolution" for their communities, advocating political militancy as a means of wresting from the establishment resources. Participants also envisioned interracial cooperation and invited students from the Black Student Union.

Incipient forms of nationalism permeated the gathering, especially when students heard about the feats of Reies López Tijerina* from those who had been at a meeting in Albuquerque sponsored by the land rights Alianza Federal de las Mercedes* earlier that year. The group then voted to support the release of Tijerina, who at this point was incarcerated for his group's raid on a court house in northern New Mexico. The students also decided to promote the grape boycott that César Chávez's* union was using to force the DiGiorgio* table grape firm to negotiate. In spite of the revolutionary rhetoric, however, the meeting was basically reformist. An indication of this was a session on how gerrymandering had broken up solid Mexican-American voting areas; this was clearly a sign that the participants had faith in reforming in the system rather than completely doing away with it. [SOURCE: Rosales, *Chicano!*, 177-178.]

UNITED STATES FOREST SERVICE

The U.S. Forest Service became a main target of the land rights movement in northern New Mexico. It issued stricter regulations on grazing, wood cutting, and water use in national forests. These restrictions caused problems for villages, who did not have enough access to natural resources. Seemingly, the Forest Service was discriminating against Hispano small farmers, as they did not revoke all grazing permits for white ranchers. While the Forest Service restricted agricultural uses of the forests, it improved trails and campsites to support recreational uses of the lands, further alienating Hispanos' access and use of the national forests. [SOURCE: Rosales, *Chicano!*, 158; Forrest, *The Preservation of the Village*, 184-190]

UNITED STATES HISPANIC CHAMBER OF COMMERCE

In 1979, Hispanic business leaders who realized the enormous potential of the Hispanic business community in the United States met in New Mexico and founded the U.S. Hispanic Chamber of Commerce (USHCC) to represent their interests before the public and private sectors. Since its inception, the USHCC, now based in Washington, D.C., has provided 1.6 million Hispanic-owned businesses with various services to support their participation in the national economic agenda. The chamber has succeeded in developing relationships with international heads of state, members of Congress, and the White House. The 130 local Hispanic Chambers of Commerce and Hispanic business organizations have become an effective network through which the USHCC effectively communicates the needs and potential of Hispanic enterprise to the public and private sector. Under its auspices, Hispanic firms can benefit from projects that foment economic development, create links to the corporate sector at the national level, enhance international trade opportunities with businesses in Latin America, obtain crucial information on legislation and programs that affect the Hispanic business community, and provide technical assistance to Hispanic business associations and entrepreneurs. The ongoing objectives of the USHCC are enhanced through two major annual meetings: the Annual National Convention and the Annual Legislative Conference. Also as part of its mission, the chamber airs "Hispanics Today," a national half-hour, weekly syndicated television show. [SOURCE: http://www.ushcc.com/about.html]

UNITED STATES SURVEYOR GENERAL CLAIMS OFFICE

In 1854, the United States Surveyor General Claims Office was established in the New Mexico territory to resolve land disputes between Hispanics and newcomers. The office was responsible for making recommendations to Congress on the legality of all claims made by Mexicans under the terms of the Treaty of Guadalupe Hidalgo.* Congress then had the final say in confirming or denying the titles. This system was even slower than the one established in California by the California Land Act of 1851. At times it took 50 years to settle just a few claims because the Surveyor General's office did not have the proper resources to carry out its charge. In the meantime, Hispanic New Mexicans were defrauded in land grabs similar to those in California. [SOURCE: Forrest, *The Preservation of the Village*, 21.]

UNITY LEAGUES

After World War II, the American Council on Race Relations provided support for the Unity Leagues in southern California. League activists made up of Mexican Americans, African Americans, Asian Americans, and sympathetic whites, forged alliances across ethnic boundaries to provide a civil rights, anti-racist agenda of activity. The rank and file, which consisted of war veterans and blue-collar workers, organized voter registration drives and supported the campaigns of candidates for public office who were either from the minority groups themselves or who would support legislation designed to improve conditions in the community. What distinguished the

Unity Leagues from previous civil rights organizations and unions is that they were not middle class in orientation and did not pursue labor issues, except peripherally. The organizations were forerunners of an important Mexican-American civil rights group, the Community Services Organization (CSO),* which a former League organizer, Fred Ross* started. Ignacio I. López, newspaper editor and one of the foremost civil rights activists in the Los Angeles area, was one of the main activists of the Unity Leagues during the 1940s. [SOURCE: Samora and Simon, *A History of Mexican-American People*, 195; www.jsri.msu.edu/museum/pubs/MexAmHist/chapter19.html]

UNIVERSIDAD BORICUA

Educator and social worker Antonia Pantoja* founded the first university created specifically to serve Puerto Ricans in the United States: Universidad Boricua. Founded in Washington, D.C., with foundation grants that Pantoja had solicited, the university was designed to provide innovative, bilingual, career-oriented programs for professionals, technicians, and workers. Pantoja served as the institution's first chancellor. [SOURCE: Pantoja, *Memoir of a Visonary;* Tardiff and Mabunda, *Dictionary of Hispanic Biography*, 653.]

URANGA, RODOLFO (?-?)

A daily columnist for *La Opinión* in Los Angeles during the 1920s, Rodolfo Uranga used his journalistic position as a forum to defend Mexicans awaiting execution or otherwise incarcerated. Uranga and his brother Lauro, who was a successful playwright in Los Angeles, were born in in the state of Hidalgo, Mexico. A conservative who opposed the anti-clerical revolutionaries in Mexico, Rodolfo Uranga was nonetheless very concerned about mistreatment and the lack of respect shown Mexicans in the United States. In one of his columns, he first announced that Ignacio Castañeda, a Detroit automobile worker, had saved a woman from drowning in the Rio Grande as he crossed at El Paso from his native Jalisco. He then wrote, "We have heroes here in the United States. Anglo Americans have no right to criticize our crime and banditry in Mexico. They have crime galore here. Look at the situation in Chicago. It is not just to brand 'inferior' Mexicans as uniquely imbued with criminal tendencies." In 1931, Uranga also wrote columns for *El Continenal,* a daily that served Ciudad Juárez and El Paso; he also became editor of *La Voz* in Ciudad Juárez. An ardent nationalist and conservative, Uranga joined a number of other like-minded ideologues in Chihuahua and helped found El Partido de Acción Nacional (PAN), in 1940, one of the most powerful political parties in Mexico today. Uranga is given credit for coining the phrase "El México de Afuera" to refer to Mexicans in the United States.

[SOURCE: Rosales, *Chicano!*, 69; http://docentes.uacj.mx/rquinter/croni-cas/1931-1940.htm]

URISTA, ALBERTO BALTAZAR, *see* ALURISTA

VALDEZ, ARMANDO (1944-)

Armando Valdez was born in Del Rio, Texas, in 1944 and moved to California with his migrant worker family in the 1950s. He was a founder of San Jose State College's Mexican American Student Confederation (MASC) in 1967 and one of major ideologues of the Chicano Movement.* Wearing a black beret and sporting a beard, which made him look remarkably like Che Guevara, he traveled around the Southwest spreading the gospel of Chicano* liberation. MASC caught the attention of Chicano students in other parts of California when in the spring of 1967 graduating seniors at San Jose State University walked out of commencement exercises and conducted their own program to protest the lack of recruitment and tutoring programs for minority students. At one of the first Mexican-American student conferences in California, held at the University of Southern California, Valdez and other northerners made a big impact on emerging Chicano consciousness in Los Angeles. The northern Chicanos exhorted Los Angeles students to take a more militant stand on issues. In the spring of 1968, Valdez had a similar impact on students at Arizona State University in Tempe. Valdez finished his degree at San Jose State University and then obtained a Ph.D. at Stanford University in Communications. He remained at Stanford as a professor and as the director of a communications research institute that focused on the impact of emerging technology on society and issues of access and equity. He now operates Valdez and Associates of Mountain View, a social marketing research firm devoted to designing and implementing community education campaigns and health promotion interventions targeted at low-income, minority, and other hard-to-reach populations. [SOURCE: Rosales, *Chicano!*, 32.]

VALDEZ, LUIS

Considered to be the father of Chicano* theater, playwright and director, Luis Valdez was born on June 26, 1940, in Delano, California. When Valdez was a boy, his parents, Francisco and Armeda Valdez, took their ten children on the migrant trail in the central valleys of California. As a consequence, the growing boy shuttled between schools until the Valdez family finally settled in San Jose. After graduating from high school in 1960, Valdez received a scholarship to San Jose State College (California State University, San Jose). In 1964, he received a B.A degree in English and then moved to San Francisco, where he worked with the San Francisco Mime Troupe, a theater group which specialized in "Guerrilla Theater" (agitation and propaganda),

V

an experience that served him well for his future endeavors. After meeting César Chávez* in 1965, Valdez formed El Teatro Campesino and staged one-act plays to dramatize the conditions confronting migrant workers and to support the workers as they struggled to build a union. The Teatro also inspired a movement known as Teatro Chicano.

Luis Valdez

Luis Valdez's career blossomed after this stint with the farmworkers. El Teatro Campesino became a touring company, based in Del Rey, Fresno, and finally, in 1971, in San Juan Bautista, California. Many of the Teatro's short plays have become classics, but in 1978, Valdez wrote, directed, and produced *Zoot Suit,* a major stage production based on the 1942 Los Angeles Sleepy Lagoon* case. The play ran successfully for two years in Los Angeles theatres, and, in 1979, it was produced at New York City's Winter Garden Theater— the first by a Mexican American to play on Broadway. In 1982, *Zoot Suit* was made into a film by Valdez. However, by far, Valdez's most successful commercial venture was *La Bamba,* a film based on the life of Ritchie Valens, the legendary Mexican-American rock-and-roller who died with Buddy Holly and the Big Bopper in a plane crash in 1958. Valdez has earned many awards, such as an Obie in 1968, Los Angeles Drama Critics awards in 1969, 1972, and 1978, and an Emmy in 1973. In 1983, President Reagan's Committee on Arts and Humanities recognized his work and Columbia College, San Jose State University, and the California Institute of the Arts have each granted him honorary doctorates. [SOURCE: http://www.galegroup.com/free_re-sources/chh /bio/valdez_l.htm]

VALLEJO, MARIANO GUADALUPE (1808-1890)

Vallejo was born in 1808 to an upper-class California Mexican (Californio) family in Monterey, then the capital of the province of Alta California. At age fifteen, barely two years after Mexican independence, he became a cadet in the Mexican army and distinguished himself as a frontier soldier, mainly in campaigns against rebellious Indians. Vallejo then became the military commander of the northern part of California and spent much of his time putting down Indian uprisings and staving off Russian settlement from Alaska. General Vallejo identified with Mexican liberals, who stressed efficient government with limited powers and the separation of Church and State. When General Antonio López de Santa Anna centralized Mexico in 1836, Vallejo supported a short-lived attempt to break away from Mexico.

Vallejo, like all Mexican liberals, admired the United States, but in 1846 General John C. Fremont lead the Bear Flag Revolt* and imprisoned Vallejo and his younger brother while Bear Flag followers looted his estates. When General Stephen Kearney, formally occupied with regular soldiers California for the United States, Vallejo's fortunes improved temporarily. He served as Indian agent for Northern California and in 1849 was one of eight Californio delegates to California's constitutional convention; he subsequently was elected to the first state senate.

In spite of having a modicum of political power and status, Vallejo suffered the same fate as most of his fellow Californios. Anglo-American squatters and speculators made claims on his vast estates, and in attempting to defend his patrimony, Vallejo spent thousands of dollars in legal fees. Finally, it became a burden which he could not sustain, and thus he lost most of his property. When he died in 1890, all he had left was a small ranch in Sonoma, California. [SOURCE: http://www.pbs.org/weta/thewest/people/s_z/vallejo.htm; Padilla, *My History, Not Yours,* 77-108.]

VALLEJO, NAPOLEÓN PLATÓN M.G. (1845-1925)

Many Mexicans who remained in the old homeland after the American takeover, accepted the new political and economic realities but at the same time regretted the passing of the old days and looked with misgivings at their declining status and fortune. Contrary to widespread belief that many higher class Mexicans completely welcomed the Anglo Americans, most were fully cognizant of their loss to the point that they often poured out their bitterness and anger through various means of communication. Dr. Napoleón Platón M. G. Vallejo, the scion of the Vallejo family of Sonoma, California, left many such lamentations. Vallejo, a medical officer who had served on the Union side in the Civil War, was born in Sonoma in 1845. His parents were General Mariano Guadalupe Vallejo and Benicia Carrillo de Vallejo. The elder Vallejo was the military chief of northern California during the Mexican period. Napoleón Platón wrote a series of letters in 1893 to William Heath Davis, bitterly lamenting the way in which Anglo historians were treating Californios and their contributions. In 1914, with practically all of the family wealth exhausted, Dr. Napoleón Platón Vallejo recounted in a newspaper series how family lands and fortune were swallowed up in suits against squatters. He died six years later. [SOURCE: Rosales, *Testimonio,* 31-32.]

THE VALLEY COALITION FOR JUSTICE

As the influx of Central American refugees into the Rio Grande Valley of Texas grew in the 1980s, the newcomers encountered problems with settlement and with immigration authorities. In 1984, immigrant rights activists responded by forming the Refugee/Immigrant Rights Coalition of the Rio Grande Valley (RIRC) in 1984. Composed of numerous organizations in a network for sharing information with each other, since its founding the RIRC's primary goal is to provide the protection of the human rights of refugees, immigrants, and the disenfranchised. The RIRC examines immigration policy and laws and advocates for changes which will positively affect refugees and immigrants; informs elected officials at all levels on border conditions; upholds constitutionally guaranteed rights for all immigrants, regardless of legal status in this country; advocates for more humane conditions in detention; educates the general public; supports refugee/immigrant self-determination projects; establishes grassroots relations with disenfranchised communities; and makes linkages with other groups and individuals to build a stronger voice. [SOURCE: http://www.casa-latina.org/links.htm]

VANGUARDIA DE COLONIZACIÓN PROLETARIA

In April 1930, a group of Mexican immigrants in Brawley, California, organized themselves into Vanguardia de Colonización Proletaria (Vanguard of Proletarian Colonization) and claimed that within two months the group had attracted 40,000 members from throughout California. Their ambitious plans were to organize the bulk of the Mexican expatriate community in the United States in order to repatriate themselves back to Mexico. The ambitious organizers hoped to raise some twelve million dollars within six months. By April, they claimed to have already collected 40 thousand dollars, which they had supposedly deposited in a Mexican bank. Alejandro Saucedo Salazar, one of the Vanguardia leaders, traveled to Mexico City to elicit support from government officials. The plan seems to have withered away, but it demonstrated the determination shown by Mexicans during the Great Depression as they tried to solve the dilemma of being stranded in the United States without employment. [SOURCE: Balderrama and Rodríguez, *Decade of Betrayal*, 161-162.]

VARELA, MARÍA (?-)

Born in Pennsylvania, María Varela came to New Mexico in 1967 after working with the Student Nonviolent Coordinating Committee (SNCC) in the American South and in Chicago. Her black civil rights activity had taken her to California and New Mexico, where she forged links with the Chicano Movement* for SNCC. On those trips, Varela met Chicano* activists, such as Luis Valdez* and Reies López Tijerina,* and had decided that her own people needed her energies more. Settling in New Mexico, she joined the Alianza Federal de las Mercedes* and helped found the Ganados del Valle Cooperative and the Tierra Amarilla Free Clinic. In New Mexico, Varela linked up with Betita Martínez,* another out-of-state activist, and together they published the famous Chicano Movement newspaper, *El Grito del Norte*

(The Northern Shout). Although many people felt this newspaper was connected to the Alianza, in reality it attempted to run an independent course. In 1982, Varela received an M.A. in rural planning at the University of Massachussets. [SOURCE: Rosales, *Chicano!*, xx, 184, 214.]

VARELA, SERVULO AND LEONARDO COTA (?-?)

In September 1846, Los Angeles Mexicans resisted the U.S. takeover by Commodore Stockton's troops and, under the leadership of Servulo Varela and Leonardo Cota, 400 signed a petition condemning the occupation by Anglo-American soldiers. The militant document threatened any collaborators of the Americans with violence, calling them traitors. [SOURCE: Rosales, *Testimonio*, 20-21.]

VARELA Y MORALES, FÉLIX FRANCISCO (1788-1853)

The longest lasting independence movement in the hemisphere was that of Spain's Caribbean colonies: Cuba and Puerto Rico. One of Cuba's first and most illustrious exiles was the philosopher-priest Félix Varela, who founded *El Habanero* (The Havanian) in Philadelphia in 1824. Subtitled

"papel político, científico y literario" (political, scientific and literary paper), *El Habanero* openly militated for Cuban independence. Varela was one of many intellectuals within the expatriate communities in Philadelphia and New York who for some twenty years had been translating the U.S. Constitution and the works of Thomas Paine and Thomas Jefferson and smuggling them into Latin America in books printed in Spanish by early American printers.

Varela, however, set the precedent for Cubans and Puerto Ricans of printing and publishing in exile and having their works circulating in their home islands. In fact, Varela's books on

Félix Francisco Varela y Morales

philosophy and education (many of which were published abroad) were said to be the only "best sellers" in Cuba, and Varela himself the most popular author in Cuba in the first third of the nineteenth century—despite there being in effect a "conspiracy of silence," in which his name could never even be brought up in public on the island. [SOURCE: Kanellos, *Hispanic Periodicals in the United States*, 10-11.]

VELÁZQUEZ, NYDIA M. (1953-)

Born in Yabucoa, Puerto Rico, in 1953, Nydia Velázquez in 1992 became the first Puerto Rican woman to be elected to the House of Representatives.

Velázquez's concern for social reform became apparent early in her life. While still in high school in Yabucoa, she organized a student boycott to protest the dangerous and unsanitary conditions of the school building until renovations were made. Much of her organizing skills were learned from her father, a sugarcane cutter in Puerto Rico who was active in labor organizing. Velázquez understood at an early age the value of education. Graduating high school early, she enrolled in college at age sixteen and graduated with high honors from the University of Puerto Rico. After winning a scholarship to study political science at New York University, she received a Master's degree in 1976 and taught at the university level both in Puerto Rico and in New York.

Nydia M. Velásquez

Velázquez was concerned about conditions in the Puerto Rican neighborhoods and decided that she could best affect change for Puerto Ricans by becoming a social and political activist. From 1984 to 1986, Velázquez served on the New York City Council and, in 1986, became director of the Migration Division of the Commonwealth of Puerto Rico, where she launched "Atrévete," a community empowerment program whose main role was to register voters. As she acquired more influence, Velázquez also put her talents to organizing a program to fight the spread of AIDS in Latino communities.

After being elected to Congress from New York City's Twelfth District, Velázquez has focused on sponsoring or voting for legislation that speaks to the rights of disenfranchised people, especially minorities, women, and children. In 1993, she helped introduce the Family Violence and Prevention Act, which established family abuse intervention services and educational programs. She also sponsored legislation to provide improved housing for low-income families in her district in New York, one of the poorest districts in the country. Congresswoman Velázquez is also an active member of the Democratic Caucus, the Hispanic Caucus, and the Women's Issues Caucus. [SOURCE: http://bio-guide.congress.gov/scripts/biodisplay.pl?index=V000081]

VELÁSQUEZ, WILLIAM C. (1944-1988)

In 1995, the Presidential Medal of Freedom was awarded posthumously to Willie Velásquez, the founder and director of the Southwest Voter Registration Education Project (SVREP).* The medal, which is the nation's highest civilian honor, was presented by President Bill Clinton to Velásquez's

William C. Velásquez

widow in recognition of the deceased activist's lifetime commitment and contributions to democracy. Born on May 9, 1944, to William and María Luisa (Cárdenas) Velásquez in Orlando, Florida, where the elder Velásquez, a union organizer, was assigned during World War II, Willie Velásquez is recognized as the single most influential organizer of Hispanics on the road to political power and representation. In an effort to continue the legacy of Velásquez, the SVREP committed itself to the most ambitious registration goal in history: one million new Latino voters for the general elections in November 1996. Velásquez was also a pioneer activist in the Chicano Movement.* He was a founder and charter member of two important Texas organizations, the Mexican American Youth Organization* and El Movimiento Social de La Raza Unida (The Social Movement of the United People). He also served as a strike worker for the United Farm Workers* in Texas and founded and became the first director of the Mexican American Unity Council in San Antonio during the 1960s. [SOURCE: Sepúlveda, *The Life and Times of Willie Velásquez.*]

VELÁSQUEZ V. CITY OF ABILENE

After passage of the Voting Rights Act Amendments of 1982, one of the first cases to challenge the dilution of minority votes was *Velásquez v. City of Abilene* in 1983. Prominent Judge Reynaldo G. Garza delivered the opinion of the Court of Appeals for the Fifth Circuit, stating that the intent of Congress was clear in cases of vote dilution. He ruled that the City of Abilene's use of at-large voting, bloc voting, and other voting mechanisms resulted in vote dilution and had a discriminatory effect on Hispanic-American voters in the city. As a result, the city of Abilene elected two Hispanics to its city council in 1991. The act and related court cases resulted in many Hispanics being elected to local positions throughout the United States. [SOURCE: Carrasco, "Law and Politics," 259.]

VENEGAS, DANIEL (?-?)

Born in northern Mexico, Venegas became a journalist, businessman, novelist, and president of Los Angeles' La Confederación de Sociedades Mexicanas (The Federation of Mexican Societies).* In the community, he emerged as an outspoken supporter of Mexicans who were treated unfairly.

He was also a talented writer who illustrated and published his own satirical weekly newspaper, *El Malcriado* (The Brat). His fictional and black-humored story about a poor Mexican immigrant who finds nothing but problems north of the border was published as a novel, *La aventuras de don Chipote; o cuando los pericos mamen.* This picaresque work, while containing much slapstick humor, also portrays the harshness of immigrant life in the United States. [SOURCE: Rosales, *Chicano!,* 69.]

Daniel Venegas

VIGIL, ERNESTO (1947-)

Ernesto Vigil, a major activist in the Chicano Movement,* played a central role in the Crusade for Justice (CFJ),* the civil rights organization founded by Rudolfo "Corky" Gonzales* in Denver, Colorado. Vigil also worked with Rosalío Muñoz* on the National Chicano Moratorium Committee* to protest the war in Vietnam and was one of the Chicano Movement leaders to refuse the induction of Chicanos* into the military. A co-founder of La Raza Unida Party (The United People's Party–LRUP)* in Colorado, Vigil played a crucial role in the historic national convention of the LRUP in 1972. In a confrontation with Denver police officers, in 1973, he was shot in the back after another CFJ member, who had wounded a policeman, was killed. A debate ensued in Denver for months over who was at fault. The police were exonerated completely, but CFJ members insisted that the police had provoked the incident. [SOURCE: Rosales, *Chicano!,* 199-200, 247.]

VIGILANTISM

In simple terms, this is the act of taking justice into one's own or a group's hands. Vigilantism is usually manifested in the actions of a committee or posse. Vigilantes have existed in the American Southwest since the mid-nineteenth century, when the United States annexed half of Mexico's northern territory under questionable terms. The acquisition of these lands provoked severe racial tensions between Anglos and the region's native inhabitants, especially Mexicans. Examples of vigilantism can be found throughout several eras, such as the California Gold Rush and the period when land grants in New Mexico inspired the rise of Las Gorras Blancas* (the White Caps). Vigilantism was implemented by both Anglos and Mexicans in the history of the Southwest. However, it was largely used against Mexicans as a terrorist expression of racial hate, particularly from the mid- to late-nineteenth century. One of the most atrocious vigilante acts occurred on January 18, 1918, when civilian vigilantes, accompanied by Texas Rangers,* converged on the town of Porvenir,* an isolated community of less than 200 Mexicans in the Big Bend region of west Texas, and selected 15 men and boys, took them to the outskirts of town and executed them because the townsmen were suspected of engaging in banditry. [SOURCE: Rosales, *Pobre Raza!*, 118-121.]

VILLA, FRANCISCO "PANCHO" (1877-1923)

Perhaps no other Mexican captured so much attention from Americans during the early twentieth century than Doroteo Arango, known to the world as the revolutionary general Francisco "Pancho" Villa. In opposing Venustiano Carranza for the presidency of Mexico, Villa courted Americans while he benefitted from a positive image in the United States. However, in 1915, President Woodrow Wilson formally recognized Carranza as President of Mexico, and Villa turned against the United States. Villa and his Villistas continued staging raids in Mexico against pro-American and Carrancista groups. Occasionally, the Villistas crossed the border to engage Americans on their own soil. The most notorious such raid was the raid on Columbus, New Mexico, on March 9, 1916. Eighteen Americans lost their lives while the Villistas suffered over 200 casualties. American General John "Black Jack" Pershing invaded Mexico in pursuit of Villa. The expedition failed to capture him and the Villistas, but it succeeded in elevating Villa to a Mexican national hero. [SOURCE: Rosales, *Chicano!*, 31-32; Katz, *The Life and Times of Pancho Villa.*]

VILLARAIGOSA, ANTONIO R. (1953-)

Antonio R. Villaraigosa, the first Hispanic mayor of Los Angeles, California, since the early 1870s, was born on January 23, 1953, in East Los Angeles. He lost his first bid for the Los Angeles mayoralty in 2001 to James K. Hahn, but defeated him in on May 17, 2005, after the incumbent's term ended. His original name was Antonio Villar, but when he married his second wife, Corina Raigosa in 1987, the two combined their names to Villaraigosa. Growing up in the Boyle Heights area of East Los Angeles, Villaraigosa experienced many difficulties as a child and even in his early adult years. Then with the support of his mother, he began to turn his life around. In 1977, he obtained a B.A. in History from UCLA and subsequently a law degree from the People's College of Law in 1980. In the 1980s, Villaraigosa worked as a teacher's union organizer and served as head of Los Angeles' ACLU office. In 1994, California voters elected Villaraigosa to the California State Assembly, where four years later, his colleagues selected him Assembly Speaker, a position that allowed him to become one of the leading liberal and Hispanic forces in California. [SOURCE: Daunt, "Early Challenges, Different Paths, Same Goal."]

VILLAVERDE, CIRILO (1812-1894)

The extent of commitment by literary figures to the exile and revolutionary press can be gauged by the example of Cirilo Villaverde, a seminal founder of Cuban literature now remembered for his novel *Cecilia Valdés* (1839), which critic William Luis considers "the most important novel written in nineteenth-century Cuba and perhaps one of the most important works in Latin America during that period." Despite his growing celebrity in Cuba as a man of letters, Villaverde who was born in Matanzas, left the island for New York in 1849, after escaping from imprisonment for his political activities; he remained in the United States until his death in 1894, working as a revolutionary journalist—"a man of action," as he put it, rather than a man engaging in the vanity of letters. Villaverde devoted himself almost exclusively to the revolutionary cause by writing for various exile newspapers; for him the revolutionary battle was to be found in the struggle to influence public opinion. One can only guess what clandestine political activities he engaged in.

Beginning in 1852, Villaverde began working for New York's *La Verdad* (The Truth), but before leaving Cuba he had already been sending dispatches and had helped to smuggle this banned newspaper into the country. In 1853, he and Manuel Antonio Marino began publishing their own bilingual newspaper, *El Independiente: Órgano de la democracia cubana* (The Independent: Organ of Cuban Democracy) in New Orleans. Villaverde was an editor and also wrote anonymously for New York's *La Voz de la América: Órgano político de las repúblicas hispano-americanas y de las Antillas españolas* (The Voice of America: Political Organ of the Spanish-American Republics and the Spanish Antilles), *La Ilustración Americana* (The American Enlightenment), and for Narciso Villaverde's monthly *El Espejo* (The Mirror), among other papers. Villaverde's political ideology was most reflected in the important filibustering publication *La Verdad*, which promoted U.S. annexation of Cuba. (Later he supported independence for Cuba.) *La Verdad* was created by a junta of Cuban exiles called the Club de Habana, who raised $10,000 for its founding, and by U.S. expansionists, such as John O'Sullivan and Moses Beach, editor of the New York *Sun*, at which facilities *La Verdad* was actually printed. The bilingual *La Verdad*'s mission was to lobby the public as well as Cubans for the annexation of Cuba, but the newspaper also supported Manifest Destiny* and U.S. filibustering expeditions in Latin America, in addition to Cuban annexation as part of the effort to create another slave state for the South. *La Verdad* called for the U.S. purchase of Cuba from Spain, and, in fact, in 1848 President James K. Polk did tender an offer of

$100 million to Spain for the island. [SOURCE: Kanellos, *Hispanic Periodicals in the United States,* 12, 205, 266.]

VISEL, CHARLES P. (?-?)

A prominent figure in Los Angeles during the 1920s, Visel held the office of the Los Angeles County Coordinator for Unemployment Relief. He, like John C. Box* in Texas and other nativists, supported restrictive immigration policy, especially in regard to Mexicans. Los Angeles at this time was a hot bed for repatriation efforts of Mexicans, and Visel stood at the center of this controversy. He worked with federal agents sent by the Secretary of Labor to apprehend and remove as many undocumented workers as possible. Their efforts, however, included the mistreatment of Mexican-American citizens. Despite this and without regard for civil rights, Visel and his minions continued these roundups. He was also a member of President Hoover's President's Emergency Committee for Employment, begun in 1931, which coordinated the voluntary repatriation of Southern California Mexicans. [SOURCE; Rosales, *Chicano!,* 50-1; Balderrama, *In Defense of La Raza,*16-18.]

VIVA KENNEDY CLUBS

At the end of the 1950s, Mexican-American political and civil rights leaders were ready to transcend regional political aspirations and obtain power at the national level. This goal seemed fulfilled during the 1960 campaign by the Democratic Party to elect the charismatic John F. Kennedy to the presidency. The cards were stacked against his winning, primarily because of his Catholic-Irish background. But Mexican Americans identified with his Catholicism and to a degree with his ethnicity. Moreover, at the 1960 convention, the Democratic Party selected as Kennedy's running mate, Lyndon Baines Johnson,* a Texas politician who early on recognized the importance of the emerging Mexican-American vote in his home state. Johnson urged Kennedy to be responsive to this constituency.

Leading Mexican-American leaders, Edward R. Roybal,* Dennis Chávez,* and organizations such as the American G.I. Forum,* Mexican American Political Association,* and the Alianza Hispano-Americana* responded to Johnson's call and formed the Viva Kennedy Clubs to deliver the Mexican-American vote for the Kennedy-Johnson ticket. Prior to this, as one historian stated, "Mexicans were not widely recognized electorally as a significant factor in national presidential elections. Mexican-American voters were taken for granted as a known but modest part of the Democratic Party constituency."

In the Kennedy-Nixon contest for the presidency, it was widely held that the Mexican-American vote was crucial in delivering Texas, a state with significant wealth of electoral votes. Texas could provide the margin of victory that Kennedy needed. For the thousands of Mexican-American volunteers who worked on the campaign, Kennedy's success also became an ethnic victory. Their leaders, who forged heretofore unseen national-level alliances, were buoyant about their political future in the United States. The wealth of experience acquired in the Kennedy campaign was subsequently parlayed into political action that would help Mexican-American candidates locally. [SOURCE: García, *Hector P. García.*]

LOS VOLUNTARIOS

Rudolfo "Corky" Gonzales* in 1963 organized a group called Los Voluntarios after becoming disenchanted with mainstream politics and the "War on Poverty" programs. The organization began protesting Denver's policy toward its impoverished Mexican-American population. The group, the precursor to the Crusade for Justice,* which acquired national fame, then took on police brutality issues and earned the enmity of Denver's law enforcement establishment. [SOURCE: Marín, *A Spokesman of the Mexican American Movement,* 10.]

VOLUNTARY RELIEF AGENCIES AND CUBANS

The initial flight to Florida of refugees escaping the July 26th Movement, the revolution that brought Fidel Castro* to power in 1959, required urgent relief. To meet the need, voluntary relief agencies, known as VOLAGs, were quickly organized by church groups, such as Catholic Relief Services, the Protestant Latin American Emergency Committee, the International Rescue Committee, and the United HIAS Service, a project funded by Jewish groups. Individual churches and synagogues also carried out their own relief efforts. The VOLAGs became so efficient that representatives met each planeload of refugees coming from Havana to inform them about the resources available to them and to distribute items which the newcomers needed immediately, such as blankets, clothing, food, and toiletries. [SOURCE: García, *Havana USA.*]

VOTER PARTICIPATION PROJECT

Many Puerto Rican activists politicized in New York City during the 1960s rejected voting as a means of achieving Puerto Rican liberation. By the 1990s, some of these same activists recognized the importance to the community of electing accountable representatives in order to confront such issues as the federal abandonment of the cities, the deepening urban crisis, and a growing right wing danger in the nation. In 1983, the Community Service Society had hired Richie Pérez to develop and run an experimental voter participation project in the Bushwick section of Brooklyn. By the early 1990s, three voter participation projects operated in Brooklyn, Manhattan, and the Bronx, the three NYC boroughs that are covered by the Voting Rights

Act. Over the years, this effort has resulted in the registration of approximately 120,000 people. [SOURCE: http://www.columbia.edu/~rmg36/NCPRR.html]

VOTERS ASSISTANCE ACT OF 1992

The U.S. Congress passed the Voters Assistance Act of 1992, which made bilingual voting information readily available. [SOURCE: Kanellos, *Chronology of Hispanic American History*, 278.]

VOTING RIGHTS ACT

In 1965, Congress passed the Voting Rights Act, an attempt to legislate protection of the rights of citizens, mainly African Americans. This act, in essence, provided all citizens with the right to vote, disallowing obstacles such as the poll taxes designed to discourage minorities and the poor from voting. Thanks to the lobbying efforts of the Mexican American Legal Defense and Education Fund,* under the directorship of Vilma Martínez,* the U.S. Congress voted to expand the Voting Rights Act to include Mexican Americans. The original act had only applied to blacks and Puerto Ricans. The act also made bilingual ballots a requirement in certain locations of the United States. [SOURCE: Carrasco, "Law and Politics," 236.]

LA VOZ DE AMÉRICA

Cuban political clubs in New York and Florida during the 1850s and 1860s made efforts to expand the revolution to include all sectors of Cuban society and to unite the separatist and abolitionist movements. A leading newspaper in this trend was *La Voz de América* (The Voice of America), under Cuban editor Juan Manuel Macías and Puerto Rican editor José Bassora. Theirs was a growing trend to challenge the elites and democratize the revolution. The publication editorially urged the inclusion of slaves not only in the revolutionary ranks but in the concept of Cuban nationality. It also actively cultivated a following among the tobacco workers. [SOURCE: Kanellos, *Hispanic Periodicals in the United States*, 12.]

LA VOZ DEL PUEBLO

La Voz del Pueblo (The People's Voice) was edited by Félix Martínez Jr.,* who openly supported the two most widespread populist movements: the vigilante Gorras Blancas (White Caps)* and the populist Partido del Pueblo Unido (United People's Party),* which opposed Anglo encroachment on the natives' lands, bias in the legal system, and a dual pay system for Anglos and Mexicans. Martínez had to pay a high cost for his stance: he was forced to leave Las Vegas and relocate to El Paso, Texas, where he published the *El Paso Daily News* and founded the *El Paso Times–Herald*. [SOURCE: Kanellos, *Hispanic Periodicals in the United States*, 82-83.]

WATTS/CENTURY LATINO ORGANIZATION

Formed in August 1990, the Watts/Century Latino Organization (WCLO) works to improve the quality of life for all Watts area residents and to ensure that the needs of the growing Latino population are met. WCLO operates a community center, a neighborhood watch program, programs to improve inter-ethnic relations, and neighborhood citizenship classes to ensure full participation in the political process. WCLO cooperates closely with the city council and other government offices so that outreach to the community is better achieved. WCLO also provides bridges between the large African-American community and Latinos. [SOURCE: http://clnet.sscnet.ucla.edu/community/wclo.html]

WELCH, SHERIFF JOHN (?-?)

During the early part of the twentieth century in Arizona, police killings of Mexicans were numerous in mining towns that had rapidly drawn thousands of Mexicans to the state's most dynamic industrial sector. Extensive labor strife characterized early formation of these worker communities; relations between company-controlled police, Mexicans and other workers was continually strained. John Welch, the half Mexican, long-time police chief in the mining town of Miami, had an especially fearsome reputation. In December 1931, Phoenix Consul Luis Castro lamented that a Cochise County grand jury had acquitted the officer after he shot to death Martín López y de la Torre. In the 1940s, labor leaders looking back at Welch's career designated him as the most villainous enemy of the Mexican working class. But his self-image was quite different. When asked by a writer about the 1920s shooting death of Juan Lugo in a gun battle, the police chief said that in the main, Miami was peaceful but "Once in a while we have a criminal who gets out of line. But this class doesn't last long." [SOURCE: Rosales, *Pobre Raza!*, 81.]

THE WHEATLAND RIOT

In August 1913, Mexican-American agricultural workers walked out of the fields at the Durst Ranch, in Wheatland, California, to protest substandard housing and low wages.

Two organizers from the Industrial Workers of the World (IWW), Herman Suhr and Blackie Ford, went to Wheatland to support the efforts by the Mexicans. But in the ensuing confrontations, the growers brought in police officers to break down the picket lines. When the police fired warning shots in the air, they purportedly were attacked by the strikers. The police fired into the crowd and four strikers died. One hundred migrant workers were arrested after the National Guard was called in, an action that ended the strike.

W

Suhr and Ford received life sentences for their part in the "riot." The tragic incident did bring about attention to the plight of farmworkers and the creation of the California Commission on Immigration and Housing, which attempted to improve the living conditions of agricultural workers. [SOURCE: Samora and Simon, *A History of the Mexican-American People,* 179.]

WHITE PRIMARY IN TEXAS

The Democratic Party in Texas employed the white primary as a private club, restricted to members who had to pass the test of having an Anglo heritage for at least three generations, before being allowed to vote in the party's primary election. The practice persisted in the early twentieth century as a way of disenfranchising African Americans, and later in south Texas, Mexican Americans. The Texas legislature established the white primary as a state law in 1923, which made voting for minorities even more difficult, since Texas was a one-party state until the 1960s. Civil rights activists, mainly African American, but also Mexican Americans, mounted numerous challenges until the white primary as a state law was ruled unconstitutional by the U.S. Supreme Court in the *Smith v. Allwright* decision of 1944. The poll tax, however, which obliged voters to pay a tax to register, continued until the 1960s. [SOURCE: http://texaspolitics.laits.utexas.edu/html/vce/0503.html]

WILCOX, MARY ROSE GARRIDO (1949-)

Mary Rose Garrido Wilcox, a descendant of a pioneer Mexican-American family, was born in Superior, Arizona, in 1949 and is a fourth-generation Arizonan. Few women in the state have attained her degree of political success; she became the first Latina to be elected to the Phoenix City Council and the Maricopa County Board of Supervisors (Phoenix area).

At Arizona State University in the 1960s, as a nineteen-year-old student she became part of a core group that organized the Mexican American Student Organization (MASO).* Within a short time, this Chicano Movement* group affectively pressured the university to be more accountable to the educational needs of Mexican Americans in the Valley of the Sun (Maricopa County). Like many of the other students, her concern for social justice graduated from reform at the university to helping the larger community gain civil rights and economic empowerment. In the 1970s, she helped numerous Mexican Americans attain political office, but Mary Rose, confident that she could serve the people directly, worked on her own political triumphs in the 1980s. With the help of her husband, Earl Wilcox, a former state legislator and justice of the peace, she served in the Phoenix City Council from 1983 until 1993, when she won a seat on the Maricopa County Board of Supervisors. In 2000 she was re-elected for a third four-year term.

In her capacity as city council member and county supervisor, Mary Rose has been instrumental in revitalizing downtown Phoenix and in instituting numerous programs for inner city youth. She has also served as a member of such organizations as the Mexican American Legal Defense and Education Fund,* the National Council of La Raza,* and the National Association of Latino Elected and Appointed Officials.* Mary Rose has received more honors than almost any other Arizona Latina/o for both her community and political work. [SOURCE: http://www.maricopa.gov/dist5/bio.asp; Rosales, *Chicano!*, 212-213.]

WILSON, THOMAS (?-?)

One of the issues that most angered the community during the Chicano Movement* was the unnecessary killing of the popular journalist Rubén Salazar.* The journalist was covering the Chicano Moratorium,* the massive anti-Vietnam demonstration on August 29, 1970. After police violence broke out, Salazar was killed by a tear gas projectile indiscriminately fired by Deputy Sheriff Thomas Wilson into the Silver Dollar Cafe, where the journalist was sipping a beer. The Coroner's Jury decided that there was no cause for criminal action against the deputy who had fired into the cafe. The decision outraged not only the community, but also many Anglos who saw Salazar as a mediating force between angry militants and a recalcitrant establishment. [SOURCE: Rosales, *Chicano!*, 203-204.]

WORKING GROUP ON MIGRATION AND CONSULAR AFFAIRS

The Working Group on Migration and Consular Affairs of the U.S.-Mexico Binational Commission has served to increase communication and coordination between Mexico and the United States on issues dealing with expatriates of each nation on each other's soil. Created in the late 1970s by Presidents Jimmy Carter and Miguel López Portillo, the Binational Commission meets annually. It currently serves as an umbrella for more than a dozen working groups that meet throughout the year. The Working Group on Migration and Consular Affairs deals with consular protection, facilitation of legal movements, and increased border cooperation. It advises on policy issues related to sanctions against the trafficking of undocumented migrants, migration legislation, and policies in both countries. The Binational Commission has also encouraged the formation of various, border-state mechanisms to facilitate or enhance the functioning of its national-level consultations. As a consequence, governors, attorney generals, and other border state officials meet regularly to discuss transnational issues, but increasingly, migration has come to dominate the agendas of these groups. [SOURCE: Martin, "Mexico-U.S. Migration," *The U.S.-Mexican Relations Forum*, http://www.ia dialog.org/publications/country_studies/immigrat.html]

XIMENES, VICENTE TREVIÑO (1922-)

Vicente Treviño Ximenes was born in Floresville Texas in 1922. He graduated from high school in 1939 and served in the military during World War II. After the war, he worked for the American G.I. Forum,* an organization of Mexican-American veterans, and became a close associate of the founder, the dedicated civil rights leader, Dr. Hector P. García.* After serving as national chairman of the Forum, Ximenes ran the "Viva Johnson" campaign in 1964 and in 1967 was appointed by President Lyndon B. Johnson* to the Economic Employment Opportunity Commission.* Later that year, after Mexican-American leaders protested that President Johnson's civil rights program excluded Mexican Americans, Ximenes was named by the president to head of the newly established Inter-Agency Cabinet Committee on Mexican American Affairs.* Ximenes continued as a stalwart of the Democratic Party and, in 1977, President Jimmy Carter appointed him to the White House Fellows Commission. After his stint at the White House ended in 1982, Ximenes returned to Albuquerque, New Mexico, and created a human rights commission, which he ran for a number of years until he retired. Concurrently, he served on the Board of Directors of Catholic College in Albuquerque and was executive director of the Democratic Party in New Mexico. Although he is now retired, Ximenes serves as chairman of the New Mexico Youth Conservation Corps. During the height of his influence as President Johnson's main advisor on Mexican-American issues, such Chicano Movement* leaders as Reies López Tijerina* and Rudolfo "Corky" Gonzales* criticized him and other "establishment" Mexican Americans for not being forceful enough in trying to end the oppression of Chicanos.* [SOURCE: Rosales, *Chicano!*, 97.]

YBOR CITY (TAMPA) STRIKE

In 1899, the first large strike in the cigar industry occured in Ybor City (Tampa), where Spanish and Cuban entrepreneurs had relocated their industry in 1886, in part to avoid labor unrest and organizing. The cigar industry relied on extensive manual-but-skilled labor by tobacco rollers. The cigar workers were one of the most radicalized and educated through a system in which they supported professional, *lectores*, or readers, who read to them all day long from world literature and newspapers while they hand-rolled cigars at their tables. The cigar rollers developed the strongest unions of any Hispanic workers and became the most influenced by socialist ideology. They struck again in 1901, 1910, 1920, and 1931. [SOURCE: Henderson and Mormino, *Spanish Pathways in Florida,* 40-45.]

YOUNG LORDS PARTY

The heyday of the Young Lords Party (YLP) in Chicago, New York, and Philadelphia was from 1969 to 1972. In 1969, Puerto Rican college students in New York City formed the Sociedad de Albizu Campos (SAC) in an effort to create an atmosphere that would make higher education institutions accountable to the Puerto Ricans in the city. But the founders felt that the Puerto Ricans in the ghetto also needed to unite with university students, so they targeted street youth and the dispossessed, guided by the belief that the "most disenfranchised segment of our community" harbored a revolutionary potential. They identified poor nutrition, lack of city services, and police brutality as issues that needed the most attention. Eventually in Chicago a Puerto Rican organization called Young Lords Party had similar objectives. The two joined using the same rubric YLP and employed tactics such as direct action and militancy, whether dealing with labor issues or making demands of church groups. The group blended political theory with civic activism in delivering free breakfasts to the poor, running lead-detection programs, supporting welfare mothers, and helping to organize hospital and health delivery system unions.

The YLP was very effective in using the media to obtain publicity and even had its own radio programs and published the bilingual newspaper, *Pa'lante* (Forward). In Philadelphia, the YLP met a great amount of repression from the police and city officials. Nonetheless, the impact of the its militancy forced the more established and moderate Puerto Rican leaders to realign their tactics and aspirations: they moved to the left more and became more forceful. Although the YLP was short-lived, it had a lasting impact on Puerto Rican politics in major urban areas, especially in Philadelphia. For the Young Lords, the homeland served as a continuing source of identity and the desire for Puerto Rican independence provided a continuous rationale for radical politics. The YLP became the Puerto Rican Revolutionary Workers Organization (PRRWO) in 1972 and shifted from a cultural-nationalist stance to a more ideological Marxist-Leninist one. That same year, the Puerto Rican Student Union allied with them to form what was considered a "mass organization." [SOURCE: Torres and Velázquez, *The Puerto Rican Movement*, 108, 113, 119, 141.]

YOUNG LORDS PARTY AND FEMINISM

When the Young Lords Party (YLP), a Puerto Rican nationalist organization of the 1970s, based in New York and Chicago, espoused a radical political agenda encompassing both feminism and nationalism, they took a unique stance in contrast to other contemporary nationalist organizations, such as the Black Panthers. High on the YLP feminist agenda was access to voluntary birth control, safe and legal abortion, quality public healthcare, free day care, and an end to poverty among Puerto Ricans and other people of color. Strong minded women in the organization, Denise Oliver, Iris Morales, and Gloria Fontanez, convinced the original male leaders of the YLP to abandon their traditional male-oriented nationalism and that women's liberation was inseparable from the liberation of people of color. [SOURCE: Nelson, "Abortions under Community Control."]

YOUNG REVOLUTIONARIES FOR INDEPENDENCE

Young Revolutionaries for Independence was founded by Juan Ramos and Wilfredo Rojas in 1967. It was one of the first Puerto Rican organizations to employ confrontational tactics and paved the way for the emergence of Philadelphia's Young Lords Party.* Inspired by the Cuban Revolution, the members "walked around with battle fatigues and Fidel Castro* buttons." [SOURCE: Torres and Velázquez, *The Puerto Rican Movement*, 112.]

YZAGUIRRE, RAÚL (1940-)

Raúl Yzaguirre has been in the forefront of a sustained drive to achieve the civil right for Hispanic Americans for more than 35 years. In 2005, he retired from the presidency of the National Council of La Raza (NCLR),* the largest national Hispanic organization. Born in the Rio Grande Valley of south Texas in 1940, Mr. Yzaguirre's initiation into civil rights activism came at the age of 15, when he organized an American G.I. Forum Juniors chapter. He then started a life-long association with Dr. Hector P. García,* the tireless activist-founder of the American G.I. Forum.* After graduating from high school in 1958, Yzaguirre joined the U.S. Air Force and served in the Medical Corps. Shortly after his discharge in 1964, he founded the National Organization for Mexican American Services. With a degree received at George Washington University in 1968, Yzaguirre became a program analyst at the Migrant Division of the Office of Economic Opportunity. The following year, he founded Interstate Research Associates, the first Mexican-American research association, which he turned into a hugely successful nonprofit consulting firm with a multimillion-dollar budget.

Yzaguirre joined NCLR in 1974. With the usual energy he employed in shaping other organizations, he parlayed it into one of the most influential and respected Hispanic organizations in the country. It now serves as an umbrella organization, working for civil rights and economic opportunities for Hispanics, and provides technical assistance to Hispanic community-based organizations that work for comprehensive community development

Yzaguirre's dedication to his work has earned him honors and awards from such venerable institutions as the Rockefeller Foundations, Princeton University, the John F. Kennedy School of Government at Harvard University and, in 1993, the government of Mexico, which awarded Yzaguirre the

Order of the Aztec Eagle, the highest honor given by to non-citizens. Many other kudos have been bestowed on Yzaguirre, including five honorary degrees. Such a profile has allowed him to become an effective and influential lobbyist on behalf of Latinos. [SOURCE: NCLR, http://www.nclr.org/; Pycior, *LBJ & Mexican Americans.*]

ZAPATA, EMILIANO (1879-1919)

Emiliano Zapata was born in Morelos, Mexico, into a family of peasant farmers. He lived his early life under great trepidation, which resulted from the economic reforms instituted by dictator Porfirio Díaz regime. He arose as a prominent figure in the Mexican agriarian movement through hard work and simple education. He assumed his role of a revolutionary leader when sugar landowners began to expand their holdings at the expense of the already destitute working class. By 1911, although Porfirio Díaz had been ousted, Zapata had written his Plan de Ayala in protest and resistance to the conservative politics of President Francisco I. Madero and continued his insurgency throughout several presidencies, including those of Victoriano Huerta and Venustiano Carranza, while maintaining a weak alliance with Pancho Villa* in the North. Zapata was murdered by federal troops, who disguised their murderous motives by pretending to defect to the agrarian cause.

In the 1960s, Chicano* militants used Zapata as a symbol of pride and as an historical predecessor of their movement, which they saw as based in working-class struggle. For Chicano Movement* activists, the Mexican Revolution and heroes like Zapata confirmed the idea that Mexicans came from a revolutionary tradition, which justified modern-day Chicano militancy. The axiom, apocryphally attributed to Zapata, "It is better to die on your feet than to live on your knees," became one of the recurrent themes of the Chicano Movement. [SOURCE: Womack, *Zapata and the Mexican Revolution.*]

Lorenzo de Zavala

ZAVALA, LORENZO DE (1789-1836)

Lorenzo de Zavala was born in Yucatan in 1789 and was a framer of Mexico's Constitution of 1824. A leading liberal ideologue, Zavala was a founder of the Masonic York Rite in Mexico City, a group that promoted democracy and free trade. As a member of the Chamber of Deputies, he was important in passing the Colonization Law of 1824, which offered incentives to both foreigners and Mexicans to settle in northern Mexico. In fact, with Vicente Filisola, he became a leader of one of the colonies and provided land contracts to eleven hundred families, most of

Z

them foreigners, in Texas. When General Antonio López de Santa Anna centralized Mexico's political organization, he attempted to close off the border of Texas to the United States. Zavala joined the Texas rebellion against the central government and became the first Vice President of the Republic of Texas, after once again having participated in the framing of a constitution. [SOURCE: Estep, "Lorenzo, Zavala De (1788-1836)," *The Handbook of Texas Online,* www.tsha.utexas.edu/handbook/online/articles/view/ZZ/fza5. html]

ZIMMERMAN TELEGRAM

During World War I, the anxiety and fear that Anglos already felt towards Mexicans because of border violence during the Mexican Revolution was exacerbated by rumors that Mexico was pro-German. Such xenophobia provoked more doubts about the loyalty of Mexicans living in the United States. Moreover, Mexican leaders Victoriano Huerta and Venustiano Carranza were suspected of having pro-German sympathies. The 1914 Yripanga incident, in which the Navy confiscated German arms bound for Huerta, convinced many Americans of his German leanings. The ultimate proof, in their eyes, was the so-called Zimmerman telegram, dispatched on January 16, 1917. In it the German foreign minister, Arthur Zimmerman, promised President Venustiano Carranza to return to Mexico the land it had lost to the United States in 1848, if Mexico would support the German effort in World War I. Intercepted, the telegram became a device of racial antagonism and justification for abuse and mistrust of both German Americans and Mexican Americans in the United States. [SOURCE: Meier and Rivera, *A Dictionary of Mexican American History,* 374.]

ZOOT SUIT RIOTS

In the Spring of 1943, with the tacit support of the press and their superiors, servicemen stationed in the Los Angeles area commandeered taxi cabs and spilled out into the streets of East Los Angeles, beating up every Mexican teenager that crossed their path. The immediate cause of the riot was conflict between young Mexican Americans and equally young American soldiers in East Los Angeles. Many Mexican youth dressed in zoot suits, a style of dress popular among young men in many urban areas, not just among Mexicans. But in Los Angeles, the dress was almost exclusively but erroneously associated with *pachuco** lawbreakers. While no one was killed, the experience served to humiliate the Mexican community, especially those members who felt optimistic about discrimination diminishing. The Los Angeles press, controlled by the magnate Randolph Hearst, provided the legitimacy for the attacks by publishing exaggerated stories about Mexican-American youth crime before the riots. Under proper discipline, the servicemen would not have been allowed such behavior—in essence permission was given to carry out the persecution of Mexican-American youths. The young soldiers were generally lauded for cleaning up Mexican areas of the so called "*pachuco* menace" by the press. After five days of violence, military authorities pressured by the CIO Central Council, began to rein in the rogue sailors and soldiers. In addition, community organizations, not just Mexican American ones, pressed for an investigation, which eventually placed responsibility on the police, local officials, and the media. [SOURCE: Monroy, *Rebirth*, 262; Mazón, *Zoot Suit Riots.*]

Chronology

1798 The Naturalization Act raises the number of years—from 3 to 5—that an immigrant has to live in the United States before becoming eligible for citizenship.

1803 France, which had acquired the Louisiana Territory from Spain, sells it to the United States, thus extending U.S. borders to New Spain.

1804 The Lewis and Clark expedition is seen by Spain as a prelude to U.S. expansion into Spanish-held territories.

1819 Following Andrew Jackson's capture of two Spanish forts in Florida, Spain is forced to sell Florida to the United States.

1821 The Moses Austin family received land grants from Spain and then independent Mexico to settle Anglo-American families in Texas.

1824 The Mexican Congress passed the Nationalization Colonization Law, opening up northern Mexico to colonization by Anglo Americans.

1836 The Republic of Texas gains its independence from Mexico. After being defeated at the battle of San Jacinto by General Sam Houston, General Antonio López de Santa Anna signs a document giving Texans their independence.

1845 Texas is officially annexed to the United States.

1846 The United States invades Mexico under the banner of Manifest Destiny.

MARCH John Charles Fremont invades California and liberates it from Mexico.

1848 The Treaty of Guadalupe Hidalgo officially ends the U.S.-Mexican War. Under the treaty, half the land area of Mexico—including Texas, California, most of Arizona and New Mexico, and parts of Colorado, Utah and Nevada—is ceded to the United States.

The Gold Rush lures a flood of Anglo settlers into California, which becomes a state in 1850.

1850 The Foreign Miner's Tax affirms the rights of Anglos to exclude Mexicans and other non-Anglos from the public domain mines of California.

1850s and 1860s Cuban political clubs in New York and Florida expand independence and abolitionist movements to include all sectors of Cuban society.

1851 Los Angeles city officials enact the first school ordinance in support of bilingual education.

Congress passes the California Land Act to determine whether land-grant holders have legitimate claims to lands they obtained prior to their annexation.

1852 The American Party, nicknamed the Know-Nothing Party, is founded to stem political inroads made by Catholic immigrants. In Texas, this group attemps to deny Mexican Catholics their rights.

1853 General Antonio López de Santa Anna returns to power as president of Mexico and, through the Gadsden Treaty, sells to the United States the region from Yuma, Arizona, along the Gila River, to the Mesilla Valley, New Mexico.

1857 Anglo freighters attack and kill Mexican cart men in the San Antonio environs to run them out of business.

1859 The Cortina War begins when Mexican landowner, Juan Nepomuceno Cortina, shoots an Anglo lawman in a street in Brownsville, precipitating border warfare between Anglos and Mexicans for the years to come.

1865 The Ku Klux Klan (KKK) is founded to violently stem the political strength of former slaves. In the 1920s, the KKK lobbies for restrictions on Mexican immigration and takes direct action on immigrants.

1870s Land speculators organize the "Santa Fe Ring" and devise schemes in which Hispanic landowners lose their farms and ranches over a period of 30 years.

1875 Carlos Manuel de Céspedes becomes Key West's first mayor. His father, who had the same given name, was the hero of the Ten Years' War in Cuba.

1880s Mexican immigration to the United States is stimulated by the advent of the railroad.

1890s Land usurpation in New Mexico leads to the formation of the "Gorras Blancas," night riders who attempt to forestall the development and modernization that threatens the Hispano way of life.

1891 Congress establishes the Court of Private Land Claims to confirm Spanish land grants. The court has jurisdiction over Arizona, Colorado, and New Mexico.

The Immigration and Naturalization Service (INS) is created by the U.S. Congress and assigned to the Department of Labor.

1894 The Alianza Hispano-Americana is founded in Tucson, Arizona, and quickly spreads throughout the Southwest.

1897 The *Rodríguez v. Texas* decision allows Mexicans to naturalize as a result of the 1848 Treaty of Guadalupe Hidalgo.

1898 **APRIL** After the the USS Maine blows up in Havana Harbor, President William McKinley declares war against Spain. As an outcome, Cuba and Puerto Rico become independent of Spain but protectorates of the United States.

1899 Cuban cigar-makers stage the first large strike in Ybor City (Tampa), where the industry had relocated beginning in 1886, in part to avoid labor unrest and organizing.

1900 *Regeneración* first appears in Mexico City, delivering a strong radical message of worker liberation to Mexicans on both sides of border. It is published in the United States after 1904.

APRIL The Foraker Act establishes a civilian government in Puerto Rico.

1903 American officials force the framers of the Cuban constitution to include the Platt Amendment, allowing the United States to intervene in Cuban affairs.

1907–1908 A recession creates conditions for the first major repatriation program of destitute Mexicans in the United States.

1910 The Mexican Revolution begins, hundreds of thousands of people flee north from Mexico and settle in the Southwest.

SEPTEMBER The first convention of Mexicans for action against social injustice, El Primer Congreso Mexicanista (The First Mexicanist Congress), is held in Laredo, Texas.

1915 El Plan de San Diego (Texas) calls upon all racial minorities to drive Anglo Americans out of the Southwest and create a separate republic.

1916 **JANUARY** Pancho Villa's men execute 17 American mining engineers at Santa Ysabel, Chihuahua, provoking anti-Mexican riots in El Paso, Texas.

1917-1919 Over 18,000 Puerto Ricans serve in the United States military during World War I.

1917 Vigilantes round up some 1,200 copper-mine strikers, many of whom are Mexican, and ship them in crowded trains without food and water to Columbus, New Mexico.

The Jones Act grants Puerto Ricans U.S. citizenship, regardless of where they were born. Puerto Ricans are not allowed to vote in presidential elections or elect congressmen or senators unless they live on the mainland.

The U.S. Labor Department arranges for Puerto Ricans to come to the mainland as guest workers during the World War I labor shortage.

An immigration act is passed by Congress, making literacy a condition for entry. During World War I, "temporary" Mexican farmworkers, railroad laborers, and miners are given a waiver to the immigration law so they can enter the United States to work.

1918 **JANUARY 28** Texas Rangers and Anglo ranchers execute 15 Mexican farmers in Porvenir, Texas, for allegedly participating in a raid on an Anglo ranch.

1920s Puerto Rican workers in New York City join La Internacional or the more radical La Resistencia with other Spanish-speaking tobacco workers.

1921 A recession provokes extreme anti-Mexican feelings. Comisiones Honoríficas Mexicanas are founded by the Mexican consular service in the United States to assist in repatriation and defense.

The Order of the Sons of America is founded in Texas to promote Mexican American participation in U.S. institutions and to achieve civil rights.

1923 Founded in New York City, the Porto Rican Brotherhood promotes mutual aid among its working-class members from Puerto Rico.

1924 The U.S. Border Patrol is organized and given the primary responsibility for curbing illegal entries from Mexico.

1926 **JULY** Puerto Ricans, the most recent arrivals in the area of Manhattan now known as Spanish Harlem, are attacked by non-Hispanic neighbors, mainly of Italian and Irish stock.

1927 La Liga Puertorriqueña e Hispana is founded in New York to increase the power of the city's Hispanic community through unification of its diverse organizations.

1928 The Confederación de Sociedades Mexicanas is formed at the urging of the Mexican government. It serves as an umbrella group for fledgling agricultural unions formed by Mexican workers in southern California.

1929 LULAC is founded in Texas by frustrated Mexican Americans who do not have access to avenues for opportunity in the United States.

1930 In the segregation suit brought on behalf of Jesús Salvatierra in Del Rio, Texas, the courts ruled that segregation of Mexican-American children is unconstitutional.

1931 A court ruling prevents the segregation of Mexican children by the Lemon Grove, California, School Board, which argued that separate facilities were necessary to achieve Americanization and English-language development.

California Assemblyman George R. Bliss introduces a bill to segregate Native American, Mexican, and Asian school children. It passes in the California Assembly but is defeated in the Senate.

1931–1932 During the worst years of the Great Depression, thousands of Mexicans are repatriated only to find themselves destitute in Mexico.

1933 Mexican farmworkers strike in the Central Valley, California, cotton industry, supported by several groups of independent Mexican union organizers and radicals.

The El Monte Berry Strike, possibly the largest agricultural strike up to that point in history, is led by Mexican unions in California.

1936 The FBI begins surveillance and repression of pro-independence elements in Puerto Rico and on the mainland.

1937 The La Folette Civil Liberties Committee investigates the "Republic Steel Massacre" in which police shot into a peaceful rally, killing ten striking workers.

1938 The Mexican American Movement emerges in southern California mostly among college students committed to uplifting Mexican Americans through education and clean living.

Young Mexican and Mexican-American pecan shellers strike in San Antonio. Emma Tenayuca is one of their leaders.

1942-1943 Mexican-American teenagers in Los Angeles are convicted of murdering another young Mexican in what is known as the "Sleepy

Lagoon Incident;" the widely publicized trial is full of racism and presided over by a biased judge.

1942 **APRIL** The Spanish-Speaking People's Division within the Office of Inter-American Affairs is created to reduce discrimination against Mexican Americans.

1943 Prompted by the labor shortage of World War II, the U.S. government forges an agreement with the Mexican government to supply temporary workers, known as *braceros*, for American agricultural work.

Mexican intellectuals and activists join the Mexican-American civil rights campaign to further better treatment through the joint membership of Comité Contra el Racismo (Comittee Against Racism).

Texas establishes the Good Neighbor Commission to improve the overall treatment of Mexicans and to offset the *bracero* embargo Mexico has placed on Texas.

U.S. military members attack young Mexican Americans in the so-called "Zoot Suit" riots in Southern California.

1945 In the *Westminster v. Méndez* case, Mexican parents in California file a suit against Orange County schools to end segregation. A federal judge concurs in 1947 that segregation is unconstitutional.

1947 The American G.I. Forum is organized by Mexican-American veterans in response to a Three Rivers, Texas, funeral home's refusal to bury a Mexican-American soldier killed in the Pacific during World War II.

The National Farm Workers Union in California goes on strike against the DiGiorgio Fruit Corporation in Kern County.

The Puerto Rican legislature establishes the Bureau of Employment and Migration to provide protection to the thousands of migrants moving to the mainland.

1948 Operation Bootstrap, a campaign for the economic development of Puerto Rico, reduces traditional agricultural employment and spurs migration to the mainland.

1950s Immigration from Mexico doubles from 5.9 percent to 11.9 percent, and in the 1960s rises to 13.3 percent of the total number of immigrants to the United States.

1952 The McCarran-Walter Immigration and Nationality Act continues the quota system stipulated in 1920s legislation but places greater restrictions on immigration from the Western Hemisphere, which had been exluded from quotas.

The *Sheely v. González* court decision abolishes segregation in Tolleson, a town in Maricopa County where Phoenix is located.

1953 69,124 Puerto Ricans come to the mainland, mostly to New York, New Jersey, and Florida, the largest migration from the island ever.

1954 In the landmark case of *Hernandez v. Texas*, the nation's highest court acknowledges that Hispanic Americans are not being treated as "whites." The U.S. Supreme Court recognizes Hispanics as a separate class of people suffering profound discrimination.

MARCH 1 Puerto Rican nationalists attack the U.S. House of Representatives in order to bring national attention to the colonial status of Puerto Rico.

1954–1958 Operation Wetback deports 3.8 million persons of Mexican descent. Very few of them are allowed deportation hearings.

1958 The Coordinating Council for the Puerto Rican Day Parade is formed to organize the parade to be held each June 9.

ASPIRA, Inc. is founded as a small nonprofit agency in New York City, specializing in counseling Puerto Rican youth. It is now a civil rights national association.

1959 The Movimiento para la Independencia is established in Puerto Rico, with affiliates on the mainland, to mobilize for Puerto Rican independence.

1960s After Fidel Castro's Revolution, voluntary relief agencies, known as VOLAGs, are quickly organized by church groups to assist refugees fleeing the revolution.

Operation Peter Pan is launched; it is a program to assist Cuban children in escaping from Communist indoctrination by coming to live in the United States.

Viva Kennedy Clubs are organized by Mexican Americans as part of the effort to elect John F. Kennedy to the presidency; the program energized many Hispanic leaders to achieve political power at the national level.

President Eisenhower authorizes the Mutual Security Act to allot one million dollars to resettle Cuban refugees fleeing the Cuban Revolution.

SEPTEMBER 8 In Miami, the first annual flotilla procession is held in honor of the patron saint of Cuba, the Virgin of Caridad del Cobre.

1961 President John F. Kennedy establishes the Cuban Refugee Program, which provides resettlement assistance to Cuban exiles.

The Puerto Rican Socialist Party (PSP) is founded in New York City as an extension of Movimiento para la Independencia.

1962 The United Farm Workers Organizing Committee in California is founded as an independent organization led by César Chávez.

1963 In Crystal City, the Political Association of Spanish-speaking Organizations (PASO) and local Teamsters (mostly Mexican Americans) unite to take over the city council for two years.

The Dade County public school system, in response to pressure from the Miami Cuban community, implements bilingual education long before the federal government provides a mandate.

OCTOBER 8 La Alianza Federal de las Mercedes (The Federal Alliance of Land Grants) is incorporated by Reies López Tijerina.

1964 Philadelphia's annual Puerto Rican Week Festival (Festival Puertorriqueño de Filadelfia) is celebrated for the first time.

The Representación Cubana del Exilio is organized by Cuban exiles in the United States to choose the leaders in a plan to oust the Communists from the homeland.

President Johnson's adminstration creates the Equal Employment Opportunity Commission (EEOC) to prevent discrimination in employment.

The Economic Opportunity Act creates the Volunteers In Service To America (VISTA) and the Job Corps. VISTA assigned volunteers to low-income areas to engage in community-action projects.

1965 Rodolfo "Corky" Gonzales is appointed director of Denver's "War on Poverty" Program.

Fidel Castro allows Cubans to leave if their relatives in the United States come to get them at Camarioca Bay. This becomes known as the "Cuban Boatlift."

SEPTEMBER 16 The National Farm Workers Association (NFWA) meets in a Delano church hall and votes to join the Agricultural Workers Organizing Committee strike.

LATE NOVEMBER–DECEMBER Chávez's NFWA begins the grape boycott, targeting Schenley Industries and DiGiorgio Corp.

1966 The Inter-Agency Cabinet Committee on Mexican American Affairs is established to include Hispanics in programs set up under President Johnson's Great Society.

Rodolfo Acuña teaches the first Mexican-American history class in Los Angeles.

The Crusade for Justice (CFJ) is founded in Denver, Colorado. It becomes the most successful organization in the Chicano Movement.

MARCH 28 At an EEOC meeting in Albuquerque, only one commissioner shows up and fifty Chicano leaders, including Corky Gonzales, walk out in protest of the lack of Mexican-American staff and efforts to address discrimination against Mexican Americans.

MARCH 17–APRIL 11 César Chávez and the NFWA march from Delano to Sacramento. It takes them 25 days and they arrive on Easter Sunday.

APRIL 29 Corky Gonzales is fired from the Neighborhood Youth Corps directorship; he promises that "this day a new crusade for justice is born." He subsequently founds the Crusade for Justice in Denver.

JUNE The farmworker solidarity march from the Rio Grande to Austin takes place. Many future leaders participate, including José Angel Gutiérrez.

JUNE 12 As Puerto Ricans in Chicago celebrate their annual Puerto Rican Parade, police provoke hundreds of Puerto Rican youths to go on a rampage, breaking windows and burning down many of the businesses in their neighborhoods.

JULY 2–4 The first Alianza public protest takes place: a three-day march from Albuquerque to Santa Fe to make demands to the governor.

AUGUST 22 The AFL-CIO executive council admits the United Farm Workers Organizing Committee, which merges from NFWA and AWOC into the AFL-CIO.

OCTOBER 15 Tijerina and 350 members of the Alianza occupy Kit Carson National Forest Camp Echo Amphitheater on behalf of the "Pueblo de San Joaquín de Chama."

The United Farm Workers (UFW) wins a contract with the DiGiorgio corporation in California.

1967 The Mexican American Youth Organization (MAYO) is formed on college campuses in Texas.

The Mexican American Legal Defense and Education Fund (MALDEF) is incorporated in San Antonio.

MARCH 13 Two hundred and fifty students representing seven Los Angeles colleges and universities meet to form the United Mexican American Students.

JUNE 5 Tijerina conducts an armed raid in Tierra Amarilla on the Rio Arriba County Courthouse to make a citizen's arrest of District Attorney Alfonso Sánchez.

AUGUST The UFW wins contracts with Gallo, Almaden, Franzia, Paul Mason, Golberg, the Novitiate of Los Gatos, and Perelli-Minetti.

AUGUST 19 The Alianza Federal de Las Mercedes changes its name to Alianza Federal de Pueblos Libres.

OCTOBER 21–22 Tijerina organizes the Alianza's national convention in Albuquerque, where La Raza Unida Party (LRUP) is discussed.

DECEMBER David Sánchez dissolves Young Citizens for Community Action to form the Brown Berets self-defense group in Los Angeles. The Berets begin a series of pickets in front of sheriffs' offices and police stations.

DECEMBER 27 More than a hundred Chicanos demonstrate at the East L.A. sheriff's substation against police brutality.

1968 The Southwest Council of La Raza is founded in Arizona; it is renamed the National Council of La Raza (NCLR) when it relocates to Washington, D.C. in 1972.

The U.S. Supreme Court rules in the *Miranda v. Arizona* case that crime suspects must be warned that they have the right to remain silent . . . in what comes to be known as the "Miranda Rights."

Betita Martínez begins *El Grito del Norte* newspaper in Española, New Mexico.

FEBRUARY 15 César Chávez begins a 25-day fast at Forty Acres, near Delano. He fasts in penitence for farmworkers' moral problems and talk of violence.

MARCH 3 More than 1,000 students peacefully walk out of Abraham Lincoln High School in Los Angeles. Lincoln High teacher Sal Castro joins them. By afternoon, 100 more students walk out of four other schools: Garfield, Wilson, Belmont, and Roosevelt.

MARCH 10–11 César Chávez breaks his fast at a mass in a Delano public park with 4,000 supporters, including Robert F. Kennedy.

APRIL 9 Seven hundred Chicano students walk out of Lanier High School in San Antonio. Soon, 600 more walk out of Edgewood High School.

APRIL 16 Denver Chicanos begin a boycott of Coors for discriminatory hiring.

MAY-JUNE The Poor People's Campaign conducts a march on Washington, D.C. to dramatize the persistence of poverty in America in spite of "War on Poverty" projects

MAY 27 A grand jury indicts the "L.A. 13" for conspiracy to disrupt the peace in organizing the school walkouts.

JUNE East Los Angeles native José Sanchez, 19, is the first Chicano to resist the military draft publicly.

SEPTEMBER 10–24 Students and parents picket Lincoln High School and the LAUSD Board of Education, demanding Sal Castro's reinstatement.

SEPTEMBER 26–OCTOBER 2 Chicanos sit in at the LAUSD Board of Education: 35 parents, students, and Brown Berets protest Sal Castro's suspension.

OCTOBER 3 The LAUSD board votes to return Sal Castro to the classroom.

NOVEMBER 4 The United Mexican American Students and the Black Student Union unite, and Rosalío Muñoz is elected UCLA student body president.

1969 to 1972 Puerto Rican militants found Young Lords Party (YLP) chapters in Chicago, New York, and Philadelphia to increase educational opportunity and to confront racism and discrimination.

1969 Cuban emigré intellectuals in the United States join in a hemispheric conference on Cuban issues at the first Reunión de Estudios Cubanos.

MARCH 27–31 The First National Chicano Youth Liberation Conference is sponsored by the Crusade for Justice.

APRIL A three-day conference is organized at Santa Barbara by the Chicano Coordinating Council of Higher Education to create a plan for curricular changes and provide service to Chicano students. Student organizations statewide change their name to El Movimiento Estudiantil Chicano de Aztlán, MECHA.

SEPTEMBER Beginning on Labor Day, Puerto Ricans in Hartford, Connecticut, stage a series riots that last two days. The causes of the upheaval can be traced to frustrations caused by years of poverty, second-class status, under-representation, and police brutality.

SEPTEMBER 16 The first "Chicano Liberation Day" is organized by Corky Gonzales.

NOVEMBER Rosalío Muñoz refuses to be drafted at the induction center in downtown Los Angeles.

DECEMBER 20 Católicos por la Raza clashes with police as it demands church programs for Chicanos in front of St. Basil's Cathedral in Los Angeles.

1970 President Jimmy Carter's reconciliation overtures to Cuba prompt some Cuban exile organizations to advocate normalizing relations with the homeland.

FEBRUARY 28 The Second National Chicano Moratorium Committee demonstration takes place in Los Angeles with 6,000 people assembled.

APRIL La Raza Unida Party (LRUP) wins four of seven seats on the Crystal City school board.

MAY 16 The first Colorado LRUP meeting takes place at Southern Colorado State College. Corky Gonzales is elected state chair.

JULY 20 The National Chicano Moratorium Committee marches in Houston, Texas drawing 5,000 people to its rally.

AUGUST 29 The third Moratorium protest in Laguna Park with close to 30,000 people. A liquor store theft provides police with the excuse to break up the peaceful gathering. Some protesters respond by throwing things at the police. At the Silver Dollar Cafe, Rubén Salazar is shot in the head with a tear gas missile.

OCTOBER 2 More than 600 Chicano students walk out of an East Chicago, Indiana, school after the vice principal says, "Mexicans are lazy and ignorant."

OCTOBER 14 Los Angeles County District Attorney Evelle J. Younger announces he will not prosecute Deputy Thomas Wilson for Rubén Salazar's death.

NOVEMBER 22 The Oakland-Berkeley chapter of LRUP has its first meeting.

1971 The FBI Counter Intelligence Program infiltrates and provokes Chicano organizations.

APRIL 2 The Deganawidah-Quetzalcoatl University, the first Native American and Chicano university, is founded near Davis, California.

MAY The Houston Chicana Conference attracts more than 600 Chicanas from 23 states.

MAY 5 La Marcha de la Reconquista, from Calexico to Sacramento, begins with Rosalío Muñoz, David Sánchez, and the Brown Berets.

1972 The Puerto Rican Legal Defense and Education Fund is founded to advocate for protection of civil rights of the Puerto Rican Community in the United States.

The National Association of Chicano Social Scientists, today's National Association of Chicana/Chicano Scholars, is founded by Chicano academicians to promote applied Chicano studies research.

The National Conference of Puerto Rican Women is founded in Washington, D.C. to increase participation of Puerto Rican women in the social, political, and economic life of the United States.

ASPIRA, Inc. brings the first suit against a school district in New York City to demand the institution of federal guidelines for bilingual education.

Cuban Americans in Washington, D.C. form the Cuban American National Council to address problems of a fast-growing Hispanic community.

Cuban-American scholars in Miami, Florida, establish the Instituto de Estudios Cubanos to study Cuba in a responsible fashion.

FEBRUARY 9 Ramsey Muñiz announces his bid for Texas governor under the LRUP banner at a press conference in San Antonio.

FEBRUARY 12 The UFW Organizing Committee charters the United Farm Worker-AFL-CIO.

AUGUST 14 The UFW files suit in Phoenix to bar enforcement of the new Arizona Agricultural Relations Act, which will prohibit harvest-time picketing.

AUGUST 28–SEPTEMBER 26 The Brown Berets invade Catalina Island and take a campsite.

SEPTEMBER 1–4 LRUP holds its national convention in El Paso with 3,000 attendees. José Angel Gutiérrez beats Corky Gonzales for the national chair in a decisive campaign that leads to the division of LRUP into two camps.

NOVEMBER 3 Ramsey Muñiz garners 6.28 percent of the Texas gubernatorial vote, nearly undermining Democrat Dolph Briscoe's victory.

1973-1976 One hundred and three bombings and 6 political assassinations are credited to hardliner Cuban exiles targeting other exiles who advocate coexistence with Castro's Cuba.

1973 The right of the Puerto Rican people to decide their own future as a nation is approved by the United Nations.

JANUARY 23 A shootout with police takes place at Escuela Tlatelolco, a Crusade for Justice apartment building.

APRIL The first meeting of the U.S. branch of the Puerto Rican Socialist Party is inaugurated in New York City; three thousand people attend.

1974 Young and radical Cuban emigrés publish *Areíto* to celebrate the revolution and dispute U.S. propaganda against the Cuban state.

The Southwest Voter Registration Education Project is established. Willie Velásquez, a former member of MAYO and LRUP, becomes its director.

At the "Congress Against Coexistence" in San Juan, Puerto Rico, Cuban exiles protest against the Organization of American States vote to lift the sanctions against Cuba.

The Comité de Intelectuales por la Libertad de Cuba is organized by Cuban exile writers in New York City for a more democratic government in Cuba.

OCTOBER 27 Twenty thousand people fill Madison Square Garden in solidarity for the independence of Puerto Rico.

NOVEMBER Raúl Castro is elected the first Chicano governor of Arizona.

1975 The Voting Rights Act of 1965 is extended to Hispanic Americans.

The National Association for Bilingual Education is founded in Dallas, Texas, to assure the implemetation of federally funded bilingual education projects.

The California State Assembly enacts the Agricultural Labor Relations Act to provide farmworkers protection.

1976 Five Hispanic Congressmen form the Congressional Hispanic Caucus to influence legislative, executive, and judicial actions affecting Hispanics.

In *Lau v. Nichols*, the U.S. Supreme Court holds that the San Francisco Unified School District has discriminated against non-English-speaking students.

1977 Fifty-five young, Cuban exiles, known as the Antonio Maceo Brigade, travel to Cuba to participate in service work and achieve a degree of rapprochement with the Cuban government.

MALDEF files suit in Tyler, Texas, to prevent the school district from charging tuition to undocumented children.

The First National Chicano/Latino Immigration Conference is held in San Antonio to oppose increased efforts to stem illegal immigration.

1978 Alan Bakke files a suit against the University of California at Davis for reverse discrimination after his application to medical school is rejected. The Supreme Court rules against the suit.

In the Cerro Maravilla incident, two young independence activists are killed by Puerto Rican policemen.

1979-1985 More than 500,000 Salvadorans, Guatemalans, and Nicaraguans enter the United States in search of political asylum as a consequence of civil war and economic disruption in their countries.

1979 The Cuban American Committee presents President Carter a petition with 10,000 signatures requesting normalization of relations with Cuba.

Large numbers of Gay Latinas and Latinos from throughout the United States participate in a historic march on Washington.

1980 In Fort Wayne, Indiana, the Cuban American Legal Defense and Education Fund is founded to advocate for equal treatment for Hispanics.

APRIL Fidel Castro allows round-the-clock evacuation of Cubans to the United States. President Jimmy Carter welcomes the new influx of exiles, who become known as *marielitos*, named after the port of their departure.

1981 Wealthy Cuban businessmen in Miami found the Cuban American National Foundation to influence President Reagan administration's policies on Cuba.

1982 **MARCH** The Sanctuary Movement begins when Tucson churches provide sanctuary to Central American refugees fleeing violence in their home countries.

1983 Puerto Rican activists begin the Voter's Participation Project in New York, registering 120,000 people since its inception.

Mexico, Venezuela, Colombia, and Panama meet on Contadora Island off the Panama coast to discuss measures to bring peace to the Central American nations and formulate the "Contadora Peace Plan."

Federico Peña becomes the first Hispanic mayor of Denver, Colorado, and is re-elected to a second term in 1987.

Inter-University Program on Latino Research is founded to employ the expanding body of knowledge on Latino communities on local, state, regional, national, and international levels.

1984 The Refugee/Immigrant Rights Coalition of the Rio Grande Valley is formed to provide human rights protection to Central American refugees.

1985 Miami elects its first Cuban-born mayor, Xavier Suárez.

1986 The Immigration and Control Act allows hundreds of thousands of Hispanic undocumented workers to obtain legal status.

1989 The Cuban American National Foundation obtains state funding for its institute at Miami's Florida International University; it is opposed by the scholarly community and not established.

Miami's Ileana Ross-Lehtinen is the first Cuban American elected to the U.S. Congress.

1990 The "Cuban Democracy Act" prohibits U.S. subsidiaries in third countries from trading with Cuba and prevents ships that had recently visited Cuba from docking in U.S. ports.

Dominicans become the second largest group of immigrants to the United States from this hemisphere (after Mexicans).

1990s-2004 The National Latina/o Lesbian, Gay, Bisexual, and Transgender Organization holds international *encuentros* to discuss issues confronting Gay Latinos.

1991 Based in Cuba, but supported by the exile community, El Comité Cubano pro-Derechos Humanos defends Cubans persecuted for protests against Cuba's state policies.

1992 The Dominican Studies Institute is founded at the City University of New York.

Cheryl Hopwood and three other white students win a lawsuit in federal court against the University of Texas Law School, claiming less qualified minority students were admitted. The appeal by the university is rejected in 1996.

December 16 The UN holds the International Conference on Central American Refugees to deal with the Central American migration crisis.

1993 The Cuban Committee for Democracy works in Washington, D.C. to advance a dialogue with Castro's government, challenging exile hardliners.

NOVEMBER California voters approve Proposition 187, denying public, social, educational, and health services to undocumented immigrants.

1996 Congress passes the Illegal Immigration Reform and Immigrant Responsibility Act to limit assistance to legal immigrants, reduce illegal immigration, and streamline the political asylum process.

NOVEMBER Proposition 209 is passed in California as a constitutional amendment to overturn all state affirmative action programs.

1997 The Nicaraguan Adjustment and Central American Relief Act provides more comprehensive immigration relief to Cubans and Nicaraguans than to other Central Americans.

NOVEMBER Gay rights activists pressure the Puerto Rican legislature to decriminalize consensual sexual relationships between persons of the same sex.

1998 **October** Hurricane Mitch devastates much of Central America, especially Honduras and El Salvador, prompting even more immigration to the United States.

1999 **September 11** President Bill Clinton gives clemency to eleven members of a Puerto Rican nationalist group after they vow to renounce terrorism.

2000 **FEBRUARY** "Dominicans 2000: Building Our National Agenda" is created in New York City to resolve issues and problems facing Dominicans in the United States.

APRIL 22 INS officers wrest six-year-old Elián González from his great uncle's home in Miami and send him back to his father in Cuba.

2002 **MAY** Latino activists meet at the University of Massachusetts, Boston, to discuss politics, health, immigration, and other issues facing their communities.

2005 **MAY 17** Antonio R. Villaraigosa is elected the first Hispanic mayor of Los Angeles in more than one hundred years.

Bibliography

Abreu, Gissell. "Second Latino Public Policy Conference Draws 600." <http://www.gaston.umb.edu/publications/gr/9xxnl/articles/latpubpol-con.html>.

Acosta, Teresa Palomo. "The Bishops' Committee for Hispanic Affairs." *The Handbook of Texas Online.* <http://www.tsha.utexas.edu/handbook/online/articles/BB/icb5.html>.

_____. "Political Association of Spanish-Speaking Organizations (PASSO)." *The Handbook of Texas Online.* <http://www.tsha.utexas.edu/handbook/online>.

_____. "Raza Unida Party." *The Handbook of Texas Online.* <http://dev.tsha.utexas.edu/handbook/online/articles/RR/war1.html>.

Acuña, Rodolfo. *Community Under Siege: A Chronicle of Chicanos East of the Los Angeles River, 1945–1975.* Los Angeles: UCLA Chicano Studies Research Center Publications, 1984.

_____. *Occupied America: A History of Chicanos,* 3rd ed. New York: Harper and Row, 1988.

Águila, Jaime. "Protecting 'México De Afuera': Mexican Emigration Policy, 1876–1928." Diss. Arizona State U, 2000.

Almaguer, Tomás. *Racial Fault Lines, The Historical Origins of White Supremacy in California.* Berkeley: U of California P, 1994.

Almaráz, Jr., Félix D. "Castañeda, Carlos Eduardo (1896–1958)." *The Handbook of Texas Online.* <http://www.tsha.utexas.edu/handbook/online/articles/view/CC/fca85.html>.

Alvarez, Jr., Roberto R. *La Familia: Migration and Adaptation in Baja and Alta California, 1800–1975.* Berkeley: U of California P, 1987.

_____. "The Lemon Grove Incident: The Nation's First Successful Desegragation Court Case." *The Journal of San Diego History.* <http://www.sandiegohistory.org/journal/86spring/lemongrove.htm>.

Aguilar, John L. "Expressive Ethnicity and Ethnic Identity in Mexico and Mexican America." In *Mexican American Identity.* Marta E. Bernal and Phyllis I. Martinelli, eds. Encino: Floricanto P, 1993. 55–67.

Andrade, Juan. "Gutiérrez Unites, Strengthens Latino Vote." *Chicago Sun-Times* (29 March 2002). <http://www.puertorico-herald.org>.

Baker, Susan, and Kenji Hakuta. "Bilingual Education and Latino Civil Rights." <http://www.civilrightsproject.harvard.edu/research/latino97/Hakuta.pdf>.

Baker, Patricia. "The Bandini Family." *Journal of San Diego History* 15 (Winter 1969): 25–27.

Balderrama, Francisco E. *In Defense of La Raza: The Los Angeles Mexican Consulate and the Mexican Community, 1929–1936.* Tucson: U of Arizona P, 1982.

_____, and Raymond Rodríguez. *Decade of Betrayal: Mexican Repatriation in the 1930s.* Albuquerque: UNM P, 1995.

Barker, Eugene C. "Mexican Colonization Laws." *The Handbook of Texas Online.* <http://www.tsha.utexas.edu/handbook/online/articles/view/MM/ugm1.html>.

Barrett, Edward L. *The Tenney Committee: Legislative Investigation of Subversive Activities in California.* Ithaca: Cornell UP, 1951.

Berkowitz, Bill. "Freedom Fighter: Remembering the National Farm Worker Ministry's Jim Drake." In *Working for a Change.* <http://www.workingforchange.com/article.cfm?ItemID=12221>.

Betten, Neil, and Raymond Mohl. "From Discrimination to Repatriation: Mexican Life in Gary, Indiana, during the Great Depression." *Pacific Historical Review* 42 (August 1973): 270–388.

Boehm, Mike. "Requiem for the Ravine." *Los Angeles Times* (18 May 2003). <http://www.artistsnetwork.org/news9/news434.html>.

Bovard, James. "The EEOC's War on Fairness." *Freedom Daily* (May 2000). <http://www.fff.org/freedom/0500d.asp>.

Bradfute, Richard W. *The Court of Private Land Claims: The Adjudication of Spanish and Mexican Land Titles, 1891–1904.* Albuquerque: UNM P, 1975.

Bridge, Durgan. "A History of Mexican Americans in California." <http://www.cr.nps.gov/history/5views/5views5h31.htm>.

Brooks, David. "Desafuero a López Obrador y comicios en el extranjero." *La jornada* (March 31 2005).

Broyles-González, Yolanda. *El Teatro Campesino: Theater in the Chicano Movement.* Austin: UT P, 1994.

Calloway, Larry. "Cultures Color N. M. Politics." <http://www.abqjournal.com/2000/nm/past/14past-19-99-html>.

Camarillo, Albert. *Chicanos in a Changing Society: From Mexican Pueblos to American Barrios in Santa Barbara and Southern California, 1848–1930.* Cambridge: Harvard UP, 1979.

Campa, Arthur. *Hispanic Culture in the Southwest*. Norman: U of Oklahoma P, 1979.

Capetillo, Luisa. *A Nation of Women: An Early Feminist Speaks Out / Mi Opinión sobre las libertades, derechos y deberes de la mujer.* Houston: Arte Público P, 2004.

Cárdenas, Gilberto, ed. *La Causa: Civil Rights, Social Justice and Struggles for Equality in the Midwest*. Houston: Arte Público P, 2004.

Cardoso, Lawrence. *Mexican Emigration to the United States, 1897-1931*. Tucson: U of Arizona P, 1980.

Carrasco, Gilbert Paul. "Law and Politics" Kanellos, *Hispanic-American Almanac* 229–286.

Carrigan, William D, and Clove Webb. "The Lynching of Persons of Mexican Origin or Descent in the United States, 1848 to 1928." *Journal of Social History* (Winter 2003). <http://www.findarticles.com/p/articles/mi_m2005/is_2_37/ai_111897839/pg_2>.

Carroll, Patrick J. *Felix Longoria's Wake: Bereavement, Racism, and the Rise of Mexican American Activism*. Austin: UT P, 2003.

Castro, Max J., and Thomas D. Boswell. "The Dominican Diaspora Revisited: Dominicans and Dominican Americans in a New Century." *Dominican American National Roundtable*. <http://www.danr.org/dominican_diaspora.htm>.

Chacón, Ramón D. "Labor Unrest and Industrialized Agriculture in California: The Case of the 1933 San Joaquin Valley Cotton Strike." *Social Science Quarterly* 65.2 (1984): 336–53.

Chapa, Jorge, et al. "The Hopwood Decision in Texas as an Attack on Latino Access to Selective Higher Education Programs." <http:www.civilrightsproject.harvard.edu/research/latino97/Chapa.pdf+%22Hopwood+decision%22&hl=en&ie=UTF-8>.

Chávez, Ernesto. *"¡Mi Raza Primero!" (My People First!): Nationalism, Identity, and Insurgency in the Chicano Movement in Los Angeles, 1966–1978*. Berkeley: U of California P, 2002.

Chávez, John R. *Eastside Landmark: A History of the East Los Angeles Community Union, 1968–1993*. Stanford: Stanford UP, 1998.

_____. *The Lost Land: The Chicano Image of the Southwest*. Albuquerque: UNM P, 1984.

Chávez, Leo R. *Shadowed Lives: Undocumented Immigrants in American Society*. Fort Worth: Harcourt Brace Jovanovich College Publishers, 1992.

Christian, Carole. "Herrera, John J. (1910–1986)." *The Handbook of Texas Online*. <http://www.tsha.utexas.edu/handbook/online/articles/view/HH/fhe63.html>.

_____. "Joining the American Mainstream: Texas' Mexican Americans During World War I." *Southwestern Historical Quarterly* 92 (April 1989): 559-595.

Coerver, Don, and Linda B. Hall. "Joining the American Mainstream: Texas's Mexican Americans during World War I." *Southwestern Historical Quarterly* 92 (April 1989): 559–595.

_____. *Texas and the Mexican Revolution: A Study in State and National Border Policy, 1910–1920.* San Antonio: Trinity UP, 1984.

Cruz, José E. "A Decade of Change: Puerto Rican Politics in Hartford, Connecticut, 1969–1979." *Journal of American Ethnic History* 16.3 (1997): 45–80.

Daunt, Tina. "Early Challenges, Different Paths, Same Goal." *Los Angeles Times* (8 May 2005).

De León, Arnoldo. *Ethnicity in the Sunbelt: A History of Mexican Americans in Houston.* Houston: University of Houston Mexican American Studies Monograph Series, 1989.

_____. *Not Room Enough: Mexicans, Anglos and Socioeconomic Change in Texas, 1850–1900.* Albuquerque: UNM P, 1993.

_____. *The Tejano Community, 1836-1900.* Albuquerque: UNM P, 1982.

_____. *They Called Them Greasers: Anglo Attitudes Toward Mexicans in Texas, 1821–1900.* Austin: UT P, 1983.

Donato, Rubén. *The Other Struggle for Equal Schools: Mexican Americans During the Civil Rights Era.* Albany: State U of NY P, 1997.

Drouin, Keith Leon. "Gerrymandering Suit." *North County Times* (11 November 2001). <http://www.nctimes.net/news/2001/20011101/55115.html>.

Durán, Isauro, and H. Russell Bernard, eds. *Introduction to Chicano Studies.* New York: Macmillan Publishing Co., 1982.

Elliston, Jon. "The Myth of the Miami Monolith," *NACLA Report on the Americas* (12 October 1995). <http://www.hartford-hwp.com/archives/43b/027.html>.

Enciso, Carmen E. *Hispanic Americans in Congress, 1822-1995.* Washington, D.C.: U.S.G.P.O, 1995

Escobar, Edward J. "The Dialectics of Repression: The Los Angeles Police Department and the Chicano Movement, 1968–1971." *The Journal of American History* 79 (March 1993): 1483–1514.

_____. *Race, Police, and the Making of a Political Identity: Mexican Americans and the Los Angeles Police Department, 1900–1945.* Berkeley: U of California P, 1999.

Espinosa, Gastón, Virgilio Elizondo, and Jesse Miranda. "Hispanic Churches in American Public Life: Summary of Findings of the Latino Religion

Center for the Study." *Interim Reports* (March 2003). <http://www.nd.edu/~latino/research/pubs/HispChurchesEnglishWEB.pdf>.

Estep, Raymond. "Zavala, Lorenzo De (1788-1836)." *The Handbook of Texas Online.* <www.tsha.utexas.edu/handbook/online/articles/view/ZZ/fza5.html>.

Fernández, Mayra. *Miriam Colón: Actor and Theatre Founder.* New York: Pearson Prentice Hall, 1993.

Figueroa, Hector. "NACLA Report on the Americas." (November/December 1996). <http://www.hartford-hwp.com/archives/43/018.html>.

Flores, William. "Francisca Flores." <http://www.clnet.ucla.edu/research/francisca.html>.

Foley, Neil. *White Scourge Mexicans, Blacks and Poor Whites in Texas Cotton Culture.* Berkely: U of California P, 1997.

Forrest, Suzanne. *The Preservation of the Village: New Mexico's Hispanics and the New Deal.* Albuquerque: UNM P, 1989.

Gamio, Manuel. *The Life Story of the Mexican Immigrant: Autobiographical Documents Collected by Manuel Gamio.* New York: Dover Publications, 1970.

_____. *Mexican Immigration to the United States: A Study of Human Immigration and Adjustment.* New York: Dover Publications, 1971.

García, Alma M. "Chicana Civil Rights Organizations." <http://www.hmco.com/hmco>.

García, David Ray, "The Romo Decision and Desegregation in Tempe." Honor's Thesis: Arizona State U, 1993.

García, Ignacio M. *Chicanismo: The Forging of a Militant Ethos among Mexican Americans.* Tucson: U of Arizona P, 1997.

_____. *Hector P. García: In Relentless Pursuit of Justice.* Houston: Arte Público P, 2002.

_____. *United We Win: The Rise and Fall of La Raza Party.* Tucson: MASRC, U of Arizona P, 1989.

García, Juan Ramón. *Operation Wetback: The Mass Deportation of Mexican Undocumented Workers in 1954.* Westport: Greenwood P, 1980.

García, María-Cristina. "Crespo, Manuel (1903-1989)." *The Handbook of Texas Online.* <http//www.tsha.utexas.edu/handbook/online/articles/view/cc/fcr/83.html>.

_____."García, Macario (1920-1972)." *The Handbook of Texas Online.* <http://www.tsha.utexas.edu/handbook/online/articles/print/GG/fga76.html>.

_____. *Havana USA: Cuban Exiles and Cuban Americans in South Florida, 1959–1994.* Berkeley: U of California P, 1996.

García, Mario T. *Desert Immigrants: The Mexicans of El Paso, 1880-1920.* New Haven: Yale UP, 1981.

_____. *Memories of Chicano History: The Life and Narrative of Bert Corona*. Berkeley: U of California P, 1994.

_____. *Mexican Americans: Leadership, Ideology and Identity, 1930-1960*. New Haven: Yale UP, 1990.

García, Richard A. "The Chicano Movement and the Mexican American Community, 1972–1978: An Interpetive Essay. *Socialist Review* 40.41 (July–October, 1978): 117–136.

Gledhill, John. *Casi Nada: A Study of Agrarian Reform in the Homeland of Cardenismo*. Albany: University at Albany, SUNY, Institute for Mesoamerican Society, 1989.

Gómez-Quiñones Juan. *Chicano Politics: Reality and Promise, 1940-1990*. Albuquerque: UNM P, 1990.

_____. *Mexican Students Por La Raza: The Chicano Student Movement in Southern California, 1967–1977*. Santa Barbara: Editorial La Causa, 1978.

_____. *The Roots of Chicano Politics, 1600–1940*. Albuquerque: UNM P, 1994.

Gonzales, Manuel G. *Mexicanos: A History of Mexicans in the United States*. Bloomington: Indiana UP, 1999.

Gonzales, Patricia, and Roberto Rodríguez. "Puerto Ricans—U.S. Citizens in Limbo." <http://www.indigenous people.net/indios2.htm>.

Gonzales, Rodolfo "Corky." *Message to Aztlán: Selected Writings*. Houston: Arte Público P, 2001.

González, Gilbert G. *Mexican Consuls and Labor Organizing: Imperial Politics in the American Southwest*. Austin: UT P, 1999.

González, José Amaro. *Mutual Aid for Survival: The Case of the Mexican American*. Malabar: Robert E. Krieger Publishing Co., 1983.

González, Luis. *San José de Gracia: A Mexican Town in Transition*. Austin: UT P, 1972.

Grillo, Evelio. *Black Cuban, Black American: A Memoir*. Houston: Arte Público P, 2000.

Griswold del Castillo, Richard, and Richard A. García. *César Chávez: A Triumph of Spirit*. Norman: U of Oklahoma P, 1995.

_____. *The Los Angeles Barrios, 1850–1890: A Social History*. Berkeley: U of California P, 1980.

_____. *The Treaty of Guadalupe Hidalgo: A Legacy of Conflict*. Norman: U of Oklahoma P, 1990.

Gutiérrez, David G. *Walls and Mirrors: Mexican Americans, Mexican Immigrants and the Politics of Ethnicity*. Berkeley: U of California P, 1995.

Gutiérrez, Felix. "Francisco P. Ramírez: Californio Editor and Yanqui Conquest." <http:freedomforum.org/publications/msj/courage.summer2000/yO3. html>.

Gutiérrez, José Angel. *The Making of a Chicano Militant: Lessons from Cristal.* Madison: U of Wisconsin P, 1999.

_____. *We Won't Back Down: Severita Lara's Rise from Student Leader to Mayor.* Houston: Arte Público P, 2005.

Hart, John Mason. *Revolutionary Mexico: The Coming and Process of the Mexican Revolution.* Berkeley: U of California P, 1987.

Henderson, Ann L., and Gary R. Mormino, eds. *Spanish Pathways in Florida, 1492–1992.* Sarasota: Pineapple P, 1991.

Hey, Jeanne A.K., and Lynn M. Kuzma. "Anti-U.S. Foreign Policy of Dependent States: Mexican and Costa Rican Participation in the Central American Peace Plan." *Comparative Political Studies* 26.1 (1993): 30–62.

Heyman, Josiah McC. *Life and Labor on the Border: Working People of Northern Mexico, 1886–1986.* Tucson: U of Arizona P, 1991.

Hispanic Americans in Congress, 1822–1995. <http://www.loc.gov/rr/hispanic/congress/contents.html>.

Hoffnung-Garskof, Jesse. "The Migrations of Arturo Schomburg: On Being Antillano, Negro, and Puerto Rican in New York 1891-1938." *Journal of American Ethnic History* 21.1 (November 1, 2001): 3–49.

Horsman, Reginald. *Race and Manifest Destiny: The Origins of American Racial Anglo-Saxonism.* Cambridge: Harvard UP, 1981.

Huntington, Samuel. P. *Who Are We?: The Challenge's to America's National Identity.* New York: Simon & Schuster, 2004.

Hutchinson, Bill. *When the Dogs Ate Candles: A Time in El Salvador.* Boulder: UP of Colorado, 1998.

Ignatiev, Noel. *How the Irish Became White.* New York: Routledge, 1995.

Jacobs, James B., and Kimberly Potter. *Hate Crimes: Criminal Law & Identity Politics (Studies in Crime and Public Policy).* New York: Oxford UP, 1998.

Jamieson, Stuart. *Labor Unionism in American Agriculture.* Washington, D.C.: U.S. Department of Labor, Bureau of Labor Statistics, Bulletin, no. 836, Government Printing Office,1945.

Johnson, Dirk. "Puerto Ricans Clinton Freed Leave Prisons." *The New York Times* (11 September 1999).

Justice, Glenn. *Revolution on the Rio Grande: Mexican Raids and Army Pursuits, 1916–1919.* El Paso: Texas Western P, 1992.

Kamp, Jim, and Diane Telgin. *Latinas! Women of Achievement.* Detroit: Visible Ink P, 1996.

Kanellos, Nicolás, ed. *Hispanic-American Almanac*. Detroit Gale Publications Inc.,1993.

_____. *Hispanic Firsts: 500 Years of Extraordinary Achievement*. Detroit: Gale, 1997.

_____. *Hispanic Literature of the United States: A Comprehensive Reference*. Westport: Greenwood P, 2004.

_____. *A History of Hispanic Theatre in the United States: Origins to 1940*. Austin: UT P, 1990.

_____. "Organizations," Kanellos, *Hispanic-American Almanac* 390–396.

_____. "Prominent Hispanics," Kanellos, *Hispanic-American Almanac* 717–740.

_____, and Cristelia Pérez. *Chronology of Hispanic American History: From Pre-Columbian Times to the Present*. New York: Gale Research, 1995.

_____, with Helvetia Martell. *Hispanic Periodicals in the United States, Origins to 1960: A Brief History and Comprehensive Bibliography*. Houston: Arte Público P, 2000.

Katz, Friedrich. *The Life and Times of Pancho Villa*. Stanford: Stanford UP, 1998.

Kerr, Louise A.N. "The Mexicans in Chicago." <http://www.lib.niv.edu/ipo/iht629962.htm>.

Kotlowski, Dean J. "Richard Nixon and the Origins of Affirmative Action." *Historian* 60.3 (Spring 1998): 523-541.

Knight, Alan. *The Mexican Revolution*. Vol. 1. London: Cambridge UP, 1986.

Kreneck, Thomas H. "The Letter from Chapultepec." *Houston Review* 3 (Summer 1981): 268–269.

_____. "Little School of the 400." *The Handbook of Texas Online*. <http://www.tsha.utexas.edu/handbook/online/articles/view/LL/kdl2.html>.

_____. *Mexican American Odyssey: Felix Tijerina, Entrepreneur and Civic Leader, 1905–1965*. College Station: Texas A&M UP, 2001.

Kushner, Sam. *Long Road to Delano*. New York: International Publishers, 1975.

Laird, Judith Fincher. "Argentine, Kansas: The Evolution of a Mexican American Community, 1905–1940." Diss. U of Kansas, 1975.

Lane, John Hart. *Voluntary Associations among Mexican Americans in San Antonio: Organizational and Leadership Characteristics*. New York: Arno P, 1976.

Larralde, Carlos. "J.T. Canales and the Texas Rangers." *The Journal of South Texas History* 10 (1997): 38–68.

_____, and José Rodolfo Jacobo. *Juan N. Cortina and the Struggle for Justice in Texas*. Dubuque: Kendall/Hunt, 2000.

Leeson, Susan M., adn James C. Foster. *Constitutional Law: Case in Context.* New York. St. Martin's P, 1992.

Lorey, David E. *The US-Mexican Border in the Twentieth Century: A History of Economic and Social Transformation.* Wilmington: Scholarly Resources, 1999.

Luckingham, Bradford. *Minorities in Phoenix: A Profile of Mexican American, Chinese American, and African American Communities, 1860–1992.* Tucson: U of Arizona P, 1994.

_____. *Phoenix: The History of a Southwestern Metropolis.* Tucson: U of Arizona P, 1989.

Lukens Espinosa, Patrick. "Mexico, Mexican Americans and the FDR Administration's Racial Classification Policy: Public Policy in Place of Diplomacy." Diss. Arizona State U, 2000.

Marchbanks, Lois Terry. *The Pan American Round Table.* n.p: Avon Behren P, 1983.

Marín, Christine. *A Spokesman of the Mexican American Movement: Rodolfo "Corky" Gonzales and the Fight for Chicano Liberation, 1966–1972.* San Francisco: R and E Research Associates, 1977.

_____. "Go Home, Chicanos: A Study of the Brown Berets in California and Arizona." In *An Awakened Minority: The Mexican Americans.* Manuel Servín, ed. Beverly Hills: Glencoe P, 1974. 226–247.

Marín, Marguerite V. *Social Protest in an Urban Barrio: A Study of the Chicano Movement, 1966–1974.* Lanham: UP of America, 1991.

Markley, Melanie. "Understanding Latino Activism: UH Class Will Reflect on History of Organizing in the Community." *Houston Chronicle* (2 February 2005). <http://www.uh.edu/ednews/2005/hc/200502/20050202 mariajimenez.html>.

Márquez, Benjamin. *LULAC: The Evolution of a Mexican American Political Organization.* Austin: UT P, 1993.

Martin, Susan. "Mexico-U.S. Migration." *Immigration in U.S.-Mexican Relations.* <http://www.iadialog.org/publications/country_studies/immigrat. html>.

Martínez, John. *Mexican Emigration to the United States, 1910–1930.* San Francisco: Arno P, 1971.

Martínez, Oscar J. *Fragments of the Mexican Revolution: Personal Accounts from the Border.* Albuquerque: UNM P, 1983.

_____. *Troublesome Border.* Tucson: U of Arizona P, 1988.

Mazón, Mauricio. *Zoot Suit Riots. The Psychology of Symbolic Annihilation.* Austin: UT P, 1984.

Masud-Piloto, Félix Roberto. *From Welcomed Exiles to Illegal Immigrants: Cuban Migration to the U.S., 1959–1995*. Lanham: Rowman & Littlefield, 1996.

McArthur, Harvey. "Puerto Rican Protestors Get Ready to Face U.S Navy." *The Militant* 63.44 (13 December 1999).

McBride, James B. "The Liga Protectora Latina: A Mexican-American Benevolent Society in Arizona." *Journal of the West* 14 (October 1975): 82–90.

McBride, Michael J. "Migrants and Asylum Seekers: Policy Responses in the United States to Immigrants and Refugees from Central America and the Caribbean." *International Migration* 37.1 (1999): 289–317.

McElroy, Martha M. "William H. Laustaunau: Menace or Martyr." Chicano Research Collection, Arizona State University Libraries, MM CHSM-324.

McWilliams, Carey. *North from Mexico*. Philadelphia: J.B. Lippincott Co., 1949.

Meier, Matt, and Feliciano Rivera. *A Dictionary of Mexican American History*. Westport: Greenwood P, 1981.

Mellinger, Philip J. *Race and Labor in Western Copper: The Fight for Equality, 1896-1918*. Tucson: U of Arizona P, 1995.

Menchaca, Martha. *The Mexican Outsiders: A Community History of Marginalization and Discrimination in California*. Austin: UT P, 1995.

Mendoza, Robert. "En el margen del Río Bravo: Catarino Garza's War with the U.S. and Mexico," *Laredos: A Journal of the Borderlands* (September 28, 2003). <http://www.laredosnews.com/archives/nov2002/lifestyle_02.html>.

Mexican American Biographies: A Historical Dictionary, 1836–1987. Westport: Greenwood P, 1988.

Miller, Yawu. "Latinos Debate Race, Identity Questions." *Bay State Banner* 37.31 (2 May 2002): 3.

Mirandé, Alfredo. *Gringo Justice*. Notre Dame: U of Notre Dame, 1987.

Mohl, Raymond A. "On the Edge: Blacks and Hispanics in Metropolitan Miami since 1959." *Florida Historical Quarterly* 69 (January 1990): 37–56.

Montejano, David. *Anglos and Mexicans in the Making of Texas, 1836–1896*. Austin: UT P, 1987.

Monroy, Douglas. *Rebirth: Mexican Los Angeles from the Great Migration to the Great*. Berkeley: U of California P, 1999.

Morales, Dionicio. *Dionicio Morales: A Life in Two Cultures*. Houston: Arte Público P, 1997.

Morín, Raúl R. *Among the Valiant: Mexican-Americans in WWII and Korea*. Los Angeles: Borden Pub. Co., 1963.

Muñoz, Carlos. *Youth Identity and Power: The Chicano Movement*. London: Verso, 1989.

Muñoz, Laura K. "Separate But Equal? A Case Study of *Romo v. Laird* and Mexican American Education." Reprinted from the *OAH Magazine of History* 15 (Winter 2001). <http://www.oah.org/pubs/magazine/deseg/documenta.html>.

Nabokov, Peter. *Tijerina and the Courthouse Raid*. Albuquerque: UNM P, 1969.

Nava, Julian. *Julian Nava: My Mexican American Journey*. Houston: Arte Público P, 2002.

Navarro, Armando. *La Raza Unida Party: A Chicano Challenge to the U.S. Two-Party Dictatorship*. Philadelphia: Temple UP, 2000.

_____. *Mexican American Youth Organization: Avant-Garde of the Chicano Movement in Texas*. Austin: UT P, 1995.

Nebbia, Gerardo, and Martin McLaughlin. "Puerto Rican Nationalists to Be Releases after Two Decades in Prison." World Socialist Web Site (9 September 1999). <http://wsws.org>.

Nelson, Jennifer A. "'Abortions under Community Control': Feminism, Nationalism, and the Politics of Reproduction among New York City's Young Lords." *Journal of Women's History* 13 (Spring 2001): 157–80.

Officer, James. *Hispanic Arizona; 1836-1856*. Tucson: U of Arizona P, 1989.

Olivas, Michael, ed. *Colored Men and Hombres Aquí: Hernandez v. Texas and the Emergence of Mexican-American Lawyering*. Houston: Arte Público P, 2006.

Orozco, Cynthia E. "Alice Dickerson Montemayor's Feminist Challenge to LULAC in the 1930s." *Intercultural Development Research Association*. <http://www.idra.org/Newslttr/1996/Mar/Orozco.htm>.

_____. "Garza, Bernardo F. (1892–1937)." *The Handbook of Texas Online*. <http://www.tsha.utexas.edu/handbook/online/articles/view/GG/fga85.html>.

_____. "Gonzales, Manuel C. (1900–1986)." *The Handbook of Texas Online*. <http://www.tsha.utexas.edu/handbook/online/articles/view/GG/fgo57.htm>.

_____. "Hernández, Maria L. de (1896-1986)." *The Handbook of Texas Online*. <http://www.tsha.utexas.edu/handbook/online/articles/view/HH/fhe75.html>.

_____. "League of United Latin American Citizens (LULAC)." <http://college.hmco.com/history/readerscomp/women/html/wh_020400_leagueofunit.htm>.

_____. "Perales, Alonso S. (1898–1960)." *The Handbook of Texas Online*. <http://www.tsha.utexas.edu/handbook/online>.

_____. "San Antonio Independent School District v. Rodríguez." *The Handbook of Texas Online*. <http://www.tsha.utexas.edu/handbook/online/articles/RR/jrrht.html>.

Ortego, Phillip D. "The Chicano Renaissance." In *Introduction to Chicano Studies*. Livie Isuaro Durán and H. Russell Bernard, eds. New York: Macmillan, 1982. 568–584.

Padilla, Genaro M. *My History, Not Yours: The Formation of Mexican American Autobiography*. Madison: U of Wisconsin P, 1993.

Pantoja, Antonia. *Memoir of a Visonary: Antonia Pantoja*. Houston: Arte Público P, 2002.

Paredes, Américo. *"With His Pistol in His Hand": A Border Ballad and its Hero*. Austin: UT P, 1958.

Pence, Richard. "The Homestead Act of 1862." <http://users.rcn.com/deeds/homestead.htm>.

Pitt, Leonard. *The Decline of Los Californios: A Social History of Spanish Speaking Californians, 1846–1890*. Berkeley: U of California P, 1971.

Preuss, Gene B. "Forto, Emilio (1856–?)." *The Handbook of Texas Online*. <http://www.tsha.utexas.edu/handbook/online/articles/view/FF/ffogu.html>.

Proctor, Ben H. "Texas Rangers." *The Handbook of Texas Online*, <http://www.tsha.utexas.edu/handbook/online/articles/TT/met4.html>.

Pycior, Julie Leininger. *LBJ & Mexican Americans: The Paradox of Power*. Austin: UT P, 1997.

Quirk, Robert E. *An Affair of Honor: Woodrow Wilson and the Occupation of Veracruz*. New York: Norton, 1962.

Raat, W. Dirk. *Revoltosos: Mexico's Rebels in the United States*. College Station, Texas A&M UP, 1981.

Radelat, Ann. "Wall Street and Business Wednesdays: Latinos Reshaping Organized Labor." *The News Journal* (21 January 2004).

Ramos, Henry A.J. *The American G.I. Forum: In Pursuit of the Dream, 1948–1983*. Houston: Arte Público P, 2000.

Reeve, Cal. *The Life and Times of Daniel De León*. New York: AIM, 1972.

Reisler, Mark. *By the Sweat of Their Brow: Mexican Immigrant Labor in the United States: 1900–1940*. Westport: Greenwood P, 1976.

Retsinas, Joan. "The International Institute of Rhode Island." *Rhode Island History* 54.4 (1991): 122–140.

Richmond, Douglas W. *Venustiano Carranza's Nationalist Struggle, 1893–1920*. Lincoln: U of Nebraska, 1983.

Ridge, John Rollin. *The Life and Adventures of Joaquín Murrieta: The Celebrated Bandit*. Norman: U of Oklahoma, 1955.

Rodriguez, Luis J. "Abelardo 'Lalo' Delgado: A Pioneering Chicano Poet Passes On to the Ancestors." *Xispas: Chicano Culture, Art, and Politics.* <http://www.xispas.com/poetry/delgado.htm>.

Romo, Ricardo. *East Los Angeles: History of a Barrio.* Austin: UT P, 1983.

Rosaldo, Renato, ed. *Chicano: The Evolution of a People.* Minneapolis: Winston, 1973.

Rosales, F. Arturo. "A Historical Overview." Kanellos, *Hispanic-American Almanac* 1–53.

_____. *Chicano! A History of the Mexican American Civil Rights Movement.* Houston: Arte Público P, 1996.

_____. "'Fantasy Heritage' Re-examined: Race and Class in the Writings of the Bandini Family Authors and Other Californios, 1828–1965." In Erlinda Gonzales-Berry and Charles Tatum, eds. *Recovering the U.S. Hispanic Literary Heritage.* Vol. 2. Houston: Arte Público P, 1996. 83–106.

_____. *"Pobre Raza!": Violence, Crime, Justice and Mobilization among Mexico Lindo Immigrants, 1900–1936.* Austin: UT P, 1999.

_____. *Testimonio: A Documentary History of the Mexican American Struggle for Civil Rights.* Houston: Arte Público P, 2000.

Rosario, Rubén del, Estér Melón de Díaz, and Edgar Martínez Masoleu, eds. *Breve Enciclopedia de la Cultura Puertorriqueña.* Río Piedras: Editorial Cordillera, 1976.

Rose-Ávila, Magdaleno. "Homies Unidos, El Salvador Peer Education with Gang Members: Protecting Life and Health." *Family Health International.* <http://www.fhi.org/en/Youth/YouthNet/Publications/FOCUS/Project Highlights/homiesunidoselsalvador.htm>.

Rosenbaum, Robert J. *Mexicano Resistance in the Southwest: "The Sacred Right of Self-Preservation."* Austin: UT P, 1981.

Ryan, Mary Ellen, and Gary S. Breschini. "Secularization and the Ranchos, 1826-1846." <http://www.mchsmuseum.com/secularization.html>.

Ruiz, Jaime. "The Marquez Equation: Knowledge x People = Power." *Random Lengths.* <http://www.randomlengthsnews.com/archive/knowledge-july 23.htm>.

Ruiz, Vicki L. *Cannery Women, Cannery Lives: Unionization and the California Food Processing Industry, 1930–1950.* Albuquerque: UNM P, 1987.

_____. *From Out of the Shadows: Mexican Women in Twentieth-Century America.* New York: Oxford UP, 1998.

Salazar, Ruben. *Border Correspondent: Selected Writings, 1955–1970.* Berkeley: U of California P, 1995.

Saldívar, Ramón. "Tomás Rivera—Author. A Biography." In *The Heath Anthology of American Literature.* 4th ed. Paul Lauter, General Editor.

<http://college.hmco.com/english/lauter/heath/4e/students/author_pages/contemporary/rivera_to.html>.

Samora, Julián, and Patricia Vandel Simon. *A History of the Mexican-American People.* <http://www.jsri.msu.edu/museum/pubs/MexAmHist/chapter22.html>.

Sánchez, George J. *Becoming Mexican American: Culture and Identity in Chicano Los Angeles, 1900–1945.* New York: Oxford UP, 1993.

Sánchez Korrol, Virginia. *From Colonia to Community: The History of Puerto Ricans in New York City.* Berkeley: U of California P, 1994.

Sandos, James A. *Rebellion in the Borderlands: Anarchism and the Plan of San Diego, 1904–1923.* Norman: U of Oklahoma P, 1992.

San Miguel, Guadalupe. "Education." Kanellos, *Hispanic-American Almanac* 287–307.

_____. *"Let All of Them Take Heed": Mexican Americans and the Campaign for Educational Equality in Texas, 1910–1981.* Austin: UT P, 1987.

Santibañez, Enrique. *Ensayo acerca de la inmigración mexicana en los Estados Unidos.* San Antonio: The Clegg Co., 1930.

Sepúlveda, Juan. *The Life and Times of Willie Velásquez: Su Voto Es Su Voz.* Houston: Arte Público P, 2004.

Sharry, Frank F. "After the Hurricane: How U.S. Immigration Policy Can Help." *InterAction.* 16.24 (21 December 1998): 23–25.

Sheridan, Thomas E. *Los Tucsonenses: The Mexican Community in Tucson, 1854–1941.* Tucson: U of Arizona P, 1986.

Shockley, John Staples. *Chicano Revolt in a Texas Town.* Notre Dame: U of Notre Dame P, 1974.

Skerry, Peter. *Mexican Americans: The Ambivilant Minority.* New York: The Free P, 1993.

Stone, Betsy. "Files Detail FBI's War on Puerto Rican Independence Fight." *The Militant* 64.23 (12 June 2000). <http://www.themilitant.com/2000/6423/642351.html>.

Suárez-Orozco, Carola Irina Todorova, and Josephine Louie. "The Transnationalization of Families: Immigrant Separations and Reunifications." Plenary session paper delivered at the American Family Therapy Academy on Friday, June 29, Miami. <http://www.gse.harvard.edu/~hip/Files/Presentations/AFTA%20Paper.doc>.

Tardiff, Joseph C., and L. Mpho Mabunda. *Dictionary of Hispanic Biography.* Detroit: Gale Research, 1996.

Taylor, Paul S. *An American Mexican Frontier: Nueces County Texas.* Chapel Hill: U of North Carolina P, 1934.

_____. *Mexican Labor in the United States: Chicago and the Calumet Region.* Berkeley: U of California P, 1931.

Telgin, Jim, and Diane Kamp. *Latinas! Women of Achievement.* Detroit: Visible Ink P, 1996.

Thompson, Jerry. "Cortina, Juan Nepomuceno." *The Handbook of Texas Online.* <http://www.tsha.utexas.edu/handbook/online/articles/view/CC/fco73.html>.

Torres, Andrés, and José E. Velázquez, eds. *The Puerto Rican Movement: Voices from the Diaspora.* Philadelphia: Temple UP, 1998.

Treviño, Roberto. "Prensa y Patria: The Spanish Language Press and the Biculturalization of the Tejano Middle Class, 1920–1940." *The Western Historical Quarterly* 22 (November 1991): 451–472.

Trueba, Enrique. *Latinos Unidos: From Cultural Diversity to the Politics of Solidarity.* Lanham: Rowman & Littlefield, 1999.

Turner, Frederick C. *The Dynamic of Mexican Nationalism.* Chapel Hill: U of North Carolina P, 1968.

Valdés, Dennis Nodín. *Al Norte: Agricultural Workers in the Great Lakes Region, 1917–1970.* Austin: UT P, 1991.

_____. "Region, Nation, and World-System: Perspectives on Midwestern Chicana/o History." East Lansing: Michigan State U Julián Samora Research Institute, 1999. <http://jrsi.msu.edu/RandS/research/ops/oc20.html>.

Varela-Lago, Ana. "From Patriotism to Mutualism: The Early Years of the Centro Español de Tampa, 1891–1903." *Tampa Bay History* 15 (Summer 1993): 5–23.

Venegas, Daniel. *Las aventuras de Don, o Chipote; o Cuando los pericos mamen.* Houston: Arte Público P, 1999.

Vargas, Zaragoza. *Proletarians of the North: A History of Mexican Industrial Workers in Detroit and the Midwest, 1917–1933.* Berkeley: U of California P, 1993.

La Voz de Aztlán Communications Network. "Heroes and Heroines of La Raza Series." (January 2000). <http://aztlan.net/default5.htm>.

Weber, David J. "Cart War." *The Handbook of Texas Online.* <http://www.tsha.utexas.edu/handbook/online/articles/view/CC/jcc1.html>.

_____. *Foreigners in Their Native Land: Historical Roots of the Mexican Americans.* Albuquerque: UNM P, 1973.

_____. *The Spanish American Frontier in North America.* New Haven: Yale UP, 1992.

Weber, Devra. *Dark Sweat, White Gold: California Farm Workers, Cotton, and the New Deal.* Berkeley: U of California P, 1996.

Weintraub, Irwin. "Fighting Enviromental Racism: A Selected Annotated Bibliography." <http://www.mapcruzin.com/EI/ejigc.html>.

Womack, John. *Zapata and the Mexican Revolution.* New York: Knopf, 1970.

Zamora, Emilio. *The World of the Mexican Worker in Texas.* College Station: Texas A&M UP, 1993.

Zielbauer, Paul von. "Hartford Bids a Bilingual Goodbye to a White-Collar Past." *The New York Times* (5 May 2003). <http://www.nytimes.com/2003/05/05/nyregion/05HART.html?ex=1053153044&ei=1&en=5a32d188a8971e1c>.

Index

298, 328, 348, 392, 422, 429, 438
environmental concerns, 278
immigrant mobilization, 9, 16, 70,
97, 108, 109, 116, 210, 214, 270,
311, 354, 379, 392, 436
immigration from Mexico, 10, 16,
97, 102, 108, 109, 270, 311, 436
La Raza Unida Party, 379
Magonistas in, 170
media, literature and arts projects,
53, 84, 189, 323, 330, 405
Mexican American Generation, 28,
42, 66, 70, 79, 106, 111, 121, 169,
203, 288, 294, 328, 338, 392, 429,
450
Mexican immigration, 100
Mexican population, 79, 100, 102,
189
nineteenth century Mexicans, 37,
117, 348, 375, 434
police relations with Mexicans, 42,
258, 270, 354
political patronage to Hispanics, 1,
79, 111, 328
repatriation from, 96, 102
Schenley Liquor Company Boycott,
424
Sleepy Lagoon Case, 28, 92, 169,
284, 407-408
social services, 50, 55, 79, 105, 150,
205, 223, 249, 271, 299, 301, 357,
422
unionization of Mexicans, 16, 70,
109, 116, 209, 222, 233, 301
Vietnam War protest, 103, 111, 185,
308, 316
women and gender issues, 81, 100,
169, 223, 233, 357
Zoot Suit Riots, 169, 338, 450-451
Los Angeles Committee for the Protection of the Foreign Born (LACPFB),
270
Los Angeles County Coroner's Jury,
395, 445
Los Angeles County Human Relations
Council, 48, 57
Los Angeles Police Department
(LAPD), 316, 383, 394
Los Angeles Team Mentoring, Inc., 271

Los Angeles Times, 79, 83, 316, 394
Los P.A.D.R.E.S, 286, 339
Louisiana Purchase, 3, 271
Lucey, Bishop Robert E. 39, 271, 272
Luna, Solomon, 272
Lutheran Immigrant and Refugee Serv-
ices, The, (LIRS), 272-273
lynching, 58, 60, 119, 173, 175, 183,
191, 192, 237, 238, 243, 273, 311,
347, 354, 370, 371, 376, 388

M
Madero, Francisco I., 234, 243, 260,
350, 417, 449
Maidique, Modesto "Mitch," 137, 138,
273
Malakoff, Texas, 195, 196
Mammoth Tank Strike, 274
Manifest Destiny, 3, 274, 369, 376,
411, 439
Mano Negra (Black Hand), 275
maquiladoras, 123, 275
Mardirosian, Reverend Vahac, 12, 153,
275, 276, 344
marielitos, 133, 273, 277, 278, 374,
375
Marquez, Jesse, 278
Martí, José, 279, 410
Martínez, Elizabeth "Betita," 280, 433
Martínez Jr., Félix, 280-281, 442
Martínez, Louis, 125, 281
Martínez, María Elena, 281
Martínez, Ray, 176
Martínez, Vilma S., 281, 282, 333
Más Canosa, Jorge, 138, 282
Massachusetts, 239, 252, 282
Massachusetts Latino Conference, 282-
283
Marxism, 11, 49, 67, 70, 102, 231, 258,
313, 380, 447
McCarran-Walter Immigration and
Nationality Act, 283, 284
McWilliams, Carey, 163, 169, 242, 284,
332, 333, 408
media, literature, and arts projects, 10,
11, 16, 21, 26, 34, 40, 53, 89, 91,
106, 115, 124, 133, 134, 141, 143,
153, 158, 165, 166, 191, 211, 219,
238, 248, 251, 253, 293, 294, 304,

U.S. Surveyor General Claims Office, 428
Unity Leagues, 106, 391, 428, 429
Universidad Boricua, 342, 429
University of Arizona, 64, 288
University of California, Los Angeles (UCLA), 308, 350, 353, 438
University of Southern California (USC), 116, 184, 284, 426, 430
Uranga, Rodolfo, 429-430

V

Valdez, Armando, 167, 430
Valdez, Luis, 11, 387, 430-431, 433
Vallejo, Mariano Guadalupe, 32, 431-432
Vanguardia de Colonización Proletaria (Vanguard of Proletarian Colonization), 433
Varela, María, 433-434
Varela y Morales, Félix Francisco, 434
Varela, Servulo, 434
Vásquez, Tiburcio, 119
Velasco Carlos, 9, 73
Velázquez, Nydia M., 434-435
Velásquez, William C. "Willie," 106, 189, 200, 292, 409, 410, 435-436
Velásquez v. City of Abilene, 436
Venegas, Daniel, 109, 205, 215, 436-437
Veracruz, invasion of, 227, 234
Vieques, Puerto Rico, 115, 116, 163, 164, 362, 363
Vietnam war, 103, 185, 188, 233, 237, 299, 316, 394, 436, 445
Vigil, Ernesto, 437
Vigilantism, 38, 237, 437
Villa, Francisco "Pancho," 48, 155, 246, 350, 401, 418, 438, 449
Villalobos, Ramón, 168
Villaraigosa, Antonio R., 114, 438-439
Visel, Charles P., 383, 440
Viva Kennedy Campaign, 13, 93, 123, 352, 440
Voz del Pueblo, La, 50, 442
Voter Participation Project, 440
Voters Assistance Act of 1992, 442
Voting Rights Acts, 441-442
Voz de América, La, 442

W

War with Mexico, 6, 12, 32, 176, 198, 267, 349, 412, 416, 432
War on Poverty, 6, 124, 151, 187, 207, 237, 332, 355, 441
Washington, D.C. and,
  lobbying and Latino elected offcials, 15, 44, 90, 113, 128, 146, 188, 207, 211, 213, 247, 279, 280, 307, 341, 347, 381, 385
  organizations in, 15, 82, 113, 115, 128, 146, 207, 210, 211, 213, 224, 238, 247, 282, 288, 291, 313, 317, 319, 320, 321, 324, 341, 385, 402, 428, 429
  protests and celebrations in, 15, 44, 162, 352, 355, 398
water rights, 182, 267, 427
Watts/Century Latino Organization (WCLO), 443
Welch, Sheriff John, 443
Western Federation of Miners, 95
Westminister v. Méndez, 285, 404, 407
Wheatland Riot, The, 443-444
White Primary in Texas, 444
Wilcox, Mary Rose Garrido, 444-445
Wilson, Thomas, 445
Wilson, Woodrow, 234, 237, 438
women and gender issues, 13, 28, 58, 61, 80, 100, 106, 115, 121, 144, 148, 166, 169, 177, 184, 192, 208, 214, 218, 226, 233, 245, 257, 259, 280, 291, 295, 300, 304, 317, 321, 331, 333, 340, 357, 359, 378, 386, 389, 395, 407, 429, 434, 435, 444, 448
Working Group on Migration and Consular Affairs, 445
World War I and,
  Latino assertiveness, 5, 38, 75, 336
  Latino veterans, 5, 75, 165, 187, 228, 336, 349, 351
  political repression, 5, 38, 91, 110, 171, 336, 349, 450
  racial discrimination, 145, 165, 187, 263, 336, 346, 349, 450
  unionization of Mexicans, 5
World War II,
  Bracero Program, 45
  Home Front support, 62